KERUX COMMENTARIES

# JEREMIAH AND LAMENTATIONS

KERUX COMMENTARIES

# JEREMIAH AND LAMENTATIONS

*A Commentary for Biblical Preaching and Teaching*

DUANE GARRETT
CALVIN F. PEARSON

KREGEL
MINISTRY

*Jeremiah and Lamentations: A Commentary for Biblical Preaching and Teaching*



Published by Kregel Ministry, an imprint of Kregel Publications, 2450 Oak Industrial Dr. NE, Grand Rapids, MI 49505-6020.



Unless otherwise indicated, the translation of the Scripture portions used throughout the commentary is the authors' own English rendering of the original biblical languages.



Italics in Scripture quotations indicate emphasis added by the authors.

The Hebrew font, NewJerusalemU, and the Greek font, GraecaU, are available from www.linguistsoftware.com/lgku.htm, +1-425-775-1130.

All photos are under Creative Commons licensing, and contributors are indicated in the captions of the photos.

Maps on pages 53, 55, 77, 272, 377, and 431 are by A. D. Riddle. Used by permission.

ISBN 978-0-8254-2567-7

Printed in the United States of America

22 23 24 25 26 / 5 4 3 2 1

# Contents

# PUBLISHER'S PREFACE TO THE SERIES

Since words were first uttered, people have struggled to understand one another and to know the main meaning in any verbal exchange.

The answer to what God is talking about must be understood in every context and generation; that is why Kerux (KAY-rukes) emphasizes text-based truths and bridges from the context of the original hearers and readers to the twenty-first-century world. Kerux values the message of the text, thus its name taken from the Greek *kērux*, a messenger or herald who announced the proclamations of a ruler or magistrate.

Biblical authors trumpeted all kinds of important messages in very specific situations, but a big biblical idea, grasped in its original setting and place, can transcend time. This specific, big biblical idea taken from the biblical passage embodies a single concept that transcends time and bridges the gap between the author's contemporary context and the reader's world. How do the prophets perceive the writings of Moses? How does the writer of Hebrews make sense of the Old Testament? How does Clement in his second epistle, which may be the earliest sermon known outside the New Testament, adapt verses from Isaiah and also ones from the Gospels? Or what about Luther's bold use of Romans 1:17? How does Jonathan Edwards allude to Genesis 19? Who can forget Martin Luther King Jr.'s "I Have a Dream" speech and his appropriation of Amos 5:24: "No, no, we are not satisfied, and we will not be satisfied until 'justice rolls down like waters, and righteousness like a mighty stream'"? How does a preacher in your local church today apply the words of Hosea in a meaningful and life-transforming way?

## WHAT IS PRIME IN GOD'S MIND, AND HOW IS THAT EXPRESSED TO A GIVEN GENERATION IN THE UNITS OF THOUGHT THROUGHOUT THE BIBLE?

Answering those questions is what Kerux authors do. Based on the popular "big idea" preaching model, Kerux commentaries uniquely combine the insights of experienced Bible exegetes (trained in interpretation) and homileticians (trained in preaching). Their collaboration provides for every Bible book:

- A detailed introduction and outline
- A summary of all preaching sections with their primary exegetical, theological, and preaching ideas
- Preaching pointers that join the original context with the contemporary one
- Insights from the Hebrew and Greek text
- A thorough exposition of the text
- Sidebars of pertinent information for further background
- Appropriate charts and photographs
- A theological focus to passages

- A contemporary big idea for every preaching unit
- Present-day meaning, validity, and application of a main idea
- Creative presentations for each primary idea
- Key questions about the text for study groups

Many thanks to Jim Weaver, Kregel's former acquisitions editor, who conceived of this commentary series and further developed it with the team of Jeffrey D. Arthurs, Robert B. Chisholm, David M. Howard Jr., Darrel L. Bock, Roy E. Ciampa, and Michael J. Wilkins. We also recognize with gratitude the significant contributions of Dennis Hillman, Fred Mabie, Paul Hillman, Herbert W. Bateman IV, and Shawn Vander Lugt who have been instrumental in the development of the series. Finally, gratitude is extended to the two authors for each Kerux volume; the outside reviewers, editors, and proofreaders; and Kregel staff who suggested numerous improvements.

*—Kregel Publications*

# AUTHORS' DEDICATION

The authors dedicate this volume:
Duane to his wife Patty
Calvin to his wife Jan
Jointly they dedicate this volume to their
mutual lifelong friend and brother in Christ,
Jesse H. Outlaw (1951–2020)

# EXEGETICAL AUTHOR'S PREFACE TO JEREMIAH AND LAMENTATIONS

In the course of writing this commentary, I have concluded that Jeremiah is the prophet for our times. I am old enough to remember well the 1970s and '80s. Those years had their difficulties, but there was much to be optimistic about. The "Jesus Movement" swept across America, and Billy Graham was at the height of his powers. He could fill large stadiums night after night with people coming to hear the gospel. It seemed we were in the midst of a new great awakening. Campus Crusade and Inter-Varsity Christian Fellowship thrived, and tens of thousands of Christian students went to the Urbana conference on missions and evangelism. On the Roman Catholic side, John Paul II was revitalizing his church. Politically, it was a time of optimism. Even those who did not like Ronald Reagan and Margaret Thatcher would have to admit that confidence, not despair, was the mood of the day. The Soviet Union collapsed, and the states of eastern Europe rapidly overthrew their communist governments. The cold war ended, and the future looked bright indeed.

A generation has passed, and the change is astonishing. The church is in serious decline in the west, nowhere more so than in America. The culture has embraced moral norms that recently were unthinkable. Society is dangerously polarized. We have encountered new and unexpected crises, and many threats seem to be on the horizon. One might be pardoned for echoing the sentiment cited in Psalm 11:3, "When the foundations are destroyed, what can the righteous do?"

In all this, we only repeat the experience of Jeremiah. He began his ministry under the great reforming king, Josiah. The shrines of the idols were removed, the law was rediscovered, the nation recommitted itself to its covenant with God, and the cycle of sin and punishment seemed to be ending at last. That great and wicked empire, Assyria, finally collapsed. But Josiah was slain by Pharaoh Neco, and under his sons Jehoiakim and Zedekiah, Judah embraced paganism with a vengeance. They demonstrated their rediscovered zeal by sacrificing their children in the Hinnom Valley. Jeremiah was cancelled; he was vilified as a traitor and heretic. He could only watch from his prison cell as Babylon sacked Jerusalem. History may not repeat itself, but it surely does have echoes.

I wish to express my deep thanks to Kregel for allowing me to participate in writing a commentary on this most timely book. And I am especially grateful that I was able to do it with my lifelong friend and dear brother, Calvin Pearson. As we Christians consider Jeremiah and Lamentations within our own perilous time, may God be with us all.

—Duane A. Garrett

# PREACHING AUTHOR'S PREFACE TO JEREMIAH AND LAMENTATIONS

Jeremiah and Lamentations are books about God's working in, through, and on His people. We live in a different century, but we have the same deceitful hearts as our spiritual ancestors, and we serve the same loving Father whose compassions and mercies are new every morning.

Anytime one preaches or teaches the Old Testament, one must keep the context of the full canon in mind. However, I would suggest that one should not turn too quickly to other passages, lest you end up preaching a passage from Ephesians and only use Jeremiah or Lamentations as an illustration. If we are not careful, we could end up preaching Ephesians and not Jeremiah.

Of course, our preaching is to be Christian. Our approach is to present the message of a pericope, knowing that the message can be more personal and more fulfilling because of Christ's work for us. The message is the same for us as it was for the ancient readers, but with Christ the understanding and application becomes richer. I often mention Jesus's work specifically, but at times it is assumed.

Sermons should have a central idea, whether it is called a theme, a main idea, or a "big idea." However, such a unifying idea is only a tool to assist in communicating the text. Our purpose is to present God's living and active Word.

My work is a starting place for effective preaching and teaching. I like to think this work is simply my sitting down with you and dialoguing about how to preach or teach a passage. I pray that as you read what we have written, God's Spirit will be at work in you. Perhaps he will use my sermonic suggestions as seeds that will help grow effective structures, illustrations, and applications for your setting.

—Calvin F. Pearson

# PREACHING AUTHOR'S ACKNOWLEDGMENTS

Without the Lord's empowerment and the impact of many people on my life, I would have never been able to write this volume.

First and foremost, is my wife of forty-six years, Jan Howell Pearson, who supported, edited, and greatly encouraged me throughout the process.

Since my area is the preaching of the text, I am greatly indebted to all those who taught me. Five stand out: Duane Litfin, Elliot Johnson, John Reed, Haddon Robinson, and Don Sunukjian. And, I thank my students and colleagues, with whom I was privileged to co-labor.

Much of my preaching skill and style was forged through the churches which God entrusted me to pastor: Calvary Baptist, Seagoville, TX; Bay Area First Baptist, League City, TX; and Hopevale Church, Saginaw, MI.

My use of the threefold movement from exegesis, to the theological focus, and then to the preaching idea was practiced and refined by two pastoral groups of which I was a part. We would meet twice a year to work not only on sermons, but also on each other's walk with Christ. Each group had a core of pastors. The first group, which met in the late 1980s, included Lane Fusilier, Andy Seidel, and Woody Woodward. The second group met during the 1990s and included Kevin Butcher, Carlton Harris, Nathan Mains, Jeff Manion, and Cecil Sanders.

Lastly, Duane Garrett's scholarship obviously forms the foundation for my homiletical contribution, but he also was a major part of the Lord's work in the foundation of my life. We grew up literally across the street from each other. We played together, prayed together, and had many teenage theological discussions, and remain close friends to this day.

Thank you, to all of these and dozens of others, for being God's tool to shape and refine my homiletics and my life. May he use this volume to bring glory to himself.

—A fellow servant of the Savior,<br>
Calvin F. Pearson

# OVERVIEW OF ALL PREACHING PASSAGES

## Jeremiah 1:1–3

**EXEGETICAL IDEA**

The superscript's reference to three named kings—from righteous Josiah to apostate Jehoiakim and Zedekiah—ending with the fall of Jerusalem gives the essential facts about the book's historical setting and implies that its theme is how and why Jerusalem, the city of David and of the temple, was destroyed.

**THEOLOGICAL FOCUS**

As evil becomes triumphant, people develop an inverted sense of right and wrong and build their lives on lies until judgment becomes inevitable, yet God provides a witness and shows the way to salvation revealed in several oracles that bring hope.

**PREACHING IDEA**

When we see God's judgment, look for and embrace his restoration.

**PREACHING POINTERS**

God wanted to dig more deeply, so most of Jeremiah's words identified sins and the consequential judgment. Motivational words without truth are meaningless and ineffective. God wanted Israel to see the depth of their sin. Then they would be ready for his forgiveness and redemption.

God wants to encourage us today. Posters of eagles soaring over mountains and dolphins jumping through waves with short motivational words have their place, but God wants to motivate people more deeply. Saying that "a journey begins with a first step" or "when the going gets tough, the tough get going" can help, but these words only deal with the surface. God wants to motivate our hearts. Jeremiah shows us that we are full of sin, but he also shows us the amazing grace and redemption that is available to us. To motivate us from our hearts, our hearts need to be changed. If we don't admit that we desperately need God's forgiveness and empowerment, we will be unprepared to live out his life in the bleak and dark world that we live in.

## Jeremiah 1:4–19

**EXEGETICAL IDEA**

Jeremiah's commission account marks him as a great prophet in manner of Moses, Samuel, and Isaiah. It also foreshadows the ordeals he will endure. The passage first describes God's call of a reluctant Jeremiah, and then declares that he must be armored by God to withstand the opposition he will face. This informs the reader that Jeremiah was genuinely chosen by

God and that the hostility he endured is a mark of his greatness; it does not imply he was a failed prophet.

**THEOLOGICAL FOCUS**

God's messengers each have a distinctive call, face specific challenges, require unique empowerment, and can be confident in proclaiming the word. But in this task, "success" is not defined by popularity or even by bringing about great changes for good. Rather, the only thing that matters is that the preacher is faithful in the face of great opposition as he receives the message and proclaims it.

**PREACHING IDEA**

God's messenger needs God's assurances and empowerment to proclaim God's message.

**PREACHING POINTERS**

This passage is often applied primarily to fellow messengers of God's truth. While this might be an acceptable application, it does not take into account that most of those who read this when it was first written were not in the role of heralds, but listeners. Jeremiah's divine appointment and message gave him courage and assurance; it also guided listeners to a submissive attitude. They needed to know by whose authority a prophet was speaking or writing. This was not the mere authority of a governor or king; this message had the highest authority.

Today God's call of Jeremiah encourages those of us who preach; but even more, this first episode of Jeremiah's narrative sets forth that this book has the authority of God. For a culture such as modern, or postmodern, America where the individual's emotions seem to carry the most authority, it is important that congregations know and remember that this message is from God—and that makes all the difference. This book is not Jeremiah's devotional thoughts; it is the very word of God. When the Bible is proclaimed, it is not the preacher's devotional words about God; it is God's authoritative word. As preachers we cannot change how a congregation listens, but we can have a level of expectation that does affect them as we view our role more seriously.

## Jeremiah 2:1–3:10

**EXEGETICAL IDEA**

A series of vivid metaphors describes how Israel's apostasy has caused the nation to be completely perverse—at the same time both self-righteous and wicked while transferring its love to stone gods and to nations that hate Israel. A series of vivid metaphors repeatedly make the points that Judah is incurably apostate and that this has robbed the nation of its identity, its good sense, its dignity, and its innocence.

**THEOLOGICAL FOCUS**

Turning from God is never done in isolation from other ethical and ideological areas of life, allowing a people to be apostate but otherwise culturally and morally healthy. Apostasy leads to immorality, cruelty, twisted thinking, misplaced affection, and a refusal to acknowledge guilt. Those who reject the truth will inevitably embrace bizarre and foolish lies.

**PREACHING IDEA**

When we give up on seeking the Lord, sin will be seeking us.

**PREACHING POINTERS**

It must have been hard for the people to hear this sermon when it was first preached. Being told that you are suffering the consequences of years of sinning is not what anyone wants to hear. The first hearers of the written form of the message could distance themselves by saying, "That is what our forefathers did; we are suffering because of their sin," and miss the point of Jeremiah's message. Jeremiah is not blaming the fathers; he is warning the children.

If not careful, we can only present this passage as a description of how bad Israel sinned and how severe the terrible consequences. The temptation is to study this from a distance, but those who first heard the sermon and those who later read, including us, are all in the same family of God. In a sense, they are our people; we are not outsiders. These words are for us, to warn and explain the tragic results of our sin and to lead us to repentance.

## Jeremiah 3:11–4:4

**EXEGETICAL IDEA**

God calls on Judah to repent, carefully defining what that means and what the benefits are, while also acknowledging that Judah is so deep in rebellion that they cannot repent. This passage, therefore, explores the meaning of repentance while also explaining why many people cannot do it. In addition, it asserts that God does not take pleasure in punishing sin but mourns over the recalcitrance of people whose hearts have turned to stone.

**THEOLOGICAL FOCUS**

God's appeals for repentance are always real, but sometimes the audience is incapable of receiving them. In such a case, the prophetic preacher must continue to explain why repentance is necessary and how the people should do it, but this does not mean that the preacher embraces any false hopes regarding his audience and the state of their hearts.

**PREACHING IDEA**

It's not enough to cry for help—we must repent.

**PREACHING POINTERS**

The caricature of the radical preacher holding a sloppily painted sign of just the one word, "Repent," gives the message of this passage an unfortunate negative barrier to overcome. To be faithful to present this passage, in a sense, requires us to do just that: hold up a sign that says "Repent." But there is more on the sign than just that one word; there are guidelines to true repentance. The better word to use might be Jeremiah's word: Return.

The passage presents what is necessary for true repentance or a true returning to the Lord, but it is not void of the same passion of the person holding the sign calling for repentance. It is serious business because our sin is a serious rejection of God. But the emotion doesn't end there. God calls for repentance in order to bless us.

## Jeremiah 4:5–6:30

**EXEGETICAL IDEA**

Judah persistently rejects correction from God's prophet and lives under the illusion that they deserve no punishment; but God persistently warns them that the Babylonians are at the gates, ready to bring his punishment down on them. This structure of this passage is driven by a lengthy series of alternating texts, first describing how the Babylonian invader is coming upon them and then asserting that the people prefer to believe lies that they are safe and will suffer no harm. These alternating texts vividly bring home the lesson that faith in a false ideology leads to ruin.

**THEOLOGICAL FOCUS**

Behavior has consequences. Sin deceives people, so that they deny both their guilt and the consequences of their deeds, but they will ultimately face the harsh reality of retribution. Jerusalem continued to think that idols, inept leaders, foreign allies, and the presence of God's temple could guarantee their safety even as the day of ruin came upon them.

**PREACHING IDEA**

Our self-deception is our most dangerous sin.

**PREACHING POINTERS**

This long passage has a constant theme that Jeremiah keeps repeating with creative and accurate descriptions of Judah's lifestyle and their unwillingness to be honest about their sin and the coming invasion. They are either ignoring or misrepresenting the truth from God's law and Jeremiah's preaching. They are deceiving themselves. In the end, this deception is so deep and so common that they no longer can even see the truth. They are "rejected silver" (6:30).

While Jeremiah is saying people can be so self-deceived that they can't respond to the truth, the application of this passage is for those who will listen and respond. It is somewhat like the unpardonable sin. If you think you may have committed it, you haven't. If one is worried or concerned that they might be self-deceived, then there is hope that they can hear and repent. But it seems that there are some whose self-deception is so deep that they cannot even hear the truth. In describing the self-deception of Judah, this passage helps us see ways that we deceive ourselves and calls us to honesty and authenticity. If we are listening, then there is hope.

## Jeremiah 7:1–8:12

**EXEGETICAL IDEA**

Judah uses religious activity, some legitimate and some illicit, as a cover for their continuing disobedience to God. Their delusions include thinking that having the temple would save them and that their idols could protect them. Against this, Jeremiah laments the coming desolation of the land and the exile of the people.

**THEOLOGICAL FOCUS**

Religious activity is no substitute for true repentance, obedience, and a living relationship with God. Those who seek to use their "religion" as a cover for a true fear of God may do some things right, but they will exaggerate its significance. They will also insert false beliefs and practices into their religious system.

**PREACHING IDEA**
The melodies of worship should change the motions in our lives.

**PREACHING POINTERS**
The sinful practices of Judah show us how important it is to examine our worship. It is good to step back and evaluate what we do in corporate worship. Most churches have a pattern or order that is followed on most Sundays. The only changes in the routines are the songs sung and the passages preached. The measure of effective worship is not how well we perform these routines that take place on Sunday morning, but how well we live after the worship.

There is a close relationship between worship and living in God's blessing. If we let the ceremonial routines be an end unto themselves, then we are exchanging the worship of routines for the worship of God. And, we are also in danger of terrible sins.

## Jeremiah 8:13–9:26

**EXEGETICAL IDEA**
This passage engages the emotional impact of the sin and suffering of Jerusalem. It is almost entirely a series of laments over what is to come for Jerusalem. This is a model for the modern believer and preacher, who must never rejoice in the sins of others, thinking they are somehow vindicated as righteous because of their neighbor's sins. We do not rejoice that God punished the unrepentant, but lament that they did not repent.

**THEOLOGICAL FOCUS**
These two things are worthy of lamentation: the godless behavior of people, and the terrible outcome of such behavior. Jeremiah grieves that the people have embraced lies, and he also grieves for the price they will pay for following their delusions.

**PREACHING IDEA**
Be ashamed of sin, but proud of God.

**PREACHING POINTERS**
This passage helps us see that shame and sadness can be the very best thing for us. Jeremiah laments with weeping for his people and the coming judgment. He is not a bystander or guest at the funeral of a distant friend; he is a participant. As he recounts the sins and the judgment, he enters the grief with vivid images that expresses his intense grief.

Hopefully our spontaneous response to sin is sadness; but sad to say, it is not always our first response. We need to choose to be upset about our sin. But it doesn't end there, because if we choose sadness for sin, that is a sign that God is working in us. We make it through these seemingly negative emotions not by running from them but by seeing God's hand at work in our lives through them. This is an odd thought: we should feel good that we feel sad about our sin, because our God is at work in our lives.

## Jeremiah 10:1–25

**EXEGETICAL IDEA**
The passage mocks idolatry to make the point that no human creation is worthy of worship. Those who do bow to the work of their own hands bring about their own ruin. This is the last passage that alternates between focus on the lies Judah follows and on the disasters their behavior will bring about. It closes with a prayer that ends this section and prepares the reader for the next section: an intense look at Jeremiah's personal pilgrimage before God, with respect to his relationship to the people of Judah.

**THEOLOGICAL FOCUS**
Everyone must choose between the true God and a man-made lie, and the consequences of that choice are enormous. The Christian too must choose between loyalty to his friends, family, and nation, and his loyalty to God. This is not a matter of becoming aloof and self-righteous, but it is a matter of choosing between following Christ and following the world.

**PREACHING IDEA**
Don't waste your worship.

**PREACHING POINTERS**
When Jeremiah describes how an idol is made and then compares that man-made carving to the Creator, the worship of idols becomes ludicrous. However, it is not just ludicrous; it is sinful and dangerous.

When we see pictures of people in tan-colored robes bowing down to a polished gold statue and throwing flowers on it, we have little or no response. It takes us a moment to realize what they are doing. We just don't see that sort of thing. Jeremiah saw it in Judah and was disgusted. But that is just not done in our western world. Thus, we have a great challenge to present this passage to our *idol-free* world. Our bodies may not bow down, but our hearts and minds regularly pay homage to something or someone other than our Lord.

## Jeremiah 11:1–23

**EXEGETICAL IDEA**
This passage examines human depravity as Jeremiah experienced it in the course of his ministry. Israel has always been unfaithful, and now its depravity is such that even Jeremiah's closest kinship group, the people of his hometown, want to kill him for his preaching. For this reason, Jeremiah with God's help will realize that the nation is incorrigible and that time for pleading that God would spare them has passed.

**THEOLOGICAL FOCUS**

This passage introduces the reader to the process whereby Jeremiah realized he could no longer intercede for Jerusalem. To understand fully God's justice and mercy, we must first understand human depravity. The horrors that accompanied the fall of Jerusalem were so great that those who honestly consider them must wonder if God was too harsh. But if one with equal honesty considers the moral depths to which the people had fallen, God's response is comprehensible. What then becomes astonishing is the promises of grace that appear later in the book.

**PREACHING IDEA**

To understand God's goodness, we must look at our wickedness.

**PREACHING POINTERS**

God's covenant with Israel was clear: worship him only, and do not worship or even make idols. They disobeyed this command almost before it was given, and then continued to disobey this part of the covenant for hundreds of years. The disobedience was so ingrained that they couldn't even hear the command any longer.

While we are not under the same covenant the Jews were under, we still serve the same God, and we still have the same kind of human hearts. Jeremiah's call to Judah and to us is to admit that our hearts are wicked. Though not explicitly stated in this passage, the warning is first to those who *do* listen. To the degree we admit that our hearts are wicked, we will see the goodness of God. The warning is also for those who *do not* listen to him. To the degree they ignore their wicked hearts, they will not see the goodness of God.

## Jeremiah 12:1–13:27

**EXEGETICAL IDEA**

This passage explores two ideas: the gravity of Jerusalem's evil and Jeremiah's awakening to the reality of the people's depravity. It speaks of how Jeremiah tried to intercede for them but got an unexpected response from God—that these people were beyond praying for. Jeremiah had wrongly supposed that only the leaders were bad, but God made him see that the whole nation was corrupt. Two object lessons illustrate this concept, and Jeremiah begins to realize that the people will not repent.

**THEOLOGICAL FOCUS**

Compassion for sinners is right and good, but it should not blind us to the severity of the corruption around us. We should not make empty excuses for sin, saying that some people are merely misled by a few bad influencers. This is not a call for arrogant judgmentalism, but an appeal for us to not mistake our own hopes for a people, often arising from our love and compassion for them, for the truth about them.

**PREACHING IDEA**

Keep your balance, while you can.

**PREACHING POINTERS**

Jeremiah's message is a terrifying warning: Judah will become incorrigible. That is, she will continue in sin to the degree that she cannot stop, and judgment will come. She was at the point of no return and did not know it. When someone is so set in their sinful ways that they won't or can't change, it is called "incorrigible." People today can become incorrigible.

How does the gymnast stay on that four-inch beam? She amazes us as she spins, flips, stands on her hands, and somehow keeps her balance, at least most of time. When she begins to lose her balance, she swings her arms, twists her torso, struggles to regain her balance, and then, unbelievably, stays on the beam. But there is a point when she cannot recover, and gravity takes control. She no longer has a choice; she will fall. In the case of a balance beam, gymnasts know very well when they have lost their balance. Can a person sin so much that he *won't* stop? Then, by continuing in sin, can he come to the point where he *can't* stop? If we are terrified by this possibility, then the message is a blessing because God's Spirit is at work in us. He is calling for repentance. If one is frightened by the warning, they are not incorrigible—yet.

## Jeremiah 14:1–15:9

**EXEGETICAL IDEA**

This text recounts three episodes in which Jeremiah prayed for Jerusalem. In each case, he received a negative response from God. Jerusalem did not fall because Jeremiah failed to pray for them or because he was unworthy; it fell because the people were incorrigibly apostate. This and similar passages exonerate Jeremiah from the charge that the fall of Jerusalem was somehow his fault.

**THEOLOGICAL FOCUS**

Prayer for sinners is the duty of the servant of God, but this does not mean that the servant can always turn aside God's wrath. Jeremiah, in particular, was a great prophet and as such, his words, so to speak, carried great weight with God. Jeremiah was not allowed to waste or misuse his prophetic authority, asking God for something that God could not grant.

**PREACHING IDEA**

We don't know who will be saved; all we know is that we should pray.

**PREACHING POINTERS**

Would that we would be more like Jeremiah. Hmm . . . *should* he be our example? He had to be told to stop praying; in fact, God took time to convince him that he must stop interceding for Judah.

In contrast, we must be convinced to start praying. We hold churchwide prayer events, promote the importance of prayer, and might even provide a meal to bolster attendance. We must be convinced to *start* praying, not to *stop*. In an ironic way, God's word to Jeremiah to not pray becomes our directive to pray. The reason is, we do not have the office of an Old Testament prophet, and God has not revealed to us who will and who will not repent. While God directs Jeremiah to not intercede, the point of this passage is that we should.

## Jeremiah 15:10–17:18

**EXEGETICAL IDEA**

This passage is a decisive turning point in the book. It explores Jeremiah's abandonment of intercession for Judah and his realization that the human heart is incurably evil. As Jeremiah awakens to this reality, he becomes more isolated and frustrated. Still, this text is a vindication of Jeremiah. A complaint against him might be that Jerusalem fell because he was not a great enough prophet to avert disaster. In fact, its destruction was delayed while he prayed for it, and he only stopped because he had to yield to God's demand to stop interceding. He also had to face the facts about the nature of his people. This was not a triumphal moment for Jeremiah; it was the occasion for bitter sorrow.

**THEOLOGICAL FOCUS**

The message that people are wicked is a hard one, and it is hard on the messenger. Perhaps more clearly than anyone in the Old Testament, Jeremiah looked fully into the corruption of the human heart. Knowing that this was true of the people he loved was especially bitter for him. The doctrine of human depravity should always be a source of grief, and not of smug self-righteousness.

**PREACHING IDEA**

A hard message is hard on the messenger.

**PREACHING POINTERS**

This seems like a very negative, downer kind of passage to preach/teach. And it would be, were it not for the promise of redemption, seen briefly in this passage (16:14–15) and reoccurring throughout Scripture.

When we grasp the wickedness of our hearts, we will be reaching for forgiveness and redemption. When the need for forgiveness and redemption is great, so the joy is great when it comes. If we only needed a little help with our hearts, then there would be little joy. It is well worth the pain of admitting that my heart is wicked in order to experience the joy of forgiveness and redemption that comes through the cross. This passage presents an insurmountable problem, with the rest of Scripture providing the solution.

## Jeremiah 17:19–18:23

**EXEGETICAL IDEA**

Judah's refusal to keep the Sabbath led to greater sins, which led to God's warning of judgment and Jeremiah's harsh imprecatory prayer. This passage includes summaries of two of Jeremiah's great sermons: the one delivered at the People's Gate, and the other at a potter's house. The sermons explore the progress of the people's apostasy and the inevitable outcome. These messages appear to have come from early in Jeremiah's ministry and illustrate how he began to realize that the people would not repent. The imprecatory prayer may come from later in his ministry, but indicates how fully he recognized that the people would not change.

### THEOLOGICAL FOCUS

Refusal to repent over little sins will lead to greater sins, which in turn will lead to facing the full fury of God. But Jeremiah realized that his people could not even do a relatively small thing, such as stop working on the Sabbath. Eventually, he saw that their wickedness had become full, and he voiced an especially severe imprecatory prayer against them. The task of a great prophet is to intercede for sinners and avert their destruction, as Moses did in the golden calf incident of Exodus 32. But sometimes this is not possible. Jeremiah did not fail, but his experience was not a happy one.

### PREACHING IDEA

Simple obedience guards against severe disobedience.

### PREACHING POINTERS

The idea of this passage could be dismissed as just being a description of a slippery slope.[1] But that is not what God is saying in this passage. Rather, it is a cause/effect. Jeremiah's two sermons can be summarized: if you sin in everyday simple matters, such as breaking the Sabbath, it will lead to greater sins, such as calling God's will meaningless, rejecting his authority, and calling sin orthodoxy.

While the slippery slope does not carry weight in a formal argument, the slippery slope of sin will carry one into deeper sin. We must remember we are not dealing with logic; we are dealing with the human heart, which is desperately wicked. Jeremiah's imprecation (18:19–23) is not explicitly stated in the preaching idea; however, the concept of *severe disobedience* implies God's wrath.

## Jeremiah 19:1–20:18

### EXEGETICAL IDEA

Jeremiah pronounced a final condemnation against his people, but was profoundly dismayed at how his life and ministry turned out. He gave a scathing condemnation of the city at the Potsherd Gate, and he cursed an apostate temple official named Pashhur. But he was so dismayed at what he had to do that he also cursed the day he was born—an expression of how thoroughly he hated that he should be put in this role.

### THEOLOGICAL FOCUS

A people can become so stubborn in their sin that there is nothing left for a minister to do but pronounce judgment, but for someone who desires to reach people for God there is no more bitter task than this. The preacher's heart will be broken by the incomprehensible, irrational evil of his people, and also by the necessity that he must curse and condemn them.

1 When trying to win an argument some will cite one bad event and say that we must stop this because it leads to something worse. In a general sense it says that because *A* happened eventually *Z* will happen. It is known as logical fallacy sometimes called the slippery slope.

**PREACHING IDEA**
There are times when it is bitter to talk about getting better.

**PREACHING POINTERS**
What Jeremiah did and where he did it are both part of his message. The place was the valley of Hinnom, where infants were sacrificed, which is the reason the nation would be shattered like a flask. Then, the personal opposition from Pashhur could have easily prompted him to deliver this message with an arrogance of self-authority, thinking, "Well, I guess I told them." But Jeremiah responds with such sorrow and grief for his nation that he cursed the day he was born.

No one likes to preach or teach about hell. But we must. This passage shows us that Jeremiah struggled with preaching about God's wrath that was coming on Judah. From his struggle we can find comfort in knowing that it is good to struggle when preaching/teaching about the coming judgment of hell. Of course, we have the luxury of preaching the good news, but we must remember that the good news starts with the bad news. If anyone will desire to be made better by God's gracious work, then the bitter portion of the gospel must be proclaimed first.

## Jeremiah 21:1–23:40

**EXEGETICAL IDEA**
A request from Zedekiah for a favorable oracle from God leads to a lengthy recital of the messages God has sent against the house of David, along with a condemnation of the false prophets. It is likely that Zedekiah had hoped that Jeremiah could provide a miraculous deliverance from the Babylonians, such as had happened in the reign of Hezekiah when the Assyrians besieged Jerusalem. To this, Jeremiah responds that the whole dynasty of David—from Zedekiah back through the reigns of Jehoiachin, Jehoiakim, and Jehoahaz—had become so corrupt that no such salvation was possible.

**THEOLOGICAL FOCUS**
If we have a history of refusing to heed the messages of warning that God has sent us, we cannot expect him to give us a message of hope. God will not extend mercy to those whose habitual apostasy and corruption has reached the maximum. The leadership of the nation, both secular and religious, bears special guilt in this regard.

**PREACHING IDEA**
Ask God for victory (intervention), but don't violate his authority.

**PREACHING POINTERS**
It is wrong to expect God to intervene for us and affirm our work when we are violating his word and worshipping other gods. Some need arises in our life, so we ask him for a victory over the problem, but what is more needed is victory over our disobedient lives and hearts. Of course, we need to ask God for victory in our lives, while being careful not to violate his authority

## Jeremiah 24:1–25:38

**EXEGETICAL IDEA**
God promises to preserve his people and his word in spite of the coming destruction of Judah's leadership and the promise of judgment against all nations. Jeremiah receives a message concerning good figs and bad figs, representing respectively those who will preserve Israel's heritage and create Judaism (the Babylonian exiles) and those who will be entirely destroyed (the people in Jerusalem). And although calamity and exile is certain, it will have an end, after seventy years.

**THEOLOGICAL FOCUS**
God's destruction of human structures and plans does not destroy his purposes or his word. God's people can become so corrupt that harsh judgment is inescapable, but God's purposes do not fail.

**PREACHING IDEA**
What basket do you want to be in?

**PREACHING POINTERS**
God gives us a choice. To use Jeremiah's image, do we choose a basket of fresh fruit or a basket of rotten fruit? Do we choose a rotten life or a good one? The choice for a good life is to submit to God's discipline and obey his clear commands.

## Jeremiah 26:1–29:32

**EXEGETICAL IDEA**
This passage explores how the most severe opposition to Jeremiah came from Judah's religious elite, the priestly officials of the temple and the popular (but false) prophets. This text demonstrates the severity of the hostility of the religious establishment toward Jeremiah. They almost killed him when he preached his great temple sermon, and they did kill another true prophet, Uriah of Kiriath-jearim. By contrast, two false prophets, Hananiah and Shemaiah, were well received as they mocked and opposed Jeremiah.

**THEOLOGICAL FOCUS**
When God's plan includes destroying an old but false tradition, many people will vigorously oppose the change. Apostate ideas create a pseudo-orthodoxy that people will fanatically and violently defend. The great tragedy is that such people believe they are defending the truth. The warning for us is to not confuse our theology with the word of God.

**PREACHING IDEA**
God, you haven't done it that way before.

**PREACHING POINTERS**
When speaking the above phrase, the intonations reveal the attitude toward God and what he is doing. The person who doesn't like or want any change is enraged when something

new comes along, even if that new something is clearly God's hand. In contrast, the person who trusts and submits to God will is encouraged when God is bringing about something new. It is pivotal that the new idea or plan is from God, for just being new does not make it of God. But when God is making changes, we not only need to accept those changes; we need to embrace them and anticipate God's good hand.

## Jeremiah 30:1–31:26

### EXEGETICAL IDEA

God will call Israel back to himself after their punishment, they will repent, and then God will fully restore them. This text is a series of messages that all seem to have come to Jeremiah in a prophetic dream. Israel will be healed of the grievous wounds it has suffered, will be brought back to YHWH and the land, and will stop wandering in search of salvation among foreign gods and foreign powers.

### THEOLOGICAL FOCUS

After repentance comes the joys of restoration. Israel, the chosen of God, had to experience severe pain as part of the process of its salvation and purification. We who are grafted into Israel and who have our own guilt to contend with should not suppose that our experience will be different.

### PREACHING IDEA

Come home to our accepting, restorative God.

### PREACHING POINTERS

Why do we hesitate to go to someone to restore a relationship? Simply put: fear. We don't know how they will respond. God made it clear to Israel, and to us, when our sin breaks the relationship with him; he wants us to know what it is like to return to him. It is a pleasant dream.

## Jeremiah 31:27–40

### EXEGETICAL IDEA

God will give Israel the new covenant to replace the Sinai covenant, in order to correct the failings of the latter. The Sinai covenant depended on Israel's ability to faithfully perform "all the words of this law that are written in this book" (Deut. 28:58). The new covenant depends on the faithfulness and compassion of God alone, as well as on his determination to bring about salvation for all true Israel. The people will acknowledge their guilt, but it will be removed from them. And unlike Sinai, the new covenant will never be terminated.

### THEOLOGICAL FOCUS

The new covenant is given to the "house of Israel and the house of Judah." But because even we Gentiles are now grafted into Israel, it belongs to all God's people, and all can celebrate this ongoing great work of God. God did not abandon Israel to destruction, and in like manner he has not abandoned the nations.

**PREACHING IDEA**
Come, join the celebration!

**PREACHING POINTERS**
The New Testament is very clear that believers in Jesus are included in the new covenant; thus, it has been inaugurated. And there is still more of the new covenant to be experienced in the future. In the past, Israel could have celebrated what God would do in the future. Today, believers celebrate what God has already started. And in the future, all will celebrate what God will have finished.

## Jeremiah 32:1–44

**EXEGETICAL IDEA**
Jeremiah purchases a piece of land, and this becomes a prophetic sign for the coming redemption of Israel. It implies that the land, which will be burnt over and trampled by foreign armies, will again belong to Israel and be fruitful.

**THEOLOGICAL FOCUS**
When things seem hopeless, a simple act can demonstrate faith that God still has a future for us. But this is not a matter of optimism, of merely hoping for the best in the face of severe danger. For Jeremiah's generation, the worst possible outcome does in fact happen. But God, who raises the dead, can bring about an astonishing and seemingly impossible reversal of the judgment.

**PREACHING IDEA**
Hope in God's future; nothing is impossible for him.

**PREACHING POINTERS**
When buying a house, we put great trust in the real estate agent. Is this a good price? Is it a wise investment? When Jeremiah was purchasing property, he had only one question. "Why should I buy a piece of land when the nation is about to be destroyed?" The answer was direct: because God told him to. This was a living illustration. What would Zedekiah and Judah think of this? It didn't make sense on the surface, so it demanded deeper thinking. Perhaps some of them would discover the deeper meaning that nothing was impossible for God. Though destruction was imminent, he still had a good future for Israel.

There are so many different stories of hopelessness in our congregations. God knows that often it is hard for us to believe that his future for us is good, so he employs a method of communication that helps us truly believe this. He tells a story and wants us to discover the meaning. When we discover a meaning or draw a conclusion, we are much more likely to believe it. Jeremiah buys land, which was investing in the future when there doesn't seem to be a future. God still has a good future for us.

## Jeremiah 33:1–26

**EXEGETICAL IDEA**

The desolate city will be restored and have a glory that surpasses anything in its past. This magnificent future that God is preparing centers on the Davidic Messiah. The historical house of David, now broken and cast down into the dust, has an enduring, eschatological future in a great act of God.

**THEOLOGICAL FOCUS**

With the death of Zedekiah, the historical Davidic dynasty came to an end. As a human institution, it never has and never will return. But God's promises are more enduring than any crisis in any historical context. A new Davidic king will give his people a kingdom not of this world.

**PREACHING IDEA**

You can't beat God's promises.

**PREACHING POINTERS**

"Call to Me, and I will answer you, and I will tell you great and mighty things, which you do not know" (33:3 NASB). This often-quoted verse has a deeper meaning when "mighty" is more correctly translated "unassailable." As Jeremiah describes the coming events of Jerusalem being gloriously restored and even a Davidic king to rule, it must have been hard for the Jews to believe. Their own lack of trust in God's power was an affront to, or attack on, the promise.

The focus of the text is God's amazing promises to Israel and to us. The correct understanding of the opening metaphor (vv. 2–3) of a fortress leads us to the awareness that though God's promises are wonderful and beyond our imaginations, they still come under attack. Opposition comes from the forces of evil, but also from our own hearts. These promises become even more real if we will acknowledge that our lack of faith in God will, in a sense, attack them. We must come to the point of surrendering our doubts and embracing belief in these glorious promises that God makes.

## Jeremiah 34:1–35:19

**EXEGETICAL IDEA**

The passage contrasts and explores the gross disobedience of the leaders of Jerusalem, who quickly broke a newly made covenant with YHWH, with the fidelity of the Rechabites, who zealously kept their ancestral traditions. Taken together, the two chapters contrast the behavior of the two groups and demonstrate how dishonest and faithless the leaders of Jerusalem had become, a matter already explored earlier in the book. These texts also illustrate how the structure of the book is more concerned with thematic continuity than with chronological sequence. The episode of chapter 35 took place more than a decade before the events of chapter 34.

**THEOLOGICAL FOCUS**

An example of simple faithfulness puts to shame the extravagant but hollow pretense of those who merely claim to be God's people. The pretense of obedience acted out by the Jerusalem nobility was impulsive and ephemeral. The determined fidelity of the Rechabites was a matter of consistent habit and deep commitment. Zedekiah and those around him had forgotten what it meant to place honor and integrity above convenience.

**PREACHING IDEA**

Don't go for a good deal; go for a good life.

**PREACHING POINTERS**

These two chapters are narratives; thus, the telling of the stories is of high importance. To make his point, Jeremiah employs a universal structure of the bad compared to the good. Zedekiah appears to be obedient, but in the end we see that he is just trying to make a deal with God. In contrast, the Rechabites are simply living out a lifestyle of a submissive heart.

Our culture is filled with a desire to make a good deal. The best deal is the win-win scenario, where both parties end up getting what they lack or need. When we try to make a deal with God, we forget that he has already won. There is nothing we have that he needs or lacks. He does, however, want our lifestyle to be one of submissive obedience.

## Jeremiah 36:1–32

**EXEGETICAL IDEA**

The incident described here, in which Jehoiakim destroyed a scroll containing an oracular message from Jeremiah, demonstrates how bitterly and completely the royal house and the aristocracy were opposed to the word of God. As described in the introduction, it also tells us how what originally was a loose collection of sermon transcripts and letters from Jeremiah began to take shape as the book of Jeremiah. It, like Jeremiah's realization that he could no longer intercede for the people, is a decisive moment in the prophet's story.

**THEOLOGICAL FOCUS**

A decisive rejection of the word of God leads to decisive ruin. Also, attempts to eradicate the word of God inevitably fail. Through his blasphemous actions, Jehoiakim showed himself to be one of the great reprobates of the Bible. When Josiah heard the Law read aloud, he tore his garments in grief and repentance. When his son Jehoiakim heard the scroll of Jeremiah read aloud, he tore up the scroll and burned it.

**PREACHING IDEA**

Rejection of the written Word of God is a rejection of God and leads to ruin.

**PREACHING POINTERS**

Baruch was to write down all the words that God gave to Jeremiah. This was no simple task; it must have taken weeks, perhaps months of work. Thus, the written copy is a very valuable and costly item. When Jehoiakim burns the scroll, it was not like the modern burning of a single copy of a book that has thousands of copies still usable. This was the only copy. Jehoiakim's rejection of God's message cannot be missed or overstated; it was as if he was trying to erase the words that had been spoken.

This story is presented in such a way as to show that Baruch's written copy of God's words to Jeremiah is equal in authority to the spoken words of Jeremiah. To reject the written words is to reject the spoken words. Of course, the application of those words in the church today will vary from the direct application for the ancient Jews. The thrust is that God's written Word is the same as his spoken words.

## Jeremiah 37:1–39:18

### EXEGETICAL IDEA

This is a tightly bound, coherent text that focuses on the differing attitudes of the nobility, Zedekiah, and Ebed-melek toward Jeremiah. The passage centers on three messages given to Zedekiah, who is not utterly wicked but is weak and yields to pressure from the nobility to silence Jeremiah. This contrasts with the faith and integrity of Ebed-melek the Cushite, who saves Jeremiah from a wretched death. In the end, it is the Babylonians who save Jeremiah from the brutal treatment he has gotten from his own countrymen and who release him after capturing the city.

### THEOLOGICAL FOCUS

In times of crisis and polarization, some will love and some will hate those who bear God's Word, while others will yield to social pressure to join in the hostility. In this passage, the foreigners recognize the authority of Jeremiah while the Jerusalem aristocracy despises him.

### PREACHING IDEA

Choose to respect, then expect to be blessed.

### PREACHING POINTERS

The passage presents the hostility of the Jewish leaders toward Jeremiah, the fluctuation of Zedekiah and the respect that comes from Ebed-melek. It begins with the prophecy of condemnation to Zedekiah and his rejection of Jeremiah. The height of the hostility toward Jeremiah comes when he is thrown into the cistern. The passage ends with Ebed-melek and the affirming prophecy given to him.

This is a tricky passage because the thrust is about attitudes toward us who are preachers and teachers. Complicating this is the difficult structure. These must not hinder the proclamation of truth. The passage presents the hostility of the Jewish leaders toward Jeremiah, the fluctuation of Zedekiah, and the respect that comes from Ebed-melek. This gives us clear examples of what our attitudes toward those who proclaim the message of God could be. This passage not only teaches that we should give respect, but that when we do we are blessed just as Ebed-melek was.

## Jeremiah 40:1–41:18

### EXEGETICAL IDEA

The violent zealotry and ambition of one man, Ishmael son of Nethaniah, destroyed the possibility of a peaceful and prosperous Jewish community continuing in the land. Although the sin was not God's doing, it fulfilled his purpose of sending all the Jews into exile, obliterating any Jewish state in the former Judah. The story also reveals the moral chaos of the exilic Jerusalem community. It was a place where, even in the midst of the calamity of the fall of the city, people could behave with a complete lack of moral principles. The most dangerous thing one could do was trust another man and take his words at face value.

### THEOLOGICAL FOCUS

God uses even human evil to fulfill his purposes. For God's redemptive purposes to be fulfilled, all that remained of preexilic Judah had to be swept away. Indeed, chapter 44 reveals that many of the Jews still in the land at the time of Gedaliah's murder were deeply committed to paganism. When the postexilic Jews returned from Babylon, they would start the community again with a clean slate.

### PREACHING IDEA

When you can't stop crying, don't stop trusting in God.

### PREACHING POINTERS

This narrative follows the tragic fall of Jerusalem and the horrific end of Zedekiah's life. The beginning of this story gives us a hint that things might get better, that Judah will survive even though dominated by Babylon. Signs of prosperity begin to grow under Gedaliah's leadership, but this ends with his murder. Since he was appointed by Babylon, the Jews expect even greater destruction because of Nebuchadnezzar's wrath. What little hope they had is gone. Judah is completely destroyed. Nothing is left in the Promised Land. Even in this continuing desolation, Jeremiah was calling Judah to trust YHWH.

It is not wrong to hope for better times, nor even to ask God to bring those times about. Often, he does. But what about when the cancer comes back, when the children and parents are not reconciled, when the addiction becomes a lifestyle, when the pain doesn't go away? Sometimes eyes full of tears can best focus on the true object of our faith: a loving sovereign Lord.

## Jeremiah 42:1–43:7

### EXEGETICAL IDEA

The Jews, in a panic over whether the Babylonians would come down upon them in severe reprisal for the murder of Gedaliah (whom Babylon had appointed as governor), asked Jeremiah to seek God's direction over whether they should flee the land and head into Egypt. They assured him they would do whatever God directed. When told to stay in the land, they immediately and angrily rejected the directive and ran for the Egyptian border. The survivors in exilic Judah thus proved to be as unreliable about their willingness to obey God as they had been before the Babylonian conquest.

**THEOLOGICAL FOCUS**
The obstinacy of people demonstrates that God's punishment is just. God's promise that the people would be safe if they stayed in the land was genuine, but in the larger theology of the book, the episode illustrates how obstinate the people were, and it shows that the exile had to be total for it to be effective.

**PREACHING IDEA**
If you ask God for help, accept his answer.

**PREACHING POINTERS**
It seemed logical that the Babylonians would severely punish Judah for killing Gedaliah. Therefore, the best course would be to flee. It would seem that the circumstances God allowed led in that direction. However, God did not send these Jews to Egypt, where they would suffer and die. Rather, they chose to reject God's offer of life.

To this day, people reject God's offer. Our attitude toward those who reject God's offer must not be that they are the enemy, nor should we look down on them in pity; rather, we should patiently proclaim God's offer of life. This rejection should also be a warning to us. While our acceptance of his gift of life through Jesus gives us a secure eternal relationship with him, it does not mean that we won't reject his expectations of us. Our disobedience does not take away the gift, but it does bring his discipline.

## Jeremiah 43:8–44:30

**EXEGETICAL IDEA**
God has repudiated the Jews who fled to Egypt: they are still under judgment, they will not create or sustain orthodox Judaism, and they will not flourish. This text condemns the exiles in Egypt in two phases. First, Jeremiah warns them that they cannot escape God's judgment by running to Egypt. Second, his confrontation with the people demonstrated that they were still devoted to pagan deities, and especially to the "Queen of Heaven."

**THEOLOGICAL FOCUS**
Those who flee, unrepentant, from God's judgment remain permanently under it. We cannot escape guilt and God's wrath by moving to a different place. And a change of location will do nothing to change our hearts. The Jews in Egypt remained as passionately devoted to the Queen of Heaven as they had been before, and they even blamed the fall of Jerusalem on a failure to honor her. This text also demonstrates that the future of the Jews lay with the Babylonian community and not with the survivors in Jerusalem (24:1–10).

**PREACHING IDEA**
Move beyond insecurity; trust God, the only true security.

**PREACHING POINTERS**
God's messages to Judah, through Jeremiah, continued even though they had exiled themselves to Egypt. This shows God's continuing grace. Judah went beyond rejecting his warning.

They had to take great initiative and effort to disobey him; it was no small task to move the remaining nation to Egypt. And in Egypt, they bowed down to the Queen of Heaven. Even so, God continued to speak. Perhaps Judah finally believed that Jeremiah's words were true when they saw the armies of Babylon invading Egypt.

This pericope has a two-part application. The first part is a theme common throughout Scripture, which Augustine wonderfully articulated years ago and has been repeated numerous times: "You have made us for yourself, O Lord, and our hearts are restless until they rest in you." The Jews were seeking safety and rest by depending upon Egypt instead of YHWH. The second application is a built-in consequence for a misplaced source of security. If our security lies in anything or anyone other than God it is sure that, one day, it will fail. The only way to get beyond insecurities is to look to God for security, and to rest in him.

## Jeremiah 45:1–5

### EXEGETICAL IDEA
This event took place in the fourth year of Jehoiakim, long before the events narrated in chapter 44. It illustrates again that the book is organized thematically and not chronologically. This comes at the end of a series of texts dealing with the trials of Jeremiah's prophetic career, and it makes the point that those who align themselves with the truth will suffer along with the heroes of the faith. Baruch was distressed over how his association with Jeremiah was costing him everything; but through Jeremiah, God reminded him that soon there would be nothing worth having in Jerusalem. Baruch's loss of prestige and outward success would matter little when the city was in flames.

### THEOLOGICAL FOCUS
Serving God in times of crisis requires focus and commitment, even on the part of those who are in a subordinate role. God rebukes Baruch for his desire to hold on to the outward trappings of success, but he also reassures him. When all of Judah was a ruin, God would still preserve the faithful scribe.

### PREACHING IDEA
Recognize God's future work, not your past accomplishments.

### PREACHING POINTERS
God's message to Baruch was twofold. God's word directed him in what he should not do, and then in what God would do for him. Often a command to not do something is followed by a positive command of what to do. This is different. God says to Baruch, and to us, "Don't seek recognition for what you have done; recognize what I will do."

One might think that the negative command to not seek great things for yourself would be followed by the positive command to seek great things for God. Perhaps we seek great things for ourselves because we think that by focusing on our great accomplishments of the past, we can somehow ensure a great future. But instead, God follows with a command to trust him with the future.

## Jeremiah 46:1–49:39

### EXEGETICAL IDEA
Each oracle represents some aspect of God's judgment against the nations. All the oracles have three things in common. First, each state, like Judah, faces God's judgment and is destined for defeat at the hands of the Babylonians. Second, each state, unlike Judah, has no hope for a future restoration. Third, Jeremiah does not engage in triumphalist gloating over the fall of the Gentile states. He views the death and destruction that will befall them as tragic and lamentable. Beyond that, each oracle has its own characteristics, as explored below.

### THEOLOGICAL FOCUS
Like Israel, the other nations of the world will be judged, and it will happen in accordance with the principles found in these oracles. Amos 3:2 says, "You alone have I known from all the families of the earth; for that reason, I will punish you for all your iniquities." It is not that Israel alone was judged, and it is not that being the chosen people confers immunity from punishment. But if judgment starts at the house of God, it will surely reach all people.

### PREACHING IDEA
Your arm is too short to box with God.

### PREACHING POINTERS
Without God's judgments, his grace and mercy are not needed. This passage helps us see that he is a God who judges. He judges not only his chosen people, his family, but he judges all. He gives us clear pictures of what and how he judges. From these nine judgments on the nations we can see some universal characteristics of his judgment that apply to us.

God's judgment will come someday, but it will come—and it won't leave any sin unpunished. And in the fuller revelation: God is merciful in his judgment, because through Christ's amazing work we can receive mercy.

## Jeremiah 50:1–51:64

### EXEGETICAL IDEA
Babylon, the enemy of God and his people, will be annihilated. The text is in two parts, with the first and very lengthy portion being a prediction that Babylon will fall and be swallowed by the sands of the desert, but that the Jews will endure. The second is a brief account of the mission of Seraiah, Baruch's brother, to deliver a symbolic act predicting Babylon's demise.

### THEOLOGICAL FOCUS
The depiction of the destruction of Babylon concerns the end of Babylon's historical dominion but also represents the complete demise of imperial power that sets itself against the kingdom of God. Babylon, from the building of the tower in Genesis 11 to the demise of the great harlot in Revelation 18, has always been always representative of the ideal of the power, wealth, and ideological dominance of the human kingdom over against the kingdom of God. The fall of historical Babylon is a sign that the ideal Babylon represents will fall before Jesus and his kingdom.

**PREACHING IDEA**
Don't take part in what God is against.

**PREACHING POINTERS**
Apparently, these prophesies against Babylon were presented to the Babylonians. That would be one tough preaching assignment. But interspersed in the judgment of Babylon are directives and affirmations to Israel. This message is not just to announce judgment on Babylon, but to give guidance to Israel and to us.

God knows that the Jews of that era and his children of today live in the midst of nations which are guilty of systemic and cultural sins. So what are we to do? God made it clear that the Jews were not to stay in Babylon any longer than they had to. He warned them not to see themselves as a permanent part of that nation. No matter the nation in which we live, all are affected by evil. Thus, we must not see any nation as the basis for our true identity. While we are to be good citizens of the physical nation in which we live, we must remember that this is not our permanent residence. We must evaluate what is around us and be careful to not be for, let alone take part in, what God is against.

## Jeremiah 52:1–34

**EXEGETICAL IDEA**
Jeremiah 52 vindicates the prophet; all his dire predictions came true. The chapter, much of it almost a word-for-word repeat of 2 Kings 24:18–25:30, describes Zedekiah's wretched fate, Jerusalem's fall, the fate of the captives, and the final gift of a bit of dignity to the aged and hapless Jehoiachin. In 2 Kings, the text narrates the sad end of the Davidic kingdom. Although it does that here too, the implied lesson is the vindication of Jeremiah's status as the true prophet of God.

**THEOLOGICAL FOCUS**
People may despise the word of God, but in the end it will be proven true. The lies by which the people lived, and which Jeremiah explores so thoroughly in the beginning of the book, inevitably brought about their ruin. All those who called him a traitor and even a blasphemer were proven wrong by the hard facts of history. Jeremiah is vindicated.

**PREACHING IDEA**
God tells us so.

**PREACHING POINTERS**
We hear again the events of Zedekiah's terrible end, the temple being burned, and the nation taken into exile. Why did God end with this summary of how his judgments of sin came to pass? Does he want to berate Israel? He does not need to build up his self-image by saying, "I told you so."

This summary reinforces that we can trust what he says. And what he says is very simple: disobey and face judgment; obey and enjoy his blessings. It really is that simple. As a reminder, our obedience does not earn God's blessings. Our obedience puts us into a position to receive and enjoy those blessings, and our disobedience separates us from them.

## Lamentations 1:1–22

**EXEGETICAL IDEA**
The passage explores the suffering of Jerusalem under the personification of the city as a woman. The poem is divided between the parts where Jerusalem herself is the speaker and those where the poet is the speaker. The personification is meant to provoke compassion and sorrow in the reader: a beautiful mother has been ravished and laid low.

**THEOLOGICAL FOCUS**
Jerusalem the beautiful city of God is fallen and destitute. Although the text does not deny her guilt, it focuses on her suffering. When a society is brought down by sin and folly, much that is beautiful is destroyed alongside the ugly. Divine wrath is just, but it is still horrible.

**PREACHING IDEA**
We are invited to feel the hurt.

**PREACHING POINTERS**
The application of this book and this first lament will stretch most pastor/teachers. The image of a widow weeping was more intense in the ancient world because much of a family's welfare was dependent upon the husband. But even with the cultural difference the feelings of pain and grief still come through. At the funeral service for a faithful husband the feelings of grief are intensified when the widow is seated.

The poet is inviting us to share Israel's pain for her sins. We are not to stand on the sidelines and say "poor Israel." Rather we, by way of the genre of poetry, are invited to feel the pain with Israel. God, through this text, is asking us to feel something, and to let the feeling become a part of how we feel about the consequences of all sin—our sins and those of others.

## Lamentations 2:1–22

**EXEGETICAL IDEA**
This poem approaches Jerusalem's calamity from a prophetic perspective, describing all that happened as the work of God. Although guilt and punishment are part of this, the focus is on God's control of events. One cannot complain to God while denying that he is the sovereign over all that happens in the world. This focus allows the poem to move toward prayer and intercession after the lament, since God remains sovereign over all things. He who struck Israel is the only one who can save Israel.

**THEOLOGICAL FOCUS**
The reader should understand that Jerusalem's fall did not come about simply because of poor leadership in Judah or aggressive enemies in Babylon. These things, too, were orchestrated by God (not in a deterministic sense, but as a response to Israelite apostasy). Appreciating

divine rule over all things, the readers can respond with a prayer for mercy, knowing that divine sovereignty does not contradict the need for prayer.

**PREACHING IDEA**
When the pain comes in, the cry should go up.

**PREACHING POINTERS**
There is no wondering about the source of Israel's pain. Clearly God is the one bringing disaster upon his people. God seems to be the enemy because the destruction is so severe. But the object of the lament is equally clear. God is the one to whom the people cry.

When we are in pain, no matter the cause or the reason, we cry out in some way. Perhaps it is a literal cry or silent cry within our minds and spirits. The passage does not explain why God allows or causes pain, but it does direct us to cry out to him. Crying out to him doesn't mean that the pain will go away. But when we cry out to him, it brings purpose and significance to our cries because he is the one who has a reason and a purpose, and we can trust him.

## Lamentations 3:1–66

**EXEGETICAL IDEA**
One single man serves as the voice of the people, and he is a paradigm of both suffering and faith. He laments over the city, expresses his extreme pain, declares his unwavering faith in God, appeals to the people to repent and pray, and himself prays in hope that God will set all things right. He is the ideal of how the devout should respond to the calamity.

**THEOLOGICAL FOCUS**
The singular man of Lamentations 3 takes on the role of the suffering servant of YHWH. In this, he is a model for all readers, in that he maintains his righteousness and devotion to God while he suffers terribly and is fully aware of how badly the people have sinned. The ideal is especially fulfilled in Jesus, but all who belong to God should imitate the model set forth in this text.

**PREACHING IDEA**
Embrace (accept) the suffering and the Savior.

**PREACHING POINTERS**
This longest of the laments is like a solo sung by a righteous man who sings while Jerusalem crumbles around him. His song doesn't gloss over his suffering; in fact, he describes it with vivid and powerful images such as teeth grinding on gravel and tears flowing like a river. But his song also has the delightful expression of God's faithfulness in 3:22–23, which is made all the more precious when we see it in light of the suffering that is expressed in this lament and in the context of the other four laments. And while it gives us hope in suffering, that is not all that God wants us to know and do when we are suffering. This lament guides us through suffering to embrace the suffering, but more importantly to embrace the Savior.

## Lamentations 4:1–22

**EXEGETICAL IDEA**

This text is an unflinching presentation of the suffering, terror, and tragedy of Jerusalem's conquest and captivity. We must see the horrors of Jerusalem's fall for what they are, and not turn our heads and move on, simply saying that the people got the punishment they deserved. Although most of us are Gentile Christians, we read this as people who have been adopted into Israel and participate in both its promises and its tragedies.

**THEOLOGICAL FOCUS**

The suffering of Jerusalem and the Jews for their apostasy is unspeakable, and yet must be spoken. We must not preach over this event coldly and clinically, and certainly not judgmentally, as though it had nothing to do with us. The poem calls on us to participate in their grief just as we would grieve some terrible shame and calamity that befell our great-grandparents.

**PREACHING IDEA**

Really? Sin can do that?

**PREACHING POINTERS**

This chapter contains some of the most horrifying images in the Bible, that of cannibalism. But the degradation plummets to depths that become unbelievably despicable: mothers boiling their children. In this lament the terrifying high cost of sin is graphically described.

The illustration of a frog in the pot of water over a flame which is gradually heated is often used to explain that little sins, uncorrected, can lead to a disaster, without the person even noticing that things are progressively getting worse. This chapter shatters the pot and lets the full heat of the results of sin come all at once. The horrific result of sin described in this passage should shock us and compel us to full obedience toward God, and to hold spiritual leaders accountable to do the same.

## Lamentations 5:1–22

**EXEGETICAL IDEA**

The poem is entirely a prayer, and it appeals to God to end the Jewish suffering. The interpreter must not emphasize ideas that are only slightly present, if present at all. The poem accurately reflects the grief and bewilderment of the Jewish people, but it says little about the apostasy that brought the disaster upon them. One should read the prayer sympathetically but not deny that something is missing in the prayer.

**THEOLOGICAL FOCUS**

The Jews will continue to suffer abuse until the great day of their redemption occurs. This is not an occasion for triumphalist boasting against the Jews. It is a sad recognition, in the spirit of Romans 9–11, that Israel's travail will continue until they look upon him whom they have pierced (Zech. 12:10).

**PREACHING IDEA**

When we suffer because of sin, seek God more than the end of the suffering.

**PREACHING POINTERS**

"Lord, remember" and "Lord, restore"—these are the two prayers of this closing lament. In between these two short prayers is the description of Israel's sufferings and their confessions of the sin that led to the suffering. Israel cries out to God for help, and she cries out to God in confession.

The ending of this book of painful experiences is not what most of us would write. When we are hurting, our loudest cry is for the pain to stop. To be sure, there is physical pain that is so intense that every part of our being—mental, spiritual, and physical—will do everything to end the pain. But when there is pain that comes from God's hand due to sin, our cry should not be "Lord, stop the pain." It should be "Lord, restore me . . . to you."

# ABBREVIATIONS

## GENERAL ABBREVIATIONS

| | |
|---|---|
| A.D. | in the year of our Lord (*anno Domini*) |
| ANE | ancient Near East[ern] |
| B.C. | Before Christ |
| DSS | Dead Sea Scrolls |
| EB | English Bible(s) |
| HB | Hebrew Bible |
| LXX | Septuagint (the Greek OT) |
| MT | Masoretic Text |
| NT | New Testament |
| OT | Old Testament |
| SP | Samaritan Pentateuch |

## TECHNICAL ABBREVIATIONS

| | |
|---|---|
| absol. | absolute (free form) |
| acc. | accusative |
| aor. | aorist |
| appos. | appositional |
| ca. | circa |
| cf. | compare (*confer*) |
| ch(s). | chapter(s) |
| com. | common gender |
| comp. | completed by |
| conj. | conjunction |
| const. | construct (bound form) |
| CV | consonant–vowel (open syllable) |
| CVC | consonant–vowel–consonant (closed syllable) |
| edit. | edition |
| ed(s). | editor(s) |
| e.g. | for example (*exempli gratia*) |
| esp. | especially |
| et al. | and others (*et alii*) |
| etc. | and so forth, and the rest (*et cetera*) |
| fem. | feminine |
| ff. | following pages |
| gen. | genitive |

| | |
|---|---|
| Gk. | Greek |
| Heb. | Hebrew |
| i.e. | that is (*id est*) |
| impf. | imperfect |
| impv. | imperative |
| inf. | infinitive |
| lit. | literally |
| masc. | masculine |
| ms(s). | manuscript(s) |
| n. | note; footnote |
| neg. | negative; negation |
| nom. | nominal/nominative |
| n.p. | no page number |
| obj. | object |
| obj. gen. | objective genitive |
| parag. | paragraph |
| part. | particle |
| pass. | passive |
| perf. | perfect |
| pl. | plural |
| ptc. | participle |
| sg. | singular |
| rev. | revision |
| § (*pl.* §§) | section(s) |
| subj. gen. | subjective genitive |
| s.v. | under the word (*sub verbo*) |
| trans. | translator(s) |
| v(v). | verse(s) |
| vol(s). | volume(s) |

## BIBLICAL SOURCES

### *Old Testament*

| | |
|---|---|
| Gen. | Genesis |
| Exod. | Exodus |
| Lev. | Leviticus |
| Num. | Numbers |
| Deut. | Deuteronomy |
| Josh. | Joshua |
| Judg. | Judges |
| Ruth | Ruth |
| 1 Sam. | 1 Samuel |
| 2 Sam. | 2 Samuel |
| 1 Kings | 1 Kings |
| 2 Kings | 2 Kings |
| 1 Chron. | 1 Chronicles |
| 2 Chron. | 2 Chronicles |
| Ezra | Ezra |
| Neh. | Nehemiah |
| Esther | Esther |
| Job | Job |
| Ps./Pss. | Psalm(s) |

***Old Testament (continued)***

| | |
|---|---|
| Prov. | Proverbs |
| Eccl. | Ecclesiastes |
| Song | Song of Songs |
| Isa. | Isaiah |
| Jer. | Jeremiah |
| Lam. | Lamentations |
| Ezek. | Ezekiel |
| Dan. | Daniel |
| Hos. | Hosea |
| Joel | Joel |
| Amos | Amos |
| Obad. | Obadiah |
| Jonah | Jonah |
| Mic. | Micah |
| Nah. | Nahum |
| Hab. | Habakkuk |
| Zeph. | Zephaniah |
| Hag. | Haggai |
| Zech. | Zechariah |
| Mal. | Malachi |

***New Testament***

| | |
|---|---|
| Matt. | Matthew |
| Mark | Mark |
| Luke | Luke |

***New Testament (continued)***

| | |
|---|---|
| John | John |
| Acts | Acts |
| Rom. | Romans |
| 1 Cor. | 1 Corinthians |
| 2 Cor. | 2 Corinthians |
| Gal. | Galatians |
| Eph. | Ephesians |
| Phil. | Philippians |
| Col. | Colossians |
| 1 Thess. | 1 Thessalonians |
| 2 Thess. | 2 Thessalonians |
| 1 Tim. | 1 Timothy |
| 2 Tim. | 2 Timothy |
| Titus | Titus |
| Philem. | Philemon |
| Heb. | Hebrews |
| James | James |
| 1 Peter | 1 Peter |
| 2 Peter | 2 Peter |
| 1 John | 1 John |
| 2 John | 2 John |
| 3 John | 3 John |
| Jude | Jude |
| Rev. | Revelation |

## HEBREW SYNTACTICAL TERMS

| Verbal Stems | Function | Voice |
|---|---|---|
| *qal* | The basic stem (no particular nuance intended) | active |
| *niphal* | passive | passive |
| *hiphil* | The so-called causative stem (nuances of agency, repetition, etc.) | active |
| *hophal* | | passive |
| *piel* | The so-called strengthened stem (active voice; intensity, repetition, etc.) | active |
| *pual* | | passive |
| *hithpael* | Reflexive | active |

| Verbal States | Basic Function | Form | Tense(s) | Mood(s) |
|---|---|---|---|---|
| Perfect (perf.) or *qatal* | Completed action | Suffixed pronouns | past | Indicative; Volitional |
| Inverted perf. or *weqatal* | Incomplete action | Suffixed pronouns | future | Indicative; Volitional |
| Imperfect (impf.) or *yiqtol* | Incomplete action | Prefixed pronouns | future; present | Indicative; Volitional;* Precative/permissive** (jussive; cohortative) |
| Inverted impf. *wayyiqtol* | Completed action | Prefixed pronouns | past | |
| Imperative (impv.) | Command | Suffixed pronouns | NA | Indicative |
| Infinitive (infin.) | Adverbial; purpose et al. | Suffixed pronouns | NA | NA |

*Verbs are indicative or volitional when stating certainty (it is, will be; I will do).
**Verbs are precative or permissive when stating possibility (it may/might or could/should be).

## EXTRABIBLICAL SOURCES

### *Apocrypha*

| | |
|---|---|
| Sir | Wisdom of Jesus the Son of Sirach (Ecclesiasticus) |
| Bar | Baruch |
| 3 Macc | 3 Maccabees |
| 4 Esd | 4 Esdras |

### *Old Testament Pseudepigrapha*

| | |
|---|---|
| 2 Bar. | 2 Baruch (Syriac Apocalypse) |
| 4 Ezra | 4 Ezra |

### *Papyrii*

| | |
|---|---|
| *P.Oxy.* | *The Oxyrhynchus Papyri* |
| *P.Par.* | *The Paris Papyri* |
| *P.Wisc.* | *The Wisconsin Papyri* |

### *Apostolic Fathers*

| | |
|---|---|
| Did. | Didache |
| Diogn. | Diognetus |
| Ignatius (of Antioch) | Syrian bishop, church father; ca. A.D. 50–ca. 110 |
| *Eph.* | *To the Ephesians* |

## PERIODICALS

| | |
|---|---|
| *AJ* | *The Asbury Journal* |
| *AJA* | *American Journal of Archaeology* |
| *BSac* | *Bibliotheca Sacra* |
| *BT* | *The Bible Translator* |
| *CBQ* | *The Catholic Biblical Quarterly* |
| *EvQ* | *Evangelical Quarterly* |
| *Int* | *Interpretation* |
| *JBL* | *Journal of Biblical Literature* |
| *JETS* | *Journal of the Evangelical Theological Society* |
| *JSNT* | *Journal for the Study of the New Testament* |
| *JSPL* | *Journal for the Study of Paul and His Letters* |
| *JTS* | *Journal of Theological Studies* |
| *MJT* | *Midwestern Theological Journal* |
| *NTS* | *New Testament Studies* |
| *PTR* | *Princeton Theological Review* |
| *SJOT* | *Scandinavian Journal of the Old Testament* |
| *SJT* | *Scottish Journal of Theology* |
| *ST* | *Studia Theologica* |
| *VT* | *Vetus Testamentum* |
| *WTJ* | *Westminster Theological Journal* |

## SERIES

| | |
|---|---|
| AB | Anchor Bible |
| ASBT | Acadia Studies in Biblical Theology |
| BNTC | Black's New Testament Commentaries |
| EGGNT | Exegetical Guide to the Greek New Testament |
| ICC | International Critical Commentary |
| JRASS | Journal of Roman Archaeology Supplementary Series |
| JSNTSup | Journal for the Study of the New Testament Supplement Series |
| JSOT | Journal for the Study of the Old Testament (Press) |
| KEK | Kritisch-exegetischer Kommentar über das Neue Testament (Meyer-Kommentar) |
| LCL | Loeb Classical Library |
| LNTS | Library of New Testament Studies |
| NAC | New American Commentary |
| NCBC | New Century Bible Commentary |
| NCC | New Covenant Commentary |
| NICNT | New International Commentary on the New Testament |
| NICOT | New International Commentary on the Old Testament |
| NIGTC | New International Greek Testament Commentary |
| NIVAC | New International Version Application Commentary |
| NTL | New Testament Library |

| | |
|---|---|
| OTL | Old Testament Library |
| PCNT | Paideia: Commentaries on the New Testament |
| PNTC | Pillar New Testament Commentary |
| PPS | Popular Patristic Series |
| SBLDS | Society of Biblical Literature Dissertation Series |
| SP | Sacra Pagina |
| THNTC | Two Horizons New Testament Commentary |
| TNTC | Tyndale New Testament Commentaries |
| TOTC | Tyndale Old Testament Commentary Series |
| VTSup | Vetus Testamentum Supplement (series) |
| WBC | Word Biblical Commentary |
| WEC | Wycliffe Exegetical Commentary |

## REFERENCES

| | |
|---|---|
| *ANET* | *Ancient Near East Texts Relating to the Old Testament*. 1969. Edited by Pritchard. 3rd ed. Princeton, NJ: Princeton University Press |
| *ANRW* | *Aufstieg und Niedergang der römischen Welt: Geschichte und Kultur Roms im Spiegel der neueren Forschung*. Part 2, Principat. Edited by Hildegard Temporini and Wolfgang Haase. Berlin: de Gruyter, 1972– |
| BDAG | Danker, Frederick W., Walter Bauer, William F. Arndt, and F. Wilbur Gingrich. *Greek-English Lexicon of the New Testament and Other Early Christian Literature*. 3rd ed. Chicago: University of Chicago Press, 2000 |
| BDB | Brown, Francis, S. R. Driver, and Charles A. Briggs, *A Hebrew and English Lexicon of the Old Testament*. Carol Stream, IL: Tyndale House, 1994 |
| *BDBA* | *The Brown-Driver-Briggs Hebrew and English Lexicon, Abridged* |
| *BHS* | *Biblia Hebraica Stuttgartensia*. Edited by Karl Elliger and Wilhelm Rudolph. Stuttgart: Deutsche Bibelgesellschaft, 1983 |
| *CTA* | Herdner, Andrée, *Corpus des Tablettes en Cuneiformes Alphabetiques: Decouvertes a Ras Shamra-Ugarit de 1929 a 1939*. 2 vols. Mission de Ras Shamra 10. Paris: Imprimerie Nationale, 1963 |
| *HALOT* | *Hebrew and Aramaic Lexicon of the Old Testament*. Ludwig Koehler, Walter Baumgartner, and Johann J. Stamm. Translated and edited under the supervision of Mervyn E. J. Richardson. 4 vols. Leiden: Brill, 1994–1999 |
| LSJ | Liddell, Henry George, Robert Scott, and Henry Stuart Jones, *A Greek-English Lexicon*. 9th ed. with revised supplement. Oxford: Clarendon, 1996 |
| *NIDOTT* | *New International Dictionary of Old Testament and Theology*. Edited by Colin Brown. 4 vols. Grand Rapids: Zondervan, 1975–1978 |
| *PGM* | *Papyri Graecae Magicae: Die griechischen Zauberpapyri*. Edited by Karl Preisendanz. 2nd ed. Stuttgart: Teubner, 1973–1974 |
| *TDNT* | *Theological Dictionary of the New Testament*. Edited by Gerhard Kittel and Gerhard Friedrich. Translated by G. W. Bromiley. 10 vols. Grand Rapids: Eerdmans, 1964–1976 |

## BIBLE VERSIONS

| | |
|---|---|
| CEB | Common English Bible |
| CSB | Christian Standard Bible |
| ESV | English Standard Version |
| HTV | [Hear] The Voice |
| JPS | Jewish Publication Society |
| KJV | King James Version |
| LXX | Septuagint |
| NAB | New American Bible |
| NASB | New American Standard Bible |
| NEB | New English Bible |
| NET | New English Translation |
| NETS | New English Translation of the Septuagint |
| NIV | New International Version |
| NJB | New Jerusalem Bible |
| NKJV | New King James Version |
| NLT | New Living Translation |
| NRSV | New Revised Standard Version |
| RSV | Revised Standard Version |

# INTRODUCTION TO JEREMIAH

## OVERVIEW OF JEREMIAH

**Author:** Jeremiah, as assisted by his scribe Baruch

**Provenance:** Jerusalem in the late seventh and early sixth centuries B.C., with the material of the book organized and edited in the early exile in Egypt and Babylon

**Readers:** The Jews of the exilic and postexilic period

**Historical Setting:** Jerusalem during the reigns of its last five kings, and then among the exilic community in Egypt

**Occasion for Writing:** The fall of Jerusalem, with the book serving as an explanation for Jerusalem's fall and as an exoneration of Jeremiah

**Genre:** Classic prophecy, with both transcriptions of Jeremiah's oral messages and accounts of key events in his life

**Structure of Jeremiah:** An extensive condemnation of Judah and the nations with, at its structural center, a promise of redemption under the new covenant

**Theological Emphasis:** Jerusalem is incorrigibly evil, and its destruction cannot be averted, but God will bring about restoration under a new covenant and a new David.

## AUTHORSHIP OF JEREMIAH

Informed readers of Daniel approach it knowing that they must come to terms with a significant critical problem: Is Daniel the account of an actual Jewish scribe who lived in Babylon during the reign of Nebuchadnezzar and who experienced miracles and saw visions concerning the future, or is the book a piece of religious fiction composed in the second century to encourage Jews in their struggle for freedom from the Seleucid Empire? Informed readers of Isaiah, similarly, must reckon with arguments seeking to demonstrate that the prophet Isaiah ben Amoz did not write much of the book that bears his name—specifically, that he did not write all of Isaiah 1–39 and wrote none of 40–66. Readers who come to Jeremiah, however, often do so with the blissful sense that at least here there are none of these problems and that even critical scholarship must recognize that the book comes from the prophet Jeremiah. This is, however, the bliss of ignorance, for there are significant problems associated with Jeremiah that call into question how much confidence we can have in the book. But the problems here are different from what we see in Daniel or Isaiah.

To be sure, there are some who have tried to apply classic source criticism to Jeremiah, but these efforts were not persuasive (for useful surveys of the history of Jeremiah source-critical scholarship, see Holladay 1989, 11–14; Carroll 1986, 38–50). Instead, the problem with Jeremiah stems from a brute fact: the standard Hebrew text of Jeremiah (the Masoretic Text or MT) is significantly different from the Septuagint (LXX), the Greek translation from roughly the second century B.C. The LXX is shorter than the MT, lacking the equivalent of about three thousand Hebrew words. In one regard, moreover, it has a different structure: the oracles against the nations in the LXX appear in the middle of the book, right after 25:13; but in the MT, they are near the end of the book, occupying chapters 46–51. Also, these oracles are not in the same order in the LXX as in the MT. How are we to explain this?

An obvious but perhaps too easy solution is that the LXX translator, for reasons of his own, shortened the book and rearranged its contents, moving the oracles against the nations from the end to the middle of the book. One argument is that the translator shortened the book by deliberately cutting out many cases of parallelism (see, for example, Althann 1983, 29, 46–47, 69, 88–89, 305–7). But this is not a characteristic of the LXX; it does not routinely omit parallel lines. It also seems surprising, and indeed unlikely, that a Jewish translator would handle the canonical text of a major prophet in such a cavalier manner, rearranging and shortening the text however he chose. In addition, a discovery among the Dead Sea Scrolls decisively speaks against regarding the LXX as a later, shortened version of the MT. The fragmentary Hebrew scrolls of Jeremiah found at Qumran included one designated 4QJer[b]. It is written in Hebrew, but in content it is closer to the LXX than to the MT (see Tov 2012, 289–92; Jobes and Silva 2000, 173–77). This implies that the LXX translation reflects an earlier Hebrew original. The LXX translator did not simply shorten and modify the text in his translation; he had a Hebrew text of Jeremiah that corresponded to the LXX as we now have it. We thus have to work with the assumption that the Hebrew *Vorlage* (a text on which a translation is based) behind the LXX was in its contents like the LXX. We cannot claim that the translator revised and shortened the text as he translated.

Another possible solution is that the Hebrew *Vorlage* the LXX translator used was rife with scribal errors, and that these errors omitted a great deal of the original Hebrew (a position taken by Lundbom 2008a, 885–87; Lundbom 2008c, 549–63). In this theory, the LXX is shorter not because the translator deliberately abridged it but because his translation was based on the Hebrew original that had been poorly copied and left out a great deal of the original text. However, this is not persuasive. If a text has many scribal errors, it will inevitably have many passages that are unintelligible. An error is by definition random, and this often causes a miscopied passage to be ungrammatical and unreadable. For example, suppose an original text says, "The house that he built is a small house, but it is very cute." A copyist, however, makes the mistake of jumping from the first instance of "house" to the second, and he omits the words in between. The result would be the ungrammatical, "The house, but it is very cute." Yet the "errors" Lundbom claims to have existed in the Hebrew *Vorlage* behind the LXX always resulted in a text that has coherent, intelligible Hebrew. It is not plausible that mistakes would unfailingly leave behind comprehensible sentences. Also, this theory does not explain why the oracles against the nations have been relocated.

The consensus today among most scholars is that the LXX Jeremiah is the earlier version and that the MT Jeremiah is a later, expanded version. The critical work here is a book done by J. Gerald Janzen, in which he argues on a case-by-case basis that when one compares the LXX to the MT, it is not likely that the LXX is the later version or that it has omitted material now found in the MT (Janzen 1973). Instead, the MT adds words to the Hebrew text that was behind the LXX.

Janzen's work is not above criticism. It covers the whole of Jeremiah and can be superficial or even forced in its analysis. One scholar, making a very close examination of a small portion of Jeremiah, demonstrates that often the situation is much more complex than Janzen allows and that simply stating that the MT is an expansion of the LXX is overly simple (Soderlund 1985, 203–46). For all that, however, the conclusion that the MT in many places represents an expansion of the LXX remains persuasive. In a more recent study, Emanuel Tov has continued the consensus, stating that the Hebrew text behind the LXX must be considered "Edition I" while the MT is "Edition II" (Tov 2012, 288). But why would a Greek translation from the second century reflect an earlier version of the book than what we now have in the Hebrew Bible? How can we explain this?

For many scholars, the explanation is that the present text of Jeremiah grew as a "rolling corpus" until it reached its present form. This means that the original book, as it came from Jeremiah and his scribe Baruch, may have been quite short. Over the course of time, however, more and more material was added, as when a snowball rolls down a snowy hill. Or, to change the analogy, the book was like a small cottage which, over the course of centuries, had various wings and other enlargements added to it until it became something of a mansion. Thus, by the time the book reached the stage at which it was translated into the LXX, it had already become much larger than it had originally been. And after its translation into the LXX even more material was added to the Hebrew text, and the placement of the oracles against the nations was changed, until at last it reached the stage at which we now find the MT. Indeed, some scholars do not believe that we can find anything in the present book that we can confidently assign to Jeremiah himself, although others do not take such an extreme position. (No two scholars understand this process in exactly the same way, but see Crenshaw 1983, 128–29; Ackroyd 1984, 47–50; McKane 1986, xv–xcix; Carroll 1986, 65–82; Aejmelaeus 2002; Allen 2008, 11, for examples of scholars who hold to some version of the "rolling corpus" theory.) Regardless, many interpreters believe that a great deal of what we have in the present book does not come from Jeremiah, that the LXX is closer to the original book than the MT is, and that even the LXX has a great deal of material that was added long after the prophet's death and that did not originate in his preaching.

This interpretation of the composition history of Jeremiah greatly reduces the book's credibility as a faithful representation of the life and preaching of the prophet. It even implies that we should use the LXX Jeremiah in our Bibles because, even if the LXX also includes many secondary expansions, it is at least closer to the original than the MT is.

Is there anything we can say in response to this? I believe there is. Untangling all the threads that make up the present book is a complex process, and this commentary, with its focus on preaching, is not the best venue for it. For a full exploration of this topic, the reader is encouraged to look to the companion volume to this commentary, *Jeremiah: Composition, Setting, and Message*. I will here only summarize the results of my research.

The book of Jeremiah is an anthology of the messages of Jeremiah interspersed with key episodes from his life. The messages are not arranged in chronological order. Originally, moreover, these messages were not part of a book but were simply the transcriptions of various messages, letters, and documents in the care of the scribe Baruch. This was no more than a collection of papers and was not in any sense a "book" of Jeremiah. A decisive event occurred in the reign of Jehoiakim, when Jeremiah was prohibited from entering the temple precincts. Instead, he dictated a prophetic sermon to Baruch, who carried it to the temple and read the scroll aloud. It contained a severe and irrevocable condemnation of Jerusalem and the prediction that Nebuchadnezzar would lay the city waste. The scroll was taken to Jehoiakim, who upon hearing it read aloud, promptly cut it to ribbons and threw it into a fire. Jeremiah and Baruch went into hiding but produced a new copy of the scroll, and in the course of time added to that scroll other oracles proclaimed by Jeremiah (this episode is recounted in Jer. 36). This document, which I call the Baruch Scroll, was the original version of the book of Jeremiah. As time went on, Jeremiah and Baruch added other excerpts from his sermons to the scroll, and they also added a list of oracles against the nations to it. I call this "Edition 0."

In the course of time, Jeremiah and Baruch had a vision for a much-expanded version of the book that included oracles not yet included in Edition 0 as well as narratives of key episodes from Jeremiah's life. They completed a first draft of this book while in exile in Egypt (Baruch was with Jeremiah in Egypt according to 43:6). This version of Jeremiah, which I call "Edition 1," was the "Egyptian" version of Jeremiah and remained with the exiles there. This became the basis for the LXX version of Jeremiah. This edition, perhaps following the analogy of Isaiah, placed the oracles against the nations after the initial series of messages against Judah (see Isa. 13–21).

Eventually Baruch made his way to Babylon to join the Jewish exiles there. (Jeremiah 45:5 implies that Baruch was destined to spend much of his life as a sojourner, and the apocryphal book of Baruch asserts that he ended up in Babylon [Bar 1:1].) I suspect that Jeremiah died in Egypt, since he was very old by this time, and the last place the book records him inhabiting was Egypt. Obviously enough, we cannot be certain about this. But Baruch carried with him Edition 1 and all the source texts used to create it. Baruch had the task, probably a charge from Jeremiah, to put together an edition that more fully and accurately presented the life and message of the prophet. The most significant change was to move the oracles against the nations to the back of the book. This gave the book a chiastic structure, as follows:

- A Prologue: The beginning of Jeremiah's ministry (1:1–19)
  - B Two anthologies against Judah (2:1–20:18)
    - C Historically contextualized messages (21:1–29:32)
      - D Eschatological salvation (30:1–33:26)
    - C′ Historically contextualized messages (34:1–45:5)
  - B′ Two anthologies against the nations (46:1–51:64)
- A′ Epilogue: The end of the house of David (52:1–34)

This move was significant because it placed the messages of salvation at the structural center of the book. Furthermore, to ensure that Jeremiah's message was adequately conveyed, Baruch inserted what now is seen as additional material in the MT. We should recall that Baruch had firsthand knowledge of how Jeremiah's words had been abbreviated in Edition 1, and he had all the original source material. He created Edition 2, and this has come down to us as the present book of Jeremiah.

Two matters of importance stand out. First, this was not a process that took centuries; it was almost certainly completed within a decade of Jeremiah's death. Second, it was not created by later generations of scribes who knew nothing of Jeremiah or his life and messages. It was the work of the man who had copied, edited, and collated all of Jeremiah's words from the very beginning. Edition 2 is the "authorized," canonical, and accurate record of the prophet's life and message. We should not be surprised that Baruch played a significant role in this process. He is by far the most prominent scribe in the Old Testament. Indeed, although all of the prophetic books were written with the aid of scribes, he is the only one of whom we have specific knowledge.

Babylon was where postexilic Judaism was created and thrived, just as Jeremiah had predicted (Jer. 24 and 29). As books such as Zechariah, Ezra, and Nehemiah attest, it was the Babylonian Jewish community that returned to Jerusalem, rebuilt the city, and conserved and completed the canonical Scriptures. For that reason, Edition 2, now represented for us as the MT, became the standard, canonical text of Jeremiah everywhere except among the Egyptian exiles, who preserved and translated Edition 1 as the LXX. But there never was a "rolling corpus," a text that got bigger and bigger through the centuries. Instead, the Egyptian community preserved Edition 1 with minimal modification until it was translated, just as the Babylonian and postexilic Jerusalem Jews preserved and propagated Edition 2 without subjecting it to continual modification. Edition 2 has come down to us in the Hebrew Bible, and it is the version we can affirm to faithfully convey the words and deeds of Jeremiah as recorded by his lifelong scribe, Baruch the son of Neriah.

## PLACE AND DATE OF WRITING

As described above, the book was written in three main stages. First, Jeremiah's messages and letters were collected during his Jerusalem ministry, going from the latter part of Josiah's reign until sometime after the fall of Jerusalem (approximately 627–584 B.C.). Second, Jeremiah and Baruch were forcibly taken to Egypt, where they completed Edition 1 perhaps by 570. Third, Baruch completed Edition 2 in Babylon.

## OCCASION FOR WRITING

The essential message of Jeremiah to his people is obvious: The Judah of the late seventh and early sixth centuries B.C. was hopelessly apostate and doomed to be destroyed by the Babylonian Empire. Most significantly, they had turned away from YHWH by worshiping idols and foreign gods. Jeremiah preached his messages to warn his people of the calamity they faced if they did not repent, and he and Baruch preserved his words and deeds as a testimony to later generations. Apart from the messages of eschatological salvation in Jeremiah 30–33, the book is entirely made up of words of condemnation and judgment.

For the Christian reader or interpreter, and especially for the preacher, this creates several difficulties. First, it makes for a very monotonous book (and a long book at that). Especially in the first twenty chapters, one may wonder why this one core message ("Jerusalem is idolatrous and will be destroyed!") must be repeated over and over. For the expositional preacher, the problem is acute: How is he to avoid preaching the same message many times over? Secondly, it is a book that is profoundly tied to its historical situation. It focuses on persons long dead and circumstances that have little relevance, it seems, to the modern world. The primary sin that Jeremiah confronts—polytheistic idolatry—is one that in its classical and literal form many Christians rarely face today. For sermons, the book might be regarded as profoundly anachronistic, and the preacher is understandably reluctant to give a series of sermons that are essentially history lessons. The interpreter, therefore, needs reckon with how the original occasion for the writing of the book relates to readers in a radically different situation. How does a series of ancient sermons declaring that Jerusalem is wicked and must be destroyed also speak to Gentile Christians today? Our answer must be faithful to Jeremiah's original message and faithfully convey it to the church, not as a lecture on the history of Judah or a biography of a prophet but as the living word of God.

## HISTORICAL SETTING

The message of the book is closely tied to the life of the prophet, but the book presents the prophet's biography in episodic snippets that are not chronologically arranged. In addition, many readers lack a basic understanding of the historical context of the book, a context that is essential to comprehending its individual episodes. To gain access to the book, therefore, one must begin with Jeremiah's life and times.

### *The Historical Context*

We begin with the last five kings of Judah: Josiah, Jehoahaz, Jehoiakim, Jehoiachin, and Zedekiah. We must also consider the two great powers of the time, Babylon and Egypt.

#### *Judah's Last Kings*

Josiah (reigned 640–609) came to power at the end of the resolutely apostate reigns of Manasseh (reigned 686–642) and Amon (reigned 642–640). In addition to the paganism of these kings, the traumatic wars with Assyria had badly scarred the nation. During the reign of Hezekiah (715–686), Assyria had obliterated the northern kingdom of Israel and its capital, Samaria. They also very nearly destroyed Judah. Although Jerusalem was saved by divine intervention (Isa. 36–37), Judah was ravaged by the invader, with many of its outlying cities destroyed and its agricultural base turned into a scorched earth (Isa. 7:17–25). Hezekiah's son Manasseh, in addition to his religious apostasy, became an abject vassal of the seemingly invincible Assyrian Empire. But Assyria's fortunes fell with astonishing rapidity. A resurgent Babylon under Nabopolassar defeated them in a major battle in 616, and in 612 a coalition of Babylonians and Medes sacked and demolished the great Assyrian city of Nineveh. It is in this context we should understand the reign of Josiah.

Josiah came to the throne as a boy in 640, and his entire reign can be interpreted as a battle against what he saw as Judah's two great enemies, the Assyrian menace and Manasseh's apostate promotion of idolatry. He dealt with the apostasy first. Soon after he took the throne, his administration shut down all the outlying shrines, destroyed pagan images wherever they found them, and required that people worship only at the Jerusalem temple under the Aaronite priesthood. He cleansed the temple of its pagan elements and refurbished the building—and in the course of this, found a copy of the Law. This gave new energy to his reformation. However, a large number of the people were not with him, believing that the Queen of Heaven was their protector (Jer. 44:15–19).

At the end of his reign, Josiah demonstrated his hostility to the Assyrians. After the fall of Nineveh, remnants of the Assyrian Empire fled to Harran in Upper Mesopotamia to make their last stand. Pharaoh Neco II marched north to assist the Assyrians, probably wanting to maintain a balance of power and hoping that the Assyrians could serve as a buffer between Egypt and Babylon. Josiah, evidently determined that Assyria should be eliminated once and for all, tried to block Neco so that he could not give assistance to the hated Assyrians. But Judah was decisively beaten by Egypt, and Josiah either fell in the battle or died soon after.

*The Death of King Josiah* by Antonio Zanchi

Josiah was devoted to YHWH and to the covenant, and he was perhaps the most consistently righteous of all of Judah's kings. Nevertheless, both of his major efforts ultimately failed. Since his reformation was from the top down and not supported by the people or nobility, Judah reverted to its pagan ways immediately after his death. Indeed, his defeat at the hands of Neco convinced many in Judah that single-minded devotion to YHWH was no guarantee of divine protection.

Assyria was destroyed. Notwithstanding Egyptian aid, Assyria's last stronghold, Harran, fell to Babylon in 609. However, this did little to help Judah. Neco, having slain Josiah, was now the dominant figure over Judah. Josiah's son Jehoahaz (also called Shallum; Jer. 22:11) was enthroned in 609 as the next king. Neco, however, quickly removed him and deported him to Egypt. Perhaps Jehoahaz had been chosen by a coalition that was anti-Assyrian and by extension anti-Egyptian. Regardless, nothing more is heard of Jehoahaz; he died a captive in Egypt (Jer. 22:10–12). Neco replaced Jehoahaz with his brother Jehoiakim. Soon afterward, moreover, Babylon became the ascendant power in the Near East. Very quickly, Babylon replaced Egypt as the power that Judah had to reckon with. With the Assyrian menace eliminated, Judah may have considered itself safe. But

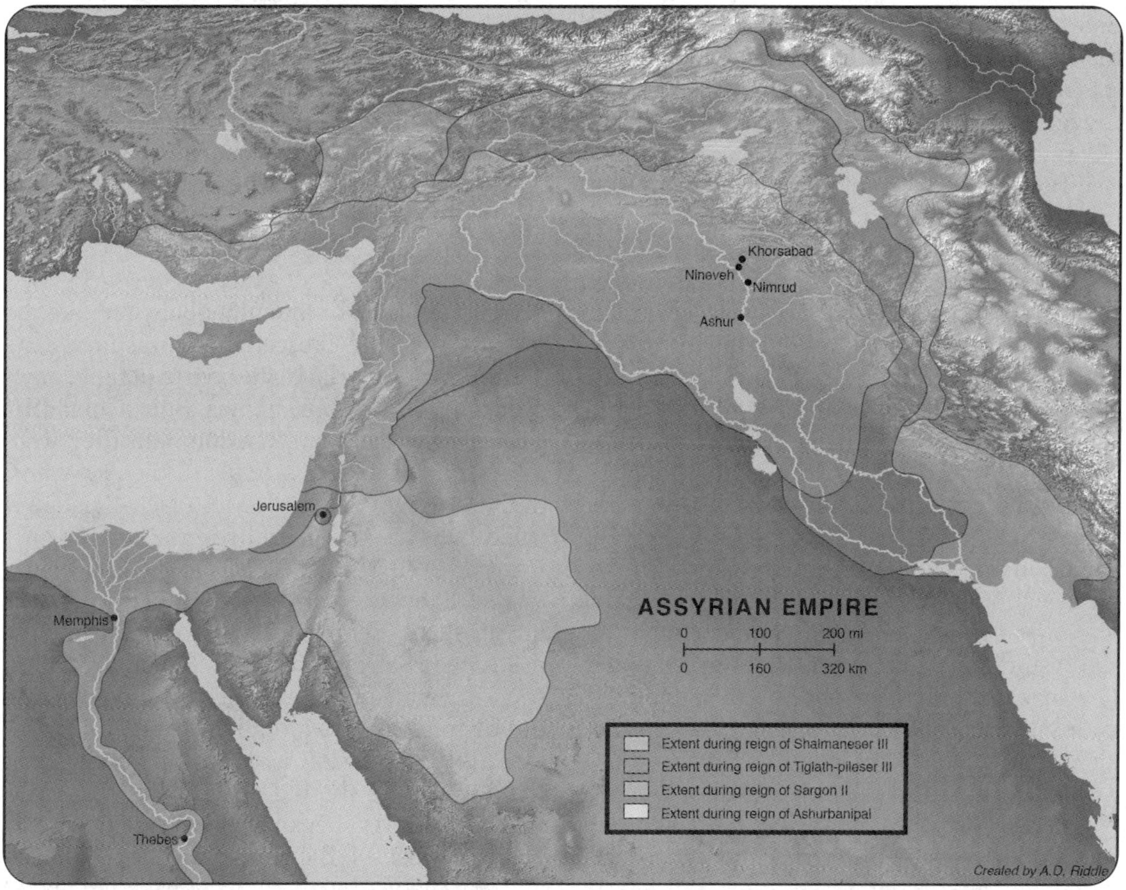


The Assyrian Empire from the ninth through seventh centuries B.C. Map by A. D. Riddle.

within a generation after Assyria's demise, Jerusalem would suffer destruction at the hands of the Neo-Babylonian Empire.

Jehoiakim (originally named Eliakim; reigned 609–598) was a subservient vassal of Neco until Nebuchadnezzar II of Babylon crushed the Egyptian forces in a major battle at Carchemish in 605. Soon thereafter, Nebuchadnezzar (who had been crown prince at the time of the battle) took the crown as king of Babylon upon the death of his father, Nabopolassar. Nebuchadnezzar marched west, and Jehoiakim of necessity swore allegiance to him. It appears, however, that Jehoiakim's sympathies were with Egypt. When Babylon and Egypt fought a bloody battle to a stalemate around early 600, Nebuchadnezzar withdrew to Babylon to refresh his battered forces. Jehoiakim then rebelled against Nebuchadnezzar and reestablished his alliance with Egypt. Nebuchadnezzar returned to Jerusalem in 598/597, and the city soon capitulated.

The end of Jehoiakim's reign is somewhat murky. According to 2 Chronicles 36:6, he was captured and taken as a captive to Babylon. Other sources, however, indicate that Jerusalem surrendered in the reign of his son Jehoiachin (for example, 2 Kings 24:8–12), implying that Jehoiakim died before the city capitulated (other sources always speak of an exile of Jehoiachin, not of Jehoiakim). Perhaps, when Chronicles speaks of the captivity of Jehoiakim, it actually means the captivity of the administration he established, Jehoiakim having died before the capitulation. While he reigned, Jehoiakim was always an implacable enemy of Jeremiah. This was, first, because Jehoiakim was a champion of the restoration of the pagan cults in Jerusalem (2 Kings 24:3), and, second, because Jeremiah counseled submission to Babylon and warned against an alliance with Egypt.

Jehoiachin (also called Jeconiah or Coniah) succeeded his father in late 598 but ruled only long enough to submit to Nebuchadnezzar. He, along with a representative group from Jerusalem's upper class, was taken to Babylon, and he spent the rest of his life there. He was evidently held under severe imprisonment for thirty-seven years, but at last Evil-Merodach (whose Babylonian name was Amel-Marduk), the son and successor of Nebuchadnezzar, eased his plight by allowing him to live in the Babylonian palace and eat at the royal table. Jehoiachin died in Babylon (Jer. 52:31).

Zedekiah (reigned 597–586) was another son of Josiah and thus the uncle, not the son, of Jehoiachin. He was only twenty-one when he became king (2 Kings 24:18) and was rather weak and vacillating, at times showing high regard for Jeremiah, but at other times yielding to pressure from members of the aristocracy who wanted to follow Jehoiakim's policies and who hated Jeremiah. He at last rebelled against Babylon in favor of a pro-Egyptian policy, and this led to the destruction of the city and end of the kingdom of Judah. Zedekiah himself was captured while trying to flee Jerusalem and blinded by the Babylonians, and he died in Babylon (2 Kings 25:1–7; Jer. 52:4–11).

### *Babylon and Egypt*

Prior to the time of Jeremiah, Babylon, like the rest of the Fertile Crescent area, was under the dominion of Assyria. In the course of time, however, a group of people known as the Chaldeans gained ascendancy in Babylon, and they were a continual source of trouble to the Assyrians. In the late eighth century, Merodach-Baladan II ruled Babylon and fought several wars against Assyria, even though he was for a time forced to flee Babylon. Conflict continued in subsequent years; Sennacherib of Assyria actually destroyed Babylon in 689. But Esarhaddon son of Sennacherib rebuilt the city because the peoples of Mesopotamia regarded the destruction of Babylon as gross impiety against the gods. Soon the old conflict between Babylon and Assyria began again. As noted above, Nabopolassar of Babylon destroyed Nineveh and eliminated the remnants of Assyrian power at Harran.

Nebuchadnezzar II, son of Nabopolassar, commanded Babylonian forces in the aforementioned battle of Carchemish just prior to assuming the crown. He reigned from 605 to 562 B.C. With Egypt beaten, he proceeded to establish Babylonian hegemony in the west. He made a show of force in the Levant and soon brought the minor regional powers there into submission. Judah was high on the list of states he wanted to dominate. With the old state of Israel (Samaria) gone, Judah was the most significant regional power controlling the land bridge between Egypt and Mesopotamia. Jerusalem quickly submitted and sent a small number of aristocratic hostages to Babylon, including Daniel (Dan. 1:1–7). This took place in late 605 or early 604. As already mentioned, however, Nebuchadnezzar's forces were somewhat ravaged in a major battle with Egypt in late 601 or early 600, and he had to withdraw to rebuild his army. This prompted Jehoiakim to rebel, and it led to the Babylonian siege and capture of Jerusalem by early 597, when Jehoiachin and leading citizens were taken captive. Nebuchadnezzar spent the following years putting down rebellions back in Mesopotamia, but when Jerusalem under Zedekiah rebelled again, he returned and destroyed Jerusalem, eliminated the kingdom of Judah, and put an end to the Davidic monarchy. Besides waging these and other wars (including a thirteen-year siege of Tyre), Nebuchadnezzar built up Babylon on a magnificent scale, making it the most impressive city of its age.

Egypt in the time of Jeremiah was not the world power it had been in the late second millennium, the "New Kingdom" era that included

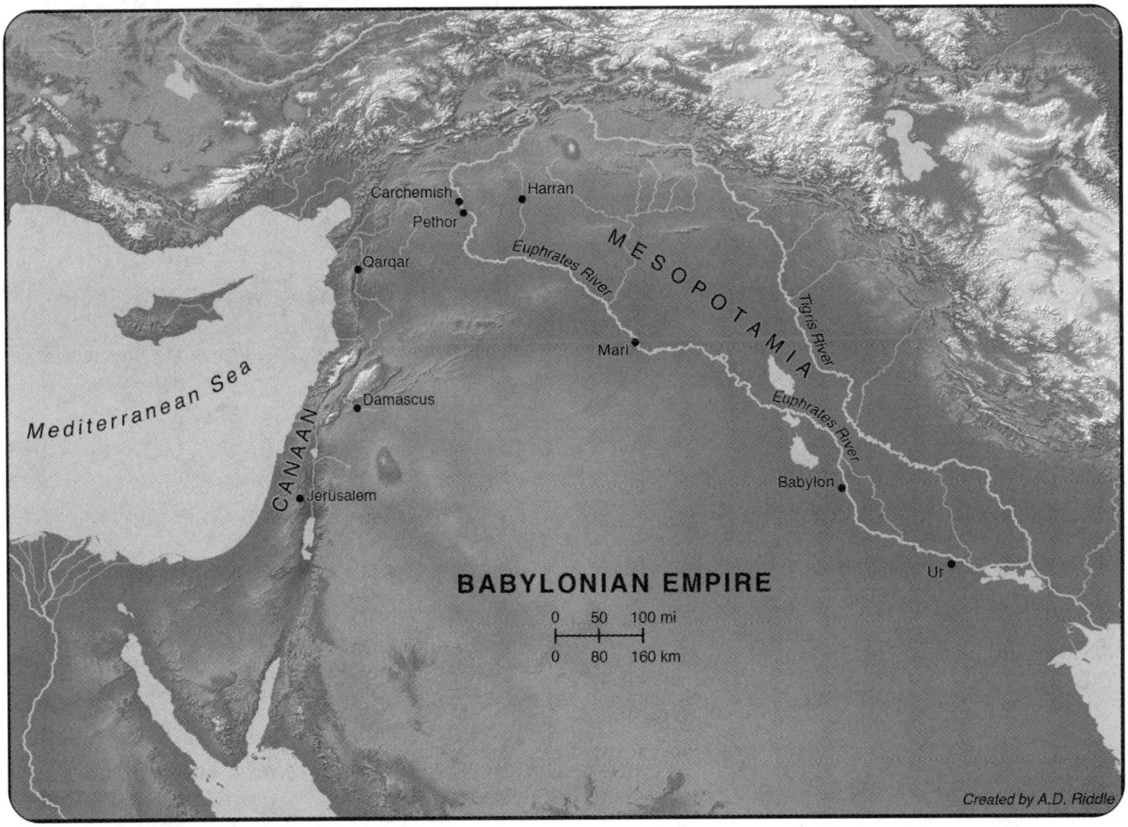

pharaohs such as the famous Ramses II. Egypt was by no means insignificant, however, and it continued to play a major role on the world stage. Israel and Judah, being physically close to Egypt and the gateway between it and Mesopotamia, could not escape its influence. An Egyptian pharaoh, whom the Bible calls "So" (possibly a ruler of the regional Twenty-Fourth Dynasty, Tefnakhte), encouraged King Hoshea of Israel to rebel against Assyria (2 Kings 17:4), a catastrophic decision that resulted in the final obliteration of the northern kingdom. From approximately 730 to 656, most of Egypt was under the Twenty-Fifth or "Cushite" Dynasty and was ruled by pharaohs from Nubia. They were deeply involved in struggles against Assyria for control of the Levant but generally fared poorly. The Assyrian Ashurbanipal actually sacked Thebes, deep within Egypt, in about 664.

Psamtik I (Psammetichus) founded the Twenty-Sixth Dynasty with its capital at Sais in the western Delta (hence it is called the "Saite" Dynasty). This dynasty lasted until Egypt was conquered by the Persians in 525. Psamtik was followed by his son Neco II who, as noted above, tried without success to prop up the remaining elements of Assyrian Empire but in the process defeated and killed Josiah. After his defeat at Carchemish, he withdrew and regrouped his forces and, as noted above, was able to inflict heavy casualties on Babylon when the latter tried to invade Egypt in late 601 or early 600, leading to Jehoiakim's revolt.

Neco II was succeeded by Psamtik II (595–589), who was in turn succeeded by Apries (589–570), known in the Bible as Hophra. It was this pharaoh who encouraged Zedekiah to throw off the yoke of Babylon and pledged to come to Jerusalem's rescue if needed. To his credit, he did try to break the siege of Jerusalem, but he only succeeded in temporarily causing the Babylonians to pull back from the city. Nebuchadnezzar repulsed Hophra's efforts and resumed the siege of Jerusalem, destroying it once and for all. Egyptian power was soon effectively broken and, although not conquered by Babylon, was confined to its borders until conquered in 525 by the Persian king Cambyses II.

### *The Life of Jeremiah*

The book of Jeremiah does not give a sequential account of his life, but it gives us many episodic vignettes, and significant portions of the book are in the first person. The story of his life plays a far greater role in his book than do the

*The Prophet Jeremiah* by Jan Mostaert

biographies of Isaiah or any of the Twelve, except for Jonah.

Jeremiah was a priest, the son of Hilkiah of Anathoth. Located a few miles north of Jerusalem in the tribal territory of Benjamin, Anathoth had significant priestly associations. It was near both Ramah, the home of Samuel, and Shiloh, the location of Israel's central shrine in the time of the judges. Jeremiah's proximity to Shiloh seems to have had a significant impact on him; he twice refers to the destruction of the shrine as an object lesson for his contemporaries (Jer. 7:12–14; 26:4–6).

He first heard the voice of YHWH in the thirteenth year of Josiah's reign (1:2, 4), in about 627 B.C. If we assume that Jeremiah was twelve or thirteen when called, he was born near the beginning of Josiah's reign in 640 (Holladay's claim that Jeremiah was born in 627 depends upon dating 16:1–4 to after 601, but this is not persuasive; see his full argument in Holladay 1989, 25–26). Jeremiah certainly knew and, as he came of age, supported Josiah's reformation. We probably see an echo of the prophet's youthful enthusiasm for what Josiah was doing in 15:16, "Your words were found, and I ate them." The finding of YHWH's words probably refers to the discovery of the copy of the Law, which happened in Josiah's eighteenth year (2 Kings 22:3–8). Thus, Jeremiah was probably about seventeen at the time, and his "eating" of the words would refer to his eager attendance at a public reading of the text. We may surmise that, with Josiah's reformation in full swing and the Law now returned to its rightful place as the code of governance for the nation, he was highly optimistic about the future survival of the nation and its adherence to orthodoxy.

At some point early in his ministry (not necessarily at his initial call), he received the vision recorded in 1:13–19. This told him that his own people would be his greatest enemies and that God would have to give him a metaphorical body of armor (or as we might say, a very tough hide) for him to endure the pain of the hostility that would be directed at him. In addition, he was commanded to abstain from marriage and the normal social activities of life (16:1–9). He would be alone, hated, and not believed. At the end of it all, Jerusalem would be destroyed. This set the pattern for the rest of his life. Despised as a traitor and, perversely, as a heretic, he was isolated and reviled. The people of his hometown, Anathoth, turned against him (11:18–12:6). He had few friends (15:17).

His youthful enthusiasm and his optimism over Josiah's reformation were quickly disappointed. Although he was YHWH's spokesman, his words also reflect his own inner dismay. He was shocked that no one believed his message: "I appointed watchmen over them [and said], 'Listen for the sound of the shofar!' But they said, 'We will not listen'" (16:7). His "temple sermon," preached early in the reign of Jehoiakim (Jer. 26), marked a singular break between himself and the majority of Judah, especially the royal house. He claimed that YHWH would abandon Jerusalem, the temple, and the Davidic dynasty to destruction—and for saying this he was banned from the temple precincts (36:4–6). To his astonishment, people blamed Josiah's reformation for the disasters that beset the nation, and they looked upon Josiah's death in battle as proof that God had repudiated him. Jeremiah thus found himself having to defend the reputation of the dead king (22:10–19).

The next decisive event in Jeremiah's ministry came when Jerusalem was occupied by Nebuchadnezzar in 597, with the result that Jehoiachin, Jehoiakim's son and successor, was taken captive to Jerusalem. The hope and expectation of the people of Jerusalem, encouraged by the lying prophets, was that God would soon break the yoke of Babylon and that Jehoiachin would return to take the throne in Jerusalem. Against this, Jeremiah proclaimed that Jehoiachin would never come back, that the Jewish captives needed to settle in Babylonia for a multigenerational stay, and that the real hope for the future of Israel lay with the captives in Babylon and not with those who remained behind in Jerusalem, whom Jeremiah viewed as hopelessly corrupt (22:24–30; 24:1–10; 27:1–28:17; 29:4–9). For the leading citizens in Jerusalem, this only confirmed that Jeremiah was a preacher of defeatism and a heretic. In the years that followed, during the reign of Zedekiah, their hostility would become much more overt and violent.

The next major incident came during the final siege of Jerusalem. When Hophra attempted to break the siege, the Babylonian army temporarily withdrew from the city to deal with the Egyptian threat. Jeremiah had pressing family business in his hometown of Anathoth, and he tried to leave the city in order to take care of it. But he was arrested at the gate on charges of treason and desertion. He was beaten, imprisoned, and eventually left to die in an empty cistern. Indeed, he would have died had not Ebed-melek the Cushite appealed to the king and received permission to rescue him. Zedekiah then put Jeremiah into protective custody. He remained a prisoner but was shielded from his aristocratic enemies, who were still looking for an excuse to kill him (Jer. 37–38).

After the fall of Jerusalem, Nebuchadnezzar released Jeremiah and gave him the choice of either staying behind in the now ruined land of Judah or joining the Jews in Babylon. He chose to stay behind. Nebuchadnezzar appointed a Jewish governor, Gedaliah, to manage what was left of the towns and populace of Judah. But a member of the royal family, a certain Ishmael, had fled to Baalis, king of the Ammonites, and so escaped deportation or death. For reasons unknown to us, he assassinated Gedaliah and then slaughtered a number of Jewish pilgrims. Perhaps Ishmael regarded Gedaliah as a traitor, or perhaps he wanted to assist Baalis in grabbing territory in the former Judah and so gain a position of authority in an expanded Ammonite kingdom. Regardless, the incident created a panic among the other Jews and they fled to Egypt, forcibly taking Jeremiah and his scribe Baruch with them (39:11–43:7).

The last thing we know of Jeremiah concerns his conflict with the other Jewish exiles in Egypt. He rebuked them for their continued devotion to the Queen of Heaven, but they reacted with great hostility, claiming that all their troubles came upon them because they had offended the goddess by not giving her the honor that she was due (Jer. 44). That is, they blamed Josiah's reformation for removing the shrines and blamed Jeremiah for his support of Josiah's program. As far as we know, Jeremiah died in Egypt.

## STRUCTURE OF JEREMIAH

Besides being almost exclusively a condemnation of Jerusalem for its idolatry, Jeremiah poses another problem for interpreters: it seems to have no structure whatsoever. Its messages are demonstrably not in chronological order, and its organizing principles have eluded readers. The renowned scholar John Bright spoke for many when he called it a "hopeless hodgepodge thrown together without any discernible principle of arrangement at all" (Bright 1963, lvi). This renders both the hermeneutic and homiletic tasks even more difficult. One cannot interpret or preach a text when one does not know how it works. The task before us, therefore, is to determine what is the context, structure, and message of Jeremiah so that we may take the individual texts and use them to create a set of authentic and relevant but distinct messages.

Happily, Jeremiah is not the hodgepodge many have considered it to be. As noted above, the book of Jeremiah has a chiastic structure. The outline demonstrates that Jeremiah has a carefully conceived structure. It is not literary chaos. The structure also resolves the two riddles about the book.

The first riddle is: Why did Edition 2 move the oracles against the nations to the end of the book? The answer is that by doing so, the editors balanced the oracles against Judah (2:1–20:18) with oracles against the nations (46:1–51:64), enabling the creation of the chiastic structure.

The second riddle is: Why do the oracles of salvation (30:1–33:26) appear suddenly at the middle of the book? Nothing prepares the reader for seeing them here, and this structure contradicts what we often see in the prophets, where messages about God's eschatological salvation of Israel are mostly clustered at the end of a book (for example, in Hosea, Amos, Ezekiel, and Isaiah). The answer, as the chiastic structure shows, is that everything on either side of 30:1–33:26 is arranged to make this section, the salvation oracles, the heart of the book.

In a more conventional, hierarchical outline, Jeremiah has the following structure:

- I. Prologue: The beginning of Jeremiah's ministry (1:1–19)
  - A. Superscript (1:1–3)
  - B. Jeremiah's commission (1:4–19)
- II. Messages against Judah (2:1–20:18)
  - A. First anthology: Illusions and reality (2:1–10:25)
    1. Introductory summary (2:1–4:4)
    2. Deluded people and their coming destruction (4:5–6:30)
    3. Deceitful religion and real lamentation (7:1–10:25)
  - B. Second anthology: From intercession to imprecation (11:1–20:18)
    1. Introductory summary (11:1–23)
    2. The end of prophetic intercession (12:1–15:9)
    3. The beginning of prophetic imprecations (15:10–20:18)
- III. Historically contextualized messages (21:1–29:32)
  - A. A failed intercession, figs, and cups of wine (21:1–25:38)
    1. Message (in 588) to the delegation from Zedekiah (21:1–23:40)
    2. Message (in 597) after the exile of Jehoiachin (24:1–10)
    3. Message (in 605) during the fourth year of Jehoiakim (25:1–38)
  - B. True prophets rejected and false prophets celebrated (26:1–29:32)
    1. Jeremiah nearly lynched: the temple sermon (26:1–19)
    2. The martyrdom of the prophet Uriah of Kiriath-jearim (26:20–24)
    3. The false prophet Hananiah and the yoke bars (27:1–28:17)
    4. The false prophet Shemaiah and letters to the exiles (29:1–32)
- IV. Eschatological salvation (30:1–33:26)
  - A. An undated message: the new covenant (30:1–31:40)
    1. The command to write the book of consolation (30:1–3)
    2. The pleasant dream (30:4–31:26)
    3. Two agricultural metaphors (31:27–30)
    4. The new covenant (31:31–37)
    5. The restoration of Jerusalem (31:38–40)
  - B. Two messages from the tenth year of Zedekiah (32:1–33:26)
    1. The redeemed land (32:1–44)
    2. Jerusalem restored under the new David (33:1–26)
- V. Historically contextualized messages (34:1–45:5)
  - A. A failed covenant and cups of wine (34:1–35:19)
    1. Zedekiah's broken covenant (34:1–22)
    2. The example of the Rechabites (35:1–19)
  - B. Jeremiah the true prophet rejected (36:1–45:5)
    1. Jehoiakim burns the scroll (36:1–32)
    2. Jeremiah the captive (37:1–43:7)
    3. Jeremiah's two Egyptian oracles rejected (43:8–44:30)
    4. A message for Baruch (45:1–5)

VI. Two anthologies against the nations (46:1–51:64)
   A. Against many nations (46:1–49:39)
      1. Superscript: concerning the nations (46:1)
      2. Concerning Egypt (46:2–28)
      3. Concerning the Philistines (47:1–7)
      4. Concerning Moab (48:1–47)
      5. Concerning Ammon (49:1–6)
      6. Concerning Edom (49:7–22)
      7. Concerning Damascus (49:23–27)
      8. Concerning Kedar (49:28–33)
      9. Concerning Elam (49:34–39)
   B. Against Babylon (50:1–51:64)
      1. The oracles concerning Babylon (50:1–51:58)
      2. The mission of Seraiah to Babylon (51:59–64)

VII. Epilogue: The end of the house of David (52:1–34)

## THEOLOGICAL EMPHASIS OF JEREMIAH

Even the most casual reader can quickly grasp what is the central message of Jeremiah, the theme that runs through the book: because of its apostasy, Jerusalem was condemned by YHWH and destroyed by the Babylonians. Even so, at the structural center of the book is a message of hope: YHWH will bring about a restoration in a great eschatological salvation.

Beyond these central ideas, however, other concepts run through the book. One that the reader may not immediately recognize is this: the book vindicates the prophet Jeremiah. He was rejected by almost everyone in his nation and declared to be a traitor and a heretic. Unlike Isaiah, at whose word the army of the Assyrian Sennacherib was destroyed, he did not call heaven's fury down on Babylon and deliver Jerusalem from destruction. And yet the book shows that he loved his people, that their downfall was entirely their own doing, and that he was a true prophet of God. Another topic that repeatedly appears in the book is the blindness, perversity, and persistence of human sin. A people in apostasy will turn to evil even when it is obviously doing them harm. They will reject the truth even when it is right before them. They will cling to false security while calling evil good and good evil. Yet another topic that winds through the book is God's sovereignty; he is judge of all the earth, and he will punish first Israel and then the nations. And because eschatological salvation is at the center of the book, this theme explores the ideas of restoration, a new covenant, and a new David. There are, of course, far too many aspects to the message of Jeremiah to summarize in a few words. But by faithfully proclaiming the book, a minister can impart to a congregation the ancient message of the book to a contemporary audience.

## OUTLINE

Jeremiah may be divided into six major sections and preached in thirty-one sermons (preaching units).

### *PROLOGUE (1:1–19)*

- Superscript (1:1–3): We suggest that the pastor preach this as an overview of the entire book. It should introduce the congregation to the book and in particular to its chiastic structure with its central focus on eschatological salvation.
- Jeremiah's Commission (1:4–19)

### *MESSAGES AGAINST JUDAH (2:1–20:18)*

- Astonishing Evil (2:1–3:10)
- An Appeal to Repent (3:11–4:4)
- Deluded People and Their Coming Destruction (4:5–6:30)
- Deluded Religion (7:1–8:12)
- A Collection of Lamentations (8:13–9:26)
- False Gods (10:1–25)
- Hardened Hearts (11:1–23)
- Failed Intercession (12:1–13:27)

- The Three More Episodes of Failed Intercession (14:1–15:9)
- The Struggling Prophet (15:10–17:18)
- How to Break a Preacher's Heart (17:19–18:23)
- The Broken Nation and the Exhausted Prophet (19:1–20:18)

### *HISTORICALLY CONTEXTUALIZED MESSAGES I (21:1–29:32)*

- A Message to the Delegation from Zedekiah (21:1–23:40)
- Messages in the Times of Jehoiachin and Jehoiakim (24:1–25:38)
- Persecuted Prophets and False Prophets (26:1–29:32)

### *RESTORATION AND THE NEW COVENANT (30:1–33:26)*

- The Restoration (30:1–31:26)
- The New Covenant (31:27–40)
- The Redeemed Land (32:1–44)
- The New Davidic King (33:1–26)

### *HISTORICALLY CONTEXTUALIZED MESSAGES II (34:1–45:5)*

- Zedekiah Compared to the Rechabites (34:1–35:19)
- Jehoiakim and the Scroll (36:1–32)
- Jeremiah's Captivity and Jerusalem's Fall (37:1–39:18)
- The Murder of Gedaliah (40:1–41:18)
- Jeremiah's Message Rejected (42:1–43:7)
- Jeremiah in Egypt (43:8–44:30)
- A Message for Baruch (45:1–5)

### *ORACLES AGAINST THE NATIONS (46:1–51:64)*

- The Subdued Nations (46:1–49:39)
- Babylon (50:1–51:64)

### *EPILOGUE (52:1–34)*

- The End of the House of David (52:1–34)

# PROLOGUE (1:1–19)

Jeremiah 1:1–19 is a prologue, giving the superscript (a brief statement on the authorship and circumstances behind the creation of the book) and an account of Jeremiah's commission to be a prophet. These texts give the reader hints about what is coming. As we make our way through the book, we see how its message and story unfold, making obvious what is only suggested in the prologue. This text is the counterpoint to the epilogue (52:1–34), which tells of the end of the earthly dynasty of David.

## Jeremiah 1:1–3

**EXEGETICAL IDEA**
The superscript's reference to three named kings—from righteous Josiah to apostate Jehoiakim and Zedekiah—ending with the fall of Jerusalem gives the essential facts about the book's historical setting and implies that its theme is how and why Jerusalem, the city of David and of the temple, was destroyed.

**THEOLOGICAL FOCUS**
As evil becomes triumphant, people develop an inverted sense of right and wrong and build their lives on lies until judgment becomes inevitable, yet God provides a witness and shows the way to salvation revealed in several oracles that bring hope.

**PREACHING IDEA**
When we see God's judgment, look for and embrace his restoration.

**PREACHING POINTERS**
God wanted to dig more deeply, so most of Jeremiah's words identified sins and the consequential judgment. Motivational words without truth are meaningless and ineffective. God wanted Israel to see the depth of their sin. Then they would be ready for his forgiveness and redemption.

God wants to encourage us today. Posters of eagles soaring over mountains and dolphins jumping through waves with short motivational words have their place, but God wants to motivate people more deeply. Saying that "a journey begins with a first step" or "when the going gets tough, the tough get going" can help, but these words only deal with the surface. God wants to motivate our hearts. Jeremiah shows us that we are full of sin, but he also shows us the amazing grace and redemption that is available to us. To motivate us from our hearts, our hearts need to be changed. If we don't admit that we desperately need God's forgiveness and empowerment, we will be unprepared to live out his life in the bleak and dark world that we live in.

# SUPERSCRIPT (1:1–3)

## LITERARY STRUCTURE AND THEMES (1:1–3)

As it is difficult to preach the superscript alone, we recommend that the first sermon on Jeremiah be an overview of the whole book. This will also allow the congregation to get a sense of what the book of Jeremiah is about. For the preacher, it will provide a foundation for the whole series. We suggest that the preacher become familiar with the chiastic structure of Jeremiah described in the Introduction, noting in particular how the message of hope (Jer. 30–33) is at the center of a book otherwise dominated by sin and judgment. This is the message of Jeremiah: evil is apparently triumphant, and as a culture embraces evil, death and ruin follow. But in the middle of it all, there is hope based in a divine work of salvation.

As is common, the superscript gives the name of the author and the years of his ministry, with the reigns of kings serving as chronological anchors (for a summary of Jeremiah's life, see the Introduction). In this case, the book only employs the names of long-reigned kings to date Jeremiah's years of service: Josiah, Jehoiakim, and Zedekiah. The two kings who reigned only a few months before being carried away into exile—Jehoahaz and Jehoiachin—go unmentioned. In Josiah, Jehoiakim, and Zedekiah, we see a sad history in outline. It goes from the devout Josiah to the apostate Jehoiakim and finally to the pathetic Zedekiah, in whose reign Jerusalem fell to Babylon.

Also, the superscript appears to say that Jeremiah's ministry ended with the fall of Jerusalem in the fifth month of the eleventh year of Zedekiah's reign, but in fact he continued to preach for some time after that, while he lived among the exiles in Egypt (see 43:8–44:30). But the superscript is not meant to be an exhaustive account of the author's life and career, and it is not surprising that some details are omitted. And because the fall of Jerusalem was the supreme vindication of Jeremiah's prophetic warnings to Judah, to speak in the superscript of his postexilic ministry in Egypt would be somewhat anticlimactic. The years of Jeremiah's ministry, not including his postexilic years, were from 622 to 587 B.C.

The structure of this passage is as follows.

- ***The Identity of the Prophet (1:1)***
- ***The Historical Setting (1:2–3)***

## EXPOSITION (1:1–3)

### *The Identity of the Prophet (1:1)*

**1:1**. The book begins with, "The words of Jeremiah . . . ." By contrast, Isaiah begins with the words, "The vision of Isaiah" (Isa. 1:1), and Hosea begins with, "The word of YHWH that came to Hosea" (Hos. 1:1). Nahum begins with, "A prophecy about Nineveh; the book of the vision of Nahum" (Nah. 1:1; see also Joel 1:1; Obad. 1; Jonah 1:1; Mic. 1:1; Hab. 1:1; Zeph. 1:1; Hag. 1:1; Zech. 1:1; Mal. 1:1). The point is that in all these books of prophecy, the first thing the reader sees is a claim that the prophet's message is of divine origin. To be sure, Jeremiah asserts that the prophet received a message from YHWH, but the book puts it in verse 2: "to whom the word of YHWH came." In opening the book by saying, "The words of Jeremiah . . . ," the superscript first focuses on the man behind the words. It implies that to understand the words, we must understand the man. It suggests that we will see a great deal of Jeremiah in this text. His story, sufferings, and the circumstances of his messages, and not just the content of his prophecies, are crucial elements in book's message. We should also remember that the Hebrew דָּבָר ("word") is not only a spoken or written "word." It can also mean an "event," the "things that happened." As such, the "words" of Jeremiah are not only what he said but also what he did and experienced.

### *The Historical Setting (1:2–3)*

**1:2–3**. Apart from learning basic chronological facts about Jeremiah and his book, the reader can draw certain lessons from the superscript. First, all the words of condemnation and warnings of impending judgment in Jeremiah were true; the prophet stands vindicated, and those who opposed him stand condemned for apostasy and deceitfulness. Second, the three kings of the superscript provide a historical outline of spiritual decay in Jeremiah's lifetime: In Josiah's reign, there was a reformation sponsored by the king. God's faithful people had high hopes for spiritual renewal. In Jehoiakim's reign, there was open repudiation of all that Josiah had stood for and disdain for Jeremiah, God's prophet. In Zedekiah's reign, spiritual delusion and hostility toward the prophet reached a high point, and Jerusalem was destroyed. Third, this is not simply a book of revelations; it is "the words of Jeremiah." It is a book about a man of God, his ordeal, his vexation, and his faithfulness. As we better understand Jeremiah the man, we better understand the book and its message. Fourth, the book moves relentlessly toward its goal, the account of the destruction of Jerusalem and its temple, and the end of the Davidic dynasty. Jeremiah tells us why and how Jerusalem fell. The superscript ends with the words, "until the exile of Jerusalem in the fifth month"; and the epilogue (52:1–34) is an account of Jerusalem's fall and the captivity. As such, this event brackets the entire book.

We should also remember, however, that in the structure of Jeremiah, salvation and the new covenant stand at the very center (Jer. 30–33; see Introduction). It would not be correct to summarize the whole of Jeremiah with the implication that it is entirely made up of condemnation and predictions of disaster. At the center of the book is the promise of eschatological restoration.

## THEOLOGICAL FOCUS

The exegetical idea (The superscript's reference to three named kings—from righteous Josiah to apostate Jehoiakim and Zedekiah—ending with the fall of Jerusalem gives the essential facts about the book's historical setting and implies that its theme is how and why Jerusalem, the city of David and of the temple, was destroyed) leads to this theological focus: As evil becomes triumphant, people develop an inverted sense of right and wrong and build their lives on lies until judgment becomes inevitable, yet God provides a witness and shows the way to salvation revealed in several oracles that bring hope.

- Every minister must go through a private pilgrimage before God. The book concerns the words and deeds of Jeremiah, and it is intensely autobiographical, providing many examples of Jeremiah's agonies.
- True ministry is inaugurated by God. Although the book is intensely personal, it was initiated by the word of YHWH to Jeremiah.
- The appearance of the triumph of righteousness in this world is an illusion, and we should not expect to see the kingdom of God in this world. The reformation of Josiah was a time of heady optimism for the righteous, but it was followed by the wickedness of Jehoiakim and the calamity of Zedekiah.
- Even when the foundations are destroyed and evil and death seem to reign supreme, God offers hope and salvation. In the structure of the whole book, the new covenant is at the center.

## PREACHING AND TEACHING STRATEGIES

### *Exegetical and Theological Synthesis*

Perhaps two passages can summarize the message of Jeremiah: "The heart is deceitful above all things, and desperately sick; who can understand it?" (17:9 ESV); and "I will put my law within them, and I will write it on their hearts. And I will be their God, and they shall be my people" (31:33 ESV). The problem is, the human heart is in rebellion against God, and his solution is a new heart. The more we see the wickedness of our hearts, the more we are amazed at his forgiveness and redemption. To deny the wickedness of our hearts is to ignore the history of humanity's cruelty and our own personal history of seeking to worship ourselves. Jeremiah helps us see both the great wickedness and the great grace. We don't want to hear bad news and we are adept at filtering out what we don't want to hear. Thus, Jeremiah says over and over again, "You have sinned, and God's judgment is coming." This sermon in a minor key is heard in forty-nine of the fifty-two chapters, but only three chapters are given to the joyful melody of the new covenant. Even the structure of the book calls us to acknowledge our sin and embrace his forgiveness and redemption.

### *Preaching Idea*

When we see God's judgment, look for and embrace his restoration.

### *Contemporary Connections*

*What does it mean?*

What does it mean that when we see God's judgment, we should look for and embrace his restoration? In Jeremiah there are basically two actors: YHWH and Israel. And, there are basically two actions: sin and the giving of a new heart. We must not confuse who does what. Jeremiah makes it clear that Israel is the one who sins, and YHWH is the one who forgives and redeems. It is imperative that the right action goes with the right actor. Israel cannot bring about forgiveness or redemption. In their, and our, fallen state we wrongly think that we can bring about forgiveness and even a new heart. That is God's action, not ours.

*Is it true?*

Is it true that when we see God's judgment, we should look for and embrace his restoration? We tend not to pay attention to warnings. When did I last read a warning label? Jeremiah's message was a warning label on the wrong behavior of Israel. The Israelites treated it like we treat the warnings to use eye protection when mowing the grass. Perhaps it was understandable that they would disregard it. When those who lived in Jerusalem heard this message of certain judgment, they perhaps thought of how God delivered them before: from Egypt, from the Philistines, and from the Assyrians. In contrast, the Jews who read Jeremiah's words on the banks of the Euphrates would perhaps embrace it more quickly and long for God's restoration. Jeremiah's message was and is a harsh warning that God will judge sin. God's purpose was always redemption; his judgment was an act of love to bring correction to his children. The people of Judah were both deceitful and self-deceived, in that they heard what they wanted to hear. Jeremiah proclaimed God's warning of certain judgment, but in their deceit and pride they disagreed with God. Jeremiah made it clear that all Jerusalem would be destroyed, but in their self-deception they thought God would not destroy his temple. They would not hear what God was really saying to them. This leads me to ask, "Do I really listen to God?"

Do I really believe that God will judge my wrongs and then restore me? When I become aware that I have let something other than him rule my life, when I check my retirement more than I check his Word, when I realize that not only have I not given anything to the poor, but it doesn't even bother me that much? Do I tear up with regret? Am I even slightly troubled over it?

Do I think that God will somehow overlook this? Are we like the people of Judah who did not heed Jeremiah's warnings? Perhaps we have forgotten that God's love means that he will, at times, discipline us. This is not only an overriding theme in Jeremiah, but it is clearly affirmed in Proverbs: "My son, do not despise the LORD's discipline or be weary of his reproof, for the LORD reproves him whom he loves, as a father the son in whom he delights" (Prov. 3:11–12 ESV).

When we finally do come to the point of sorrow for our wrongs, it then becomes equally hard to believe that God wants to bless me with a new heart. Yet this is Jeremiah's main message, as shown by his placing it in the center of the chiastic structure of the book. This new covenant promises a new heart and a personal closeness to God that went far beyond the kind of relationship Israel had under their set of laws. "For this is the covenant that I will make with the house of Israel after those days, declares the LORD: I will put my law within them, and I will write it on their hearts. And I will be their God, and they shall be my people" (Jer. 31:33 ESV).

There is no record of the Jews embracing this wonderful promise. Since it was so far from their experience and only a promise of the future, we should be sympathetic to their lack of belief. We further our wrong by thinking that we can and will have to balance our bad with good. We hear that God will give us a new heart, but we still try to live by the old one. God's salvation and our close relationship to him are his great gifts and his work in our lives.

*Now what?*

If it's true that when we see God's judgment, we should look for and embrace his restoration, why do we sometimes fail to do that? If I know that I should turn away from that which keeps me far from God and enjoy the closeness he offers me, why don't I do just that? Why didn't the people of Judah? The Jews did not think that they were that bad; they were just fitting in with those around them. While we are not as blatant as they were in the worship of pretend gods, we are subtly moving in that direction. Do we entertain ourselves with media that exalts lifestyles and philosophies that are in direct contradiction to God's guidelines?

Back in the 1980s while on a mission trip to France, I was warned about the French television lingerie commercials. Then twenty years later, while waiting in a European airport, a passionate and even pornographic love scene was projected for all to see. We can't stop this moral invasion any more than Jeremiah could stop the worship of fertility gods and goddesses by Judah. But we can turn it off in our own living rooms. It seems that this erosion of the beauty of sex within marriage has invaded our culture. Do I truly believe that God will discipline us as he did Jeremiah's hearers? While the specifics of course will be different, the same God who warned the people of Judah warns us. We hear the words of Jeremiah like we hear the words of those who warn us against global warming. While global warming is debated, there doesn't seem to be any debate that our culture is growing cold toward God—in belief in him, in dependence upon him, and in submission to him.

Jeremiah's overall message is like a sandwich: judgment on the outsides and a great and wonderful promise of restoration on the inside. We should think about Jeremiah's messages like some think about an Oreo; the best part is the creamy white center. The wafer cookies on the outside lead us to, and enhance, the sweetness of the center.

### *Creativity in Presentation*

It is good to have something in our hands that we can physically touch and take with us. Perhaps let everyone leave with a small package of Oreos, to remind them of the interesting structure of the book, but more importantly, to emphasize the sweetness of the new covenant.

The basic structure for this sermon/lesson could be presented in two different ways. The first is a two-part structure. The first major section of the sermon would combine the warning sections that are in the first (chapters 1–29) and last (chapters 34–52) parts. The second major movement of the sermon is the central part section of the book: the restoration of the new covenant (chapters 30–33). This is a structure that is familiar to our congregations. It is simply a structure of "bad news/good news." Another approach that follows the text more closely will need some additional explanation, because it is a structure that is not often seen in Western thought. The first point, emphasizing God's judgment, comes from the negative warnings in chapters 1–29, followed by the positive message of a new heart in chapters 30–33, and then back to the negative in chapters 34–52. It sounds unfamiliar: bad news/good news/bad news.

Since the entire book is the basis for this sermon, only exemplary verses would be used from the various sections. As a pastor/teacher, these could be tailored to fit your contextual needs. In one of my examples I used caring for the poor, but that might not be the best for your setting. Jeremiah gives us numerous sins from which to choose.

One needs to be careful to explain that God's judgment includes redemption. Even when he judges, restoration is at the center of God's will. There is coming a final judgment day when those without Christ's forgiveness and the new covenant will be responsible to God for all their wrongs and not living up to all that God expected of them. Depending upon the constraints of your setting, it might be a great opportunity to explicitly present the gospel.

Jesus clearly taught us that the Holy Spirit is the one who convicts of sin. As we preach this book, it is not up to us to force a person to admit that they deserve God's judgment, nor is it our job to cause them to embrace his grace. Our job is to proclaim that when we see God's judgment, we should look for and embrace his restoration.

It is important to view Jeremiah's message through the eyes of those who first heard it. This helps us present the text and yet make application that is appropriate for us. Perhaps, after the introduction, begin by presenting the text using either structure mentioned above. Then ask the congregation to imagine how three different groups would respond to the message: (1) Jews hearing Jeremiah preach in Jerusalem, (2) Jews hearing the scroll read after the Babylonian conquest, and (3) how we hear it today.

The key idea to communicate is that when we see God's judgment, look for and embrace his restoration. The passage for this preaching unit can be outlined as follows:

- Present the text
    - Setting of Jeremiah's ministry (1:1–3)
    - God judges our sinful hearts and actions (17:9)
    - God offers us a new heart (31:33)
    - God judges our sinful hearts and actions (44:10)
      *This final point is used if following a chiastic sermon structure.*

- Present the applications to the three audiences
    - Jews hearing Jeremiah preach
    - Jews hearing the scroll read after the Babylonian conquest
    - Our hearing the book today

## DISCUSSION QUESTIONS

1. What makes correction hard to receive well?

2. What difference does it make as to who is correcting us?

3. Why do you think God had Jeremiah link the extreme judgments with the extremely wonderful new covenant?

4. What does it look like to be given a new heart?

# Jeremiah 1:4–19

## EXEGETICAL IDEA

Jeremiah's commission account marks him as a great prophet in manner of Moses, Samuel, and Isaiah. It also foreshadows the ordeals he will endure. The passage first describes God's call of a reluctant Jeremiah, and then declares that he must be armored by God to withstand the opposition he will face. This informs the reader that Jeremiah was genuinely chosen by God and that the hostility he endured is a mark of his greatness; it does not imply he was a failed prophet.

## THEOLOGICAL FOCUS

God's messengers each have a distinctive call, face specific challenges, require unique empowerment, and can be confident in proclaiming the word. But in this task, "success" is not defined by popularity or even by bringing about great changes for good. Rather, the only thing that matters is that the preacher is faithful in the face of great opposition as he receives the message and proclaims it.

## PREACHING IDEA

God's messenger needs God's assurances and empowerment to proclaim God's message.

## PREACHING POINTERS

This passage is often applied primarily to fellow messengers of God's truth. While this might be an acceptable application, it does not take into account that most of those who read this when it was first written were not in the role of heralds, but listeners. Jeremiah's divine appointment and message gave him courage and assurance; it also guided listeners to a submissive attitude. They needed to know by whose authority a prophet was speaking or writing. This was not the mere authority of a governor or king; this message had the highest authority.

Today God's call of Jeremiah encourages those of us who preach; but even more, this first episode of Jeremiah's narrative sets forth that this book has the authority of God. For a culture such as modern, or postmodern, America where the individual's emotions seem to carry the most authority, it is important that congregations know and remember that this message is from God—and that makes all the difference. This book is not Jeremiah's devotional thoughts; it is the very word of God. When the Bible is proclaimed, it is not the preacher's devotional words about God; it is God's authoritative word. As preachers we cannot change how a congregation listens, but we can have a level of expectation that does affect them as we view our role more seriously.

# JEREMIAH'S COMMISSION (1:4–19)

## LITERARY STRUCTURE AND THEMES (1:4–19)

Jeremiah received a calling that echoes the calls given to great prophets from the past, and this demonstrates the legitimacy of his claim to be YHWH's prophet to his generation against his critics, who considered him to be an inferior or spurious prophet because Jerusalem was destroyed in his day. This is implicitly in contrast to a prophet such as Isaiah, who seemingly was empowered by God to turn back the Assyrian army in an earlier generation.

- ***Jeremiah Chosen by God (1:4–12)***
- ***Jeremiah Fortified Against Opposition (1:13–19)***

## EXPOSITION (1:4–19)

### *Jeremiah Chosen by God (1:4–12)*

The account of Jeremiah's commission to prophesy to Judah is in two parts, verses 4–12 and 13–19, each containing a message from YHWH related to Jeremiah's commission. It may be that the two messages came at separate times to Jeremiah, even years apart (Lundbom 2008a, 107–14).

Jeremiah's first encounter with God includes three interactions between himself and YHWH, each one initiated by YHWH. The first is a dialogue between God and his young prophet (vv. 4–8); the second is a visionary action and explanation carried out by God (vv. 9–10); and the third is a vision followed by an explanatory dialogue (vv. 11–12).

**1:4–5.** After the formulaic notice that Jeremiah received a message from God (v. 4), the text records God's initial message to Jeremiah (v. 5). It is an abrupt yet indirect command to Jeremiah to take on the duties of a prophet. It does not begin with something like, "Jeremiah, I want you to serve as my prophet," and it does not ask if he is willing to volunteer for the task (contrast Isa. 6:8). Instead, the message he received focuses on God's predestination of Jeremiah to the prophetic task, saying that God appointed him to this position before Jeremiah was born, and even before he was conceived. God's claim that he "knew" (ידע, *qal* stem) Jeremiah before his conception does not simply mean that God passively knew that Jeremiah would someday be born. It connotes God's active acknowledgment of Jeremiah as belonging to himself. Also, when God says he "consecrated" (קדש, *hiphil* stem) Jeremiah, it means he set him apart for a holy task. It is a heavenly commission. The verbs indicate that long before Jeremiah began to exist, God ordained that he would be a prophet.

This foreshadows the way the book portrays Jeremiah's experience as a prophet. The task gave him a great deal of sorrow, and at times he wanted to quit. But he was compelled to continue to preach. God's word burned in his heart and his bones, and he could not hold it in (Jer. 20:9). By opening the commission with a claim that God had predestined him to this task even before he was in his mother's womb, the text makes clear that this is, for Jeremiah, an inescapable task. He was literally born to do it.

**Jeremiah and Predestination**

The concept of predestination is difficult and divisive, but it is not a topic to avoid. Many interpreters, to be sure, take extreme views on the doctrine. This is true of almost every biblical idea, and especially of those that are hard to comprehend (2 Peter 3:16). For some, the doctrine implies strict determinism, so that we are simply lines of code in God's computer program, and we passively act out our assigned roles and respond to preordained events in precisely the manner the heavenly encoding dictated. As such, "free will" is pure illusion. Others believe that the doctrine of predestination means that God only passively knew what decisions we would make, and that he chose us in accordance with what we would freely choose. As such, God does not really predestine anything; we make all the important decisions ourselves.

Neither extreme is biblical. God desires all people to repent and come to him (2 Peter 3:9). It is difficult to see how this is compatible with a hard determinism, in which God has in effect made the decisions for us. The apostle Paul, out of a fear of God, sought to persuade people to believe (2 Cor. 5:11). This implies both that he knew that God wanted him to urge people to believe and also that people have minds and wills; they can be persuaded to come to God, and they can also refuse to be persuaded. On the other hand, he says that God foreknew, predestined, called, justified, and glorified the true members of his church (Rom. 8:29). This claim loses all meaning if it is a passive activity—that God "predestined" those whom he passively knew would believe. To the contrary, the Christian's experience of salvation is that God is active and *we* are passive. We were dead in sin and blind to the truth, but God gave us life and sight so that our believing was almost inevitable (Isa. 42:6–16; Eph. 2:1–9).

We should not maintain one great truth by jettisoning the other. God desires all to repent, and he commissions preachers to appeal to the wills, hearts, and minds of all people. Those people may stubbornly resist or may repent and believe. On the other hand, the true church is made up of people whom God predestined, called, and justified—people who in their blindness could do nothing for their own salvation, but whose hearts were strangely warmed by the grace of God.

In reality, many of the great doctrines of the faith are paradoxical and beyond human understanding. This is true, for example, of the most fundamental of all Christian teachings, that God is the Holy Trinity. There is one God in three persons. This is beyond all earthly analogy and explanation. God is not one person who takes on three roles, nor is he divided into three parts; there is but one God, not three. "One God in three persons" is a truth we can affirm, and we can grasp the meaning of the words, but we can never truly comprehend God's nature. It is beyond our experience and mental capacity. This may seem to be a great offense to reason, but it should give us comfort. God, by definition, is so far above us that we are no more able to understand his true nature than a toad is able to understand calculus. If we were inventing a religion, we would make a god that we can wrap our minds around. We would either say that there are many gods (as in polytheism), or we would say that there is a single, unitarian God (as in Islam). We can understand the "one God in one person" of Islam; this has no mystery to it at all. But the God of the Bible is a being that no human mind could invent; this fact is a mark of authenticity.

Paradox is even a feature of the great truths of nature, to say nothing of God. Insofar as we know, light is both a wave and a particle. Here too, we can grasp the meaning of the words, but we cannot truly comprehend light itself. The ideas of light being a wave and light being a particle are for the human mind irreconcilable, and yet both statements are true. Indeed, the higher physics of relativity and quantum mechanics are heavily populated with ideas and essential concepts that only a few among us are able to grasp, but that no one fully understands or can fully integrate into a unified, nonparadoxical framework. If this is true of the natural world, is it not likely that God's being and God's mind (as in the Trinity and in predestination) are beyond our grasp?

We Christians live with paradox about God all the time. We pray. We do this, seeking to persuade God to a course of action but believing that if we do not pray, God may not act. But even as we seek to persuade God to do certain things, we do not think that this invalidates God's omniscience or sovereignty. We pray for someone to repent and turn to Christ, but we do it believing both that the person has free will and that God can somehow change that person's heart. As such, we should not be offended at these truths: God has chosen some for salvation, and God wants every single person to repent and come to the truth. People are dead in sin and insensitive to the call of the gospel apart from the quickening work of the Spirit, and people have minds and free will. They come to Christ because God drew them to himself, not because they decided to choose God. And they can be influenced by arguments and examples either toward belief or unbelief, but in the end, they make up their own minds and are responsible for their decisions. These truths are paradoxical, but they reflect both our doctrine and our experience. We need to accept them even if we cannot integrate them into a single, nonparadoxical theology.

Jeremiah himself reflected the paradoxical nature of God's election. On the one hand, he was set apart for his prophetic task before he was born or made any decision on his own. And he could not escape his calling, even though it gave him great pain. He was almost a prophet against his will. On the other hand, he was fully committed to YHWH and to Israel's covenant with YHWH; and yet he was bewildered, disheartened, and angered by Israel's unbelief. His love for God and his embrace of his prophetic calling were wholeheartedly and freely given. We humans are not as unsearchably profound as the mind of God, but we too, it turns out, are complex beings.

**1:6–8**. Jeremiah's response recalls the experiences of Moses and Samuel. Like Moses when God commissioned him to lead Israel from Egypt (Exod. 4:10), Jeremiah protested that his poor speaking ability disqualified him for the prophetic office. Like Samuel, he heard God's call when only a boy (1 Sam. 3:1–14). Jeremiah's connection to Samuel is not surprising; he was from Anathoth, a town close to Shiloh and Ramah, two sites associated with Samuel. God did not directly address Jeremiah's protest that he was a poor speaker, because his lack of skill in that area was a function of his being young and inexperienced. He merely told Jeremiah not to use his youth as an excuse and ordered him go where he was directed and to speak the messages God gave him. His order that Jeremiah not fear "them" (v. 8) is quite general. The people whom he might fear are not defined, whether they would be Israelites, Gentiles, or some more specific group. Indeed, the "fear" Jeremiah experienced at this time appears to be little more than stage fright, a natural shyness about preaching to men who were older, stronger, and more experienced than himself. In all probability, Jeremiah did not yet realize the extent to which he would be persecuted. The assurance God gave to Jeremiah in 1:8, "I am with you" (כִּי־אִתְּךָ אֲנִי) is essentially the same assurance he gave to Moses (Exod. 3:12, כִּי־אֶהְיֶה עִמָּךְ).

**1:9**. Like Isaiah, Jeremiah had his mouth "touched" in a vision. Both Isaiah 6:7 and Jeremiah 1:9 have "and he touched my mouth" (וַיַּגַּע עַל־פִּי). In Isaiah, the prophet is distressed that he has "unclean lips" and is therefore unworthy to proclaim God's message, and a seraph touches his mouth with a hot coal (it was a vision, not a physical experience), symbolically purging away his impurity. In Jeremiah, the prophet is distressed that he is a youth and a poor speaker, and thus will not be able to proclaim prophetic sermons. YHWH touches his mouth, symbolically giving him the words he will speak. In both cases, the touch removes the obstacle that prevents the chosen man from carrying out his prophetic commission.

**1:10**. This verse presents YHWH's conferral of prophetic authority upon Jeremiah, and it is crucial to interpreting the whole book. It describes the scope of Jeremiah's commission with six verbs. These verbs reappear throughout Jeremiah, as indicated in the table below. To be sure, not every use of each of these verbs is a direct allusion to Jeremiah 1:10, but many are. For example, 31:28 uses all the verbs of 1:10, as well as שׁקד ("watch over") from 1:12, and as such is an obvious allusion to Jeremiah's commission. Repetition of these verbs indicates that they to a great degree informed Jeremiah's understanding of his mission and prophetic authority. The reader of Jeremiah should be on the alert for these verbs and consider how each usage may allude to Jeremiah's commission.

God "set Jeremiah over nations and kingdoms" to uproot, demolish, kill, destroy, build, and plant. At first glance, this makes it seem that Jeremiah has enormous and almost magical power, as though he could simply speak and then walls would fall down and his enemies would die. In reality, Jeremiah never had or exercised such power. In fact, no miracles at all are attributed to Jeremiah, except that several of his predictions came to pass. The verse does not confer on Jeremiah the ability to make nations fall and rise at will; it means that he is a legitimate prophet, and that his messages will in some way and in the fullness of time come true. In short, he will give genuine messages from God, and God will see to it that his messages are fulfilled.

**Six Repeated Verbs of Prophetic Authority in Jeremiah 1:10**

| Verb | Meaning | Usage Elsewhere in Jeremiah |
|---|---|---|
| נתשׁ | To uproot | 12:14, 15, 17; 18:7, 14; 24:6; 31:28, 40; 42:10; 45:4 |
| נתץ | To demolish | 4:26; 18:7; 31:28; 33:4; 39:8; 52:14 |
| אבד | To kill (*hiphil*) | 18:7; 25:10; 31:28; 46:8; 49:38 |
| הרס | To destroy | 24:6; 31:28, 40; 42:10; 45:4; 50:15 |
| בנה | To build | 7:31; 12:16; 18:9; 19:5; 22:13, 14; 24:6; 29:5, 28; 30:18; 31:4, 28, 38; 32:31, 35; 33:7; 35:7, 9; 42:10; 45:4; 52:4 |
| נטע | To plant | 2:21; 11:17; 12:2; 18:9; 24:6; 29:5, 28; 31:5, 28; 32:41; 35:7; 42:10; 45:4 |

The first four verbs are negative, implying destruction and death, while the last two are positive, implying rebuilding and life. The bulk of Jeremiah is taken up with warnings of judgment and catastrophe, but the ultimate goal is life and salvation.

### The Authority of the Prophet Jeremiah and of the Apostle Peter

As described above, God gave Jeremiah great authority. At his word, kingdoms would rise and fall. This does not mean that Jeremiah was a kind of super-magician, able to say a few words and cause a whole nation to perish, and it does not mean that God handed his authority over to Jeremiah. But it does mean that Jeremiah's words would carry great weight with God, and that God would not disregard any of Jeremiah's pronouncements. As we will see, God did not destroy Jerusalem until after Jeremiah had stopped praying for the city and instead began to make imprecations against it.

And Jeremiah's words could have great and terrible impact. Jeremiah decreed that the false prophet Hananiah would die for how he had misled the people, and he died within two months (28:12–17). This was similar to the authority Elisha displayed when he pronounced a curse against some children who were mocking him, and a bear rushed out and killed them all (2 Kings 2:23–24).

Jesus famously conferred, or appears to have conferred, special authority on Simon Peter. "You are Peter, and on this rock, I will build my church. . . . I will give you the keys of the kingdom of heaven, and what you bind on earth will be bound in heaven, and what you loosen on earth will be loosed in heaven" (Matt. 16:18–19). Roman Catholics assert that Peter was made the earthly head of the church and the Vicar of Christ, and that he was the first Bishop of Rome. Through apostolic succession, Peter's authority was conferred to each successive bishop of Rome, so that every pope down to the present day is legitimately the earthly head of the Christian church.

Protestants reject these claims for the papacy and thus have sought to counter the Catholic interpretation of Jesus's pronouncement, but their interpretations of Matthew 16:18–19 have sometimes been forced and pedantic. Some have argued that the masculine Πέτρος ("Peter") distinguishes it from the feminine πέτρα ("stone"), meaning that Peter was only a small stone, but that the rock on which the church was built was Christ himself, or perhaps that the "rock" was the faith that Peter confessed. But the proper name "Peter" was naturally put in the masculine gender (Πέτρος), while the word for "rock" is feminine. There is no implication in verse 18 that Peter and the "rock" refer to two different things. Also, Jesus probably gave the saying in Aramaic, as indicated in the Aramaic form of Peter's name, Cephas (אפיכ). In Aramaic, Jesus would have used אפיכ for both "Peter" and "rock." Even if Jesus was speaking Hebrew, it is doubtful he used two different words for "rock" and "Peter." He almost certainly did not make the statement in Greek.

Another Protestant argument is that in verse 19, the words for "bound" and "loosed" are future perfect passive participles, meaning "will have been bound" and "will have been loosed" (thus, "what you bind on earth will have been bound in heaven"). This, it is argued, implies that Peter does not have any real authority; he can only affirm what God has already done. But even if these participles are given their full grammatical force, it means only that God is ultimately in control. Peter, by virtue of having the right to declare what God has decided, still has enormous authority. And probably the Greek participles function like simple future passives ("will be bound" rather than "will have been bound"), as is typical in Hellenistic usage (Blomberg 1992, 252–55; France 2008, 257–59). Thus, it is all but certain that "on this rock" refers to Peter, and that Peter has been given the keys and the power to declare what is loosed or bound in heaven.

None of this supports the extravagant claims that the Catholic Church makes for the papacy. The New

Testament never suggests that the early Christians regarded Peter as a pope serving as the Vicar of Christ. Peter was a leader in the church, but he was subject to rebuke (Gal. 2:11–14). In the making of important ecclesiastical decisions, he was only one among equals, and not even first among equals (Acts 15, where James leads in the meeting). Peter's ability to bind and loose was conferred also on the individual congregations of the church (Matt. 18:18). Peter had apostolic authority and was held in great respect, and he was nominally the leader of the effort to evangelize the Jews, as Paul led the effort to evangelize Gentiles (Gal. 2:7). But of course, it was among the Gentiles that the church thrived, and it died among the Jews. Most importantly, Jesus never suggested that Peter could pass his authority on to a successor.

Peter's authority was analogous to that given to Jeremiah. Peter had high authority, as implied by the power to bind and to loosen, and by the "keys," just as Jeremiah was set over nations to "pluck up" and "break down." But just as Jeremiah's authority was in reality limited to certain prophetic functions, so also Peter's authority was limited to certain apostolic functions. Acts 15 demonstrates that Peter did not have the power to unilaterally make doctrinal decrees that were binding on the whole Christian church (the letter from Jerusalem regarding the Gentile churches was not issued by Peter or in his name). He certainly was not made the doorkeeper of heaven, as in popular imagination; the metaphor of the keys implies that he was given a stewardship by Christ, but he was not the only one of whom this was true (1 Cor. 4:1–2).

Like Jeremiah, Peter demonstrated that he had authority and a commission from God. Jeremiah issued a curse upon a false prophet and in two months, the man died (Jer. 28:15–17). Peter with a word healed a lame man (Acts 3:6–8), and with another word caused a deceitful husband and wife to fall dead (Acts 5:1–11). Both Jeremiah and Peter left behind writings that have become canonical texts for the Christian church. But Jeremiah had no successor to his office, and neither did Peter. Paul, similarly, could with a word cast out demons and raise the dead (Acts 16:18; 20:9–12), and his writings, too, have become canonical Scripture. The prophetic and apostolic offices are similar. Both offices went to a select few people who served as spokespersons for God, both carried great authority, both could compose canonical texts, and both offices were nontransferable. Matthew 16:18–19 asserts that Peter was a true apostle of the church, but it does no more than that.

**1:11–12.** The vision Jeremiah received is based on a paronomasia (a wordplay or pun). In the vision, Jeremiah sees the branch of an almond tree (שָׁקֵד), and God tells him that he is "watching over" (שֹׁקֵד) his word to fulfill it. The words are homonyms, words that sound the same but are etymologically unrelated. The similarities in their sound and spelling creates the pun. God will fulfill all the prophecies he gives to Jeremiah. If the prophet declares that a city will fall, then in the course of time it will fall. But there is probably a hidden lesson behind the use of the almond (שָׁקֵד) branch, apart from the pun on "watch over." An almond branch calls to mind Aaron's rod that budded in the course of the rebellion of Dathan, Abiram, and the sons of Korah—people who sought to usurp the authority of Moses and Aaron (Num. 17:8). By analogy Jeremiah, the man who stands in the tradition of Moses and Samuel, would face many challenges from false prophets and apostate priests. But in the end, God would vindicate him.

### *Jeremiah Fortified Against Opposition (1:13–19)*

In the second vision, YHWH tells Jeremiah that the main opposition he will face will come from his own people, not the Gentiles, and YHWH fortifies him to face the opposition.

**1:13–14**. Jeremiah says he received a "second" vision without indicating when it came. He could have received it on the same day as the first, after some weeks, or even after some years. But the content of the second vision is more important than its chronology; it introduces a radically new element to Jeremiah's prophetic commission. This vision, unlike that of verses 11–12, is not based on a paronomasia. Rather, elements of the vision are symbolic. A pot is boiling, analogous to how we say something like, "The people's frustration is boiling over," meaning that it is about to erupt in violence. The international crisis, in which empires and armies were on the move, was ready to break out in war and conquest. The boiling pot was tipping over "from the north." In the preexilic prophets, the "north" typically represents the great Mesopotamian powers, either Assyria or Babylon. Since Assyria's power was at this time broken, it refers to Babylon.

**1:15–16**. These verses further elaborate on verses 13–14, explaining in more detail the meaning of the vision. The "tribes and kingdoms of the north" includes Babylon with all its client states; the Babylonian army included elements from various allied and subjugated states. This massive army would lay siege to Jerusalem. It may be that the first vision, when he was told that God had set him over nations and kingdoms (v. 10), gave him the impression that he would primarily prophesy against foreign

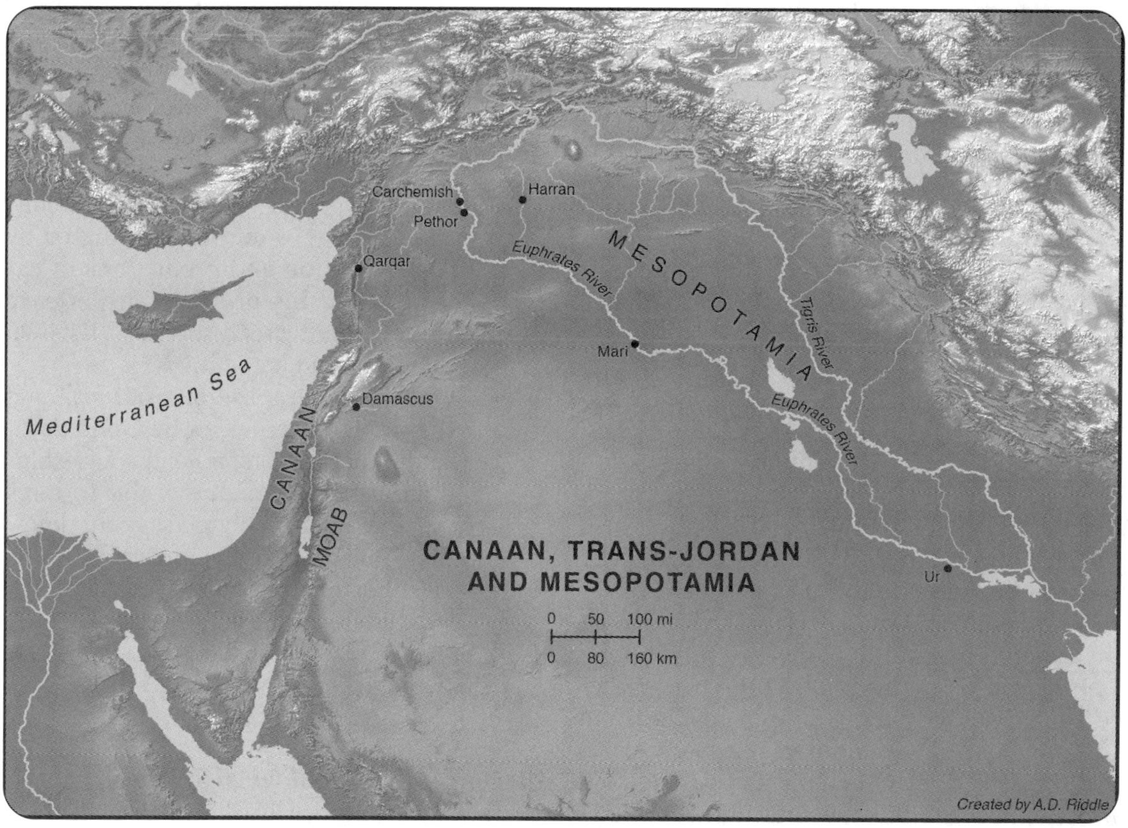

powers (as Nahum had done). He may have thought that the people of Judah would welcome his messages and that Jerusalem would rise up in triumph while all the pagan powers would crumble. When Jeremiah was first commissioned, Judah was in the midst of Josiah's reformation, and he may have been optimistic that the people would faithfully serve YHWH and see his great acts of deliverance. If so, the second vision entirely disabused him of that notion. Judah would not repent of its idolatry—and Babylon, not Jerusalem, would be the triumphant city.

**1:17–19**. This was no doubt to Jeremiah the most disturbing element of all in the second vision. It tells him that his real enemies will not be the Babylonians or any other Gentile people; it is the people of Judah who will despise his words and seek to destroy him. He must fortify himself for a bitter struggle against the prophets and priests of YHWH and the house of David, and he must be ready for hostility from his own friends and family. The secular and religious leaders in Jerusalem, along with the common people, would despise him. He would need to ready himself, in God's strength, for hatred, abuse, and violence. In the end, he would be vindicated, but his entire life would be a painful struggle.

## THEOLOGICAL FOCUS

The exegetical idea (Jeremiah's commission account marks him as a great prophet in manner of Moses, Samuel, and Isaiah. It also foreshadows the ordeals he will endure. The passage first describes God's call of a reluctant Jeremiah, and then declares that he must be armored by God to withstand the opposition he will face. This informs the reader that Jeremiah was genuinely chosen by God and that the hostility he endured is a mark of his greatness; it does not imply he was a failed prophet) leads to this theological focus: God's messengers each have a distinctive call, face specific challenges, require unique empowerment, and can be confident in proclaiming the word. But in this task, "success" is not defined by popularity or even by bringing about great changes for good. Rather, the only thing that matters is that the preacher is faithful in the face of great opposition as he receives the message and proclaims it.

- No one can choose to be God's spokesman; it is God who chooses. God commissioned Jeremiah to a prophetic task. It was a task that Jeremiah, in the sovereignty of God, was born to carry out, and he could not evade it or resign.
- God's prophets and apostles had great authority, and our confidence in canonical Scripture arises from our faith that they were truly commissioned by God. Jeremiah's words would prove true and his messages would become, for all time, canonical Scripture.
- Being a true messenger of God is no guarantee that the task will be joyful or that people will listen. Jeremiah's message would be dominated by condemnation and predictions of calamity, and his prophetic experience would entail great sorrow. His own people would hate him.
- Only a strong sense of God's call and the resilience provided by God's Spirit can prepare a person for the hardships of ministry. Jeremiah was able to carry out the calling only because he knew that God had chosen him before he was even born and because God had fortified him for the task.

## PREACHING AND TEACHING STRATEGIES

### *Exegetical and Theological Synthesis*

God's call on Jeremiah's life shows us how

important it is that the preacher/teacher be assured that they are appointed by God. How that is done will probably not happen in the same way that Jeremiah experienced his call. This calling of Jeremiah is not so much to give a pattern for how God calls people to proclaim his message, but to show us that both the messenger and the message must have God as the authority. When God's word is proclaimed, there is great authority given to the preacher by the local assembly. It might be in the role of a pastor, staff member, or a teacher of a class. Under various methods a local church gives a person the responsibility of teaching or proclaiming God's word.[1] The words of the preacher carry great weight. It is not a speech about religious topics; it is the word of God being proclaimed. That authority should affect the preacher and the listeners. God took great pains to call Jeremiah because he was to preach a message of judgment to a hostile and rebellious generation. The parallel to our times is not hard to see.

### *Preaching Idea*

God's messenger needs God's assurances and empowerment to proclaim God's message.

### *Contemporary Connections*

#### *What does it mean?*

What does it mean that God's messenger needs God's assurances and empowerment to proclaim God's message? To the degree that we respect someone, we will believe what they say. As we drive away from the policeman with our warning ticket, we drive under the speed limit and even use our blinker as we reenter the line of traffic. We respect what the officer represents, and thus the warning results in a change. Jeremiah was striving to direct the people of Judah to respect the message he was given by showing them the source. His appointment clearly highlights that his message is from God. Judah, however, did not accept him nor God's message.

Do I accept that the message of the Bible is from God? Of course—don't all evangelicals? But do my actions say something different? The prophet wanted to show the people of Judah that they should act on these warnings because they were from God. Do I let God's Word affect all areas of my life or do I hold out in some areas? All of God's Word is good for all of God's people all of the time. Jeremiah's words are a warning to us: pay attention; the message you are about to hear is from God.

The first vision shows that God will do what he says. There is a degree of comfort in that God will keep his word. What God says, will happen; no qualifiers. Even with computer enhancement, weather and economic predictions are always qualified. As proclaimers of his Word, we can be greatly assured that his message is true. However, the confidence in God's faithfulness that leads us to assurance should also lead us to weep because of his promised judgment.

#### *Is it true?*

Is it true that God's messenger needs God's assurances and empowerment to proclaim God's message? Yes, and if it is from God, why would we hesitate to proclaim it? While the above application is directed toward the readers of Jeremiah, there is also encouragement for the one proclaiming the message. We too are expected to proclaim a divine message that includes a warning of judgment. We might even want to avoid some of those topics offensive to the non-Christian such as gender issues, abortion, hell, Christian exclusivism, and clergy abuse. Biblical truths must still be proclaimed, of course, yet with graciousness (Col. 4:5–6). We

1 For a very good discussion of the authority given to the preacher by a congregation, see chapter 3, "Preaching Is Ecclesial," in Abraham Kuruvilla, *A Vision for Preaching: Understanding the Heart of Pastoral Ministry* (Grand Rapids: Baker Academic, 2015).

must not hesitate to address those topics offensive to churchgoing Christians such as greed, neglecting our bodies (obesity), stinginess, abuse of alcohol, cohabitation by millennials and senior citizens, and overzealous political allegiance.

Jeremiah could have just presented the new covenant—the happy, joyful part of God's message—but God wanted him to warn his people. God gives us a hard task in warning that judgment is coming. Just as Jeremiah needed encouragement, so do we. We must not hold back in our proclaiming God's entire message.

*Now what?*

If it's true that God's messenger needs God's assurances and empowerment to proclaim God's message, what do we need to do next? Jeremiah is not an easy book to read and understand, but if God is the source, then we need to take the effort to grasp what God wants us to hear. Perhaps for you it was in junior high or perhaps even earlier. In seventh grade I (Calvin) read my first real novel: *White Fang* by Jack London. It wasn't a picture book and it demanded more mental energy and focus than I was used to investing, but it was well worth it. Jeremiah's message will demand more from us not only to comprehend it, but to put it into practice. Warning labels on consumer products are designed to be read quickly (and hopefully without much effort) to grasp what to do or not do: "Do not use near flame," "Avoid contact with skin," or "Do not use if seal is broken." When it comes to spray paint or household insecticides, the directions are simple. But our lives are far more complicated and so are the warnings. As the study of this book begins, we need to step up our efforts to embrace this book given through Jeremiah.

### *Creativity in Presentation*

The first inclination in applying this chapter is to side with Jeremiah and take God's words to him as a foundation for God's encouragement to us. While this is a way to apply this passage, let's first and primarily view this introduction in 1:4–19 from the point of view of the people of Judah. Perhaps a skeptic in Jerusalem would ask Jeremiah, "Why should I listen to what you have to say? Why should I bother to read this book?"

Many twenty-first-century people are saying the same thing. The teacher/preacher might try painting a scene in which a skeptic, thinking out loud, rebuts Jeremiah's message. Create a scene at a workplace breakroom, where the discussion turns to Jeremiah. It would be like a discussion about Billy Graham (1918–2018), who preached the gospel of Christ in person to more than 100 million people. Imagine a coffee-break conversation: "Billy Graham was a good man, but what he said about hell. . . ." As the skeptic ponders Jeremiah's introduction his view begins to change for the positive, but just as he is about to embrace the message, the hard part comes: judgment. Leave the skeptic struggling. Then show how this text can help in this struggle. The rhetorical understating of this strategy is that you are raising and answering the questions we have about fully embracing the truth of this passage. As teachers/preachers we are helping our people accept this more fully, by dealing with their objections before they can even ask them. Most of us today believe that God sent the message, and that God performs and protects the message; we just don't believe it strongly enough.

The key idea to communicate is that God's messenger needs God's assurances and empowerment to proclaim God's message. The twofold application of the passage's main thrust can be presented in the following points:

- Being chosen by God gives assurance to the speaker and open hearts to the hearers (1:4–12).
- Being fortified against opposition

empowers the speaker and creates expectation in the hearers (1:13–19).

## DISCUSSION QUESTIONS

1. How is this (1:4–19) a good introduction to the rest of the book of Jeremiah?
2. At what points do you identify with Jeremiah? With the people of Judah?
3. Does it seem unmerciful that God will judge Judah?
4. How do you think Jeremiah felt about the message he was given to deliver?

# MESSAGES AGAINST JUDAH (2:1–20:18)

This section is a series of undated messages that accuse Judah of apostasy and foretell its destruction. It corresponds to 46:1–51:64, which is a series of undated messages against the nations. Within 2:1–20:18, 2:1–4:4 serves as an introduction. The unity of the introduction is indicated by an inclusion structure, in that it begins and ends with similar language: 2:2 contains the words, "Go and proclaim in the ears of *Jerusalem, Thus says YHWH*. . . ." and 4:3 has, "For *thus says YHWH* to the men of Judah and *Jerusalem*. . . ." (Lundbom 2008a, 250). The introduction readily breaks down into two sections. The first is an indictment of Judah (2:1–3:10) and the second is an appeal to repent and promise of restoration (3:11–4:4).

# Jeremiah 2:1–3:10

**EXEGETICAL IDEA**

A series of vivid metaphors describes how Israel's apostasy has caused the nation to be completely perverse—at the same time both self-righteous and wicked while transferring its love to stone gods and to nations that hate Israel. A series of vivid metaphors repeatedly make the points that Judah is incurably apostate and that this has robbed the nation of its identity, its good sense, its dignity, and its innocence.

**THEOLOGICAL FOCUS**

Turning from God is never done in isolation from other ethical and ideological areas of life, allowing a people to be apostate but otherwise culturally and morally healthy. Apostasy leads to immorality, cruelty, twisted thinking, misplaced affection, and a refusal to acknowledge guilt. Those who reject the truth will inevitably embrace bizarre and foolish lies.

**PREACHING IDEA**

When we give up on seeking the Lord, sin will be seeking us.

**PREACHING POINTERS**

It must have been hard for the people to hear this sermon when it was first preached. Being told that you are suffering the consequences of years of sinning is not what anyone wants to hear. The first hearers of the written form of the message could distance themselves by saying, "That is what our forefathers did; we are suffering because of their sin," and miss the point of Jeremiah's message. Jeremiah is not blaming the fathers; he is warning the children.

If not careful, we can only present this passage as a description of how bad Israel sinned and how severe the terrible consequences. The temptation is to study this from a distance, but those who first heard the sermon and those who later read, including us, are all in the same family of God. In a sense, they are our people; we are not outsiders. These words are for us, to warn and explain the tragic results of our sin and to lead us to repentance.

# ASTONISHING EVIL (2:1–3:10)

## LITERARY STRUCTURE AND THEMES (2:1–3:10)

Using a series of metaphors, Jeremiah describes how deeply Judah has fallen into apostasy. A principal metaphor here is the unfaithful wife, and the repeated idea is that Judah has fallen into a level of evil that is astonishing, surpassing even that of the pagans.

- ***Lost Love: The Bride and the Firstfruits (2:1–3)***
- ***Looking Back: Did God Fail Israel? (2:4–8)***
- ***Litigation: Israel Is Worse Than the Pagans (2:9–13)***
- ***Lost Freedom: Judah Like a Slave (2:14–19)***
- ***Long History: Metaphors for Israel's Apostasy (2:20–25)***
- ***Lowly Disgrace: Serving False Gods (2:26–28)***
- ***Love Rejected: Judah's Perverse Hostility to God (2:29–37)***
- ***Lust Without Shame: Judah's Guilt (3:1–5)***
- ***Lost Sisters: Judah's Obstinate Stupidity (3:6–10)***

## EXPOSITION (2:1–3:10)

### *Lost Love: The Bride and the Firstfruits (2:1–3)*

Israel's love for YHWH has grown cold, and thus they are no longer under his special protection. Israel is a wife who once loved her husband but does so no longer; Israel was once holy to YHWH, like the firstfruits offering, but they no longer offer themselves to God.

**2:1–2**. YHWH describes Israel's apostasy under two metaphors. The first is a bride who in the first years of her marriage showed great love to her husband. YHWH remembers the woman's former "devotion" (חֶסֶד), a word that essentially means "kindness" or "compassion" but in this context is the affection a bride gives to her husband. By implication, the bride no longer has such feelings; otherwise, YHWH would not be *remembering* it but *experiencing* it. YHWH speaks of the wilderness period as the "honeymoon" of Israel's devotion to God. Readers may be confused at this, since Exodus and Numbers record several episodes of unbelief and bitter complaining by the Israelites. However, the biblical narrative naturally focuses on important episodes and crises, and these were generally times of sin and rebellion; it does not concern itself with the day-to-day experience of the people in the forty years of wilderness wandering. Much of this was, we can presume, a positive experience of love between the people and YHWH. A strong bond formed between the two. By analogy, the first century was a honeymoon period for the church, but that time too had many troubles.

**2:3**. The second metaphor is firstfruits, the offering made when the Israelites brought the first and best parts of a harvest to present to YHWH at the sanctuary (Exod. 34:26; Neh. 10:35). By implication, Israel was the beginning of the harvest of God, and the harvest would be complete when the nations were also gathered in. Also, the grain and produce offered as the firstfruits belonged particularly to God; in the same manner, Israel specially belonged to God (Exod. 19:5) and was the "pupil of his eye" (Deut. 32:10). For that reason, God was protective over Israel and defeated all their enemies (as in the war with the Amalekites, in Exod. 17:8–16). As the first metaphor speaks of how the love of Israel the bride grew cold, the second metaphor speaks of how God can no longer give Israel the kind of special love and protection he once had, since they were no longer his.

**Israel as an Adulterous Wife**

In this part of the text, Jeremiah often employs the metaphor of Israel as an adulterous wife or promiscuous woman. In the metaphor, YHWH is the woman's lawful husband, and her promiscuity represents Israel's worship of idols and other gods. Of itself, the metaphor makes no charge against actual women—the wives, mothers, and daughters among the people of Israel. It is entirely symbolic, and in no way implies that the men of Israel were more righteous than its women. Even so, feminist interpreters are deeply offended by such language, arguing that the frequent use of the metaphor indicates a deep-seated misogyny underlying Israelite culture (Crouch 2017, 23–26). The offense taken is somewhat overwrought. The New Testament portrays the church as the beloved and ultimately glorified and pure bride of Christ, but no one takes that to mean that the New Testament holds that women are better Christians than men. In both cases, it is simply a metaphor. But even women who do not count themselves feminist may find it wearying or troubling to read so many portrayals of Israel as a promiscuous, unfaithful woman.

There is one other aspect of the metaphor that ought to encourage such female readers. The metaphor of Israel as the unfaithful wife is first fully developed in Hosea, in the story of his marriage to Gomer. Here, we do see Israel as an unfaithful wife, but she is also a mother producing children of adultery, children who have names such as Lo-Ammi ("Not my people"). Her portrayal as a mother implies that the woman is specifically the institutions and leading men of Israel—the king, the aristocracy, the priests, and the professional prophets. The "children" in the metaphor are the common people; they are the ones who have their religious ideals and behavior shaped by the leadership. As such, when Hosea and Jeremiah prosecute Israel under the metaphor of a promiscuous woman, they most specifically attack the leaders of the nation, its movers and shakers, who were almost exclusively male. As such, modern female readers can take comfort that the "adulterous woman" is in fact a male hierarchy, not a group of promiscuous women, and that it is these men whom the prophets accuse (see Jer. 2:8). Feminist interpreters who defend "woman Israel" against the prophets' charges are, ironically, defending ancient Israel's patriarchy. Readers interested in this topic can consult my commentary on Hosea, where I explore this issue in more detail (Garrett 1997, 124–33).

### *Looking Back: Did God Fail Israel? (2:4–8)*

Although YHWH had always been faithful to Israel, the people, and particularly their leaders, acted as though he had failed and so turned to other gods. And their behavior was perverse: instead of the true God, they went after worthless idols, and the priests, rulers, and prophets did the opposite of what they were commissioned to do.

**2:4–7**. The command to hear the word of YHWH (v. 4) opens this subsection. The "fathers" are a cumulative representation of all Israelites throughout their history. They have a long-established habit of not calling on God. They did not say, "Where is YHWH?" (they did not seek or call upon YHWH in times of need). Instead, when trouble came, they turned toward "worthless idols" for help. The word for idols (הֶבֶל) means "vapor" or "breath," and it connotes something that is transitory and of no lasting value. As such, it is translated as "vanity" or "meaningless" in Ecclesiastes 1:2. However, in the prophets, הֶבֶל frequently refers to idols (Jer. 14:22; Jonah 2:8 [MT 9]). The Israelites should have remembered how God had saved them from slavery in Egypt with miraculous, mighty works, and how he carried them safely through the desolation of the wilderness to a fruitful land. Instead, they forgot what God had done in the exodus and turned to inert images for help. Thus, God asks, "What fault did your fathers find in me?"

**2:8**. As verses 5–7 ask generally about the "fathers," so verse 8 asks specifically about the priests, the "shepherds" (kings and other high officials), and prophets. They, too, did not ask, "Where is YHWH?" The priests handled the Pentateuch, the texts that told of God's great works for Israel and that prescribed the laws by which they should live. They, above all people, should have known what God required, but they distorted its message. The political leaders "rebelled" (פשׁע), meaning that they used their power to usurp God's place as Israel's ultimate ruler, and the prophets gave oracles in the name of Baal. Thus, the priests twisted the Law, the "shepherds" used their authority to try to overthrow God's authority, and the prophets were spokesmen for a foreign god. Every segment of Israel's leadership perverted the roles God assigned to them, doing the opposite of what they had been charged to do.

### *Litigation: Israel Is Worse Than the Pagans (2:9–13)*

The pagans are generally faithful to their false gods, and yet Israel cannot remain loyal the true God. Their infidelity is thus as perverse as it is reprehensible. God metaphorically sues them for their crimes.

**2:9**. Because they are rebellious subjects, YHWH brings charges (ריב) against them. This is a formal accusation, analogous to a plaintiff accusing another of a wrong in a court of law (in ancient Israel, at the city gate). The accusation is directed toward Jeremiah's audience, their children, and grandchildren. In 2:4–8, he argued that Israel's apostasy and disobedience is a habitual and well-established pattern, not an aberration. Here, just as he had accused former generations, he now accuses the present and future generations. This implies that their perverse habits continue from one generation to the next.

**2:10–11**. Jeremiah tells the people of Judah to travel to Cyprus and other islands of the eastern Mediterranean (כִּתִּיִּים refers generally to the Greek archipelago, although primarily to Cyprus, as the word כִּתִּיִּים is derived from the name of a Phoenician colony on Cyprus) and also to Kedar (קֵדָר), part of the Ishmaelite confederation in Arabia. Because of the difficulty of travel (across the sea for Cyprus, and over desert and rugged terrain to Kedar), these are here regarded as distant lands, respectively, to the northwest and southeast. The implication is that they can search far and wide for a Gentile people who have behaved as badly as Judah has, and they won't find one. The question posed, "Has a nation exchanged gods?" implies that the answer is no. As a rule, pagan cults tended to be highly conservative, enduring for generations with little modification. A given people might worship the same gods and observe the same rites and superstitions for a millennium. Of course, one can find examples of a new, foreign cult coming into places and gaining adherents (as in the Roman adoption of the Greek gods and later of the cult of Mithras), but Jeremiah's question is rhetorical and concerned with general truths; it is not an examination of the history of pagan religions. The point is this: pagans can be faithful to their false gods of wood and stone for ages, but Israel cast off its allegiance to the one, true God as quickly as possible. In verse 11, the God of Israel is identified not as YHWH or simply as "God" but as Israel's "glory" (כָּבוֹד). Israel was not a great and powerful nation (Deut. 7:7). Israel had but one thing that set it apart from the other nations: this was not its empire (like the Assyrians), its monuments (like Egypt), its grand city (like Babylon), or its learning (like Greece), but its relationship to God. This alone set Israel above every other people, and yet they willingly cast aside fidelity to YHWH in favor of the artificial gods of the nations.

### *Lost Freedom: Judah Like a Slave (2:14–19)*

Israel has a long history of going to the nations for help, but it never works out well. They end up as slaves, being bought and sold among the Gentiles like cattle. Their constant attempts to gain help from the nations is another example of perverse behavior.

**2:14**. Jeremiah asks if Israel is a slave or servant born in the household (יְלִיד בַּיִת; lit., "born of the house"). The latter designation refers to someone who was born into slavery and hence has never known anything except slavery. Such persons were legally property, liable to be bought and sold like cattle. As such, stealing a slave was essentially theft of property, like taking someone's horse. By contrast, taking a free person was kidnapping, a heinous crime (Deut. 24:7). The Israelites in captivity are thus a degraded people among the nations. They have ceased to be a free people and are now the plunder of an army and property to be bought and sold on the open market. "Israel" here probably refers to all of the tribes—to the northern kingdom, which was conquered by Assyria; and to Judah, which was devastated by the Assyrian Sennacherib in the time of Isaiah and which, in the time of Jeremiah, was a prize sought by both Egypt and Babylon.

**2:15**. The nations set against Israel are like roaring lions. The roaring represents the bestial violence of Israel's enemies; they desire to devour their prey. But the metaphor of lions is not sustained through the verse. Lions do not leave a land as a desolation or devastate cities—human armies do that. Egypt and Babylon fight over Judah as for a piece of meat, and the result is that the land suffers terrible and ongoing destruction.

> *TRANSLATION NOTE FOR 2:15*
> The verb יִשְׁאֲגוּ should be translated as "are roaring," not as "have roared" (it is a *yiqtol* form). "They give their voice" (נָתְנוּ קוֹלָם) employs the *qatal*, but since it is used in conjunction with a *yiqtol*, both verbs should be regarded as present tense. The *kethiv* נִצְּתָה can be taken as a *niphal qatal* 3fs for נצה ("fall into ruin"). The problem is that the antecedent (עָרָיו, "its cities") is plural, not singular. On the other hand, use of a singular verb would not be unprecedented (Gesenius and Kautzsch 1898, §145k). The *qere* is נִצְּתוּ. This is often taken to be a *niphal qatal* 3cp from נצה ("they are in ruins"), but the form is unusual; one would expect נִצּוּ for the doubly weak verb נצה (cf. Neh 1:3). If the *qere* is followed, one should take נִצְּתוּ as a *niphal qatal* 3cp of יצת, "to be burned down," although the form of the word is somewhat peculiar. We should probably follow the *kethiv*. Thus, the verse should be rendered, "Lions roar against him / They give their voice. // And they make his land into a desolation; / His cities are in ruins, without inhabitant."

**2:16**. Since two Egyptian cities, Memphis and Tahpanhes, are said to plunder Israel, it is likely that this text comes fairly early in Jeremiah's ministry, perhaps soon after Pharaoh Neco II killed Josiah in battle. Memphis was the old capital of Egypt; it was located at the southern tip of the Nile Delta. Tahpanhes was in the eastern Delta and of some significance in the seventh century. But both are simply representative of Egypt; these particular cities do not seem to be crucial for Jeremiah's message. Egypt had a history of equipping its soldiers with the mace; this probably accounts for the claim that they are breaking the skulls of the men of Judah (see translation note below). As a side note, some expositors assert that the image of a skull being smashed invariably alludes to Genesis 3:15, the promise that the seed of the woman would crush the serpent's skull. But that clearly is not the intent here. In this case, it is the pagan Egyptians who hold the mace and crush the skull.

> *TRANSLATION NOTE FOR 2:16*
> The verb יְרֹעוּךְ is not from the root רעה, to "graze" or "shepherd," as it cannot possibly fit this context. It is probably רעע II in the *qal* stem, meaning "break," but could be רעע I in *hiphil* stem, "harm" (Holladay 1986, 51). The pointing is peculiar in either case; the tradition probably pronounced it as if it were רעה even though it is actually רעע. In any case, the word does not mean "to shave," as in the NIV. The shaving of the head would hardly be a severe punishment. In fact, Egyptians routinely shaved their own heads, and they would not regard this as a humiliation or as a brutal act to inflict on an enemy.

**2:17**. Israel is entirely to blame for the troubles they encountered, and the root of all their troubles and bad decisions is that they abandoned YHWH. The end of the verse, "at a time [when] he [was] leading you along the way" (בְּעֵת מוֹלִיכֵךְ בַּדָּרֶךְ), is not present in the LXX. Many interpreters regard the line as a gloss (not original to Jeremiah). It seems to refer to the events of the wilderness wandering in the exodus period, and this seems alien to the context, which is concerned with recent, not ancient, events (Lundbom 2008a, 272). On the other hand, the "leading" could be metaphorical, as in "YHWH has been leading you in the way you should live, but you abandoned him." And an allusion to the exodus generation is not out of place, since the context does concern Egypt. The point would be, "As you turned back toward Egypt and away from God during the exodus, so you continue to do today."

**2:18**. The prophets often condemn Israel for seeking help from the nations, their armies, and their gods. Here, "drinking water from the Nile" is metaphorical for seeking the benefits that Egypt offers. We are surprised that the text mentions Assyria as a power toward whom Israel turned for aid. It is possible that this passage comes from very early in Jeremiah's ministry, before Assyria's final collapse (Nineveh was destroyed in 612 B.C.; the empire briefly survived at Harran, but then was entirely obliterated). It is more probable that this is a historical allusion to how frequently Israel went to Assyria for help (for example, as Ahaz did in 2 Kings 16:7). Even so, the text is probably from early, before Babylon began to dominate the region (after 605 B.C.).

**2:19**. Because they have been morally evil (רָעָתֵךְ, "your evil") and theologically apostate (וּמְשֻׁבוֹתַיִךְ, "and your apostasy"), all of these troubles are coming upon them. Their actions are both "bad" (רַע) and "bitter" (מָר), the two words together meaning that they are repugnantly evil. Apostasy always leads to moral ruin and disgraceful behavior, and finally to destruction.

### *Long History: Metaphors for Israel's Apostasy (2:20–25)*

Jeremiah makes the case against Israel with a series of metaphors: Israel was like an ox released from its yoke but now unwilling to serve; it was a promiscuous woman; it was a vineyard that produced only bad fruit; it is like clothing with stains that will not wash out; and it was like a camel or wild donkey in heat. The metaphors present the nation as ungrateful, reckless, lustful, irrational, evil, and guilty.

**2:20**. Two metaphors here describe Israel's apostasy. First, although Israel was a slave in Egypt, like an ox under the yoke, YHWH in the exodus broke off their yoke and bonds, freeing them. This alludes to Leviticus 26:13, "I am YHWH your God, who brought you out of the land of Egypt, taking you from being their slaves. And I broke the bars of your yoke and made you walk upright." The verbs should be taken as first person and not as second person ("you broke"), against some recent translations (see Translation Note). By turning away from YHWH, Israel shows a gross lack of gratitude. The second metaphor is a promiscuous woman who has sex with men on every hilltop and under every tree. The hills and trees are the locations of cult shrines to various gods, and the promiscuity represents idol worship (which sometimes included actual cult prostitution).

*TRANSLATION NOTE FOR 2:20*

The verb שָׁבַרְתִּי ("I broke") could be regarded as an archaic second person, "you broke" (Lalleman 2013, 81). This is supported in the LXX, which reads the verb as συνέτριψας, "you broke apart." The LXX also has a second person, διέσπασας ("you tore apart") for the MT נִתַּקְתִּי, "I tore off." The NIV follows the LXX second-person reading. If this is correct, it describes an act of rebellion by Israel. The phrase "tear off bonds" (נתק מוֹסֵרוֹת) can refer to a rebellion against God (Jer. 5:5; Ps. 2:3), but it can also be used of God saving people from captivity (Jer. 30:8; Ps. 107:14). The same is true of "break the yoke" (שׁבר עֹל), used of Judah's disobedience in Jeremiah 5:5 but of YHWH's salvation of Judah in 30:8. In 2:20 the first person is more likely the original; it alludes to YHWH's liberation of Israel in the exodus, as in Leviticus 26:13.

**2:21**. In another metaphor, Jeremiah describes Israel as a vine grown from seed known to be of a good, productive variety. What grew of it was instead a wild vine that produced only inedible grapes. The metaphor draws upon Isaiah 5:1–7, the Song of the Vineyard. While it is possible that the "good seed" represents Abraham, the ancestor of Israel, it is unlikely that we are meant to understand the verse in terms of literal biological procreation. Rather, the "good seed" describes how God had done all he could to give Israel a good start, taking them out of Egypt through signs and wonders and then instructing them with the Law. Despite all God had done for them, they turned out badly.

*TRANSLATION NOTE FOR 2:21b*

The phrase סוּרֵי הַגֶּפֶן נָכְרִיָּה looks odd; it is literally "wandering ones of the vineyard; an alien." The text is often emended to סוֹרִיָּה גֶּפֶן נָכְרִיָּה ("foul smelling; a foreign vine") on the basis of the LXX. But סוֹרִיָּה is conjectural and otherwise unknown in the Bible. It need not be emended. The "wandering ones of the vineyard" (סוּרֵי הַגֶּפֶן) are probably invasive plants that spread among the good vines in the vineyard; we would call them weeds. The "alien" (נָכְרִיָּה) is a plant that does not belong, whether it is an inferior stock of vine or a simple weed. The line might be rendered, "How have you become to me like trash vines, or an invasive plant?"

**2:22**. In yet another metaphor, the Israelites vainly try to remove a stain from their clothing. The word for "wash" (כבס) means to launder clothes, as in Genesis 49:11, not to bathe oneself (which would require a verb such as רחץ). They can apply natron (נֶתֶר) and use lots of alkaline salts (בֹּרִית), but the stain of their sin won't come out. The metaphor refers to religious acts (sacrifices, pilgrimages, and so forth) without a truly repentant attitude. It implies that the people were aware of their guilt but sought to deal with it superficially, rather than by a true return to God. The verse also implies that only God can remove the stain of guilt.

**2:23–24**. The passage briefly steps away from its sequence of metaphors to recount the denial that the Israelites have made, asserting that they are not apostate and therefore not guilty. The denial implies that even in its most decadent state, Jerusalem's people knew that they were bound by the covenant to be faithful to YHWH, and therefore they felt obliged to assert that they had not consorted with other gods. In response, Jeremiah first speaks literally and then metaphorically. He first asks them to consider how they have behaved in "the valley," which is almost certainly the Ben Hinnom Valley in Jerusalem, where there were shrines to Baal and where child sacrifice had been carried out, as noted in 2 Kings 23:10 (Holladay 1986, 100). He then accuses them with a pair of related metaphors: Israel is a female camel or a wild donkey in heat, heedlessly rushing about for a male to mate with. Once again, the sexual metaphor portrays the lust of the people to serve other gods; it is an insatiable craving. By speaking of Israel as a camel (a large, powerful beast) or a wild donkey (an animal unwilling to submit to human control), the text implies that no one can restrain them from their apostasy. On the other hand, she is only too willing to be taken by whatever male camel or donkey desires her. Israel is stubborn toward YHWH, but compliant to other gods and the nations.

**2:25**. This section concludes with a pair of commands and Israel's response. The commands are literally, "Keep your feet from bareness and your throat from thirst," and interpreters naturally puzzle over the meaning. Probably the bare feet refer to sexual promiscuity (cf. Song 5:3), and the dry throat refers to the running and panting of the camel or donkey in heat. In both cases, the commands continue the metaphor of sexual promiscuity representing apostasy. The Israelites' response, as given in many translations, is misleading. The NIV has "It's no use" and the NRSV has "It is hopeless," both implying resignation on Israel's part, as though they would like to change their behavior but just can't. But the word in question (נוֹאָשׁ) is a blunt interjection, a refusal to comply. It means, "Forget that!" or perhaps more crudely but accurately, "To hell with that!" (*HALOT* [s.v. "נוֹאָשׁ," p. 382] gives it the translation, "Damn!"). Israel, in its determination to follow other gods, is defiant.

### *Lowly Disgrace: Serving False Gods (2:26–28)*

**2:26**. All the social classes of Judah and Jerusalem are in complete disgrace. The three classes are the common people ("the people"), the government officials ("kings and officials"), and religious leaders ("priests and prophets"). The verse almost certainly does not mean that they *feel* disgrace—clearly, they do not—but that they *are* disgraced. The verb (בּוֹשׁ, *hiphil* stem) can mean to feel shame, but it also means to behave disgracefully (Prov. 10:5), whether one feels any shame or not (see Jer. 6:15).

**2:27**. Their disgrace, the appalling thing they do, is declare that idols of wood and stone are their gods. In saying to the idol, "You fathered me," they proclaim that it created them, loves them, and cares for them just as a father cares for his children. To do this for a carved piece of wood or stone is hopelessly stupid, and it illustrates how immorality and apostasy lead to personal degradation.

> *TRANSLATION NOTE FOR 2:27*
> The *qal qatal* of ילד appears in this verse in the *kethiv* יְלִדְתִּנִי, a 2fs, and the *qere* יְלִדְתָּנוּ, a 2ms. The *qere* is preferable since the people call the idol "my father." The verb here can be translated, "You fathered me."

**2:28**. If the idols really are gods, they should prove it by rising up and saving Judah from its trouble, the way YHWH saved Jerusalem when it was under siege by Sennacherib in the time of Hezekiah (Isa. 36–37). This challenge, with its implication that Judah already felt itself threatened, indicates that this passage comes from sometime after 605 B.C., when Babylon was ascendant and beginning to threaten Judah.

### *Love Rejected: Judah's Perverse Hostility to God (2:29–37)*

Israel's apostasy has led them to behave irrationally and perversely. Though obviously in the wrong, they blame God for their troubles, as though they were blameless. They act as though God was cruel, making their lives hard and confusing, when in fact he has been clear and consistent. They turned from YHWH, their first love, and expect the nations who hate them to help them.

**2:29–30**. Far from being contrite, the people of Jerusalem blame YHWH for their troubles. It could be that the people "bring charges" against YHWH, as in the NIV, but the verb (ריב) need not refer to formal charges. It may simply mean that they habitually blame God and complain about how he has governed affairs. In response, YHWH says that the people have all rebelled (פשע) against him. Under the terms of the Sinai covenant, YHWH was Israel's sovereign. When they disobeyed the stipulations of the covenant, he was well within his rights to punish them. And being God, he is *always* within his rights if he chooses to punish. God continues his counterargument in verse 30 with the assertion that the calamities Israel suffered did not come about because God was capricious or vengeful; he was trying to bring the people to their senses, so that they would change their ways. But it was all "for nothing" (לַשָּׁוְא). Israel would not repent. Worse, they viciously attacked the prophets who rebuked them, as Jesus described in the parable of the tenants (Luke 20:9–19).

**2:31**. YHWH further responds that he has been a source of life and light to Israel; they have no right to blame him for all that has gone wrong. In a very unusual pair of metaphors, God asks if he has been a "wilderness" (מִדְבָּר) or a "land of darkness" (מַאְפֵּלְיָה) for Israel. The essential idea is that their relationship to YHWH is like travelling through a land. If the land is a wilderness or the journey is in the dead of night, it is a dangerous, confusing, and painful affair. But it has never been like that for them; YHWH saved them and provided for them, and in the Law, he always made it clear what was required of them. The demand that they worship only him was straightforward and not terribly difficult to follow. The main thing was that they had to keep away from idols. In that, their walk with God was a straight and level path on a clear day.

*TRANSLATION NOTE FOR 2:31*

The word מַאְפֵּלְיָה is a *hapax legomenon* apparently composed of מַאֲפֵל (another *hapax legomenon*, this word is found in Josh. 24:7 and apparently means "darkness") plus יָהּ, the shortened form of יהוה. Thus, it seems to mean, "Darkness of YHWH." It is generally taken to be a superlative (Holladay 1986, 108), meaning "deep darkness" or the like. The word possibly implies "supernatural darkness," that is, a darkness that is unnaturally severe or that never ends. As such, the rhetorical question would be, "Has your relationship to God been like traveling through a land where darkness never ends?"

**2:32–33**. Judah's behavior stands in contrast with what one normally sees in a faithful wife. Verse 32 asks if a virgin (בְּתוּלָה) forgets her ornaments (עֲדִי) or a bride (כַּלָּה) forgets her sash (קִשֻּׁרִים). The ornaments are in this context those worn in a wedding (Ezek. 16:11), and the sash is some kind of a garment that brides bound around themselves on a wedding day, as in Isaiah 49:18, "you bind them on like a bride" (וּתְקַשְּׁרִים כַּכַּלָּה). There are two ways to interpret this rhetorical question. It could mean, "Does a bride forget to put on her ornaments and sash when she goes to her wedding?" Or it could mean, "Does a wife forget the day of her wedding, when she wore the bridal ornaments and sash?" The latter seems preferable. In the analogy, Israel was wed to YHWH in the Sinai covenant. A good wife would treasure the memory of her wedding and keep her ornaments and sash in a special place as reminders of that day. But Israel thinks nothing of her marriage to YHWH. To the contrary, she is skilled getting out of her home and finding other lovers (Jer. 2:33). She is so practiced at it that she could instruct the worst women in the art of adultery. In the metaphor, this means that she could teach even the pagans a few things about paganism.

*TRANSLATION NOTE FOR 2:33*

The *kethiv* reads לִמַּדְתִּי (in context, "I have taught your ways to evil women"), but it is best to follow the *qere*, לִמַּדְתְּ ("You have taught your ways to evil women"). The LXX has καὶ σὺ ἐπονηρεύσω τοῦ μιᾶναι τὰς ὁδούς σου ("and you behaved wickedly to defile your ways"), apparently reading וְאַתְּ הרעות לטמא את־דרכיך. But this is not to be followed. Holladay suggests an alternative interpretation, revocalizing אֵת to אַתְּ and לִמַּדְתִּי to לֻמַּדְתְּ and taking the line to mean, "In fact you've done ill, you've been trained (in) your ways!" (Holladay 1986, 109–10). But this is not persuasive. One should simply follow the *qere*.

**2:34–35**. The people refuse to see the enormity of their crimes. They have the blood of the innocent poor on their clothes, meaning that anyone with power and influence legally entraps the poor, taking away their property and leaving them either destitute or in slavery. Such abuse was tantamount to murder, and in some cases, they actually did resort to murder, as in the famous case of Naboth's vineyard (1 Kings 21:1–14). In the face of all this, the better-off Israelites refused to acknowledge that they had done any wrong and insisted that God was not angry with them, or at least that he had no legitimate grounds to be angry with them.

**2:36–37**. In their folly, the leaders of Judah seek for help from nations that care nothing for them. The prophet asks, "Why have you been so rash (I-זלל), constantly changing your directions?" As the Israelites once turned to Assyria for help, now they turn to Egypt. But it is all useless. The Assyrians despised Israel, and in fact they destroyed the northern kingdom. Nothing is going to change; the nations will treat Israel with "contempt" (בוש is conventionally translated "be ashamed," but here it implies that nations show no respect toward Israel, and thus that Israel will be disgraced and dismayed when no help comes from these powers). Verse 37 says that their diplomats will flee these countries with their hands on their heads. Tamar, after she was raped by Amnon, went about with her robe torn, wearing ashes, and with her hand on her head (2 Sam. 13:19). The implication is that Israel's ambassadors will be treated with contempt, as Amnon did to Tamar. But it does not necessarily mean that the other nations literally abused Israel's ambassadors. It is rather that because they regard Israel with contempt, the Jerusalem leaders are fools for thinking they will find help among the nations. YHWH, moreover, completely rejects the idea that Jerusalem should place confidence in Gentile powers. Thus, even when a foreign power chose to help Judah (because it was in that nation's interest to do so), God would thwart the attempt, and Judah would be left defenseless.

### *Lust Without Shame: Judah's Guilt (3:1–5)*

Jeremiah continues to show how apostasy has produced twisted, irrational thinking among the people. Like a woman who thinks she can abandon her first husband, join herself to another man for a time, but then resume her previous marriage when it suits her, so Israel thinks it can turn to other gods but then resume its covenant with YHWH. They do not see how their apostasy has destroyed their souls and their relationship with God, and they refuse to acknowledge guilt.

**3:1**. As though seeking information on a point of law, Jeremiah asks his audience whether a man can remarry a woman whom he has divorced if in the meantime she has taken another man. The answer is no; such an act is forbidden in Deuteronomy 24:1–4. If such a thing were allowed, it would be serial promiscuity and no different from two men going to the same prostitute. Judah is under the misimpression that they can break their marriage to YHWH, the Sinai covenant, and commit apostasy with other gods, but then come back to YHWH and resume the "marriage" as though nothing had happened. Jeremiah tells them this is not so; they have broken their covenant bond with YHWH and have no claim on his protection and love.

*TRANSLATION NOTE ON 3:1*
This verse begins with the unusual, לֵאמֹר הֵן, which appears to mean literally, "to say, look!" But in this case הֵן does not mean "look" but "if," as in Jeremiah 2:10. Combined with לֵאמֹר, it poses a question and looks for a legal ruling, as in Haggai 2:11–12, "Ask for a legal ruling from the priests, as follows [לֵאמֹר]: 'If [הֵן] a man takes consecrated meat . . . .'" Thus, in Jeremiah 3:1, לֵאמֹר הֵן is an abbreviated way of saying, "Consider this question: If . . . ."

**3:2**. Jeremiah appeals to the people to look around and see how apostate they have become. In every high place and at crossroads, they have waited like prostitutes for their customers (these locations would also be likely spots for small shrines to gods). The idol worship is described as the illicit promiscuity of the prostitute, and yet, even though the sex is voluntary, the text says the woman was raped. On the literal level, sex between a client and a prostitute would have no tenderness or affection to it, and thus be more like rape than lovemaking. As a symbol for apostasy, it reveals how turning from God to serve some rival, such as an idol, ravishes the soul. Those who turn from Christ and the gospel to serve some other ideology find themselves to be spiritually, emotionally, and intellectually raped by the experience.

*TRANSLATION NOTE ON 3:2*
The *kethiv* שֻׁגַּלְתְּ ("you have been raped") has the *qere* שֻׁכַּבְתְּ ("you have been laid down"). The *qere* is a euphemism, the *kethiv* being considered too crude or harsh to read in synagogue. The *kethiv* is the correct text, but it is somewhat hyperbolic. In the metaphor, Jerusalem was not raped; she voluntarily gave herself to all her lovers (that is, to the idols). But the use of שֻׁגַּלְתְּ implies that idolatry can never be (in the metaphor of sexual union) good, joyful, or edifying. It always does damage to those who practice it. Accepting false religion is more like being raped than entering into the loving bonding of a man and woman.

**3:3**. The heavenly punishment Judah has received is further proof that their sins offend God, but they refuse to see or acknowledge it. The lack of rain demonstrates God's displeasure, and elsewhere Jeremiah speaks of a severe drought in the land during his lifetime (14:1–6). But the people, though they see the drought, refuse to make a connection between it and their sin. They have, instead, a "prostitute's forehead" (מֵצַח אִשָּׁה זוֹנָה). The words describe the facial expression of a woman who is brazenly defiant, refusing to cast her eyes down or feel shame even though the whole community knows that she is a prostitute.

**3:4–5**. These verses should be translated, "And so are you now going to call me, 'My father,' [or will you say,] 'You are my lifelong husband'? [Or will you say,] 'Are you going to hold on to anger eternally? Will you maintain [your anger] forever?' Look, [that is how] you speak as you do [all kinds of] evil. And you get away with it." (I have had to supply a number of words, indicated in brackets, for clarity.) We have no indication that ancient Israelite women called their husbands "My father" (אָבִי). Some regard this as evidence that the text is corrupt and needs emendation (Holladay 1986, 115), but this is not necessary. The two questions are not fully parallel; the one looks to YHWH as a metaphorical father, and the other looks to him as a "lifelong husband" (אַלּוּף נְעֻרַי is literally, "companion of my youth," but it refers to a woman's first and, ideally, lifelong husband). They are separate metaphors; it is not one metaphor in which a woman calls her husband "father." In verse 5, the people complain that since they are YHWH's child or lifelong spouse, he should not be severe and unrelenting in his anger. Judah is presumptuous. The people refuse to behave like a dutiful child or faithful wife, but they expect to be treated like one.

*TRANSLATION NOTE FOR 3:5*
The final verb וַתּוּכָל ("and you prevailed") is surprising for being a 2ms instead of the expected 2fs, ותוכלי. The MT may simply have dropped the י by scribal error, or it may be a case where the prior series of 2fs verbs establishes that this also is 2fs, even though it is formally 2ms (Gesenius and Kautzsch 1898, §§69r and 145t).

### *Lost Sisters: Judah's Obstinate Stupidity (3:6–10)*

Much of this text tells the story of Samaria, the northern kingdom, and specifically of its apostasy and subsequent destruction at the hands of the Assyrians in 722 B.C. But Samaria is not the real focus of this text; Jerusalem is. The point of recounting the story of Samaria's sin and destruction is that Judah had ample warning of what apostasy would do to the nation, but they followed in the footsteps of the northern kingdom anyway.

**3:6–8a**. Continuing the metaphor of the faithless wife, the text recounts how Samaria turned from God and was destroyed. The passages in Jeremiah 2–20 generally lack historical context, and even the notation "in the days of King Josiah" (v. 6) is very broad; it is not a precise marker for the date of the text. It clearly comes from the earliest stage of Jeremiah's ministry. As subsequent parts of the book make clear, Jeremiah began with some optimism about Judah's spiritual renewal. As time went by, he became thoroughly convinced that repentance was not a real possibility for his generation. This text, 3:6–10, probably represents an early message from God meant to wake him up to the reality of how deep in apostasy Judah really was. We should also recall that Jeremiah is not chronologically arranged. Some of what we see in 2:2–3:5 may come from a later stage of Jeremiah's ministry. YHWH's question in 3:6, "Do you see what apostate Israel (מְשֻׁבָה יִשְׂרָאֵל) did?" does not concern things that happened in Jeremiah's lifetime; it is purely historical. By Jeremiah's time, the northern kingdom had been gone for about one hundred years. Israel committed spiritual adultery—idol worship—on every hill and under every tree. God hoped that Israel would repent, but she did not, and Israel's "treacherous sister Judah" (בָּגוֹדָה אֲחוֹתָהּ יְהוּדָה) was watching all of this. Because of Israel's metaphorical adultery, YHWH divorced her. The divorce took the form of the armies of Assyria under Shalmaneser V (726–722 B.C.) and Sargon II (721–705 B.C.) ravaging the territory of Israel, burning down Samaria, the capital city, and taking most of the people off into exile. That is, the divorce was effectively the obliteration of the northern kingdom. Judah not only saw all this but very nearly came to the same end under Sennacherib (704–681 B.C.).

**3:8b–10**. And yet Judah learned nothing. To the contrary, Israel's "sister" Judah was unfazed by it all; "she had no fear" (וְלֹא יָרְאָה). Although the people had the example of Samaria's apostasy and destruction, they committed the same acts of apostasy and thus had all the greater guilt for it. In verse 9, the text does not specify the subject of the verbs, and some interpreters take it to be Israel (e.g., the NIV), but this is certainly wrong. It is Judah who was indifferent to the lesson of Israel's fall and continued to defile the land by her idolatry. They were frightened enough by the ferocity of the Assyrian invasion to make a pretense of repentance (v. 10), but it was all for show. They never truly turned from the idols.

*TRANSLATION NOTE FOR 3:9*
*This verse contains two translation issues*. First, its initial verb is a *weqatal* (וְהָיָה) and not, as one might expect, a *wayyiqtol*. This suggests that one should not translate the verse with simple past

tense verbs. It should be rendered, "And so it has been the case that, owing to [Judah's] indifference to [the lesson of Israel's] adultery, [Judah] has been defiling (וַתֶּחֱנַף) the land and has been committing adultery (וַתִּנְאַף) with stones and trees." The *wayyiqtol* verbs וַתֶּחֱנַף and וַתִּנְאַף continue the force of the initial וְהָיָה. Second, the expression מִקֹּל זְנוּתָהּ is a problem. It appears to say, "because of the sound of her promiscuity," but that makes little sense. The LXX renders מִקֹּל as εἰς οὐθὲν, "for nothing." Thus, probably קוֹל here is not "sound" but is a different noun, one derived from קלל, "to be slight, trifling." So understood, מִקֹּל זְנוּתָהּ is, "because of [what she regards as] the insignificance of her adultery."

## THEOLOGICAL FOCUS

When a people turn from God, it is not an isolated act. It leads to distortions of every kind. These include:

- Immoral behavior
- Intense selfishness, even if it harms others
- Deep hostility toward ideological opponents
- Preference for other religions and hostility to the God of the Bible
- Refusal to acknowledge guilt in the face of overwhelming evidence
- Blaming God for their troubles even though they have abandoned God and have no real claim on him
- A perverse preference for enemies, believing that they can be relied upon

Jeremiah 2:1–3:10 is relevant for any nation that has abandoned a Christian heritage. To cite a few examples of how it works itself out in our day, we see wide acceptance of homosexuality and transgenderism, along with a celebration of abortion. People not only practice such things but become furiously angry at those who reject such behavior. At the same time, Islam is widely celebrated in the west, even though it is the motivating force behind acts of terrorism in America and Europe and is severely prosecutorial toward homosexuals. For many people in the post-Christian west, the God of the Bible exists only as a being to blame for all their troubles.

## PREACHING AND TEACHING STRATEGIES

### *Exegetical and Theological Synthesis*

Jeremiah begins the message of this passage with two foundational sins: Israel is not loving the Lord and is not seeking the Lord. The third and largest section contains the consequences of Israel's not seeking the Lord (2:9–3:10). The last thing people today want to hear is a list of sins and the consequences that follow. God is not just giving a list of sins; he is exposing what is being lost by turning away from loving and seeking him.

One of the images that Jeremiah uses is that of trading living water for water from cisterns (2:13). When we stop loving and seeking the Lord we turn from pure living water to stagnant water. God is not just exposing sin and its consequences; he wants to bless. In this image he wants his children to have the living water. While we must not glide past the terrible consequences of sin, it might be good to show what can be gained through obedience. To leave our focus on sin and how terrible it is (which is true) is to miss the point. He wants us to change, to repent, to turn from sin and seek and love him.

### *Preaching Idea*

When we give up on seeking the Lord, sin will be seeking us.

### *Contemporary Connections*

#### *What does it mean?*

Israel stopped seeking the Lord. Jeremiah rebuked the nation for this by showing them that they had stopped asking, "Where is the

Lord?" This question, "Where is the Lord?" could be asked with various attitudes. One could be asking in frustration, "Where is the health that I used to have? Or, I asked the Lord for relief from this anger in my family? So, just where is he?" Or maybe even in anger, demanding that the Lord show up on our timetable. As in a doctor's waiting room, after an hour past our appointment time, we ask with reserved anger, "Could I ask, just where is the doctor?" While the words "Where is the Lord?" could represent a critical questioning heart, Jeremiah was directing the people to sincerely ask, "Where is the Lord?" The sense of it is that we truly need him and thus, we seek him. Am I seeking and wondering how he will answer my problems? Where is he—where is his will? I know he will act; I wonder what and when he will act. Just where is the Lord? He is not showing up when I want him to show up, nor is he doing what I expected, but I will trust him. As Gandalf says in Tolkien's *Lord of the Rings,* "Wizards are never late." If we can enjoy that concept in a fantasy, we can certainly apply it in reality to God. And, we can continually seek him.

### *Is it true?*

Jeremiah began this section with the metaphor of a newlywed bride. Most newlywed couples can't bear to be apart. They constantly seek each other. At least they should. One night a newly married husband, Bill, woke to see his wife sitting on the edge of the bed, half asleep, looking out of the window. He asked," Are you alright?" She replied, "Yes. I was just wondering where Bill was." Fortunately, it was Bill she was seeking, even in her dreams. This desire to be together faces challenges. When a young bride finds out that her husband has a habit of leaving his shoes in the middle of the living room, she could just fuss and put them up, while harboring ill will toward him. This ill will separates. Rather, she should seek him out, communicate with him—not just dream about seeking him but ask, "Where is my husband? I need to talk with him." If a young couple doesn't seek each other, it leads to diminishing love toward each other. When Israel stopped asking, "Where is the Lord?" it led to distortions in the love relationship with God.

How do we respond when it seems like God has left his shoes in the middle of our plans: when the job requires more traveling than we thought, when our teenager shows no ambition, when the close friend is rude? Perhaps, we leave our shoes in the middle of his plans for us. It is tempting to just get on with life, yet we still harbor those ill feelings toward God. We often pretend there is no problem. Jeremiah is calling us to admit there is a problem or at the least admit that there could be. We must always be asking, "Where is the Lord?" Strive to have him as a priority, to obey him, to pour our hearts out to him, to seek to understand him. Like newlyweds, we must continually work on our love relationship with him.

### *Now what?*

When do we stop seeking him? A high school teacher was required to attend a certain number of continuing education events. A conference that qualified was being held in the evening at Lone Star Auditorium. The teacher assumed that the Lone Star Auditorium was at the local community college, Lone Star College. He went to the campus, parked in a surprisingly empty parking lot, and began looking for the auditorium. He found a student running a coffee shop, and asked, "Where is the auditorium?" The student had no idea. Looking at a campus map, he tried to guess which building it would be in, but again, no success. Where was the auditorium? He found a security guard and asked her, "Where is the auditorium?" She didn't know either. Now he was really confused and frustrated. After walking around the campus for another thirty minutes wondering, "Where is the Lone Star Auditorium?", he gave up and returned home. He stopped asking, "Where is this Lone Star Auditorium ?" The next day he found out that the Lone Star Auditorium was across town—at the Lone Star Conference Center, not Lone Star College. He stopped seeking because he thought it couldn't be found. What happens when I think that the Lord can't be found? When I give up on seeking him, where does that lead me? In this case, our teacher only missed a conference. But the consequences of not seeking the Lord are catastrophic.

### *Creativity in Presentation*

The three parts to this pericope—the description of a lost love relationship (vv. 2:1–3), the reason being a lack of seeking the Lord (vv. 2:4–8) and the results of tragic distortions (vv. 2:9–3:10)—can be presented in three equal parts. However, Jeremiah gives far more attention to the distortions. Jeremiah wants us to continually ask, "Where is the Lord?" More than that, he wants us to be aware of the existing distortions, and to see clearly that we have a problem. The application is not just that we should seek the Lord, but that we must know that tragedy comes from not seeking him. The teacher/preacher needs to be careful to give time to the unpleasant descriptions of the distortions. The direct approach is not always best. In fact, Jeremiah seems to mix in accusations against the northern tribes. In presenting the distortions, it could be effective to take two passes at these: the first focusing on how we see these problems in our culture, and then the second pass to show that these distortions are often in our own backyards.

The phrase, "So, how's that working for you?" has been used is film and popularized by talk show hosts to show someone that what they are doing isn't working. Jeremiah is saying to us, if you are not loving or seeking the Lord, "So how's that working for you?" This could be used to bookend the sermon.

The wording of these three parts reflects the negative tone of the passage, but they can be presented in a positive way. Here is a possible structure presented in a positive tone:

- Seek the Lord, because sin is seeking us.
    - Seek the Lord so that our love will not diminish—diminished love is sin (2:1–3).
    - Seek the Lord even though you feel like blaming him—blaming him is sin (2:4–8).
    - Seek the Lord to avoid sins distortions—sin has drastic consequences (2:9–3:10).

## DISCUSSION QUESTIONS

1. Why does someone give up on seeking the Lord?
2. What is it about continuing to seek the Lord that prevents other sins?
3. Have you ever had a love relationship with God?
4. Have you ever lost a love relationship with God?
5. How does one's love for God diminish?

## Jeremiah 3:11–4:4

**EXEGETICAL IDEA**

God calls on Judah to repent, carefully defining what that means and what the benefits are, while also acknowledging that Judah is so deep in rebellion that they cannot repent. This passage, therefore, explores the meaning of repentance while also explaining why many people cannot do it. In addition, it asserts that God does not take pleasure in punishing sin but mourns over the recalcitrance of people whose hearts have turned to stone.

**THEOLOGICAL FOCUS**

God's appeals for repentance are always real, but sometimes the audience is incapable of receiving them. In such a case, the prophetic preacher must continue to explain why repentance is necessary and how the people should do it, but this does not mean that the preacher embraces any false hopes regarding his audience and the state of their hearts.

**PREACHING IDEA**

It's not enough to cry for help—we must repent.

**PREACHING POINTERS**

The caricature of the radical preacher holding a sloppily painted sign of just the one word, "Repent," gives the message of this passage an unfortunate negative barrier to overcome. To be faithful to present this passage, in a sense, requires us to do just that: hold up a sign that says "Repent." But there is more on the sign than just that one word; there are guidelines to true repentance. The better word to use might be Jeremiah's word: Return.

The passage presents what is necessary for true repentance or a true returning to the Lord, but it is not void of the same passion of the person holding the sign calling for repentance. It is serious business because our sin is a serious rejection of God. But the emotion doesn't end there. God calls for repentance in order to bless us.

# AN APPEAL TO REPENT (3:11–4:4)

## LITERARY STRUCTURE AND THEMES

Jeremiah 3:11–12 picks up on a theme from the previous context: the account of "apostate Israel" and "her treacherous sister, Judah." But 3:11 begins a new theme: an appeal for repentance, whereas the previous text was all accusation. It is not even certain that this passage was composed or delivered at the same time as the previous material. Jeremiah is not chronologically arranged, and the prophet and his scribe, during a later stage of the editing of Jeremiah's sermons, may have used the metaphor of the sisters as a link between the two texts.

- ***Judah Worse Than Israel (3:11–14a)***
- ***Promise of Restoration (3:14b–18)***
- ***YHWH's Lament (3:19–20)***
- ***Israel's Lament (3:21)***
- ***A Model Prayer for a Sinful Judah (3:22–25)***
- ***True Repentance (4:1–4)***

We can detect a chiastic pattern here. The complaint that Judah's sin excels that of Israel (3:11–14a) is answered by an exposition on the nature of repentance (4:1–4). The promise of restoration (3:14b–18) is answered by a model prayer to bring such restoration about (3:22–25). At the center, we have YHWH's lament (3:19–20) echoed by Israel's lament (3:21).

## EXPOSITION

### *Judah Worse Than Israel (3:11–14a)*

Under the guise of making an appeal to the exiles from Israel now scattered across Mesopotamia, this passage calls for Judah to repent while indicating that they are so deep in apostasy that repentance is impossible.

**3:11**. In saying that apostate Israel is more righteous than treacherous Judah, the text means that there is more hope that the people of the former northern kingdom might repent than there is for the southern kingdom. Judah, having seen and disregarded the lesson provided by Israel's idolatry and subsequent destruction, is unlikely to respond to an appeal. This is a rebuke to complacency of the people of Judah, who assumed that because they had the Davidic king and the Jerusalem temple, they were more righteous than the former northern kingdom. Also, the fact that the Assyrians had destroyed the Israel but had been thwarted at the gates of Jerusalem (when Sennacherib besieged the city in the time of Hezekiah), reinforced Judah's belief that they were simply better than Israel had been.

**3:12**. YHWH tells Jeremiah to go and proclaim a message "toward the north" (צָפֹ֫וֹנָה), that is, in the regions of Syria and Mesopotamia where the tribes of Israel were exiled and dispersed. It seems unlikely that Jeremiah was literally expected to journey to these regions and seek out scattered exiles and preach to them. We have no record that he did such a thing, and no indication that any Israelite exiles repented after hearing such a message. It is more likely that the text is "an indirect message to Judah" (Lalleman 2013, 87). The command to go to the Israelite exiles implies, "This is the kind of message YHWH would give you, Judah, if you were open to hearing it." In other words, the message is directed to Judah, but the rhetorical device of proclaiming the message to exiles in the north suggests that there is no point in making an appeal to Judah.

*TRANSLATION NOTE FOR 3:12*

The command to repent (שׁוּבָה) is masculine with a paragogic ה and not, as we might expect, feminine (שׁוּבִי). In this case, however, the form שׁוּבָה is used primarily because of the assonance it creates with the next word, מְשֻׁבָה ("apostate"). This is a good example of how we need to be careful not to overanalyze grammatical forms, as though every variation carried profound significance. In this case, we have שׁוּבָה מְשֻׁבָה יִשְׂרָאֵל simply because, to the Hebrew ear, it sounds better than if the feminine form were used.

**3:13–14a**. The text gives the basic elements of repentance. First, they must "return" to God (the verb שׁוב from vv. 12, 14a). Second, they must "acknowledge" (ידע) their sin—in other words, they must make confession and admit that their behavior had been wrong. The confession is specific and not general or abstract. In Israel's case, their specific sins were promiscuous idolatry and disregard for God's commands. Third, they must accept that they now belong to God and come under his authority: "for I am your lord" (כִּי אָנֹכִי בָּעַלְתִּי בָכֶם; note that בעל implies both "lord" and "husband," and it also ironically subverts their devotion to Baal, a word that also means "husband"). In Israel's case, they were bound to YHWH as his chosen people and under the terms of the covenants, and repentance was a renewal of that bond.

### *Promise of Restoration (3:14b–18)*

Anticipating the great prophecy of redemption in Jeremiah 30–33, this passage speaks of the eschatological salvation of Israel. But the promises here are not unconditionally given, as in 30–33; the whole of 3:14b–18 is a contrary-to-fact conditional situation: "This is what YHWH would do if you would repent, but of course you won't." Still, the passage anticipates the day when YHWH will change the hearts of his scattered people, bring them home, and give them the benefits of the new covenant (as anticipated in Deut. 30:1–10).

**3:14b**. There will be a great reward for Israel, if they will repent. God will regather them. God will take them "one from a city and two from a clan" (אֶחָד מֵעִיר וּשְׁנַיִם מִמִּשְׁפָּחָה). This does not mean that God will only accept a few of them; it is not remnant theology. The regathering described in 31:8 involves an enormous number of people, and no doubt it is the same here. The expression of "one from a city and two from a clan" means that God will gather them from the diverse places to which they were scattered, with some being among the Gentile cities and towns, and others in small enclaves of Jewish clans. The small numbers do not mean that only a few will be saved, but that God will find every individual, wherever he or she is.

**3:15**. Both Israel and Judah were plagued by bad leadership, as Jeremiah experienced firsthand. In the great renewal, they will have good leaders, who will manage affairs in such a way that the land and people will thrive. We see a similar promise in Micah 5:5. The essential point of the promise is that God will reverse the bad experience Israel had under its former rulers.

**3:16**. It surprises us that Jeremiah's portrait of the eschatological future includes the promise that the ark of the covenant will be absent and will not be missed. It also raises the question of whether it still existed in Jeremiah's time, and if people longed for its return. It is possible that the ark was taken away in the time of Rehoboam, when Shishak plundered Jerusalem (1 Kings 14:25–28). Or perhaps Jehoash of Israel carried it away after he defeated Amaziah of Judah (2 Kings 14:8–14). It is not included among the articles that Nebuchadnezzar II took from Jerusalem (2 Kings 25:13–17; Jer. 52:17–23). On the other hand, the absence of the ark in the lists is not definitive proof he did not take it. Josiah permanently set the "sacred ark" inside the temple, and this was presumably the ark of the covenant (2 Chron. 35:3). It is possible that the ark was lost after Josiah's time but before the fall of Jerusalem. It is possible that Neco took it after his defeat of Josiah, or even that Nebuchadnezzar II took it in 597 when he took Jehoiachin into exile. Jewish tradition says that Jeremiah hid the ark from the Babylonians, but this seems unlikely since nothing in the Bible gives the idea credibility, and because in this verse Jeremiah himself discounts the importance of the ark. Also, 2 Esdras 10:22 indicates that the ark was lost in the Babylonian conflagration. It did not exist in the second temple period (Seow 1992, 390–91), and so was definitely gone at least by the exilic era. But why does Jeremiah mention it here? Probably the ark represents the presence of God and, by metonymy, the whole temple complex. Jeremiah's contemporaries believed that Jerusalem was effectively impregnable because it had God's temple. Because YHWH dwelt in Zion, they thought, he would never let his temple and city fall. As the most sacred object in the temple, Jeremiah indicates that these things have no lasting significance. The only thing that mattered was whether the people really knew and served God.

**3:17**. Jerusalem will be holy, but not because of any sacred object within the city. Instead, its holiness will be that YHWH is there. For that reason, the nations will come and worship, as in Isaiah 2:1–4. Jerusalem will be called "The Throne of YHWH," but this is not to be taken literally, just as Jesus was not literally named "Immanuel" (Isa. 7:14). It expresses the special place of Jerusalem as the place where the one God is found. The people will know God and will no longer follow the "depravity of their evil hearts" (שְׁרִרוּת לִבָּם הָרָע; the term שְׁרִרוּת is often translated "stubbornness," but it always implies a reprobate mind).

**3:18**. The Israelites regarded the division of the twelve tribes into two separate (and often hostile) nations as a terrible tragedy, as indicated in Isaiah 7:17. In the eschatological salvation, this ancient conflict between brothers would end once and for all. The exiles, both Israel and Judah, would come back "from a northern land" (מֵאֶרֶץ צָפוֹן), that is, from Mesopotamia. Israel and Judah were carried away by Assyria and Babylon, respectively. Here, however, the statement that the exiles are in the north is more ideological than literal or historical; it represents the condition of being in exile.

**The Hope of Israel**

In interpreting the promises made to Israel in the prophets, one should keep a number of principles in mind.

- The promises are always given in terms that relate to the historical circumstances of the original audience. For example, when speaking of the regathering of Israel from its exile and diaspora, Jeremiah 3:18 implies that they are all in the "north," that is, in Mesopotamia. This does not mean that when the actual great salvation appears, it will primarily deal with regathering Jews from Iraq, Syria, and Iran.
- The promises are given in historical and contextual terms, but the great fulfillment is eschatological. Even so, there may be a limited, non-eschatological fulfillment. For example, the restoration of Jerusalem and regathering of the Jews from across Mesopotamia, especially from Babylon, in the postexilic era was a limited, non-eschatological fulfillment of the great restoration promised in passages such as Jeremiah 3:18. It was not the final and complete fulfillment, but it was a real fulfillment of the promise.
- The centerpiece of eschatological salvation in Jeremiah is the new covenant, when all of Israel and Judah's sins will be forgiven, their hearts will be changed so that they love God, and there will be no need for anyone to say to another, "Know the Lord!" (Jer. 31:31–34). Jesus established the new covenant, and we are now living in the age of the new covenant (Matt. 26:28; 2 Cor. 3:6; Heb. 8:8–13; 9:15; 12:24).

- As such, Gentiles from every nation and language find life and forgiveness in Israel's God and Messiah and in the promises that God has made. However, we "do not yet see all things made subject to him" (Heb. 2:8). All who turn to God in Christ know the Lord and have their sins forgiven, but we will not experience the full deliverance from sin that Jeremiah implies until the resurrection.
- The ultimate fulfillment of the promises to Israel is the new heaven and new earth promised in Isaiah 65:17 and Revelation 21:1. At that time, all the elect of all the nations will worship the God of Israel, will bow before the son of David, the Jewish Messiah, and will congregate at the New Jerusalem. Gentiles, seeking the word of YHWH as Isaiah prophesied (Isa. 2:2–4), adopted into Zion as the psalmist celebrated (Ps. 87:4–6), and grafted into Israel as Paul explained (Rom. 11:17–24), will bring glory to God even as they vindicate all the promises of Israel's final glorification.

Christians have differences among themselves about the meaning of various passages in the Old Testament, but we can affirm certain fundamental truths and acknowledge that in Christ all the promises of God are Yes and Amen (2 Cor. 1:20).

### *YHWH's Lament (3:19–20)*

Because of Judah's apostasy, the people are not true Israelites—children of YHWH—at all. They are the children of a foreign god, and YHWH cannot acknowledge them as his own.

**3:19**. YHWH complains that he would gladly fulfill all of the promises of the above passage, but that because of their continuing refusal to repent, he cannot. YHWH says, translating literally, "How I wish I could set you among sons!" (אֵיךְ אֲשִׁיתֵךְ בַּבָּנִים). The metaphor contrasts legitimate children with illegitimate, alien children. When Israel gave herself to foreign gods, her "children" (the people of Israel) were metaphorically the offspring of adultery, sired by someone other than her lawful husband, YHWH. It is for this reason that the third son of Gomer was named Lo-Ammi, "Not my people" (לֹא עַמִּי; Hos. 1:9). As such, the line could be translated, "How I wish I could regard you as my very own, legitimate children!" So understood, it makes sense that God would like to give them the land as their "beautiful inheritance" (נַחֲלַת צְבִי). He cannot do this, however, because they are his children in name only. The people insist that YHWH is their father, but their constant apostasy proves that it is not so. This verse anticipates Romans 9:6, that "not all who are from Israel are [truly] Israel."

*TRANSLATION NOTE FOR 3:19*

The verse contains two *kethiv* verbs, both 2mp *yiqtol:* תִּקְרְאוּ ("you [mp] call") and תָּשׁוּבוּ ("you [mp] return"). Both are 2fs in their *qere* forms: תִּקְרָאִי and תָשׁוּבִי. Either the *kethiv* or *qere* could be correct. If read as masculine plural, the verbs address all the people of Judah. If read as feminine singular, they address Judah personified as a woman. In addition, the translation of נַחֲלַת צְבִי צִבְאוֹת גּוֹיִם is disputed. Some treat the whole as one construct chain, as in the ESV: "a heritage most beautiful of all nations." The cantillation marks, however, imply that this is two separate construct chains: "inheritance of beauty, beautiful places of nations." The latter is preferable and can be more fluently rendered as "the beautiful inheritance, [indeed,] the most beautiful place of [all] the nations."

**3:20**. Returning to the metaphor of the adulterous wife, Jeremiah says Judah "behaved treacherously" (בָּגְדָה), using the same epithet that was used of Judah in 3:7–10, "her treacherous sister, Judah" (בָּגוֹדָה אֲחוֹתָהּ יְהוּדָה). This reinforces the force of the claim in 3:19 that the children are illegitimate.

### *Israel's Lament (3:21)*

YHWH is distraught because Judah's prayers for salvation are empty and self-serving. They want YHWH's help but are unwilling to change their ways.

**3:21**. Judah, in the face of the looming Babylonian attack, calls on YHWH for salvation. A key issue here is the translation of the word frequently rendered "because" or "for" (כִּי). The word has a wide range of meanings; it essentially subordinates one clause to the preceding clause. The word often is concessive ("although") rather than explanatory ("for, because"). For example, the ESV has "because they have perverted their way." If translated as "because," it means that they are facing calamity because they turned toward evil and forgot YHWH. But the preceding clause does not mention the calamity. Instead, it speaks of Judah's appeals to YHWH for help. As such, the word has a concessive meaning: "A voice is heard on the barren heights: [It is] the tearful appeals of the Israelites, *even though* they pervert their ways [and] have forgotten YHWH their God." This agrees with the previous claims that they appealed to YHWH as their beloved and their father even as they committed apostasy. Their prayers and pleas, therefore, are hollow.

### *A Model Prayer for a Sinful Judah (3:22–25)*

This passage gives a model prayer of repentance, telling Judah how they ought to respond to God's appeal.

**3:22a**. YHWH again appeals for Judah to come back (שׁוּבוּ), implying that they have in fact not yet come back. The first thing YHWH promises to do for them if they do truly come back is surprising. It is not to save them from all their troubles but to heal their apostasy (אֶרְפָּה מְשׁוּבֹתֵיכֶם). It shows that this was the true root of their problems. By analogy, when Jesus extended mercy to the paralyzed man, his first words were, "Son, your sins are forgiven" (Mark 2:5). Being paralyzed or facing an enemy invasion is terrible, but being unforgiven is far worse.

**3:22b**. In what follows, the text does not recount a prayer that they are actually making; it describes what they ought to pray. That is, it is a model for how they should repent. The opening declaration of the model prayer, "Look! We come to you!" (הִנְנוּ אָתָנוּ לָךְ), reverses their prior refusal to come to YHWH in 2:31: "We can wander as we please! We won't come to you anymore!" (רַדְנוּ לוֹא־נָבוֹא עוֹד אֵלֶיךָ). As such, it represents true repentance from a previous attitude and not the hollow appeals Israel made earlier.

**3:23**. The model of repentance for Judah begins by repudiating Baal worship. Pagan worship is a "tumultuous commotion" (הָמוֹן). Such worship might or might not include "orgies" (as somewhat misleadingly translated in the ESV); the main thing is that it was loud and disorderly. As such, הָמוֹן represents all the pagan worship that was done on the hills and mountains, whether it involved sexual acts or not. And it was a "lie" (שֶׁקֶר), since it was done in God's name but God was not involved.

**3:24**. The prayer acknowledges how their apostasy has left them devastated. They say that "The Shame" has consumed all the work of their fathers, meaning that it defeated all their efforts to build up their nation. "The Shame" (הַבֹּשֶׁת) refers to Baal. This recalls how the scribes routinely rendered the name of Saul's son, "Eshbaal" (אֶשְׁבָּעַל, "man of Baal, as in 1 Chron. 8:33) as "Ishbosheth" (אִישׁ בֹּשֶׁת, "man of shame," as in 2 Sam. 2:8). In referring to the apostasy of the fathers, the prayer does not deny the responsibility of the children, as in Jeremiah 31:29. Instead, as is clear in the next verse, it asserts that apostasy and idolatry have been besetting sins for Israel for many generations, including the present one. True repentance involves turning from the specific sins in which one is ensnared.

**3:25**. In the previous verse, "shame" (בֹּשֶׁת) was used as an epithet for Baal, but here it describes the effect of Baal worship: all who participate in paganism fall into disgrace. In saying that the people "lie down in shame," it does not connote despair, as though the repentant sinner were just waiting to die. Rather, it is a statement of utter humiliation and brokenness, as when the prodigal son purposed to say to his father, "Father, I have sinned against heaven and before you; I am no longer worthy to be called your son" (Luke 15:18–19).

### *True Repentance (4:1–4)*

Having given Judah a model prayer for repentance, YHWH tells them that they must repent in fact and not in pretense.

**4:1a**. Verse 1a is a conditional sentence, and it could be paraphrased, "If you really want to return to me, Israel, then really return to me, says YHWH." It serves to introduce the next section, which tells what "really" returning to YHWH involves.

**4:1b–2**. This is a second conditional construction, with the protasis in 1b–2a and the apodosis in 2b. The elements of the protasis are: 1) if you remove your horrible things, 2) if you do not wander away from YHWH, and 3) if you take the oath "as YHWH lives" honestly and in good faith. The elements of the apodosis are: 1) the nations will find blessing in YHWH, and 2) they will praise YHWH. The "horrible things" (שִׁקּוּצִים) are idols and shrines to other gods. The verb for "wander" (נוּד) is the same word used in 2:31, where the people declare, "We can wander [from YHWH] as we please!" Swearing falsely in YHWH's name treats God's name with gross disrespect and represents violation of the Decalogue (Exod. 20:7). True repentance, then, involves turning away from apostasy, adopting an attitude of submission to God, and showing respect for God through living with integrity. It is perhaps surprising that the promises of God in the apodosis all describe benefits to the Gentiles and not to Judah: the nations will find blessing and praise YHWH. But these things represent the fulfillment of the original election of Israel, as in Genesis 12:3, which states that all the nations will find blessing in Abraham. Furthermore, when the Gentiles submit to YHWH, Israel's God, they are at peace with Israel and treat Israel as the most honored of all nations. When the nations exalt YHWH, Israel is exalted.

**4:3–4**. YHWH calls for repentance under two metaphors, one drawn from agriculture and one from the rite of circumcision. First, they are told to prepare the hardened soil for planting by breaking it up, and that they must not sow seed among thorns. Seeds are unlikely to germinate and thrive if they are cast upon hard ground or if they emerge among thorns and weeds (this may be the source for Jesus's parable of the sower in Matthew 13:3–9). In Jeremiah, the meaning is that for repentance to be authentic and fruitful, one must come to terms with the stubbornness of the will (the hard soil) and the distraction to other things (the weeds). If one goes through the motions of seeking God's favor while refusing to confront one's inner willfulness and besetting sins, the repentance is hollow. Second, the Israelites regarded lack of circumcision to be a foul and repugnant state, as illustrated by how they used the term "uncircumcised" as a pejorative ("this uncircumcised Philistine!" as in 1 Sam. 17:26). Spiritually, lack of inner circumcision is a pollution and a sclerosis of the mind, emotions, heart, and will. It is an inner corruption, and unless one is willing to break from it, one is not truly repentant. Only God, in fact, can perform the circumcision of the heart (Deut. 30:6), but the call here in Jeremiah is for people to acknowledge their need for internal, spiritual surgery and come to God to receive it. If they will not genuinely repent, they will experience the fire of God's wrath.

## THEOLOGICAL FOCUS

This passage teaches certain salient facts about the nature of true repentance. Among these are:

- When people have been warned against turning from God and have even seen examples of what happens to those who do turn away, their guilt and their stubborn hostility toward God become all the greater.
- God's appeals for repentance always include promises concerning the benefits of repentance.
- God grieves over our spiritual perversity, but he will not pretend that we are we are more righteous than we really are. If we are not his, we will bear the consequences.
- People can cry out to God from unrepentant hearts; asking for God's help in a time of crisis is not proof of true faith. In such a case, they have little reason to expect God to answer their pleas.
- True repentance involves turning toward God and away from sins that are specific to the one repenting. Absent these, it is not repentance at all.

## PREACHING AND TEACHING STRATEGIES

### *Exegetical and Theological Synthesis*

There are three audiences—actually, four—who are listening to Jeremiah's message calling for true repentance: the first listeners to his actual message, those in exile, those who had returned, and those who have read it since it was written. With all four of these groups, there is the common problem of sin. And there is a common reaction to someone pointing it out: no one likes it. Thus, Jeremiah uses an indirect form of communication.

It is an odd thing that often when we hear someone else being corrected, we are more apt to be open to correction than if confronted directly. Part of the reason is that when confronted directly, we become defensive and deny that we need to make corrections. But when another is corrected, we listen and apply it to our lives because we choose to, rather than being told to. It is a way that God helps us discover our guilt. Jeremiah was speaking to a hostile audience, and so are we. And as the proclaimers of this passage, we must see that we are in this group resistant to repentance.

### *Preaching Idea*

It's not enough to cry for help—we must repent.

### *Contemporary Connections*

#### *What does it mean?*

Repentance is not the end result that God is seeking in this passage. He is calling us to return to the blessings that he has provided. The proverbial sign that reads "Repent" on the front should have a back side that says, "Be blessed." Repentance is not the end; it is only the beginning. Yet, the repentance must be entered into just to get the blessing. The cocky seven-year-older brother says, "OK, I've stopped hitting my sister—now what reward am I going to get?" This older brother has completely missed the purpose and point of the correction. We don't come to God with a spirit that says, "OK God, I'm sorry; now I'm forgiven, right?" The words of repentance are in verses 22–24. The big brother should be saying, "I was wrong. I should never hit my little sister. I could have hurt her." And each of us in our minds complete this picture by adding to the big brother's words, "But Dad, she hit me first." True repentance doesn't add, "But God . . ."

#### *Is it true?*

We cry out for help from God when we are in need. The spectrum runs from 9/11, the day that our nation called for help, to burning the roast at a special family dinner. Sometimes our cries for help come not from the pain of a forgetful mistake, or the harm from an outside force, but due to God's discipline. The thief justly sentenced to prison, the lazy student who fails the test, and the prideful pastor who is asked to step down are all in the pain of consequences or discipline.

God has a message of hope for us when we are in this kind of pain. However, we don't always hear his message because our cry for help is *only* so that we can be relieved of the pain of the situation. We want relief from pain, not a change in behavior. Judah was about to suffer the consequences of their tragically evil sins, and God's message of hope came through Jeremiah, but they could not hear it because they were not willing to fully repent. They were like the criminal in jail who cries out to God for help but is not repentant of the sin that put him there. The husband who is losing his marriage cries out to God but still thinks it is normal and fine to flirt with other women. A college student is put on scholastic probation and cries out to God but still sleeps until noon, skips class, and doesn't study. These people are not capable of truly hearing the message of repentance leading to great benefits, because they think that crying out to God is enough. We want the pain to stop, but we don't want to change the habits that caused the pain. Thus, we can't even hear the message for repentance and hope.

A truly tragic and sad experience is seeing someone with lung cancer refuse to stop smoking. In past years smoking was accepted and encouraged, and many became addicted. In time, many developed lung cancer. My sweet sister-in-law was one of these. When the cancer was discovered, and the directive came for her to repent of that deathful habit, she didn't even try to quit. It was as if she could not hear the doctor's message, because she had no intention of quitting. The people of Judah were the same. They wanted help for their situation, but they had no intention of truly repenting and turning away from their evil practices and turning toward God and His commands.

*Now what?*

When the consequences of our sins are heavy upon us, when our laziness results in a lack of income, when strife is in our homes because of our hot temper, when we aren't respected because we acted disrespectfully, we should cry out to God. When we cry out to God in times like these, we can hear God's wonderful message of hope because we have a willingness to truly repent. When we are ready to turn away from sin and turn in obedience toward God, then this glorious message of hope can be heard.

### *Creativity in Presentation*

Jeremiah's rhetorical device of indirect speech can be used in the structure for the sermon. He begins with a message that we are invited to listen to indirectly. It is as if we are listening to a high school graduation speaker talking directly to the graduates. We are just listening in, but often if we have a receptive spirit, that message to teenagers hits home with us as well. The preacher can present this message in similar way. Begin by saying that this message is only for a certain group; all are welcomed to listen, but to hear the message there are certain requirements. Rhetorically this heightens the desire to listen. None of us wants to miss out on something. The requirements to be able to hear the message are laid out in verses 3:13–14a. There must be a willingness to apply all the elements of repentance: returning to God, acknowledging our sin, accepting His authority. If we are willing to accept and put into practice these elements, then there is a great message for us. After this first major point, which is somewhat like an introduction, one could present the rest of this pericope: the promised blessings, the examples of prayers and laments. Let the sermon build to the fuller explanation of true repentance in 4:1–4.

The closing portion of the sermon can be a call to cry out to God with a heart that is ready to change. Depending upon your church's culture of worship, the conclusion could be a brief exhortation to action or an extended time for prayer and true repentance. Perhaps we have the pain of an ongoing depression or grumpiness due to an unsatisfied desire to always win or be better than others. Our cry to God needs to acknowledge the sin of pride and to stop thinking so highly of ourselves. Is there strife in our home because of a hot temper? Let's cry out to God for relief from the strife and stop letting anger fly so freely. Let's cry out to God, with tears for our sins and hearts ready to make changes.

It's not enough to cry for help—we must repent. Redemption is not only in the result, but even in the repentance itself. God's help not only comes after the repentance, but during it. It is a blessing to repent.

Possible presentation structure:

- Repentance admits the guilt (3:11–14a).
- Repentance deeply regrets, yet humbly receives (3:14b–21).
- Repentance speaks the shame (3:22–25).
- Repentance removes the malignant actions (4:1–4).

## DISCUSSION QUESTIONS

1. Why does the thief think he will not be caught?
2. Why do we think that the consequences of sin will not happen to us?
3. What does God include in this section besides a call to repentance and change?
4. Why should someone who asks us for our help be willing to listen to our advice?

## Jeremiah 4:5–6:30

### EXEGETICAL IDEA

Judah persistently rejects correction from God's prophet and lives under the illusion that they deserve no punishment; but God persistently warns them that the Babylonians are at the gates, ready to bring his punishment down on them. This structure of this passage is driven by a lengthy series of alternating texts, first describing how the Babylonian invader is coming upon them and then asserting that the people prefer to believe lies that they are safe and will suffer no harm. These alternating texts vividly bring home the lesson that faith in a false ideology leads to ruin.

### THEOLOGICAL FOCUS

Behavior has consequences. Sin deceives people, so that they deny both their guilt and the consequences of their deeds, but they will ultimately face the harsh reality of retribution. Jerusalem continued to think that idols, inept leaders, foreign allies, and the presence of God's temple could guarantee their safety even as the day of ruin came upon them.

### PREACHING IDEA

Our self-deception is our most dangerous sin.

### PREACHING POINTERS

This long passage has a constant theme that Jeremiah keeps repeating with creative and accurate descriptions of Judah's lifestyle and their unwillingness to be honest about their sin and the coming invasion. They are either ignoring or misrepresenting the truth from God's law and Jeremiah's preaching. They are deceiving themselves. In the end, this deception is so deep and so common that they no longer can even see the truth. They are "rejected silver" (6:30).

While Jeremiah is saying people can be so self-deceived that they can't respond to the truth, the application of this passage is for those who will listen and respond. It is somewhat like the unpardonable sin. If you think you may have committed it, you haven't. If one is worried or concerned that they might be self-deceived, then there is hope that they can hear and repent. But it seems that there are some whose self-deception is so deep that they cannot even hear the truth. In describing the self-deception of Judah, this passage helps us see ways that we deceive ourselves and calls us to honesty and authenticity. If we are listening, then there is hope.

# DELUDED PEOPLE AND THEIR COMING DESTRUCTION (4:5–6:30)

## LITERARY STRUCTURE AND THEMES

As described in the introduction, this portion of Jeremiah alternates between passages that speak of Judah as filled with deception (the sections labeled "Deceit"), and passages that speak of the coming Babylonian army and its conquest of the city (the sections labeled "Invasion"). The implied message throughout is that the lies that the leaders in Jerusalem propagate, and which the people believe, will bring the land to a catastrophic outcome: the complete destruction of the city and temple and the exile of the nation.

- ***Invasion: Sound the Alarm! (4:5–8)***
- ***Deceit: Bewildered and Corrupt Leaders (4:9–12)***
- ***Invasion: The Babylonian Storm (4:13)***
- ***Deceit: Jerusalem, Home of Evil Schemes (4:14)***
- ***Invasion: The Enemy Approaches (4:15–18)***
- ***Deceit: Senseless People and the Earth in Upheaval (4:19–28)***
- ***Invasion: The Towns Deserted (4:29)***
- ***Deceit: A Cosmetic Solution (4:30)***
- ***Invasion: The Helpless Woman (4:31)***
- ***Deceit: A Futile Search for Faithfulness (5:1–5)***
- ***Invasion: Lion, Wolf, and Leopard (5:6)***
- ***Deceit: Faithless to God and to Marriage (5:7–9)***
- ***Invasion: Ravaged Vineyards (5:10)***
- ***Deceit: Lying versus True Prophets (5:11–14)***
- ***Invasion: The All-Devouring Enemy (5:15–19)***
- ***Deceit: Houses Full of Deceit (5:20–31)***
- ***Invasion: Zion in Flight; Jerusalem Under Siege (6:1–9)***
- ***Deceit: Incapable of Hearing the Truth (6:10–11a)***
- ***Invasion: The Enemy Takes All People and All Property (6:11b–12)***
- ***Deceit: Saying "Peace" When There Is No Peace (6:13–21)***
- ***Invasion: The Cruel Army from the North (6:22–26)***
- ***Conclusion (6:27–30)***

## EXPOSITION

### *Invasion: Sound the Alarm! (4:5–8)*

An urgent call for the city watchmen to sound the alarm, telling the people that an invasion is coming, begins this section. The people must make a desperate defense of their city, but it will be hopeless because YHWH has turned against them.

**4:5a**. Verse 5 begins by addressing the watchmen on the walls of the city: "Declare [it] in Judah and make [it] heard in Jerusalem! / And say—and blow a shofar in the land! / Call out! Fill [their ears] and say!" The second line, "And say—and blow a shofar in the land!" is a case of anacoluthon (a deliberately ungrammatical construction). The point is that the prophet calls on the watchmen to sound the alarm and is about to tell the watchmen what to say, but then interrupts himself and further exhorts them to sound the alarm. The broken construction implies that the speaker is somewhat frantic and the situation urgent. The command to sound the alarm contains no less than seven verbs that mean "speak," "announce," or "blow a shofar" (נגד [hiphil, "declare"], שמע [hiphil, "make heard"], אמר [qal, "say," used twice], תקע [qal, "blow"], קרא [qal, "call"], מלא [piel "fill," with an implied object אֹזֶן, "ear," as in Eccl. 1:8]). The verbs are all imperative masculine plural, implying that the text addresses Jerusalem's watchmen, telling them to announce the coming of the Babylonian army. The multiple verbs add urgency to the command.

*TRANSLATION NOTE FOR 4:5*

Several translations (ESV, NRSV, NIV) treat the first three clauses (with נגד, שמע, and אמר) as a prose sequence: "Declare in Judah, and proclaim in Jerusalem, and say" (ESV). These verbs command some unknown group to tell the watchmen to sound the alarm. "Blow the trumpet" (וְתִקְעוּ שׁוֹפָר) thus is the first command directed to the watchmen, and it is construed to be poetry. Support for this interpretation comes from reading the *kethiv* וְתִקְעוּ as תִּקְעוּ, the *qere*. But even with the *qere*, this interpretation is not compelling. In Hebrew, a series of imperatives will often mix together verbs with and without the conjunction, but this does not imply a distinction between prose and poetry, and nothing in the text indicates that the first three clauses, unlike what follows, are prose. A stronger argument for the ESV is that אמר implies that a direct quote follows; therefore, a new, secondary set of commands must begin after the first וְאִמְרוּ. But all seven verbs are masculine plural imperatives and all demand that the addresses convey an urgent message, suggesting all are directed to the same group. The implication of the ESV and similar translations—that some unknown group must command the implied watchmen to sound the alarm—is inherently peculiar. It is more reasonable to suppose that in all seven verbs, the prophet commands the watchmen to sound the alarm. Some interpreters delete the first וְאִמְרוּ as dittography (Holladay 1986, 140), making for a more eloquent and coherent text. In my view, however, it is better not to emend. We can accept the *kethiv* while seeing the abrupt move from וְאִמְרוּ to וְתִקְעוּ שׁוֹפָר as anacoluthon, as mentioned above.

**4:5b–6a**. The watchmen are to call on the people to rush into the fortified cities. The "standard" (נֵס) they raise in Zion is a flag signaling that war has come to the city (Lundbom 2008a, 336). Men in the militia must grab their arms and get to their posts, and everyone else must seek safety within the walls of the city.

**4:6b**. YHWH then states why the watchmen must sound the alarm: he is bringing "disaster" (רָעָה) and "destruction" (שֶׁבֶר) from Babylon, here called the "north" (צָפוֹן).

**4:7**. YHWH describes the army he is bringing. It is first metaphorically a lion that comes out of a thicket, but then more literally is a destroyer of nations (מַשְׁחִית גּוֹיִם) that has come upon Judah to lay it waste. The term "destroyer" (מַשְׁחִית) will appear again as a name for Babylon (5:26).

**4:8**. Notwithstanding the call to arms given above, victory over the coming enemy is not possible. The people might as well begin their lament over their defeat. YHWH has turned against them, and escape from this disaster is out of the question.

### *Deceit: Bewildered and Corrupt Leaders (4:9–12)*

Judah's leaders will see the Babylonian conflagration with shock and dismay. The lies they clung to will be shattered. Jeremiah, however, complains that YHWH has deceived Judah and enters into a dialogue with him.

**4:9**. All the leaders of society—the priests, rulers, and prophets who in 2:8 misled the nation—will be appalled at the coming desolation. More than that, they will be "astounded" (תמה). They could not conceive of such a thing happening, as they were convinced that Jerusalem was inviolate.

**4:10**. Jeremiah responds to this prophecy of impending disaster in an unexpected manner, saying that YHWH has "deceived" the people of Jerusalem. The verb (II נשׁא, hiphil) can imply deception and enticement, luring the victim into a bad choice, as in Genesis 3:13, where Adam complains that Eve misled him. It often means that the deceived person is holding on to false hopes of safety, as when the Edomites have been deceived, thinking that they are safe because of their strongholds and the assurances of their allies (Obad. 3, 7; see also Isa. 37:10). We cannot soften the force of Jeremiah's complaint by suggesting an alternate meaning for the verb; it means to deceive someone with false hopes that all will go well. The second part of the verse summarizes YHWH's deceptive message: "You will have peace" (שָׁלוֹם יִהְיֶה לָכֶם), when in fact "a sword was about to strike [their] throat" (וְנָגְעָה חֶרֶב עַד־הַנָּפֶשׁ). To understand Jeremiah's complaint, we must consider the situation. Jerusalem's religious leaders at that time made it a point of orthodoxy that YHWH would not allow the city to fall or come to serious harm. The priests declared that the temple was inviolable with a mantra that was taken up by all the people: "The temple of YHWH! The temple of YHWH!" (Jer. 7:4). The prophets assured the people that YHWH would break the power of any nation that opposed Jerusalem (Jer. 27:14). The people believed these assurances from YHWH's spokesmen; the very idea that YHWH would permit pagans to burn, pillage, rape, and kill in his beloved Zion was, they thought, an affront to the character and word of God. As such, Jeremiah daily heard sermons from his counterparts that YHWH was sure to save Jerusalem and, knowing it was not true, declared that YHWH "deceived" the people.

In one sense Jeremiah's complaint is rhetorical and ironic, and in another sense it is literal. It is rhetorical and ironic in that Jeremiah knew that YHWH repeatedly warned Jerusalem that he was about to abandon the city to its fate—in messages delivered by Jeremiah himself. If Jerusalem was deceived, she had deceived herself. A more precise analysis would be that their false theology deceived them, not that God did it. Jeremiah knew this to be true, but in his sorrow over the folly and coming demise of the city he rhetorically presented the theological blindness of Jerusalem as YHWH's deception of the city. But Jeremiah's complaint is literal in that God did allow the priests and prophets, the heralds of YHWH, to declare that he would never allow Zion to go through such calamity. They held to a warped faith in YHWH, and it was by this warped faith that God gave the people over to the hardness of their hearts.

**4:11–12**. The interpretation of these two verses is difficult. At the outset, we must recognize that 4:9–12 is a dialogue between YHWH and Jeremiah:

- YHWH gives an oracle about the future dismay of Jerusalem's leaders (v. 9).
- Jeremiah complains that YHWH has deceived Jerusalem (v. 10).
- YHWH answers Jeremiah's complaint (v. 11).
- Jeremiah responds to YHWH's answer (v. 12).

Verses 11–12 can be translated as follows:

> 11 [But YHWH said,] "At that time it shall be said of this people and of Jerusalem:
> An unobstructed wind of the barren heights in the wilderness
> Is the way of the daughter of my people!
> And [it is] not [the kind of wind] for winnowing or sifting."
> 12 [And Jeremiah said,] "A wind too tempestuous for these [tasks of winnowing and sifting] comes against me! Now I, also, must speak judgments against them."

Verse 11 is YHWH's answer to Jeremiah's complaint that God had deceived the people, a complaint that arises from Jeremiah's desire to see Jerusalem spared. This anticipates the next major theme of the book: Jeremiah's transition from interceding for Israel to making imprecations against them. Here, instead of defending himself against Jeremiah's charge, YHWH tells Jeremiah what the prophet is really facing from the people of Judah. "At that time" (בָּעֵת הַהִיא) refers to the time when calamity begins to close in on Judah. Will the dismayed priests and leaders of Judah then come to Jeremiah in repentance? No, they will not. The "barren heights" (שְׁפָיִים) "are bare, treeless hills used for lookout points and ritualized worship" (Lundbom 2008a, 343–44). The bare hills of the Judean hinterland contrast with the modest and protected rises of the threshing floors. The soft breezes at the threshing floor takes away chaff but lets the wheat kernels fall to earth. The winds that come to the barren heights are naturally prone to stronger gusts, and as such they are useless for threshing. If someone were to try such a thing on the heights, both wheat and chaff would be carried away. This is what Judah is like; it is "the way of my daughter, my people" (דֶּרֶךְ בַּת־עַמִּי). YHWH tells Jeremiah that these are people like a strong wind; they will not leave him with any wheat, the metaphorical fruit of repentance.

Verse 12 is Jeremiah's answer, a confession that YHWH's is correct. He says, "A wind too tempestuous for these [tasks of winnowing and sifting] comes against me!" It means that they furiously rage against him. Knowing that the people are recalcitrant in their evil, he admits that he must affirm YHWH's word and that he "also" (גַּם) must prophesy against them.

*TRANSLATION NOTE FOR 4:11–12*

The word I have translated as "unobstructed" (צַח) is often translated as "sultry," "scorching," or the like. But צַח does not imply heat. In Song 5:10 it refers to a young man whose complexion is "clear and tanned" (צַח refers to a lack of blemishes). In Isaiah 32:4 it describes how a stammering tongue will be enabled to speak "clearly." It can also mean "clear" in the sense of "direct" or "unobstructed." The words חֹם צַח ("direct heat") appear in Isaiah 18:4. In context, the "heat" is a function of the word חֹם and not צַח. The Isaiah verse should be translated, "For thus YHWH says to me: 'I shall be still, so that I may look down from my dwelling, / [I shall be] like the direct heat (חֹם צַח) that comes with the daylight, [as when] the heat of late summer [burns off] the dewy mist.'" As a modifier of "wind," the word צַח in Jeremiah 4:11 implies that it is unobstructed (by trees and terrain).

The word "way" (דֶּרֶךְ) is not adverbial, against Lundbom (2008a, 341) and most translations (ESV and NIV have "toward the daughter of my people"). This passage is not comparable to a text such as 1 Kings 8:44 (דֶּרֶךְ הָעִיר, "toward the city"), where the word can be said to be used adverbially but even so concretely refers to a "road" toward a literal, geographical location. Instead, it has its common meaning of "way" as in "behavior." Also, it should not be revocalized to the verb דָּרַךְ ("has trodden") against Holladay (1986, 141, 156). When דֶּרֶךְ is in the construct form with the absolute noun referring to a person or people, it refers to a pattern of behavior. Thus, in "I have chosen him . . . to keep the way of YHWH (דֶּרֶךְ יְהוָה) by doing righteousness" (Gen. 18:19), דֶּרֶךְ יְהוָה describes upright behavior. "And he walked in all the way of Jeroboam" (וַיֵּלֶךְ בְּכָל־דֶּרֶךְ יָרָבְעָם; 1 Kings 16:26) means that he imitated Jeroboam's evil behavior. In Jeremiah 4:18, YHWH tells Jerusalem, "Your way" (דַּרְכֵּךְ) has brought these disasters upon you. So too here, the "way" of the "people" is their behavior, and it is the predicate of the sentence (רוּחַ, "wind," is the subject).

*The word "tempestuous" (מָלֵא) is literally "full."* Here, it means that the wind means is strong because it is, as it were, full of air (McKane 1986, 1.95–98).

### *Invasion: The Babylonian Storm (4:13)*

If Judah's leaders are a high wind, the Babylonians are a tornado.

**4:13**. This verse is not determinative for the meaning of verses 11–12, but it is influenced by those verses. In the previous text, the apostate leaders of Judah are like a high wind that buffets Jeremiah and does the people no good. The coming Babylonian army, however, is like storm clouds (עֲנָנִים) and a whirlwind (סוּפָה). The metaphors, along with the comparison of their horses to eagles, imply a force that is swift, destructive, and predatory.

### *Deceit: Jerusalem, Home of Evil Schemes (4:14)*

**4:14**. Jeremiah, in anguish, appeals for Jerusalem to repent and avoid this calamity. Yet he tells her that "your wicked scheming" (מַחְשְׁבוֹת אוֹנֵךְ) has found a home in her (לין can mean to lodge overnight, but it can also mean to reside permanently, as in Job 41:22, בְּצַוָּארוֹ יָלִין עֹז, "Strength abides in his neck"). Scheming, plotting, and subverting the truth are a way of life in Jerusalem.

### *Invasion: The Enemy Approaches (4:15–18)*

**4:15–16a**. Jeremiah and all of Judah are hearing reports from the region of Dan, traditionally the northernmost part of Israel, and from the Ephraim hill country, just north of Judah, that an enemy is approaching. True to form, the Babylonian enemy comes from the north. Jeremiah thus calls on heralds to warn both the local nations (Moab, Ammon, Edom, the Phoenicians, etc.) and Jerusalem that the enemy is at their gates. Babylon was the scourge not only of Judah but of all the small states of the Levant.

**4:16b–18**. The message for the heralds takes the form of an oracular poem of seven lines:

- A: "Keepers" (נֹצְרִים) come from far away (16b).
- B: They raise a clamor against the cities of Judah (16c).
- A': An army like "guards of a field" (כְּשֹׁמְרֵי שָׂדַי) surround the city (17a).
- C: Jerusalem's rebellion has brought this about (17b).
- C': Jerusalem's behavior has caused this disaster (18a).
- D: This is Jerusalem's bitter ruin (18b).
- D': It strikes the people at their heart (18c).

In the poem, lines A, B, and A' declare that an army is coming, lines C and C' say why it is coming, and lines D and D' speak of the suffering Jerusalem will endure.

The warning is that an army is coming to "besiege" (נצר) their cities (v. 16b). This verb essentially means to "keep," and thus it often means to guard or protect (Isa. 42:6; Ps. 12:7 [MT 8]). In this case, however, it means that the invading army will surround a city, preventing anyone from escaping. So too, the army is like people who protect a field of produce, keeping out animals or thieves that might damage or take the crop (v. 17a). Here, however, the army keeps the people inside the city from getting out, so that it may kill or enslave them. The clamor they raise (v. 16c) is a war cry, meant to terrify the inhabitants of the cities they besiege.

### *Deceit: Senseless People and the Earth in Upheaval (4:19–28)*

This section is in four parts, as follows:

- A: Jeremiah mourns; his world is in ruins (4:19–21).
- A': Jeremiah mourns the folly of his people (4:22).
- B: Jeremiah sees that the earth is desolate (4:23–26).
- B': YHWH governs the desolation of earth (4:27–28).

Developing the motif of God's judgment bringing about a great desolation, the text again points to the self-deception of the people. They are fools, refusing to see what is coming. They think the current order is permanent, but it will undergo complete upheaval. Everything they rely upon, even the stability represented by the life and orderliness of creation, will be upended.

**4:19**. Jeremiah is in anguish over the warfare and slaughter he sees overtaking his people. This probably is prophetic; he is overcome by a vision of what he knows will come. Hebrew regularly links a person's emotional state or character to his internal organs, as English does when it uses "heart" as a metaphor for compassion and "guts" as a metaphor for courage. Thus, "My anguish!" (מֵעַי) is literally, "My guts!" a term that refers to the intestines or stomach and that in Hebrew conveys extreme emotional distress. The translation of this verse is somewhat difficult, as described in the Translation Note. It should be rendered as two strophes of three lines each: "My anguish! My anguish! / I make the walls of my heart quiver! / My heart roars within me! // I cannot be silent, / For I hear the sound of the shofar! / My soul [hears] the war signal!"

*TRANSLATION NOTE FOR 4:19*

The *kethiv* אָחוּלָה means, "I writhe!" and is followed by most interpreters. But this leaves קִירוֹת לִבִּי hanging. The *qere* אוֹחִילָה, is generally taken to be a hiphil of יחל and so means, "I wait!" But that makes little sense in context and thus is not widely followed. However, the alternative *qere* (found in a few MSS) אָחִילָה could be parsed as a hiphil of חיל, meaning "I cause to shake!" The following noun phrase, קִירוֹת לִבִּי, is generally read as an interjection, "The walls of my heart!" (Lundbom 2008, 349). But that makes for an unusual outburst. Otherwise, it is subjected to unpersuasive emendation (as in Holladay 1986, 142). If this phrase is the object of the *qere* verb אָחִילָה, we have אָחִילָה קִירוֹת לִבִּי, "I make the walls of my heart quiver!" This is the best solution. Note that the paragogic ה on אָחִילָה is not cohortative: "Let me . . .". Instead, it implies an inner compulsion forced on Jeremiah by circumstances (Holladay 1986, 161). The second *kethiv*, שָׁמַעְתִּי ("I hear") has the *qere*, שָׁמַעַתְּ ("you [fs] hear"). But the *qere* makes for a grammatically incoherent clause. The following noun, נַפְשִׁי ("my soul"), is feminine, but if it were the subject of שָׁמַעַתְּ, the verb should be the 3fs שָׁמְעָה. The ESV and NIV follow the *kethiv* but omit נַפְשִׁי—a forced solution. The CSB follows the *qere* and translates it as "For you, my soul, have heard," a grammatically possible but implausible interpretation. A better solution is to follow the *kethiv* but read the verb שמע as doing "double duty," so that there is an implied שָׁמְעָה before נַפְשִׁי. The resultant text of two three-line strophes is plausible:

מֵעַי מֵעַי<br>
אוֹחִילָה קִירוֹת לִבִּי<br>
הֹמֶה־לִּי לִבִּי<br>
לֹא אַחֲרִישׁ<br>
כִּי קוֹל שׁוֹפָר שָׁמַעְתִּי<br>
נַפְשִׁי תְּרוּעַת מִלְחָמָה

The first strophe describes his anguish using biological language and repeats "my heart" (לִבִּי) in line 2 and 3. The second strophe concerns the sounds he makes and hears and has קוֹל שׁוֹפָר parallel to תְּרוּעַת מִלְחָמָה.

**4:20**. Jeremiah foresees one disaster following another as the Babylonian army heads south. The lamentation over "tents" (אֹהֶל) and "tent fabric" (יְרִיעָה) reflects the traditional nomadic life of the Israelites, whereby they conceived of themselves as living in tents long after they had settled into houses. Compare 1 Kings 12:16, "To your tents, O Israel!"

**4:21**. Jeremiah wonders when the nightmare of the invasion will end.

**4:22**. Jeremiah laments the reason for the disaster: his people's folly and immorality. Stacking up three words that imply stupidity ("foolish" [אֱוִיל], "senseless" [סְכָלִים], and "not understanding" [וְלֹא נְבוֹנִים]), Jeremiah shows that the people have been deceived by wishful thinking and the lies of their leaders. The root of their folly is that they do not know YHWH. They cannot do good, but they are skilled at doing evil.

**4:23–26**. In four verses, Jeremiah describes his vision of creation undone and all the earth being desolate. Each of the four verses begins with "I saw" (רָאִיתִי). In verse 23, the earth is "without form and void" (תֹהוּ וָבֹהוּ), a citation of Genesis 1:2, and there is no light (אוֹר), an allusion to Genesis 1:3. In verse 24, the mountains and hills are violently shaking about, a reversal of the idea that mountains represent solidity and permanence (Gen. 49:26; Deut. 33:15; Ps. 125:1; cf. Hab. 3:6). In verse 25, humans and birds are both absent, contradicting Genesis 1:20–21, 26–27. In verse 26, what had been an orchard (כַּרְמֶל) is now a desert (מִדְבָּר), contradicting Genesis 1:11, and the cities are desolate, contradicting the blessing and mandate for humanity to fill the earth (Gen. 1:28). This reversal of the creation narrative represents the failure of all of Judah's misplaced hopes. The creation order seems permanent, unchanging, and utterly reliable, like the "everlasting hills," but God can upend it all. The is another aspect of self-deceit of Jeremiah's people. Things that they think unchanging, including Jerusalem and its temple, are transitory.

**4:27**. Summarizing what Jeremiah saw in the preceding four verses, YHWH says that the whole land will be desolate. Jeremiah's apocalyptic vision of the undoing of the creation of earth will be in a sense locally true when Judah becomes a wasteland because of the invasion. Even so, God will not entirely annihilate it (the noun כָּלָה implies total annihilation, as when Nahum 1:9 promises the obliteration of Nineveh). Formally, this verse contradicts verse 23, which states that the earth will revert to its primordial shape of being a formless void, and this has provoked a much discussion among scholars (Lundbom 2008a, 361). But such a literal reading of the text is inappropriate, and against Holladay there is no need to alter 4:27 to bring it into harmony with 4:23 (Holladay 1986, 166–67). For those who experience the fall of Jerusalem, it will be as if the world came to an end, but in the long scheme of things, from God's perspective, all is not lost. For Jerusalem, unlike the local pagan nations, there is yet hope for a remnant and for restoration.

**4:28**. For the time being, however, that hope is a distant, secondary thing. For those of Jeremiah's generation, facing the approaching Babylonians, there is only death and destruction, and YHWH's decree that Jerusalem must fall will not change. Thus, in keeping with the theme of the reversal of the creation of earth, heaven mourns.

### *Invasion: The Towns Deserted (4:29)*

Returning to the theme of the invading army, this verse focuses on how cities will be left empty of all inhabitants.

**4:29**. We suddenly shift away from cosmic themes of creation and its apocalyptic reversal and return to human invaders and the panic they create. Cavalry and archers (פָּרָשׁ וְרֹמֵה קֶשֶׁת) are soldiers who can kill swiftly and from a distance, thus creating terror and flight among the populace. When the people forsake cities for thickets and rocks, they abandon civilization, and the world reverts to a primitive state, scarcely able to sustain life. The ideology of the city, that it represents progress from a bestial to a human state of existence, was an important element of ancient Near Eastern culture, and the invasion reverses that progress. Thus, the symbolic undoing of creation described above is matched by an actual undoing of society brought on by the invader.

### *Deceit: A Cosmetic Solution (4:30)*

The leaders of Jerusalem deceive themselves, thinking that other nations in the region will prove to be reliable allies.

**4:30**. Jerusalem is again a woman, here beautifying herself with cosmetics and jewelry. In the metaphor, the woman's adornment of herself for her lovers represents Jerusalem seeking allies among the nations. This is a hopeless act; they care nothing for Judah and will happily take part in its destruction and plunder. But there is a double act of deception here. With her cosmetics, Jerusalem presents a false image of herself, seeking the support of other states. At the same time, Jerusalem is self-deceived, not facing the fact that they will seek her life.

### *Invasion: The Helpless Woman (4:31)*

In the face of the invader Jerusalem is helpless, like a woman giving birth.

**4:31**. Staying with the image of Jerusalem as a woman, she is now in agony, as if giving birth to her first child. Jeremiah powerfully develops the metaphor: she gasps for life, she spreads out her hands, and she is exhausted. Only at the end of the verse does the language shift from the purely metaphorical to the partly literal: before her stands her killer, the invading army.

### *Deceit: A Futile Search for Faithfulness (5:1–5)*

Jeremiah describes two futile quests to find honest men in Jerusalem. He roamed the streets at God's command, looking for anyone who cared about the truth, and found none. On another occasion (not necessarily at the same time), he wrongly supposed that only the ignorant poor were so misguided, but he found apostasy in every level of Jerusalem society.

**5:1**. YHWH commands the people to roam about the streets of Jerusalem looking for a single man who does what is right. The command implicitly compares Jerusalem unfavorably to Sodom, where the angel of YHWH could not find ten righteous people (Gen. 18:32). The command uses multiple related terms: They are to "wander" (שׁוֹטְטוּ) "and see" (וּרְאוּ) "and find out" (וּדְעוּ) "and seek" (וּבַקְשׁוּ); they should look "in the streets" (בְּחוּצוֹת) and "in its plazas" (בִּרְחוֹבוֹתֶיהָ); they search for someone who "carries out justice" (עֹשֶׂה מִשְׁפָּט) and "seeks truth" (מְבַקֵּשׁ אֱמוּנָה). The implication behind all of this repetition is that people could search through the city thoroughly, looking in every nook and cranny, and find no such honest men. The claim that there is not a single righteous man in Jerusalem is not to be taken literally; it is hyperbole. Within the book, we know of men who believed Jeremiah and sought to protect him (e.g., 36:19).

**5:2**. Swearing falsely in YHWH's name seems like a relatively superficial mattered (compared, for example, the child sacrifice), but it gets to the root if Judah's sin. Using God's name to cover a lie is typical behavior for those people who deceive others, are themselves deceived, and hate the truth. In such a people, theology and mendacity come together to form a lethal mixture. To them, the truth is a life-threatening allergen.

**5:3**. The disasters that successively befall Judah have no effect on the people's attitude. Although God "strikes" them (נכה, hiphil), they feel no pain (חלה). This does not literally mean that no one suffers when they endure drought (which happened in Jeremiah's lifetime; 14:1–6) or military defeat; it means that none of it breaks through their obstinacy or drives them to repentance ("they refuse to repent," מֵאֲנוּ לָשׁוּב). In saying that they make their faces harder than stone, the text does not mean that they are exceptionally tough or resilient. But they are exceptionally stubborn and brazen. The idiom is similar to the "whore's forehead" of 3:3.

**5:4–5**. A key component of Jeremiah's story is his progress from believing that there was hope for Judah—that there was a "silent majority" who held to orthodox theology and who would in the end be faithful to God—to his complete disillusionment. He finally came to realize that Jerusalem society was rotten from top to bottom. Here, he tells how he once thought that it was only the poor, illiterate laborers who clung to paganism and superstition. Such people, he thought, did not know the teaching and requirements of the Law ("the way of YHWH [and] the justice of their God," דֶּרֶךְ יְהוָה מִשְׁפַּט אֱלֹהֵיהֶם). Surely, he supposed, those who knew the Law would pay heed to his message. But they would not. He found that the "important people" (הַגְּדֹלִים) were just as evil, deceptive, and pagan as their lower-class counterparts. It was a matter of the heart, not of class or education. The expression, "they broke the yoke; they tore off bonds" (שָׁבְרוּ עֹל נִתְּקוּ מוֹסֵרוֹת) is formulaic for obtaining freedom. In 2:20, it refers to how YHWH freed Israel from slavery in Egypt (see the translation note at 2:20); in this verse, it is Judah's determination to be free of YHWH.

### *Invasion: Lion, Wolf, and Leopard (5:6)*

As wild animals terrify and slay their prey, so the invaders will do to Judah.

**5:6**. Babylon and its vassal armies are described metaphorically as ravenous beasts. We probably should not try to unpack the lion, wolf, and leopard, looking for specific characteristics behind each metaphor (as though they represented different peoples or different units of the army). They all mean that when the invasion comes, it will be terrible and bloody, and the enemy will be as ruthless as a predatory animal.

### *Deceit: Faithless to God and to Marriage (5:7–9)*

This short passage is a three-part chiasmus:

A: God cannot forgive Judah (7a).
B: Judah is sexually depraved (7b–8).
A': God must punish Judah (9).

Faithlessness is the theme of this text, in keeping with the broader of theme of the deceit that saturates Judah. The people are faithless to God, a spiritual adultery, and as a result they are faithless to their literal marriages.

**5:7a**. God cannot forgive them; "forgive" (סלח) here does not mean to remove the guilt of the repentant but to allow the unrepentant to avoid punishment. Here again, Judah is personified as an adulterous wife, as indicated by the feminine singular suffix on "your children" (בָּנַיִךְ). The implicit metaphor is that the children are children of another father, the foreign god, and thus they turn from YHWH and swear "by non-gods" (בְּלֹא אֱלֹהִים).

**5:7b–8**. Because the nation is spiritually adulterous against YHWH, the people are also literally promiscuous and adulterous. They frequent prostitutes, an activity almost exclusively committed by men. Note that the Bible does not exempt men from the guilt of adultery; there is no double standard. There is more to this accusation, however, than going to brothels. The end of 7b does not mean that they "trooped to the houses of whores" (ESV; NIV is similar). The verb (יִתְגֹּדָדוּ) means to "gash oneself," and represents an aspect of Baal worship (see 1 Kings 18:28; cult prostitution was another aspect). This is reflected in the CSB: "they gashed themselves at the prostitute's house." Such behavior characterizes the worship of Baal; as a religion, it is no better than indulging in prostitution and perverse sexual fetishes. Returning to animal metaphors in verse 8, Jeremiah compares the men of Judah to stallions eager to mount any available filly. Faithlessness to God leads to faithlessness in marriage.

> *TRANSLATION NOTE FOR 5:7*
> Translators often follow the Targum in treating the verb יִתְגֹּדָדוּ as if it were related to גְּדוּד, "troop." But no such verb is known, and the hithpolel of גדד meaning to "gash oneself" is well attested (for example, Deut. 14:1; Jer. 16:6; 47:5). We should follow the standard meaning.

**5:9**. God not only upholds the covenant made between Judah and himself, the Sinai covenant, but also requires fidelity to the marriage covenant between a man and a woman. For both forms of infidelity, God must punish Judah.

### *Invasion: Ravaged Vineyards (5:10)*

The invading army will destroy Judah and its vineyards.

**5:10**. This verse begins with a command for an unspecified group to "go up" (עֲלוּ) and demolish the vineyards of Judah. But the addressees are not in doubt: They are the invading army, making its way toward Jerusalem. The "vineyard" is at the same time metaphorical and literal. On the one hand it is Judah, compared to a vineyard in Isaiah 5:1–10. On the other hand, it is the literal vineyards of Judah. Invading armies would sweep through cultivated land, take all they could, and burn the rest. Isaiah 7:23 describes the aftermath of the Assyrian sweep through Judah: "And it will come about that on that day, in every place where there once were a thousand vines worth a thousand shekels of silver, [the vineyards] will become briers and thorns." Jeremiah 5:10b, "Remove her branches, for they do not belong to YHWH," may be the origin of Paul's metaphor of the olive tree, in which the native branches were pruned away and wild branches grafted in (Rom. 11:17–20).

### *Deceit: Lying versus True Prophets (5:11–14)*

The people love false prophets but reject the prophets whom YHWH has sent.

**5:11–12**. Israel and Judah have "dealt treacherously" (בָּגְדוּ) with YHWH by declaring the words of his prophet to be untrue. In saying that YHWH would do nothing and would not bring an enemy against Jerusalem, they "told lies against YHWH" (כִּחֲשׁוּ בַּיהוָה). It is more than a matter of simple unbelief; it is a conscious denial and distortion of what, on some level, they know to be true.

> *TRANSLATION NOTE FOR 5:12*
> The meaning of לֹא־הוּא is uncertain and widely discussed (Lundbom 2008a, 389; Holladay 1986, 186–87). Some take it as a denial of God's existence ("He is not!"), but if that were the meaning it would almost certainly be אֵין־הוּא. Some take it to mean, "He will do nothing!" (ESV, NIV). It is probably equivalent to "Not so!" The people emphatically deny Jeremiah's message.

**5:13**. This verse is ambiguous: It could be YHWH's condemnation of the false prophets, or it could be the people's hostility toward true prophets, such as Jeremiah. But the last clause, "thus it shall be done to them" (כֹּה יֵעָשֶׂה לָהֶם), must mean, "so let what they say be done to them," as in the NIV. This implies that the speakers are Jeremiah's enemies, and that they call for the dire things he predicted to be done to him and to men like him. The false prophets, by contrast, prophesied victory and success for Judah, and thus one would not condemn them by saying that what they predicted would happen for them. Instead, Jeremiah's enemies wish that the disaster he predicts would befall him. They mock the true prophets, saying that they will become "wind" (רוּחַ). This word also means "spirit" and is perhaps a play on the prophetic claim to have the Spirit. They deny that the prophets have the "[divine] speech" (הַדִּבֵּר), meaning that their words are not from God.

**5:14**. This verse confirms that verse 13 is the people's rejection of the true prophets. God responds that since "you" have said such things

(דַּבֶּרְכֶם, masculine plural suffix, referring to the people), he will make his word "in your mouth" (בְּפִיךָ, masculine singular suffix, referring to Jeremiah's mouth) into a fire that will devour them. His word will not be mere "wind."

### *Invasion: The All-Devouring Enemy (5:15–19)*

Answering the scoffing of the people, YHWH—in the harshest and most graphic terms—describes the enemy that is set to invade Judah.

**5:15**. The invading enemy comes from far away, is an ancient and enduring nation, and speaks a language that Hebrew speakers cannot understand. Babylon was, by ancient standards, far from Jerusalem, and it was an ancient city, having been the hub of an empire as far back as the reign of Hammurabi (reigned 1792 to 1750 B.C.). Their language, Akkadian, was related to Hebrew but not close enough to be comprehensible to an Israelite, rather like English and German. This verse alludes to Deuteronomy 28:49 and implies that all of the curses of that chapter are about to be fulfilled.

**5:16**. Describing a quiver for arrows as "like an open tomb" (כְּקֶבֶר פָּתוּחַ) is peculiar. It seems to mean that as the grave has an inexhaustible appetite for the dead (see Prov. 30:16), so also the armaments of the Babylonians never have enough of killing. Also, the opening at the top of a quiver somewhat resembles a mouth.

**5:17**. Again, Jeremiah uses semiliteral language. The Babylonian army will literally consume the harvest and herds belonging to Judah, but they will figuratively eat up all in their path, including the people.

**5:18**. YHWH mitigates his judgment on Judah, saying he will not forever annihilate it (see 4:27). The nations against whom Jeremiah prophesies, however, are given no such assurance. Those nations will be destroyed but never restored.

**5:19**. When Jeremiah's mocking, skeptical audience asks why such terrible things have happened to them, the answer will be that they served other gods. That is, they did not heed Jeremiah's warnings.

### *Deceit: Houses Full of Deceit (5:20–31)*

The self-deceit of Judah exists at every level. They refuse to see evidence that the wrath of God is mounting up against them, even though they are in a drought. The enable the rich to plunder the poor by legal fraud. They gladly receive the lies of the prophets.

**5:20–21**. YHWH calls on one group to make a proclamation and give an announcement (הַגִּידוּ and וְהַשְׁמִיעוּהָ) and commands another group to listen (שִׁמְעוּ־נָא). The group that is to listen is the "foolish people" (עַם סָכָל), the inhabitants of Judah. But who is the first group? Since 5:13 describes how the people despise YHWH's true prophets, they are the ones whom he commands to make the announcement. This is a further vindication of Jeremiah and his colleagues against their enemies. The people's refusal to see and hear the truth demonstrates their self-deceit.

**5:22–23**. The verse contains a wordplay that is invisible in translation: "Do you not writhe (תָחִילוּ, from the root חיל) in fear before me, who set the sand (חול) as a boundary for the sea?" God's power is so great that he controls the most chaotic force of nature—the sea—and yet the people have no fear or awe of him. The sea is personified as a great beast that rages against the walls of its cage, but it cannot get out. But Judah's people are so obstinately rebellious that they can turn away and break free of the confines of YHWH's decrees. It is as though God himself were amazed at the tenacity with which they break his laws. Here too, there is a wordplay: They have an "obstinate heart" (לֵב סוֹרֵר, from סרר) and so "turn away" (סָרוּ, from סור) from YHWH.

**5:24**. Just as they don't learn the lesson of the seas, so they don't learn the lesson of the rains. God sends the "early rain" (יוֹרֶה [qere], rains lasting from late October to early December) and the "latter rains" (מַלְקוֹשׁ, gentle rains in March and April that do not hinder the grain harvest). God has ordained the "weeks" (שְׁבֻעוֹת) in which the rains should fall, and implicitly has also ordained the "Feast of Weeks" (Pentecost), when the people were to honor YHWH for the gifts of wheat and barley. Even though their lives depend upon YHWH's faithfulness in managing nature, they don't fear him.

**5:25**. Judah experienced a severe drought during the time of Jeremiah (14:1–6), and this message evidently came from that experience. The stubborn folly and self-deception of Judah is, in God's eyes, truly incomprehensible. Even when he withholds "these things" (אֵלֶּה, referring to the rains) from them, they refuse to admit that their own sins have brought this down upon them.

**5:26**. The sins that define Judah also cause God to withhold rain: corrupt men use legal maneuvers to confiscate the property of people who had no political connections. Unfortunately, verse 26 is very difficult, and interpreters take liberties with the Hebrew. The following paraphrase, I think, is the best one can do with the text: "For wicked men are among my people. / My people look on like fowlers. / They have set up a destroyer; / They capture men." The point is that the populace knows that there is great corruption and oppression in the land. They watch corrupt and powerful people abuse the poor, like fowlers who watch their hawks kill their prey. This provokes God's wrath, and "sets up" the destroyer, Babylon. But the main point is that the people do nothing in the face of great injustice. Since they regularly sat as jurors at the gate, they could have stopped the oppression.

*TRANSLATION NOTE FOR 5:26*

Much of this verse seems all but unintelligible in the MT. It appears to read, "For wicked men are among my people. He looks on fowlers . . . (יָשׁוּר כְּשַׁךְ יְקוּשִׁים; but the meaning of כְּשַׁךְ is unknown and thus the ellipsis); / They set up a destroyer (הִצִּיבוּ מַשְׁחִית); / They capture men." Most translations are like the ESV: "For wicked men are found among my people; they lurk like fowlers lying in wait (יָשׁוּר כְּשַׁךְ יְקוּשִׁים; the word כְּשַׁךְ is often taken to be שׁכַךְ, "subside," an infinitive with the preposition כְּ). They set a trap; they catch men." But יָשׁוּר כְּשַׁךְ יְקוּשִׁים cannot mean, "they lurk like fowlers lying in wait." The verb שׁוּר does not mean to "lurk" but "to behold," and the infinitive construction would not be כְּשַׁךְ but כְּשֹׁךְ (see Esth. 2:1). And הִצִּיבוּ מַשְׁחִית cannot mean, "They set a trap." Various emendations have been proposed (Lundbom 2008a, 406; Holladay 1986, 198), but none is persuasive. But the received text is mostly comprehensible. The first key is to recognize that the "people" (עַם) is the subject of יָשׁוּר (a collective such as עַם often takes a singular verb). Its subject cannot be the plural noun רְשָׁעִים, the "wicked men." The meaning of כְּשַׁךְ is frankly lost to us; we can only leave it as an ellipsis. The participle מַשְׁחִית means "destroying" is often used of any person who destroys, including God (Gen. 19:14), but in Jeremiah 4:7 מַשְׁחִית is the Babylonian army. This is probably its meaning here. Thus, to "set up a destroyer" (הִצִּיבוּ מַשְׁחִית) is to bring about the circumstances (that is, by behaving wickedly) that call for God to send a destroyer. Thus, the meaning is, "For wicked men are among my people. / My people look on like . . . fowlers. / They have set up a destroyer; / They capture men."

**5:27**. Following the metaphor of "fowlers," the text now uses a related but different metaphor: The people have cages full of birds in their homes. The cages are "full of lies" (מְלֵאִים מִרְמָה). The birds are their lies, which they treat as expensive, pampered pets. This is the perjury whereby they oppress people and confiscate their land through the court system.

**5:28**. Widows and orphans are naturally most vulnerable to the kind of theft through legal processes that this passage describes. The rich bring fraudulent cases against widows and orphans, and the juries do not judge the cases fairly. Thus, the rich and their friends get richer.

**5:29**. God cannot fail to bring down judgment on such a corrupt system. As verse 26 indicates, the "fowlers" and those who enable them "set up a destroyer" against Judah.

**5:30–31**. In addition to the lies in the court system, there is another set of lies that bring "desolation and horror" (שַׁמָּה וְשַׁעֲרוּרָה) upon Judah: The prophets tell lies to the people and the priests use their offices for their own benefit, and the people love it. They want to hear the reassuring lies of the priests and they are comfortable with the corruption of the priesthood. And so, they will be at a total loss when their house of cards collapses, when the nation comes "to her end" (לְאַחֲרִיתָהּ).

*TRANSLATION NOTE FOR 5:31*
The clause יִרְדּוּ עַל־יְדֵיהֶם is often taken to have the verb I רדה, "to rule," and so to mean, "(The priests) rule at their hand," that is, under the direction of the prophets. But this is an unprecedented and unlikely interpretation (Holladay 1986, 201). The verb is probably II רדה, "to scoop out," as in Judges 14:9. "They scoop with their hands" probably means they use their position to get the best for themselves, as did the sons of Eli (1 Sam. 2:22–36).

### *Invasion: Zion in Flight; Jerusalem Under Siege (6:1–9)*

In a variety of metaphors, YHWH declares that Judah is finished. The invader will thoroughly lay waste to the region, and people should flee while they can.

**6:1**. Jerusalem was in the tribal territory of Benjamin, and no doubt many of its residents were of that tribe. They too must flee the coming invader. There is a wordplay in "Blow the shofar in Tekoa!" The name "Tekoa" (תְּקוֹעַ) has the same letters as the verb "blow" (תקע). Tekoa was south of Jerusalem, and Beth-haccherem was possibly to its west. The point is that no place in Judah, whether Jerusalem or one of the outlying villages, will be safe.

**6:2**. The comparison of Zion to a lovely and delicate woman calls to mind Deuteronomy 28:54–57, which predicts that when God sends an invader against his people, even the most refined of women will cannibalize their own children.

*TRANSLATION NOTE FOR 6:2*
The verb דָּמִיתִי is usually translated, "I will destroy," based on III דמה, which means "be destroyed" in the niphal. But there is no support for a qal meaning, "destroy," and the niphal form may actually be from II דמה, which means "be silent." In other words, there may not be any root III דמה. It could be that דָּמִיתִי is an archaic 2fs. If so, the verse means, "O lovely and delicate [lady], O Daughter Zion, you have become silent!" This would mean that the city is desolate.

**6:3**. The shepherds are the enemy commanders, and their grazing sheep are the troops that surround the city. This is a strangely peaceful metaphor, but it inverts the meaning of what people normally see. They are used to seeing sheep grazing on the hills around the city—a lovely, pastoral scene. But the sheep will be replaced by enemy troops, a source of terror.

**6:4–5**. Not all of these words belong to the invader, as some translations imply. Rather, they voice the views of both camps. Invader: "Let us attack at noon!" Jerusalem: "Woe to us, for the day is ending!" Invader: "Let us attack at night!" One would think that the Babylonians would attack at early morning, as was common in ancient warfare. But the point here is that they attack at all times: in the heat of the day, at evening, and in the middle of the night. The Jerusalem forces lament as the day ends, even though this would normally be the time a besieger would desist for the night. No such respite would be given to Jerusalem.

**6:6a**. The true commander of the invading army is not Nebuchadnezzar II but YHWH of Hosts. It is he who orders the armies to put a siege mound against the city. Jerusalem therefore has no hope.

**6:6b–7**. The city must fall because it is full of evil and oppression. Once again, Jeremiah employs a counterintuitive metaphor: A well keeps water fresh, and that is a good, delightful thing. But Jerusalem keeps its wickedness fresh. This implies that YHWH is not punishing the city for some ancient sin, as though it were under a curse for crimes committed by a former generation. New sins—new reasons to punish the city—appear every day.

**6:8**. YHWH advises Jerusalem that he will turn from her in disgust (יקע, qal stem). The word is used of a lover who rejects his former partner. In Ezekiel 23:17–18, Babylon defiles Jerusalem (in a sexual metaphor) and then turns (יקע) from her because she no longer has any charm or desirability in his eyes. So also, YHWH spurns (יקע) Jerusalem because she has behaved like a prostitute.

**6:9**. Returning to the metaphor of Judah as a vineyard, Jeremiah declares that the enemy will not leave a single grape in place. That is, the Babylonians will thoroughly demolish the city and strip it of inhabitants.

### *Deceit: Incapable of Hearing the Truth (6:10–11a)*

In their self-deceit, the people are unable hear and consider Jeremiah's message. Scoffing has become for them an automatic, conditioned response.

**6:10–11a**. "Uncircumcised ears," like uncircumcised hearts, are incapable of giving heed to YHWH's word. They cannot listen to the truth about their sin and about the coming calamity, but only jeer. Jeremiah for a time remained silent, but at last could hold back no longer and gave full vent to his prophetic anger without regard to how little attention the people gave to it.

### *Invasion: The Enemy Takes All People and All Property (6:11b–12)*

God commands Jeremiah not to keep holding back, but to let the people know how thorough the destruction will be.

**6:11b–12**. YHWH tells Jeremiah to "pour out" (שְׁפֹךְ, masculine singular imperative) words of judgment against the city. It pertains to all: young and old, men and women. These merisms imply that no one will escape; everyone, regardless of age or gender, will lose houses and lands to the invading army.

### *Deceit: Saying "Peace" When There Is No Peace (6:13–21)*

Exploring the self-deception of Jerusalem, Jeremiah declares that the people persist in heinous sin, cover it with sacrifices and religious rites, and deceive themselves by saying, "Peace, peace!"

**6:13**. Judah is steeped in falsehood. Again, the text employs merisms: "from least to greatest" and "from prophet to priest." Everyone seeks for profit by fraud, and everyone tells lies as a matter of course. The word for "unjust gain" (בצע) comes from a root that originally meant to "cut off" and came to mean the unlawful acquisition of another's property (Kellermann 1974).

**6:14**. This sums up all the deceit with which the leadership beguiles the people. They claim all will be well. "Peace" (שָׁלוֹם) is not only the lack of warfare, but a state of well-being, characterized by freedom from want and from fear of enemies. In reality, Judah was surrounded by threats to their survival, and their condition was anything but שָׁלוֹם. As such, the words of the leaders only remedy the situation "superficially" (עַל־נְקַלָּה).

**6:15**. Jerusalem can commit abominations and remain completely unabashed. The nature of the "abomination" (תּוֹעֵבָה) is unspecified; the word often connotes some grossly immoral activity, such as human sacrifice (Deut. 12:31), homosexuality (Lev. 18:22), transvestitism (Deut. 22:5), or secret idolatry (Deut. 27:15). It can be used for more routine offenses, such as cheating in the marketplace (Deut. 25:16). Here, it probably does not refer to any specific offense but collectively represents all the evil done in Judah. The main point is that the people's sense of good and evil is so warped by lies that they cannot feel shame at what they do.

**6:16–17**. YHWH made every effort to draw the people back to the truth. He called on them to seek "for the ancient paths" (לִנְתִבוֹת עוֹלָם), the commands and promises that have come down to them in the Law, but they refused. He set over them "watchmen" (צֹפִים, here referring to the prophets under the metaphor of sentries on the city walls), and the watchmen implored them to pay attention to the alarm trumpets. But the people lived in denial, refusing to pay heed to the blasts of the shofar. Had they listened, they could have had "rest" (מַרְגּוֹעַ). This word is found only here, but it represents the "peace" (שָׁלוֹם) verse 14 says they vainly sought for.

**6:18–19**. YHWH announces a trial for Judah, and he calls on the nations (v. 18) and the land (v. 19) to serve as a jury. This is, of course, purely rhetorical. But in the hypothetical trial, the jurors will see that YHWH's charges against Judah are valid and that Judah's excuses are lies. The charge that Judah has rejected God's law is validated by the people's refusal to seek the "ancient ways" (v. 16).

**6:20**. Anticipating accusations that are developed in 7:1–8:12, Jeremiah speaks of how the people deceive themselves with religious acts. They suppose that God is appeased by sacrifices and expensive, exotic incense, even as they continue to commit the aforementioned abominations.

**6:21**. YHWH's judgment against Judah is to lay "stumbling blocks" (מִכְשֹׁלִים) for the "fathers and sons" (yet another merism). The metaphor of stumbling implies that the people are in darkness (Hos. 4:5), are misled by sin (Hos. 5:5; Ezek. 14:3), or arrogantly trust in human power (Isa. 31:3). This, again, speaks to their deception, except that here God causes them to stumble. This is analogous to how Paul speaks of giving people over to their own wickedness (Rom. 1:24).

### *Invasion: The Cruel Army from the North (6:22–26)*

A summary of the Babylonian invasion: The enemy is all but invincible, Judah will cringe in terror, and there will be no escape. There is nothing left to do but mourn.

**6:22–23**. The army from the north is of course Babylon. Saying that they come from "the most remote places of earth" (מִיַּרְכְּתֵי־אָרֶץ) is hyperbole, but to the Israelites Babylon was indeed far away. The army is well-armed, pitiless, a great horde (their sound is like the roaring sea), and set on conquering Judah.

**6:24**. The Babylonians "grab" (חזק, hiphil stem) bows and javelins in verse 23, but in this verse anguish "grabs" (חזק, hiphil stem) the people of Judah. They are so frightened that they are unable to move or resist the enemy, and their guts seize up like a woman having contractions. This echoes the portrait of Jerusalem in 4:31.

**6:25**. The city is under siege, and to go out from the city walls is to invite a violent death. The expression "terror on every side" (מָגוֹר מִסָּבִיב)

means that the enemy is all around, and the phrase is a favorite of Jeremiah. It appears also in 20:3, 10; 46:5; 49:29; and also in Psalm 31:13 (MT 14).

**6:26**. Lamentation often expresses repentance, but this verse is not a call to repent. It simply expresses deep sorrow of the fall of Jerusalem, an event that is now a foregone conclusion. It is analogous to the lament in Moab over the destruction of that people (Jer. 48:37–38), or the wailing over the fall of Ammon (Jer. 49:3), or the lament over burned-out villages of Judah (Mic. 1:11). Jerusalem must lament because the "desolater" (הַשֹּׁדֵד) is coming against them. The desolater is Babylon, the "destroyer of nations" (מַשְׁחִית גּוֹיִם) of 4:7 (see also the discussion of 5:26 above).

### *Conclusion (6:27–30)*

Jeremiah the refiner has tested the people by his preaching, and by their hostility to his message they have shown themselves to be dross, a worthless mineral, impossible to purify and use.

**6:27–30**. Under a metaphor drawn from metallurgy, YHWH calls Jeremiah an "assayer" (בָּחוֹן, v. 27) of his people. In this case, however, they are not refined and purified; they are found to be useless and fit only for casting away. In the metaphor, the refiner seeks for silver and gold, but the only metals he finds are iron and bronze (v. 28, representing a hardened stubbornness in the people) and lead (v. 29, perhaps here representing pseudo-silver and thus the phoniness of the people). The ore is of such poor quality that it is not worth working. The refining in this case is Jeremiah's preaching, and Judah's disdain for his message is proof of how corrupt they have become.

*TRANSLATION NOTE FOR 6:27, 29*

Verse 27 begins, in the MT, "I have made you an assayer among my people, a fortress" (מִבְצָר = "fortress"). Although YHWH does fortify Jeremiah for his task (1:18), this metaphor is out of place in this section. A commonly accepted emendation is to repoint the text to מְבַצֵּר, someone who smelts precious metal out of raw nuggets of gold ore. The word מְבַצֵּר is a hypothetical denominative piel from the noun בֶּצֶר, a noun found in Job 22:24 that appears to refer to the unrefined ore of gold. The line would thus mean, "I have made you an assayer among my people, a smelter of gold ore." The emendation is not certain but is probably the best way of handling the text. In verse 29, we have the *kethiv* מֵאֵשְׁתַּם עֹפָרֶת, which is untranslatable, and the *qere* מֵאֵשׁ תַּם עֹפָרֶת, "from fire lead is done away," meaning that it is melted and drained off. The implication is that the lead is useless for the smelter's purposes.

## THEOLOGICAL FOCUS

The alternating passages on Judah's self-deception and on the coming invasion dominate this passage. This leads to its primary theological statement: that turning from God causes people to embrace lies and to hold to a false sense of security and guiltlessness. Ultimately, reality shatters all the lies to which the sinner clings. Some salient ideas of the text are:

- Sinners refuse to believe that trouble will overtake them for what they have done, and they are shocked when it happens.
- When people refuse to believe God, they believe lies instead, and deceit becomes a prominent feature of their character.
- Self-deceit soon becomes so strong that a person simply cannot see the truth, no matter how strong the evidence.
- Eventually, a self-deceived people get a rude awakening, as when the people of Jerusalem looked out and saw the Babylonians at their gate.

## PREACHING AND TEACHING STRATEGIES

### *Exegetical and Theological Synthesis*

Judah's reaction to the accusation that they are deceiving themselves can be summarized with the simple, "No we aren't." To some degree, that is always the reaction of self-deception. If Judah had reacted with a willingness to listen, they wouldn't have been deceiving themselves. Jeremiah's message, filled with metaphor after metaphor and example after example, is so lengthy because Judah just doesn't get it. That is: they ignore the truth. Or Judah is not thinking clearly, because they misrepresent the truth. This defensive posturing is tied to self-deception. Perhaps the numerous examples were meant to break through those well-built and longstanding walls of self-deception.

We are no different in our initial rejection of the accusation of self-deception. Our walls are the same. We have either ignored the truth or we have taken the truth and reinterpreted it to support our sinful practices. God's frightful message to self-deceivers is that you can become so deceived that you can't even see the truth. This message of judgment is a grace-filled warning. God doesn't want us to be deceived. He is calling us to honesty and authenticity.

### *Preaching Idea*

Our self-deception is our most dangerous sin.

### *Contemporary Connections*

#### *What does it mean?*

The results of self-deception, while not explicitly numerated in this passage, can easily be seen. Based upon the theological emphases mentioned earlier, three possible results of self-deception are: We don't get it. We don't think clearly. We could be beyond refining.

*We don't get it.* We can be so self-deceived that when God's discipline and the consequences come into our lives, we are surprised. It is as though we didn't listen to His warnings. The Jewish leaders were shocked at the invasion, even though they had been warned (4:9). Apparently, they didn't listen to Jeremiah's warnings. Then in 6:10, Jeremiah tells the nation that they could not even listen to God's warning.

The blatant racism of the twentieth century in the USA was fostered by so-called scientific studies that declared that one race was inferior to another. This was self-deception. Even pastors of that era deceived themselves by saying it is best for all to stay segregated. They deceived themselves because it was easier to cling to traditions rather than make the hard changes. For decades many Christian leaders would not listen to the truth, and then it seemed as though they could not listen.

The church in which I grew up experienced the common situation of a changing neighborhood. I remember thinking that the church needed to embrace the new cultures that moved so quickly into the neighborhood. I knew these church leaders; they truly wanted to reach these cultures, but they kept doing church as a white Anglo church. They were bewildered as to why people of color (many colors) would not become a part of the church. The advice to let the new cultures affect the structures and leadership of the church fell on ears that could not hear. The church dwindled to a few families and moved further out of town. Today, the building is empty, and the neighborhood is full. Sometimes in our self-deception, we just don't get it.

*We don't think clearly.* When we refuse to believe God, our self-deceit can lead us to believe lies. Our thinking becomes messed up. The Jews deceit led them to the point that they didn't know how to blush (6:15). When we see on the screens in our homes a scene that presents far too much of a sexually intimate relationship, do we blush or continue to watch? When the couple decides to take their dating relationship to a new level and moves in together, though we know it is wrong we inwardly cheer. We have been deceived, and perhaps it is even self-deception. What frightens me more is that there are probably other areas in which the culture or my own flesh have deceived me, and I don't know it. Am I greedy or prideful in ways that I am unaware? Our self-deception has hurt our clear thinking.

*We could be beyond refining.* Our self-deception can tragically lead to a state to where we can't be refined. Jeremiah painted the picture of Israel being like a metal ore that is unfit for refining. Can we get to the point where the deceit is so strong that we are beyond hope of being refined? If we are concerned about being beyond hope, then that is an indication that we are not beyond refining. That should not take away the proper fear that unchecked self-deception can lead to a hardness to God's refining process.

### *Is it true?*

The problem with self-deception is that since we are being deceived, we don't know that we are being deceived. If we were aware of the deception, it would not be deception. The Israelites were deceived—and worse, they were self-deceived. God's true promises and warnings became false in their thinking. The history of God's acts among them shouted the truth of what Jeremiah was warning concerning God's judgment, but they rejected the truth to the point that it became false in their minds. They never thought that God would punish them. How could this happen? Surely people can't be deceived into thinking that what is true is false.

We see something online that we have wanted for years, but for a tenth of the price. We begin to look at it closely. We examine all the stats and pictures. Soon we see that this product is far inferior to the original item we longed for. But then, we begin to justify purchasing it. We think, "I can make it work." The pictures make it look as good as the far more expensive item, yet we know that online pictures can be deceptive. And the more we think about it, the more we allow ourselves to be deceived into thinking that this cheap imitation will be as good as the real thing. After all, it is made in Germany. We can't afford the real thing, but *this* we can afford. We get to the point that we set aside what we know and warnings from past experiences. In a moment of self-deception, we click "purchase." We buy something that, before watching the advertisements and online videos, we would not have bought. We are self-deceived, by our own choices to reject what we know as true. Foolish shopping on the internet brings the consequences of wasted time and money along with the frustration and embarrassment of being taken in. Judah's deceit and self-deception have far greater consequences.

### *Now what?*

So, what is the answer to self-deception? We need outside help. This comes from God, his Word, or his people. Certainly, God's Spirit prompts us when we sin, and his Word presents a clear standard. Somehow these are what God uses to pull me out of self-deception. I often need more help. My closest friends in God's family have been my most needed critics. Without them, I could not see my pride, my greed, my selfishness.

Years ago, there was a lie about me that turned into gossip, which fueled rumors about my character. Fortunately, due to some great wisdom of a body of deacons, the rumor was squelched. But the hurt remained. My response was minimal. After all, it was only gossip; it wasn't affecting me that much—at least, so I thought. At a gathering of pastors and wives with whom we had a very close fellowship, I shared that I was doing just fine; it was just a few gossips. A dear sister confronted me and asked why I was lying. Lying? Yes, to myself. I was hurting, and anger was festering, but I couldn't see it. To conquer self-deception, we need outside help. We must get it (be honest) and think clearly (be authentic), because self-deception is our most dangerous sin.

### *Creativity in Presentation*

Since this is a long pericope to preach, it is necessary to address the presentation before continuing with the ideas for preaching. Unless one has forty-five to sixty minutes, there is little chance of explaining every verse; and even then, there would be limited explanation. It is perhaps wiser to present the truths of this section in a summary fashion. After the introduction to the sermon and the structure of the passage, the preacher/teacher can choose four or five of the Invasion/Deceit pairs that will serve as examples of the whole passage, then present the following truths gleaned from the passage as a whole.

To get the concept of self-deception in front of our listeners, it might be helpful to start with deception. Our world today has many examples of deception. The computer world is filled with fake emails and websites that if accessed can set up ransomware for illegal profit, or destroy data and systems just for the meanness. Another form of deception is infomercials. While the products are real, the promises as to how they can give you a wonderful life are always overstated. More than likely there is someone in your church who could produce a fake infomercial. Or you can present one yourself. Have fun with it. This bit of humor could be very helpful, since this topic is quite heavy. In infomercial style, you could sell a church parking place, or rent a person to read the Bible for you. It will be important after the humor to make the turn to the seriousness of self-deception. Here is one possible structure:

- Judah's self-deception (4:5–6:21).
    - 4:5–12: ignored the truth
    - 4:13–30: muddled thinking
    - 4:31–5:9: ignored the truth
    - 5:10–31: muddled thinking
    - 6:1–11a: ignored the truth
    - 6: 11b–21: muddled thinking

- God calls us from self-deception to honesty and authenticity.
    - Instead of ignoring the truth, let's be honest with ourselves.
    - Instead of muddled thinking, let's be authentic.

- God's warning: self-deception is the most dangerous sin (6:22–30)

Another possible structure is to set up the categories of self-deception: 1) ignoring the truth, or 2) misrepresenting the truth. As you lead your listeners through the passages, ask them to decide if Jeremiah is speaking about ignoring or misrepresenting the truth. The pedagogical strategy is asking them to participate. Depending upon how formal or informal the setting, this could be done literally or rhetorically.

This very confrontive passage should ultimately lead not to guilt and shame, but to a resolve for honesty and authenticity.

## DISCUSSION QUESTIONS

1. Have you ever bought something that didn't live up to advertised expectations? Did you feel deceived? Was there some self-deception in your deciding to purchase the item?

2. What are some indicators that we are being deceived?

3. Can we recognize when we are deceiving ourselves? Why or why not?

4. Is there a progression of the results of self-deception?

5. How does transparency guard against self-deception?

# Jeremiah 7:1–8:12

**EXEGETICAL IDEA**

Judah uses religious activity, some legitimate and some illicit, as a cover for their continuing disobedience to God. Their delusions include thinking that having the temple would save them and that their idols could protect them. Against this, Jeremiah laments the coming desolation of the land and the exile of the people.

**THEOLOGICAL FOCUS**

Religious activity is no substitute for true repentance, obedience, and a living relationship with God. Those who seek to use their "religion" as a cover for a true fear of God may do some things right, but they will exaggerate its significance. They will also insert false beliefs and practices into their religious system.

**PREACHING IDEA**

The melodies of worship should change the motions in our lives.

**PREACHING POINTERS**

The sinful practices of Judah show us how important it is to examine our worship. It is good to step back and evaluate what we do in corporate worship. Most churches have a pattern or order that is followed on most Sundays. The only changes in the routines are the songs sung and the passages preached. The measure of effective worship is not how well we perform these routines that take place on Sunday morning, but how well we live after the worship.

There is a close relationship between worship and living in God's blessing. If we let the ceremonial routines be an end unto themselves, then we are exchanging the worship of routines for the worship of God. And, we are also in danger of terrible sins.

# DELUDED RELIGION (7:1–8:12)

## LITERARY STRUCTURE AND THEMES

This is the first part of 7:1–10:25, a section concerned with the religious lies the people cling to and the real pain they must face. This larger context, 7:1–10:25, demonstrates the following parallel pattern:

- Deceit: Jerusalem's perverse religious culture (7:1–8:12)
- Lamentation over a godless land (8:13–9:26)
- Deceit: idolatry versus YHWH (10:1–16)
- Lamentation over exile (10:17–22)
- Jeremiah's confession and imprecation against the nations (10:23–25)

This first section, 7:1–8:12, describes in detail how Judah has embraced theological and religious lies. It is similar to 4:5–6:30, except that it focuses on the religious lies the people believe in. It has the following structure:

- ***The Temple Sermon (7:1–20)***
- ***Orthodox Sacrifices and Disobedient Behavior (7:21–28)***
- ***Abominable Worship (7:29–8:3)***
- ***A Nation in Denial (8:4–12)***

## EXPOSITION

### *The Temple Sermon (7:1–20)*

This passage is almost certainly a summary of Jeremiah's "temple sermon." This sermon is mentioned in Jeremiah 26:1–9, which states that the prophet delivered a message at the beginning of Jehoiakim's reign in the temple precincts. The temple priests and prophets perceived the sermon to be an attack upon the temple itself. They angrily threatened Jeremiah, claiming he had no right to compare the Jerusalem temple to the Shiloh shrine, which the Philistines had destroyed (26:9). The text of 7:1–20 agrees with this account. It condemns reliance on the temple for salvation and reminds the people that God allowed the former sanctuary at Shiloh to be destroyed (7:12–14). The passage is in two parts:

- *A Summary of the Temple Sermon (7:1–15)*
- *A Private Word to Jeremiah Regarding the Sermon (7:16–20)*

Some scholars attempt to tease out a more precise history of the composition of 7:1–15, seeing here different oracles from different settings (Lundbom 2008a, 454–59), but in my view, this is a fool's errand, as evidence is too scanty for such analysis.

#### *A Summary of the Temple Sermon (7:1–15)*

**7:1.** The full, formulaic introduction in this verse implies that it begins a new, major section of the book.

**7:2.** In 26:2, YHWH tells Jeremiah to stand in the courtyard of the temple; here, he is told to stand at a temple gate. This does not mean that the two passages refer to different events. The temple complex had an inner courtyard (1 Kings 6:36) and a large outer courtyard (1 Kings 7:12). Jeremiah possibly stood at the gateway linking the inner and outer courtyards. This enabled him to address all who came to worship, as they would have to pass by him. Also, the Israelites naturally thought of a gateway as a place for public business.

**7:3**. The people must improve their ways and deeds if they want to remain in the land. Otherwise, they face exile. This is a brief, almost generic, call to repentance, but it probably summarizes a great deal of Jeremiah's sermon.

*TRANSLATION NOTE FOR 7:3, 7*

Verse 3, in the MT, calls upon the people to improve their behavior "so that I may let you live in this place" (וַאֲשַׁכְּנָה אֶתְכֶם בַּמָּקוֹם הַזֶּה), using the piel stem of שׁכן. Verse 7 also has a piel of שׁכן, "and then I will let you dwell in this place" (וְשִׁכַּנְתִּי אֶתְכֶם בַּמָּקוֹם הַזֶּה). This reading is followed by the Targum, LXX, and Syriac. However, the Vulgate and Aquila read both verbs as qal, "I will dwell with you in this place," implying respectively וְאֶשְׁכְּנָה אִתְּכֶם and וְשָׁכַנְתִּי אִתְּכֶם. Which is correct? Verse 7 requires the piel, as in the MT, since "this place" is defined as "the land that I gave to your fathers," and that implies that the focus is on whether the people continue to dwell in the land. This suggests that the piel is correct for verse 3 as well. It is possible that the piel is correct in verse 7 but the qal is correct in verse 3 (Holladay 1986, 236–37). That is, God first promises he will dwell with them (v. 3), and then promises that they can dwell with him (v. 7), if they repent. But the balance of evidence suggests that the piel is correct for both.

**7:4**. This is a centerpiece of Jeremiah's preaching, and it has a mocking tone, as Jeremiah three times repeats, "The temple of YHWH!" This is the mantra of the Jerusalem priesthood, who insisted that Jerusalem was inviolable because YHWH dwelt among them in Zion. But it was a lie (שֶׁקֶר), and this misplaced and perverted faith would lead to the ruin of the nation.

**7:5–7**. In a lengthy conditional construction, YHWH promises that the people can remain in the land if they improve their behavior. Specifically, they must carry out justice properly so that the disadvantaged (characterized as aliens, orphans, and widows) are not defrauded in the legal system. They must also curtail the widespread violence in their society, and they must not apostatize by worshiping other gods. Once again, this text is only a summary, and the specific nature of the misdeeds is not explored. For example, the condition that they not shed innocent blood (וְדָם נָקִי אַל־תִּשְׁפְּכוּ) is formulaic and general. It could include ordinary murder on the street, the judicial murder of the poor through the abuse of the courts of law, or child sacrifice. The text does not imply that the average, ordinary citizen was involved in acts of murder, but it does indicate that everyone has a duty to see to it that justice be carried out. They can do this by stopping the abuse of the legal system, by demanding that ordinary crime be properly punished, and by putting an end to human sacrifice.

**7:8**. The "lying words" (דִּבְרֵי הַשָּׁקֶר) in which the people trust are the reassurances that the temple offers them protection from all their enemies. In verse 4, the slogan, "The temple of YHWH!" is called "lying words" (דִּבְרֵי הַשָּׁקֶר). Here, their faith in the temple will give them "no benefit" (לְבִלְתִּי הוֹעִיל). The only other place where לְבִלְתִּי הוֹעִיל occurs is Isaiah 44:10 (Holladay 1986, 244), where it is used of idol-making. Although we cannot be sure that Jeremiah deliberately alluded to this passage, the comparison suggests that misguided faith is no better than idolatry.

**7:9–10**. In a rhetorical question, YHWH asks if the people think they can violate the commands of the Decalogue—here represented by theft, adultery, murder, and the worship of other gods—and be spared from wrath because they come to worship at the temple. He calls the temple, "this house, which is called by name," implying that it is both holy and closely associated with God's reputation. Jeremiah asserts that coming to the temple for worship does not provide protection. Even worse, it adds to their guilt, in that they profane the holy place. The end of the verse ironically but with embarrassing honesty lays bare their reasoning: they say, "We are saved!" (נִצַּלְנוּ), and when they show up at the temple, they do it "so that they can commit all these abominations" (לְמַעַן עֲשׂוֹת אֵת כָּל־הַתּוֹעֵבוֹת הָאֵלֶּה; the clause with לְמַעַן expresses purpose). Like contemporary Christians who believe their theology, their church activity, or their partaking of the Eucharist is a cover for an unrepentant heart, the people of Judah had a misguided notion of what it means to know God.

**7:11**. A "cave of robbers" (מְעָרַת פָּרִצִים) is a place where they can hide and be safe from facing reprisal for their crimes. That is what the temple became for Jeremiah's Jerusalem—a place that (supposedly) frees them from punishment and allows them to sin all the more. Jesus cited this verse in Matthew 21:13, but for Jesus it meant that the temple had become a place where moneychangers and merchants swindled hapless pilgrims. New Testament citations often do not relate to the same context as the Old Testament passage they allude to; words are often reapplied in a different setting with a somewhat different meaning.

**7:12–14**. What happened to Shiloh will also happen to the Jerusalem temple. Shiloh was the residence of the tent of meeting during much the period of the judges and up through the priesthood of Eli. The Philistines defeated Israel in about 1050 B.C. at Ebenezer, killing Eli's sons and capturing the ark (1 Sam. 4). Apparently, they destroyed the Shiloh shrine soon after the battle, although the Samuel narrative does not mention this. Shiloh was about thirty kilometers north of Jerusalem, close to Jeremiah's home at Anathoth. As such, he would have known the story of its fall well. Nonetheless, the suggestion that God would allow the temple to be taken and burned was, to Jeremiah's audience, blasphemy (26:9).

**7:15**. Having referred to the destruction of Shiloh in about 1050, he also alludes to the fall of Samaria to the Assyrians in 722 B.C. Samaria had been the capital city of "Ephraim," the northern kingdom. Just as the example of Shiloh showed that the temple was not a guarantee of God's protection, so also the fall of Samaria showed that the status of being Israelites and the possession of a great city would not save the inhabitants of Jerusalem.

### *A Private Word to Jeremiah Regarding the Sermon (7:16–20)*

**7:16**. Verses 16–20 are a word from YHWH privately given to Jeremiah, meant to convince him that he must preach this harsh message to the worshipers at the temple, notwithstanding their outward appearance of piety. It implies, "If you think I am being too severe on Jerusalem, Jeremiah, you couldn't be more wrong." The command not to pray for them anticipates the major theme of the second anthology (11:1–20:18).

**7:17–18**. Jeremiah often employs merism to imply that every segment of society is evil ("rich and poor," "young and old," etc.). Here, he speaks of how every member of the Israelite family is involved in paganism: Children gather wood, fathers start the fires, and mothers bake bread in honor of the "Queen of Heaven," a pagan goddess (Astarte or Ishtar). The account suggests that this was a festal family event in Jerusalem, much like decorating a house for Christmas in the Christian west. Judah's families had thoroughly assimilated pagan cult practices, implying that they could no longer distinguish what they were doing from the legitimate worship of YHWH. Indeed, even after the exile, some of them maintained the practice (Jer. 44). The pouring out of drink offerings to pagan gods was probably something done by adult men in drinking parties analogous to the Greek symposia, which always began with libations.

**7:19**. Although YHWH is appalled at the people's behavior, the end result is harm to themselves, not to him. The end of verse 19, "so that they may disgrace themselves" (לְמַעַן בֹּשֶׁת פְּנֵיהֶם), and the end of verse 10, "so that they may commit all these abominations" (לְמַעַן עֲשׂוֹת אֵת כָּל־הַתּוֹעֵבוֹת הָאֵלֶּה), are similar. As the hidden motive in their temple worship is to provide a cover for their sin, so the hidden motive of their pagan ritual is the freedom to engage in disgraceful behavior. They enjoy the debauchery that paganism allows.

**7:20**. Verse 18 portrayed the universality of Judah's paganism by listing members of the family engaged in the practices, and this verse describes the universality of YHWH's wrath by listing those who would suffer: people, animals, trees, and crops. The Babylonians would devour or destroy all the livestock and cultivated fields as they made war on Judah.

### *Orthodox Sacrifices and Disobedient Behavior (7:21–28)*

YHWH debunks Judah's false supposition that their sacrifices are a sufficient cover for their abominable behavior. It is important to see that the sacrifices described here are not attacked for being improper (such as offering a pig or a sick lamb as a sacrifice). It is not that the sacrifices in some manner violate the surface requirements of the law; the problem is their belief that the sacrifices release Israel from their moral and spiritual obligations to YHWH.

**7:21**. "Go ahead and add whole offerings to your sacrifices!" (עֹלוֹתֵיכֶם סְפוּ עַל־זִבְחֵיכֶם) sarcastically exhorts Judah to make even greater animal sacrifices, if they think that will put them in good standing with God. The following command, "and eat the meat!" (וְאִכְלוּ בָשָׂר) implies (sarcastically) that they can disregard normal ritual requirements, since people were not allowed to eat of the whole offering (עוֹלָה). If they think the mere act of sacrificing is sufficient to elicit God's favor, they should do it even more lavishly, and enjoy themselves while they are at it.

**7:22**. This remark seems strange, since in fact the law contains abundant instruction on the making of sacrifices (Lev. 1–7). The key to its interpretation is the clause "on the day that I led them out of the land of Egypt" (בְּיוֹם הוֹצִיאִי אוֹתָם מֵאֶרֶץ מִצְרָיִם). This does not refer to the very day Israel walked out of Egypt, since no laws at all were given on that day (see also verse 25, which speaks of YHWH sending prophets to Israel from the day they came out of Egypt; this, too, is not to be taken literally). It probably refers to the exodus experience from Egypt to Sinai and concerns the Sinai covenant. The original laws of the covenant were the Decalogue and Book of the Covenant (Exod. 20–23). These laws do not include any instructions on whole offerings and sacrifices. Those laws came later. The implication is that sacrifices and rituals are not the primary thing in the relationship between God and Israel.

**7:23**. This verse draws on Exodus 6:7 and Deuteronomy 5:33, and it gives a summarizing paraphrase of the original offer God made to Israel in Exodus 19:5–6. God desires maintain a consistent relationship with him characterized by obedience and love; sacrifices are valid, but they were never the main point.

**7:24**. Israel immediately went astray, as in the golden calf incident of Exodus 32. They obstinately refused to listen to God's commands.

> *TRANSLATION NOTE FOR 7:24*
> The clause וַיִּהְיוּ לְאָחוֹר וְלֹא לְפָנִים is difficult. It literally means, "And they became a back and not a face." It almost certainly does not mean that they "went backward and not forward," as in the NIV and ESV. It is probably idiomatic for turning

> one's back as an act of defiance, as in verse 26, "they stiffened their necks" (וַיַּקְשׁוּ אֶת־עָרְפָּם). Jeremiah 2:27 is analogous: "For they turned to me the backs of their necks and not their faces" (כִּי־פָנוּ אֵלַי עֹרֶף וְלֹא פָנִים).

**7:25–26**. Throughout its history, YHWH tried to call them back to himself by the ministry of the prophets, but they obstinately refused to listen. See Matthew 21:33–41.

**7:27–28**. After giving Jeremiah the message he is to preach to Judah (vv. 21–26), he adds a secondary commission in these two verses. He is to preach the initial sermon, but he is given to understand that they will neither listen nor respond. After that, he is to make a formal pronouncement over them: They are not a "nation" (גּוֹי) that will "listen" (שׁמע) to YHWH or accept "discipline" (מוּסָר) from him; "truth" (אֱמוּנָה) has perished among them and is not found on their lips. They are in effect declared to be just another pagan nation, and they will be treated as such. This is analogous to Hosea's symbolic claim that Israel is "not my people" (Hos. 1:9). They can become God's people again only by a special work of God (Hos. 1:10).

### *Abominable Worship (7:29–8:3)*

As 7:21–28 condemned Judah for thinking that orthodox but superficial worship would be sufficient to appease YHWH, this passage condemns the people for engaging in abhorrent, pagan worship. Specifically, it attacks their practices of child sacrifice (7:29–34) and astral worship (8:1–3).

**7:29**. Jerusalem, personified as a woman, is commanded to "cut off" (גָּזִּי; the imperative is feminine singular) her "crown" (נֵזֶר) and cast it away. Scholars commonly suggest that this verse concerns a woman who has taken a Nazirite vow (note the prominent use of נֵזֶר in Numbers 6, the laws of the Nazirites). If so, the implication is that she has become defiled and must interrupt her vow (Lalleman 2013, 112; Thompson 1980, 293). But context indicates that she is to cut off her hair as an act of mourning, not because of ritual defilement (see Jer. 16:6; 41:5; 48:37; Amos 8:10; Mic. 1:16). The word נֵזֶר often refers to a head ornament such as a crown or turban (Exod. 29:6; 2 Kings 11:12). In the context of the Nazirite vow, it refers to the long hair that symbolizes consecration to the vow. In Numbers 6:4, "all the days of his consecration" (כֹּל יְמֵי נִזְרוֹ) is literally, "all the days of his נֵזֶר" (this being long hair that symbolizes his consecration). Here, נֵזֶר simply refers to a woman's long hair, without any reference to a Nazirite vow. See 1 Corinthians 11:14–15, where a woman's long hair is her "glory" to cover her head.

**7:30**. Some scholars treat 7:29 as though it were a separate oracle unto itself (Lundbom 2008a, 489–92; Lalleman 2013, 112), but the word "for" (כִּי) beginning verse 30 implies that it explains the previous verse. Jerusalem must cut off her hair and mourn because YHWH rejected her (v. 29), and he rejected her because her sons did evil (v. 30). Specifically, Judah filled his house with "detestable things" (שִׁקּוּצִים), and the nature of these things is explored below.

**7:31**. The most detestable of all their acts was to sacrifice their children in Tophet, in the Ben Hinnom Valley, near the temple in Jerusalem. YHWH indignantly asserts that the thought of demanding child sacrifices never entered his mind, and this suggests that some Israelites thought that YHWH did in fact desire this. If so, they were probably misconstruing Exodus 22:29 (MT 28), "The firstborn of your sons you shall give to me," taking the verse out of context and using it to justify child sacrifice.

**7:32–33**. As punishment for sacrificing their children, God would bring about a great slaughter of the adults, turning Tophet into the "Killing Valley" (גֵּיא הַהֲרֵגָה). In their idolatrous perversity, the people thought of Tophet as holy ground, sanctified by the child sacrifices that occurred there. But during the siege, casualties would be so high that they would have to bury dead bodies there, since there was no place anywhere else in the city for burial. But eventually the bodies would stack up, remain unburied, and be eaten by the birds. The "consecrated" ground of Tophet would be entirely defiled.

**7:34**. God declares an end of all the joys of marriage and family as further retribution for the child sacrifice. People who commit such heinous crimes against the ideal of the family—child sacrifice—do not deserve to have families.

**8:1–3**. God will punish the nation for worshiping the sun, moon, and stars. The stacking of verbs in verse 2—they "loved" (אהב) the heavenly bodies, they "served" (עבד) them, they "walked after" (הלךְ אַחֲרֵי) them, they sought (דרשׁ) them, and they "worshiped (השתחוה) them—attests to how fully devoted they were to astral religion. Jeremiah anticipates that the Babylonians would desecrate Israel's royal tombs by breaking into them and scattering the bones on the ground (v. 1) and that the survivors of the conquest would be so despondent that they would give up on life (v. 3). Both of these are terrible of themselves, but the main point is that their society would be obliterated. The heritage, represented by the entombed bones of their kings, would be as dung in the field, and there would be no future because the survivors would desire to die.

### *A Nation in Denial (8:4–12)*

This passage is in two parts: the first is 8:4–7, and the second is 8:8–13. They are structured as follows:

- A: Rhetorical question over Judah's irrational behavior (8:4–5a)
- B: Answer: They embraced a lie (8:5b–6)
- A': Rhetorical question over Judah's irrational behavior (8:7)
- C: Accusation against Judah (8:8)
- D: Punishment (8:9–10a)
- C': Accusation against Judah (8:10b–12a)
- D': Punishment (8:12b)

**8:4–5a**. After the initial command to speak, the text uses a series of questions to describe rational behavior. People typically get up after they fall down (v. 4a), but Judah does not. Verses 4b–5a should be translated, "Will someone [both] return and not return? / Why does this people keep going back and forth? / Jerusalem is [in] perpetual apostasy." Normally, people genuinely return when they go through the motions of returning. Judah, however, is perpetually fallen away (v. 5a), as though they had fallen and would not get up. They are apostate, always going through the motions of returning to YHWH but never coming back to him.

*TRANSLATION NOTE FOR 8:4–5*

The clauses אִם־יָשׁוּב וְלֹא יָשׁוּב are often interpreted as, "If someone turns away, then doesn't he come back?" (Thompson 1980, 298; Lundbom 2008a, 508). If that were the meaning, however, the first clause should be אִם־יָסוּר, not אִם־יָשׁוּב. The verbatim repetition of the verb יָשׁוּב implies that there is a contrast between an apparent action and a real action. It means, "Will someone [both] return and not return?" In the beginning of verse 5, the feminine gender of שׁוֹבְבָה ("going back and forth") does not agree with the masculine noun הָעָם הַזֶּה ("this people"). But "this people" and "Jerusalem" are closely identified in 4:10–11; it appears that here "this people" stands in for "Jerusalem" and is so construed as feminine. The word שׁוֹבְבָה could be a polel *qatal* 3fs or an adjective, but it is in any case to be equated with the expression הַבַּת הַשּׁוֹבֵבָה ("O daughter who turns back and forth") in 31:22 and 49:4. Jerusalem is in "perpetual apostasy" (מְשֻׁבָה נִצַּחַת) and is always going back and forth, acting as if they are returning but never doing so.

**8:5b–6**. Judah clings to deceit (הֶחֱזִיקוּ בַּתַּרְמִית), and this is why they act the way they do. Thus, for all their apparent piety, they refuse to return (מֵאֲנוּ לָשׁוּב) to YHWH. They pretend to listen to YHWH and his prophet, but instead of relenting from evil behavior, they charge into it as cavalry charge into battle. All the while, they deny that they do any evil at all. Verse 6a should be translated, "[The people say,] 'I paid attention and I listened [to YHWH]!' Don't they speak like this? No one relents from his evil, while they keep saying, 'What have I done?'" The people's protests of innocence are contrasted with their evil behavior.

*TRANSLATION NOTE FOR 8:6*

Scholars are divided over whether the subject of "I paid attention and heard" (הִקְשַׁבְתִּי וָאֶשְׁמָע) is YHWH or the prophet (Lalleman 2013, 115). But in fact, neither makes sense, as it is not clear what YHWH or Jeremiah were supposed to be listening to or how it relates to this passage. The clause לוֹא־כֵן יְדַבֵּרוּ is usually translated, "They do not speak the truth," taking כֵּן to be I כֵּן, supposedly an adjective meaning "accurate." But the far more common word is II כֵּן, "thus" or "so." I am not convinced that there is a separate I כֵּן meaning "accurate" or "true." For example, one occurrence of I כֵּן is said to be in 1 Samuel 23:17: אָבִי יֹדֵעַ כֵּן. But this is not strictly, "My father knows [it is] accurate," but more simply, "My father knows thus," or more loosely, "My father knows this." In Jeremiah 8:6, לוֹא־כֵן יְדַבֵּרוּ is a negative rhetorical question, "Don't they speak thus?" In other words, "Isn't this the kind of thing they say?" This would then imply that "I paid attention and heard" is a claim made by the people. They say they listen to the Law and the prophets, but they do not.

**8:7**. Drawing on the migratory habits of birds, another rhetorical question portrays Judah's behavior as stupefying in its folly. The birds know when it is time to go back home, but Judah cannot recognize that they have wandered far off and must come back to YHWH.

**8:8**. Like 8:6, this verse begins with the hollow protest of the people that they are orthodox and attentive to YHWH's word. Here, "wise" (חֲכָמִים) implies that they are fully instructed in YHWH's requirements and laws; they claim that YHWH's Law is the basis of their wisdom. But Jeremiah responds that they have a distorted and subverted version of the Law. We do not know what "lie" the scribes made with their pens. Some scholars see a conflict between Jeremiah and the Deuteronomistic scribes, as though Jeremiah were opposed to Deuteronomic theology. But this is unlikely (Holladay 1986, 281–83; Craigie, Kelley, and Drinkard 1991, 134), and in my view the existence of a seventh-century Deuteronomistic school is doubtful. It is more likely that scribes found ways to distort the meaning of the book of the Law discovered in Josiah's time. Once again, the concept of deceit is prominent in this section.

**8:9–10a**. In this context, "wise men" are not a separate group of sages devoted to wisdom literature. It instead represents the priests and scribes who studied and interpreted the Law (although in this case, they misinterpreted it). Since they use their power to enrich themselves, God will take away all they have.

**8:10b–12a**. The sin of the scribes, priests, and prophets is once again that they lie to the people, saying "Peace" when there is no peace. Furthermore, they showed no embarrassment or grief over their behavior. Verse 12a should be translated, "They behaved shamefully (I-בּוֹשׁ, hiphil stem) when they committed abomination, / Even so, they were not ashamed (I-בּוֹשׁ, qal stem) at all / Embarrassment was something they did not know."

**8:12b**. The scribes and priests will suffer the same fate as the common soldiers; they will die at the hands of the Babylonians. They bear no fruit for God and must be uprooted (see Luke 13:6–9).

## THEOLOGICAL FOCUS

This passage describes how a distorted theology can give a person false assurance that he or she has no reason to fear God's judgment.

- One may have a true theology (such as faith that YHWH's name dwelt in Zion, or that justification comes by grace through faith in Christ), and yet distort what it means. If we think that it means that we have no need to fear and obey God and no reason to repent, we have missed the whole point.
- One may engage in legitimate religious practices for the wrong reasons. Offering sacrifices at the temple was not wrong, just as church attendance is not wrong. But it is no cover for sin.
- Once one has fallen into apostasy, one may adopt a theology or engage in religious acts that are horrible. In Judah, it was the terrible act of child sacrifice. We must be careful not to adopt extreme or bizarre theology and beware of adopting the world's ideology as our own.

## PREACHING AND TEACHING STRATEGIES

### *Exegetical and Theological Synthesis*

How could the same people who revered YHWH's temple and were offering the right sacrifices . . . sacrifice children to a pagan god? Why did they bother with temple worship? It seems attending the ceremonies was more important than attending to the needs of others. Sacrificing in the religious ceremony was fine with them, but sacrificing to care for others was not what they had in mind. They chose to obey some of the laws of the ceremony but ignored the laws of living. This was not only wrong but terrifying, because it led them to the unthinkable ceremony of sacrificing children. The thrust of this passage was clearly for Judah to stop the sinful practices, but also to start obeying all of YHWH's commands, particularly the commands concerning love for others. Those who read this after the fall of Judah no doubt longed for the routines of temple worship, but they had no temple. They could, however, have worship routines that became more important than fully obeying the One they worshipped.

Our worship ceremonies of course are very different, but we can struggle with the same issue. Do we love the routine of Sunday morning church more than we love the One we worship? Jeremiah's message is crucial for the church today. Sunday's gathering of the saints should be meaningful and moving; but if there is no connection to life, then we are no different than Judah. This passage does point out the danger of heartless ceremony, but we must not forget the encouraging application that worship is meaningful because it does affect and change our lives.

### *Preaching Idea*

The melodies of worship should change the motions in our lives.

### *Contemporary Connections*

#### *What does it mean?*

Going through religious activities without a heart that is focused solely on the true God is not only condemned by God but also leads to unthinkable evil. The Israelites even trained their children to worship a god whose purpose was to profit them materially. Perhaps we need to examine if our consumer-driven economy is teaching our children that the material is most important. When we feel the joy of singing "You Are My All in All" or "He Is All That I Need," we need to let it affect how we think about shopping. Yes, there is a delight in buying new things, but another new shirt or new car is not our all in all. When we joyfully sing of Jesus being the friend of sinners and of being the lamb that was slain, our view of a role model for success should change. We can teach our children that a truly successful person is not necessarily the one driving the new car and living in the big house, but the one who serves in the nursery with a grateful and willing heart. Now, that is success.

### *Is it true?*

The doctor was direct yet gentle: "I'm afraid that the test results are not favorable. There are some spots on your lungs that we need to examine more fully. You are a smoker, is that right?" The patient tried to explain, "Yes, I know it is bad, but I just didn't think about it. What I knew didn't seem to make a difference in what I did." The financial consultant asked the soon-to-be retired engineer, "So how much do you have in a retirement account?" The engineer embarrassingly responded, "I have a little. Oh, I know the numbers. I should have been saving all along, but I kept thinking that I'd start saving next year." The student, meeting after school with her teacher, tried to explain why she didn't study for the history final: "I went to the library to study, but I got distracted by some magazines. I even met some friends at a coffee shop to study, but we just talked. I guess I was just going through the motions."

Why is there this an all-too-frequent disconnect between what we believe and what we do? From not taking care of our bodies to not planning our financial future, we know the right thing to do but we don't do it. We think that somehow our actions will not really matter. Then the harsh consequences hit. The health is shot. The retirement is meager. The class is failed.

God expected the Israelites' theology to affect their lives. And on the surface, they acted religiously, but it was only a ruse. They were like the student who wants people to think that they are working, so they study at a coffee shop so others will see them. God wants us to know that there are consequences to separating our beliefs from our actions.

Yet, we can affirm beliefs in our corporate worship without letting those beliefs change the way we live. When I sing about being a child of God, my sense of being accepted should rise. Yet these religious activities can cloud our vision of sin in each of our lives. Familiar worship activity can bring back emotions of comfort, like the tune of "Amazing Grace." We like the melody, but the words are ignored. We rest in the emotion of worship that comes from the familiar. We should be worshipping a loving and all-powerful God who has expectations of His children. But our so-called worship is often nothing more than the enjoying a familiar experience and emotion. The experience of those emotions is not bad in and of itself, but to say that an emotional experience is worship is like the Jews crying out, "the temple, the temple, the temple of the Lord!" We can lift our hands in worship without lifting our hands to help others. We must see from this passage that God links true worship not only with hearts that are moved, but with lives that are changed.

### *Now what?*

The empty worship of the Israelites allowed them to hide their materialism from themselves. Even though they sang songs to YHWH, they made idols of fertility gods and goddesses. This empty worship that had as its highest value better crops and bigger herds was the worship of material things. Materialism is dangerous. It leads to greater distortions and evil. If matter is all that exists, if humans are just wet computers that act and react according to DNA and environment, then why not set aside some of the inferior or burdensome machines so that others can have a better life? The unbelievable practice of killing infants by the ancient pagan religions was done to gain material well-being. We must check materialistic tendencies.

### *Creativity in Presentation*

This passage is hard-hitting, and in our Christian preaching of it we must be careful not to take away the harshness of God's rebuke. While we are forgiven in Christ and have the joy of reconciliation to God, we still can worship with an empty heart like the Jews of Jeremiah's time. This is hard to accept and should be considered when approaching the way in which the passage is presented. One could be straightforward, walking through the passage and applying as you go through it. Or one could present the whole passage highlighting the foolishness of the Jews, being careful to present them as the bad guys. It is relatively easy to prompt a congregation to be mad at, or look down upon, an erring group. After presenting the passage and having the congregation agree that the Jews deserved punishment, make the transition to show how we can be just like the Jews. Here is one possible structure:

- First time through the passage: focusing on Judah
    - The routines of Judah's worship were just routines (7:1–20).
    - They had orthodox sacrifices but disobedient behavior (7:21–28).
    - Their focus on routines led to astonishing evil (7:29–8:3).
    - They denied that their routines were evil (8:4–12).

- Second time: focusing on application
    - The routines of our worship affect the routines of our lives (7:1–20).
    - Precision in the routines of worship does not correct routine bad behavior (7:21–28).
    - The focusing on the routines can lead to terrifying routines (7:29–8:3).
- Don't let routines keep us from seeing our sin (8:4–12).
- Are the melodies (routines) of our worship affecting the motions (routines) in our lives?

## DISCUSSION QUESTIONS

1. How does our culture worship material things instead of God? How is this belief propagated?

2. How can the game of Monopoly be used to teach materialism? Could it be used to teach a biblical view of material things?

3. What songs have we sung that contradicted our lives?

4. When is our Sunday morning worship empty? to ourselves? to God?

5. How does an emotional song, either joyful or contemplative, improve worship? How does it hinder worship?

## Jeremiah 8:13–9:26

**EXEGETICAL IDEA**

This passage engages the emotional impact of the sin and suffering of Jerusalem. It is almost entirely a series of laments over what is to come for Jerusalem. This is a model for the modern believer and preacher, who must never rejoice in the sins of others, thinking they are somehow vindicated as righteous because of their neighbor's sins. We do not rejoice that God punished the unrepentant, but lament that they did not repent.

**THEOLOGICAL FOCUS**

These two things are worthy of lamentation: the godless behavior of people, and the terrible outcome of such behavior. Jeremiah grieves that the people have embraced lies, and he also grieves for the price they will pay for following their delusions.

**PREACHING IDEA**

Be ashamed of sin, but proud of God.

**PREACHING POINTERS**

This passage helps us see that shame and sadness can be the very best thing for us. Jeremiah laments with weeping for his people and the coming judgment. He is not a bystander or guest at the funeral of a distant friend; he is a participant. As he recounts the sins and the judgment, he enters the grief with vivid images that expresses his intense grief.

Hopefully our spontaneous response to sin is sadness; but sad to say, it is not always our first response. We need to choose to be upset about our sin. But it doesn't end there, because if we choose sadness for sin, that is a sign that God is working in us. We make it through these seemingly negative emotions not by running from them but by seeing God's hand at work in our lives through them. This is an odd thought: we should feel good that we feel sad about our sin, because our God is at work in our lives.

# A COLLECTION OF LAMENTATIONS (8:13–9:26)

## LITERARY STRUCTURE AND THEMES

The prior unit, 7:1–8:12, focused on the self-deception of false religion. In keeping with the earlier pattern of heresy and apostasy being paired with impending calamity, this passage concerns the disaster that will come upon the people because of their hollow religion. Here, however, the focus is on lamentation—there is deep sorrow over the sin that brought about the calamity, and over the calamity itself.

- ***Lamentation over the Calamity (8:13–22)***
- ***Lamentation over Deceit (9:1–9 [MT 8:23–9:8])***
- ***Lamentation over the Calamity (9:10–11 [MT 9–10])***
- ***Explanation of the Calamity (9:12–16 [MT 11–15])***
- ***Lamentation over the Calamity (9:17–22 [MT 16–21])***
- ***True and False Exultation (9:23–26 [MT 22–25])***

## EXPOSITION

### *Lamentation over the Calamity (8:13–22)*

The nation faces both famine and the approach of the enemy army, and Jeremiah weeps with and for his people.

**8:13–14**. YHWH begins with a lament over the failure of the trees to bear fruit. This is in one sense metaphorical: the nation has failed God, like an olive tree that bears no fruit (8:13; see Luke 13:6–9). But it is also literal: the harvest was bad. The opening of verse 13 should be translated, "I will bring them to an end by gathering them together." The people's response (v. 14) explains this enigmatic statement. They have no reason to sit out in the countryside because there is no harvest to "gather" in. Instead, they "gather" themselves in their fortified cities to await the arrival of the Babylonians. God, by denying them a harvest to gather, is gathering them behind city walls. He will then use enemy invaders to "make an end" of them.

*TRANSLATION NOTE FOR 8:13*

The infinitive absolute אָסֹף is a gerund of means, "by gathering." The clause אָסֹף אֲסִיפֵם contains a wordplay, combining the similar roots אסף and סוּף. Zephaniah 1:2 (אָסֹף אָסֵף = "Gathering, I will make an end") is similar, and this parallel text makes it unlikely that אֲסִיפֵם should be repointed to אָסְפָּם, "their harvest," as in the NIV (following the suggested emendation in the BHS), "I will take away their harvest." Jeremiah explains the language, indicating that YHWH was driving the people into their fortified cities (gathering them together), where they would be trapped (making an end of them). Zephaniah does not explain it, implying that he is alluding to Jeremiah, where the meaning is given.

**8:15–16**. The people's prior false hopes have been shattered by the Babylonians, and now they can only lament.

**8:17**. The snakes that God will send are metaphorical for the invading army, but the image recalls the story of Numbers 21:6–9. This time, however, there will be no cure.

**8:18–19**. Jeremiah is intense pain over the suffering he sees coming upon his people. Their dismay about the fall of Zion and of the Davidic dynasty reflects their earlier false hopes that these institutions rendered their nation invulnerable. YHWH responds that this had to happen because they embraced false gods.

**8:20**. As implied in 8:13–14, Judah is facing famine. This may be in part because of the military crisis (enemy troops took or destroyed the crops) and in part because of drought.

**8:21–22**. Jeremiah voices the suffering of his people, wishing there were some way to cure it, but there is not. Gilead, on the east side of the Sea of Galilee, was known for its healing balms even in patriarchal times, as attested in Genesis 37:25 (Thompson 1980, 306). But there is no medicine that can cure the disasters facing Judah.

### *Lamentation over Deceit (9:1–9 [MT 8:23–9:8])*

Jeremiah continues his lamentation, but this time it is over the deceitfulness and evil of his people.

**9:1–2**. Verse 1 could go with either the following or the preceding section, but both verses 1 and 2 begin with the idiom מִי־יִתֵּן (literally, "Who will give," but correctly translated as an expression of a deep desire, "Oh, that . . . !" or "If only!"). This parallel suggests that the two verses belong together. Jeremiah first asserts that even if his eyes were an unfailing fountain of tears, he could not weep enough over the slain of his people (v. 1), but then he shifts his train of thought, wishing that he could get away from his people because they are so wicked. He wants a "station for travelers in the desert" (בַמִּדְבָּר מְלוֹן אֹרְחִים), a place that would be both solitary and remote. By starting both verses with the same words (מִי־יִתֵּן), he implies that it is right for him to mourn for the catastrophe that has slain so many of his people, but that it is also right for him to be deeply distressed and even disgusted by their behavior, so much so that he wishes he could get away from them and live as a hermit in the wilderness.

**9:3**. The text describes four types of evil: 1) Everyone lies to one another, using their tongues as bows to shoot at people. 2) They don't fight for truth, but for a lie: "They are powerful warriors in the land for lies and not for truth" (שֶׁקֶר וְלֹא לֶאֱמוּנָה גָּבְרוּ בָאָרֶץ; the verb גבר connotes being powerful and victorious). The ideal of what is right and true means nothing to them. 3) They become progressively more immoral, going from one evil to the next. 4) They do not know God. These four patterns of behavior reciprocally feed off and enhance one another. People who lie to each other care nothing for the ideal of truth and are ready to believe in a great lie, such as the lie that YHWH will not punish them. People who care nothing for truth become progressively immoral. When people do not know God, they embrace a lie, lose their moral grounding, and become untrustworthy.

**9:4**. Deceit is again at the heart of their evil; they believe lies and lie to one another. When hearing that every brother "is completely deceitful" (עָקוֹב יַעְקֹב), the audience could not fail to hear the name "Jacob" (יַעֲקֹב). This implies that they are offspring of a deceiver and that their racial identity as the sons of Jacob tags them as untrustworthy.

**9:5**. The word used here for "They deceive" (יְהָתֵלּוּ; a hiphil of תלל) implies that someone is playing mind games with another person. This is the word Delilah uses in Judges 16:10, 13, 14, when she accuses Samson of tricking her about the source of his strength. Here in Jeremiah, the people constantly tried to outwit one another and gain some advantage by falsehood. The social environment, in which everyone behaves evilly, is exhausting even to those who practice it. Their evil behavior wearies them.

**9:6**. YHWH tells Jeremiah, "You live in the midst of deceit, and by deceit they refuse to know me." This implies again that everyone lies to each other, that they have embraced a great lie rather than turn to God. Again, there is a reciprocal relationship between patterns of behavior such as widespread dishonesty in social interaction, the embrace of some great lie, and hostility toward God.

> *TRANSLATION NOTE FOR 9:5c–6a (MT 4c–5a)*
> At 9:5c–6a (MT 4c–5a), translations differ significantly from one another. The LXX has οὐ διέλιπον τοῦ ἐπιστρέψαι. τόκος ἐπὶ τόκῳ δόλος ἐπὶ δόλῳ ("They do not cease in order to repent. Usury upon usury! Deceit upon deceit!"). The MT has הַעֲוֵה נִלְאוּ׃ שִׁבְתְּךָ בְּתוֹךְ מִרְמָה ("They weary themselves with committing iniquity. Your dwelling is in the midst of deceit"). The LXX has read two separate words, שׁוּב ("return") and תֹּךְ ("oppression"), where the MT has one word, שִׁבְתְּךָ ("your dwelling"). The NIV follows the MT and has, "they weary themselves with sinning. You live in the midst of deception." The NRSV emends following the LXX: "they commit iniquity and are too weary to repent. Oppression upon oppression, deceit upon deceit!" The ESV is similar to the NRSV. Normally, one should stay with the MT when it makes sense, as it does here. However, the formulaic use of תֹּךְ with מִרְמָה is established at Psalm 55:11 (MT 12), which says that "oppression and deceit" (תֹּךְ וּמִרְמָה) do not depart from the marketplace (see also Ps. 10:7). This supports the LXX and NRSV rendition. The Vulgate, on the other hand, follows the MT, as reflected in the NIV. The evidence is fairly evenly divided, but lacking a compelling reason to emend, we should stay with the MT.

**9:7**. YHWH will refine and test his people, a metaphor drawn from the smelting of metals. The metallurgical process separates pure metal from mineral impurities, and the implication is that YHWH will seek out a few honest people who will genuinely fear him from the great mass of pseudo-Israelites, the people of Jeremiah's generation. Of course, smelting involves heat, and this implies calamity and suffering.

**9:8–9**. This verse echoes verse 3, demonstrating how thoroughly the habit of lying has permeated Jerusalem society. YHWH thus asks the grieving Jeremiah if there is any alternative to striking Jerusalem with a severe judgment.

### *Lamentation over the Calamity (9:10–11 [MT 9–10])*

Jeremiah again bewails the calamity that is coming upon Judah. He knows that, in answer to the rhetorical question of 9:9, God must devastate the land.

**9:10**. The "hills" (הָרִים) over which Jeremiah weeps are not mountains as we understand them. They are large hills that would have ground suitable for pastureland or for vineyards and groves of olive trees. Similarly, the "pastures of the wilderness" (נְאוֹת מִדְבָּר) are not remote deserts but regions that, although perhaps too rocky and dry for cultivation, were good for grazing sheep and goats. The Babylonian army would sweep all this away, leaving behind a land destitute of olive groves and grazing sheep. Jeremiah will raise a "lament" (קִינָה) because, employing a wordplay, the sound of cattle (מִקְנֶה) is not heard (Lalleman 2013, 122).

**9:11**. God will make not only the pastures and vineyards desolate, but also Jerusalem itself. Fleeing behind its walls for safety would not work.

### *Explanation of the Calamity (9:12–16 [MT 11–15])*

In explaining why the disaster occurred, God vindicates Jeremiah.

**9:12–16**. In a series of rhetorical questions, verse 12 asks who can explain why this has all happened. Of course, readers already know the answer: Jerusalem sinned and must be punished.

We should therefore ask why these questions are here, and not content ourselves with simply repeating the answers, valid though they are, given in verses 13–16. Verse 12 asks who is wise, able to explain all that has happened, and who has received a word from YHWH. This tells us that the issue at stake is who is the true prophet, the one who can give the valid explanation of what has happened. All of his life, Jeremiah was confronted by false prophets, deluding people with the message that Baal worship and even child sacrifice were not contrary to God's will, that Jerusalem would never fall, and that Jeremiah was a traitor and blasphemer. Even after Jerusalem fell, many people continued to blame him, saying that if only they had been more faithful in giving offerings to the Queen of Heaven, Jerusalem would not have fallen (44:18). We should not look upon this text as pointless repetition of what Jeremiah has said many times; it is an appeal for the people to ask themselves, "Who, after all, was right? Who was the true prophet?" Thus, when verses 13–14 give a familiar recitation of the sins of Judah, that they forsook the law and followed Baal, and when verses 15–16 give a familiar recitation of the trouble that will come up Judah, that they must consume the bitter food of defeat and exile, it is affirming that YHWH has revealed to Jeremiah what would happen and why it would happen. He is the wise man to whom God spoke.

### *Lamentation over the Calamity (9:17–22 [MT 16–21])*

As a mark of how great the calamity would be, Jeremiah conducts a literary funeral for the city, calling on professional mourners to bewail the city's fate. This is entirely a rhetorical, literary action; there was no actual funeral over the city. Later, after the city fell, there would be ritualized mourning for the city (Lamentations is the text for such mourning), but there is no reason to suspect that liturgical laments over the city copied funerary rites to the extent of having professional mourners perform.

**9:17**. Funerals in the ancient world were accompanied by the ritualized wailing of women, as attested in Egyptian funerary art. Jeremiah summons such professional mourners to lament over Jerusalem. While we might think of such a custom as artificial, to ancient people such demonstrations of anguish were part of the grieving process. The women may have been paid for their services, but they gave expression to the real sorrow of the bereaved.

**9:18**. The call is for the women to wail "over us" (עָלֵינוּ)—that is, over the deceased. The fallen Jerusalem and its people call for the funeral, hoping that they, now dead, will be remembered and honored.

**9:19**. The "sound of wailing" (קוֹל נְהִי) in this verse is not the lament of the professional women; it is the reason why the professional women are called to come and lament, as indicated by the introductory particle "because" (כִּי). Zion, the city of the great king, is in ruins, and its few survivors bewail what has happened as they are cast into exile. Therefore, a funeral dirge is appropriate.

**9:20**. The beginning of this verse should be translated, "Therefore, O [professional wailing] women, hear the word of YHWH!" That is, this verse calls on the women to respond appropriately to the magnitude of the disaster. Since the calamity is so great, these women must take on more staff, training their daughters and friends to join in the lamentation. The crying of just a few women will not be sufficient to demonstrate what horrors have befallen the city.

> *TRANSLATION NOTE FOR 9:19–20 (MT 18–19)*
> Verse 19 (MT 18) begins with a use of כִּי that means "because," and verse 20 (MT 19) begins with a כִּי that means "therefore." This little particle is highly flexible, and we must be careful in handling it. It often explains the prior clause (and is translated "for" or "because"), but sometimes

the clause with כִּי describes the outcome, not the cause, of the prior sentence. For example, in Isaiah 36:5b, we have, "In whom do you trust, so that (כִּי) you have rebelled against me?" It has other meanings as well ("indeed," "although," and "if" are fairly common meanings). Using context, we must analyze the flow of the words to determine which meaning is appropriate in any example.

**9:21**. Personified death has entered the streets and houses of Jerusalem, carrying away children and young men. The death of children is always especially painful, and thus they are singled out for lamentation. The latter group, the young men, were typically the pride and hope of an ancient city. They were the promise of a great future. But now that is gone. The image of death climbing through windows (חַלּוֹן) into houses and also taking "strongholds" (אַרְמוֹן) may be borrowed from Joel 2:9, where the soldiers of the northern army enter houses through windows (חַלּוֹן), and from Amos 2:5, where God threatens to burn with fire the "strongholds" (אַרְמוֹן) of Jerusalem.

**9:22**. The two metaphors for the dead here are first excrement on the ground, and then wheat cut down by a sickle but not gathered up. "Excrement" translates דֹּמֶן, a word that in the Bible always serves as a comparison to human corpses (2 Kings 9:37; Jer. 8:2; 9:21; 16:4; 25:33; Ps. 83:11). It implies how the beautiful people of Jerusalem, in their death, with bodies unburied on the ground, became foul and loathsome. The metaphor of the wheat implies waste: to cut down the grain but leave the sheaves where they fell is a great waste of food. Even so, the destruction of Jerusalem was a great waste of humanity.

### *True and False Exultation (9:23–26 [MT 22–25])*

The passage closes with a statement of what really matters to God when he looks at people: not their status or success, but whether they fear him. But the fear of God must be genuine and not a matter of hollow orthodoxy or outward show.

**9:23–24**. Since the people of Jerusalem, the city of the great king, were destined to lie like excrement in the streets, they should not boast in themselves, however powerful, beautiful, or successful they were. Their boast should be in knowing God. We normally think of "boasting" in purely negative terms—that it is always a bad thing. And indeed, the word "boast" often has a negative connotation in the Bible (1 Kings 20:11; 2 Chron. 25:19; Ps. 94:4; Prov. 27:1; Rom. 1:30). Of itself, however, boasting only concerns what someone has the most pride and joy in. If someone boasts in himself and his accomplishments, it represents a pride that tends toward evil. If someone boasts in God and does so out of a true experience with God, that boast proceeds from humility and weakness, and it draws one toward righteousness. The Psalmist says, "My soul shall boast in YHWH. / The humble shall hear it and be glad" (Ps. 34:2 [MT 3]). Paul boasted in his suffering and infirmity, knowing that this brought glory to God and was healthy for his soul (2 Cor. 11:30; 12:9).

**9:25–26**. On the surface, these two verses seem to have little to do with the preceding context, but without them one cannot grasp the full weight of the full passage. There are indeed some people who would claim that their boast is in God when in fact they are boasting of a religious practice, conviction, or identifying tag. Paul spoke of Jews who boasted in God but did not know him or live with integrity (Rom. 2:17). Many Israelites in Jeremiah's time boasted of their circumcision, thinking that this was sufficient to set them apart from all pagans and, by extension, sufficient to protect them from the wrath of God. In fact, a number of ancient people practiced circumcision. Egyptian boys were circumcised sometime prior to puberty, and we have Egyptian images of the rite being performed. Thus, it is not circumcision that makes for a true Israelite, but a genuine walk with God (Rom. 2:28–29). We can substitute anything for a genuine relationship with God, including our baptism, our faith in the truthfulness of the Bible, and our traditional moral beliefs. If our boast is in any of these things rather than in God himself, our boast is indeed hollow.

## THEOLOGICAL FOCUS

This passage explores the relationship between self-deception, sinful behavior, and refusal to heed God's warnings. It characterizes the whole package as a source of great suffering and sorrow.

- Sin provides two reasons for sorrow. One should rightly lament over both the moral decay of the sinner and the outcome of the sin: the sinner's death.
- The righteous grieve when sinners perish, but they do not pull back from seeing the connection between the sin and disaster that followed.
- At the heart of the lamentable disaster is a lie: people boast in something other than God. They have false convictions about their own adequacy and sometimes false convictions about their standing before God.

## PREACHING AND TEACHING STRATEGIES

### *Exegetical and Theological Synthesis*

Sadness is a universal emotion. Every person has been and will be sad. It is expressed differently, but there are no geographical or chronological barriers. Jeremiah's call to being distressed over sin can be applied directly to us, because this emotion is the same and so is sin. Sadness comes because of loss and sin always brings loss. Jeremiah warned Judah that they were going to suffer the catastrophic loss of the exile, and those reading his book experienced that loss. While our specific sins may be different from those of the first readers, our response should be the same.

Most of us find sadness unpleasant and strive to either avoid it or get through it as soon as we can. We don't think of it as a choice, and yet it is. Some people enjoy being down and watch movies or listen to music that promotes this emotion. There is an involuntary aspect to sadness that automatically comes when we experience loss. But even then we have a choice as to how we will handle the grief. In the case of a catastrophic loss sadness dominates a life for a time, but those who have been through this kind of loss tell us that they had to make a choice to not let the loss define them. Often emotions are more instinctive than a chosen path. When it comes to sin, sorrow is the right choice because it shows us our need and should lead to repentance.

### *Preaching Idea*

Be ashamed of sin, but proud of God.

### *Contemporary Connections*

#### *What does it mean?*

Sadness comes in varying degrees, from the sadness of a restaurant being out of the three-inch-thick center-cut pork chops that are the special of the day, to the pain of the fiancé saying that she needs some time to rethink the marriage, to the agonizing sorrow of a parent losing a child. Jeremiah and the Israelites are agonizing because of their calamity and because of their sin. God is inviting us to enter into this level of sadness because of our sin.

The level of sadness is important. As I write this, I have just come from a hospital where a family is in intense pain; the diseased body of a twenty-year-old is not responding to treatment. All that can be done has been done, but there is no medical hope. The family is in agony as they are waiting for this young life to end. The sorrow is intensified because the illness was brought on because of unhealthy practices of a sinful lifestyle. While we must not infer that a disease is God's punishment against a group of people in a sinful lifestyle, this disease was preventable. As I saw tears flow from exhausted eyes, I couldn't help but hear Jeremiah's words, "Oh that my eyes were a fountain of tears." This is the proper response to all of our sin. Not that each time we sin we shed tears, but if we have never cried because of our own sin, we are missing a great blessing. We need to let the sorrow of sin drive us to tears.

### *Is it true?*

We tend to avoid sadness. Generally, it is seen as a negative emotion that we need to get through and put behind us. But God is telling us that it is the right response to sin and to the pain that comes from sin. In some ways it is an instinctive response to our not measuring up. Children, when corrected, are not happy about it. One five-year-old boy, when hearing his father tell him, "No, you can't take that toy from your cousin," responded with quivering lip, "It's not nice to tell someone no." That reactionary sadness is how we all feel when corrected. Our culture teaches us to ignore that sadness, to pretend that it is not there, or even that the correction is not justified. Thus, we hear something like, "Don't be sad; be happy." There are even guidelines on the internet for getting over our sadness. And at times, it is good to put sadness behind us. But God is calling us to be sad for our good.

### *Now what?*

God does not leave us rubbing our eyes and grabbing for the tissues. He closes this section with a positive action to take in the midst of the tears. We should be ashamed of sin, but He counsels us to boast that we know and understand Him. Our knowledge and understanding of God can guide us through the sorrow for sin and its consequences. Sadness is closely related to loss: loss of a relationship, or some physical thing. God's counsel is to boast in that which we cannot lose. The Israelites who first read this had the consequences of sin all around them, either in exile or in a devastated homeland. When the sorrow and shame of sin surrounds us, it is God's lovingkindness, justice, and righteousness that we should boast in. The Israelites saw these attributes expressed in the sacrificial system of their day. For us, it is more clearly expressed through His death for our sins and his resurrection for our righteousness.

We love to boast in successes. When the home team wins the Super Bowl, World Series, or NBA championship, the city throws a great parade and celebration. We buy the t-shirts, hats, and banners, and boast as though we had played the game, that we made the wining point. There is nothing wrong in this kind of borrowed boasting, providing we remember it *is* borrowed boasting. When we boast in our wealth or accomplishments, even when they are good it is borrowed boasting. God calls us to boast in Him. He alone is to be praised.

## Creativity in Presentation

This passage is filled with strong metaphors that in the first readers brought out strong emotions. To help contemporary listeners experience those same emotions, scenes from appropriate movies could help. They certainly can bring a tear to our eye. It might be helpful in the introduction or even earlier in the service to present a portion of one of the following scenes. Or, rather than show one, just mention these and say, "More than likely you have shed a tear when you watched one of the following":

> *The Lion King*: When Mufasa is killed
> *Toy Story 3*: When all the toys are in the incinerator
> *Little Women*: When Beth dies
> *Bambi:* When Bambi's mother dies
> *Downton Abbey*: When Matthew dies after his son is born
> *The Cowboys*: When John Wayne is killed

As always be careful in using film clips; copyrights should be heeded. Also remember that film clips are very powerful, so be sure to use them at the right place in the sermon.

Though sadness is common in our lives, a barrier to applying this passage is the lack of personal remorse in our culture. To say that we need to cry and be deeply sorrowful for our sin to the point of anguish will probably not get a favorable response. Presenting this passage will require extra effort to help our listeners believe this. One can present each portion of the text as verifying that sorrow and shame are the right responses to sin. Then, when the congregation is on the verge of discouragement, show that shame for our sin serves as a contrast to our being proud of our God. It is through our understanding and knowing Him that we can be His delight, though surrounded by sin. Here is a possible way to present the passage:

- Lamentation over the Calamity (8:13–22): It is right to be sad when the consequences of sin are being felt.
- Lamentation over Deceit (9:1–9): It is right to shed tears when our sin is revealed.
- Lamentation over the Calamity (9:10–11): It is right to mourn when we see the effect of sin in our world.
- Explanation of the Calamity (9:12–16): It is right to have broken hearts when we see our stubborn hearts.
- Lamentation over the Calamity (9:17–22): It is right to cry when we see others hurting because of sin.
- True and False Exultation (9:23–26): It is right to be ashamed of sin, but proud of God.

Notice that this structure ends with the last point being the main thrust of the sermon.

## DISCUSSION QUESTIONS

1. When does our culture approve of sorrow that leads to the shedding of tears?
2. Can the shedding of tears for sin be faked? When have you done this, or seen this happen?
3. What are some signs that the sorrow for sin is real?
4. What is the relationship between sorrow and boasting?
5. What are some ways that we can boast in God?

# Jeremiah 10:1–25

**EXEGETICAL IDEA**

The passage mocks idolatry to make the point that no human creation is worthy of worship. Those who do bow to the work of their own hands bring about their own ruin. This is the last passage that alternates between focus on the lies Judah follows and on the disasters their behavior will bring about. It closes with a prayer that ends this section and prepares the reader for the next section: an intense look at Jeremiah's personal pilgrimage before God, with respect to his relationship to the people of Judah.

**THEOLOGICAL FOCUS**

Everyone must choose between the true God and a man-made lie, and the consequences of that choice are enormous. The Christian too must choose between loyalty to his friends, family, and nation, and his loyalty to God. This is not a matter of becoming aloof and self-righteous, but it is a matter of choosing between following Christ and following the world.

**PREACHING IDEA**

Don't waste your worship.

**PREACHING POINTERS**

When Jeremiah describes how an idol is made and then compares that man-made carving to the Creator, the worship of idols becomes ludicrous. However, it is not just ludicrous; it is sinful and dangerous.

When we see pictures of people in tan-colored robes bowing down to a polished gold statue and throwing flowers on it, we have little or no response. It takes us a moment to realize what they are doing. We just don't see that sort of thing. Jeremiah saw it in Judah and was disgusted. But that is just not done in our western world. Thus, we have a great challenge to present this passage to our *idol-free* world. Our bodies may not bow down, but our hearts and minds regularly pay homage to something or someone other than our Lord.

# FALSE GODS (10:1–25)

## LITERARY STRUCTURE AND THEMES

As described in the introduction, the second part of the first anthology (7:1–10:25, of 2:1–10:25) contains a series of contrasts between YHWH the true God and the religious lies the people believe, as well as a series of laments over the coming destruction. Chapter 10 concludes this series, marking the conclusion with a prayer by Jeremiah (vv. 23–25).

- ***Deceit: Idolatry versus YHWH (10:1–16)***
- ***Lamentation over Exile (10:17–22)***
- ***Jeremiah's Confession and Imprecation Against the Nations (10:23–25)***

## EXPOSITION

### *Deceit: Idolatry versus YHWH (10:1–16)*

This text is made up of three parts (vv. 1–5, 6–10, 11–16), with each part marked by inclusion (also called "envelope") structures, in which the first verse of each part is in some manner echoed by the last. The mockery of the folly of idolatry is a major theme of this passage.

**10:1–5**. After the heading (v. 1), this section is bounded on either side by exhortations not to "fear" the gods of the nations (vv. 2, 5b). Within this inclusion structure, the passage mocks idols and idol worship (vv. 3–5a). Jeremiah calls the people of Judah the "house of Israel" (v. 1). This was true, since Judah was all that remained of the Israelite nation, but it is a reminder that Israel the northern kingdom was destroyed for its idolatry. The "way of the nations" (v. 2) was paganism, superstition, and a constant search for omens from the gods. When the astrological signs were bad, the nations were terrified of what might happen. Both Babylon and Egypt, the two great powers of Jeremiah's time, carefully tracked what they took to be signs in the heavens (Lundbom 2008a, 583–84). But the "rules" (חֻקּוֹת) of the nations are worthless (v. 3). The word חֻקּוֹת is translated as "practices" in the NIV and as "customs" in the CSB and ESV, but it more properly means "rules," referring to all the complex rules, taboos, and religious constraints that governed astrology and paganism. Verses 3b–5a make a mockery of idolatry in the manner of Isaiah 40:18–20; 41:7; 44:9–20. How can an object made by a man, however skillfully it has been created, be a god? And yet this "god" has to be fastened in place with nails so that it does not fall over (v. 4), and it is as worthy of worship as a scarecrow (v. 5a).

**10:6–10**. This passage has as its boundaries assertions that there is no god like YHWH and that he alone is the true God (vv. 6–7, 10). Like the previous passage, this text also mocks idolatry within the inclusion structure (vv. 8–9). This section matches with previous one in that the first (vv. 2–5) asserts that the superstitions of the nations are worthless and that no one should fear them, but the second (vv. 6–10) asserts that all the nations ought to fear YHWH, God of Israel, because he is the true God. Verses 8–9 continue the mockery of the idols. Note that the issue is not that the idols are cheaply or shoddily made but that it is foolish to devote so much effort, wealth, and ingenuity to making a god.

*THE MEANING OF* מֵאֵין *IN 10:6*

The word מֵאֵין has provoked a good deal of discussion, with some emending the text to make it seem more readable (Holladay 1986, 324). For example, one suggestion is to repoint the word as מָאֵין and treat it as a double negative meaning, "There is absolutely no one like you, YHWH" (Dahood 1975). But it may be that מֵאֵין is simply the familiar אֵין plus מִן, with the מִן having an explanatory meaning. An example is Jeremiah 7:32, "They will bury their dead in Topheth, because there is no room" (מֵאֵין מָקוֹם). If so, 10:6–7 means, "Because there is no one like you, YHWH, / [and because] you are great and your name is great in might, // Who will not fear you? / For this is befitting you; / For [this is befitting you] among all the wise of the nations and in all royal domains, / Because there is no one like you."

**10:11–16.** Verse 11, distinctively, is entirely in Aramaic and not Hebrew, no doubt because it was a message for the nations and not for Judah (Aramaic was the language of international communication at this time; 2 Kings 18:26). Some regard it as a scribal addition and an interruption to the flow of the text (Thompson 1980, 330), but this is unnecessary. Jeremiah speaks of the incomparability of YHWH over against the gods of the nation, and even though the Jews are his primary audience he wants the nations to know that, despite appearances, their gods have not triumphed. Verse 16 is the counterpart to verse 11, creating another inclusion structure: The gods of the nations will perish (v. 11), but YHWH is not like them (v. 16). Verses 12–13 focus on YHWH's work as creator and especially on his power over the storms, making the point he, not Baal or any other storm god, is the giver of rains. Verses 14–16 again mock the delusion of faith in idols but also assert that YHWH, unlike the idols of the nations, is the "portion of Jacob" (v. 16; חֵלֶק יַעֲקֹב). Jeremiah clearly understands that the majority of his people are idolaters, but he implies that through the faithfulness of God, he remains identified with Israel. This speaks both of an ideal for Israel that endures, and also of a remnant who hold to the faith.

### Christianity and Idolatry

In Torah and the prophetic books, the great besetting sin of Israel is idolatry. The worship of the golden calf in Exodus 32 is the paradigm for Israel's behavior. Condemnation of this sin dominates the preaching of the preexilic prophets. Above everything else, it is the primary reason for the destruction of Israel and the Jerusalem temple (see, for example, Ezek. 8). It far less prominent in the postexilic prophets, but that seems to be because the Jews learned that lesson well. Whatever other sins they committed (as described, for example, in Malachi), they no longer served images of wood and stone. In the Maccabean wars of the second century B.C., thousands of Jews would accept death before worshiping the image set up by Antiochus IV. In the preaching of Jesus, idolatry does not appear at all. The Jews whom Jesus confronted may have been hypocritical, self-righteous, and unable to recognize the work of God among them, but they did not worship images of gods. Paul seems to have communicated very clearly to his Gentile converts that embrace of Christianity meant rejection of idols (Acts 17:16–31). To be sure, some were still tempted, but the main issue he faced was not that his converts would return to idols but that they were so opposed to idol worship that they had difficulties coping with the realities of the marketplace in the pagan, Hellenistic world. These early converts thus were becoming angry and judgmental toward each other over matters such as purchasing the meat of an animal sacrificed to a pagan god (1 Cor. 10). John, in the last verse of his first epistle, briefly exhorts the churches to avoid idolatry (1 John 5:21).

While all Christians repudiate pagan idolatry, there is considerable difference of opinion on the subject of icons—images representing God, Christ, or the saints. The Orthodox Church has fully embraced the use of icons, and to a lesser extent the Roman Catholic Church has as well. Advocates of icon usage assert that Christians venerate icons but do not worship them. The icon, they claim, has the *hypostasis* (personal presence) of the person portrayed within, albeit perhaps not in a literal sense but rather in an evocative sense. Gazing upon the icon is establishes a kind of communion with the person portrayed there and so, it is said, serves as an aid to meditation and prayer. Protestants, especially those of the Reformed variety, have strenuously repudiated these arguments, although there are exceptions. For example, Kevin Vanhoozer speaks positively of icon veneration and uses it as a model for biblical interpretation (Vanhoozer 1998, 460–67).

There is no biblical basis for distinguishing between "veneration," as applied to an image, and "worship." It is a distinction without a difference. If a Christian sets up an icon and prays toward it, bows to it, or focuses meditation upon it, such activity is indistinguishable from a Hindu who does the same before an image of Vishnu or some other god. No *hypostasis* of a person abides in an image; it exists only in the mind and imagination of the worshiper. This is dangerous because one may suppose himself to be in communion with Christ when in fact all the emotional connection is with an object. The image was created by a human, and the human who venerates the image in turn attributes personal identity and intent to the image. The image is twice-over the work of human imagination, as both the icon-maker and the one who uses it fashion God out of their desires and opinions.

Icons, like the images of ancient gods, can be beautiful works of art, and this only increases the danger. Art is powerful, shaping the minds of those who view it. If the art is "secular," this is not a great danger, because most know that the artist was a human portraying his or her personal opinions and experiences. But if the art is of the deity, one may well attribute authority to what is, in fact, a human creation.

And the veneration of images was not a feature of the early church. Paul, preaching to the Athenians in Acts 17, certainly had no notion that his converts should throw away their images of Zeus and Athena and then set to work making icons of Jesus and Mary. Icon veneration did not gain wide acceptance in the eastern churches until the sixth century—just before many of these demoralized, superstitious churches were swallowed by Islam (Harper 2017, 275–87).

What is the modern preacher to do with Jeremiah's extensive polemic against idolatry? A common strategy is to equate idolatry with greed on the basis of Colossians 3:5. While this is valid, Paul surely did not mean for us to substitute the word "greed" every time we encounter idolatry in the Old Testament. Our age is more abstract, and our idols can be more ideological than physical. If a person is a Scrooge, then truly greed is for that person an idol. But fundamentally idolatry is the substitution of a man-made god for the true God. If any ideology or practice becomes the focus of one's hope for meaning and "salvation," and becomes the thing to which one gives devotion, then truly it becomes an idol. An ideological idol may be entirely false, such as communism or fascism. An ideological idol may be essentially good, such freedom and free markets, but it can still be an idol if one thinks of it as humanity's one true hope. Addiction is close to idolatry, as the addict finds value only in the addiction. Again, it can be something that is innately evil, such as pornography, or something that relatively innocuous, such as spectator sports—basketball or football, for example. In the latter case, the emotional investment one makes in the sport determines whether and to what extent it has become a substitute religion. And, I think, the faithful Protestant should take a strong stand against icon veneration.

### *Lamentation over Exile (10:17–22)*

Again, the prior section comparing the religious delusions of the people to the reliability of YHWH and his word (10:1–16) is followed by a section lamenting the destruction soon to come. Here, Jeremiah takes on the role of the whole people, first voicing their lament (vv. 17–22) and then calling on God to show mercy (vv. 23–25).

**10:17–18**. Jeremiah exhorts Jerusalem to grab her portable possessions and flee. The city is doomed to destruction. The addressee is feminine singular (אִסְפִּי, "gather," is a feminine singular imperative), implying that it is Jerusalem personified. She (that is, the people of Jerusalem) can no longer stay in the land. This is the final act of Israel's fall and dispersal. The Jewish dispersion among the nations did not begin with the fall of Jerusalem. Israelites had already fled the northern kingdom before and after the fall of Samaria, and they were already fleeing Jerusalem before the city fell. By the time the city did fall, there was already a significant scattering of Jews around the world of that time.

**10:19–20**. Jeremiah voices the lament of Jerusalem and its people over the coming calamity. We know that the text is metaphorical, with Jeremiah serving as a stand-in for all the people, because he did not in fact have any "children" (v. 20). Also, the Israelites no longer lived in tents, but often referred to themselves as a tent-dwelling people in memory of their shepherd ancestors, as in 1 Kings 12:16.

**10:21–22**. Jeremiah laments over Jerusalem's poor leaders and the ruin they have brought upon the people. Even here, he probably does not speak for himself alone. At least some of his contemporaries felt dismay and anger over decisions made by the national leaders.

### *Jeremiah's Confession and Imprecation Against the Nations (10:23–25)*

The first anthology ends with Jeremiah's prayer. Significantly, it shows that despite all of Israel's faults, Jeremiah has not given up on praying for them. Normally, this would be a good thing. But God himself has determined that Jerusalem must be destroyed. The authority God has invested in his prophet is so great that he will dissuade Jeremiah from interceding for Jerusalem before he carries out the final, terrible punishment on the city. This passage thus serves to conclude the first anthology and to introduce the second anthology, in which the prophet moves from interceding for Judah to calling down God's wrath upon them.

**10:23–24**. In this prayer, Jeremiah speaks in the first-person singular, but he does so as a representative of Israel. He pleads not just for himself but for his nation. He affirms that a man is not in control of his own life. No one is master over the events of his generation or in control of his own destiny. This could be taken as a statement of hard determinism, that all the events of a person's life are predestined; or it could be an excuse, a way of dodging personal responsibility. Some of his contemporaries had the latter philosophy, saying, "The parents have eaten sour grapes, and the children's teeth are set on edge" (Jer. 31:29). But Jeremiah does not mean that every decision has been predetermined or that people can blame their troubles on parents or circumstances. He means that people can make plans, but God is the ruler of the world, and he can bring about success or failure. Proverbs 16:9 is similar. Jeremiah, like all Jerusalem, had plans and expectations for his life. But now the sin of Judah has caused God to bring ruin down upon them. Identifying with his people, Jeremiah calls on God to be lenient.

**10:25**. This verse is almost identical to Psalm 79:6–7. It is impossible to tell which text was written first, or if they both cite a popular or contemporary prayer. Psalm 79 is a psalm of Asaph, who was one of David's musicians (1 Chron. 16:5, 7, 37); but the psalms of Asaph

(Pss. 50; 73–82) are almost certainly from the guild of Asaph and not necessarily the individual. The date of the psalm is disputed, but it is probably from the exilic period (Kraus 1993, 133–34). The prayer for God to strike the nations who do not "know" (ידע) him seems harsh, but the word here probably implies they do not "acknowledge" that YHWH is the true God. It is not mere passive knowledge about him. They refuse to know him or to call on his name. These are nations that are relatively close at hand, since they devour Jacob and lay waste to his territory. Thus, they do not have the excuse that they never heard of Israel or YHWH. The prayer is entirely understandable: Jeremiah loves his people and is distraught to see them ravaged by their pagan neighbors. It is part of Jeremiah's pain that he will have to learn to accept the rightness of God's judgment.

## THEOLOGICAL FOCUS

When people worship the true and living God, they are not guaranteed an easy and safe life. But when someone worships an idol, whether of the ancient or modern variety, degradation and ruin are sure to follow. Emphases of this passage are:

- Every idol is a monument to human stupidity. This is true of ancient idols, gods that had to be secured so that they did not fall over, and it is true of every system we devise to serve as a substitute for salvation in God.
- Every idol will eventually be shown to be a lie.
- The nations, from Jeremiah's perspective, would someday turn from their idols to serve God. And since the coming of Christ, this has happened and continues to happen.
- A whole nation can careen into madness and serve idols, whether they are of the ancient or modern type. When this happens, those who serve God naturally mourn and pray.

## PREACHING AND TEACHING STRATEGIES

### *Exegetical and Theological Synthesis*

The ancient Jews wasted their worship by worshipping idols. For them an idol was a human creation that resembles in some way something of power or beauty upon which they focused their worship. They worshipped an image of something supposedly more powerful than humans. This power behind the image is what they worshipped, supposedly because they thought it provided comfort or strength. Human hands created the physical object (the carving of a person, or animal, or mythical creature) and the human mind created the god behind it. The sin is in the manufacturing of the false god that the image represented.

Carving a statue is not a sin in itself; it is the craving for a god which we created that is offensive to the only true Creator. Both the idol and the god it represents are made by humans, thus they are under our authority. To worship an idol or the god it represents takes that which is lower than us (the idol and the false god) and puts it above us. Idol worship is a waste because it is not only a sin against God directly; it is also a sin against his creation of human beings as the high point of his creation (Ps. 8). When idols or the gods behind them are worshipped, that worship is wasted—and those who waste their worship will be wasted. We must not waste our worship by craving for a carving.

### *Preaching Idea*

Don't waste your worship.

### *Contemporary Connections*

#### What does it mean?

*A mind is a terrible thing to waste.* This slogan created back in the '70s was effective because we easily understood it and we readily agreed to its message. This short, pithy statement communicated that every mind has so much potential that it is terrible that some minds might, or could, be wasted. Furthermore, the clear implication was that we should take action so that minds will not be wasted. No one wants to waste something of value. Thus the campaign was very effective, and this slogan is still used today to motivate us.

Picking up on the cultural belief that it is terrible for something of great value to be wasted, our worship is a terrible thing to waste. Our worship can be wasted by unknowingly worshipping a person. Not that we worship a person in the full sense of that word, but all of us have admired and put our hope in figures of authority. In high school I so admired my drama teacher that I bought a tan jacket just like he wore, and was thrilled when I was mistaken for him. But when he kicked me out of a play that he was directing, I was wasted. When Nixon ran for office in 1968, I was enthralled with his political speeches and his plans for a better America. I was wasted when he resigned in shame. And when the Astros, my home team, won the World Series what a joy—only to be wasted when it came out that there was stealing of pitching information that helped them win. When we worship anything other than the true God, we will be disappointed, let down—and even worse, we will face His discipline. We will be wasted—if not in this world, certainly when we stand before Him.

### *Is it true?*

Relative to the ancient world few of us in the western world worship idols, but we still manufacture and worship the same false gods that were behind the ancient idols.

What does worshiping a false god look like for us? Of course, there are numerous nonpersonal things that to varying degrees control our lives: finances, government, family, employers. And as I write this, the coronavirus has control over our world. To be sure, something that controls your life could well be something that in some sense is worshipped. The kind of wasted worship that Jeremiah was condemning was to a specific god, not a system or cultural construct.

The absence of idol worship in western culture makes the application of this passage more difficult than one might expect. Our first impulse is to equate misplaced priorities as idol worship. However, idol worship is not just working too many hours or letting a habit control one's life. Those are sins to be sure, but idolatry is substituting a false god for the real one. It is spiritual adultery. The metaphor is not just a husband neglecting his wife's needs because he works too much; it is him putting another woman in her place. Idolatry is personal.

### *Now what?*

So, do we have false gods in our modern age? Who is it we rely upon? Who is our Creator? Who is our sustainer? Who do we affirm? Who do we put in place of God?

The prosperity of the western world allows us to worship a personal false god that other cultures, past and present, would not think of worshipping. That false god, that idol, is self. One of the highest values in our culture is the freedom of choice, which is an expression of this self-worship. We think that we have a choice about everything, just as a god would. We tell children they can become anything they want to become, regardless of their giftedness or abilities. Our culture praises those who are brave enough to say that they don't want to live as the biological sex that they are. As gods, we think we can perform a miracle and change our gender. When our favorite sports team wins, we somehow make that win about us. Since it is *our* team, we enjoy the praise as though we had played the game ourselves. With our amazing progress we don't set up a wooden image and create a god and ask for its power to act in our favor; rather, we think that we are in control of our lives and look to ourselves for that power. It is not a cult of self-centeredness, in which we blatantly say "I am God." But, when many of us look in the mirror, we see the one who we think controls our lives. When we are honest and admit that often we worship ourselves, how foolish it sounds—and is.

### *Creativity in Presentation*

The contrast between idol worship and the worship of YHWH can be presented in somewhat formal compare-and-contrast structure. The pulpit or teaching area can be used to highlight the two very different kinds of worship. When the speaker is addressing the waste of idol worship, he/she can stand on the right side of the platform or teaching area. Then when addressing the true worship, he/she can move to the left side. As the first sixteen verses are presented, the speaker can move back and forth, to highlight the wasted worship and true worship. The last movement of the sermon would be God's judgment, which would be in the center of the teaching/preaching area, perhaps from the pulpit or lectern. Using the two areas can highlight the choice that is before our people. What side do we want to be on? Notice that the movement is from left to right, according to the congregation's perspective. This is important because there is a positive connotation in moving in the same direction that we read. The application can be driven home by asking on what side you most often find yourself.

Jeremiah closes this message against idolatry in a very personal way. He asks YHWH to correct him and then to judge the nations. Jeremiah's readers worshipped YHWH based upon the revelation available to them. They saw him in creation, they knew he spoke to their forefathers, and they experienced the sacrificial system that he ordained. Perhaps they struggled with YHWH being personal. Maybe that is why idol worship was so appealing. They could only trust that he was personal and that he would somehow, in some way, forgive and redeem them as well as judge the nations. For the Christian, the application of this passage should lead naturally to Jesus. Jesus made clear how God would, in person, forgive and redeem us. And Jesus destroys any thought that God is not personal. He is the only person we should worship.

Here is one possible structure for your sermon:

- Don't waste your worship.
  - How worship can be wasted (10:1–16)
  - When worship is wasted, we should grieve (10:17–22).
  - Worship the one worthy person (10:23–25).
    - He corrects us.
    - He judges the nations.

- Worship the only one worthy: Jesus.

## DISCUSSION QUESTIONS

1. What things vital to life are under our control? Which ones aren't?

2. What makes us think that we can fully control our lives?

3. When do we realize that we're not fully in control of our lives?

4. Why do we like to be in control?

5. Why don't we like to submit to authority?

# Jeremiah 11:1–23

**EXEGETICAL IDEA**

This passage examines human depravity as Jeremiah experienced it in the course of his ministry. Israel has always been unfaithful, and now its depravity is such that even Jeremiah's closest kinship group, the people of his hometown, want to kill him for his preaching. For this reason, Jeremiah with God's help will realize that the nation is incorrigible and that time for pleading that God would spare them has passed.

**THEOLOGICAL FOCUS**

This passage introduces the reader to the process whereby Jeremiah realized he could no longer intercede for Jerusalem. To understand fully God's justice and mercy, we must first understand human depravity. The horrors that accompanied the fall of Jerusalem were so great that those who honestly consider them must wonder if God was too harsh. But if one with equal honesty considers the moral depths to which the people had fallen, God's response is comprehensible. What then becomes astonishing is the promises of grace that appear later in the book.

**PREACHING IDEA**

To understand God's goodness, we must look at our wickedness.

**PREACHING POINTERS**

God's covenant with Israel was clear: worship him only, and do not worship or even make idols. They disobeyed this command almost before it was given, and then continued to disobey this part of the covenant for hundreds of years. The disobedience was so ingrained that they couldn't even hear the command any longer.

While we are not under the same covenant the Jews were under, we still serve the same God, and we still have the same kind of human hearts. Jeremiah's call to Judah and to us is to admit that our hearts are wicked. Though not explicitly stated in this passage, the warning is first to those who *do* listen. To the degree we admit that our hearts are wicked, we will see the goodness of God. The warning is also for those who *do not* listen to him. To the degree they ignore their wicked hearts, they will not see the goodness of God.

# HARDENED HEARTS (11:1–23)

## LITERARY STRUCTURE AND THEMES

This chapter appears to have no logical flow. It begins with a summary account of Israel's failure to keep the covenant from the exodus until the time of Jeremiah (11:1–13). Next, YHWH tells Jeremiah he must not intercede for Judah anymore (11:14–17). Finally, it speaks of how the men of Anathoth, Jeremiah's hometown, plotted to silence him by murder if necessary (11:18–23). In fact, this chapter is a summary of Jeremiah's great theological awakening. It is Jeremiah's turn away from making intercession for his people and turn toward making imprecation against them. It is somewhat hard to follow because it summarizes all of 11:1–20:18, which recounts this transformation in more detail. The people's treason against YHWH (11:1–13) and their treachery toward Jeremiah (11:18–23) together demonstrate why the prophet had to abandon the illusion that within his lifetime they might heed his message and come back to God (11:14–17).

We must not read this chapter as though the events and messages recounted in 12:1–20:18 were subsequent to the message of this chapter. Rather, this chapter proleptically gives the main point of the later chapters: that Jeremiah came to realize that his people were unflinchingly evil, and that Jerusalem's destruction was inevitable.

- ***The Covenant and Its Violation (11:1–13)***
- ***Intercession for Israel Prohibited (11:14–17)***
- ***The Treacherous Men of Anathoth (11:18–23)***

## EXPOSITION

### *The Covenant and Its Violation (11:1–13)*

Israel had a long history of covenant violation. From the day YHWH brought them out of Egypt and gave them the Sinai covenant until the time of Jeremiah they had consistently turned to idols and forsaken Torah. As such, YHWH must prepare his prophet for the hard task of announcing judgment against them.

**11:1.** This verse marks the beginning of a new section with a rather full superscript. Instead of the simple, "Thus says YHWH," it speaks more completely of how Jeremiah received a word from YHWH.

**11:2–5.** In summary fashion, this verse recalls the terms and context for the Sinai covenant and also the renewal of the covenant by Josiah. God calls on the people to hear the words of "this covenant" (הַבְּרִית הַזֹּאת), a term that appears three times in Deuteronomy (5:3; 29:9, 14 [MT 29:8, 13]). Jeremiah uses the phrase four times, all in this chapter (vv. 2, 3, 6, 8); it also appears once in 2 Kings 23:3, in the context of Josiah's covenant renewal ceremony. The phrase thus invokes the Sinai covenant, the solemn warnings given by Moses on the plains of Moab, and Josiah's reformation and attempt to end the apostasy in Jerusalem. These echoes from Deuteronomy imply that the people are still under the covenant and would be treated in accordance with its terms. The warning of verse 3, that a curse would be on anyone who did not keep the covenant, echoes the curses of Deuteronomy 27:15–26 (the phrase in Jeremiah 11:3, אָרוּר הָאִישׁ, "cursed be the man," appears at the beginning of Deuteronomy 27:15; and אָרוּר, "cursed," begins every verse of Deuteronomy 27:16–26). In addition, YHWH in verse 4 invokes the circumstances of the Sinai covenant, that he had brought them out of Egypt and at the foot of Sinai offered to them the terms of the covenant, alluding to Exodus 19:3–6. But God does not close the allusion with a threat. Instead, he reminds them of the benefits of the Sinai covenant: that he would bring them into the land of milk and honey, would be their God, and would faithfully keep all his promises. To this, Jeremiah enthusiastically responds, "Amen, YHWH!" This part of the passage probably looks back to an event early in Jeremiah's prophetic career. He was a young man at the time of Josiah's reformation, and he eagerly embraced the hope that under Josiah's leadership Judah would again be faithful to the covenant. His "Amen" voiced his hope, and probably his expectation, that the people, in obedience to Josiah, would keep the covenant and see its benefits.

**11:6–8**. These verses testify that YHWH consistently warned the Israelites—from the time of the exodus to the time of Jeremiah—that they must obey the terms of the covenant. But they, just as consistently, refused to listen.

**11:9–10**. In English as in Hebrew, the term "conspiracy" (קֶשֶׁר) generally implies a plot by a group of people against some established authority, as when a small group conspires to assassinate a political leader, or a collection of disgruntled employees conspires to have a manager fired. In 2 Kings 17:4, the king of Assyria found that Hoshea of Israel was leading a "conspiracy" (קֶשֶׁר) to revolt against Assyrian imperial authority. Although the persistent apostasy of Judah was sinful, it seems odd to call it a "conspiracy." Probably this text speaks not just of their apostasy but also of their conspiracy to silence or even to murder Jeremiah (described below in vv. 18–20). In this, they were conspiring against YHWH's lawful spokesman, and this conspiracy is representative of the long history of Israel's plots against God's prophets. Jesus, in the parable of the wicked vinedressers, also spoke of a conspiracy against himself (Matt. 21:38).

**11:12–13**. The claim that Judah had as many gods as it had towns and as many shrines as it had streets sounds like hyperbole, but it is probably closer to literal fact. Polytheistic religions tend to multiply gods and shrines excessively. Even abstract concepts could be personified as deities, as the Greeks did with the goddess Nike ("victory") and with the gods Deimos and Phobos ("panic and terror," the twin sons of Ares), and as the Romans did with the goddess Fortuna ("luck"). In a modern Hindu region, such as the Indonesian island Bali, it can be astonishing to drive the streets and see the endless number of shrines along the way.

### *Intercession for Israel Prohibited (11:14–17)*

Verse 14 forthrightly commands Jeremiah to cease making intercession for Judah, but many interpreters regard the Hebrew of 11:15–16 as all but untranslatable (Holladay 1986, 354). Part of the problem, I think, is that translators disregard the gender and person of various nouns and pronouns. "Jerusalem" in this text is feminine, but "beloved" (יָדִיד) in verse 15 is masculine, implying that it refers to Jeremiah, not to Jerusalem. Also, the standard verse division of the text is misleading. The passage makes better sense with a break at the end of verse 15a, so that all of verse 14–15a addresses Jeremiah, while 15b–17 addresses Jerusalem. The whole can then be translated with little difficulty, as follows:

> *14–15a*: And you [Jeremiah], do not intercede for this people or lift up an outcry or

prayer in their behalf, for I am not listening when they call upon me concerning their trouble. What is there in my house [the temple] for my beloved [Jeremiah] while she [Jerusalem] is carrying out her plan?

*15b–17*: The throngs of people and the holy [sacrificial] meat! They will depart from you [Jerusalem] because of your evil. Then will you be so exultant? YHWH called your name "Green olive tree made beautiful by shapely fruit." But with the sound of a great storm, he will set fire to it, and its branches will suffer. And YHWH Sabaoth who planted you has pronounced a disaster against you on account of the evil of the house of Israel and of the house of Judah, [evil that] they did of their own accord, to provoke me by making offerings to Baal.

**11:14–15a**. The abrupt command to Jeremiah to desist from praying for Jerusalem anticipates the whole of 11:1–20:18, the full account of Jeremiah's change from praying for the city to praying that YHWH would punish them. That is, this text is not in chronological order but summarizes the larger narrative, giving the reader a proleptic look at what will happen in the next nine chapters. Verse 15a, "What is there in my house for my beloved when she carries out her plan?" concerns Jeremiah ("my beloved"), who has no business going to the temple ("my house") to pray for the city while Jerusalem ("she") conspires to put him to death ("is carrying out her plan"). There is no reason to think that "for my beloved" (לִידִידִי) must refer to Israel or, more specifically, to Jerusalem. In Isaiah 5:1, the same expression (לִידִידִי) refers to God, and in Psalm 127:2, "for his beloved" (לִידִידוֹ) refers to the pious man (similarly, in Ps. 60:5 [MT 7], "your beloved ones" [יְדִידֶיךָ] refers to the righteous in the land). The word יָדִיד does not appear anywhere else in Jeremiah, and the prophets never use it as an epithet for Israel.

**11:15b–17**. These words are directed at Jerusalem. First, YHWH tells the city that God will cause offerings to cease at the temple, a prediction of the destruction of the sanctuary (v. 15bc). In 14–15a, YHWH had said that his prophet had no business being in the temple at such a time as this, and now he pronounces destruction over the temple. Second, YHWH compares the city to an olive tree, saying that although he had planted it, he will cut it down and burn it (vv. 16–17).

### *The Treacherous Men of Anathoth (11:18–23)*

These verses speak of a turning point in Jeremiah's life, when he learned of the conspiracy of the men of Anathoth to murder him and so came to understand the depth of their hostility toward God and himself. It is in two parts. Verses 18–20 are a prayer of Jeremiah, in which he thanks God for revealing the plot to murder him and speaks in astonishment at his own blindness toward their treachery, while verses 21–23 are a prophecy of destruction for Anathoth.

**11:18–20**. The opening words, "YHWH made it known to me, so now I know," serve as the title of this prayer. The rest of the prayer addresses YHWH in the second person. Verse 19a is similar to Isaiah 53:7. Jeremiah says he was like a tame lamb led to slaughter (כְּכֶבֶשׂ אַלּוּף יוּבַל לִטְבוֹחַ), and Isaiah says the Servant was like the sheep led to slaughter (כַּשֶּׂה לַטֶּבַח יוּבָל). The two are similar in that both Jeremiah and the Servant of YHWH suffered under evil men. In effect, Jeremiah, as a true prophet of YHWH, participated in the pattern of ministry and suffering set by Isaiah's messianic servant. There is a difference, however. For Jeremiah, the lamb comparison pointed to his own naivety—how ignorant he was of the plots laid against him. In Isaiah, the Servant's lamb-like quality reflected his patience and quiet endurance in the face of violence. The discovery of the treachery of the men of Anathoth was traumatic because that was Jeremiah's home, and Jeremiah believed that at least these people, some of whom were his relatives, were souls he could trust to be on his side. This experience was behind Jeremiah's discovery of the depth of human evil recounted in 17:5–10. Note that Jeremiah compares the righteous and the wicked to trees (17:5–8), just as the men of Anathoth compared Jeremiah to a tree (11:19). Also, 17:10 says that YHWH tests a man's heart and emotions (יְהוָה חֹקֵר לֵב בֹּחֵן כְּלָיוֹת), just as 11:20 says YHWH is a righteous judge who tests the heart and emotions (וַיהוָה צְבָאוֹת שֹׁפֵט צֶדֶק בֹּחֵן כְּלָיוֹת וָלֵב). This incident was a turning point in Jeremiah's life, changing forever his understanding of the human heart before God and of the impossibility of repentance among his people.

**11:21–23**. The prophecy of doom for Anathoth is similar to the destruction predicted for Jerusalem and all of Judah, except that Anathoth will have no remnant. While we cannot say how literally this prediction was meant or fulfilled, the implication is that the town would be annihilated.

## THEOLOGICAL FOCUS

This passage describes why judgment was inevitable and why Jeremiah embraced that fact. Salient points are:

- A habit of unbelief and apostasy can thrive from generation to generation, and the persistence of the apostasy will convince people that they are not apostate at all, but orthodox. Sooner or later, their apostasy will bear the fruit of depravity and destruction.
- The Old Testament prophet had great authority. His prayers mattered. As such, God could not bring his judgment down upon Jerusalem until Jeremiah stopped praying for them. God effectively limits himself by showing respect for the prophetic office of Jeremiah.
- Although the first duty of the prophet was to intercede for sinners and offer hope, Jeremiah also had to face reality. The plot of the men of Anathoth was that reality.
- Those who seek to know deeply the ways of God may have to descend into the depths of human evil and pain before such understanding comes. This kind of profound wrestling with God and people is accompanied by great sorrow, and it is not the same as self-righteous indignation, which is accompanied by great pride and anger.
- Hostility to God inevitably leads to hostility toward God's messenger.
- Those who hate and seek to silence God's messenger face a harsher judgment than the mass of people. Such bitter hostility is analogous to the blasphemy against the Holy Spirit that Jesus spoke of in regard to those who sought to silence him (Mark 3:22–30).

## PREACHING AND TEACHING STRATEGIES

### *Exegetical and Theological Synthesis*

Those Jews who were in exile or after the return were very aware that God meant what he said through Jeremiah. God said judgment was coming and it came. After this harsh discipline, they knew not to worship idols, and their practices after the exile show that they abhorred it. The postexilic Jews could proudly say that they no longer worshiped idols, but they needed to remember that idol worship was only the manifestation of the wickedness of their hearts. Jeremiah's message continues to be about the corrupt heart that lies within each of us.

The application of this is obvious; the challenge remains to communicate this to our current culture. Quoting other passages might be helpful, but this passage not only lays out the concept; it gives the example of the men of Anathoth. The principle is the same today and it is easy to point out that there are people in this world with evil hearts. Jeremiah's own self-examination from the previous pericope must be remembered. We, as teachers/preachers, need to follow Jeremiah's example and examine our own hearts. Only when I am honest about my own wicked heart can I proclaim that we all have wicked hearts.

### *Preaching Idea*

To understand God's goodness, we must look at our wickedness.

### *Contemporary Connections*

#### What does it mean?

God's warnings are prompted by our wicked hearts. The wicked hearts are seen in his children as we, unfortunately, still have wicked inclinations and actions that follow. Pastors are not exempt.

The meeting of the current pastor and his predecessor was awkward, not only because the previous pastor was still living in the area but more so because he was forced to resign due to his moral failure. The conversation was only cordial at first, but then as the trust and fraternal love grew, so did the depth of pain that was shared. The elephant in the room, the moral failure, began to be discussed. The details of the failure were not the focus; rather, the pain of the results: the loss of his job, the loss of respect, the pain and shame to his family, and the unstable future ahead. He looked at the new pastor straight in the eyes and said, "The wages of sin is indeed death." The warnings that led up to his immoral behavior had come throughout his life: the unchecked occasional viewing of mild porn, the guilty conscience after some "innocent" flirting, and the distance that grew between him and his wife. He didn't listen to the warnings, and God's loving discipline came. Today, years later, he ministers to God's people, though not as a pastor.

Far more tragic are those who refuse to give an open ear to God's offer of forgiveness and righteousness through Christ. The lack of hearing God comes in different forms. Some have made up their minds that God doesn't exist, or that if he does he really doesn't have anything to do with this world. Others readily accept God's existence, but believe that they somehow are good enough to be accepted by him. They live their lives with warnings all around them. At a funeral they hear that Jesus is the resurrection and the life. At Christmas they sing, "God and sinners reconciled." At a special program they listen to a speaker tell them about Christ's forgiveness. Even from secular musicians they hear, "Amazing grace . . . that saved a *wretch* like me." They even watch movies that invite one to put their faith in Christ. Warnings have been spoken, but did they listen?

In Jeremiah 11, God stopped listening to the prayers for the nation's salvation because of their wickedness, but he always listens to the individual's prayer of repentance, whether from one of his children or from a nonbeliever. But a day can come when the prayer will not be heard, because an individual's heart is so against God that there is no prayer. A wicked heart can mute spoken prayers.

#### Is it true?

When this was written (April 2020), the leaders of the United States and local leaders were saying that this could well be one of the saddest and hardest weeks for many Americans, because of the COVID-19 pandemic. Thousands were dying because of this highly contagious disease. Schools were closed, all sporting and entertainment events were canceled, and even churches were not meeting for corporate worship. For weeks, warnings had been issued that extreme care should be taken by all: stay home from work, no gatherings of more than ten people, at-risk people should wear protective masks in public, and continual hand-washing by everyone. These actions must be taken to prevent more deaths. These warnings were repeated numerous times every day. The government was sending written notices to every home and business; medical professionals, backed by governmental leaders from the president to local mayors, were making direct media appeals; and every newscast had special coverage about practicing social distancing. There was no doubt that the warning was going forth. Phrases which were often heard were "You must listen to what we are saying"; "Please hear that these measures are for your good"; "If you don't pay attention, more people will die." How could anyone hear this and not choose to change?

Jeremiah's listeners chose to not hear. Obviously, the sound waves entered their ears, but something happened between the ear and the mind. Perhaps the failure to listen to Jeremiah is echoed in the way some may think about the pandemic warnings. There are those who do not listen. Why? Do they not trust the leadership? Perhaps they don't think they will be infected? Or could there be an evil self-centered thought of, "People die of the flu every day; what's the big deal?" Do we respond to God's words of warning in the same way?

#### *Now what?*

Jeremiah experienced it, and we recognize it in our own lives: in our hearts we are wicked people. Not that we don't do good, but on their own our wicked hearts will not listen to God. Since we all have wicked hearts, it follows that God really will judge people, both in a disciplinary way and/or in a final judgment. This should spur us on to proclaim the great power over our wicked hearts through the cross and resurrection. In Scripture we have not just prophetic words of warning; we have words of forgiveness and true hope. Not only this, but since it is true that our hearts are wicked, the cross makes sense. But if we think that our hearts are not wicked, the cross was a mistake. Grace is amazing not because it saves a good person; it is amazing because it saves a wretch like me.

### *Creativity in Presentation*

The truth of this passage is very upsetting. Who wants to say that their heart is wicked? To those who submit to the teaching of Scripture, it is at best unpleasant. To those who are guided by secular thought, it is not only unpleasant but offensive to them. Israel Charny in *Psychology Today* writes, "Standard psychology texts imply that to be normal is to feel happy and to lead an untroubled good life—until uncontrollable lightning may strike, but this is unlikely. In their essence, life and people are good" (Charny 2018, 1). However, he goes on to say that man is good and bad; we can choose which we will be. He admits that people can be bad, but they can choose to be good.

In contrast, this passage teaches that all are basically bad. Therefore, care needs to be taken in presenting it. The passage could be presented with an introductory rhetorical question as to whether people are basically good or bad. But that forces our listeners to bring in all kinds of mental rebuttals and exceptions. It unnecessarily creates an argumentative tone. Better to present the subject as how we respond to the teaching of this passage and various ways that people respond. Some will disagree outright. Others will disagree, but because it is wrong to disagree with the Bible they will keep their objections to themselves. Others will accept it. In presenting the possible reactions, you are indirectly asking them to think about how they react. Thus, your listeners at least have to consider the teachings of this chapter. It is a way to help them be open to what God is saying. As the passage is presented, they must embrace to some degree what is being said, and perhaps truly hear it.

Most often it is good to apply the text as one teaches or preaches through the passage. It seems that this pericope is best presented in a whole, and then the application. It seems that the reason God is pointing out the wickedness in Judah's heart and in ours is not to just condemn and depress us but rather to prompt praise of his goodness, as expressed in our worship and obedience. The warnings to those who habitually reject the truth of our sin and wicked hearts must also be presented. Here is one possible structure:

- The burden of a hopelessly wicked heart (11:1–23)
    - We all have a history of hopeless depravity (vv. 1–13).
    - It can lead to a hopeless end (vv. 14–17).
        - Example: men of Anathoth (vv. 18–23)

- To the degree we admit that our hearts are wicked, we will see the goodness of God.
    - Through our admitting our sins
    - Through our trust in his salvation

- To the degree we ignore our wicked hearts, we will not see the goodness of God.
    - Through our continual rejection of salvation
    - Through the possibility of never responding to his voice

## DISCUSSION QUESTIONS

1. How do you feel toward a person who passionately presents a view contrary to a deeply held belief?

2. Do you pay attention to warning labels on products you buy? Why or why not?

3. What warnings do you wish you had listened to?

4. What warnings are you glad that you did listen to?

5. Why do we hesitate to listen to warnings?

## Jeremiah 12:1–13:27

### EXEGETICAL IDEA

This passage explores two ideas: the gravity of Jerusalem's evil and Jeremiah's awakening to the reality of the people's depravity. It speaks of how Jeremiah tried to intercede for them but got an unexpected response from God—that these people were beyond praying for. Jeremiah had wrongly supposed that only the leaders were bad, but God made him see that the whole nation was corrupt. Two object lessons illustrate this concept, and Jeremiah begins to realize that the people will not repent.

### THEOLOGICAL FOCUS

Compassion for sinners is right and good, but it should not blind us to the severity of the corruption around us. We should not make empty excuses for sin, saying that some people are merely misled by a few bad influencers. This is not a call for arrogant judgmentalism, but an appeal for us to not mistake our own hopes for a people, often arising from our love and compassion for them, for the truth about them.

### PREACHING IDEA

Keep your balance, while you can.

### PREACHING POINTERS

Jeremiah's message is a terrifying warning: Judah will become incorrigible. That is, she will continue in sin to the degree that she cannot stop, and judgment will come. She was at the point of no return and did not know it. When someone is so set in their sinful ways that they won't or can't change, it is called "incorrigible." People today can become incorrigible.

How does the gymnast stay on that four-inch beam? She amazes us as she spins, flips, stands on her hands, and somehow keeps her balance, at least most of time. When she begins to lose her balance, she swings her arms, twists her torso, struggles to regain her balance, and then, unbelievably, stays on the beam. But there is a point when she cannot recover, and gravity takes control. She no longer has a choice; she will fall. In the case of a balance beam, gymnasts know very well when they have lost their balance. Can a person sin so much that he *won't* stop? Then, by continuing in sin, can he come to the point where he *can't* stop? If we are terrified by this possibility, then the message is a blessing because God's Spirit is at work in us. He is calling for repentance. If one is frightened by the warning, they are not incorrigible—yet.

# FAILED INTERCESSION (12:1–13:27)

## LITERARY STRUCTURE AND THEMES

This passage takes us through the experiences of Jeremiah as he prayed for Judah but did so with some naivety, thinking that the sin of the people could be soon cured. These chapters repeat many charges already made against Judah, but here they serve to illustrate why Jeremiah must alter his thinking about the spiritual health of his people and understand that matters are far worse than he had imagined. As he learned more and more of the breadth and depth of their apostasy, he began to shift in his thinking. The opening dialogue with YHWH (12:1–17) is the background and setting for the passage. It includes Jeremiah's intercession and YHWH's response. Two object lessons follow. They demonstrate how sinful Judah is and what judgment awaits them (13:1–14). At the end of this text, a harsh truth is revealed: Judah simply cannot and will not repent (13:15–27). There is an inclusion pattern to this passage. The prayer and YHWH's negative response in 12:1–17 are echoed by the appeal and Jerusalem's negative response in 13:15–27. Between these are the two object lessons in 13:1–14.

- ***Jeremiah's First Intercession and Dialogue with YHWH (12:1–17)***
  - *A Prayer for Deliverance from Wicked Leaders (12:1–4)*
  - *YHWH's Response (12:5–17)*

- ***Two Object Lessons (13:1–14)***
  - *The Ruined Loincloth (13:1–11)*
  - *The Jars Filled with Wine (13:12–14)*

- ***Jerusalem Cannot Repent (13:15–27)***
  - *The Appeal to Repent (13:15–21)*
  - *Jerusalem the Incorrigible (13:22–27)*

## EXPOSITION

### *Jeremiah's First Intercession and Dialogue with YHWH (12:1–17)*

This section apparently comes from fairly early in Jeremiah's ministry. He complains to God about the success of the wicked—a complaint that carries with it the implication that the righteous do not succeed, or at least that before God they have no advantage over those who are evil. This suggests a period sometime after the death of Josiah and accession of Jehoiakim, when the righteous (Josiah) suffered defeat and the wicked (Jehoiakim) grew in power. Also, YHWH's answer in 12:14–17 implies that Jeremiah thought of certain foreign powers, such as Neco II (who slew Josiah), as among the prosperous wicked. In addition, Jeremiah's appeal for God to punish the prosperous wicked implies that he still thinks that many in Judah are not truly wicked but that a few, especially the aristocracy, lead everyone else astray. He thinks that if God would deal with the evil elite, the rest would do what is right. God corrects him, telling him that the whole of Judah is irrevocably corrupt.

#### *A Prayer for Deliverance from Wicked Leaders (12:1–4)*

This text is not a call for God to punish all of Judah. Instead, Jeremiah singles out the elite minority and calls on God to pour his fury on this small but prominent and influential segment, so that the rest of the nation might be spared divine wrath.

**12:1a**. "You are righteous (צַדִּיק), YHWH, whenever I bring a case against you (כִּי אָרִיב אֵלֶיךָ). Even so, I need to speak with you on matters of justice (אַךְ מִשְׁפָּטִים אֲדַבֵּר אוֹתָךְ)." This is how the prophet introduces his complaint against God. The clause אָרִיב אֵלֶיךָ means to bring a case against God (see Judg. 21:22; Jer. 2:29). Jeremiah acknowledges that when, in the past, he accused God of managing things unfairly, God has turned out to be in the right (צַדִּיק) and Jeremiah's complaint has failed. Even so, he must again question God's justice. The Old Testament is generally straightforward about raising such questions, not treating them as challenges to God that a truly devout person would never imagine or dare to raise.

**12:1b–3**. Jeremiah begins his complaint in general terms, asking why the wicked and treacherous prosper (v. 1b). His concern about their prosperity implies that he has the wealthy aristocracy and also perhaps foreign rulers in mind. He is not speaking about all of Judah. He describes the prosperous wicked with the metaphor of the tree, observing that YHWH planted them (נְטַעְתָּם), and that they take root (שֹׁרָשׁוּ) and bear fruit (עָשׂוּ פֶרִי). The verb נטע ("plant") recalls 1:10, where this verb implies divine favor. The growth of roots and the bearing of fruit looks ahead to Jeremiah 17:8, where the same words describe the prosperity of the righteous. And yet these people are not righteous; they only feign devotion to YHWH with their lips (12:2b). This suggests that Jeremiah primarily has in mind Israelite aristocrats and not foreign rulers, since the latter do not pretend allegiance to YHWH. He asks for this small group, the elite, to be separated from the whole herd (all the people of Judah) and singled out for destruction (12:3).

**12:4**. Jeremiah evidently gave this prayer during a time of drought, when the land was drying up. In this situation, even the wild animals suffered and became scarce. At verse 4b, the NIV has "Because those who live in it are wicked" (the ESV is similar). But this is somewhat misleading. The clause מֵרָעַת יֹשְׁבֵי־בָהּ is literally "because of the bad of its inhabitants." The word "bad" (רָעָה) can mean evil behavior (Gen. 50:15; 1 Sam. 13:16) or a calamity (Gen. 19:19; Jer. 2:3). For that reason, מֵרָעַת יֹשְׁבֵי־בָהּ could mean, "because of the calamity that has befallen its inhabitants." Also, their claim that YHWH "will not see our ending" (לֹא יִרְאֶה אֶת־אַחֲרִיתֵנוּ) does not mean, "YHWH will not see when we sin." It means, "YHWH will not see when we die." It is a statement of despair, not defiance. Jeremiah is not claiming that the common people are guiltless, but he is saying that they, like the beasts and birds, are caught up in a great calamity not of their making. To the extent that the people themselves are "bad," it is because the apostasy of the aristocracy has misled them. The political and religious leaders have brought ruin on the land.

### *YHWH's Response (12:5–17)*

YHWH responds to Jeremiah in three parts. First, Jeremiah has badly misjudged the situation and is aggrieved at a relatively small problem when, in fact, the hostility and apostasy confronting him is far greater than he knows (12:5–6). Second, YHWH speaks of how the whole land has turned against him; there is no remnant (12:7–13). Third, YHWH asserts that he will in due time deal with evil foreign powers (12:14–17).

**12:5–6**. The basic meaning of verse 5 is obvious; it is a classic argument from lesser to greater. "If you can't keep up when running with men on foot, how will you fare against horses? If you stumble when traversing level ground, how will you fair when moving through the marshes and scrub brush along the Jordan?" The question for the interpreter is this: In the comparison, what is the lesser thing and what is the greater thing? YHWH points to the answer in verse 6, when he implies that the conspiracy of the men of Anathoth is the greater thing. This, in turn, means that the lesser thing is the wickedness of the elite. Their wickedness is real, but the aristocracy is only a tiny proportion of the whole population. The conspiracy of the men of Anathoth means that even common folk out in the villages, and even Jeremiah's relatives and lifelong friends, have turned against him. In short, the whole nation is apostate against God and hostile to Jeremiah. He had thought, rightly, that the aristocracy hated him, but that turned out to be only a small part of the problem. He was, in fact, up against the entire country.

**12:7–13**. YHWH speaks this section, declaring that he must abandon Judah (called "my house" [בֵּיתִי], "my inheritance" [נַחֲלָתִי], and "the beloved of my soul" [יְדִדוּת נַפְשִׁי] in v. 7) because she has become as treacherous and violent as a lion. Verse 9 is difficult; the standard translations are difficult to justify from the Hebrew, and they actually make little sense. What does it mean to say that Judah is like "a speckled bird of prey" (NIV)? A better translation is as follows:

> Does a hyena snap at my inheritance in my behalf?
>
> Do birds of prey gather around her?
>
> Go, gather the wild beasts of the field!
>
> Bring them to eat her!

The enemy nations are likened to scavengers that come and tear at the flesh of prostrate Judah. So also, in verse 10 the enemy kings are likened to shepherds who bring their "sheep" (their armies" to consume the fields and vineyards of Judah. More literally, verses 11–13 describe the land as barren, consumed by invaders, and now with nothing to harvest.

*THE TRANSLATION OF 12:9*

The word צָבוּעַ is not attested to mean "speckled," although there is a word צֶבַע, "dyed," in Judges 5:30. Even so, the phrase "speckled bird of prey" makes no sense in context. But, as Holladay has pointed out, a better, alternative translation is possible (Holladay 1986, 387–88). The word צָבוּעַ is known to mean "hyena" in Sirach 13:18 and the Talmud. The verb עיט appears in 1 Sam. 14:32 (*qere*), 25:14; Sir 14:10; 31:16, where it seems to mean "snap at" (with the mouth) and can be used metaphorically for greed. Here, the verb is used more literally, and means that the hyenas snap at their prey, devouring it. Thus, the first occurrence of הַעַיִט in Jeremiah 12:9 is probably a copyist's error made under the influence of the occurrence of הַעַיִט found in the second line of the text. The first occurrence should be emended to היעיט, a qal *yiqtol* with interrogative ה. With this, the whole first line, היעיט צָבוּעַ נַחֲלָתִי לִי, means, "Does a hyena snap at my inheritance in my behalf?" The second line, הַעַיִט סָבִיב עָלֶיהָ, thus means, "Do birds of prey gather around her?" The metaphor is that Judah is like a dead carcass lying in a field, with hyenas and vultures dashing in to snatch pieces of meat.

**12:14–17**. Jeremiah's grief over wicked and powerful enemies could have been directed at foreign powers, such as the Egyptian pharaoh, and not just at Judah's aristocracy. As such, YHWH declares that foreigners will not escape punishment (v. 14). Although Judah is evil and God will punish her, she is still his people, and he is jealous over her. Both Judah and the nations will suffer destruction, but only Judah, God's own people, will be restored (v. 15). Strikingly, however, YHWH makes the same offer to the Gentiles that he routinely makes to Israel: if they repent, he will not destroy them (vv. 16–17). Throughout this text, Jeremiah uses verbs from his initial commission at 1:10, including נתש ("uproot" [5X, in vv. 14, 15, 17), אבד ("destroy" [v. 17), and בנה ("build" [v. 16]). God commissioned him to be a prophet not just to Israel but to the nations, and he is fulfilling that role.

### *Two Object Lessons (13:1–14)*

Using two object lessons, YHWH tells Jeremiah how thoroughly corrupted his people are and that the whole of their society is destined for ruin.

*The Ruined Loincloth (13:1–11)*

In three stages, YHWH gives a series of instructions to Jeremiah concerning a loincloth, and he carries out each set of instructions (13:1–2, 3–5, 6–7). At the end, YHWH explains the meaning of the object lesson (13:8–11).

**13:1–2**. The linen loincloth was effectively ancient Israelite underwear. It was linen, as that was far cooler and more comfortable than the alternative fabric, wool. Some interpret this to be a belt (Lalleman 2013, 144), but a belt was typically of leather. Also, Jeremiah was to put it on his "loins" (מָתְנַיִם). Although the Hebrew term can be somewhat ambiguous, here it certainly means his waist and genitals. He was not to wash it after he had worn it, probably in order to hasten its decay, as described in the following verses.

**13:3–5**. YHWH commanded Jeremiah to take the loincloth "to Perath" (פְּרָתָה). Although this could be translated as "to the Euphrates," that is almost certainly not what is meant. The Euphrates was roughly seven hundred miles away, and Jeremiah made two round trips to the location where he buried the loincloth. Perath, also called Parah, was a village about three miles from Jeremiah's hometown of Anathoth (Lundbom 2008a, 669). At Perath, Jeremiah buried the loincloth under a rock.

**13:6–7**. After an unspecified length of time, Jeremiah went back and retrieved the loincloth. The fabric, having been exposed to dirt, moisture, and changes of temperature, was ruined.

**13:8–11**. God explained the meaning of the prophetic sign. Three principal lessons are evident. First, the loincloth represented Israel's intimate relationship with YHWH. Although it seems strange to us to present it in this way, the fact that a loincloth sits up against a person's genitals is metaphorical for how Israel was close to YHWH and cherished by him. Second, Israel was arrogant about their position as the chosen people and the ruin of the loincloth showed how their pride would turn to shame. YHWH was their God, but he would repudiate them and send them away. Third, burying the loincloth at Perath symbolized their coming exile to Babylon, on the Euphrates River. Jeremiah buried the loincloth specifically at Perath (and not at some other place) because the name פְּרָת can refer to the Euphrates. As the loincloth was buried at Perath (פְּרָת), so Israel would be sent away to the Euphrates (פְּרָת).

*The Jars Filled with Wine (13:12–14)*

Using an apparently pointless truism concerning wine jars, YHWH tells Jeremiah and Judah that their total destruction is inescapable.

**13:12**. The container mentioned here (נֵבֶל) was an earthenware flask that held wine. It was not a "wineskin," because although these might burst, they would not be subject to shattering. The container appears to be a smaller vessel used for drinking, not the large containers used for long-term storage.

**13:13–14**. The statement that every wine flask would be filled with wine was a truism so obvious it was almost tautological, somewhat like the statement, "President Grant is buried in Grant's Tomb." The intent was for the people to realize that the prophet did not make pointless statements and to thus reflect over what his point might be. The text itself gives us the outline of an interpretation. First, everyone in Jerusalem, from highest to lowest, would be filled with wine. This suggests drunkenness and folly; the implication is that all the people would embrace lies and behave stupidly. It does not necessarily mean that everyone would literally become drunk, but it might imply that they would also engage in self-indulgence. Second, this calls to mind the familiar image of forcing the wicked to drink from the cup of the wrath of God (Ps. 75:8 [MT 9]; Isa. 51:17; Jer. 25:15;

Ezek. 23:32; Hab. 2:16). Third, God will smash the wine flasks against one another, shattering them. Brother will smash against brother and children against parents, suggesting great disharmony in society at the time YHWH's wrath falls upon them. Fourth, the fact that the wine jugs were full prior to being smashed suggests that the people were prosperous and falsely assumed that all would be well, when in fact they were being set up for a terrible fall.

### *Jerusalem Cannot Repent (13:15–27)*

The central problem, YHWH asserts, is not that he is unwilling to forgive; it is that the whole of Judah is hopelessly perverse and cannot repent. To this end, YHWH first appeals for them to change their way, knowing that they will not (13:15–21), and then he describes their incorrigible nature (13:22–27).

#### *The Appeal to Repent (13:15–21)*

The appeal is in four parts: a general appeal to turn back to God (13:15–17), an appeal directed to the royal house (13:18–19), a warning of calamity coming from the north (13:20a), and a warning to Daughter Jerusalem over how greatly she will suffer (13:20b–21).

**13:15–17**. This is a general appeal to all the people to repent. Pride, verse 15 implies, is the greatest impediment to repentance. The call to "give glory to YHWH your God" (v. 16) is an appeal for them to acknowledge their guilt (see Josh. 7:19; 1 Sam. 6:5; Mal. 2:2; John 9:24). The darkness that verse 16 threatens represents dark days in the sense of calamity, but it also implies that when disaster strikes, the people will stumble as though blind and not know what to do. In verse 17, it is not clear whether the one who weeps is YHWH or Jeremiah, but it probably does not matter. Both God and the prophet grieve over the people's stubbornness and ruin.

**13:18–19**. The king and queen mother mentioned here are apparently Jehoiachin and his mother Nehushta (2 Kings 24:8), implying that this message comes from the year of Jehoiachin's exile to Babylon, 597 B.C. They lost their crowns in the sense that they had been deposed from rule; Nebuchadnezzar replaced Jehoiachin with his uncle, Zedekiah. Thus, they lost all status and must abase themselves (הַשְׁפִּילוּ). The cities of the south are closed off (סֻגְּרוּ) in the sense of being under siege, with gates closed and the towns cut off from the capital. It is possible that עָרֵי הַנֶּגֶב means "store cities" instead of "cities of the Negev" (that is, of the south), indicating that all of Judah's fortified supply cities are under siege (Holladay 1986, 408). Either way, the meaning is that the royal house has lost control of its own territory. The statement that everyone has gone into exile is hyperbole; the exile in 597 was relatively small.

**13:20a**. Verse 20a is distinct from 20b–21. The former addresses the whole people, using the second masculine plural pronoun (for example, "Lift your eyes" [שְׂאוּ עֵינֵיכֶם]), while the latter uses the second feminine singular (for example, "What will you say?" [מַה־תֹּאמְרִי]). Verse 20a calls all the people to look up and see that the northern enemy (Babylon) is on the horizon.

**13:20b–21**. The Hebrew of verse 21 is very difficult, and many interpreters consider it to be corrupted beyond recovery. The standard translation (as in the NIV, ESV, and CSB) is difficult to justify, and it seems to be a case of every translation copying those that went before it. However, 20b–21 addresses Daughter Jerusalem throughout, and it seems to treat her as a shepherdess who is gripped by panic when she realizes she has lost her flock. A possible translation is as follows:

> Where is the flock that was given to you?
>
> Where are your splendid sheep?

> What will you say when [the flock] goes missing on account of you?
>
> [When] on account of you [sheep that were] docile to [you as] leader [go missing]?
>
> Haven't pains seized you as when a woman is in labor?

Daughter Jerusalem is here primarily the leadership in the community—the royal house, aristocracy, and priesthood. The metaphor as a leader as the "shepherd" of the people is very common in the Old Testament, but here the shepherd is the aristocratic rulers personified as Lady Jerusalem. They are warned that if they do not repent, they will lose everything and suffer the shame of having failed those whom they were entrusted to care for.

> *THE TRANSLATION OF JEREMIAH 13:21*
> One should repoint יִפְקֹד to the niphal יִפָּקֵד with the meaning, "it will go missing" (Holladay 1986, 413–14). Even if the qal is retained, it means "one demands an account [for the lost sheep]" and thus has the same intent as the niphal. The preposition עַל, as it commonly does, here means "on account of" (Gen. 20:3; Jer. 1:16; an especially close parallel is Ps. 44:23 [עָלֶיךָ הֹרַגְנוּ, "on account of you we are slain"]). אַלּוּף means "gentle" or "tame," as in Jeremiah 11:19, which speaks of a "gentle lamb" (כֶּבֶשׂ אַלּוּף). The expression לְרֹאשׁ ("to a head") is admittedly difficult, but רֹאשׁ often denotes leadership. So understood, אַלֻּפִים לְרֹאשׁ is literally "tame to a leader." I suggest that it means that the people, the metaphorical flock, tamely submitted to the aristocracy as their leaders.

## *Jerusalem the Incorrigible (13:22–27)*

YHWH explains to Jeremiah and his people why destruction must come to all the people. In general terms, they are a depraved people (13:22, 24–26) and well beyond any capacity to recognize their own evil and turn from it (13:23). Their specific sins, moreover, are abominable in God's sight (13:27).

**13:22**. The text again speaks of Jerusalem as a woman, and the language here is especially harsh. It says, "Your skirts are exposed; your heels suffer violence" (נִגְלוּ שׁוּלַיִךְ נֶחְמְסוּ עֲקֵבָיִךְ). But the exposure of the woman's "skirt" is a euphemism for the violent exposure of her genitals, and the "heels" are also a sexual euphemism. She will suffer violent rape (Thompson 1980, 373). This is an apt description of what happened both literally and figuratively when an ancient city was sacked by its enemies.

**13:23**. Jerusalem is incorrigibly evil and is no more likely to improve than a leopard is likely to change its spots. The metaphor of an Ethiopian being unable to change his (black) skin offends modern readers, who detect racism here. But for Jeremiah, it is merely a metaphor; it is not a condemnation of Ethiopians, as though their skin color made them evil. Racial prejudice, as we understand it, seems to have been rare or unknown in ancient Israel. They, like many peoples of the ancient and medieval world, did prefer lighter skin to darker skin, but that was an economic and class prejudice, not a racial prejudice. People who worked the fields had darker skin, and thus it marked them as peasants. In earlier times, women in places as far apart as England and Japan thus wore white makeup to try to make themselves appear more genteel. The lady of Song of Songs protests that she is "black but beautiful" and attributes her dark skin to the fact that her brothers forced her to work in the vineyards (Song 1:5–6). But there is no implication that ethnic groups with dark skin were inferior.

**13:24**. The text briefly switches metaphors: Jerusalem is now like the chaff that the winds drive away (see Ps. 1:4). Since the metaphor has changed to chaff, the text uses a third-person plural pronoun for Jerusalem (וַאֲפִיצֵם; "and I will scatter them") instead of second-person feminine singular.

**13:25–26**. Returning to referring to Jerusalem as a woman, he says that her punishment is what she gets for turning from YHWH to a "lie," referring to their idols. And again, YHWH declares he will expose her to rape, using yet another euphemism for the genitals, that he will expose her "shame" (קָלוֹן).

**13:27**. The promiscuity of Lady Jerusalem is again a metaphor for her apostasy and idolatry. She is as difficult to restrain as a mare in heat. The "hills and fields" where she prostituted herself are the shrines to the many gods she worshiped.

## THEOLOGICAL FOCUS

This passage explores the reasons that Jeremiah had to face the fact that he would not in his lifetime see Judah repentant and restored. Major emphases are:

- When we see evil that we cannot comprehend or face other issues that make us doubt God, we should take those things directly to God in prayer. It is better to complain bluntly to God than not to pray at all. And God does give wisdom, if we combine the bluntness of our questions with faith (James 1:5–6).
- We should not single out one group as the source of all evil, as Jeremiah did early in his prayers to God.
- Sometimes God forces us to see hard facts that we would prefer not to see. This is a test of faith, but it also strengthens faith.
- No person, church, or nation can presume upon God's favor. The sign of the loincloth implied that Israel had been closer to YHWH than any other nation had been, and yet God was willing to destroy them. So also, Jesus threatens to remove the lampstands of churches that turn from him (Rev. 2:5).
- Great prosperity and great folly may both be a prelude to a great destruction, as illustrated by the sign of the filled wine jars.
- People can reach the point that they simply will not repent. We should not lightly give up on people, but we should not be blind to what they are.

## PREACHING AND TEACHING STRATEGIES

### *Exegetical and Theological Synthesis*

How do we respond to God telling Israel that they no longer could repent and be saved from the Babylonian conquest? How did Jeremiah's fellow Jews respond? While this text doesn't tell us, it would seem, that collectively Israel continued to ignore God's words: solidifying God's prophecy. However, Jeremiah's message was also applicable to individuals. A person could still choose to worship and trust YHWH, even though the nation could not. In that situation it was submission to God's will, and in spite of the coming destruction he could be trusted to do what is best and right, as hard and agonizing as that may be for the individual Israelite.

For those already in exile or those reading this after the destruction, it would be easy to believe that there is point of no return because they lived in the result. Perhaps collectively they could have said, "We see it now; our nation was beyond hope, but we are still alive—perhaps we are not beyond that point, but let us never go there again." Judah's descent into evil should warn us that we too can make that descent and not even know it. So, we must daily respond to the Spirit's conviction and continuously rely upon the grace that comes through Jesus so that we will not lose our balance and fall into incorrigible sin.

### *Preaching Idea*

Keep your balance, while you can.

### *Contemporary Connections*

#### *What does it mean?*

In the classic movie *The Sound of Music*, when Maria is meeting the Von Trapp children, Curt, the eleven-year-old, says that he is incorrigible. Apparently, he was trying to frighten the new governess. However, he didn't know what it meant, for he follows up by asking, "What's incorrigible?" To be incorrigible is to be beyond correction. In the rest of this delightful family movie, we see that Curt was not incorrigible. However, ancient Israel was. That is God's message in Jeremiah 12–13. Israel was beyond the point of no return. They were incorrigible. In God's sovereign omniscience he alone knew that Israel would not repent and return to him. So, does that mean the nation no longer had a choice? The short answer is, yes. This does not mean that an individual Jew was incorrigible. God only revealed that *the nation* was at a point of no return. This seems contrary to God's love and mercy. One might think that if Israel had only strayed from the Lord for a few generations, but her disobedience was the pattern from the days of her deliverance from Egypt. Jeremiah found it hard to believe, as do we, that Israel was so far into sin that they could not repent. This does not mean that God was finished with Israel. Another prophet, who also spoke to the exiles, recorded a vision of God restoring life to dry bones. Ezekiel 37 clearly shows that God still had plans for Israel, even after the certain destruction that Jeremiah prophesied was accomplished.

God revealed this hard prophecy to Jeremiah and then reinforced it through the images of the loincloth and the shattered jars. Israel was doomed for destruction. They had reached the point of no return. In searching for a person lost at sea, a plane or ship reaches a point in its mission that there is no longer enough fuel to return to base; it is said to be *beyond the point of no return*. Before that point is reached, they must head for home. They cannot continue the search. This phrase has come to mean that there are no longer certain options available. In WWII on D-day there were numerous gliders used in the attack. An aircraft would tow the glider into the air, across the English Channel, and then the tow cable would be released. The glider would glide for a few miles and land. Once the tow cable was released there was no longer the option of returning to England. Israel had reached the point where there was no longer a choice for them; they were going to be invaded and destroyed because they would not change. It is very important for us to remember that only an omniscient God can know this.

#### *Is it true?*

It is hard to accept that a nation or a person can become incorrigible—that they simply will not repent. This is not an unusual concept. There are numerous times in life when a point of no return is reached. When a gymnast is performing those amazing routines on a four-inch-wide balance beam, it is critical that she maintain her balance. Often it seems when they land on the beam after a flip, they plant their feet, and for a moment seem to lose their balance, but they twist their torso, move an arm or leg, and stay on the beam. But other times they do lose their balance, to the point that there is no possible movement that will keep them from falling. It is a matter of gravity. When a plane lands or takes off there is a point when the pilot is committed; he can no longer abort the takeoff or landing. At a certain day in a college semester a class can no longer be dropped without receiving a failing grade. Jeremiah was beginning to understand that it was possible for the nation to reach such a point, and that point had passed. It is possible for a nation or an individual to reach the point of no return, when they no longer have a choice to repent. On the side of caution, it warrants repeating that only God knows who and when they will reach that point.

*Now what?*

How do we respond to God telling Israel that they no longer could repent and be saved from the Babylonian conquest? How did Jeremiah's fellow Jews respond? While this text doesn't tell us, it would seem that collectively Israel continued to ignore God's words, solidifying God's prophecy. However, Jeremiah's message was also applicable to individuals. A person could still choose to worship and trust YHWH, even though the nation could not. In that situation one could submit to his will, and in spite of the coming destruction trust God to do what is best and right, as hard as it would be. They would perhaps say, "If we are to survive, it will take a miracle."

For those already in exile or those reading this after the destruction, it would be easy to believe that there is a point of no return because they lived in the result. Perhaps collectively they could say, "We see it now; our nation was beyond hope, but we are still alive. Perhaps we are not beyond that point, but let us never go there again."

We must recognize that there is a point of no return. Again, this is only for God to know. But if we dismiss it, then this gracious warning is wasted. The warning is to those who have not trusted Christ: you can get to a point where you will no longer have a choice. If you choose to harden your heart again and again it becomes too hard to change. And to believers: we are secure in God's hands, but we can become so accustomed to our sin that we are insensitive to his prompting. It is living life constantly off-balance. It feels like our lives are constantly falling apart. We don't recognize that this sense of falling is his hand of disciplining love.

In this topic we must remember that whether we are thinking of the person who has not trusted Christ or the believer who has, if you are touched in any way, or remotely concerned about being beyond the point of no return, then you are not.

### *Creativity in Presentation*

Use Jeremiah's opening question as your opening question, and then move into the heart of the sermon just as Jeremiah did. Walk through the passage, examining how Jeremiah was brought to a discovery that Israel was wicked to the point of no return. This message of incorrigibility is very hard to accept, so consider presenting it in two inductive moves. The first is the point of the text. Walk through the text, presenting how Jeremiah may have struggled with the concept. At each point, he comes closer to accepting that Israel's doom is certain. It could be presented as an extension of his opening dialogue with God. Then conclude this first part with Jeremiah being resolved that destruction will happen. Yes, it is possible to reach the point of being incorrigible. The second point is also inductive: answering the question, "How do we respond?" The stating of the preaching idea could come at the end: keep your balance, while you can.

Consider using a very low child's balance beam. The teacher/preacher could try to walk on it, or have someone from the congregation come and participate. There is also value in just having the balance beam on stage. If there are pilots in your congregation, perhaps interview them about that committal moment in takeoff and landing. If they have a "close call" type of story, they could share that as well.

The following two conversations, which are based upon the text, can be presented one after the other; or the points of the second conversation could be presented with the corresponding points in the first.

1. Conversation between Jeremiah and God:

*Jeremiah*: God, I need to talk to you about this sin problem in my nation (12:1–4).
We've had some bad leaders.

*God*: It is worse than that—your nation is rotting in sin (12:5–17).

Here are two object lessons (13:1–14):
The ruined loincloth (13:1–11)
The jars filled with wine (13:12–14)
I call you to repent and humble yourselves (13:15–21).
Yet your nation will become incorrigible (13:22–27).

2. Conversation between me and God:

*Me*: God, I need to talk to you about this sin problem in my life (12:1–4).
I've had some bad leaders.
*God*: It is worse than that—your sin is rotting your life (12:5–17).
Here are two object lessons (13:1–14):
The ruined loincloth (13:1–11)
The jars filled with wine (13:12–14)
I call you to repent and humble yourself 13:15–21).
Yet, you can become incorrigible (13:22–27).

So, keep your balance, while you can.

## DISCUSSION QUESTIONS

1. Why is it hard to accept that there is a point when a person's heart becomes too hard to respond?
2. Are there other examples in Scripture where a person was beyond repentance?
3. Why can only God know who is truly incorrigible?
4. How should this truth affect our attitude toward those who seem incorrigible?
5. Can Christians become incorrigible and not lose their salvation?

## Jeremiah 14:1–15:9

**EXEGETICAL IDEA**

This text recounts three episodes in which Jeremiah prayed for Jerusalem. In each case, he received a negative response from God. Jerusalem did not fall because Jeremiah failed to pray for them or because he was unworthy; it fell because the people were incorrigibly apostate. This and similar passages exonerate Jeremiah from the charge that the fall of Jerusalem was somehow his fault.

**THEOLOGICAL FOCUS**

Prayer for sinners is the duty of the servant of God, but this does not mean that the servant can always turn aside God's wrath. Jeremiah, in particular, was a great prophet and as such, his words, so to speak, carried great weight with God. Jeremiah was not allowed to waste or misuse his prophetic authority, asking God for something that God could not grant.

**PREACHING IDEA**

We don't know who will be saved; all we know is that we should pray.

**PREACHING POINTERS**

Would that we would be more like Jeremiah. Hmm . . . *should* he be our example? He had to be told to stop praying; in fact, God took time to convince him that he must stop interceding for Judah.

In contrast, we must be convinced to start praying. We hold churchwide prayer events, promote the importance of prayer, and might even provide a meal to bolster attendance. We must be convinced to *start* praying, not to *stop*. In an ironic way, God's word to Jeremiah to not pray becomes our directive to pray. The reason is, we do not have the office of an Old Testament prophet, and God has not revealed to us who will and who will not repent. While God directs Jeremiah to not intercede, the point of this passage is that we should.

# THREE MORE EPISODES OF FAILED INTERCESSION (14:1–15:9)

## LITERARY STRUCTURE AND THEMES

This passage contains three more episodes in which Jeremiah interceded for Judah, and in each case got a discouraging word from YHWH (the first episode is in 12:1–17). Continuing the theme of the previous passage, it tracks his journey away from interceding for his nation. The following three episodes did not necessarily all happen at the same time, and they did not necessarily occur in the sequence given here. But Jeremiah has arranged the accounts in this way so that the reader can see how, despite his desire to pray for Jerusalem and see his people saved, God himself dissuaded him from continuing to hope and pray. This text repeats this same pattern three times: Jeremiah intercedes (14:1–9, 13, 19–22) and YHWH responds (14:10–12, 14–18; 15:1–9).

- ***Jeremiah's First Intercession, over Drought (14:1–9)***
- ***YHWH's Response (14:10–12)***
- ***Jeremiah's Second Intercession, over False Prophets (14:13)***
- ***YHWH's Response (14:14–18)***
- ***Jeremiah's Confession and Third Intercession (14:19–22)***
- ***YHWH's Response (15:1–9)***

## EXPOSITION

Jeremiah's first intercession concerns a drought. This was evidently quite severe, although apart this text the book only refers to it obliquely. Jeremiah obviously wanted YHWH to end the drought and alleviate Judah's suffering, but YHWH's answer was that things would only get worse.

### *Jeremiah's First Intercession, over Drought (14:1–9)*

The intensity of this drought is evident in the number of times Jeremiah refers to water, springs, rain, or the like in his messages. Evidently the shortage of water was on everyone's mind, and thus he returned again and again to the language of water: Judah abandoned YHWH, the source of living water, to go to broken cisterns or to seek water from the nations (2:13, 18). The land is parched, but the proud people do not turn to YHWH, who gives rain (3:3; 5:24; 10:13). Judah may be arid, but its evil wells up like an abundant spring (6:7). The only water YHWH gives them is bitter and unpotable (8:14; 9:15; 23:15). Jeremiah wishes his eyes were a fountain of tears (9:1), but he fears YHWH will abandon him and be to him like a stream that fails (15:18). The wicked man is like a shrub in the desert, but the righteous man is like a tree planted beside an unfailing channel of water (17:6, 8, 13). In the great day of salvation, YHWH will lead Israel beside flowing rivers of water (31:9). Babylon is blessed to sit beside many waters, but someday YHWH will dry it up (51:13, 36). In 14:1–12, however, Jeremiah speaks of the drought directly.

**14:1**. The passage does not tell us when the drought took place, but it probably happened in the reign of Jehoiakim, perhaps in late 601 (Holladay 1986, 429). The word used here for "drought" (בַּצָּרָה, evidently the equivalent of בַּצֹּרֶת, found in 17:8) is here plural (הַבַּצָּרוֹת, "the droughts"). This probably implies a lengthy, severe drought, in which several rainy seasons passed with no rain. This verse is the superscript to a psalm (vv. 2–9) composed by Jeremiah as a lament and prayer for relief from the calamity.

**14:2–6**. The psalm begins with a general description of the lamentation of the people (v. 2), and then (vv. 3–6) gives the reason for it: The land is parched. The drought afflicts first the nobility (v. 3), then the farmers (v. 4), then the vulnerable wildlife (v. 5), and finally the hardiest wildlife (v. 6). The nobility are those whose wealth normally allows them to escape the suffering that afflicts the commoners, but in this case it does not. The farmers are especially vulnerable, since their livelihood and lives depend on their crops. All people, regardless of rank, cover their heads in sorrow because they are undone (vv. 3–4; see 1 Sam. 15:30). The doe that recently fawned is particularly in need of water and grass because she needs to suckle her young, but she has none. The wild donkeys of the desert would be the creatures most capable of enduring drought, but even they are desperate for water and quickly failing. All creatures, both human and animal, suffer regardless of their resources or natural gifts.

**14:7**. Having described in detail the crisis that confronts Judah, Jeremiah calls on God's help. He first confesses Judah's sin, a necessary prerequisite to an appeal to God. The problem is that he alone is making the confession; the people do not join him in repentance. Still, this does not mean that his action is wrong. Daniel also made a representative prayer on behalf of his people, in which he confessed their sin (Dan. 9:4–19). In Daniel's case, however, Judah had already been punished; in Jeremiah's case, they had not been punished and were not repentant.

**14:8–9**. In calling on God to act, Jeremiah speaks boldly, seeming to criticize God. He uses two metaphors, first comparing God to a stranger who is passing through and only staying for the night, and thus has no real concern for the well-being of the city in which he so briefly sojourns. He then compares God to a warrior who is caught by surprise and therefore unable to resist the events that have overtaken him. The first metaphor implies that God does not care about Jerusalem, while the second implies that God is unable to save. We should understand that Jeremiah is merely voicing his anguish and frustration; he is not saying that he literally believes these things. Furthermore, Old Testament prayers are, by our standards, often very direct in their complaints (see, for example, Pss. 10:1; 22:1; 44:23–24; 74:1). Jeremiah's language reflects his disquiet and confusion; he wants to understand the justice of God's apparent indifference to Judah's suffering.

### *YHWH's Response (14:10–12)*

YHWH tersely responds to Jeremiah that he must punish Judah and that Jeremiah must stop praying for his people.

**14:10**. YHWH bluntly tells Jeremiah that the drought is punishment for the nation's sin and that he will not save them. The wandering of the feet represents how the people habitually and happily turn from YHWH and the covenant. And matters have come to a breaking point. YHWH must "now" (עַתָּה) punish them.

**14:11–12**. In an astonishing turn, YHWH tells Jeremiah to stop praying for the people. Furthermore, he will not give heed to their supplications, though they make it with fasting and sacrifice. Behind this seemingly incomprehensible command is the Old Testament understanding of the authority of the prophet. God so respects Jeremiah, as he respected the other great prophets, that he will not proceed with the punishment until Jeremiah stops praying for them. But proceed he must. We have many examples of high prophetic authority: Moses interceded for Israel when God was ready to kill them all, and God heeded his prayer and relented (Exod. 32:11–14). On the other hand, an angry and discouraged Elijah complained against the people. Although he rebuked Elijah, God commissioned three agents of death and destruction against Israel (1 Kings 19:4–18). An irritated Elisha cursed some children who were mocking him, and two bears rushed out and slaughtered them (2 Kings 2:23–24). The point here is that we should be hesitant to apply lessons to ourselves from God's command to Jeremiah. He had been given great authority (Jer. 1:10), and what was true of him is not necessarily true of us.

### *Jeremiah's Second Intercession, over False Prophets (14:13)*

Jeremiah appeals to God on the grounds that the people are being misled. In this instance, God's answer is much longer than Jeremiah's prayer.

**14:13**. On the surface, Jeremiah in this verse does no more than tell God that many of Israel's prophets promise imminent deliverance from all their troubles. But there is an implied appeal for mercy in this prayer: the people are not to blame; they only believe the people who, as far as they know, are YHWH's spokesmen. This is, therefore, another intercession for Judah.

### *YHWH's Response (14:14–18)*

YHWH answers Jeremiah in two parts, the first in prose and the second in a poetic lament.

**14:14–16**. God's prose answer is straightforward and unambiguous: The prophets who predict salvation for Judah are lying. YHWH has not spoken to them, and they will all die by the calamities that they say will never come. Apostasy causes religious leaders to embrace every manner of falsehood, and they concoct theological justification for seeing what they want to see, a "lying vision" (חֲזוֹן שֶׁקֶר, v. 14). Furthermore, the lies they speak have serious consequences: The people are indeed misled, but that will not excuse them. They will perish for having preferred these prophets to Jeremiah.

**14:17–18**. Having commanded Jeremiah not to pray for this people, YHWH gives him the words he is to speak to them. It is a poetic lament, in which Jeremiah declares that it is not for hatred of the people that he has ceased to pray for them. His heart is broken as he sees his country dying, but he can do no more than weep. He cannot use his prophetic power to make it stop. The last line of verse 18 is difficult, but I do not think it can be translated to mean that the priests and prophets will wander in a land they do not know. The line does not describe *how* God will punish them (by sending prophets and priests into exile) but *why* he must punish. The initial "because" (כִּי) implies that this line is an explanation, telling how the prophets and priests brought about the ruin of the nation. Giving the Hebrew words their conventional meanings, the line says, "Because both prophet and priest peddle [their lies] to a land, and they do not know [the truth]." The religious hierarchy are like traveling merchants, and Judah is simply "a land"—a place to find customers. "And they do not know" is purposely ambiguous. The priests and prophets speak in YHWH's name but don't know what they are talking about, and the people don't know that they are being deceived by men for whom the faith is only a way to make money.

> *THE TRANSLATION OF 14:18c*
>
> The text, כִּי־גַם־נָבִיא גַם־כֹּהֵן סָחֲרוּ אֶל־אֶרֶץ וְלֹא יָדָעוּ, explains why (כִּי) all the suffering has come to Judah. The verb סחר probably means "to trade as a traveling merchant" throughout the Old Testament (Holladay 1986, 437). It does not mean simply "to wander," notwithstanding the arguments of Speiser and others (Speiser 1974, 264–65). Also, the conjunction ו in וְלֹא יָדָעוּ goes against the standard translation "a land *that* they do not know." It means, "And they do not know (what they are talking about)." And if סחר is understood to mean that the priests and prophets "peddle" something, it is clear that what they are selling is their false teachings and visions.

### *Jeremiah's Confession and Third Intercession (14:19–22)*

In this episode, the prayer is short but follows the standard pattern for intercessory prayer in the Old Testament (14:19–22). There is nothing worthy of censure in Jeremiah's prayer. It could be considered a model prayer of intercession for his people. Even so, YHWH rejects it (15:1–9). This is not because Jeremiah was unworthy, but because the people's sin was so severe that nothing could turn YHWH aside from punishing the nation.

**14:19–21**. In another blunt prayer, Jeremiah voices bewilderment that YHWH despises Judah. Such bluntness is not problematic or unusual in the prayers of ancient Israel. It is, as it were, a way of getting God's attention and does not imply a lack of piety or respect. He admits that they have a history of sinning against God. Jeremiah fully understands that Judah's survival depends upon God's grace, and he hopes God will relent—if for no other reason than because God does not want his name and honor to fall into reproach. In this, he echoes the intercession of Moses for Israel in Exodus 32. Jeremiah's prayer is both conventional and laudable; it is the kind of prayer an Old Testament prophet *ought* to voice for his people.

**14:22**. In what is almost an appendix to his prayer, Jeremiah declares that salvation is in YHWH alone, and not in the idols of the nations. This, too, is common in such prayers; Jonah concludes his prayer of thanksgiving for salvation with a similar confession (Jon. 2:8). Here, Jeremiah declares that only YHWH can send the rain. This implies that this intercession came sometime during Judah's drought.

### *YHWH's Response (15:1–9)*

In this response, YHWH categorically declares that continued intercession for Judah will do no good. Jerusalem's destruction is decreed and will not be revoked, and all the prior blessings of being the covenant people will be turned upside down. Judah will be an accursed nation in the eyes of all people.

**15:1**. As Jeremiah did in 14:21, Moses appealed to God to forgive Israel for the sake of his honor and his promise (Exod. 32:12–13). And Jeremiah interceded persistently for Judah; in this, he was like Samuel, who said, "I will not sin against YHWH by ceasing to pray for you" (1 Sam. 12:23). Against this, YHWH bluntly declared that even if Moses and Samuel were standing before him at that moment making appeals in Judah's behalf, he would not listen. Jeremiah's prayers had no chance of changing God's mind, but this was not because of a failure on Jeremiah's part.

**15:2–3**. YHWH commanded that the people of Judah be sent away, implying that he would no longer have anything to do with them. If they should take the command literally and ask where they should go, the answer was a poetic epigram: each should go where he was destined to go—to death, the sword, famine, or exile. This means that their destruction has been decreed, and there would be no turning back from it. The list has artificially been expanded to four categories. There are only two fates (death and exile), since the sword and famine are just different forms of death. But the number four is common to apocalyptic and judgmental texts, such as Daniel 2:36–43; 7:3; Hosea 13:7–8; Revelation 6:1–8. YHWH adds another set of four apocalyptic agents of death in verse 3: the sword, the dogs, the birds, and other wild animals. Again, the list is somewhat artificial, since the sword does not fit with the other three, and the dogs (which are certainly feral) are themselves wild animals. But the meaning is that God will bring an apocalyptic calamity down upon them.

**15:4**. It is striking that this passage lays major responsibility for the fall of Jerusalem at the feet of King Manasseh (reigned 696–642 B.C.), since he died before many of Jeremiah's contemporaries were born. Like this verse, 2 Kings 24:1–4 also blames Manasseh for the calamity. Manasseh was indeed among the worst of Judah's kings, as he sponsored every type of idolatrous practice in Jerusalem, including child sacrifice (2 Kings 21:2–6). It seems odd that the people should be punished for the sins of a king who ruled when their grandfathers were young men. But probably the implication is that they continued to practice the sins of Manasseh, the archetype for their apostasy. Jerusalem never truly recovered from the spiritual damage Manasseh did.

**15:5–7**. As Jerusalem forsook YHWH, so YHWH will see to it that everyone forsakes Jerusalem. YHWH's declaration, "I am weary of relenting" (נִלְאֵיתִי הִנָּחֵם) alludes to the conclusion of Moses's intercession for Israel, in which "YHWH relented" (וַיִּנָּחֶם יְהוָה) from bringing death and disaster upon the people (Exod. 32:14). YHWH had been holding back not just since the time of Manasseh but ever since the time of the golden calf.

**15:8**. The threat to make Judah's widows more numerous than the sand on the shore alludes to the promise to the patriarchs: that God would make Israel more numerous than the sand (Gen. 22:17). The threat to send a "destroyer" (שֹׁדֵד) against Judah probably alludes to Exodus 12:23, in which God sent "the destroyer" against the firstborn of the Egyptians, although the word used there is different (הַמַּשְׁחִית instead of שֹׁדֵד). The implication is that the former blessings upon Israel would be reversed, and the great plagues that YHWH once sent upon Israel's enemies would come to Israel.

**15:9**. The "mother of seven" is a woman who normally would have no fear for her future because she has plenty of children to care for her in her old age. But now the woman (representing Jerusalem) would see her sons perish and would herself expire. "Her sun will set" means as a metaphor that her hope has failed; contrast Malachi 4:2, in which the sun rises upon Israel with healing in its wings.

## THEOLOGICAL FOCUS

The following theological points emerge from this text:

- Although Jeremiah's prayers were turned back, it is the duty of every servant of God to pray for sinners.
- We can intercede for others, but we cannot repent for them.
- Poor leaders can do great damage to a people. Still, the people are responsible for their own decisions and will not be exempted from punishment because of those who led them.
- Just as there can be a godly heritage, there can also be a sinful legacy, as illustrated by Manasseh. And such a legacy can do lasting and great damage.
- Former blessings are no guarantee of future blessings. If people become apostate, God can turn those blessings on their heads.

## PREACHING AND TEACHING STRATEGIES

### *Exegetical and Theological Synthesis*

In the last section Jeremiah discovered that Israel had gone beyond repentance. Their doom would come. Now he is discovering that God doesn't want him to pray for their welfare, which logically follows God's message that Israel was incorrigible. If their doom was sure, then Jeremiah should not pray for them. Jeremiah seems to disobey God by continuing to pray for Israel. Apparently, God is having another dialogue with Jeremiah. This time God is patiently making it firm that Jeremiah is not to intercede for Judah.

So, does this mean that we are not to pray for those whom we know or think to be incorrigible? We must remember that the unique office of the Old Testament prophet gave the prophet a level of communication with God that we do not have. Since we don't know and God has not told us who will not come to faith or are seemingly incorrigible, we must continue to pray. The point the Jeremiah was making for the exiles, and for us, is that we should pray for the lost and for those who are believers in Jesus but are not living as they should.

### *Preaching Idea*

We don't know who will be saved; all we know is that we should pray.

### *Contemporary Connections*

#### *What does it mean?*

It seems that Jeremiah struggled to not pray for his nation. It was contrary to what Jeremiah instinctively wanted to do and what prophets were supposed to do. Though the chronology may be unclear, Jeremiah had already recorded two other times that God told him not to pray (7:16; 11:14). But he still prayed. It would seem that God was being patient with Jeremiah. Since this was so foreign to Jeremiah's thinking, God listened to these three intercessions and did not correct him for still praying. This affirms that God is patient and merciful, which should cause us to continue to pray on behalf of others. While Jeremiah struggled to not pray, our struggle seems the opposite.

David Brainerd, an eighteenth-century missionary, was one who interceded for the lost: "I wrestled for absent friends, for the ingathering of souls, for multitudes of poor souls, and for many that I thought were the children of God, personally, in many distant places. I was in such agony from sun half an hour high toll near dark that I was all over wet with sweat, but yet it seemed to me I had done nothing. O, my dear savior did sweat blood for our poor souls! I longed for more compassion towards them" (Edwards, ed., Brainerd 2006, 43). His words are still exemplary.

#### *Is it true?*

This passage doesn't tell how to pray for the seemingly incorrigible—but that we should. Are we asking that God violate their free will? Of course not. We pray that their eyes would be opened, so that they can make wise decisions. S. D. Gordon, in his classic book on prayer, says when we pray for an unrepentant person, "We pray to get the dust out of his eyes so that his sight shall be clear" (Gordon 1904, 193). In the same book Gordon tells the story of an unnamed congressman from a western state who was called to be a pastor as a boy but became a skeptic. (It was the style of the early twentieth century for preachers not to mention specific names or dates.) He became a lawyer, and his career showed that he was a natural leader. He was elected to Congress for four terms and was in line to be the governor of his state. He had fully rejected God and had this reinforced by friends and fellow skeptics. One evening while in Washington, it came to his mind that God was concerned about him. He reasoned that this fleeting thought was only because he had been working too hard. He went for a walk to clear his head but he could not chase the thought away. For four months he wrestled with the thought that God cared about him. When he returned to his home state, he found out that his wife and two friends had begun praying for his salvation four months earlier. He later came to faith and returned to his calling as a pastor (Gordon, 1904, 200–205).

No doubt many who are reading this have prayed for lost friends and relatives. My wife and I prayed for a friend for years. We were eating dinner with him and his wife when the subject of belief in Christ came up. To our surprise, he clearly stated that he was a believer in Christ. We asked him, "Tell us more. How did this come about?" He answered, "John." We responded, "John? Who do you mean?" His answer was delightful, "The book, you know, John, in the Bible." He had attended a church where the pastor was preaching through the gospel of John. We are glad we didn't stop praying. Yet, at this writing I have been praying for another friend for six years. While our friendship is deeper than it ever has been, he still says that others can believe in God and he is glad that they do, but he will not. So, I keep praying.

*Now what?*

This section closes with a reference to Manasseh, perhaps the most wicked king ever to rule the Jews. Though not recorded here, the Chronicler tells us that after God's disciplining hand that sent him in to exile, Manasseh repented and was restored as king. His repentance was validated by his actions, as he tried to be a godly king, though for only a few short years. When we combine Jeremiah's recounting of his evil reign with the end of the story in 2 Chronicles 33, it gives us an example that we do not know who is incorrigible. If anyone would have been considered incorrigible, it would have been Manasseh. We are commanded to pray even for those we think are incorrigible. Perhaps there was someone who prayed for Manasseh. For whom are we praying?

***Creativity in Presentation***

A tension of this passage is that God told Jeremiah to stop praying, and yet it seems that he continued to pray. This can be used to create a tension in the sermon. After presenting the text in which God tells Jeremiah to stop praying, the question can be raised as to whether or not Jeremiah will stop. Or it could be presented as an observation: "It seems that Jeremiah is continuing to pray." These intercessions and God's responses can be presented with this tension in mind. After presenting these three intercessions and God's response, then present the explanation as to why Jeremiah kept praying and what that teaches us. This leads into the application.

There are many examples, particularly in missionary biographies, of people praying for the lost and then those very people come to faith. There are also numerous publications about how to pray for the lost. Most mission agencies have suggestions, in booklet form and online, as to how to pray for the lost. Often pastors have given out objects that reminding people to pray: plastic bracelets, bookmarkers, refrigerator magnets, etc. These are good to use, but far better is the examples from one's own life or the lives of the congregation. Depending upon your congregation, this sermon could be applied immediately by having them break into small groups of three or four to pray. Or ask your listeners to establish a relationship with a prayer partner to pray specifically for those who need to repent. Here is one possible structure:

- God patiently convinces Jeremiah to not intercede for Judah.

- Applying this to our prayer life, we must remember the uniqueness of an OT prophet.
    - OT prophets' prayers are different than ours.
    - God reveals to Jeremiah that Judah will not change.

- God invites us to intercede:
    - For the lost
    - For the wayward believer

- Let's intercede, right now (move into a time of prayer).

## DISCUSSION QUESTIONS

1. What happens in our hearts when we are consistently praying for a lost friend or relative?

2. What are some reasons that people stop praying for others?

3. Is praying for someone to turn to God hard work? Why?

4. How should we handle letting others know that we are praying for them?

5. Why are we tempted to think we know who is incorrigible?

# Jeremiah 15:10–17:18

**EXEGETICAL IDEA**

This passage is a decisive turning point in the book. It explores Jeremiah's abandonment of intercession for Judah and his realization that the human heart is incurably evil. As Jeremiah awakens to this reality, he becomes more isolated and frustrated. Still, this text is a vindication of Jeremiah. A complaint against him might be that Jerusalem fell because he was not a great enough prophet to avert disaster. In fact, its destruction was delayed while he prayed for it, and he only stopped because he had to yield to God's demand to stop interceding. He also had to face the facts about the nature of his people. This was not a triumphal moment for Jeremiah; it was the occasion for bitter sorrow.

**THEOLOGICAL FOCUS**

The message that people are wicked is a hard one, and it is hard on the messenger. Perhaps more clearly than anyone in the Old Testament, Jeremiah looked fully into the corruption of the human heart. Knowing that this was true of the people he loved was especially bitter for him. The doctrine of human depravity should always be a source of grief, and not of smug self-righteousness.

**PREACHING IDEA**

A hard message is hard on the messenger.

**PREACHING POINTERS**

This seems like a very negative, downer kind of passage to preach/teach. And it would be, were it not for the promise of redemption, seen briefly in this passage (16:14–15) and reoccurring throughout Scripture.

When we grasp the wickedness of our hearts, we will be reaching for forgiveness and redemption. When the need for forgiveness and redemption is great, so the joy is great when it comes. If we only needed a little help with our hearts, then there would be little joy. It is well worth the pain of admitting that my heart is wicked in order to experience the joy of forgiveness and redemption that comes through the cross. This passage presents an insurmountable problem, with the rest of Scripture providing the solution.

# THE STRUGGLING PROPHET (15:10–17:18)

## LITERARY STRUCTURE AND THEMES

In the previous passages, Jeremiah interceded for Judah but received no encouraging word from God. The people's sin was such that the people could not escape destruction, and Jeremiah should stop asking for the punishment to be revoked. In this text, we see the progression of Jeremiah's thought. He stops interceding, but he deeply grieves over his situation. He is a prophet to a people who are condemned by God, who bitterly resent him and his message, and who are ready to kill him. He thus enters into a somewhat angry dialogue with God. In the end, however, he affirms God's judgment and calls down God's wrath on Judah.

- ***Jeremiah Laments and Complains (15:10–21)***
- ***Two Object Lessons (16:1–9)***
- ***Jerusalem Cannot Repent (16:10–17:4)***
- ***A Meditation on the Human Condition (17:5–11)***
- ***Jeremiah's Prayer (17:12–18)***

## EXPOSITION

### *Jeremiah Laments and Complains (15:10–21)*

Jeremiah opens his dialogue with God first by offering a lament over his troubles, and then by complaining that God had failed him. In both cases, God answers Jeremiah and enables him to work through his sorrow.

#### *Jeremiah Laments His Situation (15:10)*

**15:10.** This should be translated as follows:

> Woe to me, my mother, that you bore me,
> a man of conflict and strife against the whole land!
> I have not been a moneylender and they are not in debt to me,
> but all curse me!

The third line is often translated like the NIV, "I have neither lent nor borrowed," but in fact both parts of the line compare Jeremiah to the hated moneylender. In premodern societies, people universally despised these men, as illustrated by the contempt for Shylock in *The Merchant of Venice.*

> *THE TRANSLATION OF 15:10*
>
> The verb נשא (here in a byform, II-נשה) is oddly ambiguous, meaning both to borrow and to lend. Here, the verb appears twice: first absolutely and then with an object governed by בְּ. The closest parallel is at Isaiah 24:2, כַּנֹּשֶׁה כַּאֲשֶׁר נֹשֶׁא בוֹ ("as the lender [נֹשֶׁה], so the one who borrows from him [נֹשֶׁא בוֹ]"). In Jeremiah 15:10, however, the subject is first the prophet, who has not loaned money (נשה used absolutely), and then the people, who have not borrowed money (נשה used with an object governed by בְּ). Thus, both halves of the parallel speak of Jeremiah as being treated like a moneylender.

#### *YHWH Reassures Jeremiah (15:11–14)*

These verses are very difficult in Hebrew, and the standard translations are not persuasive. A better translation, I suggest, is as follows:

> 11YHWH said, "I have in fact armored you to good purpose; I have in fact imposed the enemy on you in an evil time and in a distressing time. 12Can [your enemy] break iron—northern iron—and bronze? 13I will

give your estate and your wealth as plunder, [but] not as a price [to be paid]—neither for any of your sins, nor [for the sins committed] in all of your country. [14]And I will make your enemy cross over to a land you do not know, because a fire has been kindled in my wrath; it burns against your [people]."

*THE TRANSLATION OF 15:11–14*

In verse 11, major translations commonly take the *qere* verb שֵׁרִיתִךָ to be the piel of שׁרה with the meaning "deliver" or "set free." But this root occurs only once (Job 37:3, where in the qal it is used of God releasing lightning bolts). Also, it is not clear in what sense YHWH has set Jeremiah free. A much better explanation is that שֵׁרִיתִךָ is from a different root שׁרה, a denominative of the noun שִׁרְיוֹן, meaning "armor" (Holladay 1986, 446 note b). This is an allusion to Jeremiah's call narrative, in which YHWH armored him to face his enemies (1:18). Also in verse 11, the hiphil of פגע does not mean to "plead," whether of YHWH pleading with the enemy (ESV) or the enemy pleading with Jeremiah (NIV). The closest parallel is at Isaiah 53:6, "and YHWH imposed on him (וַיהוָה הִפְגִּיעַ בּוֹ [personal recipient with בְּ]) the iniquity of us all (אֵת עֲוֹן כֻּלָּנוּ [direct object with אֵת])." The verb פגע essentially means to impose; from that it can mean to assault someone (Judg. 8:21) or to urge someone to do something (Ruth 1:16). Thus, we have, "I have imposed on you (הִפְגַּעְתִּי בְךָ) . . . the enemy (אֶת־הָאֹיֵב)," meaning that YHWH has set the enemy against Jeremiah. Verse 12, moreover, is not an impersonal proverb about iron; the "enemy" from verse 11 is the subject. The question is not whether someone in general can break iron; it is whether Jeremiah's enemies can break the iron with which God has armored him. Verse 13 is especially difficult, and the standard translations make little sense. However, we can propose a reasonable solution. First, the message is given to Jeremiah, not to the people of Jerusalem, and it concerns him, as marked by the second-person singular pronouns in "your wealth and your treasures" (חֵילְךָ וְאוֹצְרוֹתֶיךָ). Second, in לֹא בִמְחִיר וּבְכָל־חַטֹּאותֶיךָ וּבְכָל־גְּבוּלֶיךָ, the negative לֹא governs all three phrases (Holladay 1986, 456). Also, the phrases וּבְכָל־חַטֹּאותֶיךָ and וּבְכָל־גְּבוּלֶיךָ are epexegetical of בִּמְחִיר. But וּבְכָל־גְּבוּלֶיךָ is also locative, indicating where the sins were committed, as in 17:3, בְּחַטָּאת בְּכָל־גְּבוּלֶיךָ, "for the sin in all your country."

**15:11–12**. These verses allude to Jeremiah's calling, in which God said he would fortify Jeremiah like an iron pillar against his adversaries in Judah (1:18). In verse 10, Jeremiah laments over how the whole land was set against him, and YHWH here responds by asserting that he has armored Jeremiah in such a way that they cannot touch him or break him. We are given no specifics of what the metaphor of armor implies. It at least implies that the enemies will not be able to kill him (see 15:21), and that Jeremiah will fulfill his ministry. It also implies that Jeremiah will have the spiritual resources to withstand the animosity directed toward him. He will be like Paul, who was hard-pressed and perplexed, but not crushed or in hopeless despair (2 Cor. 4:8). The armor of God does not mean, however, that Jeremiah would not suffer. Paul certainly suffered a great deal, both physically and emotionally.

**15:13**. God's armor also does not mean that Jeremiah would suffer no loss. To the contrary, he would lose almost all his earthly possessions, including his land. But he could take comfort in the fact that none of this came to him as a punishment for any sins he had committed. He was not held responsible for the sins committed in Judah, even if he suffered alongside his guilty people. This is not cold comfort. To know that one is justified before God is more precious than any amount of property.

**15:14**. God says he will deal with all those who make Jeremiah's life miserable. He will cause them to "cross over" to an unknown land. That is, his Jewish enemies will be exiles and be scattered across the earth.

### *Jeremiah Angrily Complains to YHWH (15:15–18)*

**15:15**. Jeremiah opens his complaint with a pious appeal to God and an imprecation against his enemies. He has not abandoned God, although he is sorely vexed, and his imprecation indicates the direction in which he is moving. He is coming to see that his people must be punished. This verse includes two allusions to Exodus. It opens with, "You know, YHWH." This seems odd; the word "know" almost always has a direct object, but here does not. But this unusual statement has an important parallel: after describing how the Egyptians afflicted the Israelites, Exodus 2:25 concludes, "and God knew" (וַיֵּדַע אֱלֹהִים), with no direct object. This allusion implies that Jeremiah's enemies have become as vicious as the Egyptian taskmasters. Second, Jeremiah alludes to Exodus 34:6, where YHWH is "slow to anger" (אֶרֶךְ אַפַּיִם). The grammar in Jeremiah 15:15, however, is odd. It says, translating literally, "Do not for your 'slow to anger' take me away" (אַל־לְאֶרֶךְ אַפְּךָ תִּקָּחֵנִי). Exodus 34:5–6 is the great revelation of YHWH's patience with sinners, and Jeremiah here alludes to it by citing אֶרֶךְ אַפַּיִם. But Jeremiah is not praying that God would be slow to anger toward himself; that would be equivalent to saying that Jeremiah was an unrepentant sinner. Jeremiah is concerned that God will be "slow to anger" with his enemies, and he knows that if YHWH shows such patience for too long, they will kill him.

**15:16**. Unlike his enemies, Jeremiah was devoted to God. The verse opens, "Your words were found, and I ate them" (נִמְצְאוּ דְבָרֶיךָ וָאֹכְלֵם). This probably alludes to when the Law was found in the temple during Josiah's reign (2 Kings 22:8, which uses the verb מצא). Jeremiah was a young man when that happened, and he here recalls how eagerly read from it and, by implication, how enthusiastically he supported Josiah's reformation. But Josiah died in battle, the reformation ended, and Judah descended again into apostasy. Jeremiah thus struggled against despair.

**15:17**. Jeremiah's zeal was such that he did not waste time with parties. Perhaps he considered them frivolous, or perhaps the revelry led to immorality and idolatrous practices. Even so, Jeremiah felt the pain of social isolation.

**15:18**. Jeremiah cannot understand how it is that, if God is his strength and refuge, he is so miserable and beset by pain and trouble. His complaint here is very sharp: "You really have been to me just like an untrustworthy [brook], like waters that are unreliable." This is a stream that thirsty desert travelers make their way toward only to find when they arrive that it is dry (see Job 6:15–20). Jeremiah looked for relief from God but found none. The metaphor of the unreliable brook suggests that sometimes when Jeremiah turns in prayer to God, he finds peace and relief; but at other times, he feels nothing, and his situation only seems to get worse. The words of encouragement Jeremiah received at his calling sometimes seemed to prove false. Jeremiah does not feel protected at all.

### *YHWH Rebukes and Reassures Jeremiah (15:19–21)*

Although Old Testament prayers can speak very bluntly to God, Jeremiah went a bit too far and earned a rebuke from YHWH.

**15:19**. YHWH tells Jeremiah that if he wants to continue to serve as a prophet, he must utter words that are "valuable" (יָקָר) and not "mindless" (זוֹלֵל). Jeremiah effectively called God a liar, and that could not be tolerated. Jeremiah must not become like his foolish people. "Let this people return to you"—they must learn to imitate him; he must not imitate them.

*THE TRANSLATION OF 15:19*

The word זוֹלֵל is often translated as "glutton" (in Deut. 21:20; Prov. 23:21; 28:7), but the only place where it implies gluttony is in Proverbs 23:20, where זֹלֲלֵי בָשָׂר ("mindless [eaters] of food" = "people who eat with abandon"). By context alone, therefore, זוֹלֵל in Proverbs 23:21 speaks of gluttony. But in Deuteronomy 21:20 and Proverbs 28:7, it simply refers to people who are reckless and irresponsible. Of itself, the word has nothing to do with eating. In Jeremiah 15:19, it refers to rash, thoughtless words and not to gluttony.

**15:20–21**. YHWH again speaks of giving Jeremiah the armor he needs to withstand the assaults of his people, as in 1:18 and 15:11. Specifically, God will save Jeremiah from the people who mean him harm.

### *Two Object Lessons (16:1–9)*

Abruptly, YHWH commands Jeremiah not to marry and not to attend celebrations or funerals. We should understand that these passages do not necessarily describe a single sequence of events; the prayers and oracles recounted here probably happened at different times in Jeremiah's life. They have been editorially arranged in the sequence we now see. But the arrangement in the text is logical: Jeremiah has complained about how isolated he is (15:17), and YHWH tells him that the times being what they are, his isolation is inevitable and mandatory.

#### *Jeremiah Not to Marry (16:1–4)*

**16:1–2**. The command is straightforward: Jeremiah must not marry or have children. Although celibacy has a long history in the Christian church, it is alien to ancient Israel. Moses, the prophets, and the priests were all married men. Since Jeremiah could have gotten married at a fairly young age, he must have received this command early in his life.

**16:3–4**. The Jerusalem of Jeremiah's lifetime will be no place to raise a family. It would be a time of great immorality, persecution, and suffering. This text may be behind Paul's conviction that, "because of the impending crisis," Christians should consider remaining celibate (1 Cor. 7:26–29).

#### *Jeremiah Not to Attend Funerals or Weddings (16:5–9)*

**16:5–7**. Jeremiah must not attend funerals because soon death would be so widespread in Jerusalem that the dead would not be buried. Prior to the fall of the city, death in Jerusalem would be through normal causes, and each death could be mourned individually. In the great calamity, however, suffering and tragedy would be universal, and the earlier, peaceful deaths would be enviable by comparison. By not attending funerals, Jeremiah communicated that such ordinary sorrows were insignificant compared to what was coming. Along the way, we see in this passage a glimpse of Israelite funerary rites, including a common meal, visitation to show sympathy, the interment of the deceased, and ritual self-laceration or the shaving of the head. The Law prohibits the latter two practices (Deut. 14:1; Lev. 19:27–28), but people did them anyway (Mic. 1:16; Ezek. 7:18).

**16:8–9**. Jeremiah is not to attend feasts of any kind, and specifically not weddings. Just as there are occasions when joking is not appropriate, so there are seasons when celebrations are offensive. By not joining in celebrations, Jeremiah communicates that this is such a season.

### *Jerusalem Cannot Repent (16:10–17:4)*

Jerusalem's sin demands punishment, and at this point there is no hope that it might repent.

#### *The Answer to Bewildered Jerusalem (16:10–18)*

**16:10**. God gives Jeremiah an explanation for the disasters about to befall the city, but these answers are also for Jeremiah himself, that he might understand YHWH's prohibition against further intercession for the city.

**16:11–13**. The explanation has three points: Israel has always been apostate; the present generation is even worse than their ancestors; and the only remedy is to remove them from the land.

**16:14–15**. Even so, God will redeem them. The future work of salvation will be so great that the past work, the exodus, will seem insignificant by comparison.

**16:16**. Returning to the theme of Judah's impending destruction, YHWH declares that the enemy nations, metaphorically hunters and fishermen, will seek out and remove every Israelite from their homeland, wherever they may hide.

**16:17–18**. The people behaved as though God either did not know or did not care about what they were doing. He saw their idols and considered them to be abominations, defiling his land. The exile is inevitable.

### *Jeremiah Affirms YHWH's Answer (16:19–20)*

**16:19–20**. Jeremiah responds by affirming YHWH's justice and goodness, but what he says is surprising. He does not speak of the topic that has dominated the text up until now—Judah's sin and the righteousness of God's actions against them. Rather, he speaks of how the idols are all worthless and that someday even the nations will come to recognize this. Purging Judah of its idols had been the focus of Josiah's failed reformation, and Jeremiah throughout his career fought a losing battle to get the people to abandon their paganism. He acknowledges that what God is doing now is right, but he looks forward to the time when all people would abandon the gods of the nations.

### *YHWH Reaffirms His Promise (16:21)*

**16:21**. YHWH affirms that in order to force the people to see the futility of idols, he must demonstrate his power to Judah. And this, unfortunately, requires the destruction of Jerusalem and the exile.

### *Jerusalem Is Incorrigible (17:1–4)*

The previous passage praised YHWH for the future deliverance of the Gentiles from idol worship; this passage describes the grip idolatry has on the hearts of the people of Judah. The present evil is set in contrast to the future salvation. The Hebrew of this passage is difficult, and the common translations are neither persuasive nor clear. A preferable rendition is as follows:

> The sin of Judah is written with an iron pen,
> Engraved with a stylus of flint on the tablets of their hearts.
> And [the stylus] belongs to the horns of your altars.
> 2[The engraving happens] whenever their sons remember their altars,
> And [when they remember] their Asherim at every green tree,
> On every high hill, 3[and on] my mountain, [and] in the open country.
>
> Your wealth, all your treasures I will give as plunder
> [As payment] for your high places, for sin that is in your territories.
> 4And you will drop your hand from your inheritance,
> Which I gave to you,
> And I will make you serve your enemies
> In a land that you do not know
> Because you have kindled a fire in my anger
> And it will burn forever.

*THE TRANSLATION OF 17:1–4*

In verse 1, English translations commonly state that Judah's sin is engraved on the horns of their altars. This is peculiar and unprecedented. Altar horns were not engraved and, as a metaphor, engraving sin on an altar horn has no obvious meaning. Interpreters are misled by the placement of the *athnach* with שָׁמִיר, "flint." But בְּצִפֹּרֶן שָׁמִיר ("with a stylus of flint") should be linked with חֲרוּשָׁה עַל־לוּחַ לִבָּם, "on the tablets of their hearts." The phrase וּלְקַרְנוֹת מִזְבְּחוֹתֵיכֶם ("and [it] belongs to the horns of your altars") does not describe *where* the inscription is placed. Note that the previous line uses עַל ("upon") for that, in עַל־לוּחַ לִבָּם ("upon the tablet of your heart"). The question, therefore, is what is the thing that "belongs to the horns of your altars." The best answer is the "stylus." The pointed altar horn is similar to an engraving stylus, and it is the tool that engraves sin on the people's hearts. By metonymy, the "horn" represents the whole altar, and the altar represents the paganism of the people. In verse 2, כִּזְכֹּר בְּנֵיהֶם מִזְבְּחוֹתָם ("when their sons remember their altars") seems to make no sense, and interpreters sometimes disregard the preposition כְּ (as in the NIV) or otherwise try to work around it. But the Hebrew makes perfect sense if one recognizes that the implied main clause, drawn from verse 1, is the act of engraving sin. That is, every time the people consider and are drawn toward the pagan shrines in the hills and glens of Judah, when they "remember" the altars, sin is more deeply engraved on their hearts.

Also, as in the above translation, we should disregard the verse break at the end of verse 2. Thus, the beginning of verse 3, הֲרָרִי בַּשָּׂדֶה ("[on] my mountain, [and] in the countryside") belongs with verse 2. In verse 4, וְשָׁמַטְתָּה וּבְךָ מִנַּחֲלָתְךָ is literally, "and you shall drop and with you from your inheritance," which is unintelligible. The simplest and most persuasive solution is to emend וּ בְךָ to יָדְךָ, "your hand" (Holladay 1986, 483). It is thus, "And you will drop your hand from your inheritance."

**17:1–2**. In the metaphor of verse 1, the horns of the pagan altars are engraving tools that inscribe sin on the tablets of the hearts of Judah. Every time a person of Judah engages in pagan practice or even thinks fondly about these shrines, the sin is engraved a little deeper. And the shrines are everywhere: "On every high hill, and on my mountain (the temple mount), and in the open country."

**17:3–4**. As a penalty for their idolatry, Judah will lose everything.

### *A Meditation on the Human Condition (17:5–11)*

Having just described how idolatry has taken control of the hearts of the people, Jeremiah gives us a more general statement on the human condition.

#### *The Cursed and Blessed Tree (17:5–8)*

The portrayal of the wicked and righteous under the metaphor of the tree is strikingly similar to Psalm 1. There is, however, a pronounced difference between the two texts. Psalm 1 is entirely generalized, and in that sense abstract. Although it speaks of the differences between the righteous and the wicked, it does not in any discernable way reflect a historical context. It is catechesis. Jeremiah 17:5–8, by contrast, directly reflects Jeremiah's context, as described below. Jeremiah's text is not mere instruction but is a direct response to the people he confronted on a daily basis (we, however, can read Jeremiah 17:5–8 as instruction for us). In addition, Jeremiah begins with the wicked, whereas Psalm 1 begins with the righteous. Jeremiah's meditations arise out of his conflicts with his opponents, and naturally the portrayal of the wicked is first. The psalm is an encouragement to righteousness, and so it makes the righteous to be first and more prominent.

**17:5–6**. The wicked have two qualities: they trust in human beings for help rather than in

God, and they do not flourish. They are like the scrubby, ugly plants that survive in the dry and rocky wilderness, where there is neither rainfall nor good soil. When calling them desert scrub plants, Jeremiah does not mean they are hardy or well-adapted. He means they are twisted, small, useless, and pathetic. This metaphor reflects Jeremiah's historical context in two respects. First, the leadership in Jerusalem persistently chose to trust in Egypt to save them from Babylon. That is, they trusted man and not God. Second, as noted above, Jeremiah's ministry included a time of severe drought, and he here portrays the wicked as scrawny plants that inhabit a dry wilderness.

**17:7–8**. The righteous also have two qualities: they trust in God rather than in people, and they thrive. Verse 7 seems redundant in that it pronounces "blessed" the person who "trusts" (root: בטח) in YHWH and makes YHWH his "confidence" (noun: מִבְטָח). But the second line may actually express a result: "Blessed is the man who trusts in YHWH, / so that YHWH is his confidence" (the *weqatal* verb וְהָיָה points to a result or outcome). This is sustained at the beginning of verse 8: "So that he will be (וְהָיָה) like a tree planted by water." If a person decides to trust in God, God becomes the object of that person's confidence, and over time he or she is much better able to withstand crises and trials, becoming like a tree planted by water. Note also how prominent the theme of drought is in verse 8. The tree remains green and bears fruit in the midst of drought and severe heat, and its roots are deep and stretch out toward water. This suggests that this text was created during the time of drought.

*The Secret Places of the Heart (17:9–10)*

**17:9**. This verse is a maxim expressing what Christian theology refers to as "total depravity," "original sin," or more simply, "the flesh." It asserts that the human heart has a bias to turn away from God and toward evil. The maxim is here as Jeremiah's response to his experience and environment; he had begun by praying for Judah and hoping for their recovery, and he ended bitterly disappointed. He thus drew conclusions on human nature. The heart is "deceitful" (עָקֹב, a word that sounds like יַעֲקֹב, "Jacob," a wordplay implying that the Israelites have been treacherous in their dealings with their God). The heart is also "incurably sick" (אָנוּשׁ), and this implies that depravity is fatal and not in the control of the individual. As we cannot by force of will make ourselves get well from a severe, chronic sickness, we cannot by force of will free ourselves from depravity's ravages. And like sickness, depravity disfigures and weakens people.

**17:10**. As a counterpoint and response to the previous verse, this verse asserts that God does know every human heart, as he searches them out. More than that, God rewards each person according to his or her external behavior ("according to the fruit of his deeds," כִּפְרִי מַעֲלָלָיו). This introduces an important dynamic. We Christians are inclined to reduce everything to a minimal and absolute rule: all are under depravity, and therefore the only hope is in grace and regeneration. This is true, but it can lead to an antinomian perversion, as though depravity and grace rendered works and behavior irrelevant. But God does expect us to produce fruit worthy of repentance; otherwise, our claim to have received grace will prove hollow.

*Greed (17:11)*

**17:11**. This verse contains two proverbs on greed and ill-gotten gain, in which the second proverb gives the outcome that follows from the first proverb (Proverbs 22:22–23 has a similar pattern). The verse is commonly mistranslated. It does not mean that a partridge hatches eggs that it did not lay, as though it stole eggs from other nests. A better translation is:

A partridge that broods [over its eggs] but bears no young;
[so is] one who gains riches but not by justice.
In the middle of his life [his wealth] will abandon him;
in the end, he is a fool.

The relevant verb (ילד) does not mean to "lay eggs" but to "have offspring" (Holladay 1986, 498). Partridges nest on the ground, and thus their eggs are particularly vulnerable to predation, and their nesting and brooding will have been in vain. The point of the proverb pair is that wealth wrongly acquired is quickly lost (see Prov. 10:2; 13:11; 23:5). It is somewhat surprising to find this proverb pair here, since greed is not a major theme of Jeremiah. Probably greed is here a typical manifestation of depravity. Paul, analogously, uses covetousness to demonstrate human sin (Rom. 7:7–11).

## *Jeremiah's Prayer (17:12–18)*

### *YHWH, Zion's Fountain of Living Water (17:12–13)*

**17:12–13**. These two verses have been divided improperly, and the common translation is somewhat misleading. A more accurate translation is as follows:

12 Throne of glory!
Lofty height [that has existed] from the beginning!
The place of our sanctuary!
13 The hope (and water reservoir) of Israel: YHWH!

All who abandon you are put to shame (and dry up).
And my weeds in the land will be recorded [as follows]:
That they abandoned the spring of living water: YHWH!

Notice that both strophes end with the word YHWH. In 17:12–13a, Jeremiah invokes YHWH by a series of titles, beginning with "Throne of glory!" Having recognized that his people will fail him and that trust in humans is folly, Jeremiah declares that YHWH is the only one he honors and trusts. Also, "The hope of Israel" (מִקְוֵה יִשְׂרָאֵל) could mean, "The water reservoir of Israel" (מִקְוֶה can mean either "hope" or "reservoir"). Using such a metaphor again implies that Judah was in severe drought. In verse 13bcd, those who turn from YHWH are compared to plants in a dry land, as in 17:6. In 13b, the word "be put to shame" (I-בוש) can also be interpreted as "dry up" (יבש). Without the living water that is YHWH, they are like a garden in a drought, filled with useless weeds or with plants that wither and die.

*THE TRANSLATION OF 17:13*

Three issues confuse the interpretation of this verse. First, as noted above, 13a belongs with verse 12. Second, וְסוּרַי בָּאָרֶץ alludes to 2:21 (see translation note to that verse), which refers to weeds in a vineyard. Thus, the phrase is literally, "And my wandering ones in the land," but means, "And my weeds in the land." The people are no longer a healthy vine in YHWH's land, but a sickly crop of weeds stunted by drought. Third, the verb יִכָּתֵבוּ does not go with בָּאָרֶץ, and it does not mean that they will be written in the dust or the like. Rather, יִכָּתֵבוּ כִּי עָזְבוּ go together and mean, "They shall be recorded [as follows], that they abandoned . . .". Their destruction will be recorded as punishment for apostasy.

### *Jeremiah's Appeal and Imprecation (17:14–18)*

**17:14–15**. Jeremiah felt himself wounded and endangered by his enemies in Judah, and he called on God for healing and deliverance. Readers typically assume that verse 15 is a sarcastic attack on Jeremiah, mocking his predictions of doom (Thompson 1980, 425). But it may be entirely different. Many in Jerusalem assumed that they were under God's special protection, but they were experiencing severe drought and were under threat from Babylon. As such, their question, "Where is the word of YHWH? Let it come!" may be a demand that Jeremiah produce a great miracle. Precedents would have been Elijah, at whose word rains came and ended a drought, and Isaiah, at whose word Sennacherib's army perished. If so, they were demanding that Jeremiah prove he was a "real" prophet. God had already rebuffed Jeremiah's prayers for Jerusalem because of Judah's intransience in apostasy. But the people suspected either that Jeremiah refused to intercede in their behalf out of hostility to them, or that God considered Jeremiah an unworthy prophet and refused to answer his prayers.

**17:16**. This verse should be translated as follows:

> I have not, because of an evil motive, been in a hurry to push you [to get Judah punished].
> I have not longed for the incurable day.
> You know what comes out of my mouth.
> It is right in front of you.

Jeremiah loved his people and had tried to move YHWH to save them. He had no malice, and YHWH knew both his heart and his prayers.

*THE TRANSLATION OF 17:16*

This verse is usually interpreted to mean that Jeremiah had not run away from being a shepherd, but this is a doubtful translation. The verbal root אוּץ does not mean "run away," and מֵרֹעֶה does not mean "from being a shepherd" (it means, "from a shepherd" or "from a grazing animal"). Also, it is unusual to use the metaphor of shepherd for the prophetic office. It is therefore difficult to make sense of the MT מֵרֹעֶה, and the versions have a variety of interpretations. However, Aquila, Symmachus, and the Syriac all read רָעָה ("evil"). That is preferable to רֹעֶה, "shepherd." Thus, מֵרָעָה can be taken to mean, "from (i.e., because of) an evil motive." The verb אוּץ means to hasten to try to bring about some result, often a bad one (Josh. 10:13; Isa. 22:4; Prov. 19:2; 21:5; 28:20; 29:20). If used absolutely, אוּץ often means to engage in thoughtless, hasty, or base activity, as in Proverbs 21:5b: וְכָל־אָץ אַךְ־לְמַחְסוֹר ("and everyone in haste only arrives at deprivation"). Used with a personal object, it means to push someone toward doing something, as in Gen. 19:15 (where the hiphil וַיָּאִיצוּ is used with בְּ and describes the angels urging Lot to hurry away from Sodom); Exod. 5:13; Josh. 17:15 (used with לְ). With אַחֲרֶיךָ, it means that Jeremiah has not gotten behind YHWH and in effect pushed him toward punishing Israel. The whole therefore means, "I have not, out of an evil motive, been in a hurry behind you [to get Judah punished]."

**17:17–18**. In these verses, Jeremiah prays not an intercession but an imprecation. He knew that YHWH would come not as a savior but as a terror, and he called God to afflict his enemies and not himself. This is a major turning point; Jeremiah is ready for God to unleash his fury on Judah.

## THEOLOGICAL FOCUS

This passage vindicates the justice of God and the motivations of his faithful ministers, who must often proclaim judgment and destruction.

- Those who truly love God never proclaim judgment out of spite or with joy. It breaks their hearts.
- God's ministers can become deeply discouraged, but they must not lash out at God, the source of their comfort.
- Punishment comes because people are incorrigible.
- Persistent hostility to God comes from the depths of the human heart. It is not forced on people from the outside.

- It is no sin to desire God to comfort and vindicate us when we are persecuted.

## PREACHING AND TEACHING STRATEGIES

### *Exegetical and Theological Synthesis*

Jeremiah's message to Judah was that God was going to destroy them because they had wicked practices that came out of wicked hearts. When Jeremiah's contemporaries heard his message, they wanted to kill him. When the exiles or even those who returned from exile read his words, the message was still unpleasant. It told them that though God had spared them, they still had the same wicked hearts of those to whom Jeremiah first preached.

And the message is not only unpleasant to us, it is also difficult for us to accept. Just as Jeremiah was brought through a process, so we need to be patient as we present this passage. This patience not only applies to our listeners, but also to us. Admitting that one`s own heart is evil is very hard. In fact, it won't happen because that self-centered heart is very clever at denying reality. Only by the work of the Holy Spirit will I be convicted that I have a heart like Jeremiah describes. Though this passage doesn't explain this work of the Spirit, it is important for us to depend upon him to work in us and in our listeners.

### *Preaching Idea*

A hard message is hard on the messenger.

### *Contemporary Connections*

#### What does it mean?

After years of work, the middle-aged father was taking his last test in his graduate studies, which was an oral exam. His praying wife was waiting in the university parking lot and, of course, praying for him. He passed the exam and after his supervisor congratulated him, he texted his wife, "I passed." She sent a quick email to the kids. In her hurried excitement she only put a short message in the subject line: "Daddy passed." The kids' immediate response was shock, but then each quickly realized she was referring to the oral exam. Fortunately, this was good news, but when a hard message needs to be delivered it isn't left to the subject line of an email.

It is not often but we do have to deliver hard messages in our lives. At times pastors have the heavy responsibility of communicating that a family member has died. The hardest of these is telling parents that their child has died. Years ago, when I was pastoring in a small community, a teenager was driving home from our church school when he lost control, flipped his car, and was killed. The police did not have a number for his parents, but they found papers that indicated that he went to our church school. The officers came to the church office, seeking to contact the parents. The young man's mother was a single mom, so the officer, the school principal, and I went to her place of work to tell her face to face. It was a hard message, and it was hard to deliver.

Jeremiah had a hard message. Part of his message was about a future judgment coming on the nation of Judah; the other part was about the current condition of Judah's heart. We don't have the same message about God's taking his nation into exile, but we do have the same message that the human heart is evil. That is a hard message, but it must be spoken, written, and communicated because it is true even though it is hard. Jeremiah struggled with the message that he was to deliver and so we struggle with the same message. Who wants to say to a person, "I've got some bad news for you—God says that your heart is wicked, really wicked"? If we did work up the courage to say it, we might follow up with, "Don't shoot me, I'm just the messenger." That cliché has an empty meaning, because though we might try to separate the message from the messenger, we can't. That means as we communicate to the lost world that it is lost, there will be hard feelings toward us.

God gave Jeremiah a hard message, but he also encouraged him. When I had to tell that single mom about her son, I was so glad to have two others with me. God promised Jeremiah that he would be with him, and the same very specific promise is given to us in the Great Commission.

### *Is it true?*

Obviously for us, the good news is a dominant theme of New Testament words such as "forgiveness," "justification," "reconciliation," and "eternal life." But these words have greatly diminished meanings if there is not a wicked heart that needs them. An old country preacher phrased it this way: "You can't get 'em saved until you get 'em lost." So, we must proclaim the human heart's condition, remembering that it took Jeremiah a process to accept these truths. Perhaps listeners go through a process as well, in order to agree that the human heart is wicked. When Jeremiah's readers heard his message, they wanted to kill him. When the exiles and even those who returned from exile read his words, the message was still unpleasant. It told them that though God had spared them, they still had the same wicked hearts of those taken into exile. And we have the same wicked hearts. This message is not only for us to proclaim; it is also for us to hear. It is like the COVID-19 crisis. It was hard news, but even the president was at risk because he had been exposed to this deadly virus. The words of warning by the governmental and health officials, was not that *you* have a problem, but *we* have a problem. Paul David Tripp put it well when he warned pastors and spiritual leaders about thinking that we no longer have to struggle with our wicked hearts:

> Let me say again: if you are a pastor or ministry leader, you are at the same time a person in the middle of your own sanctification. You are not yet free of sin and all its attendant dangers. You still carry around moral susceptibility. You are capable of giving way to disastrous things. You are capable of losing your way. You are capable of ungodly attitudes and dark desires. You have not been completely delivered from pride, greed, lust, anger, and bitterness. There are places where you are an idolater, where the agenda is being set by a desire for some created thing more than it is by worship of your Creator. You do not always minister as an ambassador. There are times when you do your ministry work with the attitude of a king rather than as one called to represent the King. You do not always love God above all else. You do not always love your neighbor as yourself. You are not always kind and compassionate. You are not always patient and forgiving. There are moments when you love your little kingdom of one more than you love God's kingdom. There are times when you love comfort and pleasure more than you love redemption. There are times when pride renders you unkind and unapproachable. There are times when you want your ministry to be about you. There are times when you're irritated by the very people you've been called to pastor. You are not proud of all your thoughts. You would not want your congregation to hear all your words. You do things in private moments that you would not want seen in public. (Tripp, 2012. 154)

### *Now what?*

This hard message should compel us to tell those around us that they have wicked hearts. Just like that? Just as Jeremiah did? We need to remember that Jeremiah ministered over the course of dozens of years. This was not a one-time message. The harsh message is all the more important to communicate because it is true. How terrible to not tell a family about a death. How terrible to not tell someone about their heart condition. How terrible to withhold the truth that God has revealed! We must not throw our words out like a hand grenade and let it explode on our listeners. Christ told those he sent out to be wise and innocent in their proclamation (Matt. 10:16). We are to speak the truth in love and wisdom. It was almost hidden in this section of Jeremiah's message, but there is the hope of redemption (16:15).

### *Creativity in Presentation*

If your situation warrants it, this passage could have a separate sermon, as a meditation of the human condition (17:5–11). Since it is a meditation in the midst of a story, it could well be a separate sermon, probably best presented after the whole passage is preached. While preaching the longer passage, the teacher/pastor could summarize 17:5–11 and then say that this passage will be considered in more depth the following Sunday.

This pericope (15:10–17:18) presents a process of Jeremiah accepting the hard truth that Judah was going to be destroyed and that it was God's will. Employ that concept of a process as a rhetorical device to present the passage. As part of the introduction, ask your listeners to come on a journey with Jeremiah as he fully grasps a hard message. Part of this journey is not only grasping the content of the hard message, but also understanding that it is hard to deliver that message. Present the different portions of the text as steps on Jeremiah's journey: his complaints, God's answers, the opposition, and the content of the message. It is similar to the development of a character in a story. How do the events and people around him affect his character? What changes do we see? As you move through this journey you might want to employ a spatial element to help with clarity: moving from your right to left as the journey progresses and then ending on the far left of the platform, but then moving back to the center for the application portion of the sermon.

Another possibility is to present this passage as a dialogue between God and Jeremiah. That enables you to make application throughout the sermon without giving the sense of interrupting the flow of the journey given in the suggested presentation idea mentioned above.

As Christian preachers/teachers, how could we not include in this sermon the glorious good news of Christ? He imputes his righteousness to us and gives us a new heart, though not fully realized this side of heaven. Whether you choose to present Christ's work at the beginning, middle, or end, how terrible it would be not to mention it.

Here is one possible structure: the eight points of the text could be presented *briefly*, emphasizing the progression leading up to Jeremiah accepting the reality of God's message of sure judgment and praying accordingly.

**First movement of the sermon: the text**

- Jeremiah complains: the message is hard, and it is hard to deliver (15:10, 15–18).
- God's response: I called you and I will be with you (15:11–14, 19–21).
- This message means that even weddings and funerals will be disrupted (16:1–9).
- Jerusalem will not repent—and it will be judged (16:10–13).
- But God will redeem Israel (16:14–15).
- God reaffirms that Jerusalem will be judged (16:16–17:4).
- Lesson in the condition of the wicked human heart (17:5–11).
- Jeremiah praises God and prays for Judah's destruction (17:12–18).

### Second movement: application

- Each of us has a wicked heart that needs changing.
- Accepting this is a process of God's grace, with us and in others.
- When we do accept it, we should run to Jesus.
- We need to recognize that presenting it to others will take its toll on us.

## DISCUSSION QUESTIONS

1. What are some hard messages that you've had to deliver?
2. What are some hard messages that you've had delivered to you?
3. What makes a message hard?
4. What makes a hard message hard to deliver?
5. How do you feel toward the messenger of a hard message?

# Jeremiah 17:19–18:23

## EXEGETICAL IDEA

Judah's refusal to keep the Sabbath led to greater sins, which led to God's warning of judgment and Jeremiah's harsh imprecatory prayer. This passage includes summaries of two of Jeremiah's great sermons: the one delivered at the People's Gate, and the other at a potter's house. The sermons explore the progress of the people's apostasy and the inevitable outcome. These messages appear to have come from early in Jeremiah's ministry and illustrate how he began to realize that the people would not repent. The imprecatory prayer may come from later in his ministry, but indicates how fully he recognized that the people would not change.

## THEOLOGICAL FOCUS

Refusal to repent over little sins will lead to greater sins, which in turn will lead to facing the full fury of God. But Jeremiah realized that his people could not even do a relatively small thing, such as stop working on the Sabbath. Eventually, he saw that their wickedness had become full, and he voiced an especially severe imprecatory prayer against them. The task of a great prophet is to intercede for sinners and avert their destruction, as Moses did in the golden calf incident of Exodus 32. But sometimes this is not possible. Jeremiah did not fail, but his experience was not a happy one.

## PREACHING IDEA

Simple obedience guards against severe disobedience.

## PREACHING POINTERS

The idea of this passage could be dismissed as just being a description of a slippery slope.[1] But that is not what God is saying in this passage. Rather, it is a cause/effect. Jeremiah's two sermons can be summarized: if you sin in everyday simple matters, such as breaking the Sabbath, it will lead to greater sins, such as calling God's will meaningless, rejecting his authority, and calling sin orthodoxy.

While the slippery slope does not carry weight in a formal argument, the slippery slope of sin will carry one into deeper sin. We must remember we are not dealing with logic; we are dealing with the human heart, which is desperately wicked. Jeremiah's imprecation (18:19–23) is not explicitly stated in the preaching idea; however, the concept of *severe disobedience* implies God's wrath.

---

1 When trying to win an argument some will cite one bad event and say that we must stop this because it leads to something worse. In a general sense it says that because *A* happened eventually *Z* will happen. It is known as logical fallacy sometimes called the slippery slope.

# HOW TO BREAK A PREACHER'S HEART (17:19–18:23)

## LITERARY STRUCTURE AND THEMES

This passage brings us to the climactic moment of Jeremiah's turn from intercession for his people to imprecation against them. At the end of this text, Jeremiah makes a full-throated, unrestrained appeal for God to destroy Jerusalem and bring its people to grief. It retells the story of Jeremiah's career with two samples of his sermons, one delivered at a city gate and the other at a potter's house. The first sermon evidently comes from early in his career; it is more optimistic in tone and makes light demands on the people. The second comes from sometime later, when they demonstrated an obstinate refusal to believe his words. It is much more negative in tone than the first. At the end, Jeremiah, realizing that they intend to destroy him, makes his imprecation. The account thus follows the path of Jeremiah's discouragement to his confrontation with brute facts about his people.

- ***Messages at a Gate and a Potter's House (17:19–18:17)***
  - *The Sermon at the People's Gate (17:19–27)*
  - *The Sermon at the Potter's House (18:1–17)*
- ***Jeremiah Prays a Second Imprecation (18:18–23)***

## EXPOSITION

### *Messages at a Gate and a Potter's House (17:19–18:17)*

This section includes two different sermons. We do not know if they were given near the same time, but from the content it looks like the sermon at the People's Gate came some time, perhaps years, before the sermon at the potter's house.

#### *The Sermon at the People's Gate (17:19–27)*

This sermon was probably given early in Jeremiah's career, before he became notorious in the eyes of the state and subject to severe restrictions. Also, the tone of the sermon is quite optimistic, saying that if the people will just keep the Sabbath, then both the rulers and the people will be able to keep the city indefinitely, with no fear of subjugation by a foreign empire. This implies that the oracles were given before the gravity of Judah's apostasy was apparent to Jeremiah and before he became certain that Jerusalem would fall to the Babylonians. It is even possible that this sermon was given during the reign of Josiah, very early in Jeremiah's career.

**17:19–20**. Of itself, the term "gate of the sons of the people" (שַׁעַר בְּנֵי־הָעָם; reading the *qere*) could be the name of a specific gate or it could be a more generic reference to an unnamed public gate (the latter is the interpretation of the NASB). The context, however, shows that it is the proper name of one gate (we could call it "The People's Gate"), since the verse also refers to the other gates in the city. Also, the text speaks of how the kings have made a practice of using this gate for going in and out of the city, suggesting that it was located near the royal palace. The reason for giving this message at a city gate is obvious: that was where business was transacted. The city gate in ancient Israel served as the public square for both private and public business, functioning as both marketplace and courthouse. And since Jeremiah's message concerned the conducting of business on the Sabbath, the gate was an appropriate place for him to deliver it.

**17:21–23**. The prophecy tells them, "Be careful about your lives" (הִשָּׁמְרוּ בְּנַפְשׁוֹתֵיכֶם), implying that Sabbath-breaking was a grave matter. This could allude to the episode in Numbers 15:32–36, in which a man was put to death for gathering wood on the Sabbath. The command not to carry any burden in or out of the city on the Sabbath uses a simple example of ordinary labor to serve as an example of all labor (using the rhetorical device synecdoche), and the meaning is that they should do no work of any kind. The demand that Israel keep the Sabbath was laid upon the people at the time of the exodus. The first example of a Sabbath rule for Israel is at Exodus 16:23, when Israel was in the wilderness after having escaped the Egyptian army. God said he would send them manna for six days, but the seventh day was a Sabbath when no one was to gather food. The responses of both Moses and the people indicated that they had no prior experience with a Sabbath rule and initially did not know what to make of it. Afterward, the Sabbath law was enshrined in the Decalogue at Exodus 20:8–11. Nevertheless, Israel from the beginning had difficulty keeping the Sabbath, as Jeremiah indicates in verse 23.

**17:24–26**. The promised benefits for keeping the Sabbath are quite expansive: the kings and their officials will continue to rule the city, and they will ride in and out on their horses and chariots. The example of riding obviously relates to the function of a gate, but it also implies splendor and power, and it means that the kings will rule in great honor and with national prosperity. The text also mentions all the territories of Judah: Jerusalem and the region of Benjamin, the regional cities of the ancient tribal territory of Judah, the Shephelah, the Negev, and the hill country. The implication is that the whole domain of Judah will be secure. Finally, the text mentions the whole offerings, the sacrifices, the offerings, and the incense with which the people would praise YHWH. These three categories—the splendor of kings on horses, the full territory of Judah, and the abundance of offerings for the temple—speak of how Judah could thrive before YHWH in perpetuity if they would just keep the Sabbath.

**17:27**. By contrast, the warning about the dire consequences of Sabbath-breaking, although severe, receive only brief discussion. This does not mean the warnings are less important, but the contrast suggests, again, that this sermon came during the reign of Josiah, when there was high hope that the reformation that he inaugurated would transform society and bring peace and security to the nation. Also, the enemy that would destroy Jerusalem is anonymous in this verse, suggesting again that the prophecy was delivered before the magnitude of the Babylonian threat was obvious.

### The Sabbath

To the modern Christian reader, it seems astonishing that this passage would place so much emphasis on the Sabbath, as though whether or not Israel kept it was the sole determining factor for whether YHWH blessed them or punished them. We should first note that Sabbath-keeping is an example of synecdoche in this passage, being representative for keeping all of the laws of the Sinai covenant. Sabbath-keeping was a kind of canary in the coal mine, indicating the state of Israel's heart before YHWH.

Still, we must come to terms with how heavily the passage focuses on the Sabbath. The importance of Sabbath is foreshadowed in Genesis 2:1–3, where God's rest on the seventh day sets the pattern that people should follow (and also sets the pattern for God's "rest" that people should strive to enter, per Ps. 95:11; Heb. 4:3). The initial occasion for the rule of Sabbath-keeping was the exodus. The Israelites had been slaves in Egypt, and since God had given them freedom, they should not again be enslaved again to hard, unceasing labor. Every seventh day, they, their servants, and the aliens who lived among them should take a day off and rest. The two versions of the Decalogue mention both creation and the Egyptian bondage as reasons for the Sabbath. In Exodus 20:11, it says to keep the Sabbath because God made the earth in six days and rested on the seventh; in Deuteronomy 5:15, it says Israel should keep the Sabbath because they had been slaves in Egypt.

For the ancient Israelites, Sabbath-keeping was primarily a day to rest from ordinary labor, but it was also a ritual that indicated their faithfulness to YHWH. Observing the Sabbath every week was a symbolic renewal of the Sinai covenant, whereby they demonstrated their willingness to submit to all that God had commanded. It reminded them that YHWH had saved them from the Egyptian servitude, and it was also an act of faith. By resting on the Sabbath and not working, they demonstrated their confidence in God; he would provide for them. They did not need to work ceaselessly in order to keep starvation away from their door. The ritual of keeping the Sabbath every week can be thought of as analogous to the ritual of putting on a wedding ring every day. Obviously, the reality of a wedding is in a person's willingness to maintain sexual fidelity to his or her spouse and to treat the spouse with compassion and love in a partnership through life. But the ritual of putting on the ring is significant; a man who sees that his wife has stopped wearing her wedding ring has reason to be alarmed. That is why Jeremiah 17 gives so much attention to the Sabbath; in not keeping it, Israel had effectively removed her wedding ring.

We Christians always have before us the image of the Pharisees accusing Jesus of sin because he healed people on the Sabbath, and we recoil at the burdensome rules Pharisaic Judaism imposed on the people. We also keep in mind the saying of Jesus, "The Sabbath was made for man, and not man for the Sabbath" (Mark 2:27). For us, therefore, Jeremiah 17 can be quite disturbing. But we must keep in mind that Jeremiah and Jesus spoke in radically different contexts. In Jeremiah's time, the Israelites kept the Sabbath very poorly (indeed, they had never kept it well, per verse 23). And Jeremiah did not seek to impose on them all the rules of rabbinical Judaism; he simply wanted them to desist from their ordinary, daily labor. After the exile and return, however, the Jews learned their lesson—with a vengeance. They became increasingly determined to be sure that they never violated the Sabbath in any way, and their rules became more numerous, burdensome, and exacting. Jesus addressed a religious establishment that made life miserable for its people and which missed the whole point of the Sabbath, as being something given to the Israelites for their benefit. Thus, his message strikes us as very different from Jeremiah's.

### *The Sermon at the Potter's House (18:1–17)*

This is another undated message, but it is probably later than the previous even if from relatively early in Jeremiah's ministry. Babylon is not mentioned, and the coming judgment is described in more abstract, hypothetical terms. At the same time, it is much more pessimistic than the previous passage on the Sabbath. This suggests that it comes from early in Jehoiakim's reign, when Jeremiah had begun to recognize that Josiah's reformation had not brought about true repentance and that YHWH's judgment was sure to come.

**18:1–2**. The visit to the potter's house creates a vividly acted-out parable. YHWH commands Jeremiah to go the potter but does not give him his message until Jeremiah actually arrives and observes what the potter did. This is similar to Jeremiah's visions, in which he first receives a vision and then receives a word from YHWH explaining its meaning (see Jer. 1:11–16). In this case, however, Jeremiah went to a literal potter; it was not done in a vision.

**18:3–4**. The process that Jeremiah observed was quite straightforward. The potter was making some kind of vessel from clay, but something was malformed, and the potter was unable to continue shaping it properly. Therefore, he smashed the clay back down into an unformed lump and restarted the whole process. This time, the potter was able to shape it properly, and he was pleased with the result. The properly formed vessel was ready for firing.

**18:5–6**. The above episode could be interpreted in a variety of ways, but YHWH's interpretation is of course definitive. The fundamental point of comparison is the freedom of the potter to do as he pleases with the clay in his hands. By analogy, God is free to do as he chooses as he governs nations and shapes human history. More specifically, YHWH has chosen Israel for his own purposes, and he has the right to deal with Israel as he pleases.

**18:7–8**. Although the focus of the oracle is God's working with Israel, the examples are cast neutrally, speaking of God's intent toward an anonymous, unnamed nation (גּוֹי). The effect is to turn the lesson into a universal axiom that relates to God's relationship with humanity. If God begins to punish any people and they appeal to him for mercy, God has the right to change his mind (נחם) and not destroy them. This lesson was made concrete in the experience of Jonah. We should note that verse 7 uses three verbs from Jeremiah's prophetic commission in 1:10: "uproot" (נתש), "tear down" (נתץ), and "slay" (אבד). Although we could rightly speak of God's compassion and his desire to redeem people, the point of the verse in context is God's freedom to do as he chooses with any nation. God's actions are not arbitrary or irrational. Just as the potter is not going to smash down clay that is properly forming into a good vessel, God is not going to destroy a people without cause. Still, God is to the people as the potter is to the clay. He is the master and owner, and he does as he pleases.

**18:9–10**. This is the obvious counterpart to verses 7–8. God can refrain from destroying a wicked nation that appeals for mercy, but he can also destroy a nation that he had intended to bless if they turn toward wickedness. Here, too, we see an allusion to Jeremiah's calling in 1:10 in the verbs "to build" (בנה) and "to plant" (נטע). Although the text still speaks in abstract generalities, the actual target is much more obviously Israel. God had chosen Israel to make them his "special possession" and a "kingdom of priests" (Exod. 19:5–6). He had promised them prosperity, security, and great prestige if they would obey him (Deut. 28:1–14). Furthermore, he had chosen the house of David to be an everlasting dynasty, and he had chosen Zion as the place where his name would dwell. For the people of Judah in Jeremiah's time, this meant that their position was forever secure. God would never allow the dynasty to fall or the temple to be trampled underfoot. God had made clear his intent to "plant" them and "build" them up. In their minds, God had made an unbreakable pledge, and Jerusalem could never be destroyed. But like the potter who had clay that would not be shaped into a proper vessel, Israel refused to yield to God's hand. God, therefore, had every right to smash them down and start over.

**18:11**. The lesson ends with an appeal. He has made the point that Jerusalem was not inviolable. Now they needed to take the lesson to heart and respond appropriately by repenting of their sin. The hour was late; God had already decided that his clay vessel Judah was hopeless and was preparing to smash it down.

**18:12**. This verse is badly translated in most versions. For example, the NASB says, "But they will say, 'It's hopeless! For we are going to follow our own plans, and each of us will act according to the stubbornness of his evil heart.'" This sounds truly strange, as though they really want to repent but find themselves unable to do it, and as a result, they unhappily resign themselves to their evil hearts. But this is not what we see in the book at all. Throughout Jeremiah, the people and the nobility despise the prophet and everything he says. They have no desire to change their ways, and in fact they do not think of themselves as evil. To the contrary, they think that Jeremiah is both a traitor (because he comes across as pro-Babylonian) and a blasphemer (because he said that the Davidic monarchy and the temple would fall). Instead of despairing about their spiritual condition, the people bitterly and sarcastically reject Jeremiah's words (see translation note).

*TRANSLATION NOTE: JEREMIAH 18:12*

The word נוֹאָשׁ is often translated as "It is hopeless" (NASB) or the like (see NIV, NRSV, and ESV for similar translations). It is a niphal participle of יאשׁ, a word that can speak of exasperation, or of giving up on something. In 1 Samuel 27:1, it expresses David's wish that Saul would abandon hope of ever catching David. But the word does not imply a dejected, defeated attitude; it is more often used in anger, as in the English, "Oh, forget it!" or more harshly, "To hell with this!" *HALOT* notes that the word can be an interjection, and suggests the meaning, "Damn!" Job 6:26 is somewhat difficult, but it should be translated as, "Do you suppose you can reprove [my] words, [or do you suppose you can] with wind [reprove] the speech of a man who has had all of this he can take?" Job speaks of himself as נוֹאָשׁ ("a man who has had all of this he can take"), not meaning that he is filled with despair. In context, he is angry with the three friends and considers listening to their arguments to be a waste of time. In Jeremiah, similarly, the word expresses how the people are sick and tired of listening to the prophet. Also, when the people say that they will follow the "stubbornness of their evil hearts" (שְׁרִרוּת לִבּוֹ־הָרָע), they are quoting Jeremiah's words in 16:12 verbatim. That is, they are sarcastically throwing the words of his sermon back in his face, saying that they will behave just as he said they would behave. The verse should be translated, "Oh forget that! We will just go [and do] as we intended! And each of us will carry out [what you call] 'the stubbornness of his evil heart.'"

**18:13–14**. The introduction in verse 13 implies that Israel has done something unprecedented, bizarre, and unreasonable. This provides a key for the difficulties of verse 14; it must describe something strange and unnatural, the counterpart to Israel's behavior. It is unnatural for the high mountains to be without snow or for their icy streams to run dry, just as it is unnatural for any nation to abandon its gods. But Israel has abandoned YHWH. See the translation note below.

*TRANSLATION NOTE: JEREMIAH 18:14*

This is very difficult Hebrew, but it is translatable. Scholars have suggested various emendations (Holladay 1986, 519–25) (McKane 1986, 1.429–432) (Lundbom 2008a, 821–22), but none is needed. A major problem is that Jeremiah uses words that seem inappropriate for the immediate context. However, these words do have significance in the wider context. That is, he chooses words that significantly allude to other concepts, even though they are somewhat unnatural in this verse. הֲיַעֲזֹב מִצּוּר שָׂדַי שֶׁלֶג לְבָנוֹן is literally, "Does the snow of Lebanon abandon from high country rock?" The word שָׂדָי here implies "high country," such as on the upper slopes of mountains (Propp 1987; Craigie, Kelley, and Drinkard 1991, 246–47). It seems strange to speak of snow "abandoning" a place, but the verb עזב is probably chosen for the implied comparison, that Judah has abandoned YHWH her God. Hence, the line asks if the high mountains of Lebanon are ever bereft of snow. The line אִם־יִנָּתְשׁוּ מַיִם זָרִים קָרִים נוֹזְלִים looks very odd; it literally reads, "Or are foreign, cold, flowing waters uprooted?" From context, the "foreign, cold, flowing waters" are the mountain streams in the Lebanon mountains. The word זָרִים is sometimes emended to זָבִים, "flowing," but מַיִם זָרִים ("foreign waters") occurs in 2 Kings 19:24 and thus cannot be regarded as unnatural Hebrew. In addition, the word "foreign" here implicitly contrasts the behavior of Israel with that of the nations. Foreigners do not abandon their gods, but Israel does. Finally, it is strange to speak of waters as being "uprooted," but נתש is one of Jeremiah's key words, going back to his commissioning in 1:10. "Uprooted" (נתש) is often emended to "dried up" (נשת). I would suggest that נתש is original but is also a wordplay on נשת. While a mountain stream might very well dry up (they frequently do), it is outlandish to think of uprooting it, and that is the whole point. The implication is that the foreign nations are not going to be uprooted, but Judah will be. The verse can be translated, "Is the rocky high country bereft of the snow of Lebanon? Or can [the] foreign waters [of Lebanon] be uprooted? Can [its] cold, rushing [waters be uprooted]?"

**18:15–16**. Against all precedent and in a way contrary to nature, Israel forgot their God. Worse, their God is YHWH, maker of heaven and earth, but they burn incense to useless idols. Using another metaphor for strange behavior, they have turned away from walking along a path that is prepared, built up, and easy to follow, and instead follow the confused, twisted, and dead-end paths of paganism. As a result, foreign people will someday walk through Israel's abandoned land and shake their heads in confusion and disbelief that the Israelites behaved in such a perverse manner.

**18:17**. For his part, God will turn his back on them as they turned their backs on him. When they face enemy armies, they will be scattered and flee. Once again, the coming enemy is not named in this context, suggesting that the oracle is from a fairly early period.

### *Jeremiah Prays a Second Imprecation (18:18–23)*

We recall that a major theme of 11:1–20:18 is how Jeremiah began by interceding for Judah but eventually made imprecatory prayers against his people. We do not know if the following verses come from the same time as the preceding passage (it may have come from a later period), but in the structure of the book their inclusion here makes sense, as they show how bitterly the people rejected his message and how he in exasperation turned against them.

**18:18**. The people intend to "make plans" (חשב) against Jeremiah. This could refer to a plot to kill him, although in context it appears to mean that they intend to destroy his reputation. They will strike him with their tongues, meaning that they will mock, belittle, and twist his words. This is analogous to the poisoned political discourse we see in modern times; it can be as brutal and as unjust as a physical mugging. It is important to note, however, that they consider themselves to be orthodox and Jeremiah to be the heretic. They think that they are showing faith in God and in Israel's special place before him when they insist that Jerusalem's religious life will go on as before: "The teaching of the law by the priest will not perish, nor will counsel from the wise, nor the word from the prophets." Jeremiah, who says that all of these will fail and that the nation will fall, is in their mind the one who is undermining the received faith. But of course, Jeremiah's whole point is that the priests, prophets, and sages were distorting the word of God, making their teaching more harmful than helpful. This verse does give us an insight into ancient Israelite religion, indicating that they believed that three different groups conveyed God's word: the priests taught Torah, the prophets gave oracles from God, and the sages taught wisdom, such as we see in Proverbs. Also, notice that the priests were religious teachers; they did not just make sacrifices.

**18:19**. Tired of being slandered and mocked, Jeremiah turned against the populace and called on God for justice.

**18:20–22**. This marks another decisive moment in Jeremiah's career as a prophet. Normally, it is the duty of prophets to intercede for their people, as Moses did in Exodus 32. Jeremiah had done the same, although God told him that he had to stop. Here, Jeremiah makes a bitter complaint against them. He had prayed for them, trying to turn aside God's wrath and imitating the work of Moses, but they only repaid him with schemes for his destruction. His imprecation is now against the whole people and not against the leaders alone, and the requests he makes are surprisingly harsh. He asks that their children starve to death, that their wives be left alone and defenseless, and that their men die in battle. He asks to hear cries of pain and grief rising from their houses. All of this is because they plotted against him, metaphorically digging a pit for him to fall into.

**18:23**. Jeremiah was certain that the people in fact meant to kill him and not just to destroy his reputation by slander and mockery. He declares that YHWH knows all this, meaning that God has good reason to act against them. Summarizing the prayer, he asks that God not forgive them. This, Jeremiah's climactic imprecation against Jerusalem, is a milestone in the book. It marks one of the reasons that Jerusalem fell.

**Reflection on Jeremiah's Imprecatory Prayer**

Jeremiah's imprecation against Jerusalem is extremely harsh. It is comparable to the notorious prayer of Psalm 137:8–9: "Daughter Babylon, set for destruction, / Happy is the one who repays you with the vengeance you handed out to us. // Happy is the one who seizes and shatters your children against rock." Christians have recoiled against the psalm and have tried to recast its meaning with an allegorical interpretation. Many follow Augustine's interpretation that we should take our impure thoughts and dash them against Christ (for example, Billings 2010, 190). This is impossible; clearly the psalmist did not have such a thing in mind. It is disrespectful, in fact, to take the psalmist's words and so dramatically change their meaning. It would be far better to simply reject what he says outright than to impose an alien meaning on the text.

Jeremiah's imprecation is in some respects harsher than Psalm 137. It is delivered against his own people, and he calls for the violent death of Jerusalem's men, women, and children. There is nothing in his prayer that may be so conveniently allegorized as dashing children against a rock. In both passages, we must come to terms with what the words really say. How can we deal with this?

First, these are prayers, not actions. Neither Jeremiah nor the psalmist carried out the actions described. They left it to God to determine what to do. Second, honest prayers to God about our anger and hurt over injustice is valid. The Psalter is filled with such prayers. It is an expression of our outrage, but it also helps to deal with and mitigate our outrage. Jesus told us to pray for those who persecute us, and that is a high task indeed. But it is better to pray an imprecation against those who do evil than to not pray at all. Third, the prayers of Jeremiah and the psalmist are an honest reflection of the believer's pilgrimage through a world filled with temptations, distractions, evil, and suffering. For our part, we have no idea of the kind of pain they saw or had inflicted upon them. But we know our own pain and vexation, and we should be glad to see that the Bible speaks honestly of the pain they endured and of how they responded.

## THEOLOGICAL FOCUS

This section recaps Jeremiah's journey away from praying for the people by recording two messages, one from early in his career and the other from a little later. We see how his discouragement led to a harsh reaction. Specific issues are as follows:

- Repenting from Sabbath-breaking should have been easy; all it required was resting. But the people's refusal to do even this showed they would also not obey any of the weightier commands of the Law.
- For the Israelites, keeping the Sabbath was a weekly, ritualized way of expressing a determination to keep all the commands of God in the Sinai covenant. Not keeping it seemed small, but it marked a fundamental change in direction. We too have small and perhaps ritualized habits that renew our commitment to God, and we need to see that we keep up those habits.
- Jeremiah's audience had a somewhat perverse version of what many Christians would call "eternal security," the confidence that God's election of us and his mercy toward us is everlasting. The people of Jerusalem believed that since God had chosen David and Zion, the city could never fall to an enemy. But eternal security, whether in the ancient Israelite or modern Christian formulation, was never meant to imply that we can sin so that grace may abound (Rom. 6:1–2).
- God, like the potter, enjoys sovereign freedom over his work. We should be loath to speak of putting limitations on God.
- Persistent hostility to God's minister can lead him to such grief and turmoil that he cries out to God for justice. We are not prophets like Jeremiah, and we should not assume that we have the authority to pray as he did. On the other hand, few of us have had experiences comparable to his. We may not have the freedom to pray the kind of harsh imprecation he did, but our experiences and responses can be in some measure analogous to his. As Jeremiah had done, we should try to intercede to the very end. But we too may be brought to the point of making an imprecation.

## PREACHING AND TEACHING STRATEGIES

### *Exegetical and Theological Synthesis*

Jeremiah brings two sermons together on purpose. The first is a call to obey the Sabbath, a command that is fairly simple and relatively easy to obey. He then links this Sabbath sermon to one in which God's loving sovereignty is affirmed and Israel's staggering disobedience to him is condemned, followed by the imprecation.

Those who heard these sermons in real time saw a difference between Jeremiah's early sermons calling for Sabbath obedience and his later ones, in which he was pronouncing judgment. Perhaps like ornery church members, they said, "It's high time we got a new preacher. He didn't use to preach like that." The exiles, and those of us who come after them, read these sermons together. Perhaps the message is that if we listen to and obey the first sermon, we may not need the second one—and avoid the harsh imprecation that followed.

### *Preaching Idea*

Simple obedience guards against severe disobedience.

### *Contemporary Connections*

#### *What does it mean?*

Many have taught, and rightly so, that sin is sin and that all sins are wrong in God's eye. There are no worse sins. Thus, this concept of severe sin or worse sin that is presented in this passage needs explanation. In the sense that all sins separate us from God, there is no worse or more severe sin. However, Christ did speak of greater condemnation for some sins (Luke 20:47). We all have seen that from our perspective, some sins have greater consequences. The abuse of alcohol is bad, but driving while drunk is worse.

#### *Is it true?*

Examples of one sin leading to another are easy to find in life. Adultery begins with a man making an "innocent" but inappropriate compliment about a coworker's appearance. Gossip begins with a "prayer concern" mentioned in detail to a small group, but never mentioned in prayer. Proverbs also addresses the concept of seemingly small sins leading to other larger issues, such as the sin of laziness: "A little sleep, a little slumber, a little folding of the hands to rest, and poverty will come upon you like a robber, and want like an armed man" (Prov. 6:10–11 ESV). And in great detail Proverbs 7:6–23 describes the sad example of the young man who is seduced by a prostitute. His first slippery sin is his walking down her street, and it ends costing him his life.

Over the past decades there have been great advances in understanding the brain. An article appeared in *Nat Neurosci*, a neuroscience journal, that studied the effect of lying upon the brain (Garrett et al. 2006, 1727). The authors recorded experiments which demonstrated that lying for personal gain not only leads to more lying, but also conditions the brain to lie even more. Apparently, the brain physically changes in those who consistently lie for personal gain. Neuroscience affirms that if we make sin a habit instead of obedience, it will lead to more and worse sins.

#### *Now what?*

While we are not required to observe the Sabbath in the same way as those in Jeremiah's day, the pattern that it gives to us is valuable. When we look at the guidelines set forth by God through Moses, the observing of the Sabbath was filled with weekly routines; the most obvious one was the ceasing from work. Today many cultures practice a distant version of this by seeing Sunday as a day of rest. It is a weekly routine. In every church culture that I have experienced or even know about, Sunday is the day of worship. It is a weekly habit. It is the expression of the NT command to not forsake the assembling together. Other commands of God have been expressed in what has come to be known as the spiritual disciplines. There is a habit or routine about them: daily reading of Scripture and prayer, a habit of serving, consistent giving. I have counseled dozens of pastors who have, unfortunately, failed morally. Every one of them said that not observing these daily or weekly spiritual habits was the first step toward moral failure. The purpose of the routine is to shape our hearts. The struggle is that we don't want to submit to God. The

Sabbath was a routine that called for weekly submission to God.

An athlete submits to routines that are not always pleasant, such as stretching, lifting, or running. We endure these because we trust that the routine will produce good results. In the arts it is the routine of practicing over and over again that brings about excellence, whether it is a piano piece, a solo, or lines for a play. We endure the hard and often boring work of practice because we trust that it will produce greater creativity. God gives us routines, and as we practice them he is like the personal trainer who is right there with every rep of the exercise routine or run-through of the song. While observing the spiritual disciplines we must remember that the routines are to promote our relationship with God. Routines without a conscious relationship with God can be even worse, for they can lead to pride, arrogance, and independence from God. The Sports Spectrum website, after Kansas City's Super Bowl win in 2020, reported that winning quarterback Patrick Mahomes has a routine worth noting:

> Before every game, I walk the field and I do a prayer at the goalpost. I just thank God for those opportunities, and I thank God for letting me be on a stage where I can glorify Him. The biggest thing that I pray for is that whatever happens, win or lose, success or failure, that I'm glorifying Him. (Ackerman 2020)

Of course, the foundation for this relationship is personal trust in Christ for salvation and for his sanctifying work in us through the Spirit.

***Creativity in Presentation.***

This could be a very negative sermon. There are plenty of things to tell people about that they are doing wrong and should stop. This passage begins with importance of honoring the Sabbath, which is a positive action; it is something to do. When we focus upon *not doing* the severe sins mentioned in 18:12–18, most people would say they don't struggle with those, even if they do. The goal is to not commit those sins or any sin. By focusing on the ways to honor the Sabbath or the routines of the spiritual disciplines, it gives our listeners something positive to do.

A possible way to present the closing imprecation could be as a "rest of the story" type of movement in the sermon. It is like a teacher saying toward the end of class, "And by the way, if you fail the test next week you will fail the class, so be sure to study." If we fail to observe these simple commands, we are in danger of committing more serious ones.

To provide a sense of unity for the whole, the image of the potter and the clay can be used in the first section, even though it is not mentioned in the text. It is important to show the progressive relationship between violating the Sabbath and being rejected by God.

- Let simple obedience (observing the Sabbath) shapes us into vessels God desires (17:19–27).
- If necessary, God can throw out vessels that won't or can't be shaped (severe disobedience) (18:1–23).

Idea: Simple obedience guards against severe disobedience.

## DISCUSSION QUESTIONS

1. What are some of your spiritual habits? How consistent are they?
2. What are some spiritual habits that you have observed in others' lives?
3. What is one spiritual habit you wish was part of your life?
4. What insights about God or about yourself do you gain from the image of the potter?
5. How does Jeremiah's closing imprecation make you feel?

## Jeremiah 19:1–20:18

### EXEGETICAL IDEA

Jeremiah pronounced a final condemnation against his people, but was profoundly dismayed at how his life and ministry turned out. He gave a scathing condemnation of the city at the Potsherd Gate, and he cursed an apostate temple official named Pashhur. But he was so dismayed at what he had to do that he also cursed the day he was born—an expression of how thoroughly he hated that he should be put in this role.

### THEOLOGICAL FOCUS

A people can become so stubborn in their sin that there is nothing left for a minister to do but pronounce judgment, but for someone who desires to reach people for God there is no more bitter task than this. The preacher's heart will be broken by the incomprehensible, irrational evil of his people, and also by the necessity that he must curse and condemn them.

### PREACHING IDEA

There are times when it is bitter to talk about getting better.

### PREACHING POINTERS

What Jeremiah did and where he did it are both part of his message. The place was the valley of Hinnom, where infants were sacrificed, which is the reason the nation would be shattered like a flask. Then, the personal opposition from Pashhur could have easily prompted him to deliver this message with an arrogance of self-authority, thinking, "Well, I guess I told them." But Jeremiah responds with such sorrow and grief for his nation that he cursed the day he was born.

No one likes to preach or teach about hell. But we must. This passage shows us that Jeremiah struggled with preaching about God's wrath that was coming on Judah. From his struggle we can find comfort in knowing that it is good to struggle when preaching/teaching about the coming judgment of hell. Of course, we have the luxury of preaching the good news, but we must remember that the good news starts with the bad news. If anyone will desire to be made better by God's gracious work, then the bitter portion of the gospel must be proclaimed first.

# THE BROKEN NATION AND AN EXHAUSTED PROPHET (19:1–20:18)

## LITERARY STRUCTURE AND THEMES

This account concludes the series of passages showing how it was that Jeremiah came to cease praying for his people. It includes a final, climactic sermon of judgment that included the smashing of a pottery flask as a symbol of what would happen to Jerusalem. But Jeremiah took no pleasure in doing this. He was so thoroughly disheartened that he cursed the day of his birth.

- ***The Sermon at the Potsherd Gate (19:1–15)***
- ***Jeremiah Curses Pashhur at the Benjamin Gate (20:1–6)***
- ***Jeremiah Curses the Day of His Birth (20:7–18)***

## EXPOSITION

### *The Sermon at the Potsherd Gate (19:1–15)*

**19:1–2**. Jeremiah acquired an earthenware decanter (בַּקְבֻּק), a small vessel with a narrow neck used for pouring out liquid such as water or oil. These were common in ancient Israel, and it was probably the pottery of choice for his purpose because it was small (about eight inches tall, thin, and often with a slender neck) and somewhat delicate, and therefore it was easily carried and easily broken. Against a number of translations, it was not a "jar," which could be fairly thick and cumbersome for Jeremiah's purposes. He was to take along a representative group of common people and elders and enact before them a prophetic sign-act. The event took place near the Potsherd Gate (שַׁעַר הַחַרְסִית). We do not know precisely where this was, but from the account it was obviously near the Ben Hinnom Valley, located inside the modern city of Jerusalem near what is now called Mount Zion. The name "Potsherd Gate" suggests that people would take their broken pottery pieces outside this gate and dump them there. As Jeremiah was about to proclaim that the city was going to be shattered by the Babylonians, the setting, with its mounds of detritus and potsherds, would have been appropriate. More importantly, it was near Topheth, the place where children were sacrificed to Baal.

**19:3**. Jeremiah addressed his audience, including the "kings" of Judah. This does not mean that he literally had a king present; he was sending a message to the royal house. This also explains the use of the plural; he was speaking to the dynasty and not to any one king. Jeremiah forewarned his audience that he was about to give them a harsh message; the expression "his ears will tingle" (תְּצִלֶּנָה אָזְנָיו) always introduces a message of judgment and death (1 Sam. 3:11; 2 Kings 21:12).

**19:4–6**. The reasons for the coming judgment are, first, the people are apostate, having turned to foreign gods; and second, they engage in child sacrifice. The text emphasizes two things about these sins. First, they worship gods whom their ancestors did not acknowledge or honor. That is, their behavior was contrary to their identity as the people of YHWH. Second, YHWH never commanded them to sacrifice their children; in fact, the idea never entered his head. This suggests that when the people killed their offspring, they believed they were doing God's will (perhaps based on a perverse reading of the story of the near-sacrifice of Isaac in Genesis 22). As a mark of his disdain for the practice, God declares that the place should not be called Topheth or the Ben Hinnom Valley, but the "The Killing Valley" (גֵּיא הַהֲרֵגָה). This does not mean that the name would literally be renamed "The Killing Valley" but that it would be forever infamous for the atrocities committed there.

**19:7–8**. "I make void the counsel of Judah and Jerusalem" (וּבַקֹּתִי אֶת־עֲצַת יְהוּדָה וִירוּשָׁלַם) does not refer to economic or military plans or to the advice of sages. The "counsel" (עֵצָה) in this case is their religious doctrine and more specifically the beliefs they turn to for help and security. Its use here is analogous to Psalm 14:6 (עֲצַת־עָנִי תָבִישׁוּ כִּי יְהוָה מַחְסֵהוּ), which ought to be translated, "You treat the consolation (עֵצָה) of the poor, that YHWH is their refuge, as something disgraceful." In Jeremiah, the עֵצָה is this: The people believe that they guarantee the security of Jerusalem by sacrificing their children. But God will see to it that those who committed such abominations will die by violence and starvation, and that the whole world will know of their crimes and punishment.

**19:9**. This verse is a piece of grim irony: the people are willing to sacrifice their children, believing it will give them security and prosperity, but God will make conditions in Jerusalem so bad that they will eat their remaining children to try to stay alive. The implied idea is that if they think so little of their children, they might as well eat them.

**19:10–11**. After delivering his verbal message, Jeremiah shatters the flask in the presence of the whole crowd. This is an acted-out parable representing what will happen to the city. It, like the flask, will be shattered. Verse 11 makes the interpretation of the act explicit. YHWH will irreparably shatter the city. This should not be taken too literally; YHWH will in fact bring refugees back from Babylon to rebuild Jerusalem. The irreparable shattering of the flask is a rhetorical way of saying that the city would be utterly demolished. It will not be a partial destruction, allowing survivors to remain in the city and repair it. Until the postexilic restoration, there would be no city there at all. Furthermore, just as the potsherds in the Ben Hinnom Valley formed a great, partially buried mound of rubble, so would the whole city be.

**19:12–13**. The ultimate grim irony is this: All of Jerusalem would be like Topheth. It would be filled with dead bodies and the filth and ritual uncleanness that goes with it. The ordinary homes and the dynastic palace would equally be left in flames, just as Topheth perpetually had the flames of the bodies of sacrificed children being consumed. In addition to the crime of child sacrifice, they also burned incense on their rooftops to astral deities (the roofs were flat and had small shrines upon them). Instead of the smoke of incense going up, the very houses would burn and send up smoke.

**19:14–15**. After giving his message and breaking the flask in the Ben Hinnom Valley, Jeremiah went up to the Temple Mount and delivered a similar message there. Is this message the "temple sermon" of Jeremiah 26? If so, then the events of chapter 19 took place at the same time, "early in the reign of Jehoiakim" (26:1). The account of the message here in 19:14–15 is clearly only a very brief summary; chapter 26 may give a more complete account. It looks like the whole of 17:19–19:15 recounts events leading up to Jeremiah's decisive conclusion that Jerusalem was finished. It began with the sermon on keeping the Sabbath, apparently given in Josiah's reign when there was still hope for restoration. Josiah was succeeded briefly by Jehoahaz and then by the deeply apostate Jehoiakim. The message at the potter's house, early in Jehoiakim's reign, demonstrated that the people were implacably stubborn and that there would be no revival. Jeremiah, now understanding how things really stood, made his harsh imprecatory prayer privately, consigning Jerusalem to the wrath of God. He then publicly proclaimed the coming destruction by shattering of the flask in the Ben Hinnom Valley and by giving the temple sermon. The brief account of the sermon in 19:15 focuses on a single fact: Jerusalem will fall because its people are stubborn and refuse to listen to the prophetic message.

### *Jeremiah Curses Pashhur at the Benjamin Gate (20:1–6)*

**20:1–2**. Pashhur son of Immer was evidently a priest; it is doubtful a non-priest would hold a high office in the temple. He was not the high priest, but he was apparently in charge of day-to-day affairs in the temple, including the maintaining of order there. He considered Jeremiah's sermon to be an affront to the dignity of the temple, a crime tantamount to blasphemy. Jeremiah was arrested and beaten. He was then kept overnight in stocks (מַהְפֶּכֶת), although some question whether this translation is correct and think it refers to a cramped cell in which the prisoner would remain hunched over (Thompson 1980, 454). Either way, it made for a very difficult night for Jeremiah.

**20:3**. As soon as he was released, Jeremiah gave Pashhur a new name from God himself, "Terror on every side" (מָגוֹר מִסָּבִיב). This expression appears several times in Jeremiah and elsewhere. In Jeremiah 6:25, it describes the terror of the Jewish refugees as they flee the invading Babylonians. In 20:10, it describes the mockery of the people as they listen to Jeremiah preach of the coming conquest. In 46:5, it expresses the panic of the routed Egyptian army. In 49:29, it concerns the terror of the kingdoms of Kedar and Hazor as they face the coming Babylonians. In Lamentations 2:22, it describes the devastation of Jerusalem by the Babylonians. In Psalm 31:13 (MT 14), it expresses that anxiety of the psalmist, who hears whispers of violence and of enemies all around him. In short, the term always concerns violent attacks by an enemy, and in every case except the psalm, the enemy is the Babylonian army (although the usage in 20:10 is distinctive, as described below). When Jeremiah tells Pashhur that he will be called "Terror on every side," he implies that the horrors of the Babylonian invasion will strike him personally and perhaps that people will attribute the disaster in part to Pashhur. The word מָגוֹר, we should note, plainly means "terror," since its use in every context carries that connotation. However, there are three separate roots גור, meaning respectively 1) to sojourn, 2) to quarrel, and(3) to fear. It is possible that Jeremiah associates all three meanings with מָגוֹר, because Pashhur will be terrified of all the fighting around him and he will be taken into exile (Holladay 1986, 543–44).

**20:4–5**. Pashhur will see for himself the bloody slaughter that accompanies the Babylonian invasion, and his close friends and family members will fall to their swords. Furthermore, Pashhur was a powerful and almost certainly wealthy man. He would see his possessions and the riches of the whole country carried away to Babylon.

**20:6**. Ancient people tended to be deeply rooted in the soil of their homeland, often because their family owned and occupied the same land for generations. This was certainly true of the Israelites, who also viewed the land as their "inheritance" from YHWH. Their conception of who they were and why their lives mattered was bound up with the ground they were born on, the holy soil of Israel. Thus, to be exiled and to die in a foreign land was a horrible fate. It created a profound sense of alienation, and it implied that they were unworthy to be called Israelites. This, Jeremiah says, is Pashhur's fate.

### *Jeremiah Curses the Day of His Birth (20:7–18)*

With no transition, the passage abruptly shifts from the curse on Pashhur to Jeremiah's bitter complaint to God and his wish that he had died at birth. We do not need to suppose that Jeremiah voiced the prayer while he was still standing in front of Pashhur (it is a fairly intimate prayer), but it may well have been voiced soon after the episode of the previous verses. The harsh punishment Pashhur gave him certainly fueled Jeremiah's indignation, and he links the two parts of the passage together by repeating the phrase "terror on every side" (20:3, 10).

**20:7a**. "You deceived me, YHWH, and I was deceived" (פִּתִּיתַנִי יְהוָה וָאֶפָּת) is an astonishing way to begin a prayer. The verb, from the root I-פתה (piel stem), means to deceive, to seduce, or to persuade, and it often has a negative connotation (Judg. 14:15; 1 Kings 22:20; Prov. 1:10), as it does here in פִּתִּיתַנִי. In the niphal stem, it means to be seduced (Job 31:9), or, as here in וָאֶפָּת, to be deceived or drawn in under false pretenses. It fairly appears that Jeremiah is calling YHWH a liar, speaking as though God defrauded the hapless prophet. But it is not quite as bad as it appears. The solution is not to find a different meaning for I-פתה, but to understand the context. Jeremiah understands God to be determining the whole course of his life. And he was a child of the reformation of Josiah, the king who sought to drive out paganism and restore orthodox devotion to YHWH. In his time, the temple was restored to its former dignity, the Law was found and proclaimed, and it seemed as though Judah was entering a new golden age of prosperity, security, and devotion to God. Jeremiah himself clearly participated in the enthusiasm of reformation with the joy and certainty that only youth can feel. And God had called him to be a prophet! Nothing could have been more glorious. True, God had warned him that he would need to armor him against many foes, but young Jeremiah no doubt believed he would go from triumph to triumph. But Josiah had died in battle, the reformation came crashing down, and Jeremiah soon found himself facing down the hostility of Jehoiakim, the Jerusalem establishment, and the common people. Instead of giving the word of God to eager listeners, he found himself preaching condemnation to a crowd that was not only unrepentant but considered him to be the blasphemer. The city and temple he loved were destined to come to a horrific end within his lifetime. If taken literally, Jeremiah's words call YHWH a liar, but they should not be read in that way. Jeremiah is dismayed at how his life has turned out, and he has come to look upon his prophetic calling as a great and bitter burden. What he means is, "YHWH, following your call has really turned out badly for me." It is an open and blunt statement of his exasperation and sorrow, but it is not blasphemy.

**20:7b–9**. Jeremiah had a most unenviable task: he had to preach nothing but bad news and condemnation to his people. No one wants to hear that they are evil, and people naturally recoil from that their future contains only catastrophe and misery. Jeremiah's message was ceaselessly one of "violence and destruction" (חָמָס וָשֹׁד). Consequently everyone hated him, and tried to escape the terror his words inspired by whistling past the graveyard, mocking him and his words. Even so, Jeremiah found himself unable to stop preaching. The truth of the messages God gave him, the grave danger his people stood in, the provocation their derision gave to his soul, and the sheer power of the words that the Spirit had given him made it impossible for him to retreat in silence. God had made him a prophet, and he could not escape the inner compulsion.

**20:10**. Once again Jeremiah uses the idiom "terror on every side," but this time he quotes the beginning of Psalm 31:13 (MT 14) verbatim. The verse in the psalm reads, "For I hear the slander of many (כִּי שָׁמַעְתִּי דִּבַּת רַבִּים);

[they say], 'Terror on every side' (מָגוֹר מִסָּבִיב) when they conspire together against me. They plot to take my life." This is a Davidic psalm. The verse indicates that David's enemies say, "Terror on every side" when they conspire against him, meaning that they plan to surround and attack him literally or metaphorically. Jeremiah considers himself to be, like David, the victim of a cruel conspiracy. In Jeremiah's case, however, the words are used differently. The verse means, "For I hear the slander of many (כִּי שָׁמַעְתִּי דִּבַּת רַבִּים)! [They say], 'Tell [him], "Terror on every side! (מָגוֹר מִסָּבִיב)" Let's tell him [that]!' Everyone who was at peace with me is watching for my fall. [They say,] 'Perhaps he is deceived, and we will prevail over him, and then we can take our vengeance on him.'" He has spoken of the Babylonian invasion as "terror on every side," and the people, in their mockery, use the words to deride him. They have taken the phrase as a summary of his whole message and encourage each other to throw the words back in his face. To loosely paraphrase, they are saying, "Whenever Jeremiah starts to preach, just tell him, 'Terror on every side!' Yes, we know. That's your whole message." It is possible that they adopted "Terror on every side" as a nickname for Jeremiah (Bright 1963, 132–33). If so, this may explain why Jeremiah gave the name to Pashhur, effectively saying, "You, Pashhur, are the real 'terror on every side.' Not me." In addition, Jeremiah's friends (אֱנוֹשׁ שְׁלוֹמִי; lit., "man of my peace") turn against him. But their words do betray anxiety. They say, "Perhaps he is deceived (אוּלַי יְפֻתֶּה)," using the same word that Jeremiah used when he complained that God had deceived him (I-פתה). In the mouths of his enemies, however, the words mean that perhaps the Babylonians will not conquer Jerusalem and Jeremiah will be shown to be a false prophet. Then they can fully have their vengeance on him. But the words show that they were actually afraid that he was right.

*TRANSLATION NOTE: JEREMIAH 20:10*

The interpretation of this verse is quite difficult. The opening, "For I hear the slander of many (כִּי שָׁמַעְתִּי דִּבַּת רַבִּים)" indicates that the following words are what the crowd is saying. Evidently, the crowd is saying "Terror on every side!" (מָגוֹר מִסָּבִיב), as in the psalm. The next words, הַגִּידוּ וְנַגִּידֶנּוּ, are a hiphil imperative and *weyiqtol* of נגד and mean, "Tell! So, let's tell him!" This too must be what the crowd is saying. Against many interpreters and translations, we have no grounds for translating this as "denounce" in the sense of "to publicly, verbally oppose someone." The verb is very common but is nowhere else used with that meaning. On rare occasion, it means to inform on someone, in the sense of divulging some secret to the harm of that person (Josh. 2:14, 20; Job 17:5), but this can hardly apply to Jeremiah. Who he was and what he believed was public knowledge; he shouted it out in the temple courtyard. The meaning of נגד is simply to tell, explain, proclaim, or inform someone of something. Furthermore, in Deuteronomy 32:7, where the verb is followed by a pronoun suffix (as it is here), the pronoun refers to the person who hears the message: "Ask you father, and he will tell you" (שְׁאַל אָבִיךָ וְיַגֵּדְךָ). If the suffix is third-person feminine singular, it is used abstractly for the content of the message (Isa. 44:7; Jer. 9:11), but that does not apply here. In short, the verbs can only mean that the people are exhorting one another to tell Jeremiah, "Terror on every side!" This is their response to his preaching. As described above, they are encouraging each other to mock his words by throwing them back at him. The verse, with its poetic line divisions, means:

For I hear the slander of the crowd:<br>
"Just tell him, 'Terror on every side!'<br>
  Let's tell him that!"<br>
Everyone who was at peace with me is<br>
  watching for my fall.<br>
"Perhaps he is deceived, and we will<br>
  prevail over him,<br>
And then we can take our vengeance on<br>
  him."

**20:11–12**. It is surprising to us that Jeremiah, in the middle of an outcry of despair, having just spoken of how God "deceived" him, now speaks with utmost confidence in being vindicated by God. But this is normal for Old Testament prayers. A person may in one breath seem to complain bitterly and even inappropriately against God, and in the next declare his certainty that God is with him and will save him. Besides speaking of God as his champion and declaring that his enemies will fall, Jeremiah again makes an imprecation against them, asking God to avenge him for what they have done. This is a clue to the conflicted state of Jeremiah's mind. He is truly committed to YHWH, and he believes that God will rescue him from all the enemies he has been complaining about. At the same time, his life is bitter, and the hostility of the crowd is hard to take. The really astonishing thing in this passage is not that he here praises God and expresses confidence; it is that in verses 14–18 he reverses course and curses the day of his birth. But we are here seeing two aspects of Jeremiah's character on display simultaneously: his deep faith and his extreme discouragement and sorrow.

**20:13**. The doxological call, "Sing to YHWH! Praise YHWH!" (שִׁירוּ לַיהוָה הַלְלוּ אֶת־יְהוָה) has many echoes in the Psalter and elsewhere (Exod. 15:21; Ps. 96:1, 2; 98:1; 149:1; 1 Chron. 16:23; Isa. 42:10). The proverbial clause, "He rescues the life of the poor from the hand of the wicked" (הִצִּיל אֶת־נֶפֶשׁ אֶבְיוֹן מִיַּד מְרֵעִים) also has echoes in the Psalter (Ps. 82:4; 97:10; 144:7, 11). Jeremiah is like a man who recites Scripture in the middle of a calamity that is tearing his heart out. His grief is almost overwhelming, but his faith in God is constant. Note that Jeremiah refers to himself as "poor" (אֶבְיוֹן). The term does not refer to his economic status but to his isolation and helplessness in the face of the overwhelming hostility of powerful foes.

**20:14–18**. If we had thought that Jeremiah had shaken off his gloom and was now feeling hopeful and optimistic, we are here forcibly disabused of the notion. He curses the day of his birth. The essential meaning is hard to miss: he considers his birth to be an unalloyed tragedy because his life has been so unbearably bad. Even here, his language is somewhat restrained. He does not curse God for bringing him into the world, nor does he curse his father and mother. He does, however, curse just about every other aspect of the occasion of his birth. He curses the fact that people celebrated because a son had been born (יֻלַּד־לְךָ בֵּן זָכָר; lit., "a son is born to you—a male!"). In ancient Israel, sons were expected to remain with the family and take care of their parents when they got old. Girls grew up to marry into other families, where they would help care for their husband's family. Thus, a son was much desired.

Jeremiah also curses the man who brought the news of his birth to his father. This tells us something about the domestic culture of ancient Israel. Apparently, when a woman was giving birth, she would be attended by the midwife and one or more women. A man, a friend of the father, would be nearby, perhaps in the next room or just outside the house. The father would be kept away from the birth, probably in another house. After the child was born, the midwife would tell the friend, who in turn would go and inform the father of the situation. This was probably done to provide a buffer if some tragedy occurred, such as if the child was stillborn or the mother died giving birth. In ancient Israel, this would have been more common than one would have wished. Evidently the Israelites believed it would be too traumatic for the father to be present if such a tragedy struck. For his part, however, Jeremiah curses the man who brought the news of his birth, wishing that God would do to him what he did to Sodom and Gomorrah (v. 16)! He also wishes that he had never emerged from the womb. Of course, Jeremiah is expressing himself with hyperbole. He did not literally hate the man who told his father of his birth, nor did he literally want to remain perpetually a corpse in his mother's womb, with her belly forever swollen (v. 17). The Israelites, we may be sure, knew that if a woman miscarried, the fetus was expelled. Here, as elsewhere, we need to be very careful about how we read the prophets. An overly literal interpretation will often badly skew what the speaker meant to communicate. The real meaning of Jeremiah's words comes out in verse 18: he wishes he had never had to go through so much trouble (עָמָל), sorrow (יָגוֹן), and shame (בֹּשֶׁת). But is Jeremiah's suffering sufficient to explain this extreme outburst? I believe there is more to it than that, as we see when we look at the only parallel passage, Job's cursing of the day of his birth (Job 3).

### Cursing the Day of One's Birth

Job, after having heroically refused to curse God, cursed the day of his birth (Job 3). In both of these acts, he was like Jeremiah. But the account of the cursing of the day of birth is far more complete in Job, and from it we can gain insight into what the act means. Today, scholars widely recognize that Job was alluding to the creation narrative when he cursed the day of his birth (this follows the work of Fishbane 1971). More specifically, Job *reverses* or *undoes* the acts of creation. In Job's speech we can see the following allusions:

- Job declares that the day of his birth should "be darkness," and he dissolves the distinction between day and night (3:3–6a). This reverses Genesis 1:3–4, in which God creates light, separates it from darkness, and calls the light "day" and the darkness "night."
- Job wishes to obliterate his birthday from the calendar (3:6b), breaking the regularity of days, seasons, and years God established on day four (Gen. 1:14).
- Job desires sorcerers to invoke Leviathan (3:8), a kind of demonic sea-monster, to obliterate the day of his birth. By contrast, God created great sea creatures that were "good" (Gen. 1:21–21).
- Job wishes he died in the womb and curses his birth (3:11–12, 16). This undoes God's command to multiply (Gen. 1:28), a blessing on fertility and fecundity. People should regard healthy childbirth as an absolute good.
- Job desires the rest that is the slumber of death and the tomb (3:13–15, 17–19). This is in contrast with the Sabbath, God's rest (Gen. 2:2–3). People should desire to share in God's rest, not to die as a form of rest.

Job's cursing of his birthday and his implied undoing of creation make sense in the wider context of the book. Job was a righteous man who feared God and turned from evil. Even so, God allowed him to suffer extreme affliction in order to demonstrate that he was not serving God only because God enriched and protected him. Job refused to curse God, but the event was a crisis of faith for him. Like his three friends Eliphaz, Bildad, and Zophar, Job firmly believed that the problem of evil was entirely solved by the doctrine of retribution. This states that the reason for suffering in the world is that people are evil, and God punishes them. For Job and his friends, this solution resolved any challenge to the goodness of God in his administration of the world. In their minds, all suffering comes about because God is punishing evil people. Also, they think there are no cases of the good having to suffer disasters or of the wicked escaping such ruin. By this reasoning, there is no such thing as undeserved suffering, and miscarriages of divine judgment never happen. The three friends reason that if Job suffered a terrible calamity, he must have committed some terrible sin to deserve it. The reader knows this is wrong, but neither Job nor his friends knew what God was doing. But Job knew he had not sinned and, in the terms of the doctrine of retribution, had done nothing to deserve what happened to him. Therefore, to his friends' consternation, he refused to make a hollow confession of sin in order to resolve the intellectual dilemma and save the doctrine of retribution. He continued to protest his innocence and demand a hearing from God.

But this takes us well beyond chapter 3, which is the very beginning of the dispute between Job and the three. But why does he start by cursing the day of his birth, and why does he couch it in terms of reversing or undoing the creation narrative? First, Job does not mean that he wants the whole world to be destroyed. Even though what he says reverses the creation narrative, he does not think so much of himself that he wants the entire universe to end for his sake. He sets his curse entirely against his personal existence, not against the existence of the whole world. He wants just the day of his birth to be obliterated from the calendar and be engulfed in darkness; he does not wish that the whole cosmos would go dark and that all of time would be annihilated. But Job is saying more than "I wish I were dead" or "I wish I had never been born." He did not need to invoke creation language to say that.

The creation narrative represents the fact that the world was set up in an orderly fashion by a wise and benevolent God. The world makes sense, and it is organized to make sense. It is not set up in a random, chaotic fashion. In short, the creation narrative is the opposite of a nihilistic philosophy. Virtue, purpose, order, and goodness are real things built into the very structure of the world; they are not, as in nihilism, meaningless concepts. But people see evil all the time and, worse, suffering that is apparently random, senseless, and undeserved. For this, the doctrine of retribution steps in to save the day: All suffering is the result of punishment, and indeed it always deserved punishment. Again, this is precisely what Job believed. And yet now it no longer works. He knows he is innocent (and God himself affirmed that this was true in 1:8). But the only category Job has for explaining suffering is punishment for sin. For him, therefore, the world makes no sense. Job's theology and worldview have collapsed. He has become the great counterexample to the doctrine of retribution. This is why he invokes the undoing of creation in his cursing of the day of his birth. He is saying, "The world no longer makes sense to me; it has become an arbitrary, nihilistic chaos. My life experience wrecks the whole system by which I have governed all my actions and experiences. The best thing would be to have the day of my birth obliterated from the history of creation."

Jeremiah's situation is in some respects different from Job's. Jeremiah was not dealing with the doctrine of retribution (he had no doubt that the Israelites deserved to be punished), and he was not in his own experience a counterexample to a theological postulate. Also, Jeremiah in his curse of the day of his birth does not explicitly speak of an undoing of creation in the manner of Job. But there are also significant similarities between the two. Jeremiah does give a reversal-of-creation speech in 4:23–26, where he sees the devastation to be brought about by Babylon in those terms. Jeremiah, like Job, saw himself as a man completely out of sync with orthodoxy of his peers. Job's friends believed that the doctrine of retribution was the sole and sufficient answer to problems of theodicy, but Job refused to join them in concluding that he had done something evil to deserve his punishment. Jeremiah's peers were not simply a bunch of idolaters. They believed that the Davidic Covenant and the sacred status of Zion and the temple made it inconceivable that Jerusalem could be conquered by a foreign nation. In both cases, Job and Jeremiah were regarded by their opponents as blasphemers and heretics. Finally, as Job entered his story fully believing in the doctrine of retribution, so also Jeremiah, like his opponents, believed in the Davidic Covenant, in the sacred status of Zion, and in Israel's special position as the covenant people of God.

Like Job, Jeremiah cursed the day of his birth because his world no longer made sense to him, and he was profoundly disillusioned. We cannot stress enough how significant it was that he came up during Josiah's reformation, when it seemed that righteousness had triumphed and that there was no better time to be called to be YHWH's prophet. Yet he saw Josiah die in battle and the nation revert to a perversion of the Israelite faith, being at the same time both fundamentalist about Israel's special place before God and also thoroughly paganized. Instead of ministering to his people like a beloved parish priest, he brought them nothing but condemnation and judgment, and they in turn hated him. He knew that the task of the prophet was to imitate Moses and intercede for sinners, and yet he found himself forbidden by God himself to do this and instead was calling down destruction upon his people. Like Job, Jeremiah felt that he had no place in this world.

## THEOLOGICAL FOCUS

This is a dark passage, and its core lessons are harsh and at times painful.

- Sometimes judgment is final and irrevocable, like the smashing of a clay vessel. Even though Judah returned from exile, it never recovered what it had been under the Davidic monarchy. A person or people may face a judgment that forever changes their lives, with no chance for a do-over. The ultimate final judgment is when one faces God after death.
- Paganism and apostasy lead to moral decay. In ancient Israel, this showed itself in how the worshipers of Baal sacrificed their own children.
- People can be both incurably wicked and unbearably self-righteous at the same time. The people of Jerusalem sacrificed their own children and yet branded Jeremiah a heretic for having the temerity to say that God would allow his holy city to be destroyed by Babylonians. In our day, many people abandon all forms of sexual morality but will be insufferably censorious about matters of ecology, race, and gender equality.
- Pashhur had Jeremiah beaten for saying that Jerusalem would be destroyed. Heretics often believe their doctrine fervently, and also think that they are exempted from the wrath of God.
- Sometimes those who despise the truth can be very effective at mockery and derision, making black seem white and good seem evil. But behind the ferocity of their mockery is an underlying fear that the words they hear and despise are in fact true.
- In times of crisis and when facing hostility, our prayers may seem wildly inconsistent, at times proclaiming our confidence that God will save us and at times confessing to deep despair and even impatience with God. While we need to govern our thoughts and words when speaking to God, such inner turmoil has strong precedent in the Bible.
- We may feel so dismayed that we can no longer comprehend the world and feel that we no longer belong. That too is not unusual, and in a real sense we do not belong here. But this is where God has put us, and we need to deal with it.

## PREACHING AND TEACHING STRATEGIES

### *Exegetical and Theological Synthesis*

Jeremiah shows us that it is not unusual to struggle when we must proclaim this message of sin and judgment. It was so hard for him that he even wished he hadn't been born. His prayer to God is one of great inner torment and groaning about the opposition from those around him.

We must teach and preach about sin and God's judgment, and we must struggle with it. Wayne Grudem, in his classic *Systematic Theology*, says it this way: "As long as we are in this life, and as long as we see and think about others who need to hear the gospel and trust in Christ for salvation, it should cause us great distress and agony of spirit to think about eternal punishment" (Grudem 1994, 1152).

### Preaching Idea

There are times when it is bitter to talk about getting better.

### Contemporary Connections

#### *What does it mean?*

Of course, we enjoy proclaiming the mercy and grace of the gospel. It is obviously more pleasant to proclaim the forgiveness and the life that comes through Christ. But preaching a passage that teaches about hell is personally very distasteful. The reasons are varied. People will respond negatively toward us and won't like us. The message seems out of balance: eternal punishment for seventy years of sin. Our listeners will dismiss the message and the messenger as just another "hellfire and brimstone" preacher. And besides, hell doesn't do well as a preaching topic to advertise in a pre-Easter mass mailing sent out to every home in the community. When the topic does come up in a passage, I have heard preachers, myself included, speak about the consequence of not trusting Christ as being eternal separation from God. "Eternal separation" is almost a euphemism or vague substitution for those who die without Christ and will spend eternity in hell.

If we struggle like Jeremiah when we present the truth of scriptures that teach about hell, then we are in good company. There are some preachers who don't seem to struggle with this. A friend of mine told me the reason he doesn't go to church is that at his dad's funeral the preacher didn't hesitate and showed no compassion in saying that my friend's deceased dad was burning in hell. There is something very wrong with us if we *like* to preach about God's judgment. A good parent truly means the cliché, "This is going to hurt me more than it hurts you." A good gospel witness has the same emotion.

#### *Is it true?*

Jeremiah's message could not have been clearer. Judah was going to be destroyed, completely, because of her unspeakable sins. While our outward manifestations of a sinful heart may be different, we still have the same hearts as Judah. Our sins are from a deep and twisted heart that rebels against God. There are many affirmations of the twisted human heart in our culture. Many plays and movies that have become classics are tragedies: *Macbeth, Death of a Salesman, Psycho*. To me, it is a mystery as to why these depressing stories are so popular. And yet, I remember reading *Death of a Salesman* and somehow being drawn into the story. Perhaps audiences identify with the evil that is displayed in these artistic representations of life either as victims or as those capable of such wicked actions. Jeremiah was addressing not just wickedness of hearts but the horror of the behavior that came from it: in this case, child sacrifice. Judah's real-life actions were nothing short of the gruesome images in the most extreme horror films. Jeremiah's task was to point out the repulsiveness of Judah's actions and the surety of God's coming destruction. Part of our job as proclaimers of the gospel is to point out that this same wickedness resides in each of us, and that God's judgment is coming.

#### *Now what?*

Jeremiah's struggle is not directly exemplary; rather, it is descriptive. It is like suffering. When we read of the physical and emotional struggles of the saints, are we to emulate their struggle in some kind of self-flagellation? The record of their struggle gives us comfort and lets us know that part of living for Christ is suffering. Part of being a messenger of the consequences of sin and the coming judgment is that we will struggle with that message. To develop this kind of heart, we need to be sure that we believe that God's judgment is coming. It might be wise to review biblical passages and one's systematic theology. Certainly there are different views of this, but if one takes Scripture in the most straightforward sense it is undeniable that God's judgment day is coming. Though it is natural to struggle with the message of sin and judgment, it must not be abandoned.

### *Creativity in Presentation*

This is clearly a two-part message. The first part is an extension of the conclusion from the previous section, where Jeremiah finally accepted that Judah was to be destroyed—not just conquered, but completely destroyed. It is important to present this picture of God's judgment. But the heart of the application is in Jeremiah's struggle.

When done properly, self-disclosure by a teacher/preacher is very effective. It builds identification and allows application in an almost indirect way. As our listeners hear of our struggles, they will be more apt to admit their own struggles. The self-discloser should not just end with the struggle, but also begin the process of overcoming the struggle.

This passage, along with others of Jeremiah's sermons, was delivered in a special location using an object to vividly illustrate the main idea. This gives us a precedent to be creative in the presentation. Why not shatter a small vase or pitcher? If you do, be very careful to use one made of clay or some other material that shatters in larger pieces, so that it can be cleaned up more easily. A glass vase or pitcher would be dangerous and a real pain to clean up. If a small vase or pitcher is to be used, it is imperative to try several kinds made from different materials until a manageable one is found. It is crucial to practice it. Often pastors will think through an object lesson and in their minds it works well—but only in their minds. So yes, it is good to follow Jeremiah's example of using an object, but be sure to practice it in the place you will preach.

A possible structure begins with a question that could be used to tie the passage together. Notice that the last point of the sermon comes from the greater context of Scripture. Also, this last point would be a proper place to invite people to not only embrace the bitter portion of the gospel but to trust Jesus for the better portion of it.

How do we handle the bitter portion of the gospel?

- We proclaim the bitterness with clarity (19:1–15).
- We will be opposed when we present the bitter (20:1–6).
- We will struggle with self-doubt when we present the bitter (20:7–18).
- We praise God, and thank him that the bitter can get better.

## DISCUSSION QUESTIONS

1. What do you think attracts people to watch a sad or even tragic movie?
2. When you watch a tragedy such as *Romeo and Juliet*, how does it make you feel?
3. What reality is reflected in tragedies?
4. How important is the "bad news" portion of the gospel?
5. When someone has "bad" news for you, how do you want it presented? What attitude do you want the messenger to have?

# HISTORICALLY CONTEXTUALIZED MESSAGES I (21:1–29:32)

In a series of messages dated to the reigns of Judah's last kings, Jeremiah demonstrates that the house of David has fallen into deep corruption and that the dynasty must end.

# Jeremiah 21:1–23:40

## EXEGETICAL IDEA

A request from Zedekiah for a favorable oracle from God leads to a lengthy recital of the messages God has sent against the house of David, along with a condemnation of the false prophets. It is likely that Zedekiah had hoped that Jeremiah could provide a miraculous deliverance from the Babylonians, such as had happened in the reign of Hezekiah when the Assyrians besieged Jerusalem. To this, Jeremiah responds that the whole dynasty of David—from Zedekiah back through the reigns of Jehoiachin, Jehoiakim, and Jehoahaz—had become so corrupt that no such salvation was possible.

## THEOLOGICAL FOCUS

If we have a history of refusing to heed the messages of warning that God has sent us, we cannot expect him to give us a message of hope. God will not extend mercy to those whose habitual apostasy and corruption has reached the maximum. The leadership of the nation, both secular and religious, bears special guilt in this regard.

## PREACHING IDEA

Ask God for victory (intervention), but don't violate his authority.

## PREACHING POINTERS

It is wrong to expect God to intervene for us and affirm our work when we are violating his word and worshipping other gods. Some need arises in our life, so we ask him for a victory over the problem, but what is more needed is victory over our disobedient lives and hearts. Of course, we need to ask God for victory in our lives, while being careful not to violate his authority.

# MESSAGE TO THE DELEGATION FROM ZEDEKIAH (21:1–23:40)

## LITERARY STRUCTURE AND THEMES

Jeremiah 21:1–25:38 presents three major addresses dated respectively to the three kings in which they were given: late in the reign of Zedekiah, in 588 B.C. (21:1–23:40); after the exile of Jehoiachin, in 597 (24:1–10); and fairly early in the reign of Jehoiakim, in 605 (25:1–38). As is obvious, the messages are presented in the reverse of their chronological order. Furthermore, the message to Zedekiah, Judah's last king, includes a condemnation of the Davidic dynasty with oracles originally given against Jehoahaz (22:10–12), Jehoiakim (22:13–23), and Jehoiachin (22:24–30). These three messages are cited in their chronological sequence, but they occur inside a message delivered in the time of Zedekiah. That is, the oracle against Zedekiah cites or recalls former oracles against his three predecessors on the throne. It is clear that a major function of these texts is to condemn the ruling house.

- ***The Certainty of Disaster (21:1–10)***
- ***Messages Concerning the House of David (21:11–23:8)***
    - *The Condemnation of the Dynasty Is Just (21:11–22:9)*
    - *Josiah Compared to Jehoahaz [Shallum] (22:10–12)*
    - *Josiah Compared to Jehoiakim (22:13–23)*
    - *Jehoiachin [Coniah] Is the End of the House of David (22:24–30)*
    - *The Failure and Future of the Davidic Dynasty (23:1–8)*
- ***Concerning the Prophets (23:9–40)***

## EXPOSITION

### *The Certainty of Disaster (21:1–10)*

**21:1–2**. These verses provide the background for the major series of addresses in chapters 21–23. Just prior to the climactic destruction of Jerusalem by the Babylonians, Zedekiah sent a two-man delegation to Jeremiah, seeking a message from God. The first delegate, Pashhur son of Malchiah, should not be confused with Pashhur son of Immer of chapter 20, a man who bitterly hated Jeremiah. The second delegate, Zephaniah son of Maaseiah, was also in the delegation to him mentioned in 37:3. Judging from 29:25–26, Zephaniah respected Jeremiah, regarding him as a true prophet. Thus, it appears that as Jerusalem's doom drew near, a delegation made up of men favorable to Jeremiah came to him to try to persuade him to deliver a favorable oracle, that Jerusalem would be saved. Indeed, their words in verse 2 imply that they hoped Jeremiah would bring about a repeat of the great miracle prophesied by Isaiah in the time of Hezekiah, when the angel of YHWH slew the Assyrian army (Isa. 36–37).

**21:3–7**. There will be no repeat of the great miracle against Sennacherib from the time of Hezekiah. Apparently at the time the oracle was given, the bulk of the Babylonian army had not arrived at Jerusalem and the army of Judah could still put up some resistance out in the field. The NIV translation of verse 4 should not be followed at two points. First, the text does not say that YHWH would turn the weapons of Judah "against you" (that is, against Judah, as though their own weapons would fight against them).

It only means that he will turn them and their weapons back (that is, they will be defeated and withdraw to the city). Second, the verse should not be interpreted to mean that the Babylonians were currently "besieging" you. The root I-צור can mean "encircle" or "surround," but at the time of writing the men of Judah were still out in the field. Probably the Babylonians were in process of encircling Jerusalem and preparing for a siege but did not yet have it in place. Finally, it is not clear who YHWH will "gather" (וְאָסַפְתִּי) into Jerusalem—whether it will be the defenders, who will be confined behind their walls; or the attackers, who will ultimately break into the city. Probably the ambiguity is deliberate and both are meant (Thompson 1980, 467–68). But the most important point is in verses 5–6: that YHWH is fighting against, not for, Jerusalem. Trapped inside the city, the people would suffer the ravages of "plague" (דֶּבֶר, v. 6). This was known to happen in ancient warfare. Almost 160 years later, Athens would similarly suffer a great plague while under siege by the Spartans in the Peloponnesian War (430 B.C.). Furthermore, all who survived the plague, as well as death by starvation or military violence, would be taken prisoner to Nebuchadnezzar to suffer further humiliation and death (v. 7).

**21:8–10**. God's offer to Jerusalem, that they can choose either the way of life or the way of death, is taken directly from Deuteronomy 30:15–20. Here, however, the way to life that God offers is not simply a matter of listening to him and keeping his commands—they must surrender to Babylon! The original offer of Deuteronomy and the Sinai covenant was now a dead letter; the destruction of the city and the exile of the populace had been decreed, and there was no hope that the original terms of Israel's covenant could be fulfilled by anything but death and ruin, the results of covenant violation. The glorious promise of the Sinai covenant, the rule of Israel over the Holy Land, was finished. However, people could save their own lives by voluntarily submitting to Babylon. The Jews' lives would be their only booty (v. 9; וְהָיְתָה־לּוֹ נַפְשׁוֹ לְשָׁלָל), a military metaphor meaning that survival is the best they can hope for in this war.

### *Messages Concerning the House of David (21:11–23:8)*

All of this section, along with 23:9–40, is here included in the response to the delegation from Zedekiah. This section concerns the collapse of the Davidic dynasty. It is a response to the implied belief that the dynasty cannot fall because of the promises given in 1 Samuel 7. By analogy, Psalm 89 operates from the same presupposition. The text is in five parts. First (21:11–22:9), it asserts that there can be no escape from the catastrophe, indirectly asserting that there will be no repeat of the great miracle of Hezekiah's reign (Isa. 36–37). The second (22:10–12), third (22:13–23), and fourth (22:24–30) parts recall messages given to Zedekiah's predecessors Jehoahaz, Jehoiakim, and Jehoiachin, making the point that the dynasty has acquired enormous guilt and must be terminated. The fifth part (23:1–8) reaffirms that the dynasty is finished, yet promises a future, eschatological David.

#### *The Condemnation of the Dynasty Is Just (21:11–22:9)*

This passage recites two oracles given to the Davidic house some time prior to Zedekiah's delegation, perhaps early in the reign of Jehoiakim. The two messages, respectively 21:11–14 and 22:1–9, were probably given at different times to the royal house. They are here combined and presented as evidence that God gave the Davidic kings ample warning, but they paid no heed.

**21:11–12**. The following message was specifically for the royal house of Judah (לְבֵית מֶלֶךְ יְהוּדָה). The injunction in verse 12 is a summary of God's demands, stating that the kings must be just and, in particular, stand up for those without wealth and power. Otherwise, they would face the consequences.

**21:13–14**. Jerusalem is "the inhabitant of the valley, the plateau of rock" (יֹשֶׁבֶת הָעֵמֶק צוּר הַמִּישֹׁר), which is an apt description of the city's geographical situation. It sits on elevated, rocky ground inside a basin of higher hills. So located, the people boast that their capital is impregnable: "Who can come into our lair?" (וּמִי יָבוֹא בִּמְעוֹנוֹתֵינוּ). This recalls the language of Obadiah 3, which says of Edom, "Inhabitant of the rocky clefts, dwelling on the heights, saying to himself, 'Who can bring me down to the ground?'" By implication, Judah is as evil and arrogant as the hated Edomites. But God will send fire on the city—a prophecy that was literally fulfilled.

**22:1–2**. This message was originally given outside the gates of the palace, but the date of its delivery is not specified. Here in the book, the message omits the name of any specific king, implying that it is instead a condemnation of the whole Davidic dynasty.

**22:3–5**. Like 21:12, this begins with an exhortation to do what is just and to save the poorer people from those who would exploit them. Verse 3 even uses the same language as 21:12: "Rescue the man who is getting robbed from the hand of the oppressor" (וְהַצִּילוּ גָזוּל מִיַּד עָשׁוֹק). The repetition implies that the kings had ample instruction and warning. Jeremiah no doubt made similar appeals on several occasions. But verse 3 is more expansive, listing in detail those who are most vulnerable to exploitation: aliens, orphans, and widows (וְגֵר יָתוֹם וְאַלְמָנָה). The language of verse 4 is somewhat optimistic, implying that the dynasty can have a glorious future if it will just obey God's commands. It portrays the kings, nobles, and army marching in splendid array in and out of the gates as a sign of Jerusalem's power and prestige. The word "people" (עַם) here probably refers to the army (as in 1 Sam. 14:17; see also 1 Sam. 2:26; 10:10). This suggests that this message was originally given early in Jeremiah's ministry; his message to Zedekiah in the larger context (chapter 21) is an unqualified prophecy of doom. But it is here cited in Zedekiah's time as proof that the kings received clear warning and rejected it. God said that if they did not obey, "this house" (הַבַּיִת הַזֶּה) would become a "ruin" (חָרְבָּה). In context, the "house" is concretely the royal palace and abstractly the dynasty.

**22:6–7**. The prophecy addresses the "house," more specifically the physical palace as a symbol of the dynasty. The palace was like "Gilead" and "Lebanon" because these were elevated, forested regions from which timber was imported to build the palace and temple (1 Kings 7:2–3). God says he will "sanctify destroyers against you" (וְקִדַּשְׁתִּי עָלַיִךְ מַשְׁחִתִים), meaning that the enemy army will have a divine commission to come and burn down the palace. Since the royal domain was called the "Palace of the Forest of Lebanon" (בֵּית יַעַר הַלְּבָנוֹן; 1 Kings 7:2), its destruction is described as though it were a forest being chopped down with axes and cleared by fire.

**22:8–9**. The reason for the destruction of the Davidic dynasty is given in the terms of the Sinai covenant: they abandoned the covenant in general and in particular broke its most fundamental prohibition, that they should not worship other gods. Notice that the text says nothing about the Davidic Covenant of 1 Samuel 7. That covenant, although it mentions punishment for sin, does not mention any specific terms that the Davidic kings were to keep. Instead they, like all of ancient Israel, was judged according to the terms of the Sinai covenant.

### *Josiah Compared to Jehoahaz [Shallum] (22:10–12)*

We need to recall the circumstances of the brief reign of Jehoahaz. He was the son of Josiah and, despite being younger than Jehoiakim (1 Chron. 3:15; Jer. 22:11), was named the new king after Josiah was slain by Pharaoh Neco in 609 B.C. According to 2 Chronicles 36:1, Jehoiakim was the choice of the "people of the land" to succeed his father. This may mean simply that he was popular, or the "people of the land" may have been the name of a political faction in the capital. About three months later, Neco came back from his attempt to push back against Babylon, and removed Jehoahaz from the throne, replacing him with Jehoiakim. It is not necessarily the case that Jehoiakim was more pro-Egyptian than Jehoahaz. Jehoiakim was willing to pay Neco a large sum of silver and gold, so it is more probable that Jehoiakim simply bought Neco's support and so secured the throne. Since Jehoahaz reigned for such a short time, we know very little about him beyond the fact that he "did evil in YHWH's sight" (2 Kings 23:31–35). After removing him from power, Neco took him to Egypt, where he remained until his death.

**22:10**. Since this verse exhorts its audience not to weep over Josiah but instead to grieve over Jehoahaz, it is all but certain that this message was first delivered in the tumultuous time just after Josiah had been killed and Jehoahaz had been taken to Egypt (that is, in 609 B.C.).

**22:11–12**. Jeremiah does not describe any specific sins for which Jehoahaz deserved YHWH's punishment, but his blunt assertion that he would never come back from his exile in Egypt probably implies that Jeremiah disapproved of Jehoahaz's character. The prophecy that Jehoahaz would languish as an exile and die far from his homeland is presented as a fate literally worse than death. This reflects the common view that it was a great calamity for an Israelite to die and be buried away from his homeland, in Egypt (Gen. 47:30; 50:5; Josh. 24:32; Hos. 9:6). But it implies more than that. The exhortation not to weep over Josiah but to consider the still living Jehoahaz as worse off suggests that there was a popular opinion that Josiah had died a failure. He had served YHWH faithfully and fully repudiated idols, and yet he had come to a bad end. From this, many were evidently concluding that Josiah's strategy for securing God's favor had not worked. In fact, many believed that he suffered heaven's wrath precisely because he had shut down the pagan shrines (Jer. 44:17–19). By declaring Josiah's fate to have been more enviable than Jehoahaz's, Jeremiah implied that it was the slain Josiah, not the exiled Jehoahaz, who enjoyed God's favor. This issue emerges more directly in the next oracle.

### *Josiah Compared to Jehoiakim (22:13–23)*

Although it is not clarified until verse 18, the object of this oracle is Jehoiakim. Since it portrays the death of Jehoiakim as in the future (v. 19), it is evident that within the larger answer to Zedekiah, prior oracles against earlier kings are here cited to make the point that the Davidic dynasty is morally bankrupt.

**22:13–17**. This passage condemns any aristocrat who builds a palace by oppression and extortion; in verse 18, we learn that the aristocrat in question is Jehoiakim. Verse 15 should be translated "Do you think you are behaving like a king because you have a passion for building with cedar? What about your father? He ate justice and righteousness, drank justice and righteousness, and performed justice and righteousness, didn't he? Then it went well for him" (see the translation note below). That is, Josiah lived for justice and righteousness; it was his meat and drink. Jehoiakim, by contrast, lives for self-aggrandizement through grand architecture (a common trait of tyrants everywhere and in every age). Verses 16 and 17 starkly contrast the two kings. Josiah defended the rights of the poor, but Jehoiakim used his power to squeeze every ounce of silver out of them to finance his building projects.

*TRANSLATION NOTE: JEREMIAH 22:15*

A number of translations of 22:15b are similar to the NIV: "Did not your father have food and drink? He did what was right and just, so all went well with him." But it is inherently peculiar to make a point of the fact that Josiah ate and drank, as though that were worthy of comment. The difficulty is due to the MT cantillation; interpreters interpret a minor pause between "he ate and drank" (אָכַל וְשָׁתָה) and the words "and did justice" (וְעָשָׂה מִשְׁפָּט) to imply that these are separate units in the text. The standard interpretation is that Josiah enjoyed the normal good things of life, eating and drinking, but did not let that interfere with his mission of carrying out justice and righteousness (Allen 2008, 250; Lundbom 2008b, 128). This is possible, but the grammar takes us in a different direction. Normally, a *qatal* verb is not followed by a *weqatal* for a series of separate events, as the *weqatal* is imperfective. The perfective *qatal* is typically followed by the perfective *wayyiqtol* if a simple sequence of actions is implied. As an exception to this, a *qatal* may be followed by a *weqatal* in the case of hendiadys, as is the case with "ate and drank" here. One would expect, however, that "and did justice" would employ the *wayyiqtol* if it were understood to be a separate action from the eating and drinking. Instead, we have אָכַל וְשָׁתָה וְעָשָׂה מִשְׁפָּט וּצְדָקָה, implying the three verbs function as one, and thus that "justice and righteousness" were metaphorically Josiah's food and drink. For a comparable metaphor, see John 4:34. See also (Holladay 1986, 596).

**22:18–19**. The judgment pronounced against Jehoiakim is that he will have a donkey's burial. The point here is not to compare the king to a donkey as a gratuitous insult, like calling someone a "jackass." Rather, it is that a dead donkey is a large, cumbersome carcass, and people just want to get rid of it without delay or ceremony. When the carcass is properly disposed of, people are glad to be rid of it. In the same manner, when Jehoiakim dies, people will treat his body as merely something to discard and get out of sight. He won't be missed, and his funeral will be a perfunctory affair. There appears to be some tension between this passage and 2 Kings 24:6, which says that Jehoiakim "rested with his fathers," which implies that his bones were interred in the royal family crypt along those of the other Davidic kings. But the tension is illusory. The words, "dragged off and cast outside the gates of Jerusalem" (סָחוֹב וְהַשְׁלֵךְ מֵהָלְאָה לְשַׁעֲרֵי יְרוּשָׁלָם) are what happens to the carcass of the dead donkey; it is not a prediction of what would happen to Jehoiakim's corpse. The language is metaphorical, not literal.

**22:20–23**. Verses 20 and 23 both speak of the cedars of Lebanon; these form an inclusion that sets the borders of this unit of text. They also imply that Jehoiakim and his architectural aggrandizement are still the topic of discussion. "Lebanon" and "cedar" allude to the principal building material of the royal palace, the cedars of Lebanon (see also 1 Kings 7:2). The royal court is the "inhabitant of Lebanon." Jehoiakim is implicitly compared to Solomon, who built a palace of the cedars of Lebanon and extended the borders of Israel while also making alliances with foreign states. Solomon's greater Israel collapsed soon after his death when the nation split apart, and Jehoiakim's aggrandizing pretensions will be equally vain. People in Lebanon, in Bashan to the east of the Sea of Galilee, and in the Abiram mountain range in Moab will hear of the fall of Jerusalem. Verse 22 has the unusual, "The wind will shepherd all your shepherds." The leaders of the nation, the shepherds, ought to keep the people, the sheep, safely together. Instead, the wind will drive the shepherds away into exile. Also, Jerusalem should be like a beautiful and protected maiden. Instead, she will gasp for life like a woman in hard labor.

### *Jehoiachin [Coniah] Is the End of the House of David (22:24–30)*

**22:24–27**. A signet ring, being the device whereby a man affixes his legal seal to a document, was of extremely high value. It was his signature (or to use a more contemporary analogy, the password to all his accounts). For that reason, a man would never hurl it away; it was worn as a ring on the hand to make it almost a part of his person. And yet YHWH would cast away Jehoiachin. In the analogy, the house of David is as precious to YHWH as a signet ring is to a man, and yet he is now willing cast aside the dynasty. The king and his mother will both be taken captive to Babylon. It is not clear why the curse includes Jehoiachin's mother. As queen mother, she obviously had relatively high prestige. It may simply be that his inability to protect his mother signified how weak the king was before the Babylonian onslaught.

**22:28–30**. In the analogy of verse 28, Jehoiachin is a worthless as cracked pottery jar. A broken vessel was useless, and ancient Israelites quickly disposed of them, as implied by the account of the Potsherd Gate in chapter 19. Verse 29 addresses the land; repeating the word "land" (אֶרֶץ) three times suggests that the message is particularly focused on the physical territory of Judah. The reason for this is in verse 30, which declares that the dynasty is finished—that is, the land is no longer to be under Davidic kings. Jehoiachin will be recorded as "childless" (עֲרִירִי), not meaning that he literally had no offspring (he in fact had seven sons; 1 Chron. 3:17–18) but that there will be no generation to succeed him and continue the Davidic line of kings. If there is any confusion about the meaning, the end of verse 30 makes it plain: "For no one from his offspring will ever succeed at taking the throne and ruling over Judah." Jehoiachin is described as the last of the Davidic kings because he was representative of the last generation to reign. The last actual king was Zedekiah, but he was Jehoiachin's uncle and was representative of the second-to-last generation.

### *The Failure and Future of the Davidic Dynasty (23:1–8)*

**23:1–4**. The shepherds of verses 1–2 are the royal family and the administration that governed in their name. Ancient Near Eastern literature commonly uses the shepherd as an analogy for kings and rulers. Because of their maladministration, God will take away their dynastic power. God will someday put a new administration over them (vv. 3–4). Ezekiel 34:20–31 expands upon this passage.

**23:5–6**. Jeremiah predicts a new Davidic king whom he calls the "righteous sprout" (צֶמַח צַדִּיק). The word צֶמַח is often translated as "branch," but that is misleading. The word does not mean a small limb, like a tree branch; it is a tender young sprout that comes up from a seed. It implies that something hidden and inconspicuous will rise up to become the messianic redeemer. These two verses give us a brief glimpse of the nature of the future messianic king, the one who will redeem Israel and the house of David. Jeremiah explores the concept more fully in 33:14–26. In 23:6, however, Jeremiah makes an important wordplay: he declares that the messianic king will be called "YHWH our righteousness" (יְהוָה צִדְקֵנוּ). This oracle was given in the reign of Zedekiah (צִדְקִיָּהוּ), whose name also means "YHWH [our] righteousness." What Zedekiah was only in name, the messianic king would be in reality.

**23:7–8**. These verses appear with minor variation in 16:14–15. Although it is possible that a single oracle has been cited twice in the book, it is more likely that Jeremiah had some stock expressions that he repeatedly used in his preaching ministry. The exodus from Egypt dominated Israel's identity as a people; it was the event that established who they were. In the future, the great restoration of exiled Israel will be the event that creates them as a people.

### *Concerning the Prophets (23:9–40)*

Jeremiah concludes the message to Zedekiah's delegation with a blunt condemnation of his peers, the lying prophets. The implication is that their heretical and fraudulent prophecies misled the kings and are responsible for the fall of the nation. In addition, by seeking a favorable oracle from Jeremiah, Zedekiah was in effect encouraging Jeremiah to join the ranks of the false prophets. This is why the lengthy reply to Zedekiah's embassy ends with such a robust condemnation of the prophets who predict victory for Jerusalem.

**23:9–12**. The condemnation begins with a lament. Jeremiah is so distraught he can barely function. He is himself astonished at the severity of YHWH's condemnation: "I am like a man whom wine has overcome in the face of YHWH and in the face of his holy word" (v. 9). In addition, however, he is bewildered that his people thought they could escape condemnation and continued to refuse to repent (v. 10). The land is filled with adulterers (מְנָאֲפִים): The term here probably implies both literal promiscuity and idolatry. They race down a path (מְרוּצָה) that leads to evil. The term מְרוּצָה implies a course or path that one follows when racing toward a goal (see 1 Sam. 18:27; Jer. 8:6). But God will make their path slippery, so that they trip and fall as they run (v. 12). Most specifically, however, Jeremiah is disturbed by the apostasy and immorality among the priests and prophets (v. 11).

**23:13–14**. At the time Jeremiah gave this prophecy, it had been around 130 years since Samaria had fallen to Assyria. And Samaria, like the Jerusalem of his time, was full of false prophets. The condemnation of the Samarian prophets is succinct: they prophesied in the name of Baal (v. 13). The condemnation of the Jerusalem prophets is more complete: They were adulterous (probably both literally and spiritually), they held to and propagated false teaching (וְהָלֹךְ בַּשֶּׁקֶר; literally, "and walking in the lie"), and they encouraged people in their sin rather than persuading them to repent. They were as decadent as Sodom (v. 14).

**23:15**. Their punishment will be to consume bitter food and poisonous drink. The word לַעֲנָה is traditionally translated as "wormwood" (*Artemisia absinthium*) and refers to an exceptionally bitter plant. The word רֹאשׁ in this case refers to some unknown plant that apparently had a poisonous juice. Jeremiah speaks of punishment by poison also in 8:14 and 9:15. The language is metaphorical, not literal. Here, however, it is used for a reason: the prophets had sinned by what came out of their mouths, and thus they will take poison into their mouths.

**23:16–22**. The essential condemnation of these prophets is that they proclaimed messages that were of their own invention and had not come from God (vv. 16, 21–22). The essential message of these prophets was that there would be peace and security. Again, these prophets considered themselves orthodox and Jeremiah the heretic. They may have believed that Baal and YHWH were really one and the same. They certainly believed that the presence of the temple and the house of David were guarantees that Jerusalem was safe. The reality was that a storm was about to burst over Jerusalem (v. 19), the opposite of the peace and safety they promised. And the crisis would not be an ephemeral thing; it would continue until Jerusalem was entirely destroyed and until all of God's intentions against the city were carried out (v. 20).

**23:23–24**. Numerous interpreters point out that when YHWH says he is a God both "nearby" and "far away," it implies that God is both immanent and transcendent (for example, Lalleman 2013, 196). While this is true, the ancient Israelites thought about the matter in more concrete terms. For them, the language would imply that YHWH was present not only at the Jerusalem temple but throughout all of creation. But why bring up such a thing here? Verse 24 suggests that some of the false prophets thought they could say whatever they wanted as long as they were careful about what they said in the vicinity of the temple, where YHWH might take offense. But in fact, God could see and hear them anywhere and everywhere.

**23:25–28a**. Dreams could be a valid means of obtaining revelation from God; Jeremiah himself apparently received an important message in a dream (Jer. 31:26). Claiming to have a dream from God, however, would be the easiest kind of fraud. Who could prove that you did not have a revelation from God in a dream? But God knew they were lying.

**23:28b–29**. Two metaphors contrast the true word of God with the dreams of the false prophets. First, God's word is like grain (בַּר), referring to the edible kernel of wheat; while the pretended prophecies are like straw (תֶּבֶן), referring to the desiccated stalk of the wheat or to the chaff that held the kernel. The point of the analogy is that the false prophecy has the form of the true, just as the straw is genuinely from the wheat plant, but it lacks the ability to nourish, just as the kernel can feed a person but the straw cannot. It is of no good except to spread over the floors of the stables. Second, God's word is like a hammer that breaks up rock. It may be that the false prophecy is like the rock, which is shattered by the truth, but this may be carrying the analogy too far. But the two analogies clearly indicate that God's word both nourishes like the grain and has power like a hammer. False teaching has neither quality.

**23:30–32**. Three times YHWH declares, "Now look, I am opposed to the [false] prophets! [This is] a message of YHWH!" (הִנְנִי עַל־הַנְּבִאִים נְאֻם־יְהוָה, with minor variation in v. 32). They have the appearance of being God's special servants, but in fact he considers them his enemies. Scholars have wrestled a great deal with Jeremiah's assertion that the false prophets "steal" (גנב) messages from each other (Holladay 1986, 644–45). This cannot mean that a true prophet never reuses the words of another prophet, as this is common among biblical prophets. Perhaps the most famous example is the parallel between Isaiah 2:2–4 and Micah 4:1–3 (in my view, the Isaiah text was written first). There are striking parallels between Jeremiah's oracle against Edom (49:7–23) and Obadiah. It is certainly not the case that complete originality is the mark of a true prophet. But Jeremiah's point is that the false prophets have only two sources for their oracles: exercising their imagination (v. 26) and copying each other. They never have an authentic word from God.

**23:33–36**. Jeremiah declares that God is weary of hearing the people come and ask for a prophetic message (מַשָּׂא, "burden"). In this context, מַשָּׂא refers to a divine response to an enquiry. In context, everyone was looking for a message telling them that the Babylonians would soon be driven from their lands and never return. His answer to all such enquiries is simple and to the point: "I will abandon you" (v. 33: וְנָטַשְׁתִּי אֶתְכֶם). The people will only pay heed to the message that they want to hear, and the false prophets badly muddied the waters with their unending claims to have had a divine revelation. As such, it is best to leave off all talk about prophetic messages entirely.

**23:37–40**. God only has one prophetic message for the false prophets, and it is laced with irony: stop claiming to have a message from God! They will all perish in ignominy and disgrace when their words are shown to be lies, when the Babylonians break into the city.

## THEOLOGICAL FOCUS

The historical setting for this text was Zedekiah's request for a favorable message from God that he would drive away the Babylonians. Almost certainly, the king and his men were looking for a repeat of the miraculous destruction of the Assyrian army in the time of Hezekiah and Isaiah. As such, the main focus of this text is on the prophetic oracle. Jeremiah gives Zedekiah a grim response, and then he briefly recounts oracles given against Zedekiah's predecessors Jehoahaz, Jehoiakim, and Jehoiachin. The point is that God has repeatedly condemned the house of David, and now it is certain that the dynasty will fall. The message concludes with a condemnation of the false prophets, who predicted a heavenly deliverance for the nation. Principal theological emphases are as follows:

- God will not give a message of hope to an unrepentant people. Zedekiah's search for a favorable word was pointless.
- People should not distort God's word to suit their desires. God had truly made great promises to the house of David, but they turned it into a great "get out of jail free" card, thinking they could sin with impunity and escape punishment.
- The truth of God's word is not to be judged superficially. It appeared that God had punished the pious Josiah and spared his apostate son Jehoahaz, but in fact Josiah died with honor and under God's favor, while Jehoahaz was cast from his presence.
- A true word of God will confront power and not flatter it. Jeremiah rebuked Jehoiakim for his love of luxury and grand architecture, comparing him unfavorably to his father Josiah.
- A true word from God may appear paradoxical but is always consistent. Jehoiachin was the last generation of the Davidic dynasty, which people assumed would last forever in keeping with 1 Samuel 7. But God destroyed the dynasty for its sin. The people had no understanding of how the promise of unending endurance and the abrupt termination of the dynasty would be reconciled, but it was through a Davidic Messiah whose kingdom was not of this world.
- False prophets create "God's word" out of their own imagination, proclaiming the message that they and their audience want to hear. But, too, we should fear; this can be true also of us. We are all in danger of exercising our ingenuity to find the message that we want to be true, regardless of what the text before us says. We should remember that the false teachers considered themselves theologically conservative and patriotic, and they considered Jeremiah to be a heretic and a traitor. The same can be said of the Pharisees in their relationship to Jesus.

## PREACHING AND TEACHING STRATEGIES

### *Exegetical and Theological Synthesis*

At first glance it appeared that Zedekiah's request for a favorable word from God was denied. But in God's mercy, even at this desperate stage, he gave Zedekiah and Judah a way out. It wasn't what they had in mind, but it would spare their lives: they could surrender to the Babylonians and live. They had expectations that were not in submission to God's authority. They gave God a list and told him to run to the store and pick up what they ordered. They had demands of what they wanted God to do, disregarding God's expectations for what they *should* do.

### *Preaching Idea*

Ask God for victory (intervention), but don't violate his authority.

### *Contemporary Connections*

#### *What does it mean?*

Not many of the young men who attended the small-town liberal arts college had cars. But Mike did. Because of some unexpected funds that were available to him and because of a part-time job driving a rural early morning paper route, Mike purchased a new Dodge Dart. (It was the '70s.) It was clean and smelled new. Mike was a hard worker, and he was generous. On some occasions he would let some, but not all, borrow his car. His method of vetting who got to drive his new car was one simple question. When approached to borrow his car, he would ask, "Are you going to drive it like it was your car or my car?" Often the answer would come, "Oh, I'll drive it like it was my own." That was the wrong answer. Mike wanted his friends to drive his car the way he wanted, not the way they wanted. If they wanted his transportation, they had to accept his authority. Zedekiah was willing and wanting of God's intervention to bring victory, but he didn't want, nor was he willing to submit to, God's authority.

#### *Is it true?*

Yes, there is a time when we need to be told that we have done a good job. We like to hear, "Great job! Keep it up! You can make it! Yes, if you work hard enough you can . . ." But we also need to hear, "Stop, you can't do that. What you are doing is wrong. If you don't stop, there will be terrible consequences. You won't graduate. You won't have a job. You won't have a marriage. You won't be successful." It is wrong to expect God to intervene when we are violating his word and worshipping other gods.

#### *Now what?*

We make numerous requests for God's victory, from the impulsive request to let a light be green so that we won't be late for work to the lifelong burden of praying for the salvation of a spouse. It is right to make these requests. Jeremiah did not tell the delegation that making a request was wrong, but rather that their disobedient lives were wrong. We often cite Philippians 4:8, which tells us to let our requests be known unto God. If taken out of context, this could lead to our giving God a "things to do" list. But the presenting of our requests comes after the command to not be anxious, and the directive to make the request with a spirit of supplication with thanksgiving. There is submission to God that sets the stage for making the requests. This is not *quid pro quo*—you do this for me and I'll do something for you. Rather, we should see that since God has the authority to act on our behalf, how can we not submit to the very authority to whom we are making an appeal?

It comes back to trust. Can we really trust God? Even in this passage that is filed with the promise of destruction there is the promise of a righteous branch. Those in Jeremiah's day could have responded to this promise of hope with faith in God's good hand. Perhaps the postexilic readers could have responded more easily, having seen the partial fulfillment of this encouraging word. Even with the promise of destruction and captivity in their future, God still had greater future for them than they could imagine.

As we make our requests for God's intervention, we need to be sure that we are submitting to his authority. As I write this, it is understandable that I am requesting God to intervene and grant victory in the completion of this project. As I reflected on this passage, I noticed that God's call was not only to righteousness in general but focused on justice and care for the poor. I have a practice of setting aside some cash to give to someone in need who God brings across my path; often it is a student or someone at my local church. Due to the current COVID-19 crisis my paths are very limited, so the cash is limited in its use. God's Spirit prompted me that I could put that cash to use through my church, which is actively striving to help those who have lost jobs during this crisis. I needed to put that money into the hands of those who could distribute it. I couldn't continue to ask God for intervention while not submitting to his authority. By God's gracious act in my life, I stopped my work and went to drop off the cash at the church office. May he continue to work so graciously to both convict and motivate me.

### *Creativity in Presentation*

Most pastors/teachers have a pattern of praying before or near the beginning of a sermon. Of course, this is a great practice. Our sermons should always be delivered with a conscious and voiced dependence upon God. Altering this pattern may add some verity and could more effectively present this long passage.

Sometimes a good story is a great way to start a sermon. The opening narrative of this section could be one of those stories. It is a common plot, easy to convey. A king is invaded by a superior force and asks the prophet for a victory prayer, much like it was reported that in WWII General Patton asked for a "weather prayer" from his chaplain.

The structure of this passage lends itself to a combination of an inductive and then deductive sermon. The first section is inductive. It could begin by briefly presenting story of 21:1–10, which can lead up to the main idea: ask God to intervene, but don't violate his authority. The tension is maintained in the deductive portion by asking the question, "How do we violate his authority?" Then go to prayer, asking the Father to show us. It takes the passage about making request to God and makes it an active application. Instead of just talking about making a request, one can actually make a request at that point in the sermon. Simply stop and ask God to show us how we might be violating his authority.

After the prayer, make the transition into the rest of the passage by asking, "So let's learn about how we might be violating God's authority by looking at how Judah violated his authority." Then present the rest of the passage: first about the kings rejecting his authority in their unrighteousness, and then how the prophets violated his authority by distorting his word. Since this is a long passage there will need to be a summarizing of each section, reading key scriptures as part of the summary.

The following possible structure suggests presenting all of 22:1–10, and then only selected verses that could be used to summarize the second section (22:11–23:40). There are other verses that could be used to summarize; just be sure that you as teacher/preacher grasps the meaning of each section, and then present that to your congregation.

- First section (21:1–11): Ask God for victory (intervention), but don't violate his authority.

- Second section (22:11–23:40): In making requests for God's intervention we need to:
    - Submit to his authority in our actions toward others.
        - Judah's kings did not (22:3–4, 22:14–16).
        - We should submit to his authority in every area of life.
    - Remember, not everyone will have God's victory (22:30).
    - Remember that some will have God's victory (23:5–8).
    - Trust him alone: only he knows how victory will come (23:16–17).

- Conclusion: Ask God for victory (intervention), but don't violate his authority.

## DISCUSSION QUESTIONS

1. When we submit to God's authority, how does it affect our requests to him?
2. Why do you think that in judging the kings' disobedience, God pointed out injustice and not caring for the poor?
3. What are some ways we can seek justice for others?
4. What are some ways we can care for the poor?
5. Can we obey God partially but not fully? In what ways?

## Jeremiah 24:1–25:38

### EXEGETICAL IDEA
God promises to preserve his people and his word in spite of the coming destruction of Judah's leadership and the promise of judgment against all nations. Jeremiah receives a message concerning good figs and bad figs, representing respectively those who will preserve Israel's heritage and create Judaism (the Babylonian exiles) and those who will be entirely destroyed (the people in Jerusalem). And although calamity and exile is certain, it will have an end, after seventy years.

### THEOLOGICAL FOCUS
God's destruction of human structures and plans does not destroy his purposes or his word. God's people can become so corrupt that harsh judgment is inescapable, but God's purposes do not fail.

### PREACHING IDEA
What basket do you want to be in?

### PREACHING POINTERS
God gives us a choice. To use Jeremiah's image, do we choose a basket of fresh fruit or a basket of rotten fruit? Do we choose a rotten life or a good one? The choice for a good life is to submit to God's discipline and obey his clear commands.

# MESSAGES IN THE TIMES OF JEHOIACHIN AND JEHOIAKIM (24:1–25:38)

## LITERARY STRUCTURE AND THEMES

This section contains two sets of oracles, the first delivered right after the exile of Jehoiachin and the second in the reign of his father and predecessor, Jehoiakim. The messages contain two of Jeremiah's memorable texts: the vision of the basket of figs (24:1–10), and the prediction of a seventy-year exile (25:1–14).

- ***Message (in 597) After the Exile of Jehoiachin (24:1–10)***
- ***Message (in 605) During the Fourth Year of Jehoiakim (25:1–38)***
    - *The Condemnation of Jerusalem and the Decree of a Seventy-Year Exile (25:1–14)*
    - *The Cup of YHWH's Wrath for Jerusalem and the Nations (25:15–29)*
    - *Images of the Coming Destruction (25:30–38)*

## EXPOSITION

### *Message (in 597) After the Exile of Jehoiachin (24:1–10)*

This message was given just after the short reign of Jehoiachin, who was taken to Babylon by Nebuchadnezzar in 597. It was thus early in the reign of Zedekiah, although part of its focus is on Jehoiachin and the exile that went to Babylon with him.

**24:1–2**. Jehoiachin is in this passage called "Jeconiah." He is sometimes called "Coniah." After Jehoiakim launched a rebellion against Nebuchadnezzar, he soon died, and his unfortunate son Jehoiachin had to face the oncoming Babylonian army. He quickly capitulated, and was carried off into exile and replaced by his uncle, Jehoiakim's brother Zedekiah. Along with Jehoiachin, the Babylonians took away a number of high officials (שָׂרֵי יְהוּדָה), some highly skilled workers (הֶחָרָשׁ), and some people known as הַמַּסְגֵּר, which literally means "those who shut." Some interpret these to be metalworkers, but the term is elsewhere used for a prison or dungeon (Isa. 24:22; 42:7; Ps. 142:7 [MT 8]). It may be that it refers to the king's personal guard, who would also be responsible for keeping prisoners for the king (see Jer. 37:11–15). Jeremiah sees two containers of figs in front of the temple. As this was after the exile of Jehoiachin and early in the reign of Zedekiah, it appears that the ban prohibiting Jeremiah from entering the temple district, given in the reign of Jehoiakim, had been lifted. The word for the container is דּוּד, which sometimes refers to a kettle for boiling food (Job 41:20), but it can also refer to a basket for carrying objects (2 Kings 10:7). In this case, they are probably baskets. Interpreters are divided over whether Jeremiah saw literal baskets of figs or a vision. However, since the text says they were "designated" (מוּעָדִים, the hophal particle of יעד) for placement before the temple, it appears that these were real baskets that had been set there as offerings. In this case, one of the offering baskets contained excellent figs and the other contained nasty, inedible figs (perhaps they had been attacked by insects or had gone bad before they could be used). It is not really surprising that someone had brought an offering of very bad fruit; this was a common problem for the temple. It was the duty of the priests to inspect such offerings and decide whether they could be accepted (Lundbom 2008b, 228). The good figs were "like early figs" (כְּתְאֵנֵי הַבַּכֻּרוֹת), suggesting that this was a first-fruits offering.

**24:3**. Apparently Jeremiah was stunned by the sight of a basket of excellent figs set beside a basket of disgusting figs, both meant to be offerings to God. He may have stared at it for a moment and then heard the voice of God, asking him to state what he was looking at. Jeremiah gave the simple, obvious answer.

**24:4–7**. YHWH then gave him a message, telling him that the two baskets had symbolic meaning. The good figs represented Jehoiachin and those who had been taken into exile, and the bad figs represented Zedekiah and those who remained in Jerusalem. This was a counterintuitive interpretation. One would expect that the good or fortunate ones were those who were not taken into captivity. But YHWH declared that he would watch over the exiles and bring them back into their land. More than that, he would give them "a heart to know me" (לֵב לָדַעַת אֹתִי), which signifies a disposition to be faithful to YHWH and keep his commands. YHWH would be their God and they would be his people, and they would return to YHWH with all their hearts. What does all this mean?

In one sense, it is a foreshadow of the new covenant, when God would write the law on their hearts, they would all know him, and all their sins would be forgiven (31:33–34). But the postexilic community did not truly experience the new covenant, a time when the knowledge of God would be universal and no one would ever need to exhort another to be faithful, because everyone would know God. As Ezra, Nehemiah, Haggai, Zechariah, and Malachi make clear, the postexilic community fell far short of that ideal. On the other hand, the postexilic community did learn some important lessons. They turned away from idolatry. This sin, which dominates the preexilic prophets, is conspicuously absent in the postexilic texts. Furthermore, they developed the piety that would characterize postexilic Judaism, a piety that enabled them to come through the harrowing times of persecution under Antiochus IV Epiphanes with their faith intact.

While it is true that the devotion of this community would eventually be warped and become the extreme and blinded zeal of Pharisaic religion, the devotion that characterized postexilic Judaism was fundamentally a good thing. This community produced men like Ezra and Nehemiah. It preserved the Scriptures, and for all its faults it produced the rabbinical teaching that nurtured the young Jesus. Just as the return from exile was a shadow-fulfillment of the great eschatological regathering of Israel, so also the piety of postexilic Judaism (as opposed to the gross apostasy and outright paganism of preexilic Jerusalem) foreshadowed the reign of righteousness in the new covenant. In this context, moreover, Jeremiah asserts that the true identity of the Jews as YHWH's chosen people would survive and thrive among the Jews of the Babylonian captivity. It would not thrive among the Jews who remained in Jerusalem with Zedekiah.

**24:8–10**. Just as the priests at the temple would reject the rotten figs as unsuitable for a first-fruits offering, so God would reject Zedekiah and the people who remained in Jerusalem after the Jehoiachin exile. Egypt, at this time, was already looking like a safe haven for the Jews from the depredations of Nebuchadnezzar, and apparently some had already fled there. Later, a substantial group would flee to Egypt and force Jeremiah to go with them (Jer. 43). But whether they remained or fled, God counted them all as accursed. Indeed, these Jews would experience what would become a tragic but common feature of Judaism in Diaspora, being despised and abused by the Gentiles in every land to which they fled (v. 9). They would experience no peace or security but suffer physical violence and deprivation (v. 10). The Jews in Babylon, by contrast, were treated remarkably well and became a prosperous community there; and in the end, they were liberated and allowed to refound Jerusalem. The main point of this chapter is that Judaism would survive and thrive among the exiles in Babylon; it would die among those who stayed in Jerusalem or fled to Egypt.

## *Message (in 605) During the Fourth Year of Jehoiakim (25:1–38)*

### *The Condemnation of Jerusalem and the Decree of a Seventy-Year Exile (25:1–14)*

This is the original beginning (v. 1) and ending (v 13a) of the Baruch Scroll of Jeremiah 36, together with an excerpt specifying the essential content of the scroll (vv. 2–12). The full scroll had to have been longer than what we read here because it contained multiple columns of text (36:23). Probably the scroll contained a number of undated prophecies now found in chapters 2–20. Also, the second copy of the scroll, made after Jehoiakim had burned the first copy, had more material added to it (36:32); and at some point, the oracles against the nations (Jer. 46–51 in the MT, but in the LXX found here at 25:14–31:44) were added to the Baruch Scroll. In the current form of the Hebrew text of Jeremiah, this section is a decisive repudiation of the house of David, of Jehoiakim, and of the continued existence of Jerusalem.

**25:1**. The fourth year of Jehoiakim was 605 B.C. Nebuchadnezzar became king of Babylon in September of 605, but his first full official year, as counted by the Babylonians, did not begin until April of 604 B.C. This discrepancy reflects the fact that Jerusalem at this time did not use an accession year; what the Babylonians called Nebuchadnezzar's accession year was, to Jeremiah, his first year. Thus, by Jerusalem reckoning, Jehoiakim's fourth year was Nebuchadnezzar's first year, but by Babylonian reckoning that same year was Jehoiakim's third year and Nebuchadnezzar's accession year. Daniel 1:1, written in Babylon, uses the Babylonian system. Thus, it speaks of Nebuchadnezzar as already being king in Jehoiakim's third year.

| *Approximate calendar year* | *609–608* | *608–607* | *607–606* | *606–605* | *605–604* |
|---|---|---|---|---|---|
| *Babylonian system* | *Jehoiakim accession year* | *Jehoiakim year 1* | *Jehoiakim year 2* | *Jehoiakim year 3 = Nebuchadnezzar accession year* | *Jehoiakim year 4 = Nebuchadnezzar year 1* |
| *Jerusalem system* | *Jehoiakim year 1* | *Jehoiakim year 2* | *Jehoiakim year 3* | *Jehoiakim year 4 = Nebuchadnezzar year 1* | *Jehoiakim year 5 = Nebuchadnezzar year 2* |

Note that the above table is approximate, not precise. It does not take into account the date of the new year in the ancient world in contrast to our dating the new year to January 1. The Israelites had more than one system for beginning the new year, although a king's regnal years were probably counted from Nisan, in the spring. Their reckoning of years was further complicated by their use of a lunar calendar. By our calendar reckoning, Jehoiakim probably became king in late 609, but that can be overlooked in our calculation, since our purpose is to compare the Babylonian and Jerusalem dating systems, not to give a precise chronology of the kings.

**25:2–7**. The condemnation of Jerusalem here is not specific—that is, describing sins such as child sacrifice, idolatry, and the oppression of the poor—but general, focusing on how the people refused to heed the warnings of the prophets and repent. This is well-suited to a concluding denunciation of the city, a pronouncement of impending destruction. Jesus, in the last days before his crucifixion, similarly spoke of how the Jews consistently refused to heed the prophets in his assertion that Jerusalem was doomed (Mark 12:1–11).

**25:8–10**. After the summary of the verdict against Jerusalem, the text pronounces the sentence. Jerusalem would be entirely obliterated, and all normal and joyful activity, such as weddings, would come to an end. Indeed, the land would be subject to the "ban," the total destruction of all wealth and people in the land (וְהַחֲרַמְתִּים; "and I will utterly destroy them," v. 9). This is the same word that is used for the complete destruction of the Canaanites during Joshua's conquest (כִּי־הַחֲרֵם תַּחֲרִימֵם; "for you must utterly destroy them," Deut. 20:17).

**25:11–12**. Jeremiah predicts that the captivity will last seventy years. This has caused some confusion among readers. Jerusalem fell at earliest in 587 B.C., and Cyrus II of Persia captured Babylon in 539 B.C. and issued a decree allowing the Jews to return to Jerusalem in 538. This makes for a captivity of at most about fifty years. Different parts of the Bible have different ways of accounting for the seventy years. Zechariah 1–8 focuses on the effort to rebuild the temple, and alludes to the seventy years in 1:12. Thus, Zechariah seems to reckon the seventy years from the destruction of the first temple in about 587 to the construction of the second temple, which was completed by about 515 B.C. By contrast, 2 Chronicles 36:20–23 dates the seventy years from the destruction of the city to Cyrus's decree allowing the Jews to return home—a period that, as we have noted, falls well short of seventy years. However, the Chronicler reads the number more symbolically than literally; for him, the seventy years are a time of sabbath rest for the land.

A different approach is found in Daniel 9, a prayer and revelation dated to the first year of Darius the Mede, or 539 B.C. Daniel appears to have dated the beginning of the captivity from the time he and his colleagues were carried off to Babylon in 605 B.C. (Dan. 9:2). Thus, in 539 B.C., the seventy years were almost completed, and Daniel prayed for the restoration of the Jewish nation. We can regard all of these solutions as correct, although none is precise and none is to be regarded as the singular solution. Also, it appears that the number 70 was often used as an approximation (Judg. 1:7; Ps. 90:10; Isa. 23:15; Zech. 7:5).

**25:13**. "What Jeremiah prophesied against all nations" (אֲשֶׁר־נִבָּא יִרְמְיָהוּ עַל־כָּל־הַגּוֹיִם) looks like the heading for a new section. One would expect the sentence to end with the phrase "everything written in this book" (אֵת כָּל־הַכָּתוּב בַּסֵּפֶר הַזֶּה), both because this is a more normal way to end an oracle text and because nothing in the preceding text addresses the other nations. However, "against all nations" appears to have been the original heading to the oracles against the nations now found in chapters 36–51. In the LXX, which I believe represents the first draft of the full book, those chapters appear here. All of this is to suggest that originally 25:13a constituted the ending of the Baruch Scroll mentioned in chapter 36. This document sealed the fate of Jerusalem, proclaiming YHWH's purpose to bring about the destruction of the city.

**25:14**. This verse appears to offer a commentary on the contents of the scroll: the Jews would go into diaspora among many nations and suffer much at their hands. It also serves as a bridge to the next oracle: the cup of YHWH's wrath.

### *The Cup of YHWH's Wrath for Jerusalem and the Nations (25:15–29)*

**25:15–16**. The metaphor of the cup of YHWH's wrath draws upon the familiar experience of people who drink too much wine, becoming inebriated and thus incapable of coordinated movement or intelligent speech and soon prone to sickness and vomiting. It represents the stupor and terrorized paralysis that will befall the people when they see the Babylonians at the gates. The cup metaphor represents punishment; it is not a test to determine whether a person is guilty or not, and thus it is not comparable to the adultery test of Numbers 5:11–31 (against Thompson 1980, 516).

**25:17–26**. Many nations, and not just Judah, would face the fury of the Babylonian Empire. Most of these nations are also condemned in the oracles against the nations of Jeremiah 46–51, and as noted, these oracles appear right after 25:13 in the LXX, which I believe represents the first edition of Jeremiah. It appears that in that edition, the oracle of the cup of YHWH's wrath (Rahlfs LXX 32:15–29 = MT 25:15–29) served as a conclusion to the oracles against the nations. Here in the MT, they serve as a warning to Jehoiakim that the fate of Jerusalem will be no better than that of any other nation that tries to resist Babylon.

**25:27–29**. Neither Jerusalem nor any of the other nations will have any choice in the matter: They will be forced to drink the cup of YHWH's wrath. In the macrostructure of Jeremiah, this is set in contrast to the experience of the Rechabites, who successfully refused to drink wine in the temple (Jer. 35).

### *Images of the Coming Destruction (25:30–38)*

**25:30–33**. These verses employ five powerful metaphors to communicate the horrors that are to come. First, YHWH will roar (שׁאג) like a lion (v. 30). The verb שׁאג is regularly used of roaring lions (Judg. 14:5; Isa. 5:29; Jer. 2:15; Ezek. 22:25), but the passage that is most apposite here is Amos 3:4–8, which depicts YHWH as a roaring lion on the day of YHWH. Second, YHWH is like the men who tread grapes when the vintage comes in and winemaking commences (v. 30). The crushing of the grapes and release of their juices represent the bloodshed of battle, and the celebratory shouting of the people at the grape harvest anticipates the war cries of the coming army. This metaphor is developed more fully in Isaiah 63:2. Third, the coming crisis is like a court case, in which YHWH accuses his enemies of crimes (using the noun רִיב, "lawsuit," and the verb נִשְׁפָּט, "enter into litigation") and prepares to execute them (vv. 31–32). The metaphor of YHWH formally charging the people with crimes is employed in Hosea 4:1–3. Fourth, the coming calamity is like a great storm (סַעַר) that moves across the land destroying all in its path (v. 32). This metaphor is used in Psalm 83:15 (MT 16), and it stresses how the storm of YHWH terrifies people. Fifth, the corpses of the slain troops scattered across the battlefield are represented as like dung (דֹּמֶן) in a field (v. 33). This is a common metaphor (2 Kings 9:37; Ps. 83:10 [MT 11]; Jer. 8:2;). It is also multifaceted. The bodies of the dead lie everywhere, just as a field where a herd of cattle grazed will have dung scattered across its surface. It implies that the victors have no more regard for the bodies of the slain than they would for feces on the ground, and it communicates the stench and decay of the dead bodies. The young men who were the pride of Judah are in their deaths reduced to something foul and detested.

**25:34–38**. The shepherd is a common biblical image for the leaders of the nation, including the king, the priests, the aristocracy, and the prophets. Frequently the shepherds are presented as inept or as indifferent to the suffering of the sheep, the common people (Jer. 10:21; 23:1–4; Ezek. 34:2; Zech. 10:3).

Here, the shepherds weep because YHWH has come like a lion and destroyed their flock.

## THEOLOGICAL FOCUS

This section of Jeremiah makes the categorical statement that the earthly dynasty of David in Jerusalem is finished, and that Israel's future lies with the exiles in Babylon. Particular emphases are as follows:

- Sometimes a people become so depraved that they cannot become useful to God, like the bad figs. But others can, after a period of refinement, take on great challenges and preserve the word of God.
- The summary judgment against Jehoiakim and his people in 25:1–13 represents the divine repudiation of those who refuse to listen to God's word.
- Although judgment may be delayed, God will bring it about according to his timing and purpose.
- People can be smug and scoff when all is well, but when the crisis comes they will panic like madmen and drunkards.
- Calamity from God is fearful in the extreme, as the five metaphors of 25:30–33 imply.

## PREACHING AND TEACHING STRATEGIES

### *Exegetical and Theological Synthesis*

Could Israel's exile be the blessing of God? At this stage in Israel's history, judgment was inevitable. God's message was one of judgment, but God also offered life to each Israelite. But life came in surrender to God's will, as exiles. When God's hand of discipline comes, we need to submit to his hand and trust that he is blessing us. But we can, like Zedekiah, reject God's hand and not submit. Life is found in submission to God's will.

### *Preaching Idea*

What basket do you want to be in?

### *Contemporary Connections*

#### *What does it mean?*

This passage is not teaching the oft-quoted, "When God closes a door, he opens a window." This cliché implies that we will still get what we wanted, just in a different way. But with our sovereign Lord, just the closing of the door is good—whether a window is open or not. For the Jewish exiles a door had been closed, but so much more than a window was going to open. The exiles may not have received what they wanted, but what they were going to get was a taste of the new covenant, a new heart. The Jews wanted to be rescued from the evil Nebuchadnezzar, but God had plans to rescue them from their own evil hearts. The exiles would be the ones who preserved Judaism and the written form of his Word. No windows could contain those blessings. Does this mean that God's plans are always going to mean prosperity and ease? Certainly not. But God's plans are always good, and his alternatives are always best.

#### *Is it true?*

During the winter and early spring in states that can grow citrus, fresh oranges are readily available. In the more northern states, fall brings that first frost and fresh apples. It is a joy to open a bag, cut into a piece of fruit, and have that fresh sweet flavor fill our mouths. We may respond with, "Hmmm. Now that is a good piece of fruit." But it is so disappointing and then disgusting to open a bag of oranges or apples, only to find two or three at the bottom that are mushy with greenish-white mold. Even worse is to smell something bad in the pantry, but to struggle to locate the source. After a deeper search you find, behind a bag of seldom-used specialty pasta, a rotten potato that has turned to a gooey mess. In disgust we say, "Yuck, it is rotten." God uses these contrasting images to show that the

Jews who would go into exile would have a good life, while life would be rotten for those who did not go into exile.

The exiles, no doubt, thought, "We got the wrong end of this deal. We are in exile and the others are still in Jerusalem." What seemed bad was really God's preserving hand. Jeremiah was saying to those going into exile, those in exile, and even to those who later returned from exile, "This exile is God's good hand." Several thousand years later, we can affirm this: "Yes exiles, you were the good figs; you had the good life."

Part of life is disappointments and hard times. Looking back at our own lives, we can often see that disappointments were part of God's good hand. Perhaps you were denied entrance into a prestigious college but now you realize that the smaller, lesser-known school gave you rich friendships and a personal touch to your education. which was what you needed. Was there an unhealthy engagement that was broken off? After the pain subsided and new healthy relationships began to develop, you could see how unhealthy that engagement was. Each of us could add our experiences to this list. Often, we can't see what good God is doing at the time, but looking back we see the good he was doing then.

### *Now what?*

Through Jeremiah, God gave each individual in Judah the choice for life. This choice is echoed through the Old Testament. Moses stated it clearly, "I call heaven and earth to witness against you today, that I have set before you life and death, blessing and curse. Therefore choose life, that you and your offspring may live" (Deut. 30:19 ESV). While the nation was doomed, each person still had the choice for life. This is still the choice before us. For those in Judah it was clear: Jeremiah's specific command from YHWH was to surrender. But God's will was also expressed in his written Word, the clearest list being the Ten Commandments. For us, the essence of these commands still stands and is expanded in the New Testament in passages such as the Sermon on the Mount or the latter part of Ephesians. If we want to choose life, we choose these actions, thoughts, and lifestyles that God had laid out for us in these commands.

Jim McGuiggan, a Christian educator from Northern Ireland, effectively retells the story of Helen Keller, who in spite of becoming blind and deaf at nineteen months old lived a productive and full life, largely due to the loving tenacity of her teacher, Annie Sullivan. Helen was locked in the prison of her world without sight and without words. Annie's methods almost seemed to be torments instead of teaching, as she relentlessly would spell out letters on Helen's hand. For months Helen rebelled, to the point of hating her teacher.

> Finally, it all comes to a head when Helen throws a jug of water over the teacher. Sullivan ignores the protests of the parents, grabs the jug and Helen, drags her out to the pump, forces her to fill the jug with water while she spells out W.A.T.E.R. on the girl's fingers and hands. And that's when it happens. . . . Her prison walls are collapsing; she now has a rational connection with her world—words are things. (McGuiggan 1998, 203)

To use Jeremiah's image, when Helen submitted to the authority and guidelines of her teacher her *rotten* life became good. Each one of us has a choice for life.

While it might be a parenthetical point, it is important to make clear that the foundation for the blessing of life is the cross. God's will is that each of us submits to him, by trusting the work of Jesus on our behalf.

## Creativity in Presentation

These two chapters could seem to have two very different thrusts: Israel's future, and then God's judgment on the nations. In some ways, that is true. However, the pouring out of God's wrath on the nations is a contrast to how God will redeem and restore Israel. The message begins with the two choices that are available. The choice for the good life is presented first, followed by the choice for bad. After this, the prophecy of his judgments of the nations of the world makes the choice of life through submission to his will all the more positive. It is a common and effective way of highlighting good: by showing the bad. The bad fruit makes the good fruit all the more appreciated.

Consider not leaving the sermon/lesson as only stating that to have a good life we should choose to submit and follow the Lord; give your people something specific to do, a choice to make. The Jews had Jeremiah's specific command and the Torah. We can't ask people to surrender to Nebuchadnezzar, but we can ask them to surrender to God's guidelines for life. Perhaps draw attention to one of the New Testament passages that concentrates on commands, such as Romans 12:9–21. Or, highlight the commands given in the Sermon on the Mount or the latter part of Ephesians. These could be presented on a card, you could create a bookmark for them to take home, or just list them. Depending upon your pattern of preaching/teaching, close in some type of prayer or moment for meditation, asking God's Spirit to bring to our attention one area or command that we need to choose to more fully obey.

The structure of this passage is clearly presenting a choice between good and bad. These two contrasting points can be presented in the third person. Describe, in an analytical tone, the choice that Israel had and how they chose poorly. Presenting the text in this way could encourage making a judgment call. No doubt, they will be amazed that Israel would choose God's wrath. Then make a transition into the choice that is set before us. How could we do anything but choose life? While Zedekiah made such a foolish choice, we must not. While this is not a direct application—we have not been told that exile is our blessing—the principle that God disciplines those he loves still applies. A basket of blessing of life or a basket of God's wrath—the choice is ours. Here is one possible structure:

- God's basket of blessings is filled with more than we could imagine (the exile) (24:1–7).
- God's basket of wrath has been filled up by repeated sins. (24:8–25:38).
- Which basket do you want?

## DISCUSSION QUESTIONS

1. What about rotten fruit makes it disgusting to you?
2. What about fresh fruit makes it so appealing?
3. What was God trying to stir in Jeremiah and his hearers by using the images of the rotten and good figs?
4. What are our reactions to rotten or good fruit, both emotionally and rationally?
5. How is God trying to appeal to the full person—to encourage us to obey him?

# Jeremiah 26:1–29:32

## EXEGETICAL IDEA

This passage explores how the most severe opposition to Jeremiah came from Judah's religious elite, the priestly officials of the temple and the popular (but false) prophets. This text demonstrates the severity of the hostility of the religious establishment toward Jeremiah. They almost killed him when he preached his great temple sermon, and they did kill another true prophet, Uriah of Kiriath-jearim. By contrast, two false prophets, Hananiah and Shemaiah, were well received as they mocked and opposed Jeremiah.

## THEOLOGICAL FOCUS

When God's plan includes destroying an old but false tradition, many people will vigorously oppose the change. Apostate ideas create a pseudo-orthodoxy that people will fanatically and violently defend. The great tragedy is that such people believe they are defending the truth. The warning for us is to not confuse our theology with the word of God.

## PREACHING IDEA

God, you haven't done it that way before.

## PREACHING POINTERS

When speaking the above phrase, the intonations reveal the attitude toward God and what he is doing. The person who doesn't like or want any change is enraged when something new comes along, even if that new something is clearly God's hand. In contrast, the person who trusts and submits to God will is encouraged when God is bringing about something new. It is pivotal that the new idea or plan is from God, for just being new does not make it of God. But when God is making changes, we not only need to accept those changes; we need to embrace them and anticipate God's good hand.

# PERSECUTED PROPHETS AND FALSE PROPHETS (26:1–29:32)

## LITERARY STRUCTURE AND THEMES

This is a brief report of a pivotal moment in Jeremiah's career, his "temple sermon." In this episode, Jeremiah proclaimed that he fully expected the temple to be destroyed, setting himself apart from the optimistic prophets and temple hierarchy. This publicly established him as an enemy of the religious establishment and the royal court.

- ***Jeremiah Nearly Lynched: The Temple Sermon (26:1–19)***
- ***The Martyrdom of the Prophet Uriah of Kiriath-jearim (26:20–24)***
- ***The False Prophet Hananiah and the Yoke Bars (27:1–28:17)***
- ***The False Prophet Shemaiah and Letters to the Exiles (29:1–32)***

## EXPOSITION

### *Jeremiah Nearly Lynched: The Temple Sermon (26:1–19)*

**26:1–3**. This incident probably took place early in 608 B.C., within the first year of Jehoiakim's reign, or soon thereafter. Some interpreters believe that "In the beginning of the reign" (בְּרֵאשִׁית מַמְלְכוּת) is a technical term for the period of a new king's accession to the throne, the time between the day of his coronation and the first New Year's Day of his reign (Thompson 1980, 524). Others deny this (Lundbom 2008b, 285), but it is certain that the message was delivered within the first few years of Jehoiakim's rule. Jeremiah's commission from God to speak this message is lengthy, implying that this is a vital sermon. The people's response to it will determine their future. It can be viewed as a last effort by God to get them to repent. Note that it was delivered before the delivery of condemnation found in the Baruch Scroll of 25:1–13, and about a decade before the harsh messages of judgment given to Zedekiah. Its placement here is thematically rather than chronologically determined. Chapters 26–29 all concern Judah's rejection of true prophets and reception of false prophets, providing an explanation for the severity of the judgment against them.

**26:4–6**. The report of what Jeremiah said in the temple sermon is extraordinarily brief. No doubt he said a great deal more than what is reported here, and some of the material now found in the undated material of chapters 2–20 may have come from the temple sermon (almost certainly 7:1–15 is a summary of the sermon). The text here includes only two key points: that the people consistently rejected the prophets, and that the Jerusalem temple was about to be destroyed. Shiloh had been the location of the Tent of Meeting during the time of the priest Eli (1 Sam. 1–4). First Samuel 4 tells how the Philistines captured the ark of the covenant and how Eli fell dead upon hearing of the calamity, but it does not describe the destruction of the sanctuary. But we may be confident that the Shiloh sanctuary was destroyed at that time. Afterward, the ark traveled from place to place, and no single location served as the sole legitimate shrine of Israel until worship was consolidated at Jerusalem under David and Solomon.

**26:7–9**. The people, perhaps encouraged by the priests, were outraged that Jeremiah would declare that the temple would soon be destroyed. In a mob action, they demanded his head. The situation is reminiscent of Paul's experience at the temple (Acts 21–22).

**26:10–11**. The secular officials (שָׂרֵי יְהוּדָה, "officials of Judah") took their places at the gate to render judgment against Jeremiah, and the priests took the lead in demanding that Jeremiah be put to death. Evidently the priests had no authority to hand out capital punishment and depended on the secular authorities to enforce their will. This calls to mind the public trial of Jesus, where the priests and Pharisees demanded that the Roman authorities execute him.

**26:12–15**. Jeremiah's defense was in three parts. First, he claimed that he did not speak his own opinions but proclaimed only the message that YHWH gave him (v. 12). This too has a close parallel in the experience of Jesus, who told the Jews that he proclaimed only the message sent from God, while the Jews in turn called him a demoniac and demanded his death (John 8:31–59). Second, Jeremiah declared that the calamity he had foretold need not happen; they could avoid it if they repented (v. 13). Third, Jeremiah announced that he would not resist should they choose to murder him, but that if they did so they would only compound their guilt by placing the bloodguilt for killing an innocent man—and a prophet at that—on their own heads (see Matt. 27:25).

**26:16–19**. Jeremiah, like Paul and unlike Jesus, was delivered by secular authorities from the violence of the mob and their priestly enablers. We know from elsewhere in the book that a significant number of powerful aristocrats, to say nothing of the king himself, hated Jeremiah. But he did have a few supporters (Jer. 36:25). But this episode took place fairly early in Jeremiah's ministry. It may be that the hostility of many of the nobles had not yet fully gelled and that his supporters were still able to sway the court in his favor. Within a few years, this would no longer be possible. The defense of Jeremiah given here is remarkable in that his supporters cited Micah 3:12 as precedent for Jeremiah's message. Micah lived roughly one hundred years prior to the incident recorded here. Jeremiah's supporters argued that Micah too predicted that Zion would be laid waste, but instead of killing him Hezekiah and the people listened to him and repented. If Micah was no blasphemer deserving of death, then neither was Jeremiah. This passage is significant because it implies that in the late seventh century the Israelites preserved the words of the prophets and regarded them as at least quasi-canonical. This suggests that the canonization and preservation of prophetic books began in the preexilic era, contrary to some who believe that the whole process was a postexilic phenomenon.

### *The Martyrdom of the Prophet Uriah of Kiriath-jearim (26:20–24)*

This episode, which describes the murder of the prophet Uriah of Kiriath-Jearim, is inserted here to inform the reader that the threats against Jeremiah were deadly serious. Given the opportunity, his enemies would certainly do to him what they did to Uriah.

**26:20–21**. We know nothing of Uriah beyond what is reported here. His hometown, Kiriath-jearim, was west of Jerusalem, on the edge of the Shephelah. Two facts about the man are curious. First, he shared the name of Uriah the Hittite, whom David murdered (1 Sam. 11:14–24). It may be that the reader is expected to note that both at the beginning and end of the dynasty, the house of David killed a righteous man named Uriah. Second, Kiriath-jearim was where the ark of the covenant stayed for some time after the Philistines captured and then returned it (1 Sam. 6:19–7:2). This calls to mind the destruction of the Shiloh sanctuary and end of the priesthood of Eli, an episode to which Jeremiah referred in 26:4–6. Regardless, the main point of the passage here is that Uriah preached a message very similar to Jeremiah's and had to flee for his life to Egypt. We should not condemn Uriah as a coward for this; Jeremiah and his assistant Baruch also went into hiding for a time (Jer. 36:19).

**26:22–24**. Jehoiakim was at this time a vassal of Egypt (2 Kings 23:34–35), and it appears that Egypt and Judah shared extradition rights as part of their treaty arrangements (Thompson 1980, 527). These verses mention two members of the nobility, Elnathan son of Akbor and Ahikam son of Shaphan. The former was responsible for hauling Uriah back from Egypt and the latter played a key role in saving Jeremiah from Uriah's fate, execution. Both men, along with Ahikam's father Shaphan, had played a key role in the discovery of the text of the Law during Josiah's reign and had been involved in the reformation Josiah launched (2 Kings 22:12, 14). It seems that Elnathan and Ahikam were now on opposite sides of the religious-political divide, with the former supporting Jehoiakim and the temple priesthood and the latter supporting Jeremiah. "What a dilemma the prophets of doom must have presented to the king's advisors!" (Holladay 1989, 110). Uriah was brutally murdered, and his body was cast into "the graveyard of the common people" (אֶל־קִבְרֵי בְּנֵי הָעָם). Evidently, this was a potter's field. Perhaps the aristocrats were determined to avoid his burial place becoming a shrine to his martyrdom, and so they put him in an unmarked grave. For the reader, the point that Jeremiah barely escaped alive is clear.

### *The False Prophet Hananiah and the Yoke Bars (27:1–28:17)*

**27:1**. The MT of verse 1 dates this prophecy to the reign of Jehoiakim, but this is certainly an error, perhaps based on a copyist's accidentally repeating "early in the reign of Jehoiakim" (בְּרֵאשִׁית מַמְלְכוּת יְהוֹיָקִים) from 26:1 (27:1 has מַמְלֶכֶת instead of מַמְלְכוּת, but this is only a difference of a missing ו vowel-letter, and this ו may well have been omitted in paleo-Hebrew copies of 26:1). The content of the chapter at verses 3 and 12 indicate that this prophecy took place in the reign of Zedekiah, and some Hebrew manuscripts do have "Zedekiah" here. Also, 28:1 indicates that the incident took place in Zedekiah's fourth year, not his first year.

**27:2–6**. Jeremiah wore a yoke symbolizing Judah's future servitude to Babylon and sent messages concerning the yoke to all the local nations, warning them that they faced the same fate. This is one place in Jeremiah where we see him serving as a prophet to many nations (see 1:5). Elsewhere, we see many prophecies concerning the nations (as in Jer. 46–51), but here, he actually sends messages to the nearby nations. Jeremiah gives Edom, Moab, Ammon, Tyre, and Sidon the same warning he gave to Judah: submit to Babylon, and you will survive and remain in your land; resist, and you will be destroyed. In the message, YHWH claims sovereignty over all the earth. He alone, and not the gods of the nations, causes kingdoms to rise and fall.

**27:7**. YHWH declares that Babylon will remain ascendant through the reigns of Nebuchadnezzar, his son, and his grandson, and then it, too, will fall (v. 7). This is not literally true. Nebuchadnezzar was succeeded by his son Amel-Marduk (reigned 562–560; see 2 Kings 25:27–30, where he is called Evil-Merodach). After this there was a brief period of instability under military usurpers. The last two kings of Babylon were Nabonidus, another usurper unrelated to Nebuchadnezzar, and his son Belshazzar. But the main point of verse 7 is that Babylon would fall in the second generation after Nebuchadnezzar.

**27:8–11**. Like Judah, the other nations had false prophets proclaiming that they should resist and defeat Nebuchadnezzar. Among these were "your diviners" (קֹסְמֵיכֶם, probably omen-takers), "your dream-interpreters" (חֲלֹמֹתֵיכֶם, lit., "your dreams"), "your soothsayers" (עֹנְנֵיכֶם, probably another word for those who interpreted omens), and "your sorcerers" (כַּשָּׁפֵיכֶם, the word occurs only here, but based on Akkadian cognates appears to refer to magicians). These were of course pagan nations, but Judah also had such diviners (Jer. 29:8, using קֹסְמֵיכֶם, the same word that is used of pagan diviners in 27:9). We do not know how these soothsayers carried out their trade; it probably involved looking for omens in the entrails of animals, in the stars, in the flights of birds, and so forth.

**27:12–15**. Verse 12a states that YHWH gave the same warning to Judah as he is giving to the nations, and 12b–15 is a quotation of YHWH's words to Judah. Thus, when verse 15 says of the false prophets, "I have not sent them," it is, in the most literal sense, addressed to Judah and only recited to the other nations. As far as we know, YHWH never sent messages to prophets of these nations.

**27:16–18**. Having made his case to the foreign nations, Jeremiah turns to the priests and common people of Israel to plead with them to ignore the lying prophets. It is easy to see how the false prophets had great appeal. Jeremiah, with his constant demand that they surrender to Babylon, was to them a defeatist and a traitor. Ironically, they thought he lacked faith in God. In verse 18, Jeremiah says that if any of the Jewish preachers want to be true prophets, the best they can do is to pray for the country.

**27:19–22**. Jerusalem had been traumatized by seeing the Babylonian army carry off many of the sacred objects from the Jerusalem temple along with Jehoiachin in the first exile. The false prophets kept telling them that they would all soon come back, but Jeremiah says that to the contrary, soon even the large, not easily transported items such as the bronze pillars (1 Kings 7:15–22) and the "Bronze Sea" (a large, bronze basin supported by twelve bronze bulls and used for ritual cleansing; 1 Kings 7:23–26) would be taken to Babylonia.

**28:1**. The chronological note seems confused; it first indicates that the following episode took place in "early in the reign of Zedekiah" (בְּרֵאשִׁית מַמְלֶכֶת צִדְקִיָּה), and then it says that it happened in the fourth year (בַּשָּׁנָה הָרְבִעִית). Contrary to many translations, it is unlikely that these two notations refer to the same year. "Early in the reign" would naturally refer to the first year. Few kings reigned for a long time, and Zedekiah himself only reigned c. 597–587. His fourth year was well into his reign. It is likely that some of the same textual corruption that beset 27:1 also occurred here (note the repetition of בְּרֵאשִׁית מַמְלֶכֶת from 27:1). Probably Jeremiah's sign-act involving the yoke in chapter 27 and Hananiah's counter-prophecy took place in the same year, Zedekiah's fourth.

**28:2–4**. Hananiah's prophecy was straightforward: within two years, Jehoiachin, the other exiles, and the articles taken from the temple would all be restored. As for the yoke of Babylon that Jeremiah had made so much of, it would be broken.

**28:5–9**. Jeremiah responds with what may be called semi-sarcasm and a serious argument. He calls out "Amen!" and declares that he hopes Hananiah's prophecy will come true. In one sense, this is sincere; Jeremiah would love to see all go well for Judah. On the other hand, he has no faith that Hananiah actually heard a word from God; in that sense, it is sarcasm. His serious arguments are twofold. First, many prophets have foretold times of warfare and great upheaval. He seems to have in mind the great prophets of the past, such as Isaiah, Micah, and even Moses. But one prophet (he seems to have Hananiah in mind) predicts peace. Is it likely that this man would be right and all the great prophets of the past wrong? In reality, of course, there were many false prophets preaching peace and safety, as Jeremiah frequently pointed out. But the number of false prophets is not the main point; Jeremiah is simply contrasting this upstart Hananiah with the giants of the past. Second, Jeremiah asserts that the only way Hananiah can be vindicated is if his prophecy of safety comes true. This, he implies, will not happen.

**28:10–11**. Jeremiah, as 27:2 indicates, had been wearing a yoke as a sign of what would happen to Judah and to all the other nations nearby. Hananiah sought to demonstrate the power and validity of his prophecy by removing the yoke from Jeremiah and breaking it apart. It apparently had been a fairly lightweight yoke, more symbolic than real, both because Jeremiah had been wearing it on his neck and because Hananiah could easily break it apart. Presumably the yokes that oxen wore were much larger and heavier.

**28:12–14**. Significantly, Jeremiah did not respond immediately or stand and argue with Hananiah. He replied only after he had heard a word from God. His answer was that God would put a yoke of iron on Judah's neck. The power of Babylon would be unbreakable.

**28:15–17**. Hananiah's death was both personal punishment for his presuming to make a false prophecy and a sign to everyone else. When they heard that Hananiah had died in fulfillment of Jeremiah's curse, they should have realized that Jerusalem was similarly doomed.

### *The False Prophet Shemaiah and Letters to the Exiles (29:1–32)*

This chapter describes a series of letters to and from the Jewish exiles in Babylon written early in the reign of Zedekiah. This was the exile that included Jehoiachin, and it occurred in 597. From the account we have in this chapter, the sequence of events was as follows: 1) Jeremiah sent a letter to the exiles in Babylon telling them that the exile would last seventy years and that they should build houses and settle in for the long term. Few of the original generation of exiles would ever see Jerusalem again. 2) Shemaiah of Nehalem, a high-ranking individual and reputed prophet living among the Babylonian exiles, sent a letter to Zephaniah the priest in Jerusalem, demanding that Jeremiah be severely punished and silenced. 3) Jeremiah sent a second letter to the exiles in Babylon reiterating his instructions that they should be prepared for a long stay in Babylonia and rebuking Shemaiah and other false prophets. What we have in this chapter is in effect Jeremiah's second letter, but it quotes part of Shemaiah's letter and may include portions of Jeremiah's first letter. In other words, it is not a verbatim copy of Jeremiah's second letter but a summary of the whole exchange.

**29:1–3**. These verses give the background to the sending of the letter: Jeremiah wrote it to the elders, priests, and other exiles, but notably does not include the exiled king, Jehoiachin, among the addressees. Jehoiachin was kept in close confinement until after the death of Nebuchadnezzar (Jer. 52:31), and he probably had little contact with the rest of the exiles. The letter was sent along with diplomatic mission to Babylon and was carried by Elasah son of Shaphan and Gemariah son of Hilkiah. Elasah was apparently the brother of Ahikam son of Shaphan (26:24), and Gemariah son of Hilkiah was perhaps a son of Hilkiah the high priest, a man who strongly supported Josiah's reformation (2 Kings 22:4–14). Thus, both men were probably favorably disposed to Jeremiah (Thompson 1980, 545). But it is not clear whether these verses recount the circumstances behind the sending of Jeremiah's first or second letter. Although the content of the chapter is probably mostly derived from the second letter, the heading probably concerns the first, since that was the occasion for Jeremiah's conflict with the false prophets in Babylon.

**29:4–7**. This is almost certainly not the full text of the letter. It begins very suddenly with an oracle from YHWH instructing the exiles on what they should do. A formal letter in the ancient world would have a much more elaborate set of greetings before getting into the business of the letter. Even the extremely brief "Lachish Letters" (inscribed on ostraca) do not fail to include introductory greetings and good wishes. The instructions are straightforward: the Jews will be in Babylonia for a long time and should build homes, raise families, see their children married, and nurture future generations. They should give up on hoping for a speedy repatriation to Judah. Notably, they were to pray for the well-being of Babylon (v. 7), because that was now their home.

**29:8–9**. Jeremiah had apparently heard that some reputed prophets among the Jewish exiles were predicting a speedy return to Jerusalem, hampering the task of getting the Jews settled in their new home. This is what spurred him to write. The Jews' very survival would be at risk so long as they refused to face the new reality confronting them.

**29:10–14**. The prophecy of the seventy-year exile had been given some eight years earlier, in 605 (25:11), but until the predicted period of exile was fulfilled, the Jews would stay in Babylon. Even so, God has not abandoned them. These were the "good figs" of 24:1–8; God would sustain them, and they would preserve the Jewish faith and the Scriptures. Therefore, they should not despair over the lengthy exile that lay before them. God was doing it for their good, not to destroy them. The beautiful words of this passage, "For I know the plans I have for you—a message of YHWH—plans of well-being (שָׁלוֹם) and not of ruin, to give you a future and hope" (v. 11) are given in a specific context. The Jews of the Jehoiachin exile thought that they had been singled out for punishment and that God had abandoned them, but this was not the case.

**29:15–20**. The forlorn exiles in Babylon thought that those who remained in Jerusalem were the lucky ones, and they happily listened to predictions from their pretended prophets that they would soon be able to return. To the contrary, Jeremiah says, those whom you think of as prophets among you are frauds, and harrowing times are ahead for those back in Jerusalem. They would experience all the worst that ancient siege warfare had to offer: slaughter, terror, plague, and famine. The Jews already in exile had been spared all of that. They, not the apostates back in Jerusalem, were the hope for the future.

**29:21–23**. Jeremiah names two of the false prophets among the exiles: Ahab son of Kolaiah and Zedekiah son of Maaseiah. Their primary lie was the claim that YHWH would in a short time restore the exiles to Jerusalem. Jeremiah predicted that they would be burned alive for their crimes (see Dan. 3:6 for this use of punishment in Babylonia), probably because they were regarded as plotting sedition against the Babylonian government with their prophecies. Indeed, their execution would be so famous in the Jewish community that they would become a byword and example for someone whom God had punished. It is surprising that Jeremiah mentions that they also were adulterers. Although we might attribute this knowledge to divine revelation or to rumor that had made its way back from Babylon, it is probable that

Jeremiah knew the men and their reputations while they were still in Jerusalem.

**29:24–29**. Here, Jeremiah cites the letter from Shemaiah, demonstrating that much of chapter 29 is derived from Jeremiah's second letter to Babylon. Shemaiah had written in his own name (v. 25) to the temple officials, demanding that Jeremiah be placed in stocks to prevent him from writing any further instructions to the Jewish exiles. Writing in his own name was not necessarily wrong or presumptuous; the point is that Shemaiah did not in any way try to disguise that he was the man advocating that Jeremiah be severely punished, and that he regarded Jeremiah as a raving madman (אִישׁ מְשֻׁגָּע וּמִתְנַבֵּא; "a crazy man making prophecies"; see 2 Kings 9:11).

**29:30–32**. Instead of following Shemaiah's recommendations, Zephaniah son of Maaseiah showed the letter to Jeremiah, alerting him to the source of opposition to him among the Jews in Babylon. As Shemaiah had openly opposed Jeremiah, so Jeremiah singled Shemaiah out for punishment. For making his false prophecies and opposing Jeremiah, neither he nor any of his family would have a part in all the good things that God was planning for the Jewish community. The priest Zephaniah appears several times in the book (21:1; 37:3). He was clearly respectful toward Jeremiah, much to Shemaiah's annoyance. Zephaniah came to a sad end, however. He was captured along with other senior officials when Jerusalem fell, then taken before Nebuchadnezzar and executed (Jer. 52:24–27).

## THEOLOGICAL FOCUS

The entire focus of this collection of passages is the clash between the true and the false prophets. These texts do, however, touch upon a number of different issues.

- People were infuriated that Jeremiah had said that the temple would be destroyed. This was a kind of pseudo-orthodoxy. It seemed to show profound faith in the promises to David, but it provided cover for behavior that was truly evil. Christians too can be incensed if they perceive someone to be attacking their favorite doctrine—especially if that doctrine is of dubious validity.
- Uriah and Jeremiah preached the same message, but Uriah was captured and put to death while Jeremiah, as far as we can tell, died of old age. God had a special purpose for Jeremiah; he was to create and pass on to us the book that bears his name. Uriah, by his death, served as a witness to the evil of the people of Jerusalem. God uses each of his servants for his own purposes, and it is not for us to say which man is greater in the kingdom of heaven.
- YHWH, the God of Israel, was also God of all the earth, and he judged all nations. He also offered the same warning to the other nations that he offered Judah: that they should accept Babylon as their overlord and not resist. God continues to rule all nations justly, regardless of how large their Christian population is.
- Hananiah refused to accept God's judgment on Judah, and he artfully mocked Jeremiah and his yoke. Many scoffers are excellent communicators, and they can often sway the majority of the people. But their scoffing does nothing to change God's judgment.
- Shemaiah tried to silence Jeremiah through brute force; he demanded that the state exercise its power to confine and punish him. Shemaiah failed, but many who have used this tactic have succeeded. Regardless, the word of God will not be silenced by its opponents.

- Jeremiah gave guidance and ministry to people who were far away from him, the Jewish exiles living in Babylon. He used the technology available to him, the writing of letters. Direct and personal ministry is always best, but sometimes we too have to communicate through technology, including the printed word, emails, and streamed video.
- The Jewish diaspora offers a lesson for how Christians are to live "in the world but not of the world." The Jews were to settle in Babylon, treat it as their home, and pray for its well-being. They were to never forget that they were Jews, and they were to eagerly await their redemption and restoration to their homeland. In the interim, however, they were to be good and loyal citizens. In Esther, Mordecai served as an official of the Persian state and even saved the life of the Persian king (Esth. 6:2). Christians, similarly, are to be good citizens wherever we reside, but we should never confuse loyalty to a country with our higher loyalty to God. We should think of ourselves as like the Jews of the diaspora, understanding that no earthly nation is our true home.

## PREACHING AND TEACHING STRATEGIES

### *Exegetical and Theological Synthesis*

The Jews in exile and after the exile both lived facing opposition. In exile, opposition sometimes came physically, as in the case of Esther's pleading for her people's protection. There was always cultural opposition, for they lived in a pagan land. Jeremiah facing opposition must have been encouraging to his first readers. If Jeremiah faced opposition, so could they. These readers were also faced with change. The exiles obviously experienced the change of being uprooted from the place where they were born and lived their lives. The postexilic Jews experienced the same changes. After seventy years, most of the Jews had been born in captivity and lived their lives there. Jeremiah's message was to embrace the changes that God was bringing about.

This message is so needed in every generation. Fifty years ago, I remember the tone that the old deacons used when they would not allow drums in the sanctuary even for a youth service. Now, I don't complain about drums as the old deacons did, but I find myself complaining about having fog machines with the same tone. The point is not whether we should or shouldn't have fog machines; the point is that when God does things in new ways, we need to embrace them. One area that needs to change is the racial and cultural division that exists in our churches. Clearly God wants unity. It will look different, but it is change that God is bringing about and we must embrace it. While this passage doesn't expound on what changes are of God and what changes are not of him, it does teach us that when change is of him we need to embrace it.

### ***Preaching Idea***

God, you haven't done it that way before.
*(This could be said with one of two emotions: enraged or encouraged.)*

### ***Contemporary Connections***

#### *What does it mean?*

The thrust of this passage can be applied to us in two different ways depending upon which point of view you take. From the exiles' vantage point, this narrative is wonderfully encouraging. God works in his ways, not in ours, and we can trust him. Those in exile must have thought that God was not in control, and that life as his chosen people was over. When times look terrible and we think that God is not in control, we need to hear what the exiles read in Jeremiah's letter: "For I know the plans I have for you, declares the LORD, plans for welfare and not for evil, to give you a future and a hope" (Jer. 29:11 ESV). God wasn't going to spare Jerusalem or the temple, but his chosen nation would go on and even flourish—the ultimate purpose being the coming of Christ through this nation. The hope of him working in ways they hadn't seen before encouraged them.

Another application is from the point of view of Jeremiah's contemporaries in Judah. The opposition to Jeremiah teaches us that we must not hold on to our traditions and become convinced that our ways are always equal to God's ways. These beautiful words of God's wonderful new plans were wasted on the ears of the opposition. They couldn't understand how this could be God's good hand. It didn't include Jerusalem or the temple. God wouldn't work that way. He hasn't done it that way before. The fear of him working in ways they hadn't seen before enraged them.

### *It is true?*

We need to put ourselves in the shoes of those listening to Jeremiah. Often a country will have a building that is a metonymy or an image that represents the nation, such as the White House or the Eiffel Tower. The temple carried far more emotion than these modern symbols. For more than 350 years the temple was the center of worship. It was iconic—the symbol that YHWH lived in Israel. This strikingly beautiful building was a reminder that time after time invaders came and went, but YHWH's temple still stood.

Perhaps it was in the morning when Jeremiah began to preach his temple sermon. The rising sun is just touching the top of the two tree-like bronze pillars, spotlighting the decorations carved at the top. Most of the courtyard is still in the shade. People are gathering to offer sacrifices—some to YHWH, but some worshipping at altars set up to other gods. Jeremiah climbs the steps, and stands in front of the doors that used to be covered with gold but now are just wood. He is recognized as a prophet and a small crowd gathers, including priests and other prophets. And there Jeremiah proclaims that the temple and Jerusalem will be destroyed, and that those taken into exile are the ones blessed by God.

Imagine a pastor standing in the shadow of the Washington Monument, saying that Washington would be destroyed by a hostile power. While we must not make a theological parallel between Israel and the United States, the emotional parallel can help us feel the anger that the Jews had toward Jeremiah. Superhero films often play on this type of emotion, as when the bad guy's flag is seen flying over the White House. No wonder they wanted to kill Jeremiah. To them, his message was heresy. They must have thought and perhaps even said, "YHWH will not let that happen. This temple will always be here. How could exiles be the ones blessed? Don't you think God can protect us? God rescued us in the past; surely, he will rescue us again. What do you mean that the temple will be destroyed? How can that happen? Take us into exile and bless us there? That's crazy. God hasn't done it that way before."

The stage is set for three reactions to Jeremiah's message: the people want to kill him, Hananiah seeks to refute him, and Shemaiah tries to get the authorities to put Jeremiah in irons because of a letter Jeremiah sent to the exiles containing the same message.

### *Now what?*

Back in the 1970s Ralph Neighbour published *The Seven Last Words of the Church*; its subtitle was *We Never Did It That Way Before*. Jeremiah's opponents only slightly alter this, to "God never did it that way before." On the other hand, the seven last words of the church today could be, "Let's try something new; it might work." Churches are going through some amazing changes: worship styles, multisite congregations, cowboy churches, home groups instead of Sunday school, multiple preachers, coffee lattes in the sanctuary, and the list could go on. It is neither good nor bad simply because it is new.

In 1933 the pastor of First Baptist Lubbock, Dr. Robert Campbell, printed a sermon series. *Modern Evils* was published by Revell, and to give credibility it was endorsed by the head of the Southern Baptist Mission Organization. One of the modern evils that Campbell condemned was attending movies. He called them a "commercialized menace" (p. 46). To be fair, Dr. Campbell was opposing the industry more than the actual medium of film, but the outcome was that it was a sin to go to a movie, any movie. Yet, less than fifty years later the publishing arm of the SBC was producing and selling movies. Could God use movies? He hadn't done that before. A wonderful pastor in South Carolina confided in me that he had preached against the use of Facebook and other similar social media technologies. But during the COVID crisis he found himself using the very thing he had preached against. New methods of ministry must be evaluated and guided by Scripture, but we must not restrict our trust in God by thinking he will always work in the same way.

### *Creativity in Presentation*

A way to help the congregation follow this long passage is to present it as scenes from a movie. (I hope Dr. Campbell doesn't mind.) Jeremiah presents God's message three times in three different ways, followed by opposition. The temple sermon is the first scene with opposition coming from the people, who intended to kill him. There is a short flashback of Uriah's death to add tension. Scene two is the yoke image presentation of the message, with Hananiah's opposition. Scene three is the letter presentation of the message, followed by Shemiah's opposition. Using this format, this long narrative can be more easily presented because our listeners are familiar with this kind of structure. Of course, not every verse can be read, but key verses can and should be read as the scenes are unfolded. Here is one possible structure:

- Four ways to respond when God works in new ways:
  - Kill the idea (26:1–24).
  - Refute the idea (27:1–28:17).
  - Stall the idea (29:26). (This opposition is embedded in the next scene but logically can be presented here.)
  - God's directive: embrace the new idea (29:1–32).
- God, you haven't done it this way before.

## DISCUSSION QUESTIONS

1. What changes have you seen in churches in the past 10, 20, 50 years?
2. What is it about change that makes it hard to accept?
3. What guidelines, beside Scripture, do we use to evaluate changes?
4. What new ways of ministry have you seen God bless?
5. How might one's background affect their view of change?

# RESTORATION AND THE NEW COVENANT (30:1–33:26)

Standing at the structural center of the book, this section promises a regathering of Israel under the new covenant and an eschatological Davidic Messiah.

# Jeremiah 30:1–31:26

**EXEGETICAL IDEA**

God will call Israel back to himself after their punishment, they will repent, and then God will fully restore them. This text is a series of messages that all seem to have come to Jeremiah in a prophetic dream. Israel will be healed of the grievous wounds it has suffered, will be brought back to YHWH and the land, and will stop wandering in search of salvation among foreign gods and foreign powers.

**THEOLOGICAL FOCUS**

After repentance comes the joys of restoration. Israel, the chosen of God, had to experience severe pain as part of the process of its salvation and purification. We who are grafted into Israel and who have our own guilt to contend with should not suppose that our experience will be different.

**PREACHING IDEA**

Come home to our accepting, restorative God.

**PREACHING POINTERS**

Why do we hesitate to go to someone to restore a relationship? Simply put: fear. We don't know how they will respond. God made it clear to Israel, and to us, when our sin breaks the relationship with him; he wants us to know what it is like to return to him. It is a pleasant dream.

# THE RESTORATION (30:1–31:26)

## LITERARY STRUCTURE AND THEMES

Jeremiah places four chapters promising eschatological restoration at the center of the book. Just as the whole book separates undated from dated material, so also the salvation oracles contain first undated and then dated messages. A common theme and repeated content hold the whole unit together. The material in 30:1–31:40 broadly parallels that of 33:1–26. Each part contains the following four elements:

- Introduction to the oracles (30:1–3 and 33:1–3). Both begin with Jeremiah receiving a word from YHWH, and both speak of a significant new revelation:
    - 30:2: "Write all the words that I speak to you on a scroll."
    - 33:3: "I will tell you great and unassailable things."
- Desolate Jerusalem will again thrive (30:4–31:26 and 33:4–13). Both passages speak of the reversal of the desolation of Jerusalem.
    - 30:18–20: "The city shall be rebuilt upon its mound . . . and thanksgiving and the sound of people playing will go forth from them . . . their children will be as before, and the population will be established before me."
    - 33:10–11: "In the towns of Judah and the streets of Jerusalem, [once] made desolate by lack of people or inhabitants or livestock, there will be the sound of celebration and the sound of joy, the sound of groom and of bride, [and] the sound of those who say, 'Praise YHWH!'"
- Israel will be under an eschatological regime (31:27–34 and 33:14–18). These are, respectively, the new covenant and the eschatological David:
    - 31:31: "I will make a new covenant with the house of Israel and the house of Judah."
    - 33:15: "I will make a righteous shoot to flourish for David, and he will carry out justice and righteousness in the land."
- Restored Israel to be as enduring as the heavens (31:35–40 and 33:19–26). Both use the analogy of the heavens to describe how eschatological Israel will endure:
    - 31:35–36: "Thus says YHWH, who gives the sun for light by day and the laws governing [the procession of] the moon and the stars for light by night: If these laws vanish before me, then also the offspring of Israel will cease to be."
    - 33:20–21: "If you could break my covenant, the day, and my covenant, the night, so that there would no longer be day and night at the appropriate time, then also my covenant with David my servant could be broken."

The parallels between 30:1–31:40 (which speaks of a new covenant) and 33:1–26 (which speaks of a new David) creates an inclusion structure, with 32:1–44 at the center describing the redemption of the land.

Jeremiah 30–31 is the "Book of Consolation." After the initial command to write it

(Jer. 30:1–3), significant boundary markers appear in the text at five places. One of these is the comment about Jeremiah's awakening from a dream (31:26). The other four employ the expression, "days are coming." These are at 30:3 (which ends the introductory command), at 31:27 (which begins a new major subdivision after the dream notice of 31:26), at 31:31 (which introduces the New Covenant oracle), and at 31:38 (which introduces the restoration of Jerusalem). For this unit, we deal only with 30:1–31:26, which describes Jeremiah's dream of Judah's restoration. We will deal with the new covenant in the next unit.

The structure of the first section, The Restoration (30:1–31:26), is as follows:

- ***The Command to Write the Book of Consolation (30:1–3)***
- ***The Pleasant Dream (30:4–31:26)***
  - *Introduction to the Pleasant Dream (30:4)*
  - *The Reversal of Military Calamity (30:5–11)*
  - *The Healing of the Incurable Wound (30:12–17)*
  - *The Rebuilding of the Desolate Cities (30:18–31:1)*
  - *The Return of the Refugees (31:2–14)*
  - *The Return of Rachel's Lost Children (31:15–17)*
  - *The Forgiveness of Ephraim's Sin (31:18–20)*
  - *The Way Back for Wandering Israel (31:21–25)*
  - *Jeremiah's Awakening (31:26)*

## EXPOSITION

### *The Command to Write the Book of Consolation (30:1–3)*

**30:1–4**. This section introduces the whole of chapters 30–31. It includes both the command to write (vv. 1–2) and a brief summary of the message (v. 3). The introduction is unusually long, suggesting that what follows was conceived to be a major addition to the writings of Jeremiah. It is significant that the command in verse 2, "Write all the words (כְּתָב־לְךָ אֵת כָּל־הַדְּבָרִים) that I have spoken (אֲשֶׁר־דִּבַּרְתִּי) to you on a scroll (אֶל־סֵפֶר)," echoes the vocabulary of 25:13, "I will bring on that land all my words (אֶת־כָּל־דְּבָרַי) I have spoken (אֲשֶׁר־דִּבַּרְתִּי) against it, all that are written on this scroll (כָּל־הַכָּתוּב בַּסֵּפֶר הַזֶּה)." See also 36:4, 28, 32. I have suggested that 25:1–13 is the conclusion to the Baruch Scroll mentioned in chapter 36 and that this scroll was the original core of Jeremiah. It was entirely a work of condemnation and announcement of judgment. The Book of Consolation, chapters 30–31, was at some point added to it to provide a promise of final salvation, a counterpoint to contents of the original scroll.

### *The Pleasant Dream (30:4–31:26)*

What follows is a series of short oracles describing the restoration of Israel. They were apparently all given in a dream, as 31:26 implies.

#### *Introduction to the Pleasant Dream (30:4)*

**30:4**. Although this verse could be considered part of the general introduction in 30:1–3, it probably relates specifically to the Pleasant Dream oracles of 30:5–31:26.

#### *The Reversal of Military Calamity (30:5–11)*

For the people of Israel and Judah, the first and most obvious issue was that they endured calamitous defeat at the hands of Assyria and Babylon. This is, therefore, the first matter addressed.

**30:5–7**. The calamity is described under three headings: First, abstractly, Israel must endure a time of terror (v. 5). Second, concretely, their soldiers are gripped by panic and unable to fight (v. 6). Israel's fighting men are so terrified that their bowels spasm and they grab their abdomens, looking like women going into labor.

Third, this is the terrible Day of YHWH (v. 7). Amos 5:18–20 declares that the Day of YHWH is dark and dreadful, and that Israel will not escape it (see also Joel 2:11 and Zeph. 1:14–18). The term is eschatological, but it can also be manifested in historical events. The people of God are not spared the Babylonian scourge that strikes the rest of the nations.

**30:8–9**. The last two words of verse 7, "But [Israel] will be saved from it" (וּמִמֶּנָּה יִוָּשֵׁעַ), belong at the beginning of verse 8 and serves as a general, abstract promise of salvation. Verse 8 concretely describes their deliverance, with YHWH breaking the yoke on their necks and the fetters on their limbs and releasing them from servitude. Verse 9 then introduces a glorious future: Israel will serve YHWH and their Davidic king, the latter being a messianic figure. This eschatological glory is in contrast to the terrors of the Day of YHWH described in verse 7. As such, verses 5–7 and 8–9 have a similar pattern: An abstract introduction is followed by a concrete promise and a final outcome that draws upon eschatological language in the Old Testament. The salvation in 8–9 is the counterpart to the disaster of 5–7.

**30:10–11**. This concludes the initial promise of deliverance from exile among the nations. God will return his people to their land and give them peace and security, but he will destroy the nations. It contains language that is standard among the prophets for such promises. The people are encouraged not to fear (see Isa. 41:14); YHWH will recover them from all the lands to which they were driven (see Jer. 29:14); they will live in peace (see Isa. 35:9); God will be with Israel but will punish the nations (see Jer. 46:28).

### *The Healing of the Incurable Wound (30:12–17)*

**30:12–14**. This passage uses the metaphor of the lawsuit: Judah is being accused or sued in court, and no one bears witness in its defense (v. 13). It also uses the metaphor of the abandoned consort: Judah is like a woman who has taken many lovers, but in her time of need they all abandon her (v. 14). Both metaphors speak of how Israel suffered under the Babylonian onslaught, but no former ally came to their rescue. The dominant metaphor of this text, however, is the incurable wound. A soldier has taken a severe wound in battle; it is infected, and the soldier can now only wait to die. YHWH himself has struck down Judah, condemning it to death.

**30:15**. The first line should be translated, "Why do you cry out about your being shattered, [and about] your injury, that it is incurable?" A rhetorical question such as this implies that they should not cry out. Obviously, a person with a broken leg or a deep and festering laceration will often groan or even scream in pain; the point is not that they should stoically endure the agony and keep silent. The implied outcry is not simply the groaning of one in pain; it is the demand of a sufferer to know why this has happened. The passage says that there is no need to ask why such agony has come upon them because they already know the answer: it is because they abandoned the covenant and are being punished for it. Furthermore, their sins were so abundant (רֹב) and so grave (עָצְמוּ; literally, "they were strong"). Note that 15b repeats 14b verbatim.

**30:16–17**. Verse 16 begins, "Therefore (לָכֵן), all who consume you will be consumed." The word "therefore" appears odd, as the sentence seems to create a contrast, and for that reason some translations render it as "but" (NIV) or "nevertheless" (CSB). "Therefore," however, is the accurate meaning of לָכֵן. The word is used because the suffering inflicted on Israel was a divine punishment (Babylon was only God's instrument). God may use the nations to carry out his verdict, but the nations did not have the right to exploit Israel's degradation. When they did so, they maliciously took advantage of God's punishment of Israel, and therefore they would themselves be punished with the same calamities that befell the Jews. Israel, in turn, would receive full healing and restoration. The passage gives us an illustration, on a very large scale, of Proverbs 24:17–18: "Do not rejoice when your enemies fall, and do not let your heart celebrate when they stumble, or else YHWH will see it and it will be evil in his eyes, and he will turn away his anger from them."

### *The Rebuilding of the Desolate Cities (30:18–31:1)*

**30:18**. This verse serves as a general introduction to 30:18–31:1, asserting that the demolished cities will be rebuilt. This perspective does not necessarily imply that the oracle came from after the fall of Jerusalem, since throughout his ministry Jeremiah predicted that it was destined for destruction. The passage speaks of four restorations: the "tents of Jacob" (אָהֳלֵי יַעֲקוֹב), its "dwelling places" (וּמִשְׁכְּנֹתָיו), the "city" (עִיר), and the "citadel" (אַרְמוֹן). The "tents" refer to the homeland of the people, the whole of Israel, using language that recalls their shepherding origin. The "dwelling places" are any inhabited settlements. The "city" is Jerusalem, and the "citadel" is the royal palace in the city of David, the small hill that was the original Jerusalem. The language moves from the broadest domain ("tents of Jacob") to the smallest ("citadel"), and it implies a restoration under a son of David.

**30:19–22**. This text again proceeds from a broad, general account of the restoration (the people will celebrate, they will be numerous and not few in number, they will worship in God's presence, they will be honored by the nations, and they will be safe from all their enemies [vv. 19–20]) to a much narrower matter (their future leader [v. 21]). It closes with the most important element in the restoration: they will be YHWH's people (v. 22). The elements of the prophecy relate closely to the experience of Jerusalem in defeat and exile, and the future celebration answers their current pain and sorrow, as expressed in Lamentations. The predicted great number of people answers their pitifully small population at the time of the exile (see Jer. 52:28–30). The renewal of their worship, when "the congregation is established before YHWH," answers the destruction of the temple. The honor predicted for them and the punishment of their oppressors answer their current disgrace, that they were both despised and defeated by Gentile powers. The coming leader reverses the demise of the Davidic dynasty. Verse 21 predicts that this coming ruler will be Jewish and not Gentile, a matter that answers their humiliation of being under the thumb of foreign empires and kings. It also predicts that the ruler will have a priestly function, having the freedom to approach God directly. Although this does not contradict the notion that the future ruler would be Davidic, it implies that he will greater than the Davidic kings of old, who were not free to approach YHWH, as illustrated by the experience of King Uzziah, who tried to offer incense in the temple (2 Chron. 26:16–21). It also points toward Psalm 110 and the use of the psalm in Matthew 22:41–46. Jeremiah's conclusion, that they would be YHWH's people and YHWH would be their God (v. 22), restores what is most fundamental to the identity of Israel. It recalls the promise of Exodus 6:7, and reverses the curse of Hosea 1:9 where Israel was declared to be "not my people."

**30:23–31:1**. Like 30:19–22, this segment of the text concludes with the promise that Israel will again be celebrated as YHWH's people (31:1). However, 30:23–24, perhaps somewhat surprisingly, describes this as a work of God's anger (we might expect it to be a work of his compassion). In this context, the anger arises from YHWH's jealousy for Israel (Joel 2:18; Zech. 1:14; 8:2). God looks upon Israel as his own possession, and he is furious at how the nations have abused his people.

### *The Return of the Refugees (31:2–14)*

**31:2**. The Hebrew of this verse is difficult, but it is a general introduction to the theme of the return of the refugees. It draws upon the exodus tradition, implying that there will be a great deliverance from captivity, just as there was from slavery in Egypt.

> *TRANSLATION NOTE: THE MEANING OF 31:2*
> Jeremiah 31:2b, הָלוֹךְ לְהַרְגִּיעוֹ יִשְׂרָאֵל, is difficult to unravel. It is literally, "An act of going (infinitive absolute of הלך) to provide him with rest (לְהַרְגִּיעוֹ), Israel (יִשְׂרָאֵל)." Interpreters differ over whether Israel is in search of rest (Lundbom 2008b, 414–15; Smothers, Keown, and Scalise 1995, 106) or YHWH is coming to give rest to Israel (NIV), and several translations depend upon emendation of the Hebrew. But one can make sense of the text without emendation. The masculine suffix on לְהַרְגִּיעוֹ probably has the noun עַם ("people") as its antecedent, and יִשְׂרָאֵל is probably pendant, parallel to שְׂרִידֵי חָרֶב ("survivors of the sword") and defining עַם. Furthermore, the subject of the action in 2b is neither YHWH nor Israel; it is the infinitive הָלוֹךְ, here meaning something like "journey." The whole verse thus means, "Thus says YHWH: / 'A people find grace in the wilderness; [they are] refugees from the sword! / It is a journey meant to provide them rest; [they are] Israel!'"

**31:3–5**. YHWH appears to Israel from far away; they are in exile, but God, from the Promised Land, will call them to himself. God here promises a series of blessings for Israel. First, God loves them and will demonstrate to them how great his love is. Second, he will draw them back to their land with his kindness (חֶסֶד). Third, he will rebuild their cities. Fourth, they will celebrate in the streets. Fifth, they will plant vineyards and enjoy the wine; foreigners will not take it. God will reverse the curses of captivity.

**31:6**. Watchmen in the hill country of Ephraim will call out that it is time to journey to the temple to worship God. This is in contrast to Jeremiah's time, when they were on the lookout for enemy troops on the horizon. The verse also indicates that in the future Ephraim will come to the Davidic temple, Zion. There will be no heretical temples such as those in Dan and Bethel, shrines that led the northern tribes into apostasy.

**31:7–9**. God calls on Israel to rejoice over their coming salvation. He will gather them from the north (Babylonia, the land of their enemy) and from the most distant places on earth. That is, no place is so hostile or distant that the scattered Jews will not be found and returned. He will gather the blind, the lame, and the pregnant. In other words, no one will miss the great regathering because of a physical infirmity. They will come with weeping and prayer, meaning that he will draw them to repentance. He will bring them on level, straight paths that run alongside streams of fresh water, implying that their journey will not be unduly harsh. He is their father and will bring them back to himself—a message that recalls Hosea 11:1, 8–9.

**31:10–11**. These verses are addressed to the nations. Israel's captivity had been its shame and disgrace before the whole world, but that shame will be removed. The nations will learn that God has loved his people and redeemed them from slavery.

**31:12–14**. This summarizes all of 31:2–14. Israel will rejoice in Zion, their own land, for their captivity will be over. They will have eternal prosperity, as implied by the wine, oil, and flocks. No one will be left out: male and female, young and old, and priests and laity will participate. All will have a share in the abundance YHWH will provide.

### *The Return of Rachel's Lost Children (31:15–17)*

**31:15**. Ramah of Benjamin was the home of Samuel, and it was also the town closest to the burial place of Rachel (1 Sam. 10:2). Rachel was the mother of Joseph and grandmother of Ephraim and Manasseh, as well as the mother of Benjamin. These tribes, especially Ephraim, dominated the northern territory of Israel (the northern kingdom is sometimes simply called "Ephraim"). Therefore, even though she was not the literal mother of all the northern tribes, she functions as their matriarch. From her tomb near Ramah, the spirit of Rachel weeps over the slain of the northern tribes of Israel after the calamity of the destruction brought about by the Assyrians. The destruction was so thorough and so tragic that, metaphorically, their matriarch was weeping over them from her tomb.

**31:16–17.** YHWH encourages Rachel to stop weeping. He will restore and multiply her children. They will return from their captivity and become more numerous than ever before.

### Jeremiah 31:15 and the Slaughter of the Innocents

Matthew 2:17–18 cites Jeremiah 31:15 with the assertion that Herod's massacre of the baby boys in Bethlehem "fulfilled" Jeremiah's word. This is problematic because the contextual meaning of the Jeremiah text is that the northern kingdom of Israel has suffered destruction and exile under the Assyrian Empire. The spirit of the deceased Rachel, in a vivid metaphor, weeps over them. By the time Jeremiah wrote these words, the fall of Samaria (722 B.C.) was already more than a century in the past. Nothing suggests that the passage is a prediction of a future event involving a literal slaughter of children, nor that it is messianic. How can we account for this?

One could argue that, based on Genesis 35:19 and 48:7, Matthew believed that Rachel's tomb was in Bethlehem and thus that her tomb was very close to the terrible slaughter of children Matthew describes. This, however, is not a good solution. The passages in Genesis do not assert that Rachel was buried in Bethlehem; in fact, they exclude that possibility. Genesis 35:19 states, "And Rachel died and was buried on the way to Ephrath (that is, Bethlehem)." Ephrath was the area in Judah occupied by the Ephrath clan, and its most significant town was Bethlehem. Thus, the verse identifies Ephrath for readers who may not know the territory by referring to its most significant and famous town. It does not say she was buried in Ephrath; it says she was buried while on the way to Ephrath (in other words, before she got to Ephrath). Genesis 48:7 confirms this, saying that she died a short distance away from Ephrath. She was not buried in or near Bethlehem.

To locate Rachel's tomb, the reader should have in mind a north-to-south line of towns and regions within the hill country of Ephraim, Benjamin, and Judah. At the top is Bethel (in Ephraim), the sojourning site of Jacob and later an Israelite shrine. South of that is Ramah, the home of Samuel; and south of Ramah is Gibeah, the home of Saul. South of Gibeah is Jerusalem. Ramah, Gibeah, and Jerusalem are all in Benjamite territory. South of Jerusalem is the old clan territory of Ephrath of Judah, and at the southern end of Ephrath is Bethlehem. South of Bethlehem, and deep inside of Judah's territory, is Hebron.

Jacob and his family were traveling from north to south. They started at Bethel (35:16) and were on their way to Hebron (35:27), but in the middle of their trek, while just north of Ephrath, Rachel died (35:19). The region that was just north of Ephrath was Benjamin, where Ramah was located. She thus died near Ramah, where she was buried (1 Sam. 10:2). She was not in Ephrath, and she was nowhere near Bethlehem, at the southern end of Ephrath. In 1 Samuel 10, when Saul left Ramah to return his home in Gibeah, he would have headed south, and the first place he would have passed by was Rachel's tomb (v. 2). For his part, Matthew never alludes to the Genesis texts or suggests that Rachel was buried near Bethlehem. The only location he mentions is Ramah and the only text he cites is Jeremiah 31.

We are thus left needing to explain why Matthew says that the slaughter of the innocents "fulfilled" Jeremiah 31:15, since the Jeremiah text is a poetic metaphor referring to historical circumstances (that the tomb of Rachel was near Ramah and that the Assyrians had slaughtered her "children," the tribes of the northern kingdom). Jeremiah 31:15 is not a prediction, and it does not speak of a slaughter of literal children in Bethlehem of Judah.

In Matthew, however, "fulfill" often does not mean that a specific prediction has come about. It means that a theological pattern has come to its ultimate realization in Christ. The specific pattern here is that the people of Israel and especially their children suffer brutality at the hands of the nations. The pattern had its first instance in the Egyptian persecution, when Pharaoh attempted to murder all the newborn boys of Israel (Exod. 1). Other texts that follow this theme are not hard to find. For example, "For these things I weep; / My eye, my eye runs down with water; / Because a comforter, someone to restore my soul, is far from me. / My children are lost, / Because the enemy has won" (Lam. 1:16; see also Jer. 6:10–12; 18:21; 38:23; Lam. 4:2; Ezek. 9:6; Hos. 1:6; Amos 1:13; Mic. 1:16). Matthew asserts that the massacre of the innocents in Bethlehem repeated the pattern of Gentile cruelty toward Israel's children. Herod's atrocity brought this theological theme to its ultimate realization. Herod was a terrible oppressor in the pattern of Pharaoh, and Jesus would come out of Egypt to bring about a new exodus. In Matthew's account, the matriarch Rachel, who had wept from her tomb over the destruction of Ephraim in the eighth century, wept again over the slaughter of Jewish children at Bethlehem. As in Jeremiah, this is metaphorical. The actual meaning in Matthew is that the terrible pattern of Gentile rulers murdering Jewish children was fulfilled again in the lifetime of Jesus.

### *The Forgiveness of Ephraim's Sin (31:18–20)*

**31:18–19**. Ephraim is here represented as a young man who has grievously sinned. He had been like a wild young bull that refused to be domesticated and did great damage. Like the prodigal son of Luke 15:11–32, he came back to his father and pleaded for mercy. After he came back and was instructed, his mortification over his past behavior was all the greater. The closer he got to his father, the more he realized what a wicked fool he had been.

**31:20**. This verse strongly echoes Hosea 11:8–9. Israel is his son; God cannot give up on him. His heart yearns for Israel's return, and he is determined to restore him.

### *The Way Back for Wandering Israel (31:21–25)*

**31:21–22**. As described in the translation note above, this text has nothing to do with God creating a new thing defined as a woman surrounding a man. The verses concern the wandering of Israel, and it exhorts her to return home, where YHWH will initiate the new covenant. The wandering is metaphorical, even though it does have a somewhat literal historical application in how the kings of Judah sent emissaries to various nations, especially Egypt, seeking their help. Also, the Jews in diaspora wandered among the nations. But the primary meaning is that the people should return to YHWH and stop seeking for support from other sources, whether they be foreign nations or foreign gods.

**The Meaning of Jeremiah 31:22**

As it stands in the major translations, Jeremiah 31:22 is unintelligible. Verse 22b is the conundrum: כִּי־בָרָא יְהוָה חֲדָשָׁה בָּאָרֶץ נְקֵבָה תְּסוֹבֵב גָּבֶר. The ESV translates the full verse as "How long will you waver, O faithless daughter? / For the Lord has created a new thing on the earth: a woman encircles a man." This substantially agrees with other major English translations such as the KJV, NIV, and NRSV, as well as standard translations in French or German. The LXX is anomalous. It has ἕως πότε ἀποστρέψεις, θυγάτηρ ἠτιμωμένη; ὅτι ἔκτισεν κύριος σωτηρίαν εἰς καταφύτευσιν καινήν, ἐν σωτηρίᾳ περιελεύσονται ἄνθρωποι ("How long will you turn away, dishonored daughter? For the Lord has created salvation as a new planting; people will go about in salvation"). It is highly unlikely that this represents a different Hebrew *Vorlage*; it is more likely that the translator, trying to make sense of the Hebrew, gave the text a very loose and expansive paraphrase. The LXX translation is of no value for unraveling the Hebrew. The Vulgate essentially supports the MT, albeit giving it a translation that cannot be justified. It translates the end of the verse as *femina circumdabit virum*: "A woman will put [something] around a man." Interpreters have tried to come to terms with this difficult verse in various ways.

Perhaps the closest thing to a plausible interpretation is that the phrase "a woman encircles a man" means that the woman will protect the man (Lundbom 2008b, 451–52). The CSB similarly paraphrases the line as, "a female will shelter a man." This fails for two reasons. First, the verb סבב does not mean "protect." It means to walk about, to go around, or to surround. One human cannot "surround" another, and a woman walking in circles around a man makes no sense. Some cite Deuteronomy 32:10 and Psalm 32:10 as examples of סבב having this meaning, but in these texts, the significance is derived from context; the verb סבב of itself does not imply protection or shelter. In Deuteronomy 32:10 the subject is God, who (unlike a single human) can surround a person: "[YHWH] found [Israel] in a wilderness, / in a barren, howling desert. / He surrounded him (יְסֹבְבֶנְהוּ), / he took thought for him (יְבוֹנְנֵהוּ), and he protected him (יִצְּרֶנְהוּ) like the pupil of his eye." The idea is that YHWH was all around Israel, protecting the nation from all enemies as carefully as a man would protect his eye. Apart from the context (particularly the verbs יְבוֹנְנֵהוּ and יִצְּרֶנְהוּ), the verse would be incomprehensible, saying only that YHWH "went about" Israel. In Psalm 32:10, YHWH's mercy (חֶסֶד) goes about a person in the sense that wherever he is and whatever he does, the compassion of God is with him. This, again, is strictly a work of God. Nowhere in the Bible is סבב used of one human sheltering or protecting another. Second, the idea of a woman protecting a man in this context makes no sense. That is, the interpretation has no relationship to the rest of Jeremiah 31, and one cannot give a plausible explanation for why the text would say such a thing.

Another interpretive translation is, "A woman is turned into a man" (McKane 1986, 2.806–807). This has nothing to commend it linguistically, and it is hard to see how turning a woman into a man is a good thing.

A more common interpretation is that the woman will become the initiator in love, as in "A female courts a man" (Allen 2008, 343). This is taken to mean that the Israelites will love YHWH spontaneously and aggressively. But the interpretation is not credible. The word סבב simply cannot mean to "court" or to "aggressively love."

Some take it to mean that the woman will defeat the man in combat, suggesting that this implies that Jerusalem will defeat her enemies (Holladay 1989, 195). But again, סבב does not imply victory in battle. Also, Babylon, like Jerusalem, is routinely personified as a woman. There is no basis for thinking that the woman is Jerusalem, but the man is the enemy.

Some take the verse to mean that the genders will swap roles, so that the woman behaves like a man and the man like a woman (Sawyer 1999; Kruger 2008). Once again, סבב cannot possibly have this meaning. It is very doubtful that the Israelites would regard a reversal of gender roles as a good thing, and the idea has no coherent meaning the context of Jeremiah 31.

Another view is that the woman will dance around the man as a metaphor for Israel's joy in the love of YHWH (Unterman 1987, 51). Yet again, this saddles סבב with a meaning it cannot bear. Also, it is not clear how the celebration of Israelites could be the "new thing" that YHWH "creates in the land," since they routinely celebrated before YHWH in their worship.

An older interpretation is that a woman surrounding a man refers to pregnancy; it is the gestation of a male baby in the womb. In traditional Christian interpretation, this is taken to refer to the virgin birth, although some modern interpreters take it to mean that Israelite women will give birth to healthy boys (Smothers, Keown, and Scalise 1995, 121–23). But the claim that סבב, "to walk about, to surround," refers to pregnancy is far-fetched. And women giving birth to baby boys is scarcely a "new thing on the earth" (on the implausibility of taking the verse to refer to the virgin birth, see Feinberg 1966; Feinberg 1967). Also, although it is true that a woman "surrounds" the male organ in sexual union, this has no bearing whatsoever on the context and is certainly not a "new thing" (and it would be a bizarre use of סבב).

Some interpreters hold to the standard translation but frankly admit that it is a hopeless enigma, having no discernible meaning (Bright 1963, 282; Carroll 1986, 605).

All of the above interpretations are based upon the standard view that "A woman will surround a man" is the literal meaning of the last clause, נְקֵבָה תְּסוֹבֵב גָּבֶר. I believe that this translation is wrong. As explored above, the notion that a woman will surround a man has no plausible interpretation. Furthermore, it has no discernable connection to 21–22a, which speaks of the wandering of Jerusalem, the faithless daughter. Also, the first words of 22bα, although easy to translate, are problematic: כִּי־בָרָא יְהוָה חֲדָשָׁה בָּאָרֶץ ("For YHWH has created a new thing in the land"). It is not clear how this "surrounding" of a man by a woman is a "new thing" that God has created, and the prepositional phrase בָּאָרֶץ ("in the land" or "on the earth") has no discernible function in this context if one follows the conventional interpretation. Is a woman "surrounding" a man supposed to be a new act of special creation on earth, like the sudden creation of a new species? Or is it something that God will specially do in the land of Israel?

To make sense of this, we should begin by observing that the word נְקֵבָה is more precisely "female," and that the word גֶּבֶר refers to a man in the prime of life and vigor; it could be translated as "hero" or "warrior." These are not generic man and woman. The term "female" focuses on female gender identity and social behavior as understood in ancient Near Eastern society, and it is set in contrast to the vigorous man in the prime of life.

Furthermore, סבב is here in the polel stem. The polel of סבב most commonly means "walk about," as when something—a person, a wild dog, or a personified force—walks back and forth inside a city (Ps. 59:6, 14 [MT 7, 15]; 55:10 [MT 11]; Song 3:2), or a worshiper walks about an altar (Ps. 26:6). It can describe an undersea current swirling about a drowning man (Jonah 2:3, 5 [MT 4, 6]). It means "surround" when the subject is God (Deut. 32:10) or a crowd of people (Ps. 7:7 [MT 8]).

When we consider the context, the best translation of 31:21–22 is as follows:

> Set up signposts! Put road marks in place!
> Focus your attention on the route—on the road you will travel!
> Come back, Virgin Israel,
> Come back to these your cities!
> How long will you wander afar,
> O Daughter who keeps turning about?
> YHWH is creating a new thing in the land,
> O Female [who] wanders around [like] a man in his prime!

Verse 21 establishes the metaphor: Israel is like a woman wandering far from home. This follows the common prophetic theme of Israel being a wayward wife who seeks help from her "lovers," the foreign nations and their gods. Here, she is out on the highways in faraway lands going from place to place looking for sanctuary and safety, and the prophet exhorts her to come back home. Verse 22a obviously continues the metaphor: she has wandered far, turning this way and that. Verse 22bα then gives the reason she should return home: YHWH has created something new in the land, which in this context must refer to the land of Israel (and not the whole earth). Verse 22bβ, נְקֵבָה תְּסוֹבֵב גָּבֶר, is not the new thing YHWH is creating. It directly addresses the woman, reasserting that she is a woman wandering far from home: "O Female [who] wanders around [like] a man in his prime!" This translation of נְקֵבָה תְּסוֹבֵב גָּבֶר is based on the following considerations.

- Verse 22bβ is parallel to הַבַּת הַשּׁוֹבֵבָה in 22aβ, "O Daughter who keeps turning about." This implies that both have the same rhetorical function of directly addressing the metaphorical woman.

- The noun נְקֵבָה is here understood to be vocative and not the grammatical subject of תְּסוֹבֵב.

- The words תְּסוֹבֵב גָּבֶר form a relative clause with an implied אֲשֶׁר, "who." The omission of אֲשֶׁר is so common, especially in poetry, that it needs no comment. Thus, נְקֵבָה תְּסוֹבֵב means "O female [who] wanders around" and not "A female wanders around."

One may object that a vocative in Hebrew generally has the definite article, but this is not decisive. The article is often absent from vocative nouns: "The person (or the thing) that is addressed (vocative), since it is always determinate, should always have the article; in fact the article is often omitted, especially in poetry or in lofty prose" (Joüon and Muraoka 2006, §137g). The vocative function of the noun is already established by the parallel in 22aβ. In the very next verse (Jer. 31:23), moreover, we have a pair of vocatives in which the first is indefinite and the second definite: "O Righteous pasture, O Holy mountain!" (נְוֵה־צֶדֶק הַר הַקֹּדֶשׁ).

Similarly, the preposition בְּ is implied before גֶּבֶר. Omission of small, inseparable prepositions is also common in poetry. For example, Jeremiah 19:5 has, "And they build the high places of Baal in order to burn their sons in the fire [as] whole offerings to Baal (עֹלוֹת לַבָּעַל, omitting בְּ)."

Grammatically, the translation proposed above is unobjectionable. In context, it makes perfect sense. Jerusalem is a female who runs from place to place as though she were a man in his prime, heedless of the risks. In ancient Israel, women were somewhat sequestered and did not roam alone in the streets of their own cities, much less out in the highways in foreign lands. Typically, only a vigorous and relatively young man would dare do such a thing; even older men tended to stay indoors because of "dangers in the streets" (Eccl. 12:5). Furthermore, the "new thing" (חֲדָשָׁה) that YHWH creates "in the land" (בָּאָרֶץ) is also evident in context. It is the "new covenant" (בְּרִית חֲדָשָׁה) mentioned in verse 31. The "land" in question is Israel. The prophet exhorts the woman stop her wandering and to return home because that is where God is at work, making a new covenant in the land of Israel to redefine the relationship between God and his people.

**31:23–25**. These verses further define the significance of YHWH creating a new covenant in the land of Israel. The land and its cities will be blessed and joyful. All peoples will recognize this to be the abode of the true God and will pronounce blessings upon it (v. 23). Under the new covenant, people will be safe both in the towns and out in the fields with their flocks (v. 24). And there will be no more want (v. 25). The "new thing" God creates will truly be glorious, and the wandering female should come home to enjoy it.

*Jeremiah's Awakening (31:26)*

**31:26**. After having had so many oracles from YHWH that were filled with condemnation and calamity for Judah, Jeremiah had at last received in a dream a message that gave him joy. His sleep, therefore, had been pleasant to him.

## THEOLOGICAL FOCUS

This portion of the book, having promises of restoration rather than threats of judgment and destruction, is refreshing to readers who may have found the first twenty-nine chapters of Jeremiah wearisome. At the same time, it also exhorts the readers to repentance. Main theological emphases are as follows:

- Scripture contains hard texts that speak of our sin and punishment, but it also has the hope of deliverance, as illustrated by how the introduction in 30:1–3 alludes to the Baruch Scroll and the judgments it contains.
- We should not delude ourselves into thinking that the Day of the Lord is, for us, all glory and no suffering, as many in Israel did. But if that day is a time of fiery wrath, even for us, it is ultimately the day of our redemption. We should both fear and hope.
- God regards Israel as the pupil of his eye, something to be protected at all costs. So too, we who have been grafted into Israel are under that same love. Those who persecute the church bring destruction on themselves.
- Only the messianic son of David can take away Israel's reproach. The Messiah himself, however, first shared their reproach. We, as Christians, share in

the reproach Christ endured so that we may share in his glory.

- For ancient Israel, true worship required coming to the true temple. It still requires that, except that the true temple is now the person of Jesus.
- The true Davidic Messiah is more than a king; he is both a king and a priest. He is sovereign, but he also stands in our place to intercede for us.
- Hostility to God leads to unimaginable evil. The nations tried to destroy Rachel's children Israel, and a depraved king killed all the baby boys in Bethlehem.
- Repentance is a process. It involves turning from sin and returning to God, but often the repentant sinner has only the most superficial understanding of the gravity of sin. Like Ephraim, the sinner will have a deeper abhorrence of his own actions as he grows in grace. But along with the deepening remorse, there is also a deepening awareness of the mercy of God.
- We, like foolish Israel, run from place to place seeking truth, security, and hope. But these things are found in our own "land," in the new covenant that we now partake of.

## PREACHING AND TEACHING STRATEGIES

### *Exegetical and Theological Synthesis*

Restoration is not always offered—and if it is, what does it look like? God is not only promising to return Israel to their land, but he gives a picture of that coming restoration. Perhaps those hearing Jeremiah proclaim this were confused, for they didn't even realize that their relationship to YHWH was broken. But some did trust in YHWH and realized that judgment was coming. For these believing ones who heard Jeremiah, and then for those who later read Jeremiah's words, either in exile or after the exile, these words of glorious promises brought joy and hope. God was not only inviting his people to return to him, but he was laying forth the conditions of this renewed relationship—and what a glorious picture. It was like a dream.

These seven pictures of God's promises are filled with delight and joy, and yet there is also a strong undercurrent of the necessity of the people's repentance and God's disciplining hand. The focus is on God's wonderful restoration, but repentance must not be forgotten.

### *Preaching Idea*

Come home to our accepting, restorative God.

### *Contemporary Connections*

#### *What does it mean?*

When conflicts result in a relationship being destroyed or hurt, the conditions of restoring that relationship is very important. This can be seen across a spectrum, from global conflicts to interpersonal relationships.

Toward the end of WWII, the Red Army was moving quickly into Germany from the east, and the western allies were moving in from the west. Within Germany, during the last days of the war, there was a mass movement of German soldiers toward the west. This was not because of an order by generals; rather, this was from the soldiers. They wanted to surrender to the US and Britain because the hoped-for restoration from the US and UK was thought to be far better than that of the Soviets. Would they, as German POWs, be treated by rules of the Geneva Convention? Would they be killed? Would they be allowed to eventually return home?

Even in personal relationships the conditions of restoration are important at a level that fits the moment. Rich and Mary had been dating for six months. Rich told Mary that he couldn't come to a gathering of her family because he wasn't feeling well, when really he simply didn't want to go. Instead, he went to shoot some hoops with friends. In time his lie became known to Mary and she broke off the relationship. Rich didn't want to end the relationship, so he decided to talk with Mary. How would she respond? If they could restore the relationship, what would it look like? Would she hold it over his head? Would she truly forgive? How could he show he was truly repentant?

*Is it true?*

Jeremiah's picture of renewal applied directly to Israel and it applies to us as well, though more abstractly. When we stray from the Lord, we might hesitate to return to him because of some past attempts at mending human relationships that went badly. Perhaps we wanted to restore a dating relationship but we were left heartbroken. Likewise, we hesitate to come back to God because our emotions are telling us, "Careful, don't get hurt again." Or we think that God will hold a grudge over our heads and never let us forget that we blew it. We think that he may take us back, but it will be with a price. God wants us to know that his mending of our relationship is grand and glorious; we need not fear coming back to him. Part of this glorious picture of restoration was a future mystery to those of Jeremiah's time, but it is crystal-clear to us. What could be more joyful than the restoration that comes though Jesus—restoration and reconciliation in ways that ancient Israel couldn't even imagine?

*Now what?*

God is inviting each of us to return to him. But often we think that we don't need to return to him because we never left him. One of the hardest things to see is how our own sin separates us from God. That is why Jeremiah spent twenty-nine chapters showing Israel her sin. We need to listen to what he said. The idolatry in Judah was obvious. They physically bowed down to a carved image, trusting it to bring them fulfillment. When we purchase some major item, car, vacation, big flat-screen TV, new home, or even a small item like a Belgian chocolate bar, it gives us a scene of well-being, at least for a moment. However, we often are disappointed when that delightful feeling fades all too quickly. That disappointment reveals our idolatry. While we are not bowing down to a new TV or a new house, we are putting our trust in these things to give us fulfillment. Our worship is off just as much as Israel's. God is calling us back to him. When we see how he will receive us, how can we not return to him? The process is very simple: admit before God that we are sinful, trust that through our faith in Christ's work that he has forgiven us, and then rejoice in his restoration of our being at home with him.

### *Creativity in Presentation*

As a preaching professor, I was often asked, "How many points should a sermon have?" My answer was always, "As many points as the passage has." In this case there are seven distinct sections of Jeremiah's dream of restoration. These can be presented in one sermon, but extra care will need to be given to be precise and efficient. A possible structure could be to move through each section using a repetitive pattern. By using the same pattern, it is easier for the listeners to follow and even anticipate how the sections will be developed. Perhaps summarize each passage, read one or two key verses, and state how Israel would have heard this. Then move to what this passage tells us about the kind of restoration God offers to all. Here are how the first two sections might look:

1. The reversal of military calamity (30:5–11)
   V. 10: Don't fear, Israel; the Lord will ultimately save you.
   God has power over the forces that are against us.

2. The healing of the incurable wound (30:12–17)
   V. 17: The deepest wound of Israel's sin is forgiven.
   He will forgive our deepest of sins.

Continue with this pattern, remembering that the overriding goal is to appeal for a return to the Lord, based upon how he will restore us. Keep that call to return to him in front of us by asking at the end of each section something like, "Why not return to him?" Or, "Our God always wants to restore us; let's repent of our sin and turn to him today." Another possibility would be to expand this pericope into a seven-part sermon series on our amazing, restorative Lord.

Style (word choice) used in this sermon is particularly important. Some words are particularly inviting because of their connotation. One could say, "Come back to God" or "Come home to God." The feeling that the word "home" engenders is clearly significant. The songs that were used in some evangelical settings for what was called an invitation hymn are filled with marvelous word choices for God's call to return to him. It could be helpful to check out the wording:

- Ye who are weary, come home ("Softly and Tenderly")
- He will embrace me in his arms ("I Will Arise and Go to Jesus")
- Thou wilt receive, wilt welcome, pardon, cleanse, relieve ("Just as I Am")
- I am welcomed with open arms (Travis Cottrell's version of "Just as I Am")

## DISCUSSION QUESTIONS

1. What role does repentance play in restoration of a relationship? What are some ways you have seen people restore their relationships?
2. Is restoration a one-sided action?
3. Is forgiveness a one-sided action?
4. What role does anger play in restoration?
5. How does forgiveness fit into restoration?

## Jeremiah 31:27–40

**EXEGETICAL IDEA**

God will give Israel the new covenant to replace the Sinai covenant, in order to correct the failings of the latter. The Sinai covenant depended on Israel's ability to faithfully perform "all the words of this law that are written in this book" (Deut. 28:58). The new covenant depends on the faithfulness and compassion of God alone, as well as on his determination to bring about salvation for all true Israel. The people will acknowledge their guilt, but it will be removed from them. And unlike Sinai, the new covenant will never be terminated.

**THEOLOGICAL FOCUS**

The new covenant is given to the "house of Israel and the house of Judah." But because even we Gentiles are now grafted into Israel, it belongs to all God's people, and all can celebrate this ongoing great work of God. God did not abandon Israel to destruction, and in like manner he has not abandoned the nations.

**PREACHING IDEA**

Come, join the celebration!

**PREACHING POINTERS**

The New Testament is very clear that believers in Jesus are included in the new covenant; thus, it has been inaugurated. And there is still more of the new covenant to be experienced in the future. In the past, Israel could have celebrated what God would do in the future. Today, believers celebrate what God has already started. And in the future, all will celebrate what God will have finished.

# THE NEW COVENANT (31:27–40)

## LITERARY STRUCTURE AND THEMES

This passage is the centerpiece of Jeremiah—the great promise of hope around which the whole book is structured.

- *Two Agricultural Metaphors (31:27–30)*
- *The New Covenant (31:31–37)*
- *The Restoration of Jerusalem (31:38–40)*

## EXPOSITION

### *Two Agricultural Metaphors (31:27–30)*

Jeremiah here inserts two metaphors that are both agricultural but that have different functions. The first speaks of the great blessing God will give to Israel, and the second speaks of Israel's guilt.

**31:27–28**. The metaphor of verse 27, sowing the land of Israel with the seed of men and beasts, seems peculiar, but it only means that God will repopulate the land and restore the agricultural prosperity, a mark of which is an abundance of livestock. The metaphor draws upon the language of Jeremiah's call at 1:10, in which YHWH declared that through Jeremiah's prophetic ministry God would "uproot and tear down, destroy and overthrow, and build and plant." For this reason, verse 28 repeats all six of these verbs from 1:10, and it also speaks of God "watching over" (שׁקד) Israel and Judah, using the same verb found in 1:12. The implication is that all YHWH had announced concerning the full scope of Jeremiah's ministry was coming to pass. However, since the destruction of Israel and Judah was now all but complete, there remained the task of planting and rebuilding. Jeremiah's new covenant prophecy addresses the crisis of the exile, indicating that the land would be restored in the postexilic community, but it also anticipates a greater eschatological salvation.

**31:29–30**. The cited proverb, "The fathers have eaten sour grapes and the sons' teeth are set on edge," is the second agricultural metaphor. It draws on the common experience of an unpleasant feeling in one's teeth when eating sour fruit. It implies that the children suffer for the misdeeds of the parents. It is, in fact, undeniable that the sins of parents can have terrible repercussions on their children, and the Bible does not deny this (Lam. 5:7). However, in Jeremiah's time, this proverb had become the means for avoiding responsibility. People claimed that the sin of previous generations was the only reason they suffered so much. Ezekiel 18, citing the same proverb, explores the issue in detail. The point in both Jeremiah and Ezekiel is that the generation that experienced the fall of Jerusalem had enough sin and guilt on their hands to account for all that befell them. In the present context, Jeremiah's use of the proverb makes the point that when God changes the hearts of the people and brings in the blessings of the new covenant, it will entirely be a work of grace. It will not be because the people were innocent and did not deserve punishment. Everyone who experiences God's grace will know this to be true, and not seek to evade admission of guilt.

### *The New Covenant (31:31–37)*

**31:31**. Jeremiah dramatically inserts the new covenant prophecy at this point, introducing it with הִנֵּה (traditionally, "behold") to mark it as a sudden and prominent moment in the larger context. The time for the new covenant in the indefinite future: "days are coming" (יָמִים בָּאִים). This is a favorite idiom of Jeremiah (he uses it fifteen times). The formula announces some future act of God. Sometimes, as in this case, it refers to an eschatological event. The recipients of the new covenant are the "house of Israel and the house of Judah." This language speaks of the twelve tribes of Israel as divided into two states, the kingdoms of Samaria and Jerusalem. It clearly relates to ethnic Israel; it concerns a specific people with a specific history. It is not a generic term for "the people of God" or the like. Any interpretation of this text and of the covenant it describes must take this into account.

**31:32**. The new covenant will not be like the covenant YHWH made with Israel at the time of the exodus, that is, the Sinai covenant. This was bilateral in the sense that it depended on human obedience. If Israel kept it, God would bless and protect them; if Israel broke it, God would strike them with plagues and disasters and ultimately drive them from the land. The new covenant would be a unilateral covenant in the sense that it was a pledge from God, and God himself would see to it that it was fulfilled.

**31:33–34**. The essential element of the new covenant is the renewal of the human heart, an act that is again a unilateral work of God. To have God's law written on the heart is to be free from the law of sin and death, whereby people are impulsively and of necessity sinful. This is a transformation that no human can bring about. In addition, the transformation will be universal, so that there is no need for one person to encourage another to love God. Under the new covenant, every person will love God freely and fully.

**31:35–37**. This is a pledge from God that Israel will continue and, implicitly, that it will one day thrive under the new covenant. It is a simple analogy, comparing the certainty of God's pledge to natural certainties with which we are all familiar. Every morning the sun rises, and every night there are stars in the heavens. Every month the moon goes through its cycle. The waves of the sea constantly crash against the shore. In the same way, God's pledge to preserve Israel and to revive them under the new covenant is eternal and unchanging. Similarly, just as it is inconceivable that humans could measure the heavens or search out the subterranean realm, it is inconceivable that God could abandon his pledge to Israel (v. 37).

### *The Restoration of Jerusalem (31:38–40)*

**31:38–40**. At first glance, this seems to be describing a rebuilding program for the city. This, considering all the eschatological language of the previous context, seems incongruous and anticlimactic. Some take it to be a secondary text, inserted from the time of reconstruction under Nehemiah (Holladay 1989, 199, "The setting for this passage, like vv 35–37, is doubtless in the time of Nehemiah"). Indeed, the "Horse Gate" and the "Tower of Hananel" mentioned here also appear in Nehemiah (Neh. 3:1, 28; 12:39). Even so, Jeremiah 31:38–40 is unlikely to be a later interpolation. Jeremiah was distinctively concerned about the defilement of the Hinnom Valley due to the child sacrifice that took place there (Jer. 7:31–34; 19:1–15). This text refers to the Ben Hinnom Valley as "all of the valley, the corpses and the ashes" (Jer. 31:40). Nehemiah, however, does not show evidence of concern over the defilement of Hinnom. For his generation, that was well over a century in the past; it was no longer a live issue. The places mentioned are all in Jerusalem, although the precise locations are in part lost to us. The Tower of Hananel (31:38) was probably in the northwest corner of the Temple Mount (Eskenazi 1992). It apparently existed in preexilic Jerusalem, destroyed by Nebuchadnezzar II, and rebuilt by Nehemiah (Ritmeyer 2006, 200–01). The locations of the Gareb Hill and Goah are unknown. The "Horse Gate" (31:40) was on the east side of the outer wall (Liid 1992). Jeremiah may be describing a circuit about the city, but his focus is on the defiled places of Hinnom Valley and the fields of the Kidron Valley, which were in Jeremiah's day polluted by pagan cult objects that had been dumped there (2 Kings 23:4–6). Even these defiled places, Jeremiah asserts, will be "sacred to YHWH" (v. 40). This prophecy was fulfilled in token form in the postexilic period when the city was purified and rebuilt under Haggai, Zechariah, and a little later, Ezra and Nehemiah. The ultimate fulfillment is the New Jerusalem, which will never be defiled.

### The Fulfillment of the New Covenant

Jeremiah makes the following claims regarding the new covenant:

- It is for Israel.
- It will bring about a transformation of the heart, enabling people to love God and keep his commands.
- It is universal, meaning that under the new covenant every person knows God. Evangelism will be unnecessary.

On the other hand, the New Testament assures us that we are in the new covenant now. Hebrews 8:8–12 quotes Jeremiah's new covenant prophecy in full. Clearly, the author believed that the new covenant is currently in effect, as that is his whole basis for telling his readers that they should not turn (or return) to Judaism and the laws of the Sinai covenant. The latter is obsolete after the arrival of the new covenant in Christ (Heb. 8:13). Other New Testament texts have the same perspective. Paul claimed to be a minister of the new covenant (2 Cor. 3:6), and Jesus declared that he was ritually inaugurating the new covenant in the original eucharist (Matt. 26:28; Luke 22:20; 1 Cor. 11:25). We are thus left with the following problems related to Jeremiah's original promises:

- If the new covenant is for Israel, how is it now enjoyed by Gentiles?
- If we are under the new covenant now, how is it that we are still drawn into evil? Doesn't the transformation of the heart imply that people willingly and wholly love and obey God?
- If the new covenant is operational now, how is that most people do not know God? Why is evangelism a primary duty of the church?
- Thus, in sum, how and when is the new covenant fulfilled?

These are weighty questions, and they impact the whole structure of biblical interpretation and major elements of Christian theology. Traditionally, evangelical theology has handled this issue in one of two ways.

Covenant theology, in its various forms, has generally treated the new covenant as defined generically as between God and "the people of God," or as defined more specifically as a covenant between God and Jesus, who is understood to be the true Israel, as it were, incarnate in the one person. Alternatively, or additionally, the church is thought to have superseded Israel, so that the latter's place in the plan of God has been taken over by the worldwide body of Christ. Thus, the new covenant rightly belongs to the church. Israel is no longer the chosen people. The church is now the true locus of the "people of God." Although "covenant theology" as such is a product of Reformed theology, much of the Christian church through its history has held to principles found within this system. Most churches regard Israel's role as complete and Christianity as its replacement. Roman Catholicism, for example, has long considered itself to be the true successor of Israel, with its priests taking over the intercessory role once provided by the Aaronic priesthood.

It is difficult to see, however, how Jeremiah 31:27–30 can be brought into agreement with covenant theology. As stated above, when verse 31 speaks of the "house of Israel and the house of Judah," this can only be read in its ordinary sense of the Israelite nation—the Jews. Indeed, the initial promises of verses 27–28, that God would restore Israel and Judah, specifically refer to the destruction of Samaria and Jerusalem at the hands respectively of the Assyrians and Babylonians. That is, they relate to a specific people with a specific history. The reunification and restoration of the Israelite tribes is at the heart of the promise. The promise cannot be transferred in any coherent manner to the church, and Israel cannot here be redefined either as the "people of God" or as Jesus.

In addition, covenant theology (in its classic, Reformed form) asserts that the new covenant is part of a series of covenants that are all integrally tied to one another as part of the "covenant of grace." But this is problematic because Jeremiah 31:32 says that the new covenant is "not like" the older covenant, that is, the Sinai covenant. But if the new covenant in integrally bound to Sinai as successive developments of the "covenant of grace," in which the one is simply a more advanced stage of the other, the two cannot be said to be unalike. Covenant theology is not a satisfactory solution.

Dispensationalism proposes a radically different solution. It sets a wedge between Israel and the church, declaring them to be two separate peoples with separate agendas from God. In dispensationalism, a generic "people of God" does not exist at all. All of the promises of the Old Testament belong to Israel, and the church is a parenthetical age, unforeseen in the Old Testament. The age of Israel existed throughout the Old Testament era and through the time of Jesus, but it was interrupted when the church age began at Pentecost. The age of Israel resumes after the rapture of the church and continues through the seven-year tribulation and into the millennial kingdom. At that time all of the promises of glory and prosperity for Israel, including the promise of the new covenant, are fulfilled. There is thus no question about the identity of the "Israel" of Jeremiah 31: it is ethnic Israel. Dispensationalism has no difficulty with the nationalistic nature of the promises to Israel in Jeremiah 31. That is what they appear to be, and that is precisely what they are.

Even so, the dispensational solution also faces insuperable difficulties. First among these is the unavoidable insistence of the New Testament that the church is under the new covenant now. If that is not so, then the book of Hebrews, with its citation of *the entire new covenant prophecy* in chapter 8, makes no sense. The argument of Hebrews wholly depends upon the premise that the Sinai covenant, with all of its rituals and requirements, is now obsolete under the new covenant. And Paul does more than declare himself to be a minister of the new covenant. He declares that the "pedagogue" (the Sinai covenant with its regulations) has now been terminated since "faith" (the fulfillment of the promises under the new covenant) has come (Gal. 3:17–4:7). It is hardly persuasive to insist that the experience of salvation by grace through faith, along with the pouring out of the Spirit and the submission of the Gentiles to the Messiah of Israel, is something other than the new covenant. It is an indefensible proposition. The Christian experience in the New Testament is not something *like* the new covenant; it *is* the new covenant.

In addition, the millennium makes for a poor fulfillment of the new covenant. As already noted, according to 31:32, the new covenant is explicitly "not like" the Sinai covenant that it replaces. And yet, in traditional dispensational teaching, the millennium is precisely a return to old covenant practices, with a temple of stone in which animal sacrifices are offered by an Aaronic priesthood. This simply cannot be; the Sinai covenant cannot be replaced by a new and different covenant and at the same time be reestablished as the law of the land and the rule of true worship.

We need a new solution, one that is neither dispensationalism nor covenant theology. Other recent solutions, such as "new covenant theology" and "progressive dispensationalism," are too closely bound to prior, unsatisfactory solutions and do not offer a way forward. The former, despite a few minor tweaks, restates the essentials of covenant theology. The latter jettisons the heart of dispensationalism (the separation of Israel from the church) while holding to its outer form (the rapture, tribulation, and millennial kingdom). But the idea of a separate rapture for the church makes no sense when the core distinction between the two peoples of God is abandoned.

We must begin by setting aside a dispensational distinctive: that the church is a parenthesis in the age of Israel and is not foreseen in the Old Testament. Psalm 87:4–5 states, "I will record Rahab and Babylon as those who acknowledge me. / Indeed, of Philistia and Tyre, and Cush, too, [it will be said,] 'This one was born in Zion.' // And of Zion it will be said, 'This one and that one were born in her,' / and the Most High will establish her." Isaiah 2:2–4 asserts that the Gentiles will make their way to Zion to learn from Israel's God, and 42:4 declares that distant peoples will put their hope in YHWH's servant. These and many other passages speak of the coming of the Gentiles to Israel's God. James's citation in Acts 15:16–17 of Amos 9:11–12, a prophecy that God would draw Gentiles to himself, makes little sense if he did not believe it was fulfilled in Paul's work in evangelizing the Gentiles (a fact acknowledged by a prominent progressive dispensationalist; Saucy 1993, 79). The church in which people of every nation, tribe, and language bow before the Jewish Messiah and affirm that Israel's God is maker of heaven and earth, that the gods of their ancestors were worthless idols, and that the Son of David is King of kings and Lord of lords is surely the fulfillment of the Old Testament hope. In the present age, the nations have come to Zion. The New Testament, moreover, is incompatible with the "two peoples" hypothesis, that the church and Israel are separate peoples with separate programs. In Christ there is no longer Jew or Greek (Gal. 3:28). There is only one people of God and one plan of God, not two.

But who are the "people of God"? In answer to this, the Bible is clear: "Salvation is of the Jews" (John 4:22). *There is one people of God, and it is Israel, and the new covenant belongs to Israel.* How then do the Gentiles partake of it? Here too, the Bible is clear: believing Gentiles have been grafted into Israel (Rom. 11:17). We of the nations were wild olive branches that God grafted onto the great tree that is Israel. Or, to switch metaphors, the wall of division (the Law) that separated Israel from the Gentiles has been broken down, and we are one people of God in Christ (Eph. 2:11–20). In short, covenant theologians are wrong to think that the church has superseded Israel, and dispensationalists are wrong to think that they are two separate peoples. Rather, to know the glories of the covenant and promises of God, a person must belong to the one people of God, Israel. Gentiles belong by being grafted in (Rom. 11), by having been adopted into Zion (Ps. 87), and by virtue of the wall of division being broken down (Eph. 2). All of this is done through faith in Christ.

We thus can answer our first question, *If the new covenant is for Israel, how is it now enjoyed by Gentiles?* Gentiles do not obtain it by becoming proselytes into Judaism (the solution offered by Paul's

Jewish opponents); instead, by God's grace, they are adopted into Zion. The church does not push aside Israel, as in covenant theology. There are certainly differences between the New Testament church and Old Testament Israel. Even so, they are not separate peoples, as in dispensationalism. The differences are accounted for by the change in covenants. Ancient Israel was under the Sinai covenant, not the new covenant.

We are now in a position to answer our other questions: If the new covenant is in effect now, why do believers still struggle with evil, and why do we need to evangelize? How and when is the new covenant fulfilled?

The answer, as has often been said, is that the new covenant is now and not yet. Its ultimate fulfillment is in the new heaven and new earth, when all the saints in resurrected bodies will be forever free from the bondage to sin. There they will experience and enjoy God forever. And, of course, the new earth will be inhabited only by those who belong to God, so that, as Jeremiah says, no one will need to say to his neighbor, "Know the Lord!" In that sense, the full experience of the new covenant is "not yet." By analogy, Jesus is now Lord, but "at the present, we do not yet see all things submitted to him" (Heb. 2:8).

On the other hand, the new covenant is in effect now, as the New Testament indicates. Nevertheless, believers are still in the flesh and in the world. Because we are in the flesh, and not yet risen in bodies like that of Christ, we still experience the pull of sin. For this reason, we are exhorted to consider ourselves dead to the flesh and to sin (Rom. 6:11–13). Regeneration and the gift of the Spirit, however, is a genuine experience of the blessings of the new covenant in the present age. Because we are in the world, we still regularly encounter people who do not "know the Lord," and the duty to evangelize is still very real. A Christian church is ideally a body composed entirely of people who know God, a kind of outpost for the new covenant in this world until its fullness is realized in the new earth.

We can therefore assert that the new covenant has been inaugurated in the present age and will be fully realized in the eschatological new earth. We may ask whether the millennium might serve as an intermediate stage between the two. While this is conceivable, I would argue that it is unnecessary and, in some interpretations, genuinely unbiblical. The most cogent argument for arguing in favor of a literal millennial kingdom is that various Old Testament prophecies speak of a utopian future in which people enjoy great prosperity, longevity, and security. It is said to be a future in which the lion and lamb will lie peaceably beside one another, and a small child will safely play among cobras (Isa. 11:6–8). Dispensationalists understandably reject all "spiritualizing" interpretations of such passages, whereby the peaceful kingdom is interpreted to be the gentle and kindly moral characteristics of people who have submitted to Christ.

But we need not consider a purely metaphorical or absolutely literal interpretation to be our only choices. More probably, these are descriptions of the new earth given in terms meaningful to human beings, and specifically to ancient Near Eastern humans. It is an act of condescension, whereby the glories of the age to come are described in terms comprehensible to the readers. By analogy, Psalm 87 speaks of the future adoption of Gentiles into Zion by asserting that God would include Babylon and the Philistines among those who know him. Those nations disappeared long ago, but they are representative of people who were hostile to Israel when the psalm was written. The literal meaning is not the point, but the passage is not to be "spiritualized." It describes a very real eschatological event, the admission of people from all over the world into the true Israel.

Analogously, in Revelation 21 the New Jerusalem is a great cube of approximately 2,200 kilometers on each side. It has a wall with twelve gates (named for the tribes of Israel) and twelve foundations, each foundation made of a precious stone (and named for the apostles). The wall is made of jasper, each gate is made of a single pearl, and the streets are paved with gold. The new earth will have no sun because God and Christ will provide its light. We do not know what the New Jerusalem will "really" be like. But Revelation describes the city's glory in terms that are meaningful to us. The language is not necessarily literal, but it is not a metaphor either. It truly speaks of the future city of God, telling us that it will have no imperfections (as indicated by its cube shape, which lacks any asymmetry), that it will have room for all (as indicated by its huge size), and that it is founded on the teaching of the apostles (as indicated by the twelve foundation stones). The only gateway into it is through adoption into Israel (the twelve gates), and God will forever be the light, joy, life, and love of those who dwell there (the lack of a sun). Passages like Isaiah 11 similarly speak of peaceful conditions of the new earth, using language meaningful to its readers.

But as mentioned above, some interpretations of the millennium are incompatible with biblical teaching. In standard dispensational doctrine, the millennium will effectively restart the Sinai covenant, with animal sacrifices offered by Levitical priests in a Jerusalem temple. But it is difficult to believe that Jeremiah's prophecy, which envisages a new covenant that is "not like" Sinai and is a replacement for it, will in fact be fulfilled by the Sinai regulations coming back into full force. Such an idea is not compatible with the New Testament, where the whole priestly system is but a shadow of the work of Christ and is now made obsolete and ready to disappear (Heb. 8–10). It is not sufficient to say that the sacrifices will be a "memorial" of the work of Christ (a standard dispensational response), because the sacrifices were always but a shadow, incapable of truly removing guilt. Calling them a "memorial" is simply a way of restarting their shadow function. But the point of Hebrews is that because they are obsolete, they should no longer be offered at all (Heb. 8:13).

But to give a single, specific example, we may consider the dispensational interpretation of Ezekiel 40–48 as a literal, millennial temple. In the vision, the Shekinah Glory, the manifestation of God among his people, returns to his temple and inhabits it (Ezek. 43), just as the Shekinah inhabited the Tent of Meeting and Solomon's temple. For the Christian, a literal interpretation of this is impossible. Since the incarnation, the glory of God has resided in Jesus, the true and eternal temple of God (John 2:21). One may not plausibly suggest that the Logos, the presence of God, would simultaneously reside in Jesus and in a physical building. The time for temples of stone and wood is over. The remainder of Ezekiel 40–48 is also rich in symbolic meaning, but we cannot explore it here. But it is not meant to be a literal building.

In summary, Jeremiah predicts an eschatological future in which Israel would enjoy God forever under the new covenant. In its fullness, all people will know God, and sin will be no more. Although Jeremiah does not in this text mention the inclusion of the Gentiles, many other passages do speak of this as part of the eschatological salvation. Paul explains that Gentiles, like wild olive shoots, are grafted into Israel to partake of its blessings of life and the love of God. Thus, the promise that all the nations would find blessing in Israel (Gen. 22:18) is fulfilled. Moreover, the new covenant has been inaugurated now, and people from every nation and language that Israel's Messiah is Lord of heaven and earth. Thus, Gentiles enjoy the knowledge of God by the power of the Spirit. Even so, we are for now in the flesh and the world, and the duty to strive against sin and to exhort neighbors to know the Lord remains in force.

## THEOLOGICAL FOCUS

Obviously enough, the new covenant is at the center of this text. In order to proclaim the passage to a Christian congregation, we need to combine its message with related elements of biblical theology. For Christian teaching, the following points stand out:

- God does not abandon his people to suffering. Often there is intermediate relief, as when God brought the Jews back from the Babylonian exile and enabled the rebuilding of Jerusalem and the temple. God's ultimate salvation is when he gathers us to himself in the resurrection.
- The salvation God offers is predicated on true repentance. No one who turns to God can speak a modern counterpart to "The fathers have eaten sour grapes, and their children's teeth are set on edge." A true work of God involves recognizing how we have sinned and by God's grace turning from the sin.
- Although the new covenant was promised to Israel, all the peoples of the world are invited to share in its blessings through Christ.
- Although we belong to God and live under the new covenant, we are still in the flesh and experience the power and bondage of sin. Our lives in the flesh should be dedicated to sanctification, whereby we become more Christlike even while in this world. As we reckon ourselves dead to sin and alive to God, through the power of the Spirit we experience freedom. In the resurrection, we will experience pure and eternal freedom.
- Every church is a new covenant outpost where those who know God gather to create communities that anticipate the coming glory, when we will all stand before Christ. In the meantime, we are in this world and must tell others, "Know the Lord!"
- As surely as God maintains the working of the sun, moon, and stars, so surely will God maintain this promise: We will dwell with him forever and be without fear, guilt, or death.
- The Jews experienced something unique. Their city and nation were destroyed, and the people were scattered, but God brought them back to rebuild their city and preserve their identity. No other ancient people can make such a claim. When the Moabites, Edomites, Ammonites, or Philistines had their cities sacked and their populations killed or scattered, those nations simply disappeared. But the Jews came back to Jerusalem. This was God's down payment—a sign that the New Jerusalem would one day be the eternal city of God.

## PREACHING AND TEACHING STRATEGIES

### *Exegetical and Theological Synthesis*

In presenting the joyful blessings of the New Covenant we must remember what surrounds this chapter—God's fierce judgment of Israel's sins. This passage shines like a jewel on black velvet. God is promising the new covenant because we, as sinful beings, desperately need God to act on our behalf. The joy of forgiveness is heightened by showing our guilt. The excitement of a new heart is welcomed when we acknowledge the propensity of our old heart toward sin.

We can celebrate the new covenant because: 1) It is unilateral. Our salvation is God's work, not ours. We simply receive it. 2) It is transforming. Our hearts are being transformed through repentance and obedience. God is enabling us to love and obey him even more. 3) It is unifying. A day is yet to come when all who are present under the new covenant will know the Lord. We can look forward to the unity of the special future community. In that day we won't argue over the details of how the new covenant will be completed, because we will all be living in it. 4) It offers forgiveness. God will remember our sins no more. Would that we could forget our own sins; God does. 5) It is sanctifying. The Hinnom Valley, where the most heinous idolatry was practiced, will be made a sacred place. No matter how sinful our lives were in the past, with the new covenant God will make our lives sacred to him.

### *Preaching Idea*

Come, join the celebration!

### *Contemporary Connections*

#### *What does it mean?*

On August 14, 1945, joy erupted in towns and cities across the globe. WWII was over. This meant that the millions in the armed services were going home and that those in the heat of the war zones now had hope for life rather than death. Celebrations broke out everywhere. The emotion of the moment was captured in an iconic photograph taken in Times Square of a sailor kissing a nurse in celebration of the end of that tragic and terrible scar on the human race. My mother-in-law was a teenager when she heard the news. She and her sister jumped on a bus to join the celebration in downtown Houston, which from her description was not that different from what happened in New York. As I listened to her description of thousands who took to the streets overflowing with joy, I grew in my understanding of what that war cost. I am honored that my father fought in that war, and in my home hangs his officer's hat. Looking at that, I try to imagine what it was like to have been there and hearing, "The war is over!" How would we have reacted if we had been there when Jeremiah told the Jews that God would give them a new heart, a new life, a new covenant? Are we left to our imagination? No, this is different. We are not just observing history; we are included in the new covenant. We are in the event itself, not just in the celebration of it.

#### *Is it true?*

What Jeremiah said to the Jews should have brought great joy to them, even to the point of celebrating. God was promising something new and wonderful, and offering it unilaterally. It was not the bilateral wilderness agreement between two parties. This was God's new work. It was what God would do for Israel: the new covenant would be for all the tribes; he would transform their hearts; their sins would be remembered no longer; somehow God would use the ground that was the place of wicked worship of false gods and make it sacred. The Jews had much to celebrate about God's future for them, although the postexilic community did have the fulfillment that they were back in the land. If God could bring them back from exile, then this new covenant would be possible as well.

#### *Now what?*

Years ago, in our premarital counselling our pastor, Dr. Presnall Wood, told us that we must plan and work hard to celebrate. The hard times need no planning or initiation, they just come; but celebrations need to be planned. God, through Jeremiah, gave Israel something to celebrate: the new covenant. To be sure, it was a delayed celebration for those of Jeremiah's day. And even for the returning exiles the celebration was muted. For these ancient Jews, the promise of a new covenant must have seemed far off and almost incomprehensible. But even just being given the promise was cause to celebrate. For us who are living in the inauguration of the new covenant, we have even more cause to celebrate. So, how do we?

We need to acknowledge that the specifics of the fulfillment of the new covenant vary according to one's theological perspective.

Hopefully, the following general application can fit into most theological interpretations.

Because it is *unilateral,* we can praise God for his work and rest in the security that our salvation is his work. Because it is *transforming,* we can seek this transforming work each day through repentance and obedience. Because it is *unifying,* we need to embrace each other as being in the same family. All believers are included: the premillennialist and the amillennialist; those who hold to elder rule and the congregationalist; even First Baptist and Second and Third Baptist churches. Are all included in the new covenant. Someday our heavenly Father will work out the differences. Because it offers *forgiveness,* we should overflow with thankfulness. What words could be more pleasant to hear? To extend Jeremiah's anthropomorphic metaphor, when we come to God with a repentant heart and ask him for forgiveness, his response is, "What sins?" He remembers them no more. What words could bring greater gratitude? Because it is *sanctifying,* we can start over, daily if needed. *All of us have a worm in our past that could devour our future.* (This quote comes from a 1998 A&E film version of C. S. Forester's *Horatio Hornblower.)* God wants us to know that if he can take that place where the most wicked and terrible acts were performed in Israel and make it sacred, then he can do the same for us, no matter how evil our past. O hallelujah! We need to step into what he is making us today, and leave our debilitating guilty feelings at his sanctifying cross.

### *Creativity in Presentation*

What a wonderful passage to call people to repentance and faith by inviting them to be part of the celebration: celebrating what God has done; what he will do; and what he is doing right now in our lives. It could be a call for an unbeliever to turn to belief in Jesus, for a renewal of faith, or to repent and return to faith. God is inviting each of us to celebrate that we are part of the new covenant.

Billy Graham often began his sermons by letting the listeners know that God was inviting them into a relationship with him. His introductions sounded almost like his conclusions. This passage could be presented in the same way. Begin by saying that there is a celebration to which each of us is invited. More than that, we are invited to be part of what is being celebrated. It is like going to a graduation celebration and being the one who is graduating, or to a birthday party and it's our birthday. We are celebrating the new covenant of which we are, or can be, a part. We are not observers of the celebration; we are participants in what is being celebrated. This hopefully will help listeners want to better understand the new covenant and fully participate in it.

The following possible structure includes transitional questions that lead into the next point.

- Join the celebration because:
  - God will restore (31:27–28).
    - Who needs restoration?
  - Each person needs restoration (31:29–30).
    - What will it look like?
  - The new covenant restores with forgiveness and a new heart (31:31–37).
    - Can God really do this?
  - God's restorative power can make the worst the best (31:38–40).

- Come and join the celebration of God's restoration of you.

## DISCUSSION QUESTIONS

1. The above metaphor mentioned a jewel on black velvet. That is an example (or metaphor) using sight. What could be another example using sight or other senses to illustrate that sin and God's judgment is the setting for the new covenant ?

2. How would you list the elements or parts of the new covenant ?

3. Of these, which do you think was most meaningful to the Jews who first heard it?

4. Which is the easiest to believe will happen?

5. Which part is the most challenging to grasp and believe?

## Jeremiah 32:1–44

### EXEGETICAL IDEA

Jeremiah purchases a piece of land, and this becomes a prophetic sign for the coming redemption of Israel. It implies that the land, which will be burnt over and trampled by foreign armies, will again belong to Israel and be fruitful.

### THEOLOGICAL FOCUS

When things seem hopeless, a simple act can demonstrate faith that God still has a future for us. But this is not a matter of optimism, of merely hoping for the best in the face of severe danger. For Jeremiah's generation, the worst possible outcome does in fact happen. But God, who raises the dead, can bring about an astonishing and seemingly impossible reversal of the judgment.

### PREACHING IDEA

Hope in God's future; nothing is impossible for him.

### PREACHING POINTERS

When buying a house, we put great trust in the real estate agent. Is this a good price? Is it a wise investment? When Jeremiah was purchasing property, he had only one question. "Why should I buy a piece of land when the nation is about to be destroyed?" The answer was direct: because God told him to. This was a living illustration. What would Zedekiah and Judah think of this? It didn't make sense on the surface, so it demanded deeper thinking. Perhaps some of them would discover the deeper meaning that nothing was impossible for God. Though destruction was imminent, he still had a good future for Israel.

There are so many different stories of hopelessness in our congregations. God knows that often it is hard for us to believe that his future for us is good, so he employs a method of communication that helps us truly believe this. He tells a story and wants us to discover the meaning. When we discover a meaning or draw a conclusion, we are much more likely to believe it. Jeremiah buys land, which was investing in the future when there doesn't seem to be a future. God still has a good future for us.

# THE REDEEMED LAND (32:1–44)

## LITERARY STRUCTURE AND THEMES

This text contains a historical problem. It speaks of an event during the tenth year of Zedekiah, while Nebuchadnezzar was besieging the city and Jeremiah was imprisoned at the court of the palace guard (32:1–2). Zedekiah asked the imprisoned prophet why his messages were always pessimistic, and in reply Jeremiah told the king of a message from YHWH that had recently come to him. YHWH revealed that his cousin Hanamel would soon arrive and tell him to purchase a piece of land in Anathoth. Jeremiah was the nearest relative and so had the right and obligation to do this. Soon thereafter, Hanamel did show up and Jeremiah, from his prison cell, carried out the purchase in the presence of legal witnesses (32:3–13). Based on this transaction, Jeremiah told Zedekiah that although he and Jerusalem faced certain destruction at the hands of the Babylonians, there was yet hope for the Jewish people. Jeremiah's purchase of land was a sign-act foreshadowing YHWH's redemption of Israel (32:14–44).

Against this, 37:11–14 tells a related but somewhat different story. It describes how Jeremiah, during a break in Nebuchadnezzar's siege of Jerusalem, tried to go to Anathoth to acquire a piece of property but was arrested on charges of attempted desertion. He was then imprisoned on the palace grounds. It is certain that these two accounts refer to the same incident (Holladay 1989, 287–88; Lundbom 2008c, 57), but we need to reconcile the differing details. The most reasonable solution is as follows.

- In accord with 37:11–15, Jeremiah knew that he had to redeem the property and tried to get to Anathoth when Nebuchadnezzar's siege was briefly lifted. He was detained while trying to leave the city and then charged and imprisoned.
- The imprisoned Jeremiah all but despaired of being able to perform this duty, but YHWH revealed to him that Hanamel would soon arrive and that they could settle the matter, and this took place (32:6–15).
- Zedekiah questioned him (32:1–5), and Jeremiah replied as recorded in 32:6–44.

We must ask why the book arranges the material concerning Jeremiah's imprisonment, the redemption of the land, and the eschatological promise in such a convoluted manner, giving some details in chapter 32 and some in chapter 37. Although the two chapters concern the same events, they overlap very little. It would have been simpler to tell the story in a single, sequential narrative, as I briefly did above.

In fact, despite the abundance of detail, neither text has the purpose of providing a coherent biography of Jeremiah. Chapters 37–38, as described below, are in a context that concerns Jewish unbelief. They omit entirely the hope for eschatological redemption given in chapter 32 but focus on the persecution Jeremiah suffered and on other immediate matters—for example, on Jeremiah's advice that Zedekiah should surrender to Babylon (38:17). Chapter 32, by contrast, omits all the details about how Jeremiah was wrongfully arrested, beaten, imprisoned, and cast into a cistern. It does not mention that he had tried to go to Anathoth. It is instead a prophetic sign-act depicting eschatological salvation. Details about Jeremiah's personal history, such as those in chapter 37, would have confused things.

The details of a single incident from Jeremiah's life have therefore gone through a literary bifurcation, with one set of data going to Jeremiah 32 and another set going to chapters 37–38. This separation of material demonstrates that the editor deliberately isolated the messages of salvation and set them at the book's center.

- ***The Purchase of Land (32:1–15)***
- ***Jeremiah's Prayer (32:16–25)***
- ***God's Response (32:26–44)***

## EXPOSITION

### *The Purchase of Land (32:1–15)*

**32:1–2**. The date for this episode is given with unusual precision, correlating it to the regnal years of two different kings, Zedekiah and Nebuchadnezzar. The year in question is approximately 587 B.C. Furthermore, Jeremiah was under arrest and imprisoned at this time on charges of treason and desertion, as described above. He was kept in the royal precincts, and thus Zedekiah had easy access to him. The siege of Jerusalem had already begun. We learn from chapter 37 that the Babylonian army had temporarily pulled back from the city in order to repel the army of Egypt, and that it was at this time that Jeremiah had tried to leave the city and was apprehended. By the time of the episode here in chapter 32, the Babylonians may well have returned and again surrounded the city.

**32:3–5**. This passage gives the ultimate but not immediate cause for Jeremiah's arrest. The immediate cause was that he was caught trying to leave the city in order to take care of family business in Anathoth and was accused of treason; the ultimate cause, and the reason he was subject to so much suspicion and hostility, was that he had consistently preached that Nebuchadnezzar would capture and destroy Jerusalem. The challenging question for Jeremiah in this text comes from Zedekiah, and no doubt the king was vexed with the prophet over his message. But in reality, the question represents the hostility of almost all of Judah's aristocracy. It is important to note that Jeremiah's enemies did not misunderstand or misrepresent his message. Their summary of his prophecy—that Babylon would capture Jerusalem, that Zedekiah would be taken as a prisoner to Nebuchadnezzar, and that no strategy could save them from this fate—accurately recapitulates Jeremiah's predictions.

**32:6–8**. These verses do not answer the question posed in verses 3–5; to the contrary, verses 3–5 simply set the context for the following episode, stating that Jeremiah was in prison because he faithfully spoke about the disaster to come. The account of the episode actually begins in verse 6. It may seem surprising to us that God would reveal to Jeremiah that his cousin was coming to him on family business; we would not think that the prophet would receive a special word from YHWH over such a mundane business matter. However, this ordinary transaction would be the basis for a great oracle of salvation. Hence, God alerted him to what was coming. Jeremiah had the "right of redemption" (מִשְׁפַּט הַגְּאֻלָּה) to acquire the land. According to Leviticus 25:25–31, a man had the right and even obligation to purchase the land of a near relative that was in danger of being lost to the family. The ideal was that Israelite families had gained possession of plots of land at the time of the conquest under Joshua and that this land belonged to the families in perpetuity. But if the owner fell into dire poverty or died without an heir, there was a danger that the plot could be lost to the family forever. Therefore, a near-relative would "redeem" the property by purchasing it to keep the estate within the family. Evidently, such a situation had developed among one of Jeremiah's close relatives in Anathoth, and he was asked to take care of the matter. And Hanamel, Jeremiah's cousin, showed up at his jail cell just as

YHWH had predicted. Then Jeremiah "knew that it was a word from YHWH," meaning not just that he knew that YHWH was the source but also that the event would have special significance. In other words, what otherwise would have been a mundane transaction was now a prophetic sign-act, analogous to Hosea's marriage to Gomer (Hos. 1) or Jeremiah's wearing of a yoke on his shoulders (Jer. 27).

**32:9–11**. Jeremiah bought the land for seventeen shekels (about 11.5 grams) of silver. There was no coinage at this time, and so purchases were made by barter or by weighing out specified amounts of silver or gold, as was done here. The text gives us the price so that we may understand that the purchase was entirely legal and was dutifully transacted. Apart from this, we should avoid speculating about the transaction. We do not know how much money Jeremiah had, and so we do not know whether the purchase was a financial hardship for him. We do not know how large the property was, and so we do not know if it was cheap or expensive. We do not know what the purchasing power of seventeen shekels of silver was at this time, and so we do not know if this represented much or little money. Even if we had some way of determining the general purchasing power of a shekel of silver in the early sixth century, Jerusalem was in great upheaval due to the Babylonian siege of the city, and prices were probably badly out of kilter. What matters is that everything was done according to strict legal requirement: the specified amount of money was paid, deeds of purchase and other legal documents were drawn up in the presence of witnesses, and the terms of the sale were accurately recorded. It was a lawful and complete transaction. It is also significant that Jeremiah entrusted all of his legal documents to Baruch (v. 12). As suggested in the Introduction to this commentary, Baruch played a crucial role in the ministry of Jeremiah and managed all of his documents, including the texts that made their way into the book of Jeremiah. This passage indicates what high confidence Jeremiah had in Baruch.

**32:13–15**. Comparing verse 11 to verse 14, it is evident that the legal documents included at least two specific texts: the "sealed" (הֶחָתוּם) document and the "open" (הַגָּלוּי) document. The latter would have been kept by Jeremiah and the former would have been kept with public records as a safeguard against fraud. Jeremiah, however, did something unusual. In the presence of all the parties, he ordered Baruch to take both copies, place them inside a clay pot, and bury the pot somewhere. The pot would have had a lid that was sealed in place to make it relatively impermeable. Jeremiah had no personal concern about the land; he was old, and Jerusalem would soon fall to the Babylonians, rendering land ownership insignificant. Soon the Jews would be carried into exile, and all the land would belong to Babylon! But the preservation of the documents in a clay pot was a symbolic act, indicating that someday the Jews would return and claim their land. As verse 15 says, the time would come when the Jews would again have houses and farms here. For Jeremiah, the preservation of the documents was a prophetic sign-act representing God's promise to Israel; it was comparable to his other sign-acts, such as the burial of the loincloth (Jer. 13). It did not mean that Jeremiah would personally come back and reclaim the land (and being unmarried and childless, he had no expectation of descendants who would claim it). Also, verse 15 is a proleptic indication to the reader of what was coming later in the chapter, a foreshadow of the significance of the event. As verse 25 indicates, at the time of purchase, Jeremiah himself did not know why God wanted him to buy the land.

### *Jeremiah's Prayer (32:16–25)*

The prayer is in two parts: a preamble, which speaks of God's power and former works (vv. 16–23), and an implied request for enlightenment, in which Jeremiah describes the current situation and implicitly seeks a revelation of what lies ahead for Israel (vv. 24–25).

**32:16**. Specifying that Jeremiah prayed after he had turned over the legal documents of the purchase to Baruch, this verse implies that Jeremiah recognized that the event was a sign relevant to the current crisis in Judah. He thus prayed concerning the punishment Judah was enduring and asked God for further clarification of the meaning of the land purchase.

**32:17–19**. All of verses 17–24 are a preamble; the actual request is not given (and that only by implication) until verse 25. As is common in Old Testament prayers, Jeremiah begins at the very beginning, praising God as maker of heaven and earth. This only demonstrates, he says, that YHWH can do whatever he pleases (v. 17). Hence, God can still do a great work of salvation for Judah. Also, he alludes to the great revelation of God's compassion and justice in Exodus 34:4–7, implying that although God punishes sin, he remains merciful and will act according to his character (v. 18). He also declares that God examines the behavior of every purpose and rewards or punishes accordingly. Even so, God's plan is "great" (גְּדֹל) and his ways "manifold" (רַב), implying that he has purposes that are hidden and beyond human understanding.

**32:20–23**. After the creation, the other event most cited in preambles to Old Testament prayers is the exodus. Jeremiah speaks of the "signs and wonders" (אֹתוֹת וּמֹפְתִים) that God did in Egypt, focusing on how God by his power manipulates the nations as he pleases. Furthermore, God continues to do great works in the world (v. 20). The actual events of saving Israel from Egypt (v. 21) and giving them the Promised Land (v. 22) are cited as events that demonstrate God's faithfulness and kindness to his people. This creates a contrast with their flagrant disobedience to the terms of the Sinai covenant as given in the Law (v. 23). By implication, the punishment they receive is richly deserved.

**32:24**. Jeremiah next speaks of the current crisis: The siege of Jerusalem has come about in fulfillment of all the warnings God gave to the nation, an allusion to Deuteronomy 28 and to Jeremiah's own many prophecies.

**32:25**. Jeremiah finally comes to the nub of his prayer: in spite of the imminent destruction of the city and exile of all of Judah, God told him to purchase a piece of land and to be sure that the sale was legally witnessed and documented. The implied question is, "Why did you have me do this?" Buying land in a country that is about to be conquered is analogous to buying stock in an insolvent company only days from going out of business. It makes no sense. Jeremiah was thus asking God for the meaning of what he had just done.

***God's Response (32:26–44)***

**32:26–27**. God responds to Jeremiah with a preamble of his own, an echo of Jeremiah's prayer in verse 17: nothing is too difficult for God. Thus, everything that has happened to Judah, and everything that will happen, is in God's control. What to Jeremiah seemed an absurd waste of time and money, buying land in a dying country, makes sense if one understands the wider plan of God.

**32:28–29**. First, if Jeremiah were harboring any illusions that God might turn back the Babylonians so that the land he had just purchased would not be lost, God assures him that this is not the case. God will indeed "give this city into the hand of the Chaldeans." All the property of every Jew will be lost, Jeremiah's newly acquired estate included. Most assuredly, the king of Babylon "will take it" (וּלְכָדָהּ). Not only that, but they will also burn all the buildings and leave the city as a heap of rubble. As the Israelites have burned incense and made libations to other gods on the roofs of their homes, so YHWH will demolish those homes. Because the guilt of Israel is so great, the destruction of the nation cannot be avoided.

**32:30–33**. YHWH metaphorically depicts Israel as a person who has been intractably evil ever since youth. In this case, the "youth" refers to the time when Israel first entered the land in the conquest, and it alludes to the idolatry and immorality of the time of the judges. But the move to a monarchy did not improve things. Jerusalem has provoked God's anger "from the very day they built it" (לְמִן־הַיּוֹם אֲשֶׁר בָּנוּ אוֹתָהּ; v. 31). This does not refer to the original founding of Jerusalem in the Chalcolithic period nor even to the occupation of the city by the Jebusites, as none of that would have provoked God to destroy the Israelite city. It refers to the city under Israelite control, which was first captured by David and then dramatically expanded by David, Solomon, and their heirs. The "holy city," and more specifically its temple, did more to provoke God's anger than to assuage it. This alludes to how Solomon set up shrines to foreign gods (1 Kings 11:4–6), an act that was imitated by many of his successors. Furthermore, the evil was not the act of a few bad leaders. Everyone, from the highest ranks of society to the lowest, participated in the apostasy (v. 32). Also, the apostasy was not done in ignorance. God had given them instruction from the very beginning of the nation, an allusion to the giving of the Law at Sinai and to the subsequent work of the prophets (v. 33). Their apostasy was willful, and they have no excuse.

*TRANSLATION NOTE: JEREMIAH 32:33*

The words וְלַמֵּד אֹתָם הַשְׁכֵּם וְלַמֵּד are literally, "And teaching them, arising early and teaching." The form לַמֵּד could be a piel infinitive construct, but in context is to be regarded as infinitive absolute. There is no subject given, and this makes translation somewhat difficult. The implied subject is the instruction and warning the people received from the Law and prophets, and the verbs are perhaps best rendered as virtual passives. The repetition of לַמֵּד implies that the teaching was done consistently and not sporadically. The metaphor of arising early (הַשְׁכֵּם) implies that God instructed them at the birth of the nation at Mount Sinai. The words could be paraphrased, "Even though they have been persistently taught ever since the very beginning of the nation."

**32:34–35**. The people defiled the temple by placing all manner of idols in and around it. This is explored most fully in Ezekiel 8. Besides mere idolatry, they committed in the Ben Hinnom valley the great abomination (הַתּוֹעֵבָה) of child sacrifice (v. 35). Jeremiah explores this sin more fully in 7:30–8:3. It is perhaps surprising to us that the text would make a point of asserting that God never commanded child sacrifice and that indeed such a concept never entered his mind (לֹא־צִוִּיתִים וְלֹא עָלְתָה עַל־לִבִּי). It is unlikely that the passage would go to such lengths to deny that YHWH commanded such things, except for the likelihood that in Jeremiah's time many were claiming that YHWH did in fact demand child sacrifice. Probably some Jews took such passages as the near-sacrifice of Isaac (Gen. 22) and the assertion that the firstborn child belongs to God (Exod. 13:12) as justification for arguing that the practice was orthodox and indeed the will of God.

**32:36**. God now addresses all the people and not just Jeremiah, using the plural "you" (אַתֶּם) and not the singular. They were saying that YHWH had handed the city over to their enemies and its people to death by violence, famine, and disease. What they were saying was not incorrect, but they drew from that the wrong inference, that God had abandoned them and their city forever.

**32:37**. Despite all appearances, Israel was not finished. This is the meaning of the sign of Jeremiah's land purchase. People make investments because they have faith in the thing in which they invest. They believe it has a future. Jerusalem will fall, but it is not finished. God will regather his people and enable them to live with confidence that they are safe (לָבֶטַח). This would take place in a limited, token form in the postexilic community and come to its complete fulfillment in the eschatological future of the New Jerusalem.

**32:38–40**. Jeremiah once again speaks of the new covenant. It would fulfill the ancient promise that Israel would be his people forever as he would forever be their God (v. 38; Lev. 26:12; Hos. 1:11). Their hearts would be changed so that they would love and fear God and never again disobey (v. 39). The new covenant, unlike the Sinai covenant, would endure forever (v. 40).

**32:41–44**. God will restore Israel joyfully and not grudgingly, as though under compulsion or with resentment over their past sins. This wholehearted embrace of Israel's restoration is implied by the phrase "with all my heart and with all my soul" (בְּכָל־לִבִּי וּבְכָל־נַפְשִׁי; v. 41). It means that God will, as it were, have no mental reservation about redeeming and restoring them. Their coming redemption was no less certain than their impending destruction at the hands of the Babylonians (v. 42). The city and land would indeed become a desolation filled with rubble, a ruin so great that people who saw it would despair of it ever coming back. Nevertheless, it would be rebuilt, and people would again buy and sell property there, because it would once again become valuable land (vv. 43–44). This aspect of the prophecy was quite literally fulfilled in the postexilic period.

## THEOLOGICAL FOCUS

Although this passage, like much of Jeremiah, contains a great deal about Judah's sin and coming destruction, it is fundamentally a message of hope.

- When people despair about the future, they no longer care about long-term plans, prudent behavior, or investments. One does not buy stocks if the market is in shambles and showing no signs of recovery. By purchasing land in the middle of the Babylonian siege of the city, Jeremiah showed he had hope for the future of the country. It was an act of faith. Jeremiah did not live to see the restoration, but his hopes were not in vain. Before the sixth century ended, a new Jewish community made up of returnees from Babylon were rebuilding Jerusalem.
- God's promise came at Jerusalem's darkest hour, when the Babylonian siege was in process and the destruction of the city imminent. God gives hope when we need it most.
- Jeremiah had tried to go out to Anathoth to buy the land, but was arrested as a traitor. What seemed to be an unmitigated evil turned out for good. Instead of conducting the business in an isolated village, he conducted it in the heart of the royal palace grounds and was able to relate to all the significance of the act. Even when things go terribly, we should not lose faith in the providence of God.
- The whole point of Jeremiah's prayer was, "God, you had me buy this plot of land just before the whole nation is obliterated. Why?" Yet he begins his prayer with a lengthy preamble praising God for the creation and the exodus. This is a model for how we should approach God.
- Even though God is gracious, there is no avoiding judgment for persistent evil.
- God is gracious, and he will preserve his people through disaster and ultimately redeem them from all their troubles.

That should enable them to stand up to the crises of life.

## PREACHING AND TEACHING STRATEGIES

### *Exegetical and Theological Synthesis*

Jeremiah's prophecy is filled with the kind of hope that is in the new covenant. It is focused upon God restoring the Jews to their homeland that would, one day, flourish again. The application of this passage requires careful thought. Believers in Jesus today are included in the new covenant, but the promises of cities being rebuilt and fields producing an abundant harvest were spoken to the Jews.

While Jeremiah is not giving us promises regarding our cities of the twenty-first century, he is telling us about the God who promised these specifics to Israel. The kind of hope that God offered to Israel through Jeremiah's sign-prophecy is offered to us. God is faithful to provide a grand future for all his children.

### *Preaching Idea*

Hope in God's future; nothing is impossible for him.

### *Contemporary Connections*

#### *What does it mean?*

On December 17, 1927 off the coast of Cape Cod, a tragic submarine accident took place that resulted in greatly improved submarine rescue technology. This was during the early stages of submarine development, and as with other new areas of new technology, accidents happened. Submarines were so new that this one didn't even have a name other than S-4. Naval historian Joseph A. Williams, in his 2015 book *Seventeen Fathoms Deep*, gives the details of this tragedy. The sub was struck by a surface vessel, sending it to the floor of the ocean with a crew of forty, most of whom perished within seconds. Six crewmen were alive but trapped in the forward torpedo room. In their last moments on this earth, before losing consciousness because of a lack of oxygen, they tapped on the hull of the ship in Morse code, "Is there any hope?" (Williams 2015).

Is this what the Israelites were asking? It might be what we are asking today; or if not asking, thinking it; and if not thinking it, feeling it. It might be a desperate cry, like those in Jerusalem surrounded by an enemy, or the hopelessness that comes when we look at our empty bank account. Perhaps it is a feeling that comes over us after watching the evening news reporting on the petty name-calling in an election year. Is there any hope for rescue? Is there any hope out of this hole I'm in? Is there any hope for the future of our nation?

Those living in Jerusalem at the time of this prophecy were terrified because the army of the world-dominating Babylonians surrounded them. They were doomed. There was no hope. They saw Jeremiah buying a piece of land and making sure that the documents would be secure over time. They no doubt asked why. Even Jeremiah asked this. God's answer was that he was going to restore Israel, because nothing was too hard for him. Those in exile who read about Jeremiah's sign-prophecy had to cope with the hopelessness that comes from confusion and insecurity. They were in a new land: new customs, new food, new climate, and new ways of worshipping YHWH. Everything was unfamiliar. Was there any hope? And the answer was yes—find comfort and security in YHWH; he will restore the land because nothing is too hard for him. The Jews who later returned to the land and read Jeremiah's prophecy had a huge task: to rebuild the nation. It was not only hard physical work, but they had to protect themselves from enemies while doing it. Other prophets such as Haggai and leaders like Nehemiah were sent to motivate and lead them to work. Apparently, the work was so hard they wanted to quit. They perhaps asked, "Is there any hope that we will ever get the work done?" And the answer was still, "Yes there is hope, because nothing is too hard for God."

*Is it true?*

Financial experts have told me that the stock market rises and falls because of emotions. It is what caused people to hoard toilet paper at the onset of the COVID-19 crisis. This fear was based on feelings, not fact. We are often driven by our emotions. The sign-prophecy of Jeremiah buying a piece of land when the city was about to fall is not only trying to help us understand something. God is also trying to get us to *feel* something: hope. Often advertisers will show someone enjoying a product, with the intention of us drawing the implication that if we use this product we will also be happy. The persuasion is more powerful because we make the connection within ourselves as though we came up with the idea, though it is probably subconscious. The Jews observed what Jeremiah was doing and could draw their own conclusions. If Jeremiah is making an investment in the future, then he must know something about God's plan that we don't. He gave them a sign and picture, and the implications had potential to produce the emotion of hope.

Can we truly believe that God has good in store for us in the future? Observe what God did through Jeremiah, through Jesus's death and resurrection. Observe what God has done in other lives, in our own, and draw your own conclusion. What does he want you to discover?

*Now what?*

Sometimes we are hopeless and despairing due to a family situation, health, finances, and many other situations. God offers us hope. It doesn't mean that our idea of relief and hope is what is in store for us. God's plan is probably different, but it is still good. It may well be that we need to take some actions; if so, we should. But in our hopelessness, God wants us to know that nothing is too hard for him.

Sometimes we are confused, uncertain, and insecure. Our job may be on shaky ground because the company has just been sold. Or, our church is changing leadership. Perhaps, we just moved to a new area. There seems to be change all around us. In the midst of feelings of hopeless insecurity there is something that doesn't change. God has a grand future for us. What is it? He doesn't give us the details, but it will be good because nothing is too hard for him.

Are we weary and tired of life being so hard? It is not so much that we are saying or even feeling hopeless directly, but life just seems so hard—having to work long hours, the constant demands of caring for children or others with special needs, the weariness that comes from the ever-increasing pressure of starting a new business or ministry . . . it just seems endless. Is there any hope that what I am doing is making a difference or has any purpose? The answer is still that God has a grand future for you, because nothing is too hard for him.

### *Creativity in Presentation*

The story of this chapter could be presented as a whole to show the thrust of the passage. To help with application, three sets of Jews can be considered: those in Jerusalem, those in exile, and those after the exile. These three groups would have different needs and levels of hopelessness, and thus see the prophecy from different perspectives. All three groups could be presented as a unit, followed by specific applications for today. Or, after each group of Jews with their particular needs is presented, the application is made for us today, with similar needs.

The unequaled example of God giving us hope because nothing is too hard for him is our salvation. The foundation of hope is not just in hope itself, but in the one who is the object of our hope. In my guilt I was hopeless before a holy God, but nothing is too hard for him. He demonstrated this on the cross when the judgment for my sin was placed on Jesus; and in his resurrection, I was given righteousness and a new life.

Here is one possible structure:

- First movement or point: Present the story of the text.
    - The buying of the land (32:1–15)
    - Jeremiah's response (32:16–25)
    - God's response (32:26–44)

- Second move: Present three possible Jewish responses to Jeremiah's message.
    - In Jeremiah's presence: Babylon's power is great. We might trust God, or not.
    - In the exile: We are defeated. How stupid for Jeremiah to buy land. How can we trust God?
    - After the exile: Jeremiah was right. I guess we can trust God.

- Third move: Our response to Jeremiah's message to us
    - Sometimes we trust God but not fully, because of uncertainty.
    - Sometimes when life falls apart, we are in despair and think that we can't really trust him.
    - But, God will come through; he will keep his promises. We can trust him.

- Hope in God's future; nothing is impossible for him.

## DISCUSSION QUESTIONS

1. What are some words that we associate with "hopeless"?

2. What are some words that we associate with "hope"?

3. What kinds of things do people put their hope in?

4. When have you felt hopeless?

5. What might be the relationship between hope and belief? How does one lead to the other?

## Jeremiah 33:1–26

### EXEGETICAL IDEA

The desolate city will be restored and have a glory that surpasses anything in its past. This magnificent future that God is preparing centers on the Davidic Messiah. The historical house of David, now broken and cast down into the dust, has an enduring, eschatological future in a great act of God.

### THEOLOGICAL FOCUS

With the death of Zedekiah, the historical Davidic dynasty came to an end. As a human institution, it never has and never will return. But God's promises are more enduring than any crisis in any historical context. A new Davidic king will give his people a kingdom not of this world.

### PREACHING IDEA

You can't beat God's promises.

### PREACHING POINTERS

"Call to Me, and I will answer you, and I will tell you great and mighty things, which you do not know" (33:3 NASB). This often-quoted verse has a deeper meaning when "mighty" is more correctly translated "unassailable." As Jeremiah describes the coming events of Jerusalem being gloriously restored and even a Davidic king to rule, it must have been hard for the Jews to believe. Their own lack of trust in God's power was an affront to, or attack on, the promise.

The focus of the text is God's amazing promises to Israel and to us. The correct understanding of the opening metaphor (vv. 2–3) of a fortress leads us to the awareness that though God's promises are wonderful and beyond our imaginations, they still come under attack. Opposition comes from the forces of evil, but also from our own hearts. These promises become even more real if we will acknowledge that our lack of faith in God will, in a sense, attack them. We must come to the point of surrendering our doubts and embracing belief in these glorious promises that God makes.

# THE NEW DAVIDIC KING (33:1–26)

## LITERARY STRUCTURE AND THEMES

Jeremiah 33 is closely tied to chapter 32, since it concerns a "second" oracle to Jeremiah while imprisoned in the royal courtyard (33:1). More specifically, it is a second divine response to Jeremiah's prayer of 32:16–25, as YHWH's words in 33:3 indicate: "Call to me and I will answer you." Jeremiah did call on YHWH—and YHWH gave him a very complete answer.

The key to understanding chapter 33 is in verses 1–6. Unfortunately, the Hebrew is difficult, and the standard translations take significant liberties with the text in order to present a coherent reading. This is not necessary, however. One can give the text as it stands a meaningful interpretation if one recognizes where it is elliptical and implicitly alludes to chapter 32. A full translation of verses 2–6 is presented below. The structure of this text is as follows:

- ***YHWH Will Tell Jeremiah Unassailable Things (33:1–3)***
- ***Desolate Jerusalem to Be Filled with Life (33:4–13)***
  - *The City Healed (33:4–9)*
  - *Joyful Sounds in the City (33:10–11)*
  - *Flocks of Sheep in the Countryside (33:12–13)*
- ***Israel to Be Ruled by David's Righteous Shoot (33:14–18)***
  - *The Advent of David's Righteous Shoot (33:14–16)*
  - *Houses of David and Levi to Thrive Forever (33:17–18)*
- ***Restored Houses of Israel to Endure Like the Heavens (33:19–26)***
  - *Covenants with David and Levi as Enduring as the Sun (33:19–22)*
  - *Offspring of David and Jacob to Endure Forever (33:23–26)*

## EXPOSITION

*THE TRANSLATION OF JEREMIAH 33:2–6*

The full translation is as follows:

> Thus says YHWH who made [the earth], YHWH who formed it in order to establish it—YHWH is his name: [3]"Call to me and I will answer you, and I will tell you great and unassailable things that you did not know." [4]For thus says YHWH the God of Israel:
>
> Concerning the houses of this city and concerning the houses of the kings of Judah that are to be demolished;
>
> Concerning the siege ramps and concerning the sword, [5][the forces] coming with the Chaldeans to fight [the men of Jerusalem] and to fill [the Jerusalem houses] with human corpses, [people] whom I struck in my anger and my rage;
>
> And as for the fact that I have hidden my face from this city because of all their evil:
>
> [6]I hereby announce that I will restore health and healing to her! And I will heal them, and I will show them an abundance of peace and security.

In verse 2, "the earth" is the implied meaning of the pronoun suffix on עֹשָׂהּ, "her maker." Interpreters are annoyed that the text only says that YHWH made "it" without specifying what he made. But the verse alludes to 32:17 and concerns how YHWH made the earth, or more generally, all of creation.

The Hebrew of 33:4–5 appears quite difficult, but it is much easier to follow if one recognizes what is happening in three consecutive statements:

- As is commonly done, one should take עַל in עַל־בָּתֵּי הָעִיר הַזֹּאת וְעַל־בָּתֵּי מַלְכֵי יְהוּדָה to mean "concerning." Thus, it is "Concerning the houses of this city and concerning the houses of the kings of Judah."
- The word אֶל in the phrases אֶל־הַסֹּלְלוֹת וְאֶל־הֶחָרֶב also means "concerning." As *HALOT* notes, אֶל "often alternates with עַל" (Ludwig et al. 1994, 51). The common rendition of the verse, "the houses of this city and the houses of the kings of Judah that were torn down to make a defense against the siege ramps and before the sword" (NRSV), is impossible grammatically and makes no sense historically. Jerusalem already had a wall; it is unlikely that the Jews would attempt to gain additional protection against siege ramps and towers by demolishing their houses and trying to pile up debris on their walls. The effort would be obviously futile. Furthermore, Jeremiah 32:29 says that the Chaldeans would burn the houses of Jerusalem, not that the Jews would destroy their own houses. As a matter of historical record, the houses of the people and the royal house were indeed destroyed by the Babylonians (Jer. 39:8). Thus, one should not take הַנְּתֻצִים ("the torn down [houses]") to mean that the Jews torn down their own houses prior to the fall of the city. The verb נתץ ("to tear down") is formulaic in Jeremiah for YHWH's judgmental decrees. See 1:10 and the subsequent usage at 4:26; 18:7; 31:28; 39:8.
- Similarly, the word אֲשֶׁר in וַאֲשֶׁר הִסְתַּרְתִּי פָנַי means "that," and in context means, "and as for the fact that I have hidden my face."

The above three parts of the text point to three matters (from chapter 32) that YHWH alludes back to: the destruction of the buildings of Jerusalem, the siege ramps and warfare that the Chaldeans have brought upon the city, and YHWH's wrath. Because verses 4–5 are a series of allusions to a previous context ("concerning . . . concerning . . . and as for the fact that . . .") the text contains sentence fragments and appears ungrammatical.

In verses 4–5, the destruction of Jerusalem is described as an accomplished fact even though, as of the time of the oracle, it was not yet finished. Also, in verse 5, the participle בָּאִים refers to all the siege machines, infantry, and other forces that have come with Babylon to attack Jerusalem. לְהִלָּחֵם ("to fight") refers implicitly to fighting against the men of Jerusalem, and the suffix on וּלְמַלְאָם ("to fill them") refers to the houses of Jerusalem.

In verse 6, הִנֵּה, as is common, announces a solemn declaration (for example, Gen. 1:29: "I hereby give you every plant" [הִנֵּה נָתַתִּי לָכֶם אֶת־כָּל־עֵשֶׂב]). Thus, הִנְנִי מַעֲלֶה־לָּהּ אֲרֻכָה, means, "I hereby announce that I will restore health."

Verses 2–6 allude back to chapter 32 and to the judgments pronounced against Jerusalem, making that point that although the judgments will come about, God will someday reverse the judgments and bring about a great salvation. The following table demonstrates how fully chapter 33 echoes chapter 32 (keywords found in both texts are marked with italics).

| Jeremiah's Prayer and YHWH's First Answer in 32 | YHWH's Second Answer in 33 |
|---|---|
| "Alas Lord *YHWH*! You *made* heaven and *earth* by your great power. . . . *YHWH* Sabaoth *is his name*!" (32:17–18) | "*YHWH* who *made* [the *earth*], YHWH who formed it in order to establish it—*YHWH is his name*" (33:2) |
| "Look! *Siege ramps come* to the *city* to take it! The *city* is lost to the *Chaldeans* who *fight* against it because of the sword and the famine and the plague. . . . The *Chaldeans* that *fight* against this city will come and they will set fire to this city and burn it and the *houses* upon whose roofs they offered incense to Baal." (32:24, 29) | "Concerning the *houses* of this *city* and concerning the *houses* of the kings of Judah that are to be demolished; concerning the *siege ramps* and the *sword*, [the forces] coming with the *Chaldeans* to *fight* [the men of Jerusalem] and to fill [the Jerusalem houses] with human corpses" (33:4b–5a) |
| "This city has been to me a matter for *my anger* and *my rage* from the day they built it until this day, so that I must get it out of *my face*." (32:21) | ". . . [people] whom I struck in *my anger* and *my rage*, and as for the fact that I have hidden *my face* from this city because of all their evil" (33:5b) |

In summary, we should take Jeremiah 33 to be a second, additional response to Jeremiah's prayer in chapter 32. It expands the main point: even though YHWH has condemned Jerusalem to destruction at the hands of the Chaldeans, he will again fill it with life and activity.

This chapter is important for Christian readers for another reason: except for brief references to a future David in 23:5–6 and 30:9, it is the only salvation oracle in the book that is explicitly messianic in focus.

### *YHWH Will Tell Jeremiah Unassailable Things (33:1–3)*

**33:1**. The superscript to this chapter tells us that it took place while he was still imprisoned with the royal guard. This is important, because it suggests that the context for chapter 33 is the events related in chapter 32. As described above, 33:2–6 at significant points alludes to chapter 32.

**33:2**. As noted above, "Thus says YHWH its maker" (כֹּה־אָמַר יְהוָה עֹשָׂהּ) alludes to Jeremiah's prayer at 32:17: "YHWH, you made heaven and earth by your great power and outstretched arm; nothing is too wonderful for you!" The allusion here means that God, because he is the almighty creator, can also do wondrous things for Israel. Also, "YHWH is his name" alludes again to Jeremiah's prayer in 32:18, and beyond that alludes to the revelation of the name to Moses in Exodus 3:14–15. The meaning is that YHWH and no other god is the source of Israel's salvation.

As he saved them in the exodus, so he will do in recalling them from exile.

**33:3**. God promises to do "great and unassailable (וּבְצֻרוֹת) things" in response to Jeremiah's prayer. Although this is an invitation to continue praying, it also alludes to Jeremiah's prayer in chapter 32. The noun בָּצוּר ("unassailable, fortified") generally refers to fortified cities (Deut. 1:28; Josh. 14:12; 2 Kings 18:13; Hos. 8:14). In Jeremiah 15:20, however, God promises to make the prophet himself into an "unassailable wall of bronze" (חוֹמַת נְחֹשֶׁת בְּצוּרָה), meaning that Jeremiah will withstand all the criticism, unbelief, and hostility the people hurl at him. Thus, when God promises "unassailable things," he means that the promises will effectively speak to people despite all the scoffing and anger Jeremiah's enemies may throw at him. Also, in the face of all opposition, they will be fulfilled.

## *Desolate Jerusalem to Be Filled with Life (33:4–13)*

### *The City Healed (33:4–9)*

**33:4–6**. For the translation of these verses, see the translation note above. Against a number of English translations, this passage does not mean that the people of Jerusalem tore down their own houses to use the debris for the defense of the city. It alludes to Jeremiah's prayer and YHWH's response in chapter 32, which spoke of how the Babylonians would bring their siege works against the city, take it, and destroy all the houses within. In these two verses, YHWH affirms that all of that is true, but implies that the fall of Jerusalem is not the end of the story. In the face of all that destruction, YHWH solemnly declares that he is giving them a revelation of restoration and healing.

**33:7–9**. The clause וְהֲשִׁבֹתִי אֶת־שְׁבוּת יְהוּדָה, often rendered as "I will restore the fortunes of Judah" (NASB), can also mean, "I will bring back the captivity of Judah." Thus, just as the nation is about to go into exile to Babylon, YHWH announces their restoration to their own land. This is clearly the focus, since God adds that he will rebuild (בנה) the city. In addition, God will forgive all their sin (v. 8) and Jerusalem will become a place of joy, so that all the nations will turn to the God of Israel. This plainly recalls the promise of a new covenant in chapter 31. Here, as is common, Jeremiah blends together several elements of how God's promise will be fulfilled. The Jews will come back and rebuild Jerusalem, as they did in the postexilic community, and people from all the nations will come and worship Israel's God, as is done now under the new covenant. Jerusalem will be a place of happiness, peace, and glory, as will be the case in the New Jerusalem.

### *Joyful Sounds in the City (33:10–11)*

**33:10–11**. At the time this oracle was given, Jerusalem was a city in turmoil, surrounded by a massive, irresistible army. Soon after it was written, Jerusalem would be an empty wasteland, having little more than a few burned-out buildings and great heaps of rubble. It was, to all appearances, a complete obliteration of the city and an elimination of Jewish society. Jeremiah promises that it will again be filled with laughter and joy. There will be wedding songs, a sure sign that people are optimistic about the future. Above all else, there will be songs of praise to YHWH. This will happen because God will "restore the fortunes of the land." As already noted, כִּי־אָשִׁיב אֶת־שְׁבוּת־הָאָרֶץ can also mean, and probably primarily means, "bring back the captivity of the land."

### *Flocks of Sheep in the Countryside (33:12–13)*

**33:12–13**. The Israelites were historically a shepherd people, and their livestock represented both their wealth and their culture. To be deprived of their animals, as most were in the exile experience, represented a loss of their identity. The land itself, bereft of the sheep and cattle that grazed upon it, ceased to be traditional Israel. Barren lands that would be restored include the hill country of Judah (הָהָר); the gentle slopes of the Shephelah, near the Mediterranean coast (הַשְּׁפֵלָה); the Negev, the wilderness region of southern Judah (הַנֶּגֶב); and the vicinity of Jerusalem in the traditional tribal land of Benjamin (וּבְאֶרֶץ בִּנְיָמִן וּבִסְבִיבֵי יְרוּשָׁלַםִ). This is the territory of the state of Judah, the southern kingdom. This was the center of the postexilic community, especially in the early period, when very few Jews lived in the north. The fulfillment of this part of the passage is primarily in the postexilic community; it is not eschatological.

### *Israel to Be Ruled by David's Righteous Shoot (33:14–18)*

Apart from 23:5–6, chapter 33 has the only explicitly messianic prophecy in Jeremiah.

#### *The Advent of David's Righteous Shoot (33:14–16)*

**33:14**. Introducing the promise of the Davidic savior, Jeremiah speaks of "the good word I have spoken" (אֶת־הַדָּבָר הַטּוֹב אֲשֶׁר דִּבַּרְתִּי), implying that Jeremiah is recalling earlier prophecies of a messianic king from the line of David. Examples of such prophecies are at Hosea 3:5, which speaks of the people coming back to "David their king," and Amos 9:11, which speaks of restoring "David's fallen hut." This promise, notably, is for both "the house of Israel (בֵּית יִשְׂרָאֵל) and the house of Judah (בֵּית יְהוּדָה)," using the same phrases as are found in the new covenant prophecy at 31:31. The shift from a promise of restoration for Judah only (in vv. 12–13 above) to a promise for both Israel and Judah implies that the prophecy has shifted toward the eschatological future.

**33:15–16**. The messianic term here is often translated as "branch" (צֶמַח). But that is misleading; in English, "branch" generally connotes a small limb of a tree growing out from a larger limb. The word צֶמַח means "shoot" or "sapling," such as the young sapling of a tree or a tender plant shooting up from the soil. A good example is in Isaiah 61:11, which like Jeremiah 33:15 uses צמח in both its noun and verb forms: "For as the earth sends forth its sprout (צִמְחָהּ), and as a garden causes what is sown in it to sprout up (יַצְמִיחַ)." The "sprout of righteousness" (צֶמַח צְדָקָה) in verse 15 is not one branch among many growing out from a large, established tree; it is new life springing up from a seed in the ground. In the metaphor, the house of David has perished; it died when Jerusalem fell and the dynasty ended. But God will make what seemed dead and buried to live again. The promise that the messianic king would execute "justice" (מִשְׁפָּט) and "righteousness" (צְדָקָה) may allude to the messianic promise of Isaiah 9:7, which uses the same two words. Verse 16 promises that the eternal Jerusalem would be known by the name "YHWH is our righteousness" (יְהוָה צִדְקֵנוּ) need not be fulfilled literally. Old Testament prophecies involving names often describe the character of the thing or person so named; they do not mean that the thing or person will literally have that name. Thus, for example, the name Immanuel ("God with us") speaks of the character of the son to be born (Isa. 7:14), but Jesus was not literally named "Immanuel." However, the name "YHWH is our righteousness" is highly significant; it is a wordplay on the name Zedekiah (צִדְקִיָּהוּ), which also means "YHWH [is our] righteousness." Zedekiah was the last king of the line of David; in his reign, Jerusalem fell. Calling the New Jerusalem "YHWH is our righteousness" implies that the meaning of Zedekiah's name would finally be fulfilled and that the disgrace that took place in his reign would be forever erased.

#### *Houses of David and Levi to Thrive Forever (33:17–18)*

These two verses address the two catastrophic events that befell Jerusalem when Babylon took the city: the royal dynasty of David ended and the temple fell, taking with it the legitimate function of the Levitical priesthood. The loss of these two institutions would cause the Jews of the exile to despair, because everything upon which they had set their hopes was lost. This text tells us that they will endure.

**33:17**. As a historical reality, the Davidic dynasty did end and there has never been another earthly king ruling over the state of Israel. Nevertheless, this verse asserts that the promise of 1 Samuel 7 has not failed and that the throne of David will not be vacant forever. It is an answer to the despairing cry of Psalm 89. The fulfillment is in the eternal reign of Jesus.

**33:18**. The fulfillment of this passage is problematic because in the new covenant, the Levitical priesthood serving at a physical building is obsolete. Even dispensationalism—which expects a new, earthly temple to be built in Jerusalem after Jesus returns and sacrifices to be resumed there—cannot find a literal fulfillment to the prophecy: The millennium only lasts for a thousand years, but this verse says that the priests and Levites would serve before God and make offerings "forever." Clearly, if the reign of the Davidic king of verse 17 is to endure eternally, we would expect that the priestly ministry of the priests and Levites would as well, since verse 18 is set up as a parallel to verse 17. And in eternity, in the New Jerusalem, there will be no temple (Rev. 21:22), and so the Levitical priests cannot continue to serve there as they had in the Old Testament. But perhaps verses 17 and 18 are not as different as they first appear. Although Jesus will fulfill all the promises made to the house of David, it will not simply be a restoration of the old order of things. The earthly kingdom of David is well and truly finished, and Jesus's kingdom is not of this world (John 18:36). All the promises will be fulfilled, but all will be made new. As the ideal of the Israelite king is realized in Jesus in the new earth, so also the ideal of Israelite worship is fulfilled there, where all will praise Israel's God perfectly. Everything that the Levitical priests foreshadowed will be fulfilled in Jesus, who is a priest forever after the order of Melchizedek (Ps. 110:4; Heb. 6:20–7:17).

### *Restored Houses of Israel to Endure Like the Heavens (33:19–26)*

Just as one may rely upon the heavenly bodies to go through their courses in the sky above, so one may be sure that God's promises to Israel will be fulfilled. This comparison indicates that the fulfillment of the promises of this chapter is in the new covenant (see Jer. 31:35–37).

#### *Covenants with David and Levi as Enduring as the Sun (33:19–22)*

**33:19–21**. This section is a metaphor that links the regularity of day and night to the faithfulness of God. "My covenant—the day, and my covenant—the night" (אֶת־בְּרִיתִי הַיּוֹם וְאֶת־בְּרִיתִי הַלָּיְלָה) speaks of day and night as if they were covenants because their analogical counterpart is a literal covenant, called "my covenant" (בְּרִיתִי) with David. As God faithfully maintains the regularity of day and night, so he faithfully maintains his covenant with David. But this does not mean that day and night are literal covenants. A covenant is an agreement between two sentient parties that governs their relationship, and this obviously does not apply to the day and night.

**33:22**. A second comparison links the high number of stars in the sky and of sand on the shore to the future large number of the "offspring of David" (זֶרַע דָּוִד) and of the Levites. The prophecy anticipates the demise of the house of David, Zedekiah being the last king of that dynasty. Thus, to all appearances, the line of David would cease to exist, with the biological descendants of David being absorbed into the larger population and losing their identity as a royal line. The Levites, similarly, were facing a complete elimination of their purpose and identity. Lacking any temple, they lacked any purpose for existing, so that even if they had physical descendants, they would be no more than the descendants of people who once had a special purpose in the religion of Israel. While one might speak of the descendants of David in the genealogy of Christ as a kind of fulfillment, and one might similarly speak of the rebuilding of the temple and recovery under Ezra and Nehemiah as a limited fulfillment of this promise concerning the Levites, this text clearly anticipates an enormous multitude of descendants that endures forever. Therefore, these cannot be literal, biological offspring. The best interpretation is the New Testament assertion that all who believe in Jesus are heirs with Christ who will reign with him forever. Similarly, all who believe in Jesus will stand before God forever to worship and praise him, fulfilling the role once taken on by the Levitical priests and choirs. There is ample precedent for this understanding of offspring in the Old Testament. For example, Isaiah 54:1 states, "'Sing, barren woman, who has not borne! / Break forth into singing, and shout out loud, / You who have never been in labor! / For the children of the desolate woman are more than those of the married woman,' says YHWH." These children of Zion are not biological offspring, but the great number of the redeemed, particularly the Gentiles, who populate the New Jerusalem (see Gal. 4:26–28).

### The Messianic Hope in Jeremiah

For Christian readers, the sparsity of explicit messianic statements in Jeremiah may seem surprising. In addition, it may seem disturbing, in light of some Christian interpretations of the Old Testament, that Jeremiah ties its messianic theology strictly to a future Davidic king and not to other things we have come to expect. For example, there is no allusion to the "seed of the woman" of Genesis 3:15, nor is there any reference to a suffering Messiah who brings about atonement and redemption. On the other hand, Jeremiah does give us a glimpse into how pious Israelites actually framed their messianic hope.

Many passages that Christians today routinely take as messianic prophecy seem to have made little impact on ancient Israelites. For example, it is difficult to find any certain allusion to Genesis 49:10 (concerning the scepter not departing from Judah until "Shiloh" comes) in the Old Testament, and there is no indication that people cited this verse as messianic prophecy. Even 1 Samuel 7, the great promise to the house of David, never alludes to this verse, even as it does allude to other passages (for example, there is allusion to the exodus narrative in 1 Samuel 7:6, 23). If David thought that Genesis 49:10 predicted the royal line of Judah and indeed a messianic king, one would have expected him to say something about it in his response to God in 1 Samuel 7. The same can be said for the "star and scepter" prophecy of Balaam in Numbers 24:17. Christians generally see this as a messianic prophecy, but we do not have evidence that the ancient Israelites read it in that way. Some second temple–era Jews did interpret this passage as messianic, but they believed that the "star" and "scepter" were two separate messiahs! In short, we need to take seriously the fact that much messianic prophecy is in "mystery" form, its true significance not recognized until after Jesus came. After all, even Jesus's disciples were bewildered at his claim that the Messiah had to suffer and die. No one expected such a thing.

First Samuel 7 and subsequent events are the actual wellspring for a popular messianic expectation such as it existed in ancient Israel. The earliest Israelites, in the time of the judges, did not have a king. To the contrary, they had deep qualms about the appropriateness of a king, as illustrated by Gideon's refusal of a crown: "I will not rule over you, nor shall my son rule over you; YHWH shall rule over you" (Judg. 8:23). When the Israelites finally decided to seek a king in imitation of the other nations, the act was condemned by YHWH and his prophet, Samuel (1 Sam. 8:4–19). First Samuel 7, however, marks a watershed moment. In promising an eternal dynasty to David, God as it were redeemed the institution of kingship and placed it at the center of Israel's hope of eschatological salvation. Henceforth, promises concerning the ultimate redemption of Israel in the aftermath of the fall of Israel and Judah would almost invariably focus on the future David, a messianic king.

The destruction of Jerusalem at the hands of the Babylonians was the great crisis precipitating Israel's messianic hope. Psalm 89 explicitly and exhaustively describes their dismay; God had made promises of an everlasting dynasty to David, and yet the people saw Jerusalem and the Davidic throne cast down and crushed under the great empires of earth. How could such a thing happen? Had God forgotten his promises? In response, the prophets spoke of the future Davidic king. The two great prophets at the time of Jerusalem's fall, Jeremiah and Ezekiel, present Israel's glorious future as the coming of a new David (Jer. 30:9; 33:15–26; Ezek. 34:23–24; 37:24–25).

We should not be surprised at how the Israelites of this time thought of a future savior. Their messianic expectation reflected the context in which they found themselves. God had chosen David's line as their eternal dynasty and had promised him great dominion, and God had chosen the temple of the house of David as the place where his name would dwell and where priests would lawfully serve him. Now they saw all of this ending in a nightmare before their eyes. Their temple was burnt to the ground and the last Davidic king, Zedekiah, was taken away tortured and left to die in ignominy as a prisoner of a foreign empire. We should not be surprised that their messianic hope focused heavily on the restoration of the Davidic monarchy and the institutions it created. Their expectation was not wrong, but it was incomplete. Also, we should understand that these passages are set in language that reflect the times in which they were written. The ancient Jews would be no less surprised than Jesus's disciples and John the Baptist at what the messianic king would actually do when he came (Matt. 11:3).

*Offspring of David and Jacob to Endure Forever (33:23–26)*

**33:23–24**. The main question in this text is whether "this people" (הָעָם הַזֶּה) refers to Jews who are complaining that God has rejected them or to a Gentile people, such as the Babylonians, who are celebrating because they think that God is finished with Israel and has written them off. Secondarily, who are the "two clans" (שְׁתֵּי הַמִּשְׁפָּחוֹת) YHWH has supposedly rejected? It is unlikely that YHWH would say that Jews "spurn my people" (וְאֶת־עַמִּי יִנְאָצוּן) as unworthy to be considered a nation. In all probability, therefore, it is the Babylonians who regard Israel as a rejected entity and now a non-people. Also, it is unlikely that the two "clans" are the houses of David and of Levi. The Babylonians would have little interest in the demise of Levi, and it would be odd to call the royal family a "clan" (מִשְׁפָּחָה), a term that is generally used for larger population bodies as in Genesis 10:5. It is much more likely that the two "clans" are the northern and southern kingdoms of Israel: Samaria and Judah.

**33:25–26**. This passage returns to the comparison of the endurance are reliability of YHWH's promises to the heavenly bodies. As God will not break the laws that govern the heavens, so he will not reject Israel or David.

## THEOLOGICAL FOCUS

The primary focus of this passage is the certainty of the eschatological restoration of

Israel and the permanence of the new Israel under the new covenant.

- God always answers the prayers of his people. Jeremiah lived through a terrible crisis, and at his death Israel was destroyed, the monarchy was finished, and the people were still in exile. Even so, his prayers received a favorable answer, and they were fulfilled in Jesus and the beginning of the new covenant, and they will yet be fulfilled in the new earth.
- God's promises are "unassailable" (33:3). Many people may attack and mock them, and circumstances may seem to disprove them, but they will come to pass.
- The kingdom of heaven is, in the eyes of many, easy to despise. Jeremiah 33:15 promises that a "sprout" would come up out of the barren, scorched earth of Jerusalem after the fall of the city. A sprout is a small, tender young plant that would appear to have no future, being so weak and small. By analogy, Jesus said that a mustard seed is the smallest of all the seeds, but from it comes a great tree that the birds of the air can nest in (Mark 4:30–32).
- The hope of Israel, the promises to the patriarchs, and the glories of the new covenant are all centered upon the person of Jesus, the true son of David.
- The Davidic kingdom of the Old Testament and the priestly worship of the Levites in the temple were but shadows of the glory to come. Those who belong to Christ will reign with him forever and praise him forever.
- As surely as the sun rises in the east and sets each evening in the west, so we can be sure that God's promises will not fail.

## PREACHING AND TEACHING STRATEGIES

### *Exegetical and Theological Synthesis*

For the Israelites the idea that Israel would be destroyed and then rebuilt was certainly not a pleasant one, but at least they could conceive of the idea. The rebuilding part certainly fits into their view of God's intention for their nation. In their minds, the land and the physical kingdom was the focus. This prophecy affirms that, but then takes it to another level when God speaks of David's line and the Levitical line enduring forever. In a sense, the question is not "Is it true?" but "Is it conceivable?" It must have been hard for the besieged Jews to believe that God would restore their land, and from the way they treated Jeremiah not many did believe. But even more challenging to their faith was their believing that God had plans for Israel that would go beyond the physical kingdom into an eternal kingdom.

When we teach our respective view of God's future restoration of the earth, it is hard to imagine what that will be like. No doubt the Jews must have had the same difficulty in grasping the extent of these glorious promises of a eternal righteous king. We can see that God's fulfillment through Jesus is far better than the OT Jews could have imagined. Whatever nuance our theological system may place upon God's promise of a glorious restoration of the earth and our lives, his work will be far greater than our imaginations.

### *Preaching Idea*

You can't beat God's promises.

### *Contemporary Connections*

#### *What does it mean?*

The prophecy of the righteous sprout is filled with the overtones of growth. Its beginning is very different from that full-grown plant. The Israelites were only told of a spout. On this side of the first advent, we are privileged to see the growth of the spout, the Davidic Messiah: his incarnation, his teachings, his coming to atone for our sins, his rising from the grave, his ascension, and his promise to come again. The Jews of Judah were left to look forward to his coming, though filled with many questions and misconceptions. It strikes me that we, as well, are left to look forward to his coming—again. And like the Jews, we have many questions and more than likely some misconceptions. One thing was clear for them and is clear for us: he will return, and he will reign forever, and ever, and ever. Hallelujah!

### *Is it true?*

An American pastor was preaching in Poland through a translator. Things were going along just fine, until the pastor told a story about a father and son in the South who were estranged and had not spoken or seen each other in years—until the day the dad visited a church, not knowing it was the church his son attended. In God's great plan the father sat in the row just in front of the son. During the meet-and-greet time, as people turned to each other, the dad turned around and in the southern style of greeting grabbed the outstretched hand of the young man sitting behind hm. It took a moment, but as the recognition came, the handshake turned into an embrace. As the pastor told this story, the translator was so struck that he turned directly to the pastor and said, "Really?" He couldn't imagine this happening. Perhaps the Israelites said the same thing about the kingdom of Israel continuing forever. Really? Though it is hard to conceive, it is still true. To be sure, exactly what it will look like is greatly debated. But even though we may not have agreement as to the vision of *what* it will be, it is clear that it *will be*. And as God told Jeremiah, it will be great.

### *Now what?*

What is our response to this promise? As with any narrative, the application is difficult because there are no imperatives or direct commands, but God gave us this story and he is doing something with it. But what? Let's take a clue from the introduction to this prophecy. God is going to tell Jeremiah great and unassailable things. The greatness of this prophecy is apparent: the restoration and enduring forever of Israel under an eternal Davidic king. Using the image of a fortified city, God says that it is unassailable which affirms that the promise will endure, and it assumes that it will be attacked. Who is attacking it? What is opposing our accepting this prophecy?

The attack might come because of limited imaginations. God saying to Israel, "A king is coming who will rule forever," stretched their imaginations. But a fuller picture of the incarnation was perhaps beyond their imaginations. How does our imagination handle the second coming and the eternal state? Psalm 40:5 implies that God's plans for us are beyond what we could speak of. Ephesians 3:20 tells us that God is able to do far more than we could ever ask or think. Perhaps we unknowingly attack God's promises because we limit him to our imaginations.

*Anne of Green Gables* is the delightful story of a young girl growing up on Prince Edward Island. Because of her harsh childhood in and out of orphanages in the late 1800s, she developed an amazing imagination just to survive. But then in the security of family who accepted and loved her, this imagination brought abundant delight. She saw a costal lagoon that was not much more than a marsh and called it "The Lake of Shining Waters." God's plans for Israel and for us are far better than we can even imagine. So when he says that Israel and we, by way of the new covenant, will reign forever with him, let's not limit our imaginations. We must not attack God's future plans for us with our limited imaginations.

The attack could come from those who proclaim a plan different from God's promises of the future. Jeremiah already encountered this. The false prophets were not only wrong in saying that God would not destroy Israel, but they were also wrong in that they didn't even have a hint of a Messiah who would reign forever. They left out the wrath and apparently had no clue about the glorious redemption. It seems that the prevailing worldview today is that of materialism. I've heard it described that human thinking and being are nothing more than tissues and chemical reactions—just a wet computer. In this view our future is the same as the future of my first computer, a Fat Mac. It no longer exists; its drives are empty, and its screen is dark. Materialists see our future as just turning off the switch. Views that deny that judgment is coming for the unrighteous and that a glorious future is in store for the righteous are attacks on God's promises. These opposing views of our future will fail, so we must not embrace them.

Another futile attack could come from stubbornness. I hung on to my flip phone for far too long. I just didn't like the idea of a tapping, double tapping and sliding my figure across a screen rather than the simplicity of punching buttons. On what became a pivotal day, I left my beloved flip phone on top of my car while I put a box of books in the back seat. That phone is still somewhere on the streets of Fort Worth. I was stubborn in my accepting that there might be a better phone. I had a phone that worked for me. I knew what was best, or at least I thought I did. Now I can't imagine trying to send an email on a flip phone. The attack on God's plan can come from thinking that our plans are better than his. Instead of saying, "God, I don't want your plan because it doesn't look like what I had in mind," we should rather say, "Lord, I didn't have this in mind, but I trust your good hand."

### *Creativity in Presentation*

Chapter 32, through the image of Jeremiah buying land, emphasized hope because nothing is impossible for God. This section is an extension of that hope, but the object of hope focuses not on God's omnipotence but on his immutability. Nothing can change his plans.

A possible strategy in presenting this passage is to highlight the four major sections presenting them as an absolutely glorious future plan from God. Again, one's personal theology will affect the specificity of the description. The important thing is to present it in such a way that no one could possibly be against it. This is wonderful news that everyone should welcome. Then move to God's opening words to Jeremiah, pointing out that God's use of the image of a fortified city implies opposition. How could anyone be opposed to God's good plans? The Jews were, and perhaps we might be as well, though unknowingly. Then as you move through the possible "attacks" the message of the text will be revisited, giving attention as to how we can truly trust our immutable, unchanging Lord.

Below is a suggested structure. The last point differs from the second, though the wording is similar. Point two emphasizes life, while point four emphasizes life's eternality.

- First move or section: the text and current application
    - YHWH will tell Jeremiah unassailable things (33:1–3).
        - God's promises are solid and withstand any attack.
    - Desolate Jerusalem is to be filled with life (33:4–13).
        - We are promised life eternal.
    - Israel is to be ruled by David's righteous shoot (33:14–18).
        - We have a righteous king: Jesus.
    - Restored houses of Israel are to endure like the heavens (33:19–26).
        - We will have life forever.

- Second move or section: What attacks our belief in God's promises? (The list below serves as a springboard into your own list of things that attack God's promises.)
    - Limited imagination of what God will do

    - Promises that are contrary to God's
    - Stubbornness

- God's promises are so good and wonderful—who would want to attack or not believe them?

## DISCUSSION QUESTIONS

1. How does thinking about the future benefit the present?
2. When is it hard to think about the future?
3. Who has the most level of success in predicting the future—weather reporters, financial analysts, medical personnel, etc.?
4. How do we show our belief or lack of belief in what these professionals predict for our future?
5. What is your favorite part of the future that God describes in this passage?

# HISTORICALLY CONTEXTUALIZED MESSAGES II (34:1–45:5)

This section tells of Jeremiah's experiences during Jerusalem's harrowing last days, making the point that the generation that stayed behind after the Jehoiachin exile was consistently hostile to the prophet both before and after the destruction of the city.

## Jeremiah 34:1–35:19

### EXEGETICAL IDEA

The passage contrasts and explores the gross disobedience of the leaders of Jerusalem, who quickly broke a newly made covenant with YHWH, with the fidelity of the Rechabites, who zealously kept their ancestral traditions. Taken together, the two chapters contrast the behavior of the two groups and demonstrate how dishonest and faithless the leaders of Jerusalem had become, a matter already explored earlier in the book. These texts also illustrate how the structure of the book is more concerned with thematic continuity than with chronological sequence. The episode of chapter 35 took place more than a decade before the events of chapter 34.

### THEOLOGICAL FOCUS

An example of simple faithfulness puts to shame the extravagant but hollow pretense of those who merely claim to be God's people. The pretense of obedience acted out by the Jerusalem nobility was impulsive and ephemeral. The determined fidelity of the Rechabites was a matter of consistent habit and deep commitment. Zedekiah and those around him had forgotten what it meant to place honor and integrity above convenience.

### PREACHING IDEA

Don't go for a good deal; go for a good life.

### PREACHING POINTERS

These two chapters are narratives; thus, the telling of the stories is of high importance. To make his point, Jeremiah employs a universal structure of the bad compared to the good. Zedekiah appears to be obedient, but in the end we see that he is just trying to make a deal with God. In contrast, the Rechabites are simply living out a lifestyle of a submissive heart.

Our culture is filled with a desire to make a good deal. The best deal is the win-win scenario, where both parties end up getting what they lack or need. When we try to make a deal with God, we forget that he has already won. There is nothing we have that he needs or lacks. He does, however, want our lifestyle to be one of submissive obedience.

# ZEDEKIAH COMPARED TO THE RECHABITES (34:1–35:19)

## LITERARY STRUCTURE AND THEMES

These two chapters could be handled separately; they concern separate incidents. However, they have been intentionally set together. They contrast the fickleness of the Jerusalem nobility, who in chapter 34 quickly violated their covenant to release all of their Jewish slaves, with the steadfast fidelity of the Rechabites, who in chapter 35 maintain their family tradition of drinking no wine. In the structure of the book, chapters 21–25 are balanced by 34–35.

- Chapters 21–23 describe how Zedekiah sought to have Jeremiah intercede for Jerusalem by asking YHWH, in a repeat of Hezekiah's Sennacherib miracle, to drive away Nebuchadnezzar. Jeremiah refused, and he pronounced in detail the sins of the house of David and of the Jerusalem aristocracy.
- Balancing this, chapter 34 describes how Zedekiah and the leading citizens sought YHWH's favor during the Babylonian crisis by entering a covenant to grant manumission to their Hebrew slaves. This failed because the Jerusalem aristocracy broke their covenant by enslaving again those whom they had manumitted.
- Chapter 25 contains a prophecy that Jerusalem and the nations would have to drink wine from the cup of YHWH's wrath whether they were willing or not (25:15–29).
- Balancing this, chapter 35 contains the narrative of an event that took place during the reign of Jehoiakim. Jeremiah took a group of Rechabites to a chamber in the temple precincts, set cups of wine before them, and commanded them to drink it. They refused, saying that drinking wine was a violation of a tribal taboo.

The structure of this text is:

- ***Zechariah's Broken Covenant (34:1–22)***
  *An Oracle for Zedekiah (34:1–7)*
  *The Broken Covenant (34:8–22)*
- ***The Example of the Rechabites (35:1–19)***

## EXPOSITION

### *Zedekiah's Broken Covenant (34:1–22)*

The oracle for Zedekiah comes from early in Nebuchadnezzar's siege of the city, probably in January of 588 (34:1, 6–7). It first declares that the city will fall, and that Zedekiah will go as a captive to Babylon (34:2–3). Verses 4–5, however, look like a blessing on Zedekiah. It significantly mitigates the decree of verses 2–3, and it asserts that Zedekiah will die "in peace" (בְּשָׁלוֹם תָּמוּת, v. 4). This is a problem because Zedekiah's demise appears to have been anything but peaceful. Against this, we could claim that this was fulfilled historically. Zedekiah was captured and died in Babylonia, presumably not by execution. Josephus claims that he had a state funeral (Josephus, *Antiquities* 10.154), although this is late testimony, and it may be a tradition created specifically to vindicate this prophecy. But this solution is unappealing. If losing your kingdom, seeing your city burned to the ground and your children cut down by the sword, having your eyes gouged out, and perishing in prison constitutes dying "in peace," then any death could be said to be such (see 39:5–7). Furthermore, there is reason to believe that his imprisonment was not a quiet confinement ending in a decent burial. Instead, he very well may have been set to slave labor, grinding grain in a Babylonian workhouse alongside common criminals, and dying there in ignominy (see commentary on 52:3b–11 below).

### *An Oracle for Zedekiah (34:1–7)*

**34:1–3**. Verse 1 emphasizes the hopelessness of the odds against Judah: "Nebuchadnezzar the King of Babylon and all his army and all the kingdoms of his imperial domain and all [their] ethnic groups were fighting against Jerusalem and all its towns." Judah, its capital city, and a handful of small towns stood against the world. In this situation, God spoke to Jeremiah. Verse 2 states unequivocally that the city will fall and be destroyed. The miracle of Isaiah and Hezekiah will not be repeated, and there is no conditional offer of reprieve. Similarly, verse 3 offers no route of escape for Zedekiah personally. He would be captured, be brought as a prisoner before Nebuchadnezzar, and be taken as a captive to Babylon. But this does not mean that his fate had to be what in fact did transpire—that the last act he would witness before being blinded was the execution of his sons. There was still the possibility that things could go reasonably well for him, albeit in the condition of a defeated, captive, and now deposed king.

**34:4–5**. The transitional line in verse 4 ("Yet hear the word of YHWH!") is ambiguous. It could simply mean that YHWH has something more to say. Or it could imply a condition, as if it said, "But things will be better for you if you give heed to what YHWH says." Together with 21:8–9 and 38:17–18, one implied condition might be that Zedekiah surrender to the Babylonians (Holladay 1989, 233–34). More generally, the condition is that Zedekiah must show fidelity to YHWH and give heed to Jeremiah's admonitions. Zedekiah at times did this, and the prophetic blessing acknowledges positive aspects of his behavior. Still, we should not isolate this text from all the warnings and exhortations Jeremiah gave Zedekiah.

The king would not die by the sword but die in peace (לֹא תָמוּת בֶּחָרֶב: בְּשָׁלוֹם תָּמוּת; vv. 4–5). This is probably not an unconditional guarantee. The Hebrew *yiqtol* (imperfect) is not always future indicative in meaning; it is often more subjunctive, and לֹא תָמוּת בֶּחָרֶב could mean "You need not die by the sword" rather than "You will not die by the sword." Even seemingly irrevocable promises can be called back in the face of gross disobedience. An example is the address to Eli in 1 Samuel 2:30: "Therefore YHWH God of Israel says, 'I did in fact say that your house and the house of your father would walk before me forever.' But now the message of YHWH is: 'Far be it from me; for those who honor me I will honor, and those who despise me shall be treated badly.'" The following factors help us to understand what is meant by the conditional promise to Zedekiah and why, in the end, things went so badly for him.

First, as mentioned above, we must interpret dying "in peace" against the story of Josiah, Zedekiah's father. Huldah promised that Josiah would die in peace, but he in fact was slain while fighting Pharaoh Neco (2 Kings 22:20; 23:29). Josiah's death was said to be "in peace" because he did not live to see Jerusalem fall and because he ended his life with courage and in faith. Jeremiah asserted that Josiah died in God's favor and contrasted his life and death with those of his sons (Jer. 22:10–23). With the allusion to Huldah's prophecy, Jeremiah gave Zedekiah the opportunity to share his father's fate. In fact, verses 4–5 offers nothing less—and nothing more—than a good death. Zedekiah should have resisted his officials and shown obedience to YHWH by surrendering to Babylon, by preventing the people from reclaiming their slaves, and by openly opposing the hostility to Jeremiah. He did none of these things. If he had, the analogy to Josiah is no promise of a long life. Like his father, he would have perished with his honor intact. His experience before Nebuchadnezzar would have gone far differently, and his captivity and death would have been peaceful. He could have ended his life being treated well by his captors, as Jehoiachin did, and with his countrymen recognizing that he had done the right thing by surrendering to Nebuchadnezzar and sparing the city much bloodshed. They would have mourned him with the words, "Alas [for our] lord [king]!" (הוֹי אָדוֹן).

Second, Zedekiah's moral weakness played a role in the story. He did some good things, seeking to protect Jeremiah and making a covenant with the nation for the manumission of all Jewish slaves. But he feared and submitted to the aristocratic hatred of Jeremiah, and his manumission of the slaves backfired when the upper classes rounded up and forced their recently freed slaves back into servitude. This final failure meant that Zedekiah's demise was truly terrible and ignominious.

Third, the account of the broken covenant, described in verses 8–22, sheds light on verses 4–5. Covenant-breaking was heinous, and the reversal of the manumission showed that Zedekiah and company had no regard for even a freshly made covenant, to say nothing of the hoary Sinai covenant. The leaders of that generation, by repudiating their covenant to release their claims on their slaves, showed that no promises made to God had meaning for them.

Fourth, verse 13, in which YHWH speaks of how he redeemed Israel from the land of slavery, recalls the whole account of the exodus. In the narrative, Pharaoh first released the Hebrews but then regretted his actions and tried to recapture them, losing his whole army to the Red Sea in the process (Exod. 14). Zedekiah failed to restrain his nobles from doing the same, and he too would suffer a horrible defeat.

In summary, 34:4–5 should not be regarded as an unconditional promise of salvation for Zedekiah. Defeat was already certain, but the king had the opportunity to die with honor. Through his moral unsteadiness, he lost that opportunity.

**34:6–7**. Jeremiah gave the message to Zedekiah while the noose was tightening around Jerusalem. All the outlying towns except Lachish and Azekah had fallen, and these were under siege. Both towns were fortified centers on hilltops in the Shephelah. Lachish had once before been besieged and taken by Sennacherib in 701; and now, in 588, it faced the Babylonians. Among the small missives inscribed on potsherds found there, the "Lachish Letters," number 4 states that the men at Lachish can no longer see the fire-signal from Azekah, implying that at the time of writing it had already fallen (see Hallo and Younger, Jr. 2003, 3.80). One can visit Tel Lachish National Park in modern Israel today.

### *The Broken Covenant (34:8–22)*

The leaders of Jerusalem attempted to win YHWH's favor by retroactively doing what they should have been doing through all their history, that is, providing manumission for their Jewish slaves. The text does not imply that God had said that if they did this, the siege would be lifted and they would be saved from the Babylonians. The idea appears to have originated with Zedekiah. But as it turns out, the point is moot, because they quickly reneged on the manumission and brought the Jews back into slavery.

**34:8–10**. Zedekiah's covenant and its subsequent reneging was the occasion for the prophecy; God did not command Zedekiah to make this covenant. The covenant was a mutual pledge before God that they would release their slaves. Legally, there was no need for a covenant; it was just a matter of keeping the commands of the Law. Perhaps the king thought that if he had the people enter into such a covenant they would adhere to its terms and not enslave again those they had freed. Verse 10 says that both the officials and the people agreed to this. That is, every person of means—anyone who could afford to own slaves—joined the process. The passage says that they would "release" their slaves (שׁלח, the same word regularly used for the release of the Hebrews from Egypt in Exodus). It is possible that the release was done informally, without legal documentation of manumission. Otherwise, one wonders how they could have so easily forced them back into bondage.

**34:11**. The owners then "went back" (וַיָּשׁוּבוּ) on the deal. The root שׁוב can be used of repentance, but here it refers to going back on a promise. They "subjected them" (וַיִּכְבְּשׁוּם) again to servitude. The word כבשׁ means to forcibly (often by violence) bring someone into compliance and submission. It can be used of rape (Esth. 7:8; Neh. 5:5), but it is also used of enslaving people (Neh. 5:5; 2 Chron. 28:10) or of conquering a land (Num. 32:22; Josh. 18:1).

**34:12–13**. The word from YHWH first refers to the Egyptian bondage, because that was the great reproach from which God had delivered Israel. Because of the exodus event, the very idea of Israelites being kept in slavery should have been repugnant to all the people. It was a repudiation of the greatest event in their history.

**34:14–16**. The prophecy cites the command first given in Exodus 21:2–6 and repeated in Deuteronomy 15:12–18, the gist of which is that an Israelite slave should be released in the seventh year; none should serve more than six years. But this law had long been ignored. The recent act of manumission was a good and proper if belated step in the right direction. The covenant was, so to speak, a nice touch, although not strictly necessary. The covenant did, however, make their guilt even more extreme. They went back to their former disobedience and, on top of that, violated a solemn oath before God.

**34:17**. In a highly sarcastic turn of phrase, YHWH declares that since Jerusalem refused to give "freedom" (דְּרוֹר) to their slaves, he would give Jerusalem the "freedom" to experience defeat, plague, famine, and terror.

**34:18–20**. Sadly, everyone in Jerusalem (including the slaves) would experience the terrors of the siege, but God promises special punishment to the covenant violators. This passage is important for understanding ritual and its meaning in ancient Israel. It tells us that a common manner of enacting a covenant was to cut a sacrifice into two halves and to walk between the pieces. The implied meaning of the act was that if a man were to go through the ritual but break the oath, he too should be violently slain just as the sacrifice had been. The meaning conveyed was, "If I violate this covenant, may what happened to this animal be done to me." The people of Jerusalem did violate the covenant, and God promised that they would fare no better than the calf whose pieces they had walked between. Their bodies would be torn asunder and left for the beasts to devour.

**34:21–22**. We learn an important piece of background information in verse 21. The leaders of Jerusalem broke their covenant and took back their slaves because they thought the danger to them had passed. Pharaoh Hophra's army appeared on the scene and forced Nebuchadnezzar's army to break off the siege and move away to face the threat. People thought that the danger was over, that the Babylonians would soon have to withdraw to their homeland, and that Jerusalem was free to behave with impunity before God. But the Egyptians quickly withdrew, and Babylon came back to resume the siege. By then, the people had broken their covenant, and they had only increased their guilt before God.

### *The Example of the Rechabites (35:1–19)*

During the reign of Jehoiakim, a nomadic people called the Rechabites fled to the vicinity of Jerusalem because Nebuchadnezzar of Babylon had "invaded the land" (35:11). Jeremiah took a group of these Rechabites to a chamber of the temple and tried to persuade them to drink wine. They refused, citing a taboo handed down from their ancestor Jehonadab son of Rechab (35:6–8).

The Rechabites were a subgroup of Kenites (1 Chron. 2:55). They were pastoral nomads, traveling from place to place with their flocks. For them, drinking wine was emblematic of embracing the life of the settled farmer. After they rejected the wine, Jeremiah gave a sermon comparing the stubborn disobedience of Jerusalem to the stubborn loyalty of the Rechabites, and promising that YHWH would bring disaster upon the city (25:12–17). They approached Jerusalem while heading toward the south because they wanted to avoid coming into proximity with military forces that were operating in the north. Their livestock would have been tempting and easy prey for any army they crossed (and armies in the ancient world were always hungry for provisions). While they were at Jerusalem, Jeremiah took them to the temple area and tried to get them to drink wine. They refused because this was against rules handed down from their ancestors. Their fidelity to their ancestral rules stood in contrast to Jerusalem's disregard for the rules of the Sinai covenant. There is, however, a historical problem.

The story indicates that Jeremiah still had access to the temple, but he was excluded from the temple in 604. However, the Rechabites say that they were fleeing Nebuchadnezzar's army. This seems to imply that the episode of Jeremiah 35 took place in around 598, during the first siege of Jerusalem (this siege resulted in the Jehoiachin deportation in 597). This creates a contradiction because Jeremiah at this time should not have had access to the temple.

The best solution is that the incident took place before Jeremiah was excluded from the temple. We know that Nebuchadnezzar conducted a campaign in "Hatti land" (the area of Syria, Lebanon, and Israel) in 605–604 B.C. We also know that Jehoiakim made a formal submission to the Babylonians at this time, sending hostages to Babylon in around 605 B.C. (Dan 1:1). This act of submission does not imply that Jerusalem had been under siege by Babylon; it only means that Babylonian forces were in the region and that as a matter of prudence Jerusalem offered the formal tokens of obedience to Babylon, which included hostages (with Daniel among them). The Rechabites, as indicated, had been somewhere in the north and, not wanting to be caught with their livestock near any troop movements, headed south. Along the way, they passed by Jerusalem. However, Jeremiah 35 does not imply that there was fighting in the immediate neighborhood when they were at Jerusalem, much less that the city was under siege. The Rechabites were simply staying prudently far away from any military activity. They pitched their tents at (not inside) the city, had their meeting with Jeremiah, and moved on. In short, the event took place around 605, before Jeremiah was excluded from the temple. There was no fighting and no army outside the walls when the Rechabites were there. They were merely intent on keeping as much distance as possible between themselves and combatant forces. The event did not take place in 598, during the siege that resulted in the captivity of Jehoiachin, but happened in 605, when Jeremiah was still free to enter the temple district. For a full exploration of Jeremiah's life and times, see the companion volume, *Jeremiah: Composition, Setting, and Message.*

The whole episode was an object lesson: the Rechabites obey the rules handed down from Jehonadab, but the Jerusalemites do not obey YHWH. Three other aspects of the narrative are noteworthy:

- Jeremiah took the Rechabites to the temple to offer them wine. We might not expect the temple to be the place to do this. But symbolically the temple (Zion) was the counterpart to Sinai, the place of the giving of the covenant. The setting thus reinforced the contrast between the fidelity of the Rechabites to their traditions and the infidelity of Israel to the covenant.
- According to 2 Kings 10:15–23, "Jehonadab son of Rechab" was an ally of Jehu when he slaughtered the house of Ahab and the priests of Baal. The name and episode resonated in the new context. It implied that another slaughter of wicked Israelite rulers and priests was imminent.
- The Rechabites refusal of an offer of wine from YHWH's prophet contrasts with the prophecy that YHWH would force the nations to drink the wine of his wrath (Jer. 25:15–29).

**35:1–5**. Jeremiah received a word from YHWH during Jehoiakim's reign. At God's behest, the prophet invited Rechabites to one of the rooms along the side of the temple. We know little about the precise layout of the temple; we only know that it had a series of chambers along the two long sides of the sanctuary. The specific information the text provides, that the chamber was "next to the chamber of the officials, which was over that of Maaseiah son of Shallum" (v. 4) is of little help to us. We also know nothing about Jaazaniah son of Jeremiah beyond what is in this passage; he was apparently the leader of the Rechabites.

**35:6–10**. The Rechabites refused Jeremiah's offer of wine because they lived under the rule of their forefather Jehonadab, which made wine taboo. It is not likely that drunkenness was the reason for the prohibition. Instead, it is that wine production requires a lengthy process of cultivation, harvest, preparation, fermentation, and aging of the juices of the grapes. This absolutely required the establishment of permanent settlements, but the chosen life of the Rechabites was that of the nomadic shepherd. From verse 7, which forbids the building of houses and the cultivation of any kind of crop, it is clear that this, and not intoxication, was the main concern. Wine, however, is an intensely attractive and enticing product; it could easily draw the people toward a sedentary way of life (the cultivation of a vineyard requires years of work and preparation even before a usable grape harvest comes in). Thus wine, but no other agricultural product, was prohibited. The main point of the rule is that they were to live in tents as "nomads" (גָּרִים).

**35:11**. This verse does not imply that the Babylonian army was outside the gates at the time of this incident. The Rechabites say that they fled toward Jerusalem "when Nebuchadnezzar came up into the land" (בַּעֲלוֹת נְבוּכַדְרֶאצַּר מֶלֶךְ־בָּבֶל אֶל־הָאָרֶץ). The phrase "the land" (הָאָרֶץ) does not imply that the Babylonian army was in Judah. If "the land" refers to Israel, it could easily refer to the traditional northern parts of the land, the region around Dan and the Sea of Galilee. But in fact, it need not refer to Israel at all. It simply denotes wherever the Rechabites were when they fled south. Also, appearances notwithstanding, the text does not imply that Nebuchadnezzar was personally present with the army they fled from. The Bible routinely speaks of Nebuchadnezzar as the conqueror of Jerusalem, as though he were present with the army when it fell, when in fact he was far away in Syria when his army conquered Judah.

**35:12–17**. The oracle from YHWH draws attention to the contrast between the Rechabites and the people of Jerusalem, with the former being faithful to the rule of their forefather and the latter being unfaithful to the Law and the prophets. This added only one more reason that the city would fall.

**35:18–19**. When God speaks of having a man "to stand before me" (עֹמֵד לְפָנָי), it generally implies priestly or prophetic service (Deut. 4:10; 10:8; 1 Kings 17:1; 18:15; Jer. 15:19). But it is unlikely that this is what God was promising Jehonadab, who was not even an Israelite. It probably means that the Rechabites would always have among their people those who knew and served YHWH. We have little certain information about what became of the Rechabites after this episode. Nehemiah 3:14 mentions that a certain "Malkijah son of Rechab" did work on the Dung Gate at Jerusalem in Nehemiah's time.

## THEOLOGICAL FOCUS

Each of chapters 34 and 35 has significant lessons on its own, but together they create a powerful contrast. Major emphases are as follows:

- Zedekiah inherited a very bad situation, and a glorious and triumphant reign was never a possibility for him. But he could have ended well and died with honor; he need not have come to such a horrible end. But he was weak and lacked courageous faith. For many of us, a long, peaceful, and blessed life is out of reach, but if we are faithful, we can live and die well.
- Zedekiah and his peers in Jerusalem made a sudden and convulsive effort to appease God by making a covenant and releasing the slaves. But those who serve God faithfully need do none of this. For such people, obedience is a long habit, and the taking of oaths to God is superfluous. Oath-taking is more likely among the unrighteous than the righteous.
- But if one does take an oath before God, it is a terrible thing to break it. Such behavior only compounds one's guilt.
- The people of Jerusalem despised Israel's heritage and the great work of God in the exodus when they kept their own people as slaves. Slavery is a degrading condition, but for the Israelites it was almost a repudiation of the exodus. We too should be zealous for the dignity and freedom we have in Christ.
- The fidelity of the Rechabites put the behavior of the people of Judah to shame. We too may at times see members of other religions and denominations and feel that our theology is far superior to theirs, and yet be shamed by their faithfulness and integrity.
- The vow of the Rechabites to abstain from wine has importance for us who enjoy the freedom of Christ. The Rechabites were absolutely consistent in keeping their tradition, but they did not demand that others keep the same rule. As far as we can tell, they did not consider the Israelites immoral for drinking wine or living in houses. But the Rechabite rule was necessary for them to maintain the nomadic and pastoral life that they cherished. In Christ, we have the freedom to live by rules and restraints that we impose on ourselves. Someone who wastes enormous amounts of time watching television may go on a temporary or permanent "fast" from television or movies. Someone who struggles with pornography may abstain from using the internet, or may live by other rules, such as never being online alone. From a variety of convictions and personal needs, one may adapt rules regarding food and drink. Such "taboos" can be very helpful in learning to adopt a disciplined life and to free oneself from addictions. But unless something is forbidden in Scripture, we must not make what is a rule for us into a universal rule, demanding that everyone follow it. We do not all fight the same battles.

## PREACHING AND TEACHING STRATEGIES

### *Exegetical and Theological Synthesis*

Jeremiah is structured purposely to put these two stories together. Zedekiah seems to be bargaining with God. He obeys God to a point and apparently thinks that he has had enough obedience to warrant God's favor. This a is a great misunderstanding of how we are to relate to God. We can never buy God's favor. We can't cut a deal with God. Jeremiah doesn't leave us with what *not* to do. He gives us the positive example of the Rechabites. Their lifestyle of submission to authority is what our lives should be like.

God desires us to have a life of obedience and submission to him. We don't make deals with him; rather, we live our lives with him and in submission to him. Our acts of kindness are not sporadic. Our seeking reconciliation is not conditional. We daily put our hope in his good hand. We seek to serve others. Obedience and submission to God is how we live. For those of us under the new covenant, that begins with our trust in Christ and continues by his empowerment to live such a life.

### *Preaching Idea*

Don't go for a good deal; go for a good life.

### *Contemporary Connections*

#### *What does it mean?*

Zedekiah wasn't submitting to God—he was trying to make a deal with God.

Years ago, I heard this story that parallels the thoughts and actions of Zedekiah and the Israelite aristocracy. Two men were traveling in a small airplane run by a local airline that used smaller planes. They cordially chatted about where they lived, family, and work. One talked about his manufacturing business that was doing very well and expanding each month. It was clear that he perceived himself as being skillful at making deals. Before the other man, a pastor, could describe his work, the conversation suddenly ended due to unexpected turbulence. It was not only troublesome but downright scary. Seat belts were fastened even more tightly. The cabin crew buckled down and didn't even have time to pick up the plastic cups and empty snack wrappers. Between the bumps, drops, and sudden uplifts the businessman said, just barely above a whisper, "Lord, if you will get me down on the ground safely, I'll give you half of everything I make."

After what seemed hours but was only a few minutes, the pilot changed altitude, the turbulence began to ease, and the plane made a smooth landing. As they were waiting for their luggage, the pastor stepped over to the businessman, handed him his card, and said. "I heard the promise you made to God. That is really generous of you. And if you need help in knowing how and where to fulfill that promise, let me know."

The businessman responded, "Tell you what, parson; I made God a better deal. I told him if I ever fly in that small an airplane again, he can have it all." It was clear that his promise was made out of fear, not out of submission.

Zedekiah followed this same pattern. We could modernize Zedekiah's conversation: "OK God, here's the deal: we will obey you and free the slaves like we should have done, and you will save us from Nebuchadnezzar. . . . Oh wait, God, the danger has passed, so we really don't need to obey you. But thanks anyway."

In contrast to Zedekiah's action is that of the Rechabites. They obeyed the tradition laid out by their forefather. They weren't trying to make a deal. They were motivated not by fear but by respect for the authority of their forefather. They had a lifestyle of submission to authority; in their case it was human tradition, possibly linked to their lifestyle. They listened to—that is, they submitted to—their forefather's authority. One must remember that this narrative is illustrative—not of the object of their submission but their ongoing submissive lifestyle. If one uses this as a command to not drink wine, then one must also agree to live in tents. The point that is being affirmed is the attitude and lifestyle of submission.

*Is it true?*

Our world admires someone who can make a good deal, but deals are made between parties that both need something. We want a deal that is "win-win," with both parties feeling that the deal met their needs. But how can we, with our great needs, negotiate with one who has no needs? God wants us to win, and for us it comes through a lifestyle exemplified by a submissive, obedient heart.

*Now what?*

Is our obedience more of making a deal with God, like Zedekiah? Perhaps not as overtly, we make emotional deals. We expect to feel good when we do good things. We assume that when we take some food to a family in a crisis, we will feel appreciated. Perhaps our deals are more in the area of material things; we know it is right to give a percentage to the church, so we give assuming that if we do this our finances will improve. How about relational deals? It could be in the context of a marriage, a work relationship, or a friendship. A conflict results in some kind of separation, so we go to God saying that we're going to do our part, expecting this relationship to improve. We don't consciously think about it as a deal with God, but our obedience might come not out of a submissive spirit but out of a fear of losing a relationship, or out of a desire to gain something. In short, we try to make a deal with God. God doesn't play *Let's Make a Deal.*

I was blessed with a very generous father. It wasn't something he did occasionally; it was his lifestyle. A friend and I had been on an overnight trip to Mr. Haygood's farm, where he let us drive the tractor and hunt in the woods. Mr. Haygood was dropping me off at my home late one Saturday evening. As my dad thanked him for his kindness, Mr. Haygood asked if my dad happened to have an extra three-pronged electrical plug. He needed it and it was too late to buy one. I'll never forget what my dad did. First, he said, "Sure." Then, he went into the garage, and without Mr. Haygood seeing it my dad cut the plug off a perfectly good extension cord and gave it to him. Afterward, I asked my dad about what he did. He responded in a matter-of-fact way, "The man needed a plug. I can always get another one." It was a lifestyle.

### Creativity in Presentation

As with other pericopes, these two chapters can be presented more clearly using the pulpit or stage area. After introducing the sermon, move to the right side (speaker's right) of the area to present the story of Zedekiah. Use the left side for the story of the Rechabites. Then move to the center areas to show the contrast and the application. By using the two sides of the platform, one can draw the parallels more clearly. For example, stand on the left side when highlighting that the Rechabites received Jeremiah's command in the temple. Then move to the right side, highlighting that the Israelites received God's commands at Sinai. Bring these two different settings together by standing in the center to point out that both places were very sacred.

In the application portion, the two sides could be referred to by asking on which side we find ourselves. Sometimes people will put up the excuse that they could never live a life of total submission to God and dismiss the application as being too difficult. A great way to encourage our people is to ask them to at least take a step toward the correct side: weekly attendance, giving consistently, or committing to prayer every morning. Our Lord is worthy of a lifestyle of submission to him.

The text clearly has two parts, which can be presented in a straightforward manner:

- Don't try to make a good deal with God (34:1–22).
- Live the good life he offers, through a lifestyle of submission to him (35:1–19).

Another structure can be to present both stories and then compare and contrast, which can lead into the application:

- Present the two stories (34:1–35:19).
- Compare and contrast:
  - Zedekiah tried to make a good deal.
  - The Rechabites lived a submissive life.
- Application: Don't go for a good deal; go for a good life.

## DISCUSSION QUESTIONS

1. What are some secrets to negotiating a deal—for example, in business or with your child?
2. When have you been involved in making a deal?
3. What kind of listening takes place in negotiations?
4. What kind of listening takes place in submitting to God?
5. What are some ongoing acts of submission in your life toward God?

# Jeremiah 36:1–32

**EXEGETICAL IDEA**

The incident described here, in which Jehoiakim destroyed a scroll containing an oracular message from Jeremiah, demonstrates how bitterly and completely the royal house and the aristocracy were opposed to the word of God. As described in the introduction, it also tells us how what originally was a loose collection of sermon transcripts and letters from Jeremiah began to take shape as the book of Jeremiah. It, like Jeremiah's realization that he could no longer intercede for the people, is a decisive moment in the prophet's story.

**THEOLOGICAL FOCUS**

A decisive rejection of the word of God leads to decisive ruin. Also, attempts to eradicate the word of God inevitably fail. Through his blasphemous actions, Jehoiakim showed himself to be one of the great reprobates of the Bible. When Josiah heard the Law read aloud, he tore his garments in grief and repentance. When his son Jehoiakim heard the scroll of Jeremiah read aloud, he tore up the scroll and burned it.

**PREACHING IDEA**

Rejection of the written Word of God is a rejection of God and leads to ruin.

**PREACHING POINTERS**

Baruch was to write down all the words that God gave to Jeremiah. This was no simple task; it must have taken weeks, perhaps months of work. Thus, the written copy is a very valuable and costly item. When Jehoiakim burns the scroll, it was not like the modern burning of a single copy of a book that has thousands of copies still usable. This was the only copy. Jehoiakim's rejection of God's message cannot be missed or overstated; it was as if he was trying to erase the words that had been spoken.

This story is presented in such a way as to show that Baruch's written copy of God's words to Jeremiah is equal in authority to the spoken words of Jeremiah. To reject the written words is to reject the spoken words. Of course, the application of those words in the church today will vary from the direct application for the ancient Jews. The thrust is that God's written Word is the same as his spoken words.

# JEHOIAKIM AND THE SCROLL (36:1–32)

## LITERARY STRUCTURE AND THEMES

Jeremiah 36:1–45:5 contains a series of narrative episodes recounting how Jeremiah and his message were rejected and indeed hated by his people, and describing the final result of that process: the destruction of Jerusalem and the fall of the Davidic dynasty. Within the narratives are interspersed various messages given by Jeremiah. The series of episodes is loosely chronological, proceeding from the reign of Jehoiakim to that of Zedekiah and the fall of the city, and then to the experience of Jeremiah with the Jewish refugees in Egypt. In many details, however, the account is nonsequential, with various episodes moved out of their chronological position for structural purposes. The series begins with Jehoiakim's burning of Jeremiah's scroll in the fourth year of his reign, an event in which Baruch was intimately involved (chapter 36); and it ends with an oracle from Jeremiah to Baruch that was given in that same year (chapter 45). These two events bookend the whole series.

As described in the Introduction, Jeremiah 36 is crucial for understanding the history of the composition of the book of Jeremiah. It is the account of the writing of the "Baruch Scroll," which Jehoiakim burned. As I have argued above, I believe that the scroll contained some (but not all) of the prophecies contained in Jeremiah 2–20 and that it ended with Jeremiah 25:3–13a. Furthermore, this was the very earliest version of a compiled "book" of Jeremiah. Various oracles were added to it, including the oracles against the nations (now located at Jer. 46–51). The scroll was the core of what finally became our present book.

Jeremiah 36 is also of great theological and structural significance, as it marks the decisive repudiation of Jeremiah and his prophecies by the king, and by most of the nobility and common people. From that point forward, the destruction of Judah was a foregone conclusion. Thus, chapters 36–45 recount that process.

- ***The Background to the Reading of the Scroll (36:1–8)***
- ***The Scroll Read in the Temple Precincts (36:9–10)***
- ***The Scroll Read in the Palace (36:11–19)***
- ***The Burning of the Scroll (36:20–26)***
- ***Jeremiah and Baruch Produce Another Scroll (36:27–32)***

## EXPOSITION

### *The Background to the Reading of the Scroll (36:1–8)*

**36:1–2.** The writing of this scroll was in a sense the culmination of Jeremiah's preaching ministry to Judah, even though it came about long before he completed his work. The event took place in about 605 B.C., and Jeremiah would continue to preach and interact with the people and their rulers through to the fall of Jerusalem and after, until perhaps 570 B.C. But at the time of receiving this command, Jeremiah had already been preaching through the latter years of Josiah's reign and into the beginning of Jehoiakim's. Many of the oracles of chapters 1–20 came from this early period of his ministry. His message had been decisively rejected, and the contents of the scroll presented in detail the sins of the nation and the final judgment God had decreed against it. Although there would still be appeals for repentance, the decree was final. Jerusalem would be destroyed, the temple would be burned down, and the dynasty of David would fall. Everything that came after the reading of this scroll was in some measure anticlimactic.

**36:3**. The possibility of repentance described here is not disingenuous, but it does not imply that the decree of Jerusalem's destruction that is to follow is subject to cancellation. It is a statement of God's character—that he always wants to forgive and relent from punishing. With God, of course, there is no "perhaps" (אוּלַי) in the literal sense. We have seen already that God forbade Jeremiah from continuing to make intercession for Judah, the reason being that God knew they were incurably apostate and were no more capable of repentance than a leopard was of changing its spots. Nevertheless, it is in God's character to continue to hold out the possibility of revival and restoration. God's decree was irrevocable not because God was stubborn but because his people were.

**36:4**. Jeremiah's trusted scribe Baruch would of course be the one to write out the scroll. Translations regularly indicated that Jeremiah dictated the words of the scroll; the text literally says, "And Baruch wrote from the mouth of Jeremiah (מִפִּי יִרְמְיָהוּ) all the words of YHWH that he had spoken to him on a scroll." The common translation "dictated" is not incorrect, but it may lead readers to believe that the scroll contained a verbatim and complete account of everything Jeremiah had preached up to this point. In reality, what we have in Jeremiah 2–20 can only be a short summation of his messages. Instead of saying that the Spirit inspired Jeremiah to remember everything over the years verbatim, it is better to say that the Spirit inspired him accurately and adequately give the gist of his sermons.

**36:5–8**. We do not know precisely when or why Jeremiah was excluded from the temple precincts. The most probable cause was his preaching of the "temple sermon" of 7:1–15. Jeremiah 26:1–9 indicates that the prophet delivered this message at the beginning of Jehoiakim's reign in the temple precincts. He preached from the courtyard of the temple, and his message declared that this temple was no better than the Shiloh sanctuary, which the Philistines had destroyed (7:12; 26:6). The people had a superstitious faith that the mere presence of the temple made Jerusalem inviolable; they recited the chant "the temple of YHWH" as a talisman against any destruction coming upon them, even though they had not repented of their idolatry and immorality (7:4–10). Goaded by the priests, they were so enraged at Jeremiah's rebuke that they wanted him put to death (26:7–9). This, it seems clear, would have led to prohibiting Jeremiah from again coming near the temple. Thus, here in chapter 36, Jeremiah sent Baruch as his proxy. Jeremiah told Baruch to read the scroll "on a day of fasting" (בְּיוֹם צוֹם). This was not done on a prescribed, regular fast day but on the fifth day of the ninth month of the year, probably December of 605. For some unknown reason, the authorities had called for a fast on that day. We can imagine at least two reasons Jeremiah wanted the scroll to be read that day. First, as a fast day, it was a ritual of repentance—but the people had no genuine repentance in their hearts, and the scroll reminded them that a superficial turn to YHWH had no value. Jeremiah, at least formally, held out the hope that the message of the scroll could change their ritualized repentance into a real revival (36:7). Second, a large crowd would have been present on this day, and Jeremiah wanted the message to be heard by as many as possible. Baruch did as he was told and read the entire scroll (36:8). Baruch evidently had some prestige, both because of the prominence of his family and because of his status as Jeremiah's scribe. He was thus able to get an audience and read the message.

### *The Scroll Read in the Temple Precincts (36:9–10)*

**36:9–10**. As expected, a very large crowd was present from all over Judah. He read it from the chamber of Gemariah son of Shaphan, "at the upper courtyard" (בֶּחָצֵר הָעֶלְיוֹן) of the "new entrance of the gate of YHWH's house." Our knowledge of the layout of the temple is limited, but it appears that this chamber had something like a balcony overlooking the "new entrance," and that this was the primary gateway for people to enter. Thus, Baruch was able to address the whole assembly. Thematically, moreover, reading the scroll of condemnation from this location was highly significant. Shaphan had been a high official in Josiah's reign and been entrusted with overseeing the restoration of the temple. When a scroll of the Law was found, it was reported to Shaphan, who in turn read the scroll to the king (2 Kings 22:3–10). Thus, Shaphan father of Gemariah read to King Josiah the Law of Moses, with its warnings of punishments the nation would endure if they broke their covenant with YHWH. Baruch, in turn, in the reign of Jehoiakim son of Josiah, standing in the chamber of Gemariah, read YHWH's decree of the destruction of Jerusalem—a decree that had been given through Moses's counterpart, Jeremiah the prophet.

### *The Scroll Read in the Palace (36:11–19)*

**36:11–12**. Micaiah, son of Gemariah and grandson of Shaphan, recognizing the significance of the words Baruch read, quickly made his way from the temple precinct to the royal palace (that is, he went from the temple mount south to the old Jebusite Jerusalem, the area called the "city of David" in modern Jerusalem). As Gemariah's son, he obviously had access to the chamber of Gemariah, from which Baruch read the scroll (he may have been standing beside Baruch while he read it). In the palace, he found a group of senior officials and told them that Jeremiah's scribe had read a message of harsh condemnation within the temple grounds and by that had effectively circumvented the prohibition against Jeremiah's coming within the gates of the temple court. As far as we can tell, Micaiah did not act out of hostility to Baruch and Jeremiah. Verse 19 indicates that he and his colleagues urged Baruch and Jeremiah to go into hiding, and Micaiah's father Gemariah later urged the king not to burn the scroll (v. 25). Why then did Micaiah hasten to report what had happened? There was no doubt, first of all, that word of the incident would soon reach Jehoiakim; there was no avoiding that. It is likely that Micaiah sought out a few like-minded leaders to try to map out a strategy for damage control. They wanted to manage how the news reached the king.

**36:13–16**. Baruch, having finished reading the scroll, may have stayed in the temple area to interact with people, or (as is more likely) he may have gone home. Whichever it was, the officials with whom Micaiah conferred were able to locate him quickly and bring him to their office. The men who had not been at the temple would have wanted to hear its contents for themselves, and thus they had Baruch read the whole thing over again in their presence. When they heard it, they were "filled with dread" (פָּחֲדוּ). What was the source of this dread? Two answers present themselves, and both may be true. First, Jeremiah had claimed in God's name that the final judgment on Jerusalem was near. An unthinkable event, the fall of the city, would soon take place amid starvation and warfare. Second, they knew that Jehoiakim would react to this scroll with rage, lashing out at the prophet and creating a new crisis in the city's internal social life. When the officials declared that they had to report this to the king (v. 16), it was again not as though there were any chance of hiding it from him. They at least showed that they were not slack in doing their duty to the king.

**36:17–19**. The purpose of the interrogation of Baruch is not difficult to fathom. The officials had to be sure that the words of the scroll actually came from Jeremiah and that they were not fabricated by Baruch. For all the antagonism directed toward Jeremiah, he was still widely recognized as a true prophet, as shown by how Zedekiah sought him out for a word from God (as at Jer. 38:14). Thus, the question of whether the words of condemnation came from Jeremiah was a matter of utmost seriousness; they could not be lightly dismissed. Some people in Jerusalem regarded Baruch as the evil genius behind Jeremiah, prompting the prophet to issue messages of judgment against the people (Jer. 43:3). But Baruch assured them that the words were Jeremiah's own; Baruch had only acted as a secretary, faithfully writing down no more and no less than what Jeremiah had said. Convinced that the scroll represented the true prophecies of Jeremiah, the officials urged both prophet and scribe to go into hiding, for they knew that the king's anger would know no limits. Knowing how extensive Jehoiakim's network of sycophants was, they told Baruch to let no one know their hiding place.

### *The Burning of the Scroll (36:20–26)*

**36:20–21**. Elishama is here called "the scribe" (הַסֹּפֵר), but the word here evidently refers to the chief scribe of the kingdom; it is sometimes translated "the secretary." Elishama occupied the same office that had once been held by Shaphan, father of Gemariah and grandfather of Micaiah. Being the royal keeper of records, Elishama was naturally entrusted with Baruch's scroll. Jehudi was sent to fetch the scroll and bring it to the king. Jehudi was evidently a scribe as well, since he was the one who read out the scroll before the king (v. 23). It is curious that Jehudi's genealogy goes back to his great-grandfather Cushi (v. 14). The name Cushi (כּוּשִׁי) means "Cushite man," and the name Jehudi (יְהוּדִי) means "Jewish man." It is thus possible that Jehudi was descended from an immigrant from Cush, with the name Jehudi referring to his status as a fully naturalized citizen (Berridge 1992b). Another official at the palace, Ebed-melek, was also a Cushite (Jer. 38:7).

**36:22–26**. It being the "ninth month" (Kislev, late November and early December), Jehoiakim was in the royal winter quarters. Scholars differ over whether this was a separate wing of the palace or a different building altogether (Lundbom 2008b, 604). Regardless, it was probably constructed to be less open to breezes, and it had some kind of fire pit or brazier (מְבֹעֶרֶת, lit., "burning place") for heating the chamber. The full scroll was read for the third time that day. This suggests that it was fairly short (Thompson 1980, 627). We may speculate that this, the very first version of the book of Jeremiah, contained no more than the equivalent of five chapters of our current book. Jehoiakim showed his contempt for Jeremiah's prophecies by systematically burning the manuscript as Jehudi read through it. The material was probably papyrus and not leather, and thus it burned easily. The knife in question probably belonged to Jehudi, as he was apparently a scribe. Jehoiakim and his courtiers showed no fear of YHWH and did not tear their garments in grief at the words of the prophecy. This dramatically contrasts with his father Josiah's response when he heard the words of the Law read out. He not only tore his robes but called on the prophetess Huldah for a fresh word from God (2 Kings 22:11–13). Jehoiakim sent for the prophet Jeremiah—but only to arrest him, not to seek a word from YHWH. Of all the nobility, only Elnathan, Delaiah, and Gemariah appealed to the king to respect the prophecy. Of course, Baruch had originally read the scroll from Gemariah's chamber, and this latter action further indicates that Gemariah was favorably disposed toward the prophet. Jehoiakim in turn sent three nobles to arrest Jeremiah, one of them being "Jerahmeel, a son of the king." This man was not Jehoiakim's son; the king was only about thirty years of age and too young to have a son capable of such responsibilities. He may have been another son of Josiah, or "the son of the king" may be an honorific title. Considering how Jehoiakim had treated the prophet Uriah (Jer. 26:20–23), it is evident that he wanted to kill Jeremiah and Baruch. "But YHWH hid them" (וַיַּסְתִּרֵם יְהוָה). We know that the prophet and his scribe had hidden themselves at the urging of the sympathetic nobles (v. 19). The point of verse 26 is evidently that God made their efforts to hide successful, thwarting the efforts of the government officials to find them.

### *Jeremiah and Baruch Produce Another Scroll (36:27–32)*

**36:27–28**. Jeremiah, at God's direction, had Baruch make another scroll like the first one. The scroll was not simply a miscellaneous collection of prophetic oracles, however important that would be in its own right; it was the first edition of a canonical book of Scripture. Thus, the fact that God commanded a new copy to be made attests to the abiding status of the book of Jeremiah. Jehoiakim was not the last to try to obliterate the Bible by fire; but like all the others, he failed.

**36:29–31**. God gave Jeremiah another oracle specially for Jehoiakim. We do not know when or how he delivered the message; obviously he could not take it to the king in person, since Jeremiah had a price on his head. Because he refused to believe, Jehoiakim would suffer two punishments. First, his son would not succeed him on the throne. This has an obvious difficulty in that Jehoiachin did in fact take the throne after his father. However, Jehoiachin held the throne for only about three months (2 Kings 24:8); he was deposed by Nebuchadnezzar and taken into exile to Babylon, where he died. The brief reign and hasty removal of Jehoiachin should be seen as a fulfillment of the prophecy rather than as a violation of it. Second, Jehoiakim's dead body would be cast out to the elements, where it would be exposed to the heat of summer and the cold of winter. We have little information on the death of Jehoiakim and therefore cannot speak to how literally this prophecy was fulfilled. Second Kings 24:6 simply says that Jehoiakim slept with his fathers (i.e., he died). Josephus (*Antiquities* 10.6.3) says that Nebuchadnezzar had Jehoiakim killed and cast outside the walls of Jerusalem. Second Chronicles 36:6, however, suggests that he was taken in chains to Babylon. Josephus's account may be simply a later tradition that was based on Jeremiah 36:30 (Berridge 1992a). Regardless, the curse on Jehoiakim is profound and appropriate. He had been in the winter apartments and had thrown (וְהַשְׁלֵךְ, v. 23) the pieces of the scroll into the fire. As punishment, his body would be thrown (מֻשְׁלֶכֶת, v. 30, from the same root) out to the heat of summer and cold of winter. As he had rejected and tried to eradicate the word of God, so he would be rejected by God and men and abandoned to oblivion.

**36:32**. This verse does not imply that Baruch immediately created a version of the scroll that was significantly longer than the original. It means that the copy of the original became the core text of the expanding book of Jeremiah, a process that took many years. As described in the Introduction, I believe that one of the first additions to the original core was an early version of the oracles against the nations. But as Jeremiah preached more messages and went through more harrowing experiences, ever more material for the expanding book was available.

## THEOLOGICAL FOCUS

The focus of this text is on the importance of the written Word of God, as it recounts the perilous journey of the very first version of the book of Jeremiah. It demonstrates that people can be as hostile to God's Word as they are to God's people.

- There have been many Bible burnings throughout history. Jehoiakim's may have been the first. But the Word of God cannot be hindered or eradicated by physical violence.
- Some of the nobility knew that what Jehoiakim did was wrong, and in vain they tried to stop him. But it was impossible because Jehoiakim and his close associates had no fear of God at all. A culture can become so perverted and depraved that those who do fear God can do little more than helplessly stand by and watch the fires burn. A people can be beyond saving.
- There is a reciprocal relationship between the leaders of a society and its people. The leadership, by its oratory and example, will drive the attitudes of the people. At the same time, the leaders will reflect the prevalent attitudes and strive to run to the front of any parade. Jehoiakim's terrible act no doubt emboldened many people toward open hostility toward Jeremiah. At the same time, Jehoiakim was himself being swept along in the river of popular opinion. Jehoiakim's position of authority gave him greater culpability, but he was not solely responsible for the popular hatred of the prophet.
- After Jehoiakim burned the scroll, Jeremiah and Baruch had to produce another. The writing was done by hand, using what we would consider primitive materials; it also required strenuous mental effort, since Jeremiah had to recall the words of the previous scroll. Defending the Word of God can be labor-intensive. Today, there are still physical attacks on the Bible; in some countries, the only Bibles are those that have been smuggled in. More often, however, attacks on the Bible are intellectual. Responding to these attacks (apologetics) also requires strenuous effort in the form of research, speaking, and writing. It also requires honesty, fairness, insight, and prayer.

## PREACHING AND TEACHING STRATEGIES

### *Exegetical and Theological Synthesis*

The reading of this scroll took place three times, emphasizing that the reading of Jeremiah's words is the focal point of the story. The climax takes place as Jehoiakim deliberately and systematically burns the scroll, section by section. The event is easy for us to visualize. It would be like a person reading a book, and as each page is read it is torn out and put through a shredder. Perhaps Jehoiakim watched the section burn before the next section began, or as one section was burning the next was being read. It is important to note that he had the words read aloud and then destroyed that copy of them. He was demonstrating his rejection of their authority, and further he demonstrated his false assumption that he could destroy God's promises.

It is easy for us to distance ourselves from this blatant rejection of God's Word. We would never burn even the preface pages of a Bible. However, when we fail to try to understand a difficult passage, or when we dismiss the genealogies as only valuable to the ancients, or when a clear command is obeyed but only partially or not at all, we are rejecting God's Word. We would never destroy the portions of his Word that contain promises of blessing, but are we, in some ways, trying to destroy the warnings of God by ignoring them? We need to remember: his Word will endure forever.

### *Preaching Idea*

Rejection of the written Word of God is a rejection of God, and leads to ruin.

### *Contemporary Connections*

*What does it mean?*

This distain for God's Word is unthinkable for many Christians today. As a child I was taught not to put another book on top of a Bible out of respect. For years I've kept a box of Bibles that my dad used that I can't bear to part with, not only because they were my dad's but also, I can't just throw them away; perhaps I could give them away, but certainly not throw them into a recycling bin. It wasn't Jehoiakim's physical act of burning a scroll with writing on it; rather, it was what he was showing by doing that. He could have just ignored Jeremiah's words by not even giving any attention to them. He could have just had the whole scroll destroyed or just sent it back to the archives. He was making a point by having the scroll read, word by word, and then burning each section. He went beyond ignoring, to rejecting, and then to putting himself above God's words.

Three recently graduated mechanical engineers did something similar with a set of instructions. They were sharing a house as roommates and bought a piece of furniture from a popular Scandinavian company that requires assembly. They descended upon the project with their newly affirmed engineering skills in place and, of course, set aside the instructions. They decided that the first piece didn't have the hole in the right spot, so they drilled a new one. This resulted in the next piece not quite fitting, and so on. Finally, they set aside their pride, consulted the instructions, and completed the project. Fortunately they had just ignored the instructions and hadn't burned them. Jehoiakim didn't just ignore God's instructions; he burned them. He repudiated them.

*Is it true?*

Of those who have received the message which God spoke to Jeremiah, very few actually heard Jeremiah speak God's words. By far, most have either read them or heard them read. What kind of authority do these written words have? For the Jews in exile and those living in the land after the exile, who heard the words being read, perhaps some thought that their authority was diminished. They easily could have thought, "Yes, it is good to hear these words read—but it is not like being there when Jeremiah spoke these words from God." Today Jeremiah's written words are more than 2,500 years distant from the actual event. Do these written words have authority today?

*Now what?*

Rejecting God's Word in such a blatant and dramatic way is far beyond what we would do, but the rejection of God's written Word can come in other forms. How is this done today?

The establishment clause of the U.S. Constitution has been used to separate God's Word from much of our culture. This trend in our culture is to say that the Bible doesn't have a place in courtrooms or classrooms. This cultural mindset of regulating God's written Word to only religious settings can lead believers to compartmentalize the Bible, as something that has authority in the church but not in our daily lives. Are we really to forgive others, even in business? Are we to care for the poor, even at the cost of a hefty retirement fund? We don't burn God's Word, but are we rejecting it by separating it from having authority over every part of our lives? In the area of racial relationships, do we tear out the section about loving our neighbors as ourselves and, through our disobedience, place it in a shredder?

Our rejecting the authority of God's written Word can be veiled in an academic pursuit of focusing on what the text says without submitting to its authority. A pastor veils his rejection of God's Word when he continues flirting with a church staff member while writing articles about a biblical view of divorce. He might as well tear out God's clear commands about marriage and burn them. We must always strive to understand what the text is saying and what it means, accompanied by a submissive spirit to obey.

Could our traditions be held to so strongly that we burn up our ability to obey God's Word? Tragically, for many years the tradition of segregation led many who claimed to be submissive to God's Word to actually preach that God taught that segregation was his ordained way for civilizations to function. It was as if the pages of Scriptures that taught justice, reconciliation, love for all, and our being one in Christ were being cut out and burned. It seems that the smoke from those times still lingers in the body of Christ to this day.

We could take James's teaching that to disobey one command is to be guilty of all, and alter it to say, "Because I obey in one area, I can disobey in another." We'll sacrifice to go on a mission trip to evangelize those in another country and feel very good about "going into all the world." But we can't build relationships with our neighbors, so that we can "go" to them with this same message of Christ's work on their behalf.

All of us would admit that at times we have unintentionally or unknowingly disobeyed God's Word. To think about it as burning that portion of his Word might help us to think more deeply about our disobedience. For me, I have not taken seriously enough God's directives on fasting. Not that I have ignored or rejected it; in fact, I have even taught on the subject. But I just haven't been intentional as I should be about fasting. Perhaps I haven't been burning those passages, but I sure have laid them close to the fire.

Not only was Jehoiakim rejecting God's warnings; he was rejecting God's offer of life. God's offer of life still comes to us through the incarnate Word. How tragic it is for anyone to reject the Word of God, who became flesh and died and rose again on our behalf.

### *Creativity in Presentation*

In retelling the story, the drama of the burning of the scroll needs to be highlighted. As this narrative is told it is very important to show that the scroll, in a sense, is a central character. It would be relatively easy to make a scroll to use as a physical illustration or prop. Sheets of old-fashioned manila paper used in kindergarten can be glued together to form a scroll that is not too different from what Baruch's looked like, at least for stage purposes. However, I would strongly recommend not burning it. Unintentional reactions could take place in our listeners, not to mention the safety hazards. Just having a physical scroll in the pulpit would help ensure the centrality of the written Word.

This story could be told from the perspective of Baruch, since he was present for every scene. If there is time, and one has the background, the preacher/teacher could take on the character of Baruch and tell the story from a first-person point of view. (Torrey Robinson's *It's All in How You Tell It* and Reg Grant's and John Reed's *Telling Stories to Touch the Heart* give important advice for this type of sermon.) In a similar way but not as demanding, the text could be read and expounded using the perspective of Baruch. I wonder how he felt when he saw his labor being burned. Here is one possible structure:

- Present the story. (Note: the three times the scroll is read are the pivot points to the plot.)
    - Jeremiah commanded to write (36:1–4).
    - Baruch sent to the temple and reads the scroll to the people (36:5–8).
        - Micaiah reports him to the king's officials (36:9–12).
    - Baruch reads the scroll to the officials (36:13–19).

        - The officials report to the king (36:20).
    - Baruch reads the scrolls to the king (36:21–22).
        - The king burns the scroll (36:23–26).
    - Jeremiah and Baruch rewrite the scroll (36:27–32).

- Application (these lists can and should added to and nuanced for each contemporary setting)
    - Ways we can metaphorically burn God's written Word:
        - Ignore it
        - Reject it
        - Repudiate it
    - Ways to respect it:
        - Read it
        - Obey it

- Rejection of the written Word of God is a rejection of God.

## DISCUSSION QUESTIONS

1. What do you think Jehoiakim was thinking as he watched the scroll burn?

2. What do you think Baruch was thinking as he watched the scroll burn?

3. What are some differences in hearing something read and silently reading it?

4. What seems to have more authority, something written or something spoken? Why?

5. Of the ways that we can reject God's Word, which is the most subtle?
    a. Setting it aside
    b. Studying without submitting
    c. Obeying one part and ignoring other parts

## Jeremiah 37:1–39:18

**EXEGETICAL IDEA**
This is a tightly bound, coherent text that focuses on the differing attitudes of the nobility, Zedekiah, and Ebed-melek toward Jeremiah. The passage centers on three messages given to Zedekiah, who is not utterly wicked but is weak and yields to pressure from the nobility to silence Jeremiah. This contrasts with the faith and integrity of Ebed-melek the Cushite, who saves Jeremiah from a wretched death. In the end, it is the Babylonians who save Jeremiah from the brutal treatment he has gotten from his own countrymen and who release him after capturing the city.

**THEOLOGICAL FOCUS**
In times of crisis and polarization, some will love and some will hate those who bear God's Word, while others will yield to social pressure to join in the hostility. In this passage, the foreigners recognize the authority of Jeremiah while the Jerusalem aristocracy despises him.

**PREACHING IDEA**
Choose to respect, then expect to be blessed.

**PREACHING POINTERS**
The passage presents the hostility of the Jewish leaders toward Jeremiah, the fluctuation of Zedekiah and the respect that comes from Ebed-melek. It begins with the prophecy of condemnation to Zedekiah and his rejection of Jeremiah. The height of the hostility toward Jeremiah comes when he is thrown into the cistern. The passage ends with Ebed-melek and the affirming prophecy given to him.

This is a tricky passage because the thrust is about attitudes toward us who are preachers and teachers. Complicating this is the difficult structure. These must not hinder the proclamation of truth. The passage presents the hostility of the Jewish leaders toward Jeremiah, the fluctuation of Zedekiah, and the respect that comes from Ebed-melek. This gives us clear examples of what our attitudes toward those who proclaim the message of God could be. This passage not only teaches that we should give respect, but that when we do we are blessed just as Ebed-melek was.

# JEREMIAH'S CAPTIVITY AND JERUSALEM'S FALL (37:1–39:18)

## LITERARY STRUCTURE AND THEMES

The book abruptly jumps from the fourth year of Jehoiakim to the end of Zedekiah's reign and the fall of Jerusalem. In the narrative flow, the movement from Jeremiah 36 to 37–39 shows that the direct outcome of Jehoiakim's burning of the scroll was the fulfillment of all the dire prophecies that the scroll contained.

Jeremiah 37:1–44:30 is the longest generally sequential unit in the book. It goes from Jeremiah's arrest and confinement to the fall of Jerusalem and then to his last message, given in Egypt to a group of Jewish refugees.

Chapters 37–38 make up the first major segment of this unit. They form a coherent and tightly bound collection of passages, with various verbal markers employed to indicate individual segments. References to the king's "servant(s)" mark the beginning, middle, and ending of this text. The word עֶבֶד ("servant") is strategically placed at 37:2 (where it refers to the king's officials) and at 38:7 and 39:16, in the name of one Cushite official, Ebed-melek (עֶבֶד־מֶלֶךְ; "King's servant"). At the beginning, the passage states that neither the king nor "his servants" would listen to the words of YHWH (37:2). The center and turning point of the narrative is when Ebed-melek saves Jeremiah from death in a cistern (38:7–13). At the end, Jeremiah blesses Ebed-melek with a promise from YHWH (39:15–18).

The passage is also separated into smaller segments by various cues. Several end with the clause "and [Jeremiah] stayed" (וַיֵּשֶׁב יִרְמְיָהוּ). A statement that Jeremiah had a word from YHWH initiates two of the segments. In another two places, a phrase that we should translate as "And so it was" (וְהָיָה) marks the beginning of a segment. Thus, the structure requires some extra explanation beyond a bare outline.

The individual segments are as follows:

- ***Introductory Summation (37:1–5)***
  This summarizes Zedekiah's reign and the people's refusal to believe Jeremiah, and it describes the initial state of affairs for the narrative given in chapters 37–38.
- ***A Prophecy for Zedekiah That Jerusalem Is Doomed (37:6–10)***
  The beginning of this unit is marked with, "And there was a word of YHWH to Jeremiah" (וַיְהִי דְּבַר־יְהוָה אֶל־יִרְמְיָהוּ).
- ***The Officials Disbelieve and Imprison Jeremiah (37:11–16)***
  The beginning of this unit is marked with "And so it was" (וְהָיָה). An account of Jeremiah's arrest and imprisonment follows. The ending is marked with, "And Jeremiah stayed" (וַיֵּשֶׁב יִרְמְיָהוּ) in prison for many days.
- ***A Second Prophecy Given to Zedekiah; Jeremiah Is Transferred (37:17–21)***
  Jeremiah gave Zedekiah another prophecy, and he pleaded for more lenient treatment. They moved him to another, apparently less harsh, place of confinement. The text ends, "And Jeremiah stayed (וַיֵּשֶׁב יִרְמְיָהוּ) at the court of the guard."
- ***The Officials Disbelieve and Abandon Jeremiah to Die (38:1–6)***
  They accused Jeremiah of demoralizing the troops with treasonous talk. They forsook him to die at the bottom of a muddy cistern. "And Jeremiah sank into the mud" (וַיִּטְבַּע יִרְמְיָהוּ בַּטִּיט), marks the end of this

unit. As a unit division marker, this has the same weight as the repeated clause, "And Jeremiah stayed" (Lundbom 2008c, 52).

- ***Ebed-melek Saves Jeremiah (38:7–13)***
  Ebed-melek pleaded for Jeremiah and saved his life. Verse 13 concludes the episode with, "And Jeremiah stayed at the court of the guard" (וַיֵּשֶׁב יִרְמְיָהוּ בַּחֲצַר הַמַּטָּרָה).
- ***A Third Prophecy for Zedekiah (38:14–28a)***
  Jeremiah gave Zedekiah a third prophecy, and he only escaped death by lying to the Jerusalem officials about his reason for speaking to the king. The text ends with the same words as the previous text, "And Jeremiah stayed at the court of the guard (וַיֵּשֶׁב יִרְמְיָהוּ בַּחֲצַר הַמַּטָּרָה) until the day Jerusalem was captured."
- ***The Fall of Jerusalem; Jeremiah Freed (38:28b–39:14)***
  The beginning of this unit is marked with "And so it was" (וַיְהִי). A full account of the fate of Zedekiah and the end of Jerusalem follows. Jeremiah was freed at Nebuchadnezzar's orders, and the text ends, "And [Jeremiah] stayed (וַיֵּשֶׁב) among the people."
- ***A Prophecy for Ebed-melek (39:15–18)***
  The beginning of this unit is marked with, "And to Jeremiah there was a word of YHWH" (וְאֶל־יִרְמְיָהוּ הָיָה דְבַר־יְהוָה). Jeremiah gave a prophetic blessing to Ebed-melek.

We can thus see, after the introductory verses (37:1–5), a chiastic structure to the larger unit:

A "And there was a word of YHWH to Jeremiah" (37:6–10)
  B "And so it was" (37:11–16)
    C "And Jeremiah stayed at the court of the guard" (37:17–21)
      D "And Jeremiah sank into the mud" (38:1–6)
    C' "And Jeremiah stayed at the court of the guard" (38:7–13, 14–28a)
  B' "And so it was" (38:28b–39:14)
A' "And there was a word of YHWH to Jeremiah" (39:15–18)

In the narrative, Jeremiah's situation gets progressively worse until he is abandoned to die in the cistern, the center point of the chiasmus. After that, his situation improves: Ebed-melek saves him, he is placed under better confinement at the court of the guard, the Babylonians fully release him, and there is a blessing on Ebed-melek.

## EXPOSITION

### *Introductory Summation (37:1–5)*

**37:1–2.** This is purely a summary, stating that Zedekiah became king and that he and his people continued to defy God's warnings through Jeremiah. The historical setting is important. First, Zedekiah replaced Jehoiachin (here called Coniah), who after a very brief reign was taken captive to Babylon. Second, Nebuchadnezzar placed Zedekiah on the throne. These two facts demonstrated that Babylon's power over Judah was absolute. Zedekiah should have recognized that he was incapable of resisting and abandoned any thoughts of rebellion. Verse 2, however, states that both the king and the people rejected God's messages given by Jeremiah (who advocated submission to Babylon). Hence, Judah under Zedekiah's rule were certain to continue to do the wrong thing.

**37:3–5.** The initial episode of the narrative sequence took place while Jeremiah was still a free man in Jerusalem. The text makes it appear that Zedekiah's reign was off to a great start, as he seems to have begun by asking Jeremiah to pray for the city. In fact, however, this request came very late in his reign, during the final Babylonian siege of the city. Still, the appearance given by the text that Zedekiah began his reign with a pious appeal to Jeremiah is deliberate. It implies that some of the king's sensibilities were good and that, unlike Jehoiakim, he could have been a devout ruler. But he would prove to be weak and inconsistent. Verse 4 speaks of Pharaoh Hophra's attempt to relieve the siege of Jerusalem. He would draw the Babylonians away from the city for a short time, but he would be driven back to Egypt and so allow the assault on Jerusalem to continue.

Many commentators treat this episode and the delegation mentioned in 21:1–2 as two separate events (for example, Smothers, Keown, and Scalise 1995, 216). While this is technically correct, we should think of 21:1–10 and 37:3–10 as parts of a single episode that took place in different stages, like an extended negotiation between two parties. The process continued on through two more interviews. The events were as follows:

- The Babylonians invaded Judah; and Zedekiah, through emissaries, asked for Jeremiah's prayers (21:2). Jeremiah declared that Jerusalem would fall to the Babylonians (21:3–10).
- Pharaoh Hophra's army came out of Egypt, and Nebuchadnezzar's forces temporarily lifted the siege in order to confront Hophra.
- Zedekiah tried again: he sent the delegation of 37:3 and again asked Jeremiah to intercede for the city. Jeremiah, however, repeated his prior prediction that the Babylonians would destroy Jerusalem. Hophra would fail, and Nebuchadnezzar would come back (37:6–10).
- Jeremiah tried to leave Jerusalem to take care of family business in Anathoth, but he was arrested, charged with treason, and imprisoned (37:13–15).
- After Jeremiah's imprisonment, Zedekiah wanted to keep his contact with Jeremiah private and secret (37:17; 38:24. His third appeal to Jeremiah, therefore, was done in person (37:17–20).
- After this, Jeremiah was thrown into the cistern and would have died had he not been rescued by Ebed-melek (38:4–13).
- Zedekiah then had a fourth interview with Jeremiah (38:14–26).
- This implies that Zedekiah four times sought a favorable oracle from Jeremiah:
    - After the siege had begun and while Jeremiah was still a free man (21:1–10)
    - While the Babylonian army was drawn away and Jeremiah was still free (37:3–10)
    - After his initial arrest and while the Babylonian army was still away (37:17–20)
    - And, after his time in the cistern (38:14–26)

Through the whole process, Zedekiah was seeking to have Jeremiah declare that God would destroy the Babylonian army in the same manner as he had destroyed the Assyrian army in the time of Isaiah and Hezekiah (Isa. 37). The give-and-take between the king and the prophet was a single, extended conversation centered on Zedekiah's efforts, like Balak with Balaam, to obtain a favorable word from God.

We should say a word about the delegations to the prophet. Jeremiah 21:1–2 mentions the names of two delegates, Pashhur son of Malchiah and Zephaniah son of Maaseiah. Although the delegation of 37:3 included Zephaniah, instead of Pashhur it had Jehukal son of Shelemiah. Judging from 29:25–26, Zephaniah appears to have been well-disposed toward the prophet. Jehukal, mentioned in 37:3, accused Jeremiah of treason in 38:1–5, and in this he was joined by a certain Gedaliah son of Pashhur (evidently this Pashhur was Pashhur son of Immer of 20:1–6, a man who despised Jeremiah). Thus, Zephaniah and Jehukal were in different factions, the former being sympathetic to Jeremiah and the latter hating him.

### *A Prophecy for Zedekiah: Jerusalem Doomed (37:6–10)*

**37:6–8**. Jeremiah warned the king that the Egyptians under Hophra would not be able to give any lasting relief to Jerusalem. He maintained his consistent message that Jerusalem would be destroyed.

**37:7–10**. YHWH has decreed the destruction of Jerusalem; nothing could avert it. The illustration that even the walking wounded of the Babylonian army could bring down Jerusalem is obvious hyperbole. But its purpose is not to show how weak Judah was in comparison to their enemy (even though that was true). The point is that even if the defenders of the city somehow by superhuman courage and brilliant strategy defeated the Babylonians in a major battle, they would still lose the war because God was against them.

### *The Officials Disbelieve and Imprison Jeremiah (37:11–16)*

As described above, this is connected to the episode of chapter 32. That passage concerns how the imprisoned Jeremiah was able to redeem property in Anathoth that was connected to his family by proxy. This passage, by contrast, tells how Jeremiah tried to go out to Anathoth while he was still free but was arrested while leaving. Obviously, therefore, the events of chapter 37 took place prior to those of chapter 32.

**37:11–12**. Jeremiah set out to take care of a property matter in his hometown of Anathoth. The town was close to Jerusalem; both cities were in Benjamin. We learn in chapter 32 that he had to "redeem" some land. Perhaps some near relative of his had died and he needed to purchase the real estate so that it would remain within the family.

*TRANSLATION NOTE: לַחֲלִק in 37:12*

The word לַחֲלִק is difficult somewhat to interpret. The root חלק is well attested, but it appears nowhere else in the hiphil stem (and here it is a defectively spelled hiphil). In the qal, it means to "divide" (1 Sam. 19:30; Neh. 13:13), and it has essentially the same meaning in the piel (1 Kings 18:6; Ps. 22:18 [MT 19]). The niphal and pual are both passive, "to be divided," and one hithpael appears, with the meaning "and they shall divide it among themselves" (וְהִתְחַלְּקוּ; Josh. 18:5). The hiphil לַחֲלִק would seem to mean "to make a division," but this makes little sense in context. But since the hiphil appears only here, we cannot be sure. Perhaps לַחֲלִק should be emended to לָקַחַת חֵלֶק, "to receive a portion" (Holladay 1989, 288). At any rate, the verse almost certainly means that Jeremiah was to receive a portion of the family estate.

**37:13–14**. Jeremiah was accused of desertion and treason. The text goes out of its way to identify the officer who arrested and accused Jeremiah: Irijah son of Shelemiah son of Hananiah. This was an infamous deed, and it seems that the book is not content to leave the guilty party anonymous. Curiously, Irijah's name (יִרְאִיָּיה) means "YHWH sees," although the text does not focus on that. His office, בַּעַל פְּקִדֻת, literally means "master of supervision" or "master of the mustering [of troops]," but the title appears only here, and we do not know what duties it entailed.

**37:15–16**. Jeremiah was beaten and placed in confinement. There was no reason for such brutality, and the text states that several officers (הַשָּׂרִים) were involved in his maltreatment. This implies that among the junior officers there was a high level of hostility to Jeremiah, as they considered him a traitor. Like many junior officers, they had a nationalistic zeal that far outstripped their wisdom. Ancient Jerusalem probably had no jails (people were not punished by imprisonment but by fines, beating, or death), and thus the house of the secretary Jonathan was used as a temporary holding area for an enemy of the state such as

Jeremiah. The house must have been substantial, because it had its own cistern in a small building called the בֵּית הַבּוֹר ("cistern building"). This was probably not, as some translations have it, a "vaulted cell" (NIV) or a "dungeon" (ESV). It was more likely a shed covering the opening of the shaft of the cistern; the prophet would have had to sit and sleep at the edge of the shaft. Jeremiah was confined there a long time (יָמִים רַבִּים; "many days"). The wretched conditions would have made the time seem extensive, even if was in reality only ten days or so. We do not know how long it actually was.

### *A Second Prophecy for Zedekiah; Jeremiah Transferred (37:17–21)*

**37:17**. Jeremiah, although now under harsh confinement, refused to modify his answer to Zedekiah regarding YHWH's message. This verse is probably just a summary of their discussion and of Jeremiah's report of the word from God. The principal reason for recording this encounter was to convey to the reader Jeremiah's plea for release from his harsh confinement.

**37:18–19**. Jeremiah pled his case, saying that he had not deserved such severe punishment. He had only told the truth. The other "prophets" who had predicted that war would never reach Jerusalem were subject to no retaliation or mistreatment. When supposed experts, intellectuals, and religious leaders say what people want to hear, they are not held responsible even when their claims and predictions turn out to be catastrophically wrong.

**37:20–21**. Jeremiah, who was apparently being starved, asked that the conditions of his confinement be changed. Zedekiah, not for the first time, showed himself to have some respect for the person and authority of Jeremiah. He commanded that the prophet be moved to better conditions at a military compound called the "courtyard of the guard" (חֲצַר הַמַּטָּרָה) and that he be given food as long as any was available. But the king would soon show his weakness and inconsistency.

### *The Officials Disbelieve and Abandon Jeremiah to Die (38:1–6)*

**38:1–3**. This is something of a flashback. Four of the most powerful men in Jerusalem demanded that Jeremiah be put to death for his preaching. It is certain that this is not the first time these men had heard of Jeremiah's dire predictions for Judah. The implication is that they had a long-standing hostility toward the prophet. The seemingly treasonous words that they cited (vv. 2–3) may well have been truly spoken by Jeremiah, but they were wrenched from context to make him look as bad as possible. The trick of selectively quoting one's political opponents continues to be used today. Jeremiah's point was that because God had irrevocably turned against Jerusalem, the only path to survival lay in surrender. They made it sound as though he were simply voicing Nebuchadnezzar's propaganda, discouraging the army and populace from further resistance. They may have likened Jeremiah to the Assyrian propaganda minister (רַב־שָׁקֵה), who in the time of Hezekiah declared that God had handed Jerusalem over to Sennacherib (Isa. 36). In the minds of the four nobles, Jeremiah was a terrible prophet. Isaiah had brought about the divine destruction of the enemy, but Jeremiah took on the role of the enemy's propaganda minister! What they failed to consider, however, was that Hezekiah and the men around him had sincerely turned to God in repentance (Isa. 37). Isaiah, had he been alive at the time of Zedekiah, would have joined Jeremiah in his condemnation of Jerusalem.

**38:4–6**. Too weak to resist the demands of the aristocratic opponents of Jeremiah, the king gave them permission to kill him (from their words in verse 4, it was clear that this was their intent). To bring about his death, they lowered him into another cistern, this one being dry except for a layer of mud at the bottom. They intended to starve him to death. One wonders why they did not kill him outright. At least two answers present themselves, and both may be correct. They may have had scruples about slaying the prophet by direct violence, fearing that God would punish such an act but thinking they could avoid punishment if Jeremiah simply died through neglect. Or, they may have wanted Jeremiah to suffer and die slowly.

### *Ebed-melek Saves Jeremiah (38:7–13)*

**38:7–9**. Ebed-melek was a "Cushite" (כּוּשִׁי). "Cush" or "Cushan" is generally taken to the territory immediately south of Egypt, and thus "Cushite" is often translated as "Ethiopian." The region of Cush was also called Nubia, and it is to be identified with northern Sudan. There was also a Mesopotamian Cush as implied in Genesis 10:8–12, a people probably to be identified with the Cassites of the second millennium B.C. (Baker 1992). In the vast majority of cases, however, biblical "Cush" is the African region. The Bible describes these Cushites as tall and beardless (Isa. 18:2) and implicitly dark-skinned (Num. 12:10; Jer. 13:23). Moses's second wife was a Cushite (Num. 12:1), and a Cushite soldier served in David's army during his civil war with Absalom (1 Sam. 18:21). Cushites were often associated with Egypt and its military (Isa. 20:3–5). During the 25th Dynasty (747–656 B.C.), a series of Cushite pharaohs ruled Egypt. It seems certain that Ebed-melek was from African Cush (for further information, see Sadler, Jr. 2006).

Ebed-melek means "king's servant." It is probably a titular name and not his given name. Since he was a foreigner, it may be that the Israelites found his original name hard to pronounce and so they simply called him "king's servant." The term "servant" (עֶבֶד), however, does not necessarily imply that he was a menial slave doing household chores. Indeed, he was apparently not a household slave at all, since he was the leader of a group of men in the rescue of Jeremiah. In the Bible, moreover, the highest-ranking officials in a kingdom are normally called the king's "servants" (Gen. 40:20; Exod. 7:10; 8:31; 1 Sam. 28:7; 1 Kings 1:2, 47). Ebed-melek is called a סָרִיס, which refers to someone with an official function in the king's palace. The term can refer to a eunuch, a castrated man who was in charge of the royal harem (Esth. 2:3), but it is often used of men who were almost certainly not castrated and had different offices (Gen. 39:1; 2 Kings 18:17; 25:19). Ebed-melek was able to approach the king directly and in some haste, implying that he had routine access to the king's person. This could mean that he was a personal attendant to the king, or it could mean that he occupied a special place in the bureaucracy. He could have been the king's personal guard (kings have often employed foreigners to be their bodyguards because they wanted guards with no ties to local political factions). But we should be careful about speculating over his office. We do not have enough information about this, just as we do not know how a Cushite came to be in Zedekiah's service.

Unlike many Israelites, however, Ebed-melek had faith in YHWH (39:15–18) and believed the words of Jeremiah. He knew that the prophet would surely starve if left in the cistern. The people of Judah did not have enough to feed themselves; they certainly would not toss food down into the cistern.

**38:10**. Zedekiah, with an abrupt change of heart, decided he could not allow Jeremiah to be put to death. This shows us again the tragedy of Zedekiah, that he generally meant well but had a weak will. He was not like his brother Jehoiakim who simply despised Jeremiah, but he could not consistently do what was right.

**38:11–13**. The starving and weakened Jeremiah would scarcely been able to hold on to a rope while being pulled up, and if the rope were secured to his body, it could give him severe rope burns. But the resourceful Ebed-melek found a solution to the problem. Clothing and fabric were very expensive and would not be thrown away. People would find a use for them until they were entirely used up. Thus, the palace had a storage place for old clothing and rags. He took some of these to enable Jeremiah to be brought up safely. Jeremiah was still a prisoner, but was no longer abandoned to perish.

### *A Third Prophecy for Zedekiah (38:14–28a)*

**38:14–16**. Zedekiah again sought a message from God through Jeremiah. We do not know where the "third entrance" to the temple was; it may have been a private entrance reserved for the king. Zedekiah's injunction to Jeremiah, that he must not "hide" (אַל־תְּכַחֵד) anything from him, is strikingly similar to Eli's demand that Samuel not "hide" (אַל־נָא תְכַחֵד) anything (1 Sam. 3:17). In both cases, the prophet brought a message of doom to the high official making the demand. But Jeremiah, now doubly wary of being put to death for his words, sought assurance from the king that there would be no retaliation for his message.

**38:17–18**. Jeremiah told the king that defeat was inevitable but that he could avoid complete disaster if he surrendered to the Babylonians immediately. Zedekiah could not expect complete leniency; he had rebelled against Babylon's suzerainty and forced Nebuchadnezzar to go to the expense and trouble of bringing an army to besiege Jerusalem. He probably would have been deposed and taken as a captive to Babylon, but his life would be spared, and by implication his ordeal would not be extremely severe. Most importantly, the city would be spared, and as king, that should have been Zedekiah's first concern.

**38:18–20**. Zedekiah, true to form, was driven by fear. A number of the Jews of Jerusalem, members of the "pro-Babylonian party" as opposed to the more powerful "pro-Egyptian party," had already abandoned the city and handed themselves over to the Babylonians. Zedekiah considered these men to be his political enemies and feared they would persuade Nebuchadnezzar that he was untrustworthy and an implacable enemy of Babylon. Zedekiah thought he would be tortured and perhaps killed. Jeremiah assured him that no such thing would happen and explicitly assured him that he would be treated well.

**38:21–23**. As he commonly did, Jeremiah included a warning of what would happen if Zedekiah refused to surrender. This time, however, he focused on what the women would say and what would happen to them. He mentioned the women in order to recall the traditional duty of men to protect their women, and in particular of the king to protect the women of the city. Their sharp words of condemnation would mark Zedekiah as a failure. The king's own wives and daughters would be subjected to use and abuse by the Babylonians, so that his loss would be personal as well as reputational. The taunt the women would give to the king, "Your feet are sunk (טבע) in the mire," recollects Jeremiah's experience in the cistern, when he sank (טבע) into the mud" (38:6). But for Zedekiah, there would be no rescue.

**38:24–27**. By a bit of subterfuge, Jeremiah was able to evade further reprisals from the hostile nobility. In the king's explanation, the men who had earlier tried to kill Jeremiah were certain to press him to see if he was continuing to prophesy disaster or had learned his lesson. They would demand to know what message he had given and say, "Do not hide it from us" (אַל־תְּכַחֵד מִמֶּנּוּ), echoing the king's words and the earlier words of Eli (38:14; 1 Sam. 3:17). But Jeremiah did hide it from them. To be sure, Jeremiah's evasive answer was in obedience to the king, and he wanted to save himself from further violence. But by implication, the nobles were no longer worthy to hear the words of the prophet (compare Acts 28:24–28). Zedekiah and Eli before him stood condemned, but these men were much worse.

**38:28a**. Although still in confinement, Jeremiah was able to spend the last days before the city fell in relative peace, at least knowing that his own people were not trying to kill him. There is some irony here: Jeremiah was trapped in Jerusalem by the city leaders, but the city leaders and Jerusalem itself were trapped by the Babylonian army. At the heart of the city was the man who proclaimed the word of God, and outside the city was the fulfillment of his word. The Jews were caught between the two.

### *The Fall of Jerusalem; Jeremiah Freed (38:28b–39:14)*

**38:28b–39:3**. The account of Jerusalem's fall is astonishingly concise; we are given only the dates of the beginning and end of the siege. The precise dates and the length of the siege are in dispute. Most interpreters take it to be from January 588 to July 587, about eighteen months (Thompson 1980, 646; Holladay 1989, 291; Smothers, Keown, and Scalise 1995, 230). Lundbom argues that the siege lasted for thirty months, until about July of 586 (Lundbom 2008c, 84). Regardless, it was a prolonged and terrible experience, and it culminated in the unthinkable: the city of God, the seat of YHWH's house, fell to a pagan army. The account jumps from the moment the walls were breached (v. 2) to the end of the battle, after the city was secured and the high officials of Babylon took their seats in the Middle Gate of the city to pronounce judgment on the survivors (v. 3). It seems strange to us that the text would list the names of these officials, but this is in keeping with the annalistic nature of ancient historiography, which is often more interested in giving a list of kings and rulers involved in an event than in, for example, giving a blow-by-blow account of a battle. Also, the seating of Babylonian officials in authority over Jerusalem conveys in powerful terms that the city is truly fallen and that the Davidic dynasty and the state it ruled no longer existed. Notably, Nebuchadnezzar is not listed among those who sat in authority at the city gate; he was away at Riblah, north of Damascus.

> *TRANSLATION NOTE: The Meaning of 38:28b*
> The clause וְהָיָה כַּאֲשֶׁר נִלְכְּדָה יְרוּשָׁלָ͏ִם is difficult. The particle כַּאֲשֶׁר normally means "when," as in Genesis 32:2 ("And Jacob said when [כַּאֲשֶׁר] he saw"); or "just as," as in Deuteronomy 2:14 ("the entire generation perished . . . just as [כַּאֲשֶׁר] YHWH had sworn"). Jeremiah 38:28b could be a dependent clause, "And so it came about that when Jerusalem was captured," but this is highly unlikely. Lundbom regards Jeremiah as the subject of וְהָיָה, translating, "And he was there when Jerusalem was taken" (Lundbom 2008c, 6). This is grammatically possible but improbable. A clause-initial וְהָיָה ought to have both an explicit subject and an explicit particle "there" (שָׁם). Holladay simply excises כַּאֲשֶׁר נִלְכְּדָה יְרוּשָׁלָ͏ִם as a corruption (Holladay 1989, 268). This solves the problem but is not compelling. It is noteworthy that we have the *weqatal* וְהָיָה instead of the common *wayyiqtol* form, וַיְהִי. Thus, it does not simply mean, "And it came about" (as in Exod. 32:19, וַיְהִי כַּאֲשֶׁר). It probably means, in effect, "And things developed as follows when Jerusalem was captured." Compare also the NIV translation, "This is how Jerusalem was taken."

**39:4–7**. The details of Zedekiah's flight and capture are also recorded in 52:7–11, where the account of the fall of the city is given in more detail (see the commentary below on chapter 52 for further exposition). In contrast to chapter 52, this chapter focuses heavily on the sad plight of Zedekiah. It describes the outcome of his vacillating policy and unwillingness to fully embrace Jeremiah's message.

**39:8–10**. The city was burned to the ground and its walls were broken down. The people, except for the very poor who would henceforth scrounge for survival in the hill country of Judah, were taken away. To put it simply, the city of Jerusalem no longer existed.

**39:11–14**. The account of Jeremiah's release is given in more detail in 40:1–6 (see commentary below on that text for further exposition). Nebuchadnezzar evidently knew about Jeremiah and respected him. Ancient kings, like modern states, were keen on getting intelligence about their enemies, and Nebuchadnezzar already had a large community of Jewish exiles in Babylon who were in regular communication with Jeremiah. Thus, it is not surprising that the Babylonian king knew about the prophet and was aware that he had advocated surrender to his people. For that reason, and also because he respected Jeremiah's office as a prophet, he wanted him to be treated well.

### *A Prophecy for Ebed-melek (39:15–18)*

**39:15**. This prophecy is chronologically out of place, since it was given before the city fell and while Jeremiah was still in confinement.

**39:16–18**. Jeremiah assured Ebed-melek that the city would fall to the Babylonians. This was not good news to Ebed-melek. After all, he too was a resident of the city and in fact attached to the royal court. He was as likely to be killed or enslaved as anyone else. But Jeremiah did have good news: because he had shown both fear of God and human decency in rescuing Jeremiah, Ebed-melek would not be killed or abused. He would survive and, we presume, enjoy some level of prosperity.

## THEOLOGICAL FOCUS

We see in this passage different attitudes toward the word of God and God's prophet, as epitomized in the nobility, Zedekiah, and Ebed-melek.

- The nobility believed that their theology and nationalistic zeal was wiser than the words Jeremiah received from YHWH. They therefore rejected all that he said, hated him, and sought to kill him. The worst forms of hatred and persecution comes from those who fervently believe that they are right and that all others are traitors and liars.
- Zedekiah had respect for Jeremiah and wanted to hear God's word, but he tried to bend it to his own desires through extended negotiations. He hoped that Jeremiah (or God) would modify his harsh position over the course of their discussions. There is a time and place for intercession, when one seeks to persuade God to relent. But that is always based in repentance and submission to God's will. Simply trying to get a better deal from God while refusing to accept his plain and direct judgment is never a good idea. That, coupled with his weakness before the nobility, led to Zedekiah's horrible end.
- Ebed-melek not only believed Jeremiah but acted upon it, rescuing the prophet when he knew that this would enrage powerful nobles and could lead to his own death.
- The Gentile Ebed-melek believed in YHWH and in his prophet Jeremiah when the majority of the Jews did not. This anticipates the experience of Jesus, who would be rejected by his own people but would predict that many Gentiles would come from east and west to enter the kingdom of God (Matt. 8:11).

## PREACHING AND TEACHING STRATEGIES

### *Exegetical and Theological Synthesis*

The three attitudes that are expressed are the hostility of the nobles, the fluctuation of Zedekiah, and the favor of Ebed-melek. The nobles wanted to kill Jeremiah, Zedekiah couldn't make up his mind, and Ebed-melek rescued him from death.

The parallel for us is our attitude toward our pastors and teachers of God's Word. This is not a one-to-one application. Pastors and teachers are not speaking the words of God as Jeremiah was. But they *are* presenting the message of God. They are helping us see what God is saying in his written Word. Our attitude toward the pastor/teacher is a choice that greatly affects what we receive.

### *Preaching Idea*

Choose to respect, then expect to be blessed.

### *Contemporary Connections*

#### *What does it mean?*

Few of us have hostility toward a pastor or teacher, but it can and does happen. It could start with a mild disrespect toward the pastor/teacher because of a missed handshake, or a facial expression that we took as disapproval or some other perceived offense. A wall of resentment begins to build.

Perhaps more subtle is the attitude that seems to waver. Zedekiah's attempts to make up his mind about Jeremiah had the same effect as the nobles' attitude of hatred. In his vacillation he, like the nobles, put himself in judgment over Jeremiah. When there is a lack of respect for the messenger, the blessing of the message is lost. The preaching and teaching that was always a blessing are somehow not as helpful as they once were. We think the preaching changed, when really it was our attitude that changed.

I've experienced this on both sides of the pulpit. When I assumed a pastorate by a vote of the congregation, those who voted against my coming continued in their disapproval, finding fault in every sermon. Their attitudes degenerated until they were even praying for my salvation. After many conversations and much prayer that group respectfully left the church, even though that was not the best for Christ's body. On the other side of the pulpit, I was a member of a local body in which the pastor was a decent preacher, but I was in graduate school and he wasn't quite academic enough for me. While I did not want to throw him into a cistern, I still had chosen a critical attitude toward him. By God's gracious action, I was confronted by a good friend that my attitude was wrong. God began to put a new heart in me, and I chose to have a good attitude toward the pastor—and amazingly his preaching "improved." Our attitude toward a preacher/teacher is our choice and it affects how we receive the message. Unfortunately, there are situations in which a pastor/teacher needs to be confronted morally or theologically, but that is not the focus of this passage.

#### *Is it true?*

The attitude toward the speaker or messenger greatly affects what listeners will receive. Rhetoricians call it ethos, from Aristotle's triad of ethos, pathos, and logos. James McCroskey, in his textbook on rhetoric that has endured into its ninth edition (McCroskey 2006, 83), makes the point that ethos is the most important.

I don't remember why I didn't respect my eleventh-grade English teacher, but I know I didn't learn very much from him. It may have been a judgmental spirit in me, or perhaps he truly was a poor teacher. But in contrast to him was Lawrence Smith, my senior English teacher. Because of him, a love and fasciation for literature and writing was planted in me. My positive attitude toward him and the amount I learned went hand in hand. Ethos comes into play even with our Lord. When Jesus was in his hometown, those listening to him missed great blessings because they saw him as just another kid who grew up in Nazareth. The attitude of the listeners matters.

Certainly, our attitudes are affected by many sources, but ultimately our attitude is our choice.

The three attitudes expressed in this narrative were choices. The message itself, of course, was an influence. The nobles and the king didn't want to lose their positions, but neither did Ebed-Melek. Speech teachers encourage students that an introduction should strive to establish good will from the listeners, so that they will be open to the message. But if listeners have already made up their mind to oppose this speaker, communication breaks down. The mindset toward the speaker is a choice. The rejection of the message was clearly illustrated in the previous pericope when the scroll was burned. This section focuses on the choice of attitudes toward Jeremiah.

*Now what?*

Ebed-melek sets a clear example for us. He not only had a favorable attitude toward Jeremiah, but he acted upon it. This is a delicate point in the sermon or lesson because the application is to work on building a favorable mindset toward one's pastor or teacher. It could sound like a hurt little child wanting everyone to like them. A way to approach this is for the pastor/teacher to mention those to whom they are accountable, and mention the pastors or teachers to whom they listen. Perhaps mention a struggle that you overcame in respecting an authority or teacher. It would seem best to not mention negative attitudes toward you, even though they may exist. Rather, take this opportunity to affirm their support.

### *Creativity in Presentation*

This is a long and, at first glance, very complicated story line. Be sure that you look closely at the commentary to thoroughly understand the chiasmus structure. This structure is foreign to most of us, but it is the structure of the text so it should be followed. As in other sermons, the platform area can be utilized to help clarify and demonstrate the structure. As part of the introduction, give a very brief lesson on chiastic structure. Then tell the story using a physical space to illustrate the outline. Start by stepping down from the stage area to the right and present the first prophecy to Zedekiah (A in the outline). Then move up and toward the center point, presenting that Jeremiah was imprisoned (B). Move a little closer to the center point for the second prophecy to Zedekiah (C), then in the center point at the pulpit or lectern cover Jeremiah's sinking into the mud (D). The second half of the chiasmus then mirrors the first half, only on the left side starting with Jeremiah's third prophecy to Zedekiah (C').

A possible structure is to first present the story of the text using the following story outline. One will need to summarize the longer passages and read key verses in each section. The second part of the sermon could use the three reactions to Jeremiah as a picture of what our attitudes toward preachers/teachers could be. To help with the telling of the story, here is the chiastic outline with the major events included.

- Present the text:

  A "And there was a word of YHWH to Jeremiah" (37:6–10; 1st prophecy to Zedekiah)
    B "And so it was" (37:11–16; Jeremiah imprisoned by nobles)
      C "And Jeremiah stayed at the court of the guard" (37:17–21; 2nd prophecy to Zedekiah)
        *D* "And Jeremiah sank into the mud" (38:1–6; nobles throw Jeremiah into the cistern)
      C' "And Jeremiah stayed at the court of the guard" (38:7–13, 14–28a; 3rd prophecy to Zedekiah)
    B' "And so it was" (38:28b–39:14; Jerusalem falls, Zedekiah taken)
  A' "And there was a word of YHWH to Jeremiah" (39:15–18; prophecy for Ebed-melek)

- Application: attitudes toward pastors/preachers/teachers.

- Correct attitudes of hostility and fluctuation
- Strive for, and maintain, respect
- Choose to respect, then expect to be blessed.

## DISCUSSION QUESTIONS

1. Who were some of your favorite teachers?

2. What did you learn from them?

3. What about them caused you to choose to have a positive mindset toward them?

4. What steps can be taken to start changing a negative attitude toward a pastor/teacher into a positive one?

5. How does our attitude toward a pastor/teacher affect our attitude toward God's Word?

## Jeremiah 40:1–41:18

### EXEGETICAL IDEA

The violent zealotry and ambition of one man, Ishmael son of Nethaniah, destroyed the possibility of a peaceful and prosperous Jewish community continuing in the land. Although the sin was not God's doing, it fulfilled his purpose of sending all the Jews into exile, obliterating any Jewish state in the former Judah. The story also reveals the moral chaos of the exilic Jerusalem community. It was a place where, even in the midst of the calamity of the fall of the city, people could behave with a complete lack of moral principles. The most dangerous thing one could do was trust another man and take his words at face value.

### THEOLOGICAL FOCUS

God uses even human evil to fulfill his purposes. For God's redemptive purposes to be fulfilled, all that remained of preexilic Judah had to be swept away. Indeed, chapter 44 reveals that many of the Jews still in the land at the time of Gedaliah's murder were deeply committed to paganism. When the postexilic Jews returned from Babylon, they would start the community again with a clean slate.

### PREACHING IDEA

When you can't stop crying, don't stop trusting in God.

### PREACHING POINTERS

This narrative follows the tragic fall of Jerusalem and the horrific end of Zedekiah's life. The beginning of this story gives us a hint that things might get better, that Judah will survive even though dominated by Babylon. Signs of prosperity begin to grow under Gedaliah's leadership, but this ends with his murder. Since he was appointed by Babylon, the Jews expect even greater destruction because of Nebuchadnezzar's wrath. What little hope they had is gone. Judah is completely destroyed. Nothing is left in the Promised Land. Even in this continuing desolation, Jeremiah was calling Judah to trust YHWH.

It is not wrong to hope for better times, nor even to ask God to bring those times about. Often, he does. But what about when the cancer comes back, when the children and parents are not reconciled, when the addiction becomes a lifestyle, when the pain doesn't go away? Sometimes eyes full of tears can best focus on the true object of our faith: a loving sovereign Lord.

# THE MURDER OF GEDALIAH (40:1–41:18)

## LITERARY STRUCTURE AND THEMES

This passage sets the stage for the self-deportation of the last meaningful Jewish community in the land. The passage is in two parts, with the first telling how Jeremiah chose to stay in the land (40:1–6) and the second giving the background explanation for the decision of all the other Jews to abandon it (40:7–41:18).

- ***The Oracle Announcement and the Background Material (40:1–6)***
- ***Gedaliah's Murder and the Flight of the Mizpah Community (40:7–41:18)***

## EXPOSITION

### *The Oracle Announcement and the Background Material (40:1–6)*

**40:1**. This verse presents us with an enigma. It is a typical oracle superscript of the kind we regularly see as a heading to a message of Jeremiah, and yet the message that follows is uttered not by Jeremiah but by Nebuzaradan. But the Babylonian's words in verses 2–3 sound exactly like a typical message of Jeremiah. There are several ways we might account for this. It could be that Nebuzaradan is thought to be the agent of YHWH's word; God spoke through him to Jeremiah. Although unlikely, this is not impossible (see 2 Chron. 35:22). Second, it could be that the phrase serves as a heading for a message from Jeremiah that comes later in the book, in 42:7. However, that message is removed quite far from the heading. A third possibility is that it is simply titular. The phrase "the word of YHWH that came to Jeremiah" (הַדָּבָר אֲשֶׁר־הָיָה אֶל־יִרְמְיָהוּ) typically comes at the head of a major unit of text; it appears at 7:1; 11:1; 18:1; 21:1; 30:1; 32:1; 34:1; 34:8; 35:1; 40:1; 44:1. Thus, it could be that instead of introducing a specific speech by Jeremiah, it only introduces a new section of the book.

**40:2–4**. English has a somewhat confusing ambiguity in that its second person ("you") makes no distinction between singular and plural. Thus, when Nebuzaradan says "you sinned" (חֲטָאתֶם) and "I am freeing you" (פִּתַּחְתִּיךָ), it is not apparent in English that the former has the plural and the latter has the singular. Using the plural, Nebuzaradan asserts that all the people of Jerusalem sinned; using the singular, he says that he is freeing Jeremiah. We do not know who chained Jeremiah; it could have been the Jewish authorities in Jerusalem, or it could have been some Babylonian soldiers who chained him up for exile not knowing who he was. But since the whole narrative up to this point has been focused on Jeremiah's captivity at the hands of his own countrymen, we are probably meant to understand that it was the Jews, not the Babylonians, who had put him in chains.

But the most surprising thing in this text is how closely Nebuzaradan's indictment of the people of Jerusalem mirrors Jeremiah's preaching. It is not too surprising that a Babylonian authority would attribute the destruction of Jerusalem to the work of a god; this was common in the ancient Near East. Also, it was common to assert that a city had fallen because its patron deity had become angry at the offenses of his or her people. The famous Sumerian Lament over Ur declares that the city fell because most of its gods abandoned it. It is still surprising that Nebuzaradan sounds so much like Jeremiah himself. It is of course possible that the Babylonian commander was influenced by Jeremiah; he obviously respected the prophet. However, we do not necessarily have the *ipsissima verba* of Nebuzaradan. The Bible often gives summarizing, somewhat paraphrased accounts of what characters said and not verbatim quotations. It is enough that Nebuzaradan affirmed that YHWH had abandoned Jerusalem because of its apostasy. What is significant, however, is that this passage presents the pagan Babylonian as a stark contrast to Jeremiah's countrymen. He affirmed Jeremiah's prophecies after the Jews had rejected them. He freed Jeremiah after the Jews had imprisoned him.

**40:5–6**. Jeremiah 39:14 mentioned that Gedaliah son of Ahikam was entrusted with the confinement of Jeremiah during the last days of Zedekiah's reign, but this is the first the reader has seen that Gedaliah was appointed by the Babylonians as governor over the territory of the former state of Judah. It appears that Gedaliah had been sympathetic to Jeremiah and thus would have had a more pro-Babylonian political position than most of his colleagues, who were stoutly pro-Egyptian and anti-Babylonian. Gedaliah was thus chosen as the governor over the province, and his administrative center was at Mizpah. There were no less than six different places called Mizpah in or near the land of Israel; this one was in Benjamite territory north of Jerusalem. It had a dark history in biblical narrative; this was where a concubine was raped and murdered, an event that triggered a bloody civil war in the time of the judges (Judg. 20–21). After the nation was split between Israel and Judah, Mizpah was a fortified city defending Judah from the northern tribes (1 Kings 15:22). As noted in this passage, Mizpah was the administrative center for the Babylonian Empire, and it continued to have that function for the Persian Empire (Neh. 3:15). Judas Maccabeus used Mizpah as a rallying point for his army in his war with the Seleucids (1 Macc. 3:46). Earlier scholars placed Mizpah at Nebi Samwil, but it is now thought to have been at Tell en-Nasbeh (Arnold 1992; Rainey 1979).

Nebuzaradan gave Jeremiah complete freedom of movement: He could stay in the land, go to Babylon, or go wherever he wanted, and he was given provisions to enable him to make his choice without being constrained by a lack of means. He chose to stay in the former Judah with Gedaliah. His decision is set up as a contrast to the next narrative, which tells why the rest of the remaining Jews fled the land. The total emptying of the land was not what Jeremiah wanted; he would have much preferred to see the remaining Jews stay there and thrive. But human ambition and fear got in the way, and soon the land of Judah was all but devoid of Jews.

### *Gedaliah's Murder and the Flight of the Mizpah Community (40:7–41:18)*

**40:7–8**. The remaining nobles, soldiers, and civic leaders—men who had hidden out "in the hinterland" (בַּשָּׂדֶה) in advance of the advancing Babylonian army—heard that one of their own, Gedaliah, had been appointed as governor over the province. This was good news, as it would allow them to return things to a state of affairs that at least resembled former times. Most of them no doubt intended to lend their support to the creation of a Jewish state and hoped that better times lay ahead. It is easy for the modern reader to miss the significance of this. If all the Jews had been of a good will and had behaved responsibly, they could have continued on as a Jewish state, albeit a province of the Babylonian Empire. In this situation, Judah would not have been entirely eradicated and the exile would not have been complete. God did not cause the events that followed, but those events did lead to what God intended: the total annihilation of a Jewish state in the land, with the result that the people were entirely in exile.

**40:9–10**. Gedaliah assured the men who came to him that they had nothing to fear from the Babylonians, and he swore an oath to them to that effect. They would be allowed to settle back in the land and reestablish their communities. Some of these men had perhaps led guerilla resistance to Babylon (Thompson 1980, 655). If so, Gedaliah needed not only to reassure them but also to dissuade them from trying to stage an insurrection against the Babylonian authorities. He wanted them to lay down their arms and take up an agricultural life. This would ensure the survival of the people and lay the groundwork for a larger restoration of Jewish settlement in the land.

**40:11–12**. In addition to those in the hinterland of the former Israel and Judah, some Jewish refugees had fled to Moab, Ammon, and Edom. These too sensed that the violence of the war was over, and that they could return to the land and take up the task of rebuilding a Jewish society there. We do not how many of these there were; some Edomites had shown extreme hostility to the Jewish refugees (Obad. 10–14). But there are always some refugees who, through luck or personal connections, manage to find shelter even in hostile areas. These too came back to assist in rebuilding the new community, and as Gedaliah suggested, they set about gathering what crops they could find. Since they collected grapes, olives, and "summer produce" (קַיִץ), it was late summer when they returned. It is perhaps surprising that they were able to glean a "great abundance" (הַרְבֵּה מְאֹד) of these crops, since the land would have been ravaged by the invading Babylonians. But armies can never totally eradicate agricultural fields (to do so takes an enormous amount of labor, and the troops were preoccupied with the siege of Jerusalem). Also, the surviving Jewish community was very small, and the gleaning was enormous in proportion to their modest needs. The language is deliberately idyllic (Lalleman 2013, 265), suggesting that the Jews had a legitimate opportunity to reestablish themselves as a flourishing community in their ancestral land.

**40:13–16**. Gedaliah comes across in the account as both decent and naïve. He wanted to believe the best of the men who were with him, but he could not see that there was a serpent in their midst. Also, Ishmael was of the royal blood (2 Kings 25:25; Jer. 41:1), and this may have persuaded Gedaliah that he could not possibly serve as an assassin and upend the hopes of the Jewish community. The man who warned Gedaliah, Johanan son of Kareah, was himself fairly ruthless; he was willing to murder Ishmael secretly, and in 43:2–7 he rejected a message from YHWH and forcibly took Jeremiah with him to Egypt. Even so, Johanan correctly identified Ishmael as an assassin, and hoped to thwart his plot and enable the Jews to remain safely in the land.

**41:1–3**. Ishmael murdered Gedaliah's through foul treachery. Sharing a meal with a man and then suddenly killing him obviously implies a complete lack of moral scruples, but in an ancient Near Eastern culture it was especially heinous, given the great importance placed on hospitality. Thus Psalm 41:9 (MT 10) complains, "the friend who shared my bread lifted his heel against me." The murder took place in the seventh month, in September or October, soon after his initial meeting with Gedaliah. The Bible only gives us the barest hint of Ishmael's motive, implying that he killed Gedaliah because he had been appointed by the king of Babylon (v. 2). We know this much about Ishmael: he was a member of the royal family, head of a faction of Jews (the ten men who were with him in the murder), tried to take to Ammon a group of captives (including women who were of the royal family), and was a willing agent of Baalis king of Ammon (40:14). It is possible that King Zedekiah, in his flight east from Jerusalem (39:4–5), was headed toward Ammon. If so, Baalis may have been strongly anti-Babylonian.

All of this suggests that Ishmael wanted to continue, by insurrection, the fight against the Babylonians. When he assassinated Gedaliah, he also killed whatever Babylonians he found. He appears to have been stridently nationalistic, and perhaps wanted to avenge Zedekiah. He perhaps wanted to be recognized as the legitimate Davidic king; having women from the royal family would have strengthened his claim, particularly if he were to marry one who was closer to the line of succession than himself. Baalis was perhaps willing to sponsor Ishmael's claims, knowing that if Ishmael were widely regarded as the true heir of David, Baalis would be all the stronger for having Ishmael as a client. Ishmael almost certainly regarded Gedaliah as a collaborator, traitor, and perhaps as an obstacle. As such, his murder of the governor was thoroughly political.

But this does not tell the whole story. Besides killing Gedaliah and his staff, Ishmael carried out a slaughter of Jewish pilgrims from the north (41:4–9), people who surely could not have been considered collaborators with the Babylonians. This suggests a more pathological and irrational frame of mind. It may be that in his extreme zeal and anger, he saw traitors everywhere and began to murder indiscriminately. If so, he was by no means unique in the history of guerilla warfare and resistance movements. Perhaps he looked on all northerners as traitors to the house of David. If so, his actions were singularly insane; there was hardly any point to maintaining old animosities now that both the northern and southern kingdoms were in ruins. But again, a high level of rationality is not a quality associated with zealotry.

**41:4–10**. A group of pilgrims arrived from the north, the former kingdom of Israel. They lived in what had once been great or important cities that had been conquered and left in ruins. Shechem is the city that Simeon and Levi ravaged in the time of Jacob (Gen. 34); but more recently, in 724, the Assyrians had laid waste to the city. The Assyrians had also destroyed Samaria, the capital city of the northern kingdom, in 722. Shiloh during the time of the judges had been the site of the Tent of Meeting, but the city had been ravaged and the central sanctuary destroyed (Jer. 7:12–14). It was fitting that survivors of the holocaust of the northern kingdom came south to mourn Jerusalem and its temple. The pilgrims may have come for the Feast of Booths, as it was the seventh month, but they intended to make ritual mourning over the destruction of the temple.

Ishmael's appeal to the pilgrims is literally, (בֹּאוּ אֶל־גְּדַלְיָהוּ בֶן־אֲחִיקָם; v. 6) "Come to Gedaliah son of Ahikam." The invitation was obviously meant to put them off their guard; they would think that all was well and that they were about to have an audience with the governor. But it is also grimly ironic: Gedaliah was dead, and the pilgrims would "come to Gedaliah" in the sense that they would soon join him. Ishmael and his cohort murdered the eighty pilgrims, all except for ten men who bought their lives with a stash of food. If Ishmael had any patriotic zeal, he was now shown to be no more than a common brigand. He tossed the bodies into a cistern, apparently because he wanted to conceal the deed for a time, giving him the opportunity to carry out his plan to find and kidnap some residents of Mizpah before he was detected. The cistern is identified as one that Asa of Judah had dug when he controlled Mizpah and used the city as a defensive bulwark against Baasha of Israel (1 Kings 15:16–22). We do not know how many captives Ishmael tried to take away to Ammon, but it was probably a small group since Ishmael had only ten men with him. But as suggested above, the women of the royal household may have been his real target.

> *TRANSLATION NOTE: The Problem of the Cistern in 41:7, 9*
> The passage twice speaks of throwing the corpses of the pilgrims into a cistern (vv. 7, 9), but in both cases, there are textual problems. Verse 7b has the ungrammatical, "And Ishmael son of Nethaniah slaughtered them to the middle of the cistern" (וַיִּשְׁחָטֵם יִשְׁמָעֵאל בֶּן־נְתַנְיָה אֶל־תּוֹךְ הַבּוֹר). There is evidently a textual corruption. The Syriac and two manuscripts of the LXX (Codex Venetus and a Lucianic recension) add the equivalent of "and threw them" (וַיַּשְׁלִיכֵם). Also, the LXX lacks תּוֹךְ. Thus, the line should be translated, "And Ishmael son of Nethaniah slaughtered them and threw them into the cistern." Verse 9a is also difficult; it literally reads, "Now the cistern where Ishmael threw all the bodies of the men whom he had killed by the hand of Gedaliah" (וְהַבּוֹר אֲשֶׁר הִשְׁלִיךְ שָׁם יִשְׁמָעֵאל אֵת כָּל־פִּגְרֵי הָאֲנָשִׁים אֲשֶׁר הִכָּה בְּיַד־גְּדַלְיָהוּ). This is clearly impossible. Some modern translations render בְּיַד־גְּדַלְיָהוּ as "along with Gedaliah" (NIV, ESV), but this is forced; the Hebrew cannot mean that. Instead of בְּיַד־גְּדַלְיָהוּ, the LXX reads φρέαρ μέγα, "a large cistern," evidently translating an original בּוֹר גָּדוֹל. This should be followed. So emended, verse 9a reads, "Now the cistern where Ishmael threw all the bodies of the men whom he had killed was a large cistern."

**41:11–16.** Ishmael took his captives and went from Mizpah to Gibeon. This is strange, because his destination was Ammon, east of the Jordan, but Gibeon is a few miles southwest of Mizpah. Some have suggested that he detoured to Gibeon to recover the stash of supplies mentioned in 41:8, or simply to evade pursuers (Lundbom 2008c, 121). Johanan son of Kareah was evidently not too far from Mizpah. He got word of what had happened soon enough for him to gather his forces and then find and overtake Ishmael. Two factors in this passage suggest that Ishmael was indeed making a play to be recognized as the true heir to David's throne.

- First, verse 12 mentions that Johanan's force caught up with Ishmael "somewhere near the abundant water at Gibeon" (אֶל־מַיִם רַבִּים אֲשֶׁר בְּגִבְעוֹן). The words do not necessarily mean they were right beside the pool; they were reasonably close to it. But it seems that the narration intentionally locates the conflict here. During David's rise to power after Saul's death, an important skirmish was fought here between some of David's men and a remnant of Saulide forces under Abner. The skirmish was part of a larger conflict to see whether David or a member of Saul's family would become the next king, and although it was not the final, decisive battle, the Saulides lost and fled (1 Sam. 2:12–16). This suggests that we readers are meant to see the parallel between the two battles at the pool of Gibeon. Ishmael, like Abner, lost and fled. And as the Saulides failed to claim the throne, so did Ishmael.
- Second, the text goes out of its way to say that the captives were happy to see Johanan arrive and that they got away from Ishmael as quickly as they could (vv. 13–14). Furthermore, verse 16 tells us that the captives were made up of soldiers, women, children, and eunuchs. We know that the women were of royal blood; this suggests that the soldiers in the group were palace guards and that the children were also of the royal family. Eunuchs would be associated with the harem and palace administration. Once again, it seems to be a small group, almost entirely made up of people associated with David's palace. These were the people Ishmael wanted, and yet they escaped him as quickly as they could. This would suggest that none of them supported Ishmael and his objectives. If any of the royal family

> still had any hopes for a restoration of the Davidic throne, they did not think Ishmael was the man to do it.

Ishmael only lost two men in the fight (he came with ten and returned with eight), but if he had a plan to make himself the new Davidic king, he failed.

**41:17–18**. Johanan, having gotten the captives from Gibeon back to Mizpah, collected all the Jews in the area and took the now sizable group down to Bethlehem. They were certain that the Babylonians would not sit still at the news that their governor and some of their soldiers had been murdered. They expected the Babylonians to slaughter every Jew they found, killing first and asking questions later. Their only hope, they thought, was to flee to Egypt.

## THEOLOGICAL FOCUS

Unusually for a prophetic book, this text is entirely narrative, and most of it does not directly concern the life of Jeremiah (unless he was one of the captives whom Ishmael seized, an unlikely development since the book would probably have mentioned such a thing). We must therefore approach this passage as narrative rather than as prophecy. It tells a story, and we must determine the meaning of the story. At the heart of it is a seeming tragedy. The Jews who remained in the land were fairly well treated by Nebuchadnezzar; they had the opportunity to rebuild their community under the governance of one of their own. This man, Gedaliah, was a decent man who desired the best for his people and encouraged them to rebuild their lives and communities. A brutal and ambitious zealot, however, destroyed all of this when he murdered the governor. The ultimate outcome would be the self-deportation of the remaining Jews, leaving the land effectively desolate. But the careful reader of Jeremiah knows that this was God's purpose. In perhaps Jeremiah's most important message, the scroll read out in Jehoiakim's fourth year, he declared, "This whole country will become a desolate wasteland" (Jer. 25:11). In addition, we learn from chapter 44 that apostasy was still deeply rooted in the Jews who remained in the land. The exile was to be a comprehensive event, and there could be no thriving Jewish community in the land the time of deportation ended. Specific theological lessons are as follows:

- Nebuzaradan showed better understanding of why Jerusalem fell than did most of the Jews. He also freed Jeremiah, whereas the Jews repeatedly kept him in captivity. Sometimes outsiders show more integrity, compassion, and theological acumen than those who are, nominally at least, the people of God.
- Jeremiah's devotion to his people was never in doubt. He could have taken what probably would have been a comfortable retirement in Babylon, but he chose to stay in the now-desolate land with the Jews. A true spokesman for God continues to serve those to whom he is sent, even when he has been reviled.
- We must learn to read people carefully. Ishmael gave signs of being fully on Gedaliah's side, but he murdered the governor. Johanan had his faults, but in one important matter he was right. Looking at the matter from a purely practical point of view, Gedaliah should have believed the harsh-talking Johanan and not the oily Ishmael.
- Ambition and zeal make for a dangerous combination. Ishmael apparently acted for his own benefit, desiring to elevate himself to the status of a king. His zeal against perceived traitors justified his treachery and violence, deadening the voice of conscience, but

his ambition guided his zeal, driving him to do what was for his own benefit.

- A man driven by ambition and zeal may commit heinous and irrational acts, as when Ishmael slaughtered the pilgrims.
- The Bible does not tell us what became of Ishmael. It is perhaps enough for us to know that his plans failed and that he, although of the royal family, died in obscurity. Perhaps his years of wasting away at the court of Baalis was punishment enough.
- We should look at events, as it were, through bifocals, able to function in the historical present and yet also able to perceive God's hand for more distant purposes. On the one hand, it was right for the remaining Jews to try to rebuild their lives, and it was right for Johanan to try to thwart Ishmael's murder of Gedaliah. We should do our best to build an upright and peaceable community. On the other hand, it was God's will for the preexilic community of Judah to be thoroughly eradicated. They could not continue on in the land, for otherwise the lessons of exile would never be learned and they would continue in their idolatry (as chapter 44 demonstrates). It is right to mourn the evil committed by Ishmael and its repercussions, and it is also right to see hand of God at work for greater purposes.

## PREACHING AND TEACHING STRATEGIES

### *Exegetical and Theological Synthesis*

The story leads us to envision hope for Israel. Even though the nobles and king have been defeated and the temple destroyed, there are still some Jews who under the good leadership of Gedaliah can rebuild Israel. There is even a bountiful harvest. Through the tears for Israel's defeat we can see God's hand. Israel is not totally destroyed. But then even this little bit of hope comes crashing down when the naive Gedaliah is killed by the evil Ishmael, resulting in the Jews planning to exile themselves to Egypt.

Wait, what happened to the happy ending? There is one, but this passage doesn't present it. This side of heaven, there is no guarantee for happy endings. God is always faithful, but in this case his good and faithful hand is conducting Israel's total destruction.

### *Preaching Idea*

When you can't stop crying, don't stop trusting.

### *Contemporary Connections*

#### *What does it mean?*

What is the object of our faith? Of course, we trust Christ's work on our behalf to bring us into the new covenant with God and give us new hearts. This passage helps us focus that faith in him with more accuracy. Is our faith in God alone, or is our faith in what we hope God will do for us? Are we trusting that a pleasant result will come out of hardship, or are we trusting a sovereign God no matter what he does? Through our tears, we are looking for God's good hand. The intense emotion has produced a number of songs that speak to this, filled with phrases of God's blessing coming through tears. These are wonderful songs and we have been blessed by them. Often God does bring about a delightful result from hardship, but not always. So, what is the object of our faith? Are we looking to a happy ending, or are we submitting to a sovereign Lord?

#### *Is it true?*

We in our very comfortable western world we tend equate "good" with "easy." If it is hard, then it is not what we had in mind. We ask God for good but in our hearts what we are really asking for is comfort. This story shows us that God can bring his purpose out of something that is very hard. His ultimate purpose was for Israel to be in exile, with no national presence in the Promised Land. So, God's plan was to thoroughly eradicate Israel from the land? Yes. Without the exile his nation would continue in their idolatry. In our application we must be careful not to equate all pain as a result of sin. The pain in the passage is the direct result of sin, both Ishmael's murder and the centuries of Israel's sins of idolatry. Sometimes the pain in our lives is the result of sin, but often it is not. Not all the pain in our lives comes from sin, but all our pain can bring about God's good purpose.

Jerry Sittser has the right to speak about pain. In one horrible traffic crash he lost his mother, his wife, and his youngest daughter. Several years after this catastrophic loss, he wrote *A Grace Disguised*. His intent was to "show how it is possible to live in and be enlarged by loss, even as we continue to experience it" (Sittser 2004, 18). The rest of the book presents that the only way to truly do that is through a relationship with the Lord Jesus. This must-read book shows that God uses pain to accomplish good. God used Israel's pain and he uses ours.

*Now what?*

There is an old hymn by John Newton, "I Asked the Lord," readily available on numerous websites, which captures the application thrust of this passage. The hymn or poem traces the journey of one seeking to know God more. The opening stanza is a prayer.

> I asked the Lord that I might grow
> in faith and love and ev'ry grace;
> might more of his salvation know,
> and seek more earnestly his face.

After five stanzas describing great struggles and burdens put on the poet by God, he closes with God's answer to his prayer.

> These inward trials I employ
> from self and pride to set thee free,
> and break thy schemes of earthly joy
> that thou may'st find thy all in me.

We are to find our all in God, not in what he does. There is a subtle form of idolatry that we must caution against. Is the pleasant outcome of hard times what we trust in, or is it God alone?

Some friends have written and performed a play called *The Day Between*. It is the struggle that Mary, the mother of Jesus, had during those hours between the crucifixion and the resurrection. Of course, we listen with ears that have heard the hallelujahs of the resurrection, but in the play Mary is in the deepest sorrow and confusion. Many of those to whom we preach and teach live their lives in an in-between world. The pain is real, and the resurrection seems so far off that its future joy doesn't diminish the current pain.

### Creativity in Presentation

It is hard for me to write about trusting God alone when the tears are flowing. What right do I have to give direction to those whose lives are pain upon pain? I am trying to paint a picture of a truth that could help, but I am not in the picture like they are. They know constant pain. Others cry each day for a son or daughter who is far from them and far from God. We teachers/pastors must remember that we are not presenting truths from our lives; we are presenting truths that God has revealed. Now, if you have suffered a great loss or are enduring a constant pain, it could be wise to be transparent about it; of course, good judgment must be exercised. Some things should not be public. Even if your loss or pain seems minor compared to others, being transparent can help in presenting the truth of this passage. People always identify with our struggles far more than our successes.

Sometimes a narrative can be told in sections, giving application along the way. It would seem best to preset this whole story before applying it, because the truth emerges out of the bigger picture. A way to create tension is to tell the story as though the application were to come at the point in the story of Gedaliah coming to power and the harvest being plentiful. We see that God has come through again. Israel is going to continue, but that is not the end of the story. When stories have twists, they are more interesting, so capitalize upon this twist and upon our assumption that this story will end with "they lived happily ever after."

Depending upon the teacher/pastor this passage can be presented with a strong evangelistic appeal at the end, because ultimately there is a very happy ending for those who receive the great gift of forgiveness and righteousness that comes through Christ. This promise of life is as sure as God's promise of the destruction of Israel.

Others may choose to conclude by staying focused upon the not-so-pleasant but very necessary truth that our trust must be as accurate as possible. It is most accurate when our faith is centered upon God himself, even when great evil surrounds us and there seems to be no joy in life.

Here is one possible structure:

- Present the whole story:
    - Introduction to the story (40:1–6)
    - Rebuilding begins under Gedaliah (40:7–12)
    - Gedaliah wrongly trusts Ishmael (40:13–16)
    - Ishmael's murder of Gedaliah and treachery against Israel (41:1–10)
    - Johanan's rescue of the people (41:11–16)
    - Plans to flee to Egypt (41:17–18)

- Analysis of the story
    - This set into motion the complete deportation by Nebuchadnezzar, which was God's plan.

- Application of the story
    - When you can't stop crying, don't stop trusting.

## DISCUSSION QUESTIONS

1. Take time to pray, by name, if possible, for those who are hurting with chronic physical pain.

2. Pray for those who are in constant emotional pain due to broken relationships.

3. When a situation brought great pain into your life, describe some of the emotions you felt. What helped you keep to trusting in the sovereign Lord?

4. How do you think God could use can some of the evil we see in our nation?

5. If appropriate and only if you are comfortable sharing, tell how God has used evil in your life to grow your relationship with him.

## Jeremiah 42:1–43:7

**EXEGETICAL IDEA**

The Jews, in a panic over whether the Babylonians would come down upon them in severe reprisal for the murder of Gedaliah (whom Babylon had appointed as governor), asked Jeremiah to seek God's direction over whether they should flee the land and head into Egypt. They assured him they would do whatever God directed. When told to stay in the land, they immediately and angrily rejected the directive and ran for the Egyptian border. The survivors in exilic Judah thus proved to be as unreliable about their willingness to obey God as they had been before the Babylonian conquest.

**THEOLOGICAL FOCUS**

The obstinacy of people demonstrates that God's punishment is just. God's promise that the people would be safe if they stayed in the land was genuine, but in the larger theology of the book, the episode illustrates how obstinate the people were, and it shows that the exile had to be total for it to be effective.

**PREACHING IDEA**

If you ask God for help, accept his answer.

**PREACHING POINTERS**

It seemed logical that the Babylonians would severely punish Judah for killing Gedaliah. Therefore, the best course would be to flee. It would seem that the circumstances God allowed led in that direction. However, God did not send these Jews to Egypt, where they would suffer and die. Rather, they chose to reject God's offer of life.

To this day, people reject God's offer. Our attitude toward those who reject God's offer must not be that they are the enemy, nor should we look down on them in pity; rather, we should patiently proclaim God's offer of life. This rejection should also be a warning to us. While our acceptance of his gift of life through Jesus gives us a secure eternal relationship with him, it does not mean that we won't reject his expectations of us. Our disobedience does not take away the gift, but it does bring his discipline.

# JEREMIAH'S MESSAGE REJECTED (42:1–43:7)

## LITERARY STRUCTURE AND THEMES

The people who remained after Gedaliah's assassination begged Jeremiah to pray for them and to give them a word from YHWH to guide them in the matter of whether they should remain in the land or flee to Egypt. They were terrified that Babylon would bring a terrible retribution down upon them for the assassination. Jeremiah came back with a lengthy message from God telling them that they must remain in the land, and that if they did so he would protect them and restore their prosperity. If they fled to Egypt, however, he would destroy them. The people, despite having solemnly sworn to do whatever YHWH commanded, angrily rejected the message. They not only fled to Egypt, but they took the unwilling Jeremiah with them.

We may well wonder why this passage is part of the book. The intent, it seems clear, is to show that the complete deportation of the Jews from the land was not an arbitrary or cruel act of God. Even if it was God's will that the exile be comprehensive, it came about because of the foolish and disobedient acts of the people—acts that they committed of their own accord. They chose exile for themselves, and through their defiance of God and of Jeremiah they brought about their own ruin. This passage demonstrates that destruction and exile was for the Jews a self-imposed fate. It also proves that the Egyptian Jewish community was a continuation of the apostate Jerusalem community that existed prior to the exile. Israel's true remnant was in Babylon, not Egypt. This fulfilled the prophecy of Jeremiah 24, which promised that the Jews taken to Babylon were the "good figs," but that those who remained in Jerusalem or who fled to Egypt were the "bad figs," a people destined for destruction.

- *The Request and Vow (42:1–6)*
- *YHWH's Message (42:7–22)*
- *The Response (43:1–7)*

## EXPOSITION

### *The Request and Vow (42:1–6)*

**42:1–3**. It appears that officers of the army of Judah, now a defunct organization, took the leadership role in the small community of exiles. Johanan son of Kareah had led the rescue of the people Ishmael had kidnapped, and thus he was at this time undoubtedly the ranking member of the community. Jezaniah son of Hoshaiah in 43:2 is called Azariah ben Hoshaiah. In the LXX of 42:1 (where it is numbered 49:1), he is called Αζαριας ("Azariah"), suggesting that there may be a scribal error in the MT. He too was evidently a leading citizen. But men of no rank also came to Jeremiah, as implied by saying that people "from the least to the greatest" stood before him. Their decision to seek out Jeremiah was by common consensus. Their request, in verses 2–3, is to listen to their concerns and then take them to YHWH to obtain an answer. Their appeal is based on their very small number: unless God directs us and shows us his favor, they imply, we are sure to vanish from the face of the earth. Forebodingly, their request is almost identical to that of Zedekiah in 37:3: "Pray for us to YHWH our God" (הִתְפַּלֶּל־נָא בַעֲדֵנוּ אֶל־יְהוָה אֱלֹהֵינוּ). Johanan said, "And pray for us to YHWH your God" (וְהִתְפַּלֵּל בַּעֲדֵנוּ אֶל־יְהוָה אֱלֹהֶיךָ). Zedekiah's request began a series of events that led to Jeremiah's imprisonment, and Johanan's request led to Jeremiah being taken captive to Egypt.

**42:4–6**. Jeremiah promises to pray for them and seek direction from God, but he is careful to point out that he will relay to them all that YHWH says. What they make of God's directives will be up to them (v. 4). The Jews in turn swear an oath that they will do whatever Jeremiah, delivering God's message, tells them to do. Their oath is especially strong because they invoke God as their witness (v. 5). They further swear themselves to unconditional obedience, saying that they will follow God's directions, "whether good or evil" (אִם־טוֹב וְאִם־רָע). This expression appears to mean whether the advice seems to them to be good or bad. Their oath is strong, detailed, and binding.

### *YHWH's Message (42:7–22)*

**42:7–9**. Verse 7 literally says, "And it came about after ten days that there was a word of YHWH [belonging] to Jeremiah" (וַיְהִי מִקֵּץ עֲשֶׂרֶת יָמִים וַיְהִי דְבַר־יְהוָה אֶל־יִרְמְיָהוּ). Does this mean that Jeremiah received YHWH's word at the end of ten days, or could he have received YHWH's word some time earlier but only delivered it after ten days? Most readers presume that it is the former, but the Hebrew is somewhat ambiguous on this point; it could be the latter. Interpreters note that there is no explanation or clear precedent for the ten-day waiting period (Lundbom 2008c, 131). It could be, as some suggest, that Jeremiah needed time to be sure that he was getting the true word from God and not simply expressing his own opinion and desire (Thompson 1980, 665); or it could be, as many suppose, simply that he got no response from God until the tenth day. But if he received YHWH's answer earlier, waiting ten days before giving it to the people may have been a deliberate imposition of a "cooling-off" period. Immediately after the murder of Gedaliah and the kidnapping attempt, the Jews would have been traumatized and in something of a panic. By waiting until the tenth day, Jeremiah gave them a chance to settle down and assess the situation.

Whatever the correct explanation, Jeremiah on the tenth day summoned the leaders and the whole community, wanting to be sure that everyone heard his message in its entirety and that they got nothing secondhand. His opening words contain both the standard formula that the following words come from God ("Thus says YHWH, the God of Israel") and a reminder that the Jews were receiving instructions from God in response to their direct request. This was to remind them of their duty to obey, both because the message was from God and because they had voluntarily brought this divine directive upon themselves.

**42:10–12**. In several statements, YHWH reassured the Jews that they would be safe if they remained in the land.

- Recalling the language of Jeremiah's call (1:10), YHWH told the Jews that if they stay, he will build them up and not destroy them, and that he will plant them and not uproot them. This allusion reinforces the authority of Jeremiah, and it implies that God has the freedom either to heal or to harm. They should, therefore, do as they were told, knowing that God was now reversing much of what he had previously said through the prophet—that he would destroy and uproot rather than build and plant.
- Astonishingly, YHWH also told the Jews, "I regret the disaster that I have brought upon you" (נִחַמְתִּי אֶל־הָרָעָה אֲשֶׁר עָשִׂיתִי לָכֶם). This language closely follows the words of YHWH to Moses in Exodus 42:14, "And YHWH relented concerning the disaster that he had said he would bring upon his people" (וַיִּנָּחֶם יְהוָה עַל־הָרָעָה אֲשֶׁר דִּבֶּר לַעֲשׂוֹת לְעַמּוֹ). This has the purpose of communicating that God's compassion for his people has been reawakened. It does, however, raise certain issues, as are explored below.
- In general terms, he told them that they need not fear Nebuchadnezzar,

because God would deliver them from his hand (v. 11). This addressed their fear directly, as they believed that the king would retaliate for the deaths of his governor and men both brutally and indiscriminately. This promise could be misunderstood, however; the people might have thought that God would destroy the Babylonian king and his army.

- As clarification, YHWH assured them that he would provoke Nebuchadnezzar to show compassion on the Jews (v. 12). There would be no retaliation against them. God would see to it that the king understood that the remaining survivors had nothing to do with the assassination and that it was not in his interest to punish them for Ishmael's actions.

What does YHWH mean by saying that he "regretted" or "relented" from his previous decision to obliterate Jerusalem (v. 10)? In normal English usage, "regret" means that someone has decided that his previous actions were wrong, and "relent" means to turn away from what one has been doing. In Genesis 6:6, for example, God states that he regretted ever making human beings (וַיִּנָּחֶם יְהוָה כִּי־עָשָׂה אֶת־הָאָדָם). This would seem to imply that YHWH had come to believe that he should never have allowed Nebuchadnezzar to take Jerusalem, or at least that he would allow no more such events. And yet the entire thesis of chapters 40–44 is that YHWH was determined to eliminate the entire Jewish community from the land. He had to do this because, as the events of these chapters show, the Jews were incorrigibly apostate. The only way to heal the land and change the people was to make a clean slate, and this involved a complete exile.

Careful consideration of the language gives part of the answer. The Hebrew word נחם, like the English "regret," can have a range of meanings. Although it can mean that a prior action is now viewed as mistaken, it can also mean to be grieved at having to take an action, even if one believes that the action is necessary and right. Thus, an employer who grieves at firing an underperforming employee does not believe that the action is wrong but is sorry at having to do it. In verse 10, YHWH does not mean that destroying Jerusalem was a mistake, but he does mean that he took no pleasure in it. God's "regret" for his prior actions is a vivid anthropopathism, implying that he did not act out of animosity and that he hated having to do it.

But what are we to make of his promise to grant the Jews safety and prosperity if they remain? This is somewhat surprising, again, because the whole point of the narrative is that the exile must be thorough. No meaningful Jewish community was to be allowed to remain in the land. The promise was genuine, and the people could have had a thriving Jewish community in the land in the immediate aftermath of the fall of Jerusalem. But the validity of the promise, somewhat paradoxically, does not contradict the reality of God's purpose to eliminate any Jewish community in the land. This paradox is characteristic of many divine offers. In every case, there is the genuine possibility of salvation even when it is God's purpose is to carry out judgment. If the Jews had chosen to remain in the land, in obedience to Jeremiah's message, would God have protected them and enabled them to thrive? Yes. Similarly, the preaching of Jesus to the Jews of his generation was a genuine appeal for repentance and offer of salvation even though, in the hidden purposes of God, the Jews would not believe, Jesus would be crucified, and the message of the gospel would go out to the Gentiles.

*TRANSLATION NOTE: A Scribal Error in 42:10?* The MT אִם־שׁוֹב תֵּשְׁבוּ בָּאָרֶץ הַזֹּאת is unusual for having the infinitive absolute of שׁוּב ("to return") followed by the *yiqtol* of ישׁב ("to stay"). The Greek reads, Ἐὰν καθίσαντες καθίσητε ἐν τῇ γῇ ταύτῃ ("If staying, you stay in this land"), suggesting that its *Vorlage* reads יָשׁוֹב, the infinitive absolute of ישׁב,

instead of שׁוב. Many interpreters believe that the LXX is the better reading and emend the MT accordingly. Holladay, however, prefers to keep the MT and translate it as, "If you go back and stay in this land" (Holladay 1989, 274). This implies that they should go back from Bethlehem to Mizpah and stay there. On the other hand, שׁוב sometimes means "to do again" or "continue to do." For example, in Judges 19:7, וַיֵּשֶׁב וַיָּלֶן means, "and he continued to lodge." Ecclesiastes 1:7b says, "To the place where the rivers go, there they continue to go" (שָׁם הֵם שָׁבִים לָלָכֶת). Thus, it is possible that the unamended text of Jeremiah 42:10 means, "If you continue to stay in this land." Although emending the MT to agree with the LXX appears to be the obvious solution, it may not be correct.

**42:13–18**. This passage gives the alternative—what will happen if the people refuse to obey and head for Egypt. Verse 13 describes the motivation for their flight to Egypt—it is (an understandable) fear. They have had enough of war, and they are terrified of ever hearing again the signal trumpets of the Babylonian army. They have experienced siege and the accompanying famine, and they never want to go through that again. Nevertheless, the truth was counterintuitive. If they stayed in what was now a minor province of the Babylonian Empire, they would flourish and never again hear the sounds of battle or feel the gnaw of hunger. In Egypt, however, they would remain under God's judgment, and the recent nightmare would continue. We speak of the four horsemen of the Apocalypse, but in Jeremiah there are three agents of punishment and death: the sword, famine, and disease (v. 17). These accompanied every siege; and for the surviving Jews, if they should flee to Egypt, those terrors would never end. Their experience in Egypt would be a continuation of the judgment on Jerusalem (v. 18). Again, counterintuitively, the Egyptian who were their allies in the war against Babylon would revile them as refugees in their midst. Their Babylonian conquerors would leave them in peace. But to accept these counterintuitive truths, they had to have faith in God and his prophet.

**42:19–20**. Having given the Jews YHWH's message, Jeremiah adds a personal note of warning. Verse 20 should be translated as follows: "For you made an error to your own harm when you sent me to YHWH your God with the words, 'Pray on our behalf to YHWH our God. Tell us everything that YHWH our God says, and we will do it.'" It is surprising that Jeremiah declares that they made a serious error when they asked him to pray for them and convey to them YHWH's instructions. But the following verse (21) indicates that Jeremiah, even before they answered him, was sure that they would reject his message and violate their vow. Asking God's prophet to pray for them and to seek God's will was, of itself, not an error. But it was an action that only compounded their guilt when they refused to listen. Their vow was similar to the covenant Zedekiah and the leading citizens made in chapter 34 promising to release their slaves—a covenant that they promptly broke. Both the covenant of chapter 34 and the vow of chapter 42 would have been good if the people had done as they promised. But their violation of the promises only made their standing before God that much worse.

*TRANSLATION NOTE: The Meaning of 42:20*

The words הִתְעֵיתֶם בְּנַפְשׁוֹתֵיכֶם have caused some trouble (we are here following the *qere* הִתְעֵיתֶם). The words literally mean, "You have led astray with/by/in your selves." Some follow the Vulgate *decepistis animas vestras*, "You have deceived your souls," but it is unlikely that the preposition בְּ marks the direct object (for a full discussion of this problem, see Holladay 1989, 301). Probably the preposition should be regarded as a בְּ of price, meaning, "You have gone astray at the cost of your own lives." But there is another problem in this verse. It can be rendered in two different ways. The first is represented by the ESV: ". . . you have gone astray at the cost of your own lives. For you sent me to the LORD your God, saying, 'Pray for us to the LORD our God, and whatever the LORD our God says, declare to us and we will do it.'" In this version, the clause "you have gone astray" (הִתְעֵיתֶם) is a general warning that they are making a grave mistake if they disobey God. What follows, "For you sent me" is a merely secondary appeal, reminding them that they were the ones who initiated the inquiry to YHWH. Against this, the NIV translates the verse, "you made a fatal mistake when you sent me to the LORD your God and said, 'Pray to the LORD our God for us; tell us everything he says, and we will do it.'" In this version, the clause "you made . . . a mistake" (הִתְעֵיתֶם) is not part of a general warning but is a specific claim that the very act of making an inquiry to YHWH through Jeremiah was a serious error. This is a case where Hebrew linguistics cannot resolve the problem; from the standpoint of normal Hebrew grammar, either the ESV or the NIV is defensible. Only context can settle the issue. On the surface, and supporting the ESV, it would seem odd to claim that asking Jeremiah to pray was problematic. Verses 21–22, however, indicate that Jeremiah already knows that they will not obey his message. This implies that verse 20 means that commissioning Jeremiah to seek God's will was indeed a "fatal mistake." Before God, they would have been better off had they simply headed to Egypt without ever seeking his directions than to have first asked and then disobeyed.

**42:21–22**. Jeremiah here speaks as though they have already answered and have refused to obey God. He thus pronounces a judgment on them: the sword, famine, and pestilence that they seek to escape by fleeing to Egypt will overtake them there. We do not need to assume that Jeremiah required a special revelation from God to know that they would reject his message. From the time the request was made, he had ten days among them to hear their gossip and gauge their mood. It would have been clear that the delay in getting a response had only increased their fear of reprisal and made their determination to flee all the more urgent. He could sense the panic and anger growing among the people. Instead of cooling off during the delay, they became all the more agitated.

### *The Response (43:1–7)*

**43:1–2**. Jeremiah's audience, apparently unanimously, accused him of being a liar. It is difficult to know exactly how events transpired, but it seems that as he spoke, the community leaders and some of the more hotheaded members of the crowd, "all the arrogant men" (וְכָל־הָאֲנָשִׁים הַזֵּדִים), began to shout him down, "You are telling a lie!" (שֶׁקֶר אַתָּה מְדַבֵּר). Soon the whole crowd was angrily denouncing the prophet. If there was any minority report from people who thought that Jeremiah spoke the truth and should be obeyed, the text does not mention them. Either they were cowed into silence or there simply weren't any. Significantly, in their minds they were not disobeying God, for they believed that God had not sent this message by Jeremiah. But that was only self-justification. They had previously recognized Jeremiah as God's prophet and had pledged to follow whatever directions he gave.

**43:3**. This is perhaps the strangest thing in the whole passage. Why would they think that Baruch, Jeremiah's scribe, controlled the content of the message? Surely, they recognized that Jeremiah was the authoritative figure in the relationship and that Baruch was the subordinate. Jeremiah would not parrot whatever words Baruch gave to him. One possible explanation is that they were afraid to attack Jeremiah personally and so blamed everything on the lesser figure, Baruch (Thompson 1980, 668). But in the previous verse, they had vigorously attacked Jeremiah as a liar. Also, we do not elsewhere see a prophet being attacked through his scribe or followers. Certainly, Jesus's and Paul's opponents did not attack them by blaming their disciples and subordinates. This is unique in the Bible. To all appearances, everyone recognized that Baruch's position vis-à-vis Jeremiah was exceptional. It was not that Baruch was in charge or even had undue influence over Jeremiah, but that he was much more a partner of the prophet than we see with any other amanuensis. Furthermore, being a man from a powerful family, the people naturally saw him as an active agent and not just as a subordinate. Finally, Baruch had been the one to read out Jeremiah's severe denunciation of Jerusalem and pronounce that Babylon would overwhelm the city (Jer. 36). They blamed Baruch because they regarded him as a powerful enemy, because they knew that he was closely involved in Jeremiah's ministry, and because claiming he had helped to shape the message agreed with their predisposition to believe that a conspiracy was afoot against them.

**43:4–7**. These four verses are a good example of an inclusion structure in a biblical text. At the front end, verse 4 says that Johanan and the rest of the people "did not obey the voice of YHWH" (וְלֹא־שָׁמַע . . . בְּקוֹל יְהוָה) that they should stay in the land. At the back end, verse 7 says that they "did not obey the voice of YHWH" (לֹא שָׁמְעוּ בְּקוֹל יְהוָה) and that they went to Tahpanhes. The two bookends repeat the point that they did not obey YHWH and together explain the geography of their disobedience—both their refusal to stay in the land and their flight to Egypt. In between these two verses, the passage lists all who went to Egypt (vv. 5–6). It included those who had scattered to nearby states and then returned, as well as the men, women, and children whom the Babylonians who had left behind in the former Judah. In other words, it included everybody. By their own decision, the Jews had made the exile complete, leaving the land empty and in ruins. They had broken their vow and disobeyed God—and to make even that complete, they forced Jeremiah and Baruch to come along.

## THEOLOGICAL FOCUS

This passage, ironically, is the ultimate vindication of Jeremiah. It is ironic because one would not expect the prophet to be vindicated by having the people angrily and absolutely reject his message. But the entire burden of the book is that the people were incurably apostate and that, because of this, Judah would become a wasteland, without people, towns, or cultivated ground. What is even more striking is that they left of their own accord, even though God had promised to protect them if they stayed. The exile was not God's fault or even Jeremiah's; the people had chosen that path. The very perversity of the people showed that Jeremiah had been right about them all along.

- When an apostate people are offered life, they will choose death, thinking that they are taking the only path that will save them.
- God makes genuine offers of salvation even to people who are sure to reject it, and even when he has already made it his purpose to bring about their destruction.
- If people are faithless, their vows are meaningless. But they will be held accountable for breaking their vows.
- When people turn from the truth, they embrace conspiracy theories and are quick to cast about accusations, just as the Jews did with Baruch.
- Although God is the agent of judgment, people ultimately bring their ruin on themselves.

## PREACHING AND TEACHING STRATEGIES

### *Exegetical and Theological Synthesis*

How did this story change the way those in exile or those in the land after the exile viewed YHWH? Certainly, they witnessed his authority, for the land was devastated just as he said it would be. The Jews who returned after the exile saw this most vividly. They could have easily blamed God for the destruction. He did allow it, and even promised that it would happen. But this story clearly shows that it was brought on by the wickedness of the Jews. They flatly rejected God's offer of life, over and over again. This pericope makes it clear who was at fault.

This story should change the way we think about those who reject God's offer: we should be disappointed but not see them as the enemy. It should also change the way we think about God's wrath. It is not God's fault that people chose and still choose to reject his offer of life. Both of these lessons, while important, lead us to a more personal application. What the Jews did with God's word from Jeremiah is a warning to us.

### *Preaching Idea*

If you ask God for help, accept the answer.

### *Contemporary Connections*

#### *What does it mean?*

Did God send these Jews to Egypt where they would suffer and die? No, they chose to reject God's offer of life. And to this day, people reject God's offer of life. To better grasp what God is teaching us in this narrative, it can be helpful to put ourselves in the place of those who first heard Jeremiah's words.

The exiles in Babylon, when they read or heard of this, must have been amazed that those in the land of Israel would go against God's offer for life. The exiles, to some degree, knew that life would go on, and that God's hand was still with them. Perhaps they shook their heads and thought, "Why would those in Israel still reject the offer of life?" This narrative should change our attitudes toward those in our world who reject the offer of life given to them today. They are not the enemy; rather, they are rejecting an amazing offer. Ours is not to judge them, but rather feel sorrow that they are not accepting this amazing offer of salvation. The Jews in exile did not see their fellow Jews as the enemy, but surely they were disappointed that their fellow Jews rejected this offer of life. Seeing this should affect the way we present the gospel, and how we view those who reject Christ.

When I was in my twenties, I was invited to go snow skiing. It was going to be expensive and take quite a bit of time to drive from south Texas to the slopes. And besides, it seemed like a tourist trap—and what's more, I didn't know how to ski. So I declined. My friend's response was, "You don't know what you're missing." He kept encouraging me and saying how refreshing it was. Finally, and still hesitantly, I gave in. Sure enough, the car broke down on the way, delaying us a full day, and the accommodations were below par. I was not impressed. Then the ski school for beginners was humiliating. The first day was frustrating: falling, snow in the gloves, boots that felt like a vise. But then, that second day when I found myself sailing through a pine forest by myself with only the sound of the snow swishing under my skis, I thought, "Wow, my friend was right; I didn't know what I was missing." My friend was never angry at me for rejecting his offer to take me skiing—disappointed, yes, but not angry. I'm glad he persisted.

#### *Is it true?*

In the world of education, it is a stated goal that no one be left behind to fail. But what if that's their choice? Graduating from high school is a given rather than something that is earned. Educators have a great challenge. Sometimes, a student staying behind in a grade that they failed creates more problems than letting them move on with peers to the next grade. Educators are trying to help those who struggle with academics and hopefully, help our society. I admire their efforts. But it seems that mindset has also affected some employment situations. In some large bureaucratic settings, being fired is very rare. If one has a proven record of incompetency, the employee is simply moved to a new department. It is hard to get fired. Again, employers are trying to help or perhaps avoid a lawsuit, but the mindset that is created is dangerous. We tend to think of God is the same way.

After Gedaliah was killed, the Jews looked to Jeremiah for a word from God. He gave it to them, and they didn't like it, and once again they would not submit. Their rebellious hearts were made obvious. This passage shows us that there is a judgment day, and when it comes the truth of our record of rebellion against God will be made clear. He offers life through our faith in Jesus's work for us. We can submit to his way of salvation and have life, or not. We are responsible to God, and his wrath will come upon those who have not submitted to his way to forgiveness and new life through Christ. For those who have submitted to his offer of life, we must remember that we can still reject his commands and be disciplined. Perhaps we think that when God's word comes to us and we reject it, we will not be held responsible. We wrongly think that somehow, we will get transferred, or we will still get to graduate.

### *Now what?*

Many of God's promises and directions are still in place. The specific commands to stay in the land and not flee to Egypt obviously do not apply directly to us, but many other commands and promises of God are directly applicable. This is story is a negative example of what happens when God's guidelines are not followed.

Mike was very infatuated with a new start-up manufacturing company. The owners were aggressive businessmen who had a proven record of making money. While they were ethical, they did seem to push the decency envelope when it came to their competition. He was affirmed when they contacted him joining the company. As Mike prayed about it, he kept sensing that God did not want this relationship to go forward. But Mike wanted to work for a company like this. He spent a several weeks in prayer before the final interview. They made him a great offer and Mike asked if he could take a day or two to pray about it. The CEO said, "Sure, if you are into that kind of thing, but we keep our religion private around the office." As Mike drove home, he again asked God for guidance, hoping that God's answer would have changed. Instead, a Scripture came to mind about not being unequally yoked. Just then he received a phone call from the CEO, saying that they needed a decision that day. What would Mike do? Would he be like the Israelites who asked God for direction, only to reject the direction when it came? Would he choose God's offer of life through obedience?

It is not just in the big decisions that we can ask God for guidance and then reject it. The seemingly smaller everyday type of directives from God can be rejected as well: being a servant to someone who doesn't appreciate us, taking the time to listen to someone who never seems to listen to us, being generous when others are not, being faithful in marriage when the temptations are strong. When we seek God's direction, and through his Word it is clear or becomes clear, what will we do? This story affirms that rejecting his will is always costly.

### ***Creativity in Presentation***

This story is quite simple in its plot: The remaining Jews ask Jeremiah to seek God's will. Jeremiah does so and reports. The Jews reject what he says and go to Egypt. It seems the writer is raising the tension in the lengthy appeals and responses. Therefore, the content of the requests and responses needs to be highlighted. This section could be presented in parts, pausing to ask how different groups may have responded. The first two are those people actually listening to Jeremiah, and then the exiles who are in Babylon or the postexilic Jews. An imaginative step can be taken to ask how we might have responded had we been there.

This allows the teacher/preacher to highlight the content of the dialogue.

Often it is best to present the whole narrative before one makes an application. This passage lends itself to present the three parts of the story and apply each one before moving on to the next. The reason for this is that the plot is simple and easy to follow: the request for help, the answer, the response. Here is one possible structure:

- God, we need your help.
    - Israel's request and vow (42:1–6)
    - Our requests and vow
- Here is the answer:
    - Jeremiah's answer to Israel (42:7–22)
    - God gives us his direction for:
        - Salvation
        - Direction in life
- Will we submit?
    - Israel did not (43:1–7).
    - Will we?
- If you ask God for help, accept the answer.

## DISCUSSION QUESTIONS

1. What might have been some reasons that the remaining Jews wanted to go to Egypt?
2. What did God offer to the remaining Jews?
3. Why was it hard for the Jews to obey?
4. When is it hard for us to obey?
5. Is it wrong to ask God for direction? Why or why not?

## Jeremiah 43:8–44:30

**EXEGETICAL IDEA**

God has repudiated the Jews who fled to Egypt: they are still under judgment, they will not create or sustain orthodox Judaism, and they will not flourish. This text condemns the exiles in Egypt in two phases. First, Jeremiah warns them that they cannot escape God's judgment by running to Egypt. Second, his confrontation with the people demonstrated that they were still devoted to pagan deities, and especially to the "Queen of Heaven."

**THEOLOGICAL FOCUS**

Those who flee, unrepentant, from God's judgment remain permanently under it. We cannot escape guilt and God's wrath by moving to a different place. And a change of location will do nothing to change our hearts. The Jews in Egypt remained as passionately devoted to the Queen of Heaven as they had been before, and they even blamed the fall of Jerusalem on a failure to honor her. This text also demonstrates that the future of the Jews lay with the Babylonian community and not with the survivors in Jerusalem (24:1–10).

**PREACHING IDEA**

Move beyond insecurity; trust God, the only true security.

**PREACHING POINTERS**

God's messages to Judah, through Jeremiah, continued even though they had exiled themselves to Egypt. This shows God's continuing grace. Judah went beyond rejecting his warning. They had to take great initiative and effort to disobey him; it was no small task to move the remaining nation to Egypt. And in Egypt, they bowed down to the Queen of Heaven. Even so, God continued to speak. Perhaps Judah finally believed that Jeremiah's words were true when they saw the armies of Babylon invading Egypt.

This pericope has a two-part application. The first part is a theme common throughout Scripture, which Augustine wonderfully articulated years ago and has been repeated numerous times: "You have made us for yourself, O Lord, and our hearts are restless until they rest in you." The Jews were seeking safety and rest by depending upon Egypt instead of YHWH. The second application is a built-in consequence for a misplaced source of security. If our security lies in anything or anyone other than God it is sure that, one day, it will fail. The only way to get beyond insecurities is to look to God for security, and to rest in him.

# JEREMIAH IN EGYPT (43:8–44:30)

## LITERARY STRUCTURE AND THEMES

Two oracles of Jeremiah are recorded from his time in Egypt. The first (43:8–13) took place at the point of entry to Egypt, Tahpanhes, and asserts that Egypt will prove to be no refuge for the Jews. The second (44:1–30) concerns the Jews' continued devotion to the goddess called the "Queen of Heaven." These two episodes complete the story arc begun in chapter 40. The Jews who fled to Egypt are shown to be as apostate as they had been prior to the fall of Jerusalem. Even in exile, the wrath of God is still turned against them.

Jeremiah gave two oracles to the refugees in Egypt. The first, 43:8–13, warns them that fleeing to Egypt will not protect them from the power of the Babylonians (and by implication, from the wrath of God). The second, 44:1–30, warns them that they have not repented of the sins that brought down Jerusalem and therefore face yet more divine punishment.

- ***A Second Babylonian Conquest (43:8–13)***
- ***The Queen of Heaven (44:1–30)***
    - *The Debate (44:1–23)*
    - *The Final Denunciation (44:24–30)*

## EXPOSITION

### *A Second Babylonian Conquest (43:8–13)*

**43:8–9**. Jeremiah gives a message from YHWH accompanied by a sign-act, the burial of large stones beneath a brick pavement. Tahpanhes was a city on the extreme eastern edge of the Egyptian Delta; it was probably the first Egyptian town one would see when entering Egypt from traditional Israelite land. At this point, the Jewish refugees had barely gotten inside Egypt. The building where Jeremiah was to bury these stones is sometimes translated as "Pharaoh's palace," but בֵּית־פַּרְעֹה is more literally Pharaoh's "house" or "building." Located on the frontier of Egypt at Tahpanhes, it almost certainly was not a palace, at least not the grand residence that the term implies to modern readers. It was probably some kind of government building, perhaps a garrison headquarters, an administrative center, or the equivalent of a customs and immigration office. It may have served all these functions, and the pharaoh may have stayed there when he was in the area. The early archaeologist W. M. F. Petrie dug at Tell ed-Defenna, the probable location of Tahpanhes, in 1887. He found a fortress and brick pavement, and he believed that these were the places mentioned in Jeremiah. Objects associated with the pharaohs Neco II, Psamtik II, and Hophra were found here (Jones and Fiema 1992), demonstrating that the site was indeed occupied and in service at the time of Jeremiah. The stones Jeremiah buried marked the location where Nebuchadnezzar would set up his throne (v. 10).

**43:10–13**. Jeremiah predicts a Babylonian attack upon Egypt. Nebuchadnezzar would ravage the land so that it would suffer pestilence, captivity, and slaughter in the course of military defeat (v. 11). He would also burn down their temples and carry away the Egyptian gods. In a vivid metaphor, he would go through Egypt picking away every bit of plunder like a shepherd picking through his cloak to get every flea (vv. 12–13). To the shepherd, the fleas are a nuisance but not a real threat, and that is how Nebuchadnezzar views Egypt.

Unfortunately, we have little specific knowledge about the latter years of Nebuchadnezzar's reign. There is evidence, however, that he led a punitive expedition against Egypt near the end of his life. Reconstruction of the historical facts is difficult, and we cannot be sure that we fully understand the course of events. It appears that in 570 B.C. an Egyptian general known to us as Ahmose II (Amasis II) overthrew Pharaoh Hophra (Apries) and seized the throne. Hophra, with Babylonian assistance, tried to retake the throne, but he was killed in battle (an alternative view is that Ahmose captured Hophra after the battle and strangled him). Nebuchadnezzar appears to have taken part in this campaign: he marched against Egypt in the thirty-seventh year of his reign (LaSor 1979, 507), approximately 567 B.C., to subdue Ahmose and, it seems, to restore Hophra to power. We know that Hophra died in or soon after the battle; it may be that Ahmose made a show of obeisance to the Babylonian Empire, ending the war. It is clear, however, that Egypt was not utterly crushed because Ahmose continued to reign until 526 B.C. He was succeeded by his son Psamtik III, who was soon deposed by Cambyses when the Persians conquered Egypt (Shaw and Nicholson 1995, 19). All of this poses a bit of a problem: Jeremiah's prophecy seems to state that Nebuchadnezzar would march through Egypt and leave it prostrate. From our limited knowledge of events, it appears that he simply made a show of force, made Ahmose acknowledge his supremacy, and took away some plunder.

Jeremiah's language probably is an example of hyperbole, speaking of Egypt's military inferiority to Babylon in dramatic terms. But what Nebuchadnezzar did was enough to vindicate Jeremiah's claim that Egypt was not immune to Babylonian power. Also, it is fully credible that Nebuchadnezzar set up his throne outside the fortress of Tahpanhes, as this was the gateway to Egypt. The main point of this passage is that the Jews who thought they were safe in Egypt were mistaken; Babylon could come there too. Certainly Jews who remained in Tahpanhes, where Jeremiah gave this oracle, would live to see the arrival of Nebuchadnezzar and his army.

### *The Queen of Heaven (44:1–30)*

This chapter describes Jeremiah's conflict with the Jewish exiles in Egypt over their continued allegiance to the goddess called the "Queen of Heaven." It is divided into two parts. The first (44:1–23) is an account of Jeremiah's initial confrontation with the exiles and their response, in which they contended that all of their suffering came about because they failed to honor the goddess with sufficient sacrifices and libations. This part takes on the character of a debate, with each side making their case. The second part (44:24–30) is Jeremiah's final denunciation of the exiles. Verse 30 indicates that the events of this chapter took place while Hophra was still the pharaoh, meaning that it happened prior to 570 B.C.

#### *The Debate (44:1–23)*

**44:1–6**. Of the four places mentioned in verse 1, two are on the eastern edge of the Delta (Migdol and Tahpanhes), one is at the southern tip of the Delta (Memphis), and one is a broad term describing all Upper Egypt, the region south of Memphis and extending to the first cataract at Aswan (Pathros). Thus, the oracles are addressed to all the Jews in Egypt, although Migdol, Tahpanhes, and Memphis may be where many of them were concentrated. Verses 2–6 establish the premise for all that follows: Judah broke its covenant with YHWH by worshiping other gods, and YHWH in turn obliterated Judah and Jerusalem.

**44:7–10**. In light of the premise given above, the Jews in Egypt are behaving with astonishing foolishness, repeating the very sins that brought about the fall of their country. They "provoke" (כעס, v. 8) YHWH in Egypt the same way they provoked (כעס, v. 3) him in Jerusalem. As their previous apostasy caused the deaths

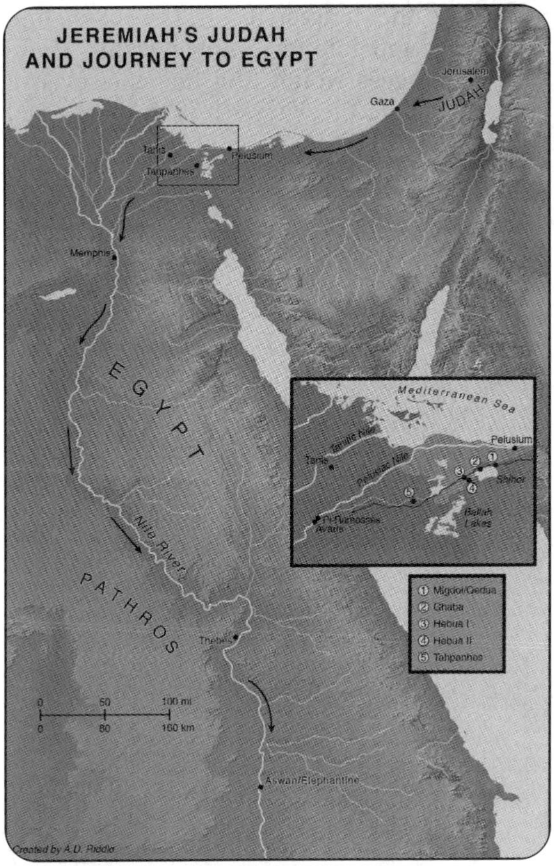


of men, women, and children of Judah, so their continued apostasy will cause the same result for the Jews in Egypt (v. 7). Their current sins, like all sin, is self-destructive; the prophet asks, "Why do you do this great evil against yourselves?" (v. 7, literally "against your souls," אֶל־נַפְשֹׁתֵכֶם). Verse 9 mentions the guilt of the king and the commoners, the ordinary men of Judah, implying that the idolatry was rampant in all classes. But it also mentions the royal wives and the wives of the commoners, something one does not normally see in judgment oracles such as this. The implication is that the wives are deeply involved in the apostasy, or that they practiced a kind of idolatry that especially appealed to women. The extent of the women's commitment to such religious behavior is made clearer below. Verse 10 says the people were not "made contrite" by the intense retribution they received for their behavior. More literally, however, it can be translated that they were "not crushed" (לֹא דֻכְּאוּ). This cannot mean that they were not militarily or politically crushed; clearly, they were. It means that their hearts were not broken in such a manner that they decisively abandoned their former ways. By analogy, massive destruction and death within Germany through the course of the Second World War "crushed" the Germans, not only in the sense that they were thoroughly beaten but in that they renounced Nazi ideology. But the people of Judah, although militarily crushed, did not renounce the paganism that had brought this upon them.

**44:11–14**. Because they have not forsaken their previous idolatry, Jeremiah in YHWH's name pronounces a severe judgment on the refugees. They will never return to their land but will die in Egypt, and their deaths will be violent: by the sword, by pestilence, and by famine. Indeed, *all* of them will die in this manner (although verse 14 does allow that a few refugees will stagger back to Judah). Furthermore, the Jewish refugees in Egypt would be universally despised as the hapless exiles of a fallen state.

This passage presents us with another historical problem in that it is difficult to square the prophecy with what we know of the Jewish community in Egypt. It is of course possible that Jeremiah is speaking exclusively of the Jews who abducted him and carried him off to Egypt; and for all we know, that relatively small group may have all come to a bad end. However, the oracle introduction in verse 1 gives the impression that he is speaking of all Jewish refugees in Egypt, and indeed verses 11–14 repeatedly speak of the Jews throughout the whole country. The Israelites had a long history of going down to Egypt in times of trouble (1 Kings 12:2; Jer. 26:21–23). It is possible that some Israelite refugees made their way to Egypt after the fall of Samaria, and certainly a significant group would have fled there during the Babylonian catastrophe, as Judah had an alliance with Egypt. In subsequent years Jews had a significant presence there, most famously at a settlement in Elephantine, in the far south of the country. This colony existed prior to the Persian conquest of Egypt, meaning that it was established, in all probability, by refugees from the fall of Jerusalem. A very important collection of Aramaic texts from this community, the "Elephantine Papyri," were found there. To be sure, the Jews were not always welcomed; a syncretistic temple to YHWH at Elephantine was destroyed by Egyptians in about 410 B.C., and the Jewish community there vanished. Sometimes Jews in Egypt suffered under local pogroms. But the Jews continued as a significant expatriate group within Egypt. There was a large Jewish community during the Ptolemaic period, especially at Alexandria, and these were the Jews who translated the Old Testament into Greek. Jews maintained a major presence in Egypt under Roman rule; Philo (c. 20 B.C. to c. A.D. 50) was an Alexandrian Jew, as was the Christian teacher Apollos (Acts 18:24). Jews maintained a sometimes quite large presence in Egypt long into the Muslim period—although in the modern era, as a result of Islamic anti-Zionism, they seem to have been eliminated from the country. It is thus not the case that the Jews were exterminated from Egypt in ancient times. What then are we to make of this prophecy?

- Scholars have noted that this passage is similar to the prophecies of Jeremiah 29:18–19 and 32:29–35, two texts that speak of God's judgment on Jerusalem through Babylon. The implication is that the judgments of 44:11–14 are meant as continuations of the judgment on Jerusalem and its inhabitants, implying that those refugees would find no relief even if they fled to Egypt. It is this—the fact that YHWH's wrath was still turned against them, and not the number of their casualties—that is the point.
- The syncretism and collapse of the Jewish Elephantine community can be seen as an example of the fulfillment of the prophecy. This is not to imply that the Jews in Elephantine were part of the same group that kidnapped Jeremiah, or that all the Elephantine Jews were slaughtered.
- The harsh language of the prophecy—that everyone would die by the sword, by pestilence, and by famine—is somewhat formulaic and was not necessarily meant to be taken literally. The main point is that Egypt would not be the place where Judaism would survive and thrive; YHWH repudiated those Jews. This agrees with Jeremiah's letter of chapter 29, telling the Jews in Babylon that they should build homes and have families there as they wait for YHWH to deliver them. And it was the Babylonian Jewish community, not the Egyptian, that established the contours of orthodox Judaism for centuries to come.
- The main point of this text, therefore, is that the Jews who have fled to Egypt were still under YHWH's curse. The Judaism of Egypt was not the Judaism of Haggai, Zechariah, Malachi, Ezra, or Nehemiah; these all came out of Babylonian Judaism.

**44:15**. The place where this meeting occurred is obscure. Verse 15 speaks of all the Jews of Pathros, but this is an enormous geographical region, including all of Upper Egypt from Memphis to Aswan. It is not necessarily the case that the meeting took place somewhere within Pathros; the last time we saw, Jeremiah was in Tahpanhes, located in the eastern Delta. He probably received some delegates from Jews who lived in various places throughout Pathros. It is possible that the bulk of the crowd with which he spoke was made up of Jews living near Tahpanhes, but that what was said in the exchange applied equally to Jews throughout Egypt. What is clear, however, is that a significant number of women were present and that these women had taken the lead in certain pagan rituals.

**44:16–19**. The people flatly tell Jeremiah that they will not listen to him. The declare that they will continue to observe the rituals associated with the Queen of Heaven, and in fact, they turn Jeremiah's messages on their head. They declare that instead of their paganism being the cause of their ruin, their failure to participate in pagan rituals brought about their ruin: "But from the time we ceased to burn incense to the Queen of Heaven and to pour out libations to her, we have lacked everything and have perished by sword and famine" (v. 18). They were probably referring to Josiah's reformation and to his closure of all the pagan shrines and high places in Judah. Even with Josiah's death, apparently, many pagan sanctuaries remained abandoned, and open shows of devotion to the goddess never returned to its pre-Josiah level. At least, that is how it seemed in popular imagination. Now that they were refugees and, they supposed, had been chastised by the goddess for failure to honor her, they had no intention of cutting down on their offerings.

But who is the Queen of Heaven? Most likely, she is Astarte, commonly known in the Bible as Ashtoreth (עַשְׁתֹּרֶת), a deliberate distortion of her name to make it sound like the word for "shame" (בֹּשֶׁת). Astarte is the Canaanite/Phoenician version of the ancient Sumerian goddess Inanna, known in Akkadian as Ishtar. The goddess was ubiquitous in the ancient Near East, worshiped in various forms throughout Mesopotamia, the Levant, and Egypt. She was an astral deity, and thus was known as Queen of Heaven in both Mesopotamia and Egypt. She was also a goddess of both fertility and warfare, giving the paganized Jewish women reason to think that because they neglected her, they had suffered both famine and military defeat. The women baked sacred cakes for her called כַּוָּנִים (v. 19), and this term is derived from the Akkadian *kamanu*, which refers to cakes baked for Ishtar (for further information, see Ackerman 2006; Schmitz 1992; Day 1992).

In a sense, what the women said was irrefutable. No one could prove by pure logic and rhetoric whether their troubles had come about because they had made sacrifices to the goddess, as Jeremiah contended, or if the disasters had happened because they had failed to honor her, as the women contended. People cannot see what God or the gods are doing, and thus no one can prove that Judah's troubles were punishments brought on by YHWH or by the Queen of Heaven. This does not mean that Jeremiah cannot give any logical reason whatsoever that the women's claim is false. In the next passage, Jeremiah will make several points to refute them. But this does demonstrate an important fact about apologetic arguments: On the one hand, we can and should give logical reasons for our beliefs. On the other hand, we cannot give direct, empirical evidence that God is real and is acting, because that would require that everyone in some sense "see" God. Adherence to biblical orthodoxy is a matter of both faith and reason.

**44:20–23**. Jeremiah makes several counterarguments against the women's assertion that they suffered for failure to honor the Queen of Heaven.

- Jeremiah refutes the women by denying their premise: They had not failed to honor the Queen of Heaven. In fact, they made offerings to her on every street corner in Jerusalem (v. 21). It is hard to see how she could have felt offended.

- There is a principle implicit his claim that YHWH, not the Queen of Heaven, obliterated Jerusalem and left it desolate (v. 22): YHWH was understood to be the true owner of the land of Israel (2 Chron. 7:20; Isa. 14:25; Jer. 2:7; 16:18; Ezek. 38:16; Joel 1:6). It was his to protect or to destroy, and it never belonged to the goddess. Therefore, they should not attribute their suffering to her indignation.
- The destruction of the land was a violation of Israel having broken the covenant with YHWH (vv. 22–23). Israel had always been constituted as the people of YHWH. He had brought them out of Egypt, and they were in covenant with him. Nowhere in their tradition was there any hint that the Queen of Heaven had led them through the wilderness and into Canaan, and she certainly made no covenant with them. They owed her no devotion. Also, in Deuteronomy, Israel was given ample warning that disobedience to the covenant would bring upon them famine, disease, and military defeat (for example, Deut. 28:21–68). These threats came from YHWH, not the Queen of Heaven.
- Jeremiah had repeatedly been proven correct in his prophecies. This argument is present throughout the book and implied in his prophetic denunciation of the worshipers of the Queen of Heaven. In the past, he had warned that Jehoiachin's exile would last a long time, that Nebuchadnezzar would defeat Jerusalem and take the city, and that the temple would be destroyed. At every point, he had been correct. The false prophets, who opposed Jeremiah, had been wrong every time.

But there is one argument he does not make: that the Queen of Heaven simply is not real. Jeremiah certainly did not believe she was real, but making such an argument gets deeply into presuppositions, and Jeremiah sticks to concrete, historical facts. Thus, we see that a defense of the faith involves making clear and reasonable arguments—but that there is still a need for faith. For many, the disposition of the heart will prove decisive. And these women were not disposed to abandon their goddess.

### *The Final Denunciation (44:24–30)*

Since the people have made plain that they will not abandon their devotion to the goddess, Jeremiah concludes the discussion with a final denunciation from YHWH. This is in three parts. In the first, YHWH gives them over to their apostasy, effectively washing his hands of the affair (vv. 24–25). In the second, he pronounces a judgment upon them, declaring that no one would pronounce his name in Egypt (vv. 26–28). In the third part, he gives them a sign that what he has predicted will come about (vv. 29–30).

**44:24–25**. Jeremiah tells the Jews to go ahead and fulfill their vows to the goddess by making offerings and pouring out libations to her. Jeremiah obviously does not approve of their actions, but what he says is not quite sarcasm, as though he did not mean what he said. It is, rather, resignation. He has seen that arguing with the people is hopeless and so he gives up on them, handing them over to do what they are determined to do. It is analogous to the theology of sin in Romans, in which God gives people over to their passions (Rom. 1:24). Jeremiah is through arguing with them. He will let them exercise their free will.

> *TRANSLATION NOTE: Jeremiah 44:25*
> The end of 44:25, הָקֵים תָּקִימְנָה אֶת־נִדְרֵיכֶם וְעָשֹׂה תַעֲשֶׂינָה אֶת־נִדְרֵיכֶם, "completely fulfill your vows and completely perform your vows," is perhaps somewhat surprising for its repetition of "your

vows" (אֶת־נִדְרֵיכֶם). The Greek lacks the second occurrence of "your vows," and a few Hebrew manuscripts replace נִדְרֵיכֶם with נִסְכֵּיכֶם, "your libations." Holladay adopts the former solution, simply omitting the second נִדְרֵיכֶם; he translates the line, "Do confirm your vows and do perform (them)" (Holladay 1989, 280). The latter solution is followed in the NRSV: "By all means, keep your vows and make your libations!" Most modern English versions, however, follow the MT. Against the NRSV, the verb עשׂה is never used with נֶסֶךְ as its object. Normally, and frequently in Jeremiah 44, the verb נסך is used with the noun נֶסֶךְ. One rarely sees עשׂה used with נֶדֶר, but see Judges 11:39. This indicates that the MT should be retained and that the second נִדְרֵיכֶם should not be omitted or emended.

**44:26–28**. YHWH's judgment against the Jews in Egypt is in three parts. First, no Jew in Egypt would ever again pronounce his name there. YHWH's name is "great" (גָּדוֹל), and for an Egyptian Jew to speak it, especially in an oath, would simply be to blaspheme it (v. 26). Second, YHWH will give special attention to the matter of destroying them, seeing to it that they all die by the sword and by famine (v. 27). Third, the very few who do survive will make their way back to Judah and will have to confess that YHWH's word, not theirs, was true. Their claim that their suffering was due to neglect of the Queen of Heaven will finally be shown to be false. As discussed above, this is not to be pressed for a literal fulfillment, as though almost every Jew in Egypt would die a violent death and none of them would be able to say the word "YHWH." The meaning is that Judaism would not flourish there, that God repudiated the "Jewishness" of the refugees, and that events would vindicate Jeremiah and not vindicate those who honored the Queen of Heaven.

**44:29–30**. Jeremiah says that the Jews will know that Jeremiah's words are true when they see Pharaoh Apries (Hophra) slain. As noted above, Hophra was dethroned by a general known to us as Ahmose II in about 570. Hophra had tried to subdue the Greek colony of Cyrene in Libya, but his army had been defeated, creating discontent with his leadership in the Egyptian military. At this point, Ahmose II deposed him and Hophra fled the country. He then sought to regain the throne, and he appears to have had the support of Nebuchadnezzar, who perhaps thought he would be a more submissive vassal than the upstart Ahmose. But Hophra either died in battle or was captured and strangled by the year 567 (for an account of the reign of Hophra/Apries, see Redford 1992). Once again, the words of the prophecy might mislead the casual reader. We might take verse 30 to mean that God would give Hophra "into the hand" of Nebuchadnezzar, who would then slay him. That is not what happened, but that is also not what the passage says. It says that Hophra would be slain by "his enemies," but it does not claim that the enemies who slew him were necessarily the Babylonians. The verse states that Nebuchadnezzar captured and slew Zedekiah, but the verse mentions this only an analogy for what would happen to Hophra.

## THEOLOGICAL FOCUS

The episodes of this section are the last recorded events of Jeremiah's life. To all appearances, it was a bitter way for him to end his ministry. Nevertheless, his last confrontation with a hostile and unbelieving Israelite audience is instructive for us.

- A faithful ministry is no guarantee that people will respond. Jeremiah fulfilled his commission from the time he was a boy in Anathoth until his death in Egypt. He suffered terribly, was falsely accused, imprisoned, and nearly executed, and he died as an unwilling captive in a foreign land. He lived in celibacy and isolation, hated even by friends and family from his hometown. In many respects,

Jeremiah was the most Christlike of all the Old Testament prophets. But for all his exemplary conduct, he was not able to persuade his audiences, even when the audience had seen his earlier predictions fulfilled. We should not equate success in ministry with God's approval.

- If people flee from the wrath of God but do not repent, they will never find refuge or peace. The Jewish refugees made it as far as Tahpanhes, but soon Nebuchadnezzar would come there as well. Even those whom he did not slay remained under God's curse. For them, ruin was inescapable.
- When people have had their values warped, no amount of contrary evidence can convince them that they are wrong. The refugees who took Jeremiah down to Egypt had no rational reason to think that failure to honor the Queen of Heaven was the cause of their suffering. But they had long ago committed themselves to a pagan cult and their hearts were permanently hardened.
- One should not be quickly shaken when an Old Testament narrative or prophecy appears to be different from apparently established facts of history. There is always a great deal that we don't know, and often the rhetorical purposes of the prophetic text account for language that at times seems problematic.
- The Jews are the people of God, but the Jews in Egypt effectively forfeited their status as Jews by their behavior. That being the case, God will certainly cut away Christians who fall into apostasy (Rom. 11:17–21).
- When confronting unbelief, we should give rational, reasonable, and historically based arguments. Those arguments are meaningful and can have an impact on people. But still, only God can break a human heart and give faith.

## PREACHING AND TEACHING STRATEGIES

### *Exegetical and Theological Synthesis*

This narrative is a very unpleasant one. There seems to be no hope here at all except for a brief reference to the remnant. Egypt will be destroyed, and those who will not humble themselves before God and rely upon Egypt will suffer and die. This is a summary and a culmination of God's judgment on Israel. Not a happy narrative.

But the purpose is not to discourage us by the reporting of tragic news; rather, it is to encourage us not to do what these Jews did. It is tragic that they once again rejected God's will and lost the life God offered. We need to be discouraged when we realize that our security lies in this world, but as we turn from that insecurity to the sure foundation of our Lord, we can find joy.

### *Preaching Idea*

Move beyond insecurity; trust God, the only true security.

### *Contemporary Connections*

#### *What does it mean?*

Where are we looking for rest and peace or fulfillment? It is not wrong to want these important ingredients of security in our lives. But their importance makes it crucial for us to look for them in the correct places. Even a country-western song grabs hold of this theme of having a right source, in terms of relationship: "I was looking for love in all the wrong places."

There are many sources from which we can sense a temporary feeling of security. For most of us, our home is a place of rest. When we are away from our homes, whether it's due to a pleasant vacation or a difficult hospital stay, we are eager return to home. Home gives us rest. When the car begins to make funny noises, the extensive warranty that came with the car gives us peace.

When everything is clean and in place—the dishwasher is emptied, the floors mopped, the furniture dusted, the yard mowed—it gives us a temporary fulfillment. These certainly are not bad things. So, what does it look like to seek rest and peace and fulfillment in wrong places?

Often, during a time when these everyday sources have run dry or have been taken away, the true source of our security emerges. When the Jews saw that Babylon might retaliate against them for the murder of Gedaliah, they sought security—not from YHWH, but from Egypt. When our homes are destroyed by natural disasters or relational disasters, where do we find rest? When the car warranty has expired, where do we find peace? When we can't complete a task due to health or circumstances, where do we find fulfillment? From where does our security come? Do we escape into entertainment? Our unresolved anger might come to the surface. Perhaps a sullenness or self-pity becomes our theme of daily life. These unsettling emotions might well indicate that our source of security isn't as secure as we had thought.

Finding a temporary feeling of security in these situations is not wrong. But true security, true rest, true peace, true fulfillment only comes from placing our lives and our trust in the hands of YHWH. Trusting that his way is the best and submitting to his will is the only source of true security. The sources for the temporary sense of security are not wrong, but when we desire an unshakeable security, it can only be found in trusting YHWH. This is ultimately expressed in our trusting Christ, that he forgave our sins and grants us his righteousness.

As I write this, the COVID-19 pandemic is preventing the traditional gathering together of the saints. Certainly, the church physically gathered is a source of security and strength, yet the lesson the church is learning is that God is the source of our security. As wonderful as gathering together may be, it is a gift *from God*; God himself is the source. Fortunately, we are discovering new ways of gathering together. I have been surprised at how meaningful an internet prayer meeting can be. While God uses many different means of granting us a feeling of security, the ultimate and the only permanent source of that security is God and God alone.

### *Is it true?*

This is only half the application. The Jews were looking for security in the wrong places, and Jeremiah warned them that there were severe consequences for doing so. The same is true for us. When we seek a permanent and deep security from anything other than God, we are not only setting up ourselves for disappointment but also for his wrath. God not only wants us to rely upon him for our security, but there are harsh consequences when we do not. We need to hear the words articulated by Augustine, that our hearts are restless until they rest in him. But we also need to hear that if we seek that rest from anywhere else, there are terrible consequences. The Jews who sought security from Egypt were set aside from God's work; they became an obscure footnote in history, instead of being used in God's plan to bless the world.

When we place our hope for security in that which is insecure, there are consequences from God. Some of the consequences are very logical: homes are damaged or destroyed, cars break, tasks will not always be completed. It is as if God built in consequences for trusting in the insecure for our security. Our false security vanishes—not if they fail, but when. So, God's wrath may come in what seems to be a logical result of looking for security in all the wrong places. However, for the Jews it was more than just the inevitable failing of the Egyptian Empire; God's wrath was expressly setting them aside from his work as part of his chosen people. When we seek true unshakeable security in anything or anyone other than God, we become the objects of his wrath. What that may look like is as varied as the people and situations that call for it. But we must not just say that we should look for security in the right place; we must also say that when we don't, God's wrath will be upon us.

*What now?*

It is important to articulate that there is a great difference between those who have trusted Christ and those who have not. Those who have trusted Christ and live in a relationship with God do experience God's wrath in the form of discipline and consequences—but only here, in this life. But for those who have rejected Christ and his offer of forgiveness, the consequences of seeking security in the wrong place are eternal.

This is again an opportunity to invite people to trust Christ as their savior. To the nonbeliever, the appeal is the offer of a solid security of eternal life. To the believer, it is an offer to return to the sense of security that comes though daily submission to God's wonderful will.

### *Creativity in Presentation*

As I write this (August 2021), the ravages of Hurricane Ida are just becoming known. In most settings there is a current or recent natural or man-made disaster that one's congregation is familiar with or has experienced. Using that crisis is an effective tool to remind us that nothing in this world is secure. The twofold application of this passage offers us a creative structure for this sermon. It is almost like two sermons. Consider beginning the sermon as though the first application was all that was going to be presented, affirming that we should find our security and satisfaction only in God. Verses 43:8–13 could almost serve as a short sermon on only finding rest in God. One could even move into what sounds like a conclusion, at only one-third of the time given for the sermon. This could build tension, because listeners would be intrigued (hopefully not relieved) that the sermon was ending so soon. Then present the rest of the story, giving adequate time to tell the story of chapter 44. Here is one possible structure:

- Don't look for security in the insecure.
  - For Israel: Egypt cannot provide security (43:8–13).
  - For us: the world cannot provide security.
  - We must find our rest in God.

- The false securities of this world will always disappoint and bring terrible consequences.
  - Israel will suffer in Egypt (44:1–30).
  - Every so-called security of this world is ultimately insecure.
  - If our rest is not in God, we have no true rest.

- We can get beyond our insecurity by resting in God.

## DISCUSSION QUESTIONS

1. What does security feel like? What are some things that help us feel secure?

2. What experiences have made you feel very insecure?

3. What are some consequences of placing our security in something insecure?

4. What are some things that you once thought were secure, but now you see they are not as secure as you once thought?

5. What does it look like to only trust in God for our security?

## Jeremiah 45:1–5

### EXEGETICAL IDEA

This event took place in the fourth year of Jehoiakim, long before the events narrated in chapter 44. It illustrates again that the book is organized thematically and not chronologically. This comes at the end of a series of texts dealing with the trials of Jeremiah's prophetic career, and it makes the point that those who align themselves with the truth will suffer along with the heroes of the faith. Baruch was distressed over how his association with Jeremiah was costing him everything; but through Jeremiah, God reminded him that soon there would be nothing worth having in Jerusalem. Baruch's loss of prestige and outward success would matter little when the city was in flames.

### THEOLOGICAL FOCUS

Serving God in times of crisis requires focus and commitment, even on the part of those who are in a subordinate role. God rebukes Baruch for his desire to hold on to the outward trappings of success, but he also reassures him. When all of Judah was a ruin, God would still preserve the faithful scribe.

### PREACHING IDEA

Recognize God's future work, not your past accomplishments.

### PREACHING POINTERS

God's message to Baruch was twofold. God's word directed him in what he should not do, and then in what God would do for him. Often a command to not do something is followed by a positive command of what to do. This is different. God says to Baruch, and to us, "Don't seek recognition for what you have done; recognize what I will do."

One might think that the negative command to not seek great things for yourself would be followed by the positive command to seek great things for God. Perhaps we seek great things for ourselves because we think that by focusing on our great accomplishments of the past, we can somehow ensure a great future. But instead, God follows with a command to trust him with the future.

# A MESSAGE FOR BARUCH (45:1–5)

## LITERARY STRUCTURE AND THEMES

Scribes in the ancient Near East were men of high status and often held important positions in government. Jeremiah's scribe Baruch appears to have been from an important family and would have been destined for success among the Jerusalem aristocracy, had he not attached himself to the outcast prophet Jeremiah. This was not an easy path for Baruch to follow, and as both warning and encouragement he received a private word from God.

- ***The Background and Setting (45:1)***
- ***Baruch's Complaint and YHWH's Response (45:2–5)***

## EXPOSITION

### *The Background and Setting (45:1)*

**45:1**. The episode took place in the fourth year of Jehoiakim, and the narrative specifically recalls the major event of that year, as told in chapter 36. At that time, Jeremiah dictated to Baruch a prophecy announcing Jerusalem's imminent destruction. Since Jeremiah could not enter the temple court, Baruch took the scroll and read it to the people there. News of the event soon reached the king, and the scroll was taken to him. As it was being read in his presence, the king took it, cut it into pieces, and threw the pieces into a fire. Baruch and Jeremiah had to go into hiding. Jeremiah then dictated his message again to Baruch, who wrote it out on a replacement scroll.

It is not clear at what stage of these events the episode of chapter 45 took place. It could have happened after Jeremiah had dictated the first scroll and commissioned Baruch to read it before a crowd outside the temple. If so, Baruch's distress probably came from worry over what would happen to him if he so publicly aligned himself with the politically unpopular prophet, a man who had even been expelled from the temple. It may be that chapter 45 took place after Jehoiakim had burned the first scroll and Jeremiah set about making a new copy. If so, then Baruch had fully realized how much the king hated Jeremiah and that by serving as his representative, Baruch had made himself *persona non grata* with all the powerful and influential people in Jerusalem. Either way, Baruch saw that his prospects were ruined and that even his life was in danger (see Jer. 36:19).

Indeed, on the professional level, Baruch's public association with Jeremiah had cost him a great deal. Baruch's brother Seraiah was a high-ranking member of a delegation to the king of Babylon (51:59); this implies that they were from a prestigious family. But Baruch would now see all his paths to advancement blocked. On a personal level too, he had no doubt lost a great deal. Everyone in Jerusalem who mattered—all of his social peers—would now shun Baruch, leaving him as socially isolated as Jeremiah himself. In such a situation, Baruch was understandably distressed, and he received a private message from YHWH.

### *Baruch's Complaint and YHWH's Response (45:2–5)*

**45:2–3**. In Baruch's complaint, he multiplies synonyms of distress to demonstrate the severity of his anxiety. He experiences "grief" (יָגוֹן) on top of "pain" (מַכְאֹב), he "struggles" (יגע) with "sighs" (אֲנָחָה), and he has not found any "relief" (מְנוּחָה). This redundancy implies lengthy, ongoing sorrow and a creeping shadow of despair.

Surprisingly perhaps, he attributes his trouble to YHWH. But Jeremiah himself spoke similarly (4:10; 15:17–18). The two men believed God was ultimately in control of all things, and thus they believed that he had led them into the distress in which they found themselves. This does not mean that they excused themselves or the people around them, nor does it imply a fatalistic view of divine foreknowledge and sovereignty. It is the outcry of a faithful man of God who does not understand why that faithfulness has only given him pain and anxiety. Perhaps a modern analogy would be a pastor who, beset with opposition and problems in his church, cries out, "God, why did you lead me to a ministry such as this?"

**45:4**. YHWH speaks of the crisis that he is bringing about on earth. His words recall the commission given to Jeremiah in 1:10: "Look, I have appointed you this day over nations and over kingdoms, to uproot (נתשׁ) and to break down, to destroy (הרס) and to overthrow, to build (בנה) and to plant (נטע)." YHWH now tells Baruch that he is about to "destroy" (הרס) what he "built" (בנה) and "uproot" (נתשׁ) what he "planted" (נטע). This allusion to Jeremiah's call, coming in a message not for Jeremiah but for Baruch, is highly significant. The book several times alludes to the verbs of 1:10 in order to tie some oracle to Jeremiah's initial calling. For example, two messages of hope for Israel do this (31:28; 42:10). Here, the same language of Jeremiah's prophetic call is applied to his scribe. This implies that Baruch is a highly significant character in the book's narrative. He was much more than a mere copier of texts. I argued in the Introduction that Baruch played an important role in the formation of the book of Jeremiah. Although this chapter does not speak directly to that function, it does tell us that Baruch should not be regarded as no more than one out of the crowd of anonymous copyists. He had a special calling and mission.

The last line of the verse (וְאֶת־כָּל־הָאָרֶץ הִיא) is grammatically unusual, but it is not hard to translate. To loosely paraphrase, it means, "[and by this, I mean that I will destroy and uproot] the whole land." But there is significant ambiguity in כָּל־הָאָרֶץ, since it can mean either "the whole land [of Israel]" or "all the earth." This raises the question of whether YHWH refers only to disasters he is about to bring upon Judah, or if he is speaking of disasters to come upon all the nations. In favor of it referring to Judah alone, other allusions to 1:10, as noted above, concern the future God has planned for Israel (31:28; 42:10). Also, God's uprooting of what he had planted seems naturally to connect to the frequent metaphor of Israel as God's vineyard, fig tree, or crop, as in the Song of the Vineyard (Isa. 5). Furthermore, the events of chapter 45 are set in the historical context of Baruch's reading of the scroll that prophesied the imminent destruction of Jerusalem and exile of the Jews (Jer. 36). On the other hand, chapter 45 in the MT is immediately prior to the oracles against the nations in chapters 46–51, implying that 45:4 speaks of international conflict and conflagration. Also, 1:10 speaks of "nations and . . . kingdoms," not just of Israel. One can argue for either interpretation. In my view, however, there is no need to consider the two to be mutually exclusive; the ambiguity of כָּל־הָאָרֶץ is intentional. It does primarily refer to Judah, implying that Baruch need not worry about impressing or offending important people in Jerusalem. Soon, most of those people would be either prisoners or dead, and Jerusalem would be a smoldering ruin. Beyond that, however, the whole world was about to be engulfed in flames. That being the case, Baruch's concerns about making a name for himself and gaining success are fairly pointless. However, such upheaval is coming, and Judah is about to go through terrible trauma. It will soon experience the most important event in its history since the exodus (and indeed will experience a reversal of the exodus—a return to captivity). For this reason, Baruch needs to focus on fulfilling his task as Jeremiah's co-laborer. This, not his loss of status, should occupy his thoughts.

**45:5.** YHWH both rebukes and encourages Baruch. He tells him not to waste his time "seeking great things." Recognition and promotion would do Baruch no good, and even wealth might do no more than make him a target. If you are on a sinking ship, there is little point in checking to see if you have been invited to dine at the captain's table. However, God promises that even though Baruch will see death all around him, he will survive the violence, famine, and privation that will engulf the world. Furthermore, God will keep Baruch safe in all his travels. Although the passage says nothing about where Baruch would go, we know that he went to Egypt with Jeremiah. I have suggested in the Introduction that he finally made his way to Babylon, which after the exile became the center of Jewish life and culture.

## THEOLOGICAL FOCUS

Baruch serves as a paradigm for the average believer who is called to faithful service to God in extraordinary times.

- Baruch experienced distress and doubts at a time of crisis, when he had to read Jeremiah's scroll and so make a break from high Jerusalem society and publicly align himself with the prophet. Times of crisis demonstrate the reality of one's faith or lack thereof.
- Distress, fear, and hesitation are part of a believer's life. No one transcends such things and goes on as though untouched and unconcerned.
- No one wishes to live in times of upheaval, but such events demonstrate that seeking prestige is pointless.
- In a time of turmoil, we should seek to serve God and our neighbors all the more.
- God can see us through difficult events, even if we seem to be left as vagabonds who have lost everything. But those who seem to be the world's great successes will lose everything.

## PREACHING AND TEACHING STRATEGIES

### *Exegetical and Theological Synthesis*

Baruch's complaint is general. God's response to him gives us an indication that he was seeking something great for himself. Seeking to be great in Jerusalem in this time of Babylonian domination and destruction would have ignored reality. Why be great in a country that is falling to an enemy? In fact, being great in that context could get you killed. Few of us aspire to being great. Oh, we all want to succeed at something, but very few of think that we could become a national figure, a champion, or a winner of a gold medal. We want to be a great mom or dad, a great employee, a great teacher, and so on. By "great," we usually mean that others recognize our abilities or accomplishments. Perhaps Baruch just wanted that level of recognition.

But God told him instead of seeking to be recognized by others, he needed to recognize that God was giving him life. For Baruch, it literally meant that he would not die in the destruction of Jerusalem. God tells followers of Jesus that we can an abundant life This specific promise of life given to Baruch is an expression of a theme that runs throughout the Bible, and is given new vitality when Christ says that he came to give us life and that we would have it abundantly.

### *Preaching Idea*

Recognize God's future work, not your past accomplishments.

### *Contemporary Connections*

#### *What does it mean?*

This chapter is not just an exhortation to humility and to a willingness to accept the loss of prestige; God is giving us the reason why seeking great things for ourselves is futile. Each of us seeks to have a level of prestige. We hope that people would respect us enough to ask for our advice and even heed it, that they would see us as being important. Perhaps you have been part of a committee discussion and it seems that every time you want to speak someone else speaks over you, and the group ignores this discourteous action. Then, when you do speak, your ideas or opinions are dismissed as irrelevant. We either get hurt or disengage, or we work harder to speak our minds. We often want people to think we are at least great enough that they would want to listen to us.

Perhaps the greatness we seek is in the future. We hope we can accomplish something of value and that people would remember our contribution—not that a building would be named after us, but that people would talk about the good we accomplished, and not just at our funeral. Do we hope that the legacy we leave behind will be great enough that they will remember it came from us?

We could be seeking a level of affirmation. We would not see it as seeking greatness for ourselves. We would simply see it as at getting some appreciation from those whom we serve. We want people to think that even if we aren't great, at least they know we are putting forth a great effort.

#### *Is it true?*

"In 1492 Columbus sailed the blue." For years in the United States, this little phrase helped schoolchildren remember both the date and the person that culture identified as a metonymy for Europeans coming to the Western Hemisphere. Over the past few years that discovery has been more fully reported as having many wrongs associated with it. The trajectory of this thought has seen the Columbus Day holiday no longer being promoted and even his statues being removed, by vote and in some cases by angry protesters. To past generations this would have been unthinkable. But it has happened.

This trend in tearing down past heroes has even touched what was thought to be a permanent structure that would never be torn down or replaced: the Jefferson Memorial in Washington DC. This massive monument to a central framer of the Declaration of Independence is being shaken by Jefferson's descendants, some of whom have suggested his image be removed. Again, it is not because of the good that he did but because of his wrongs that were ignored. Just as a past generation could not conceive of Christopher Columbus falling from prominence, so too it is hard to imagine that the United States culture would no longer honor Thomas Jefferson. The point of this is not to say that this trajectory is right or wrong; rather, it is to show that greatness given to someone by a culture is never permanent.

Though we don't like to think about it, no nation or culture lasts forever, and the greatness that a culture gives to a person will also fall away. For Baruch, the greatness he might have sought in Israel would fade almost immediately. Dr. Garrett's comment in the commentary above is worth repeating here: "If you are on a sinking ship, there is little point in checking to see if you have been invited to dine at the captain's table."

Often the fickleness of greatness is apparent at the beginning of a pastorate. Church members, eager to affirm their recent selection of a pastor, could brag that their new pastor is a great preacher and leader. After a few years, or sometimes only months, reality sets in and this once great preacher and leader is not so great. To be fair, in a similar way pastors often see a new congregation as being great, but that greatness also fades with time.

*Now what?*
Our desperately wicked hearts are always vulnerable to seeking to be seen as great in the eyes of our culture and those around us. We must set aside this desire to seek greatness for ourselves because it is futile. When it rains, the car wash closes. Oh, you could get a car wash while it was raining, and it would look great . . . until you drove the car back into the rainy streets. The greatness we receive from this world or anyone it in it will not last. So don't seek greatness any more than you would seek a car wash in the midst of a thunderstorm.

When those hurt feelings come because our great ideas are being ignored, we need to set aside our desire for prestige. When we worry about how others will think of us when we are gone, we need to notice how little we think about those who have gone before us. When we feel like no one notices how hard we work, or when our great sacrifice is not appreciated, we must see this as our seeking great things for ourselves.

On my insecure days, I find that I want people to know about my academic accomplishments and my ministry experiences. I want to be recognized, but I know I shouldn't seek it. Here is what I have done to try to get around the command to not seek great things for myself: When I first meet a fellow pastor or ministry leader, I ask them about their schooling and experience. Then, I politely and genuinely listen—hoping that they, in turn, will ask me about mine. Instead of seeking recognition, why don't I recognize what God has promised me? Instead of wanting others to recognize my past accomplishments, I should focus on God's accomplishments.

### *Creativity in Presentation*
A quick search can give the teacher/preacher numerous examples of past "heroes" in sports or politics or science who have been forgotten. This could be tailored to fit your situation. Most communities have schools, parks, streets named after heroes of the past who have been forgotten. For example, Dr. Garrett and I both attended a high school in Houston named after Charles H. Milby. I have no idea who he was, and during my three years at the school named after him neither he nor his contributions were ever discussed.

Since this passage is so much shorter than any of the other passages that have been covered thus far, it could affect the length of the sermon or lesson. We tend to think that the sermon must be a certain length. Since this passage is short and can be explain fairly easily, let the sermon reflect that. If you are in a situation where a time slot must be filled due to broadcasting the service or some other constraint, then be creative with the time, perhaps adding more music, a discussion, or testimonies. This is not suggesting that the content be minimized. The content is still powerful and life-changing, but God's own presentation of it is shorter than other sections of Jeremiah.

The main thrust of this passage can come at the beginning of the second point. It is an inductive/deductive sermon. The first point leads up to the main thrust, and the second point expands upon it. Here is one possible structure:

- Present the text:
  - Baruch's complaint (1–3)
  - God's response (4–5)
    - Don't seek recognition of your past work.
    - Recognize the promise of God's future work.

- Application: Recognize God's future, not your past.
  - How have we sought recognition?
  - How should we respond to God's offer of life?
    - Accept it.
    - Live in obedience.

## DISCUSSION QUESTIONS

1. What are some great things we want for ourselves?
2. What do you see as the difference between great things and great things *for us*?
3. How is greatness different from just being effective?
4. What makes seeking great things for ourselves futile?
5. Of those in your high school who were voted "most likely to succeed," how did they do?

# MESSAGES AGAINST THE NATIONS (46:1–51:64)

As the counterpoint to the messages against Judah in 2:1–20:18, here the book delivers a series of messages against the nations. This unit has two distinct major sections. The first is a series of oracles against various nations contemporary with Jeremiah. Most but not all were neighbors of Israel or closely involved in the history of Israel (46:1–49:39). The second major section is dedicated to a prophecy about the fall of Babylon (50:1–51:64).

## Jeremiah 46:1–49:39

### EXEGETICAL IDEA

Each oracle represents some aspect of God's judgment against the nations. All the oracles have three things in common. First, each state, like Judah, faces God's judgment and is destined for defeat at the hands of the Babylonians. Second, each state, unlike Judah, has no hope for a future restoration. Third, Jeremiah does not engage in triumphalist gloating over the fall of the Gentile states. He views the death and destruction that will befall them as tragic and lamentable. Beyond that, each oracle has its own characteristics, as explored below.

### THEOLOGICAL FOCUS

Like Israel, the other nations of the world will be judged, and it will happen in accordance with the principles found in these oracles. Amos 3:2 says, "You alone have I known from all the families of the earth; for that reason, I will punish you for all your iniquities." It is not that Israel alone was judged, and it is not that being the chosen people confers immunity from punishment. But if judgment starts at the house of God, it will surely reach all people.

### PREACHING IDEA

Your arm is too short to box with God.

### PREACHING POINTERS

Without God's judgments, his grace and mercy are not needed. This passage helps us see that he is a God who judges. He judges not only his chosen people, his family, but he judges all. He gives us clear pictures of what and how he judges. From these nine judgments on the nations we can see some universal characteristics of his judgment that apply to us.

God's judgment will come someday, but it will come—and it won't leave any sin unpunished. And in the fuller revelation: God is merciful in his judgment, because through Christ's amazing work we can receive mercy.

# THE SUBDUED NATIONS (46:1–49:39)

## LITERARY STRUCTURE AND THEMES

The messages here are directed against nations that were subdued by Babylon. But in examining the individual oracles, one fact stands out: the messages are not all the same. They differ considerably from each other regarding what aspect of judgment and conquest they focus on. Each one has a specific and distinct emphasis. Together, these oracles create a complete picture of what divine judgment on the nations means. Thus, the reader should seek to determine what is the specific purpose or emphasis of each, and then draw all these themes together into a unified interpretation.

- ***Superscript: Concerning the Nations (46:1)***
- ***Concerning Egypt (46:2–26)***
- ***Concerning Israel (46:27–28)***
- ***Concerning the Philistines (47:1–7)***
- ***Concerning Moab (48:1–47)***
- ***Concerning Ammon (49:1–6)***
- ***Concerning Edom (49:7–22)***
- ***Concerning Damascus (49:23–27)***
- ***Concerning Kedar (49:28–33)***
- ***Concerning Elam (49:34–39)***

## EXPOSITION

### *Superscript: Concerning the Nations (46:1)*

**46:1**. This superscript is a heading to all of 46:2–49:39. Its counterpart, the heading to the judgment on Babylon, is at 50:1.

### *Concerning Egypt (46:2–26)*

This oracle is in two parts. The first is a taunt song over the defeat of Egypt at the hands of the Babylonians at the Battle of Carchemish in 605 (46:2–12). The song is not dated, but it probably was first sung soon after the battle. The second part (46:13–26) prophesies that Egypt is destined to suffer further defeat and humiliation in its wars with Nebuchadnezzar. This part is not dated at all; it may have been written soon after the taunt song or many years later. For Jeremiah's audience in Jerusalem, this oracle was a warning against reliance upon Egypt. But the theological focus is on how military might cannot save a people from divine judgment.

**46:2**. This verse is a superscript to the song in verses 3–13. It implies that the song was composed after, not before, Carchemish. It is not a prediction. The song is in part a celebration over the defeat of Pharaoh Neco II, who had slain King Josiah in 609.

**46:3–9**. Verses 3–4 are a sarcastic call for the Egyptians to prepare for battle. They can go through the motions of arming and equipping themselves for facing the Babylonians, but it will do them no good. Verses 5–6 jump from the pre-battle preparations to the scene at the end of the Battle of Carchemish: the terrified Egyptian army is routed. The expression "terror all around" (מָגוֹר מִסָּבִיב) is used in Jeremiah 6:25; 20:3, 10 to describe how the Babylonians will terrify Jerusalem. This implies that the judgment that will befall Judah has also struck Egypt. Verses 7–9 jump back in time to when Egypt was preparing to advance into the northern Euphrates Valley to confront Nebuchadnezzar. The Egyptians had thought that they would move through like a river in flood stage, as the Nile does in its annual inundation, sweeping away all that was in their path and seizing control of Syria (the metaphor of an invading army as a flooding river appears elsewhere; see Isa. 8:7–8). But their campaign would not go as they had hoped.

**46:10–12**. Verse 10 declares that Egypt's defeat at Carchemish was for them the "day of YHWH," the time when they had to face the wrath of God. Amos 5:18 warns the Israelites not to think that the day of YHWH was for the nations only and not also for Israel, but here it is directed against Egypt. In verse 11, the Egyptians are sarcastically told to seek healing in Gilead, famous for its balm (Jer. 8:22 refers to the balm of Gilead when speaking of the destruction of Judah). No medicine can restore Egypt's prominence on the international stage, because all the world now knows that Egyptian power is broken (v. 12).

**46:13**. This is the superscript to 46:14–26. It does not have any clear indication of when this message was given, although verse 17 suggests that it was written in the time of Hophra. The most difficult aspect of this passage, however, is that it appears to predict that Babylon would successfully invade Egypt and carry away the people into exile. It mentions several Egyptian locations (Memphis on the southern tip of the Egyptian Delta; Migdol and Tahpanhes, both on the eastern side of the Delta; and Thebes, far to the south in Upper Egypt), implying that these places must be prepared for a Babylonian attack (vv. 14, 25). Verse 19 indicates that Memphis would be sacked and warns the Egyptians, "Prepare your gear for [going into] exile!" It appears that Nebuchadnezzar did attack Egypt in 568 in order to put down a revolt by Pharaoh Ahmoses. To do this, he certainly would have had to overcome Egyptian outposts in the eastern Delta, but we do not know if Babylon sacked Memphis or penetrated as far south as Thebes. Clearly, Nebuchadnezzar did not take Egypt into exile, beyond perhaps putting some prisoners of war into slavery. We should be careful about taking prophecies such as this too literally, however. They use conventional military language to describe the defeat of a nation, but that does not mean that the prophet expected everything to happen exactly as the text might seem to imply. Babylon broke the power of Egypt, and that is the main point of the prophecy. Within a few decades, after the Persians seized control of Babylon, Egypt was entirely conquered by the Persians and was thereafter dominated by foreign empires.

**46:14–15**. Verse 14 warns the garrisons of various Egyptian cities to prepare for a Babylonian siege. Verse 15 may describe how Egyptian forces would be routed, but it probably describes the capture of the Apis, a sacred bull associated with the god Ptah and housed at Memphis (this was a live bull; when one died, it was associated with Osiris, god of the underworld, and a new bull was chosen to take its place in the shrine).

*TRANSLATION NOTE FOR 46:15*

Verse 15 reads מַדּוּעַ נִסְחַף אַבִּירֶיךָ לֹא עָמַד כִּי יְהוָה הֲדָפוֹ, which might be translated, "Why have your mighty ones been washed away? He did not stand, for YHWH has pushed him." But this is odd because it has a plural subject (אַבִּירֶיךָ) with a singular verb (נִסְחַף). Also, it seems strange that the Hebrew would have just the two words לֹא עָמַד as an independent clause, "He did not stand." The LXX, however, has διὰ τί ἔφυγεν ὁ Ἆπις; ὁ μόσχος ὁ ἐκλεκτός σου οὐκ ἔμεινεν ὅτι κύριος παρέλυσεν αὐτόν ("Why has the Apis fled? Your chosen bull did not endure, because the Lord has undone him"). This suggests that the Hebrew read נָס חַף for נִסְחַף. The word חַף is the equivalent of the Egyptian word for the Apis, so that נָס חַף means, "Apis has fled." The word אַבִּירֶיךָ could be a plural of majesty for "your powerful [bull-god]." Or אַבִּירֶיךָ could be a scribal error for the word *abrek* (אַבְרֵךְ) found in Genesis 41:43 (Holladay 1989, 328–29). This is an Egyptian term of high honor, perhaps meaning something like "Majesty" and used of a person before whom one should bow. The word אברך was probably used both for an exalted official (such as Joseph) and for a god, such as the Apis. This explains the LXX, which loosely

> translated "*abrek* will not stand" (אברך לֹא עָמָד) as "Your chosen bull did not endure." While it is impossible to be certain, it looks like the MT has been corrupted and that the LXX more accurately represents the original.

**46:16**. By the time of the 26th (Saite) Dynasty, Egypt was heavily dependent on foreign mercenaries, especially from Greece (Shaw and Nicholson 1995, 250). Thus, in this verse, the soldiers of Egypt's defeated armies flee back to their home countries.

**46:17**. The last words of this verse are, "He has missed the opportunity" (הֶעֱבִיר הַמּוֹעֵד). The word for "he has missed" (הֶעֱבִיר) may be a play on the name Pharaoh Hophra (spelled חָפְרַע in Jer. 44:30; he reigned 589–570). If so, it dates 46:13–26 to the latter part of the reign of Zedekiah.

**46:18–19**. Nebuchadnezzar will come upon Egypt like Tabor and Carmel, and so the Egyptians should prepare for exile. These mountains are both dominant over the local terrain and represent the dominance of the Babylonian army.

**46:20–21**. Ephraim is metaphorically called a heifer (עֶגְלָה) in Hosea 10:11, as Egypt is here. In both cases, the nations are represented as beautiful but stubborn and rebellious. A horsefly will come upon the heifer that is Egypt and send it into paroxysms. However, in verse 21 Jeremiah takes the metaphor of a heifer in a different direction: Egypt's mercenaries are lazy and overfed like fatted calves and are useless for battle.

**46:22–24**. The text moves through a dizzying series of metaphors to describe Egypt's fall. The snake (v. 22a) could refer either to Babylon, as a dangerous aggressor; or to Egypt, as a treacherous, lowly enemy. But it is probably the latter. The uraeus cobra (called in Egyptian the Wadjyt) was a standard symbol of Egyptian power; a flaring Wadjyt was at the center the pharaonic crown, worn just above the forehead. Next, Egypt is like a forest that men will come upon with axes and cut down; the woodsmen will be more numerous than locusts, and they will clear-cut the land just as locusts devour fields (vv. 22b–23). Egypt had no literal forests, but the term is metaphorical for a nation's wealth and splendor (see Isa. 10:33–34; Jer. 22:7). Finally, Egypt is a young woman given into the power of the "northern people," the Babylonians (v. 24).

**46:25–26**. YHWH prosaically declares that he has set himself against Egypt and her gods and rulers, and that Nebuchadnezzar will be his agent for destroying them.

### *Concerning Israel (46:27–28)*

Although it is possible that one could regard this as a part of the Egyptian oracle, 46:26 closes with a standard way of ending an oracle, "But after that, [Egypt] will be inhabited as before, says YHWH" (compare 48:47; 49:6, 39). Thus, 46:27–28 is a separate oracle. We are surprised to see an oracle concerning Israel here among the nations, but it is a message of comfort and restoration and so stands out from the other oracles against nations.

**46:27–28**. This passage is a doublet of 30:10–11; much of it is a word-for-word repetition. Although we cannot be certain, it seems likely that the passage was originally composed for chapter 30, the "Book of Comfort," and then copied into the oracles against the nations in order to press home two points. First, although Israel must be punished, God is not being unfair. The other nations will also have to face God's justice. Second, Israel will be restored fully. This is not something one can say for many of the nations listed here. Israel thus remains God's first and chosen people. Implicitly, the salvation of the Gentiles depends upon Israel.

### *Concerning the Philistines (47:1–7)*

Annihilation is predicted for Philistia. The passage does not name any sin for which they are punished, nor does it name who would attack Philistia. Verse 1 does mention an Egyptian attack on Gaza, but it does not say that this one Egyptian attack would also be directed at all the other Philistine cities or that it was the occasion for their fall. But that is not the most important issue. Although the passage uses a great deal of military language, its real point is that Philistia would soon disappear. The text does not concern itself with the time or the means but only with the end result: the Philistines would soon be gone forever. The implied reason for this is the historic aggression of Philistia against Israel.

**47:1**. This superscript dates the oracle to sometime prior to an anonymous pharaoh's attack on Gaza. However, since we do not know which pharaoh is meant and since we have no other record of such an attack, the information is of no help to us (for a survey of opinions, see Smothers, Keown, and Scalise 1995, 299–300).

**47:2–3**. Using fairly conventional language for military defeat (see 6:24; 46:7–8; 50:43), Jeremiah predicts the demise of Philistia. This does not imply that every Philistine city would suffer military annihilation, but it does mean that they would be helpless before conquerors and would, in the course of time, disappear.

**47:4–5**. Neither the Phoenician cities (Tyre and Sidon) nor Caphtor (Crete) would be able to help the Philistines. The Philistines have been abandoned by all.

**47:6–7**. Even the prophet laments the ferocity of YHWH's sword, but it cannot be put away until it has obliterated Philistia. The biblical narrative is replete with accounts of the animosity of Philistia toward Israel (for example, that they dishonored Israel's first king, Saul, after his death in battle [1 Sam. 31]). The implied lesson is that nations that behave viciously toward Israel will not endure.

### *Concerning Moab (48:1–47)*

We are not surprised that the oracles concerning Egypt and Babylon are lengthy, but it is extraordinary that the text devotes so much space to Moab as compared to Ammon, Edom, or Philistia. We should recall, however, that the oracles were not composed at the same time and originally were not a collection. The length of one message should not be compared to another, as though they were all part of a single literary plan. The focus in this oracle is on the thoroughness of the destruction YHWH sends on his enemies.

**48:1–47**. Although it is lengthy, this oracle is best taken as a whole. Three facts stand out.

First, it has an astonishing number of geographic names. It reads like a catalogue of all the places in Moab: Nebo, Kiriathaim, The Fortress (v. 1); Heshbon, Madmen (v. 2); Horonaim (v. 3); Luhith (v. 5); Dibon (v. 18); Aroer (v. 19); Arnon (v. 20); The Tableland, Holon, Jahzah, Mephaath (v. 21); Dibon, Nebo, Beth-diblathaim (v. 22); Kiriathaim, Beth-gamul, Beth-meon (v. 23); Kerioth, Bozrah (v. 24); Kir-heres (v. 31); Jazer, Sibmah (v. 32); Heshbon, Elealeh, Zoar, Horonaim, Eglath-shelishiyah, The Waters of Nimrim (v. 34); Kir-heres (v. 36). In almost every case, the places mentioned are destroyed or are in great distress.

Second, the passage uses a variety of metaphors and images to portray the annihilation of Moab: the god Chemosh and his priests will go into exile (v. 7); Moab has long been at peace, like wine settled on its dregs, but YHWH will pour out the wine and smash the wine jugs (vv. 11–13); all the warriors of Moab will be slaughtered by "the destroyer" (vv. 14–20); Moab's arrogance will be brought down and it will be like a pathetic drunkard (vv. 26–30); all the heads will be shaved and the land will be filled with lamentation (vv. 37–39); the Moabites will flee, but it will be as if their land were filled with pits and snares for them to fall into, and everyone will be taken captive (vv. 43–46).

Third, Jeremiah grieves deeply over the fall of Moab: he wails and weeps (vv. 31–32), and his heart mourns like a flute (v. 36).

The exhaustive geographic catalogue and the variety of metaphors all indicate that Moab will undergo massive destruction. It is so severe that the prophet, representing YHWH, expresses great sorrow. Even so, some reprieve is promised in verse 47. Moab, like Ammon in the next oracle, was part of the empire of David, and the restoration of Israel's fortunes will also mean a restoration for Moab. Theologically, it points toward a general salvation for the nations.

### *Concerning Ammon (49:1–6)*

The conflict between Ammon and Israel is portrayed as a conflict between YHWH and the god Milcom. YHWH's victory would put an end both to Ammon and to the depravity associated with Milcom worship, but an eschatological renewal is promised. The focus here is on how the Ammonites and their god were rivals to Israel and YHWH, and were therefore destined to fail.

**49:1–5**. This oracle condemns Ammon for a specific sin against Israel: the occupation of the territory of Gad (the tribe of Gad occupied land on the east side of the Jordan, adjacent to Ammonite territory). Gad was part of the northern kingdom of Israel, a nation that had disappeared long before the time of Jeremiah; it had not been under Davidic rule since the time of Solomon. While it is true that ancient people could have very long memories about grievances against another nation, there is more to the condemnation of Ammon than ancient Israelite hostility toward occupation of what they believed was their territory. It represents the larger dispute over who really owns the land, YHWH's people Israel or Milcom's people Ammon. Milcom (also called Molech) was the deity of Ammon (there is some debate about whether Milcom was the god of Ammon, but 1 Kings 11:7, 33 does not leave the issue in doubt). The cult of Milcom included child sacrifice (Lev. 18:21; 20:2–5). The time was soon to come, Jeremiah promised, when the Ammonites would be obliterated and the images of Milcom would become plunder.

**49:6**. The Ammonites under the Tobiad family persisted as a people, albeit subject to foreign empires, into the second century B.C. After that, they disappeared from history. YHWH's promise to restore the Ammonites could refer to their survival during this period, but it probably views them as a part of the historic empire of David. The eschatological renewal of Israel would include its former dominion. In this, the Ammonite restoration probably refers to the inclusion of the Gentiles in greater Israel, as is the case for Edom in Amos 9:11–12.

### *Concerning Edom (49:7–22)*

The oracle against Edom is similar—and at many points identical—to the prophecy of Obadiah. This naturally raises the question of which passage came first. *Prima facie*, it is more likely that the Jeremiah text is earlier. Obadiah is almost certainly an exilic book, written in the years after the fall of Jerusalem. While this could be true for Jeremiah's oracle against Edom as well, the majority of Jeremiah's prophecies are preexilic. Furthermore, Jeremiah does not include the complaint mentioned in Obadiah 10–14, that the Edomites abused and despoiled Jewish refugees after the fall of Jerusalem. Thus, it appears that Jeremiah prophesied before Jerusalem's fall and that Obadiah, writing after that event, borrowed from Jeremiah when he denounced the viciousness and greed of Edom. This does not diminish the value of Obadiah. Originality is not a necessary aspect of inspiration. The message here in Jeremiah combines several themes, including the thoroughness of God's judgment and the fact that geographical isolation and lofty fortifications will not save a people from God's fury.

**49:7–8**. Edom was reputed to have a tradition of great wisdom. They should show wisdom by abandoning their territory and hiding from the calamity to come.

**49:9–11**. This is an analogy from lesser to greater: A harvester or thief will only take so much, leaving the rest behind, but the conqueror that YHWH sends will leave Edom with nothing. Verse 11, notwithstanding how it appears, is not an offer of mercy. Instead the conqueror, before killing the Edomite men, promises to take the women and children away into slavery.

**49:12–13**. Using the familiar metaphor of the cup of YHWH's wrath, the text draws another lesson from lesser to greater. It asserts that even some nations that were relatively innocent had to face the fury of divine judgment (in the form of the Babylonian army). That being the case, the treacherous Edomites would have to drink of the cup that much more. Bozrah was Edom's capital city.

**49:14–16**. Using the image of a herald sent from one nation to another to make a declaration of war, YHWH warns the Edomites to prepare for a desperate battle. As was common, the herald announces his disdain for the defenses of the nation he confronts, telling them that their hope that their defenses will protect them is in vain (see the speech of the Assyrian herald in Isaiah 36:4–10).

**49:17–22**. YHWH portrays himself as a ferocious lion or giant eagle attacking the sheep of Edom (in the metaphor, the "shepherd" is Edom's leadership, and the sheep are the people). YHWH's language is unusually harsh and even sounds boastful (v. 19), but that is a function of the metaphor—a conqueror (here portrayed as a lion) brags about his ferocity and terrifies his victim. Edom has no future. YHWH will utterly obliterate it.

### *Concerning Damascus (49:23–27)*

Damascus in its day had been one of Israel's greatest enemies, but in Jeremiah's time the Syrian kingdom was a shadow of what it had been. Prophecies of its demise had already been and were still being fulfilled. The focus here is on how prophetic denunciations made generations earlier have not expired.

**49:23–26**. Damascus, Hamath, and Arpad had all at one time been major Syrian cities, but by the time of Jeremiah all had fallen into relative insignificance after repeated wars with Assyria. With the Assyrian Empire gone, Babylon moved in to control the region. Jeremiah does not refer to any sin of Damascus, but in earlier times it had often fought and come near to destroying Israel. The armies of the weakened Syrian states are now helpless before the Babylonian onslaught, Jeremiah says.

**49:27**. This verse is strikingly similar to Amos 1:4: "And I will send fire against Hazael's palace, and it will consume Ben-hadad's citadels." Both verses end with וְאָכְלָה אַרְמְנוֹת בֶּן־הֲדָד ("and it will consume Ben-hadad's citadels"). Ben-hadad had been a scourge of Israel around 790 B.C. (2 Kings 13:3). The allusion implies that the judgment issued by Amos in the eighth century was still being fulfilled in Jeremiah's time, about two hundred years after Ben-hadad.

### *Concerning Kedar (49:28–33)*

The destruction of the distant Arabian tribal people of Kedar demonstrates the power and reach of the Babylonian army. The focus here is that being remote and isolated will not allow a people to escape divine judgment.

**49:28–33**. Kedar, a north Arabian tribe, had no history of conflict with Israel, and this passage attributes no specific sin to Kedar. The Kedarites flourished from the eighth to the fourth centuries. They carried out raids to the north, to Mesopotamia, and so came into conflict with both Assyria and Babylonia. In 599, Nebuchadnezzar carried out a major expedition against Kedar, and this passage seems to refer to that event. Jeremiah 2:10 refers to Kedar and Cyprus as two places respectively in the extreme southeast and extreme northwest. Therefore, 49:28–33 apparently draws attention to Kedar because it was so remote and yet still fell to the Babylonian army. Also, this passage gives much more attention to Nebuchadnezzar than we see in the other oracles against nations. The point is that the Babylonian conquest extends to the most distant parts of the world. They are God's instrument of judgment, and their power is irresistible.

*TRANSLATION NOTE: THE MEANING OF* חָצוֹר

The word חָצוֹר in 49:28, 30, 33 is usually taken to be a proper noun, Hazor. This is not the familiar city of the Galilee region that flourished in the Bronze and Iron Ages. Instead, it is usually taken to be an otherwise unknown Arabian city. The difficulty is that there is no other evidence, literary or archaeological, that an Arabian Hazor ever existed. Also, 49:29–31 portrays the Kedarites as a seminomadic shepherd people who, when stationary, live in unwalled villages. This too contradicts the idea that "Hazor" was a major city, perhaps the Kedarite capital. Furthermore, there is a common Hebrew word חָצֵר, which can refer to an unwalled settlement. It seems likely that although חָצוֹר functions as a proper noun in this text, it is not a specific city but is a variant of חָצֵר and refers to the Kedarite mode of living in small, unwalled communities. *HALOT*, under II חָצוֹר, suggests the meaning "the resident Arabs," and this is perhaps analogous. The people were able to maintain their seminomadic lifestyle since these villages could be easily or temporarily abandoned. They apparently relied on their remoteness for their security. If this is correct, then 49:28a should be translated as, "Concerning Kedar and the Kingdoms of the Unwalled Village" (see also Holladay 1989, 382–83, but I do not think his translation "settled folk" is the best).

### *Concerning Elam (49:34–39)*

Elam represents a distant, ancient nation that is nevertheless still under YHWH's rule and subject to his judgment. The focus of this oracle is that Elam's downfall is a work of God.

**49:34–39**. Elam, located just east of the lower Tigris River at the western edge of modern Iran, was an ancient culture, dating back to at least 3200 B.C. It played a major role in the history of the great Mesopotamian cultures, but it declined significantly during the period 1000–539 B.C., especially under pressure from the Assyrians. By 539, the Elamites were absorbed into the Persian Empire and persisted only as a minority population. But they had little or no interaction with Israel and certainly were not engaged in conflict with Israel and Judah except that perhaps some Elamites, as vassals of Assyria or Babylon, may have been included among the troops that attacked Samaria or Jerusalem. But Jeremiah says nothing about there being any Elamite troops in the campaigns against Israel, and thus this is not likely to be essential to his message. The notable feature of this oracle is how theological it is: YHWH declares that he will fight against Elam, scatter them to the four winds of heaven, and place his throne in their territory. God, in the account, deals directly with Elam. This suggests that the main point is that God rules over all the nations, even the most remote. It may also explain the promise of Elamite restoration in verse 39: as God rules even the most distant Gentiles, so also he will one day bring them salvation (this theme is prominent in Isaiah, as at 41:1, 5; 42:4, 10, 12, 15; 51:5).

## THEOLOGICAL FOCUS

As noted in the introduction, each oracle has a focal point and each one contributes an element to a larger theological portrait. Taken together, they make the following assertions about divine judgment on the nations:

- Some of these nations have had a long history of hostility against Israel, and had oracles delivered against them by previous biblical prophets. The implication is that all the ancient prophecies against these nations will be fulfilled to the uttermost. The predicted disaster may seem to tarry, but it will come.
- Nations that sought to destroy Israel will be punished with great severity.
- Although judgment begins with Israel, it will also come to the nations, and they will suffer the same calamities that Israel goes through. The messages reassure Israel that they are still God's chosen, just as they also make the point that Israel's election does not exempt it from divine wrath. As Israel was first to receive God's favor, it is first to receive God's punishment. But the other nations will not escape.
- These nations are all presented, implicitly or explicitly, as victims of Babylon. This means, on the one hand, that God's reach is very long and that he uses Babylon to repay the nations for their sins. But on the other hand, it means that Babylon is an aggressive, ruthless empire, acquiring a great mass of guilt. Babylon is the agent of God's wrath, but that does not excuse its cruelty. Its arrogance and violence will bring about its own downfall, as described in 50:1–51:64.
- Ultimately, the judgment on the nations is a work of God. Babylon is only the instrument. YHWH, the God of Israel, is the judge of all the earth.
- When the calamity comes, it will be massive, causing great loss of life and intense suffering.
- The gods of the nations will all disappear.
- A nation's military power, fortifications, or isolation will not avert the coming destruction.
- Although God judges the nations, he does not hate them. His prophet, Jeremiah, weeps over them.
- Just as the nations were judged along with Israel, so God will extend mercy to them. This will happen when they are drawn into Israel's great salvation.

## PREACHING AND TEACHING STRATEGIES

### *Exegetical and Theological Synthesis*

Who would hear or read these prophecies? When Jeremiah first proclaimed his messages, the Jews living in Judah must have been delighted. God was going to punish all the other nations. They failed to realize that his judgments are not only for other nations; he judges his own people. They failed to realize that they too would be judged because of their continual rebellion against him—and they didn't seem to grasp that their wicked hearts fueled this rebellion.

When the exiles returned from Persia, they witnessed many of these nine prophecies already having been fulfilled. Would these judgments affect them? History shows us that the Jews at least stopped their idolatry, but would they submit to all of God's commands? The postexilic prophets still had to address other sins; and then, the development of the pharisaical laws that later emerged shows that they learned little from these nine prophecies.

Which leads to the question: Will *we* learn from these prophecies? How could God's message to nations, most of which no longer exist, teach us anything? The thrust of this passage comes when we see the characteristics of God's judgments. He is still the same God, and he still judges.

### *Preaching Idea*

Your arm is too short to box with God.

### *Contemporary Connections*

#### *What does it mean?*

The application of each of these messages as individual applications can be overwhelming. In a sense it would become a nine-point sermon. However, it is important not to miss the subtle differences that God presents to us. Thus, an application for each message will be briefly presented, as well as key verses that help encapsulate the message of that section. Then, for the purposes of effective communication, these nine messages will be compiled into three major and universal characteristics of God's judgment.

*Egypt (46:3–5).* The Egyptians trusted their military might. No matter how much we take care of our bodies, they will not win the battle of age and of living in a world filled with physical dangers. Taking care of our bodies is always right, but we must not trust our physical strength to keep us from facing God at our death.

*Israel (46:28).* Everyone will be judged or disciplined. It would be easy for Israel to think that God's judgment is only on other nations. Though his judgment on Israel was for the purpose of discipline, his judgment still comes on those of his chosen race and royal priesthood.

*Philistines (47:2–4).* Those against Israel will not stand. To oppose Israel was to oppose God's plan for him to bless the world. God has seen fit to bring the church into his plan to bless the world, and to oppose it is to challenge God's plan. Not that it doesn't need correction at times, but to reject the church is to reject God's plan.

*Moab (48:42–43).* You can't be higher than God. We can justify disobeying God by thinking that it is acceptable to disobey him in certain situations. When we justify sin, we are putting ourselves above God.

*Ammon (49:3).* Man-made gods will fail. When something or someone becomes more important to us than God, we are creating a god of our creation. No matter how great the cause or the person, it or they will not last. All man-made gods will fail.

*Edom (49:14–16).* Physical structures can't protect you. While we don't set up fortresses to hide in, we do set up financial fortresses that can become our source of trust rather than God. For some, having a secure place to live in, such as having a house paid for, can become the focus of our security. No matter how strong your fiscal or physical structures are, they will not last.

*Damascus (49:23–24).* God will do what he says. The Israelites saw this happen. Since we live in an age of wanting things to happen quickly, from deliveries of purchases to our home to the preparation of meals, we could think that since God's judgment hasn't come yet, it might not come. How very wrong this is.

*Kedar (49:28–29).* Isolation from God is impossible. While we know that we can't truly separate ourselves from everyone, some people try and "go off the grid," living with as few connections as possible. But just as no one can truly exist without contact, we can't escape judgment from God by trying to sever our contact with him.

*Elam (49:35–38).* You can't hide from God. In a similar way as above, people try to isolate themselves from others by living as remotely as they can—not only off the grid, but off the roads. No matter now far away from civilization one may live, there will still be some kind of contact. We know that we can't move away from God physically; after all, this is his world. But we can move away from him emotionally and mentally, to the point that we could feel hidden from him. But we can't hide from God.

### *Is it true?*

When the exiles returned from Persia, they witnessed many of these prophecies already having been fulfilled, including the message that follows these regarding Babylon (Medo-Persia had conquered Babylon). James Weldon Johnson wrote a series of poems in the early part of the twentieth century based upon the style of African American preachers, compiled in his book *God's Trombones.* In one of his sermon/poems he uses the phrase, "Your arm is too short to box with God," to affirm that God's judgment is sure and complete (Johnson 1969, 21). These nations couldn't box with God, and neither can we.

The nine messages Jeremiah gives regarding the nations articulate different ways that people try to challenge God. This challenging of God may not seem like a direct confrontation, though in some cases it is; rather, when people disobey God in any form, they are challenging him. When people certainly have gone against his authority and the judgment is delayed, it can create a mindset that one can challenge God and get away with it. But God's judgment will come. To those in the family and household of God, this judgment is in the form of discipline. Those of us on this side of the cross are trusting in the forgiveness that comes through faith in Christ. Though the exiles did not fully understand the means of salvation they, through their faith in God's provisions, shared the same standing. Those who choose to reject the offer of forgiveness will receive God's righteous judgment.

### *What now?*

No matter what our standing before God, each of us at times thinks that we can challenge God. At first, we might think that we would never challenge God. How could anyone, how could any nation, challenge the living God? These judgments not only teach us about the sins and judgments of nations, but also reveal to us the sinful subtleties of our own hearts and God's judgment upon these sins. In the wickedness of our hearts, each of us is in danger of trying to box with God.

These nine judgments show the many ways our hearts rebel against God. One could leave the application there but I, along with Dr. Garrett, suggest that we draw summary characteristics of God's judgment from these nine. It is much easier to expand three applications than nine. Here are three that I suggest:

- God's judgment is sure. Judgment will come someday, but it will come.
- God's judgment is complete. He won't leave any sin unpunished.
- God is merciful in his judgment. Through Christ's amazing work, we can receive mercy.

### ***Creativity in Presentation***

This complex sermon will be more effective if it begins and ends with an image or story that bookends the sermon. The image of your arm being too short to box with God may not fit you as a teacher/preacher and may not be best for your congregation, but strive to find an image that creates the feeling of competition and of challenging an opponent. An image from another sport, game, or even business could be effective.

Another helpful tool is to compile the diverse messages into major themes. We can help our listeners stay engaged through this long passage by asking them to look for characteristics of God's judgments. What general principles can we see in these nine specific judgments? Tell them up front that going over the judgments has a purpose; this will help them stay with you as you go through this lengthy passage. I am suggesting the following three themes, but there could be some variation; one could have four, two, or even just one. Here is one possible structure:

- Present the text.
    - See the list of nine judgments above.
- Identify three characteristics of God's judgement.
    - God's judgment is sure.
        - Judgment will come someday, but it will come.
    - God's judgment is complete.
        - He won't leave any sin unpunished.
    - God is merciful in his judgment.
        - Through Christ's amazing work, we can receive mercy.
- Your arm is too short to box with God—so rather than box with him, trust in his mercy.

## DISCUSSION QUESTIONS

1. Describe a time when you were judged in a presentation setting: for example, a speech or music class, a business presentation, or doing a math problem in front of the class:
    a. What did it feel like before you presented?
    b. Whose opinion mattered most?
    c. What did you try or hope to get out of the presentation?
2. What might make people think that they can escape judgment?
3. What kind of judgments do people try to avoid?
4. When are people successful at avoiding human judgments?
5. What difference does it make as to who is doing the judging?

# Jeremiah 50:1–51:64

## EXEGETICAL IDEA

Babylon, the enemy of God and his people, will be annihilated. The text is in two parts, with the first and very lengthy portion being a prediction that Babylon will fall and be swallowed by the sands of the desert, but that the Jews will endure. The second is a brief account of the mission of Seraiah, Baruch's brother, to deliver a symbolic act predicting Babylon's demise.

## THEOLOGICAL FOCUS

The depiction of the destruction of Babylon concerns the end of Babylon's historical dominion but also represents the complete demise of imperial power that sets itself against the kingdom of God. Babylon, from the building of the tower in Genesis 11 to the demise of the great harlot in Revelation 18, has always been always representative of the ideal of the power, wealth, and ideological dominance of the human kingdom over against the kingdom of God. The fall of historical Babylon is a sign that the ideal Babylon represents will fall before Jesus and his kingdom.

## PREACHING IDEA

Don't take part in what God is against.

## PREACHING POINTERS

Apparently, these prophesies against Babylon were presented to the Babylonians. That would be one tough preaching assignment. But interspersed in the judgment of Babylon are directives and affirmations to Israel. This message is not just to announce judgment on Babylon, but to give guidance to Israel and to us.

God knows that the Jews of that era and his children of today live in the midst of nations which are guilty of systemic and cultural sins. So what are we to do? God made it clear that the Jews were not to stay in Babylon any longer than they had to. He warned them not to see themselves as a permanent part of that nation. No matter the nation in which we live, all are affected by evil. Thus, we must not see any nation as the basis for our true identity. While we are to be good citizens of the physical nation in which we live, we must remember that this is not our permanent residence. We must evaluate what is around us and be careful to not be for, let alone take part in, what God is against.

# BABYLON (50:1–51:64)

## LITERARY STRUCTURE AND THEMES

The following text is in two parts; 50:1–51:48 is an oracle poem against Babylon and 51:59–64, a passage dated to the fourth year of Zedekiah, is a commission Jeremiah gave to Seraiah to take to Babylon a scroll containing a message of judgment against Babylon. The commission to Seraiah is dated to 594 B.C., but the main oracle is undated and may be a composite of earlier prophecies.

A noteworthy feature of the main oracle is that in any text in which it identifies the agent of Babylon's destruction, that agent is always the Medes (51:11, 28). During the lifetime of Jeremiah, the Medes were the dominant power in the Medo-Persian coalition. However, Cyrus II of Persia came to the throne in 559, and he soon established himself as the ruler of the coalition, making the Persians the dominant power. For that reason we speak of the Persians, not the Medes, as the conquerors of Babylon. This implies that the oracles authentically come from the time of Jeremiah and are not a secondary addition to the book composed after the rise of Persia. Some scholars believe that there are numerous secondary additions to this material (small, "midrashic" comments made by later editors), and thus not all of the oracle poem is authentically from Jeremiah (for example, see Holladay 1989, 402–15). But these claims are arbitrary and unpersuasive; the whole poem can be regarded as Jeremiah's.

This does not mean that the material is easy to deal with. It is an extremely long and somewhat repetitive passage. In it, YHWH declares his absolute hostility to Babylon and his determination to destroy it to avenge the destruction of Jerusalem. It is fairly easy to grasp the surface meaning of the passage; it is much more difficult to know what to do with it. What is one to make of the "theology" of this lengthy diatribe?

To answer this, we must ask another question: Why is the oracle against Babylon so long and so severe? The obvious answer is that Babylon destroyed Jerusalem, and on one level this is true. The Jews had a grudge against Babylon beyond what it felt toward any other nation (Ps. 137). But this answer is not adequate. In Daniel, Babylon is the first of the great world empires, the beginning of Gentile domination over many nations and peoples and especially the Jews. Each world empire is a counterfeit kingdom of God, with the imperial king standing in for God. In Revelation too, Babylon is symbolically the center of Gentile political and economic power. The oracle against Babylon does announce YHWH's vengeance on the historical destroyer of Jerusalem; but in that role, Babylon represents the political, cultural, religious, and economic domination of the imperial power over the people of God.

- ***The Oracles Concerning Babylon (50:1–51:58)***
- ***The Mission of Seraiah to Babylon (51:59–64)***

## EXPOSITION

### *The Oracles Concerning Babylon (50:1–51:58)*

Some translations treat some of the verses as prose, but there is no compelling evidence in favor of this; it is entirely poetic. Interspersed among the verses, however, are prose subheadings that declare what follows to be the word of YHWH (for example, 50:18: "Therefore this is what YHWH Almighty, the God of Israel, says"). Sometimes these prose declarations indicate a response to an issue raised in a previous verse. Thus, 50:17 declares that Assyria and Babylon have scattered Israel; but in 50:18, after the prose subheading, YHWH declares that he will punish Babylon just as he punished Assyria. Similarly, in 51:34–35, Jerusalem laments how she has been swallowed by Babylon; and in 51:36, after the subheading, YHWH declares that he will take up Jerusalem's case and leave Babylon desolate.

**50:1**. This is the superscript to the oracle against Babylon (50:2–51:48), and serves to set the oracle against Babylon as the counterpart to the oracles against the other nations.

**50:2–3**. This is a general introduction to the poem, announcing that Babylon has fallen and its idols have been taken away. Babylon was captured by the Persians, whose domain was east of Babylonia. But Jeremiah says the enemy is from the "north." In the Old Testament, however, "north" is simply shorthand for distant kingdoms in Syria, Mesopotamia, and regions beyond. It is not meant to be geographically specific. "Merodach" is Marduk, the patron god of Babylon.

**50:4–5**. As Babylon falls, the Jews will return to their land and to YHWH. They will seek for Zion, and not merely in a geographical sense. They have learned the lesson of the exile and will turn to their God and not idols.

**50:6–7**. The Jews had been misled by their leaders and abused by the nations. In the metaphor, the Jews are sheep; their shepherds (the Israelite leadership) had left them wandering in the hills, and the wild animals (the nations) devoured them.

**50:8–10**. All the residents of Babylon, particularly the Jews, should abandon the city. It cannot resist the warriors who will come against it. This is strikingly different from the advice in Jeremiah's letter to the Jehoiachin exile, which exhorted the Jews to build houses, raise families, and settle in for a long (seventy-year) captivity (29:1–10). But the circumstances are different. The earlier letter contradicted a false claim that the exile would be short-lived and that Jehoiachin would soon retake the throne in Jerusalem (he would in fact never return). Jeremiah 50–51 anticipates the future demise of Babylon, when the Jews would finally be able to leave (prior to that event, they could not have left if they wanted to). It also tells future generations of Jews that Babylon is not the place for them. When Cyrus of Persia took control of the city and released the Jews from captivity, many preferred to stay put since they had built prosperous lives for themselves there. In the early postexilic era, Zechariah was still exhorting Jews in Babylon to come home (Zech. 2:6–7). Yet another group of Jews came back with Ezra much later, during the reign of Artaxerxes (reigned 464–424; see Ezra 8:1). Jeremiah's appeal was meant to tell the Jews that they should not consider Babylon their permanent home and should come back as soon as possible.

**50:11–16**. In a vivid series of metaphors, the celebrations of the Babylonians over all their victories are portrayed as a skipping heifer. But their city (the metaphorical mother) will be put to shame when the enemy arrives and Babylon experiences utter defeat.

**50:17–20**. Assyria and Babylon were like lions that scattered a flock of sheep (Israel and Judah). But God will answer the violence of Assyria and Babylon. Assyria has fallen, and Babylon will fall, but Israel will again feed upon the pastures in their own land.

**50:21–27**. YHWH commands the destruction of Babylonia, here also called "Merathaim" and "Pekod" (v. 21) and "the land of the Chaldeans" (v. 25). Like the spilling of grain on the ground when a granary bursts, the bodies of the slain Babylonians will be dumped on the earth (v. 26). The population is to be totally annihilated; the text twice uses the root I-חרם, to "obliterate a people," to describe what will happen to the Babylonians (vv. 21, 26).

**Jeremiah's Oracle and the Historical Fall of Babylon**

Here we must confront a significant problem: the oracle against Babylon predicts a military conquest with massive casualties for the defenders and citizens of Babylon—a complete genocide. It also speaks of a conflagration of the city and of a plundering of the idols of the local gods (see 50:2–3, 10, 13–15, 21–23, 32, 36–37; 51:4, 14, 29–32, 43, 58). In fact, this did not happen. Babylon was not destroyed by Persia at all, and there was no slaughter of the population or plundering of the temples.

Cyrus II did come upon the city with a sizable army, but the conquest of the city was nearly bloodless. There seems to have been only minor skirmishing on the night the city was taken, with very few deaths (among them the co-regent of Babylon, Belshazzar). And the Persians did not make a mockery of Marduk and Babylon's other gods, carrying them into exile. To the contrary, Cyrus presented himself as the liberator of Babylon. He claimed he had been called by Marduk to come and put an end to the blasphemous reign of Nabonidus and to restore the prestige of Marduk's temple in Babylon. The Babylonian populace received their new Persian overlords with little distress or disruption. The city continued to thrive in the years after the Persian conquest, as illustrated in Daniel 6. For them, it was little more than a change of government, and many officials (Daniel among them) who had served under the Chaldean administration now served the Persian administration.

And the city endured for a long time. Babylon was still a major urban center in the time of Alexander the Great, who died there in 323 B.C. A large Jewish community was still in Babylon during the Christian period; the Babylonian Talmud was composed there around A.D. 200. In the course of time, after the Muslim conquest, the city was abandoned and became the empty ruin it is today, but this was not because of anything Cyrus's army did in 539 B.C. What are we to make of this?

First, this problem does indicate that the prophecy was authentically written in the preexilic era. If it had been composed by a scribe in the postexilic years, it certainly would not have described Babylon's fall in this manner. Everyone living under the Persian Empire knew that the city was doing well and had not been destroyed.

Second, it looks as though the oracle against Babylon is modeled on the fall of Nineveh, which did suffer a violent destruction with widespread slaughter and looting. That is, the fall of Nineveh served as an archetype for the fall of a great empire. The prophecy of Nahum against Nineveh exemplifies this model. This implies that a prophetic vision of the demise of a great, thriving state will typically follow a canonical model and so employ stark and bloody military terms, even if the actual event was not so cataclysmic. Or a destruction oracle may follow the model of the obliteration of Sodom and so describe a place that comes under God's judgment—as, with Sodom, a lifeless desert scorched by the fire of God (Isa. 13:19; Jer. 50:40; Amos 4:11; Zeph. 2:9). Jeremiah, in fact, looks to the destructions of both Sodom and Assyria as patterns for Babylon's destruction (49:18; 50:17–18, 40). But his use of these models does not imply that the city's fall will involve a sudden conflagration, whether by an enemy army or by fire from heaven. Instead, the earlier calamities at

Sodom and at Nineveh provide a theological pattern or ideal—namely, that God will bring judgment upon any state that does a great evil. Sodom and Nineveh are types for the judgment of God upon a Gentile state. But it is the complete demise of an evil state, not the literal details of how it fell, that is the message.

Third, just as the account of the fall of Babylon is based on a literary pattern or theological type—the destructions of Sodom and Assyria—so also Babylon is itself a type for the ideal of imperial power. The great empire that dominates the nations is the antitype to the kingdom of God. This pattern appears numerous times in the Bible, most famously in Daniel's presentation of Babylon as the first of the four world empires (Dan. 2:38) and in Revelation's portrayal of Babylon the Great Prostitute (Rev. 17:5). The ideal appears in other places as well. Habakkuk 1–2, for example, looks upon Babylon as the ideal of the world conqueror. Thus, the extreme length of Jeremiah's oracle, the great violence against Babylon, the claim that it would fall never to rise again, and the mockery of Babylon's gods all have a purpose not immediately evident on a surface reading of the words. As the archetype of the blaspheming world empire, what Christians might call the ideal of the Antichrist, the text portrays the violent annihilation of all that Babylon represents, particularly its cultural and religious ideology (the latter signified by its idols). The oracle against Babylon points toward the triumph of the kingdom of God over the kingdoms of this world. In the stream of biblical theology, Babylon is more than the historical city. It is the concrete form of the carnal ideology of conquest, oppression, decadence, arrogance, and false gods. This culture dominates the nations and is destined for destruction.

Finally, we should note that the Persian conquest, if not a particularly violent event, was in fact a turning point in Babylon's history. With Cyrus's victory, the Babylonian Empire disappeared. Henceforth, the city would be governed by foreign empires until it finally disappeared beneath the sands.

And there is one other matter: if Cyrus had carried out a massive slaughter of the inhabitants, the Jews would have been in a terrible bind, as they were trapped there until after the Persian conquest was complete. It is doubtful that the Persian troops would have distinguished indigenous Babylonians from expatriates.

**50:28**. Jewish fugitives return to Zion and declare that Babylon is fallen. This text personifies Zion (a common practice in the Bible). Broken and prostrate, she hears the welcome news that her oppressor has been slain.

**50:29–30**. Unnamed heralds receive the commission to summon an army to destroy Babylon for what it did to Judah. There is no need to try to identify the heralds as angels, prophets, or the like. The command to summon an army functions as a virtual passive ("Let archers be summoned").

**50:31–32**. YHWH declares he is against Babylon. The city is twice called "insolence" (זָדוֹן). Arrogance, including indifference to the suffering of others, characterizes the world empire. Babylon embodies this ideal.

**50:33–34**. Babylon has held Israel and Judah captive, but YHWH will redeem them. This implicitly compares the fall of Babylon and liberation of the Jews to the exodus. Like Pharaoh, the Babylonians refused to "release" their captives (note the use of the piel of שׁלח, "release," in v. 33 and in Exod. 3:20; 4:21, 23; 5:1–2; 6:1, 11; 7:2, 14, 16; etc.).

**50:35–38**. A series of curses against Babylon declare that a sword will slay her citizens, officials, scholars, omen-takers, infantry, cavalry, and chariot corps, and that it will burst open her treasuries. That is, all of Babylon's resources will fail. A final curse declares that a drought will consume her waters in retribution for her idolatry. It is not necessary to identify the sword (for example, that it represents Persia). As is common in a curse, the agency of the destruction is anonymous. Verse 38 suggests that Babylon is symbolically the fountainhead of idolatry.

**50:39–40**. In Mesopotamian ideology, a city such as Ur, Uruk, Akkad, or Babylon represented human civilization and culture. The great city stood in contrast to the savagery of the wilderness and its beasts (we see this ideology, for example, in The Epic of Gilgamesh). But Babylon, jewel of Mesopotamia, will revert to pre-human chaos. In addition, Jeremiah employs the proverbial desolation of Sodom to depict Babylon's cultural obliteration (see also Jer. 49:18). These verses also draw upon Isaiah 13:19–22 (Holladay 1989, 395).

**50:41–43**. This passage repeats with modification 6:22–24, which predicts that the Babylonians, the people from the north, will come down upon Jerusalem and lay it waste. Now, Babylon will suffer what they had done to Judah. The text is not inauthentic; Jeremiah could reuse his own material (against Holladay 1989, 395). But redirecting an oracle originally against Jerusalem toward Babylon carries an implied message: Israel, God's chosen people, are the first to be judged, but the same judgment will overtake Babylon.

**50:44–46**. As in the oracle against Edom (49:19–21), this passage portrays YHWH as a lion coming upon a flock to drag away its lambs. In both passages, the lion boasts of his ferocity, terrifying his victims, and in both the earth trembles. It is impossible to tell whether 49:19–20 or 50:44–46 was written first. One difference, however, is noteworthy. In 49:21 the sound of Edom's fall echoes in the *Yam Suph* (the Gulf of Aqaba), the sea to the south of Edom, implying that the calamity has implications in the immediate region. But in 50:46 the sound reaches all nations, signifying that the whole world is astounded that the great empire is fallen (cf. Rev. 18:9–19).

**51:1–5**. Using a variety of rhetorical devices, the passage predicts military disaster and annihilation for Babylon. In verse 1, YHWH will bring a wind on Babylon to slay its armies. The "destructive wind" is probably a metaphorical whirlwind, although it could mean "destructive spirit." "Leb Qamai" is an *atbash*, a cipher, that refers to Babylon (there is no place called "Leb Qamai"). The letters לב קמי correspond to כשדים, "Chaldeans," the dominant race of the Babylonian Empire. In verse 2, enemy soldiers called "foreigners" will winnow the Babylonians as one winnows grain. There is a wordplay linking "foreigners" (זָרִים) to "and they shall winnow it" (וְזֵרוּהָ). One should not emend "strangers" to "winnowers" (זֹרִים) as some do (e.g., ESV), as this misses the wordplay. In verses 3–4, without any metaphor, the foreign soldiers are commanded to slay the Babylonians. Judah has already been punished for her sins; and now Babylon, whose sins are far greater, must face judgment (v. 5).

*TRANSLATION NOTE: THE MEANING OF 51:3*

The MT of 51:3 has two untranslatable phrases, אֶל־יִדְרֹךְ and וְאֶל־יִתְעַל, which respectively mean "unto he will bend" and "unto he will raise himself up." Lundbom repoints אֶל as אֵל, "God," and so translates them as "God will bend" and "God will raise himself up" (Lundbom 2008c, 434). No ancient version takes it this way, but Jeremiah 32:18 and 51:56 do use the word אֵל. Even so, this is not persuasive. More commonly, אֶל is emended to אַל, "not," giving the meanings, "Let him not bend" and "let him not rise up." This is supported in the Syriac, Vulgate, and Targum. The interpretation is that the Babylonians should not bother stringing their bows or putting on armor, since defeat is inevitable. However, treating the Babylonians as the subjects of the first two clauses seems forced; nothing suggests the text is addressing the Babylonian army here. It goes against context, because it requires that the next clause, וְאַל־תַּחְמְלוּ, "and do not pity," abruptly change subject from Babylonians to foreign enemies even though this clause has the same grammatical structure as the previous clauses. This makes for harsh disruption in the discourse; if אַל is used three times, the reader expects the three clauses to be roughly parallel. The LXX has ἐπ᾽ αὐτὴν τεινέτω, "Against her [i.e., Babylon], let him bend." This implies that for אַל the Hebrew originally read אֵלֶיהָ. This, in my view, is the best solution. Thus, one should translate, "Against her, let the one who bends a bow bend it, and against her, let him raise himself up in his armor. And do not pity her young men."

**51:6**. The Jews must flee Babylon because it is under God's wrath.

**51:7–9**. Using the familiar metaphor of the winecup of God's wrath, this text asserts that Babylon was God's agent of judgment. But Babylon now faces God's judgment, and all other nations should pull away from her. The passage does not indicate who tried to heal Babylon. Probably the image of a nation having an incurable wound is just a stock metaphor, as in Micah 1:9 (Holladay 1989, 422), and no specific agent of healing is intended.

**51:10–12**. The fall of Babylon vindicates Zion, as opposed to the Babylonian temples, as the true domain of God. The command for the enemy warriors to prepare their arrows (v. 11) further suggests that the archers of verse 3 are the Medes, not the Babylonians.

**51:13–14**. Babylon was situated on the great Euphrates River and thus was said to dwell upon waters. The metaphor of enemy soldiers swarming over Babylon like locusts appears again in 51:27.

**51:15–19**. YHWH, the Creator, is over the waters of Babylon and its idols. This passage is very nearly a verbatim repetition of 10:12–16. As he does elsewhere with repeated oracles, Holladay regards all of 51:15–19 as inauthentic (Holladay 1989, 397, 405). But we know that a prophet sometimes borrows a whole section from another prophet (compare Isaiah 2:2–4, which is probably the original, to Micah 4:1–3; and compare Jeremiah 49:7–22 to Obadiah). There is no reason Jeremiah could not have reused his own material. In this case, because it fits the context of chapter 10 so well, 10:12–16 is probably in its original location. But because it contributes to the theological significance of the fall of Babylon, the passage was copied into this oracle as well. YHWH, not Marduk or the other gods of Babylon, is maker of heaven and earth. When Babylon defeated Jerusalem, Marduk had seemingly defeated YHWH, but this was in fact not the case. It was YHWH who chose to punish his people; it was not a work of the Babylonian deity. When Babylon falls, the idol-makers will be chagrined that their gods of gold could not save the city.

**51:20–24**. God has a battle-mace (מַפֵּץ) with which he smashes all those he condemns. The language of this verse is exceedingly violent; the mace smashes not only kingdoms, warriors, and high officials but also entire populations, including women, children, and the elderly. The mace is not identified. Three options scholars regularly suggest are Israel, Babylon, and Cyrus of Persia (this latter suggestion is tentatively made, but without any argumentation, in Huey 1993, 422–23). In favor of Israel, Jeremiah uses a different word, not מַפֵּץ, when describing Babylon as God's war-hammer (פַּטִּישׁ in 50:23). Also, verse 24 in context is most reasonably taken to mean that God will use his mace to smash Babylon, obviously implying that the mace is not

Babylon (Holladay 1989, 405–07). Scholars who take the mace to be Babylon (Lalleman 2013, 309; Smothers, Keown, and Scalise 1995, 369–70; Lundbom 2008c, 451–52) also argue that the repeated *weqatal* verb וְנִפַּצְתִּי could be translated as "and I have smashed," meaning that God in the past used Babylon as his instrument in the past but now will repay Babylon for its crimes. And against the Israel identification, it is difficult to see in what sense Israel is expected to fulfill the role of being the mace that strikes Babylon. The Jews played no part in the overthrow of the city. Against the Babylon identification, the pronoun for "you" in verse 20 is masculine (אַתָּה), but Babylon is regularly portrayed as feminine. More importantly, the translation of וְנִפַּצְתִּי as "and I *have* smashed" is certainly wrong. The *weqatal* rarely has a perfective sense (typically only when in hendiadys with a *qatal* verb). It means, "and I *will* smash." The verbs show that YHWH's "mace" must be some future entity, and in context Jeremiah declares that the Medes will overthrow Babylon (51:11, 28). The masculine "you" could be the unnamed future king of the Medes and Persians, Cyrus, although I think it more likely that the singular "you" is simply a personification of the Medes as a people. It is thus most likely that the Medes are the mace by which God will destroy Babylon.

**51:25–26**. YHWH is against Babylon, "the destroying mountain." Since the city was located on a flat plain, this is purely metaphorical and has nothing to do with geography. The mountain metaphor implies great prominence (Egypt also, situated in another flat alluvial plain, is compared to mountains in 46:18). The meaning is that grand Babylon will be brought down.

**51:27–32**. YHWH summons the Medes to lead their vassal nations to smash Babylon's army. "Ararat is the Assyrian *Urarṭu*, a people centering around Lake Van in what is now eastern Turkey. . . . The Minni were the Manneans, centered just south of Lake Urmia in what is now northwest Iran. . . . Ashkenaz are to be identified with . . . the people later known as the Scythians" (Holladay 1989, 427). The implication is that Babylon will face a massive coalition. In reality, it was the Persians under Cyrus who led the coalition, but the prominence of the Medes in this text tells us that it was written before Cyrus became dominant over Media.

**51:33–44**. A series of metaphors and highly descriptive portraits tell how YHWH will bring justice to Babylon for its treatment of Jerusalem. These metaphors at times contradict each other if taken together literally, but that is not the intent. Instead, they depict in differing ways the sin and fate of Babylon.

- Babylon will be harvested like grain and threshed (v. 33). In the ancient world, grain was spread over a threshing floor and a heavy, spiked sledge was dragged over it, crushing it to separate the kernels from the chaff. Babylon will thus be crushed and shredded.
- Babylon has taken everything from Jerusalem, drinking her blood like a man draining down wine from a goblet, or as when a sea monster (תַּנִּין) swallows a whole fish. Jerusalem cries out for vengeance (vv. 34–35). The תַּנִּין was a mythical sea serpent, analogous to the more familiar Leviathan.
- God, in turn, will dry up the sea and leave the monster wallowing in the mud (v. 36), and he will put the Babylonians into a drunken stupor from which they will never rise (v. 39). He will make the sea monster spew out the captives it has taken, allowing them to return to their homes (v. 44).
- Bel in verse 44 is a Babylonian deity, probably to be identified with Marduk. In Babylonian mythology found in the cuneiform myth *Enuma Elish*, Marduk slew the water-monster deity Tiamat.

But here, Babylon/Marduk is the sea monster that YHWH will slay.

- Babylon will be a desolate desert, inhabited only by hyenas and shunned by people (vv. 37, 41, 43). The term Sheshach in verse 41 is an *atbash* cipher, according to which the letters ששך, "Sheshach," represent בבל, "Babel."
- Although Babylon is a desert, it will also be flooded. It will be covered by the waters as in the great deluge (v. 42).
- The Babylonians have been like a pride of lions among the nations, but God will drag them away like lambs to the slaughter (vv. 38, 40).

**51:45–50**. The boundaries of this text are set by an inclusion structure, with both verses 45 and 50 encouraging the Jews to get out of Babylon. This, again, is quite different from the letter of 29:1–10, which exhorts the Jews to settle into Babylon for a multigenerational sojourn. It is difficult to know what circumstances this text addresses, with its exhortations not to be alarmed at various rumors about troubles and upheavals (v. 46). Some think that it addresses political crises in Babylon after the death of Nebuchadnezzar (Holladay 1989, 430; Lundbom 2008c, 485). But it is not clear that what amounted to Babylonian palace intrigue would have been of great concern to the Jewish exiles, or that they would have even known much about it. It seems more likely that "the land" about which rumors would have swirled among the exilic Jews was their own homeland, Israel. They would have feared that it was dominated by foreigners or in hopeless chaos, and they would have preferred to stay put in Babylon. This was certainly what Zechariah 2:7 confronts. It appears, therefore, that this passage looks to a more distant future, when the Jews are free to leave Babylon (something they could not do until after the Persian conquest) but are fearful of doing so. The prophecies that Babylon would be destroyed (vv. 47–49), therefore, mean that even after the Persian takeover, the city continued to be under God's curse and was no place for God's people. In short, this passage anticipates the early postexilic situation and tells the Jews that Babylon is forever an accursed place. They should return to Jerusalem and rebuild it.

**51:51–53**. The focus of this text is more on the exilic Jews perhaps in the early days of their captivity, lamenting the brutal treatment they received from their conquerors. The gods of Babylon seemed to be the triumphant powers behind an invincible empire. But no matter how high Babylon rises, YHWH will bring it down.

**51:54–58**. As a final word of assurance, the oracle asserts that Babylon's days are numbered, and its military might will fail. Babylon's walls will be demolished, and the city will be burned to the ground. All efforts to defend it will be futile. The oracle thus closes with an unadorned account of the fall of the city, almost entirely free of metaphor, asserting as plainly as possible that God will bring justice to the wicked empire.

### *The Mission of Seraiah to Babylon (51:59–64)*

Unlike the above oracle, this passage is precisely dated and concerns a single, specific event.

**51:59–60**. Identified as the son of Neriah and grandson of Mahseiah, Seraiah was the brother of Jeremiah's scribe Baruch (see 32:12). The delegation took place in 594. It appears that he carried Jerusalem's tribute to Babylon. Ironically, Jeremiah had him also take along another "tribute" for Babylon: a word from YHWH prophesying the city's downfall.

> *TRANSLATION NOTE: SERAIAH'S OFFICE*
> It is not clear what Seraiah's office was; in the MT, he is called the "chief of the resting place" (*שַׂר מְנוּחָה*). This peculiar term appears nowhere else in the Old Testament. Some interpreters emend מְנוּחָה either to מַחֲנֶה ("camp," so that the office is

"commander of the camp") or to מִנְחָה ("gift," so that the office is "chief of tribute"). The latter is supported in the Targum and the LXX; the Greek reads ἄρχων δώρων, "chief of gifts." The Vulgate, surprisingly, has *princeps prophetiae*, "chief of prophecy," a translation that "derives from a post-biblical understanding of 'resting-place' as 'inspiration,' an interpretation based on Isa. 11:2" (Holladay 1989, 434). But it is highly unlikely that the Jerusalem administration had such an office. Today, שַׂר מְנוּחָה is routinely left unemended and translated as "quartermaster" (ESV, NRSV); but as Holladay says, it is hard to see why someone with this office, charged with providing food and equipment to troops in the field, would be part of a delegation to Babylon, and he prefers to emend to מִנְחָה (Holladay 1989, 434). Lundbom translates the unemended text as "caravan prince" (Lundbom 2008c, 507), but this is highly speculative and should not be followed. Since the emendation is very minor (from מְנוּחָה to מִנְחָה) and is supported in two ancient versions, it seems best to emend to שַׂר מִנְחָה and take it to mean, "official charged bringing tribute [to Babylon]."

**51:61–64b**. Seraiah was charged with carrying a text of a prophecy against Babylon to the city and reading it aloud, although it is not clear precisely where or to whom he was to read it. If he read it before Babylon's high officials, or even before Nebuchadnezzar, then he was a brave man indeed! Of course, Daniel told Nebuchadnezzar (at least by implication) that his empire was destined to fall to another (Dan. 2:37–39). The oracle Seraiah carried with him may have been substantially identical to 50:1–51:60, but this does not mean that Jeremiah gave this entire oracle for the first time in the fourth year of Zedekiah. He could have compiled it just prior to Seraiah's departure from earlier oracles against Babylon. Casting the document into the river means that Babylon would, in similar fashion, sink and never again rise. But since it is the text of a prophecy, the act perhaps also implies that its words cannot be altered. No one could retrieve the document and change what it says.

**51:64c**. This is a colophon, a concluding notice to a text. It indicates the end of the record of Jeremiah's prophecies. The following, final chapter of Jeremiah is an epilogue, not an account of the ministry and messages of the prophet, and thus the colophon is appropriate. This line is not present in the LXX, where the passage is in the middle of the book (MT 51:64 = LXX 28:64). The colophon is appropriate to Edition 2, but not Edition 1 (see Introduction).

## THEOLOGICAL FOCUS

The prophecy of Babylon's demise had obvious significance historically: the nation that destroyed Jerusalem would fall. But theologically, the annihilation of what Babylon represents is of more significance for the modern Christian reader.

- God uses the empires of the world for his purposes, but that does not exempt them from judgment for their violent rapacity.
- Although Israel may face judgment first, it will come to Babylon as well. The godless may rejoice over the fall of God's people, but they will soon experience the same ruin.
- The exodus and the fall of Babylon both serve as examples for the persecuted church. God will vindicate and deliver his people.
- The fall of Jerusalem seemed to imply that YHWH had failed and Marduk was triumphant. But this was not the case. Even so, the apparent failure of Christianity in the west does not mean that the plan of God has failed.
- As Jeremiah exhorts postexilic Jews to get out of Babylon, so Christians should be careful not to let themselves

be polluted by the ideals of the culture in which they live.

## PREACHING AND TEACHING STRATEGIES

### *Exegetical and Theological Synthesis*

This passage is clearly about Babylon being destroyed, but that is not all. There are also the directives to Israel sprinkled throughout. The more prominent theme of the destruction of Babylon and the evil system it represents needs to be presented, but not in a revengeful way. Revenge is part of the very system that is being destroyed. It is deep in this world's culture. We see it in the ever-popular retribution plots of movies. It could be the classic western of the good guy whose family is killed by the bad guys and how the good guy gets his paybacks, or the more modern version of that plot in which an unethical big business is brought down by the wife of an employee who was wronged. These plots do well in the box office because our culture values revenge and even enjoys it.

The application that we need to make is not to lead our people to feel good about the bad guys being punished; rather, we must listen to God's directives to Israel about living in the midst of a world filled with evil. Yes, evil will be judged, but until it is we must live counterculturally to evil. Only through the powerful grace-filled work of God can we do this.

### *Preaching Idea*

Don't take part in what God is against.

### *Contemporary Connections*

#### *What does it mean?*

We need to guard against the influence of living in this world of sinful nations. We must not let national practices cause us to personally sin. When I was in my late teens, a godly friend and I began to work in construction during the summer. We benefited by learning the value of a hard day's work, but we also began to pick up some new vocabulary. It was difficult to keep those crass and vulgar expletives out of our minds because we heard them all day long. Once, at a crosswalk, we were in that moment of indecision when the light was about to turn. Should we, or should we not step into the intersection? My friend made up his mind and uttered a cuss word: "Oh _____, let's just go." I was amazed not so much that he cussed, but that it didn't bother me.

We also need to be aware that these national cultural and systemic sins will affect us in ways that create feelings and mindsets that are sinful. But they seem natural and not sinful because it was the way we were raised. One of these is racism. Our culture has made many changes, but there is still an underlying racist way of thinking. As a young child I remember seeing two water fountains in stores: colored and white. That image put in my little mind that races should not share the same water source. I'm sure there were many other any things that were imbedded in my malleable mind, and they don't leave easily. God's warnings to Babylon are warnings to me that as the Spirit of God exposes these sinful thoughts about race, I must repent and turn from them.

There are numerous other sins that our cultures and nations pass on to us that we must be careful not to be a part of, and when possible, take action to curb those sins in our culture: volunteer at a pregnancy center; be intentional about developing real relationships with people of other races; avoid the lure that having more things brings more fulfillment.

#### *Is it true?*

This full description of God's wrath against Babylon could be seen in a similar way that we see the monsters being destroyed in some fantasy movie. As the beasts are being destroyed, the militaristic victory march is being played. There is jubilant rejoicing that the space invaders have fallen and the earth is saved. God's wrath is certainly just, and we can take comfort in knowing that his wrath will be poured out upon evil. But Babylon and those like her are not space invaders, nor are their sins from another system. God's wrath is being, and will be, poured out on national patterns and systems that, like Babylon's, are in opposition to his rule. Yes, God used Babylon to discipline Israel, but Babylon was still responsible for what it had become. And so, we could read this description of God's wrath not only against the literal nation of Babylon, but against all the national systemic wrongs in our world, and take comfort that justice will be done. These modern Babylonian types of nations will be judged: nations that make Christianity a crime, nations that punish evangelistic actions by death, nations that forbid the education of women, nations that regulate churches to the point of control, nations that have not only allowed but provide for abortions, nations that refuse to acknowledge the long-term effect of the heinous sin of slavery. Nations like the United States.

Though "In God We Trust" is written on our government-issued currency, it does not mean that God governs the cultural mindsets and actions of the United States. For the systemic sins of abortion and racial injustice, and others, God will judge the United States. It would be wrong to say that the United States or any other nation is the modern Babylon, but just as Babylon was judged for her sin so will every nation. What that judgment will look like is hard to articulate, for it lies in the metaphors of Jeremiah's prophecy. But it is clear that judgment will come—and it will be harsh.

### *What now?*

Again, there are numerous sins that our cultures pass on to us that we must be careful to avoid, and perhaps even help prevent. The first part of this is to be aware of those cultural sins and turn from them. There are the big categories of racism, materialism, epicureanism (pleasure-seeking), and others. It is important not to leave these in general terms because people do not identify with broad terms. Rather, paint some specific pictures, such as those mentioned in the "What does it mean?" section above.

It will also be helpful to give specific ways to counteract these cultural sins. We can volunteer at a pregnancy center. We need to be intentional about developing real relationships with people of other races, by having these new friends over for dinner and listening to their stories. We must avoid the lure that having things brings fulfillment; one way to do this is to give generously to ministry causes. If we aren't giving about ten percent, or at least striving toward that goal, then perhaps money is too important to us. These specifics may and probably should vary depending on your setting, but it is important to give enough details that our listeners can form a picture of obedience.

### ***Creativity in Presentation***

Begin with the closing paragraph of this section. Using a little imagination, recreate the scene in which this Jewish scribe, Seraiah, was reading this prophecy against Babylon to some group of Babylonian leaders. It will be important to create a tension in the congregation of wanting to know what is in this prophesy. A way to create this tension is to have the scribe arguing with himself about not wanting to present the content. He could ask himself questions like: Why do I have to present this? They aren't going to like it at all. What are they going to do to me? Will my diplomatic immunity protect me? This revealing of the scribe's internal struggle can help the congregation want to know what is in the prophecy. Then, present the highlights of the 110 verses found in these two chapters. The point is to help the congregation pay attention to what God is saying to Babylon. After presenting the judgment against Babylon, take the time to carefully show that Babylon is representative of any nation that has a systemic sin against God, including one's own nation, be it the USA or another country. This leads into God's directives to those of his household, contained within these two chapters to his children. The distinction between those who are God's children and those who are not should lead to a brief gospel presentation. This could be done at the midpoint in the sermon, almost as a parenthesis in the sermon/lesson.

Start the sermon with a normal kind of introduction; make the subject and need clear. Then transition by asking listeners to go with you back to Babylon. Present the scribe Seraiah, who has the task of reading Jeremiah's prophecy (50:1–51:58) to the Jews. Then depending upon your setting and propensities, you could take on the role of Seraiah and read it as though you were Seraiah. Or you may be more comfortable simply reading it and interjecting how Seraiah must have felt.

After the text is presented, step out of the character and move into application. Depending upon time constraints, one might have to summarize portions of the text and read representative verses. Here is one possible structure:

- Introduction
  - Subject: living in an evil world
  - Need: Our complex culture makes it hard—so, how do we live in this evil world?
  - Transition: Set the stage for Seraiah's reading of the prophecy (51:59–64).

- Present the Text
  - Read portions of the judgments and directives (50:1–51:58).

- Application
  - Avoid the influence of evil cultures.
  - Take positive steps to help correct evil when you can.

- Don't partake in what God is against.

## DISCUSSION QUESTIONS

1. What cultural norms of your country would you like to see changed?

2. What are some acceptable sins in your culture?

3. What are some ways that we can guard against falling into cultural sins?

4. In what ways have you seen the culture negatively affect the church?

5. In what ways have you seen the culture negatively affect you?

# EPILOGUE (52:1–34)

As the prologue told of the commissioning of Jeremiah to be YHWH's prophet, so the epilogue tells of the final vindication of his message: the destruction of Jerusalem.

# Jeremiah 52:1–34

## EXEGETICAL IDEA

Jeremiah 52 vindicates the prophet; all his dire predictions came true. The chapter, much of it almost a word-for-word repeat of 2 Kings 24:18–25:30, describes Zedekiah's wretched fate, Jerusalem's fall, the fate of the captives, and the final gift of a bit of dignity to the aged and hapless Jehoiachin. In 2 Kings, the text narrates the sad end of the Davidic kingdom. Although it does that here too, the implied lesson is the vindication of Jeremiah's status as the true prophet of God.

## THEOLOGICAL FOCUS

People may despise the word of God, but in the end it will be proven true. The lies by which the people lived, and which Jeremiah explores so thoroughly in the beginning of the book, inevitably brought about their ruin. All those who called him a traitor and even a blasphemer were proven wrong by the hard facts of history. Jeremiah is vindicated.

## PREACHING IDEA

God tells us so.

## PREACHING POINTERS

We hear again the events of Zedekiah's terrible end, the temple being burned, and the nation taken into exile. Why did God end with this summary of how his judgments of sin came to pass? Does he want to berate Israel? He does not need to build up his self-image by saying, "I told you so."

This summary reinforces that we can trust what he says. And what he says is very simple: disobey and face judgment; obey and enjoy his blessings. It really is that simple. As a reminder, our obedience does not earn God's blessings. Our obedience puts us into a position to receive and enjoy those blessings, and our disobedience separates us from them.

# THE END OF THE HOUSE OF DAVID (52:1–34)

## LITERARY STRUCTURE AND THEMES

Jeremiah 52 is virtually identical to 2 Kings 24:18–25:30, with the following differences. First, Jeremiah lacks the material in 2 Kings 25:22–26 which describes Ishmael's murder of Gedaliah, the governor Nebuchadnezzar had appointed over what had formerly been Judah, and the subsequent flight of the local Jewish population to Egypt; this episode is covered in more detail in Jeremiah 40–42. Second, the account of the Babylonian despoiling of the metallic objects of the temple is more detailed in Jeremiah 52:17–23 than in 2 Kings 25:13–17. Third, Jeremiah 52:24–30 gives a more complete account of the Jewish captivity than does its counterpart in 2 Kings 25:18–21, in that the latter lacks the equivalent to Jeremiah 52:28–30, the number of people taken in the various deportations (although 2 Kings 24:14–16 does give numbers for the deportation of Jehoiachin).

We naturally wonder which text was written first, the account in 2 Kings 24–25 or the one in Jeremiah. *Prima facie,* we might suppose that the Kings text is the source for Jeremiah, since Kings is primarily concerned with the history of the kings of Israel and Judah, whereas this is only a secondary concern in Jeremiah. But that conclusion may not be correct. The composition of Kings and, beyond that, the composition of the whole historical narrative from Joshua to Kings, are highly complex issues. It is clear that the histories, covering at least some five hundred years, used sources. We do not know how or in what stages these books were created. If, as it surely did, Kings incorporated material from other source texts into its narrative, Jeremiah 52 may have been one of the texts it made use of. The Jeremiah narrative, as noted above, is more detailed than the one in Kings (apart from the fact that Jeremiah, for good reasons, skipped the account of the Gedaliah episode found in 2 Kings 25:22–26). One could argue that, where Jeremiah is longer, it expanded upon what was found first in the Kings account (and thus that it is the later version). But it equally plausible to argue that Kings has abbreviated the earlier account in Jeremiah. We have no way of knowing. But it may be that neither view is precisely correct.

The Talmud, at *Baba Batra* 15a, attributes Kings to Jeremiah. Although it is beyond the scope of this commentary to make the argument here, I have always found this tradition to be appealing and plausible. If in fact Jeremiah and Baruch are responsible not only for Jeremiah but also for Kings, neither Jeremiah 52 nor 2 Kings 24:18–25:30 need be regarded as the "original." It may be that the original text was a single composition, but it was adapted for use in two separate locations: one at the end of Jeremiah and the other at the end of Kings. Or it may be that there was no "original" version. Using the same sources, Jeremiah and Baruch constructed two separate but parallel accounts in Kings and Jeremiah.

- ***Summary of Zedekiah's Reign (52:1–3a)***
- ***Zedekiah's Failed Rebellion Against Babylon (52:3b–11)***
- ***The Plundering of Jerusalem (52:12–23)***
- ***The Captives (52:24–30)***
- ***Jehoiachin Shown Respect (52:31–34)***

## EXPOSITION

### *Summary of Zedekiah's Reign (52:1–3a)*

**52:1–3a**. This is a summary of Zedekiah's reign, such as we routinely see in Kings. Zedekiah was the full brother of Jehoahaz, the successor of

Josiah. Hamutal of Libnah was the mother of both Jehoahaz and Zedekiah (see 2 Kings 23:31). But Jehoiakim was Zedekiah's half-brother; his mother was Zebidah of Rumah (2 Kings 23:36). The summation of his reign is both terse and bleak: Zedekiah did evil, and for this reason God cast the Jews out of the land.

### *Zedekiah's Failed Rebellion Against Babylon (52:3b–11)*

**52:3b–11**. The only historical event with which the narrative is concerned is Zedekiah's attempt to break free of Babylon and its disastrous results. The passage tells us nothing else of his reign, and even in this account the focus is entirely on the fall of Jerusalem and what happened to Zedekiah. Jeremiah does not figure in this narrative at all, even though he had personal interactions with the king during Jerusalem's last days. The precise chronology of events is disputed; some date the ninth year and tenth month of Zedekiah to January of 588, implying that the city fell in June or July of 587. Others date the fall of Jerusalem to a year later (on the basis of verse 12, which dates the fall of the city to Nebuchadnezzar's nineteenth year). The Babylonians built a "siege work" (דָּיֵק) against Jerusalem. Outside of the parallel text in 2 Kings 25:1, this word appears elsewhere in Ezekiel 4:2; 17:17; 21:27 (English 21:22); 26:8. A דָּיֵק was almost certainly a siege wall, as it was built "around" (סָבִיב) Jerusalem (v. 4). This was a temporary wall a besieging army built around a fortified city in order to entrap the inhabitants and to defend against sorties from the city. Verses 6–7 imply that the precipitating factor in the capture of Jerusalem was that starvation forced a group of Jewish troops to burst open gates near the king's garden and attempt a desperate sortie to escape the dying city. That is, the first breach in the defenses was made not by the Babylonians but by Jews desperate to escape. King Zedekiah was among those trying to flee. They attempted to make their way to the wilderness east of Jerusalem, the "ascent of Adummim," which drops steeply down to the Jordan Valley. Zedekiah may have been trying to get to Ammon (Holladay 1989, 292), or he may have simply been running toward wild country where he hoped to lose his pursuers. The sortie did make it past the siege wall and toward Jericho, but the Babylonians came after them. At some point, with the Jewish troops well into the rugged wilderness and the Babylonians on their heels, it became every man for himself. The soldiers around Zedekiah scattered, his escape failed, and he was captured and brought before Nebuchadnezzar at Riblah. This was a crossroads city located far to the north, on the Orontes River in eastern Syria. Thus, we learn that Nebuchadnezzar himself was not at the siege of Jerusalem.

Nebuchadnezzar's punishment on the king was brutal: Zedekiah's sons and officers were slain before his eyes, and then Zedekiah himself was blinded. But this did not end his suffering. He was imprisoned in the "house of punishments" (בֵּית־הַפְּקֻדֹּת, v. 11), which of itself sounds like a place of torture, although it could simply mean "prison," as *HALOT* suggests. But the Greek says, "And they placed him in the mill house" (καὶ ἔδωκεν αὐτὸν εἰς οἰκίαν μυλῶνος). This suggests that he was, like Samson, set to grinding grain after he was blinded. He would have been set in a workhouse, an *ergastulum*, where he would have spent his last days pushing a millstone in circles, crushing grain into flour. In such a workhouse, "inhabitants formed a heterogeneous group. The authorities apparently made no attempts to segregate them, despite the differing reasons for their confinement. Prisoners of war could thus find themselves in the company of distrainees, local criminals or defaulting debtors. . . . Throughout the first two millennia B.C., from Babylon to Palestine, defeated enemies were confined in *ergastula,* where many had to live out their lives as grinders" (Toorn 1986, 250–51). In such a manner the last Davidic king of Jerusalem, perhaps surrounded by criminals, prisoners of war, and debt-slaves, ended his days. As for Jerusalem itself, the breach made by the fleeing Zedekiah enabled the Babylonian troops to storm into the city and fall upon the hapless, starving inhabitants.

### *The Plundering of Jerusalem (52:12–23)*

**52:12–16**. As Nebuchadnezzar, the king, was far away in Riblah, the Babylonian commander in the field at the siege of Jerusalem was Nebuzaradan. His title is often given as "commander of the imperial guard" (NIV), "captain of the bodyguard" (NRSV), or the like. The word טַבָּח can mean "cook" (1 Sam. 9:23) or "guard" (Gen. 37:36, where שַׂר הַטַּבָּחִים means "captain of the guard"). But in Jeremiah 52, where Nebuzaradan is the commanding general of a large field army carrying out the siege of Jerusalem, the title רַב־טַבָּחִים does not describe his rank or function. It is an honorific title, meant to describe a high official who has direct access to the king. The officer who had the actual function of commander of the king's personal bodyguard, much less his chief cook, would not be commanding a full army in a major campaign. When verse 13 says he set fire to the temple, it obviously does not mean that Nebuzaradan personally torched the building. But it does mean that he gave the command that the temple be burnt to the ground. The destruction of the temple was not an accident or the work of a few hotheaded private soldiers; it was an intentional act carried out at the direction of the Babylonian high command. Similarly, the Babylonians methodically demolished Jerusalem's walls, an act that was probably carried out some time after the city was taken (v. 14). Having burnt down the temple and demolished the walls, they then carried out their policy toward the inhabitants of the city (vv. 15–16). This was to take away a significant part of the population, including some of the poor, so that there would not be enough people to rebuild and reestablish Jerusalem as a political entity. For the same reason, skilled workers and natural leaders were taken away. Only a small number of impoverished peasants, people who could never set up an independent state, were left behind. This seems to contradict the portrait we have in Jeremiah 40–43, where at least some of the people are leaders in the community and apparently came from the higher levels of society. But no government policy is carried out with complete efficiency and thoroughness; it is to be expected that some people of higher prestige did not go into exile. Also, the passage tells us that all who deserted to the Babylonians during the siege were taken into exile. As we do not know how they were treated or what became of them, we should not make moral judgments. Also, these deserters were more faithful to Jeremiah's admonitions than were the leaders of Judah.

**52:17–23**. The account gives a surprising amount of attention to the metallic objects and architectural decorations plundered from the temple. Why is this?

- The objects had significant financial value. This is obviously true of the gold and silver, but even the bronze, especially in objects as large as the two pillars, would be valuable. But the account gives no attention to the monetary worth of the plundered objects, and it is only concerned with objects taken from the temple. The Babylonians certainly took a great deal of rich plunder from the homes of the nobility and the royal palace, but the text is silent about this.
- It possible that the account of the plundering of the temple points to the impiety of the Babylonians. They plundered YHWH's house of its sacred objects; and later, Belshazzar would use the sacred vessels to demonstrate his disdain for YHWH (Dan. 5:2). But this chapter does not indict the Babylonians for impiety against YHWH, and some of the objects, although

attached to the temple, were not sacred, cultic objects (such as the two pillars). This suggests that the Babylonians' offense against YHWH is not the primary concern of the passage.

- The most likely explanation is that this text echoes 27:19–22, which predicts that Nebuchadnezzar would carry away the pillars, the bronze sea, and all the other temple objects he did not carry away when he took Jehoiachin into exile. That is, 52:17–23 marks the fulfillment of 27:19–22 and vindicates Jeremiah as a true prophet.

### *The Captives (52:24–30)*

**52:24–27**. In addition to King Zedekiah, a number of other high officials were taken before Nebuchadnezzar and executed at Riblah. These ranking men were from all the branches of leadership in Jerusalem. They included priests and religious leaders (v. 24, "the chief priest Seraiah, the second priest Zephaniah, and the three guardians of the threshold"), a ranking military officer (v. 25, "an officer who commanded the fighting men"), highly placed political leaders from the nobility (v. 25, "seven men who had direct access to the king"), and a military administrator (v. 25, "a scribe who was head of the department for conscripting the people of the land into the army"), and more mysteriously, "sixty men from the people of the land who were found in the city" (v. 25). This could represent sixty unfortunate members of the poorest class who were chosen for transport to Riblah and execution. But this seems unlikely. "People of the land" (עַם הָאָרֶץ) does not necessarily mean "the poor peasants." On the other hand, it certainly does not refer to the "landed gentry," the wealthy elite (against, among others, Smothers, Keown, and Scalise 1995, 381). It probably refers to freemen generally, regardless of economic status. The sixty could have included some peasants or poor day laborers, but it could have also included artisans and property owners from the higher ranks of society. In short, they were just sixty ordinary citizens. They were probably a token, representing all the Jewish people. As is well known, the Babylonians used a sexagesimal (base-60) mathematical system, as represented in cuneiform numerals. As such, it is not surprising the Nebuchadnezzar had sixty random citizens executed as representatives of the nation. In summary, the executed men included a small group who were singled out because of their high rank: religious leaders, military commanders, and leading aristocrats. But it also included sixty randomly chosen citizens whose deaths served as a token for the whole people.

**52:28–30**. The text gives us a kind of census of people taken into exile under Nebuchadnezzar. It tells of three deportations: the deportation of Jehoiachin (597 B.C.), in which 3,023 Jews went into exile; the deportation after the fall of Jerusalem (587/586 B.C.), in which 832 men went into exile, and a third deportation (582 B.C.), in which 745 people went into exile, for a total of 4,600 men. This passage does not include the deportation of those who went to Babylon along with Daniel (Dan. 1:1; c. 605 B.C.). But this was more a taking of hostages than a true exile. The numbers given here are surprisingly low—4,600 men for all three major deportations. The number of deportees given in 2 Kings 24:14–16 is of itself confusing, but it certainly represents a higher number than in Jeremiah. It lists, for just the Jehoiachin exile, ten thousand deportees, and then speaks of seven thousand soldiers and one thousand artisans deported. This could mean that there was a total of eighteen thousand deportees in the Jehoiachin exile, but it probably means that the ten thousand includes the eight thousand soldiers and artisans along with two thousand other miscellaneous deportees. Even so, the figure of ten thousand is far more than the 3,023 given in Jeremiah 52:28. This cannot be explained by asserting that the Jeremiah text includes only the adult men (Lalleman 2013, 317), since the numbers in Kings clearly represent adult men (as in the seven thousand soldiers). But understanding numbers in the Bible is often challenging; we frequently do not know how they compiled their figures. It appears that Kings gives round figures for the total number of male deportees, but that Jeremiah, for reasons we do not grasp, gives much more specific numbers for more select, smaller groups of deportees. It may be that Jeremiah includes only people of rank (Wray Beal 2014, 519–20). The Kings passage at least tells us that the total number of exiles was not as tiny as the Jeremiah text seems to imply.

### *Jehoiachin Shown Respect (52:31–34)*

**52:31–34**. In what amounts to an epilogue to the epilogue, a kind of final postscript, the narrative tells how Jehoiachin was taken from his prison cell and treated with respect during the brief reign of the Babylonian king Evil-Merodach, the son and successor of Nebuchadnezzar. His Babylonian name was Amel-Marduk, "Man of Marduk," and he reigned 562–560 B.C. The "days" that Jehoiachin spent dining as a favorite guest of the Babylonian king were apparently not very many. The text mentions his presence at Evil-Merodach's table only, and it does not say that he dined with any subsequent ruler. This of itself would not be overly significant, but Evil-Merodach was murdered by his brother-in-law Neriglissar in 560. It is unlikely that Neriglissar honored the favorites of the man he murdered. Thus, Jehoiachin probably lived only a short time under Evil-Merodach's favor, whom he probably predeceased. For this reason, it is not unreasonable to postulate that Jehoiachin died around the year 561.

But why does the narrative include this detail? It could serve as a token indication that someday the house of David would be restored. However, Jeremiah himself had prophesied that Jehoiachin would never have a descendant recorded to him or a man to sit on David's throne (Jer. 22:24–30). It is highly unlikely, therefore, that the book would close with a hint that Jehoiachin's line would be restored. An obvious parallel to Evil-Merodach's treatment of Jehoiachin is David's treatment of Mephibosheth son of Jonathan, who ate at David's table. On David's part, this was an act of kindness and a fulfillment of his oath to Jonathan. On the other hand, it also represented the fact that the house of Saul was utterly broken and could never challenge David's rule. David had nothing to fear from Saul's grandson, and the house of Saul would never rise again. In the same way, Babylon had nothing to fear from Jehoiachin. Thus, if the parallel to Mephibosheth is intentional, it does not necessarily imply a good future for the Jewish monarchy.

But probably the postscript was added simply to close the book, which had been fairly bleak throughout, on a positive note. For all his sins, and for all the sins of his people, Jehoiachin of the house of David still died with his dignity intact.

## THEOLOGICAL FOCUS

As an epilogue to Jeremiah, this chapter is meant serve as a concluding reminder that Jeremiah was a true prophet of God and that all his unheeded warnings came to pass. Other specific lessons include:

- God's punishment can be severe, as illustrated by the wretched fate of Zedekiah.
- When a nation turns from God, every part of society suffers. But the leadership bears the greatest guilt.
- Even in specifics, such as the prediction that the bronze pillars would be taken from the temple, the word of God proves true.
- As illustrated by the dignity given to Jehoiachin in his last days, God can be gracious even in judgment.

## PREACHING AND TEACHING STRATEGIES

### *Exegetical and Theological Synthesis*

In a sense, this last chapter is God saying to the exiles and postexilic readers, and to us, "I told you so." God told the Jews that if they continued to worship other gods and not follow his commands, they would be destroyed. In this closing historical narrative Jeremiah reminds Israel of their king's bitter end and the painful dismantling and destruction of the temple. The governmental and cultural hearts of Israel were both destroyed, just like God said they would be. And, through Jeremiah, God repeatedly told the Jews that they should surrender to the Babylonians, because it was those in exile who would be blessed. The brief anecdotal example of Jehoiachin being blessed in exile is yet another way of God saying "I told you so."

### *Preaching Idea*

God tells us so.

### *Contemporary Connections*

#### *Is it true?*

"I told you so." No one likes to hear these words. Often they are spoken to shame us or to inflate the speaker's ego. But even when spoken in the form of a simple fact, we don't like to hear them. They remind us that we should have listened to someone who tried to warn us. "I told you so" is embarrassing because these words expose our pride. We thought we knew best and didn't need another's input. We bristle when we hear this admonition because it puts us in a position of acknowledging that we were wrong and someone else was right. They are particularly painful when we rejected the advice or warning out of a stubborn heart that chose a course of action, just to spite the one who gave the warning.

What is our response when we hear those words? If the one speaking them is being rude, we could return the rudeness with a snarky "Who made you the authority?" Or, we could just smile and say, "I know, I know."

Our response can vary from, "Thanks, I appreciate you trying to warn me" to "Don't you start preaching to me." If we know the person had our best interests in mind and not their own self-gratification, then hopefully we learn from the experience. Those painful words could actually be some of the best words we could hear.

#### *What does it mean?*

Many evangelicals' functioning view of God and our own lives was coined in the little booklet *Four Spiritual Laws*: "God loves you and has a wonderful plan for your life." While this is true, it can lead to an incomplete view of God. Part of that wonderful plan is his judgment of my sin. One cannot read Jeremiah and miss that God's wrath is against sin and against those who sin. Jeremiah teaches us that God is a God of wrath and that he hasn't changed. His wrath will come against those who have rejected his offer of life. It will come in discipline against his children when we sin. Yes, we can sing that God is a "Good, Good Father" and that "God Is So Good." But we also need to remember his character includes his wrath.

#### *Now what?*

We have every reason to obey. Jeremiah is telling us that we should be motivated to obey God not only because of his love and grand plans for our lives, but we should also be motivated to obey him because of his wrath. That does not mean that God wants to spoil our fun and that we should walk in fear that at any minute he will bring down thunderbolts of his wrath. That is defining God's wrath in terms of human rage. God's wrath is his just action toward sin.

There is a healthy motivation that can come from fear. The fear of failing a class compels us to study. The fear of hurting our spouse causes us to be careful of our words. The fear of not having resources in retirement causes us to begin saving early in life. Even as I write this, there is a storm brewing in the Gulf of Mexico. The fear of losing power causes me to buy gas for our generator. If we fail to take action in scenarios like these, it is easy to visualize those words being spoken, perhaps to ourselves, "I told you so." The fear of God's discipline should move us to obedience. Unfortunately, we often see our sins as forgiven, which they are—but we forget that, as the Westminster Confession states, our sin brings on "fatherly displeasure."

And for those who haven't accepted the offer of forgiveness in Christ, it is not wrong to let the fear of God's wrath motivate them to consider accepting the gift of forgiveness. We must not present this as a "get-out-of-jail-free card." Life is not a game in which we might get caught in our sin, so let's keep that card if we need it. This is the holy God of the universe—the all-knowing, ever-present God who will judge every sin. If we understand, at least at some level, his intense wrath against sin, our accepting his gift of forgiveness will lead to a life of thankful submission to his will.

When we went into a new class with a new teacher, we didn't know how hard the tests would be. Sometimes upon taking a test for which we studied little, we found ourselves saying, "If I had known how hard the test would be, I would have studied more." We know how hard the test will be. God tells us so.

Will God judge sin and bless obedience? He tells us so.

### *Creativity in Presentation*

God has revealed himself through a narrative, a story, so it is important that that story be clear. There are several ways that the story could be presented. Since the main point comes not from the individual parts but from the whole, it seems best to present the story as a whole. This can be done by reading portions, or even every verse. It could be helpful to give a preview of the two areas of destruction (the king and the temple) and the anecdotal example of blessing, so that as the story is told the congregation can have a grid with which to follow the story. The difficulty will be giving the congregation a reason to listen to this story. What is the tension that will make them want to listen? One possibility is to have the congregation ask themselves: Why did God choose to end this book with a vivid description of the destruction of the king, the temple, and the nation? And what about the short little story about Jehoiachin being blessed? Why these portions? This will ultimately lead into the application.

Or another way of creating tension is to begin by asking, "How angry was God at the Jews?" This description comes from verse 3, in which God's anger is his response to Judah's sin. So, what is his anger going to look like? By asking the congregation to be looking for something in the text, one can promote listening to the story.

This building of tension leads into application. God wants us to know that he will keep his word. He will bring wrath against sin, and he will bless obedience. That should motivate us to believe what he says and obey. Here is one possible structure:

- Present the story:
  - Destruction of the king (52:1–11)
  - Destruction of the temple (52:12–23)
  - Destruction of the nation (52:24–30)
  - Blessing of Jehoiachin (52:31–34)

- Application
  - He will bring wrath against sin, and he will bless obedience. He tells us so.

## DISCUSSION QUESTIONS

1. What applications could come from this story? How does drawing our own applications affect our reception of the truth?

2. What do Jeremiah chapter 1 and this closing chapter have in common?

3. Describe a time when fear motivated you.

4. When someone says, "I told you so," what difference does it make who says it?

5. Contrast how being motivated by fear is different from being motivated by blessing.

# INTRODUCTION TO LAMENTATIONS

## OVERVIEW OF INTRODUCTORY ISSUES

**Author:** Traditionally Jeremiah, but the Hebrew book is anonymous

**Provenance:** Either Babylon or the ruins of Jerusalem

**Readers:** Jews living in the aftermath of the fall of Jerusalem

**Date:** Either the sixth or fifth century B.C.

**Historical Setting:** The poetry sets the reader in the context of the fall of Jerusalem.

**Occasion for Writing:** To provide a liturgy to mourn the intense suffering of the Jewish people during and after the fall of Jerusalem in 586 B.C.

**Genre:** Acrostic poetry to be used for remembrance and mourning

**Theological Emphasis:** The significance of the suffering of the Jewish people in salvation history

## AUTHORSHIP OF LAMENTATIONS

Lamentations is anonymous in the Hebrew text. The LXX, however, contains the following superscript: "And it came about after Israel was taken captive and Jerusalem was left desolate that Jeremiah sat down weeping and made this lament over Jerusalem, and he said" (Καὶ ἐγένετο μετὰ τὸ αἰχμαλωτισθῆναι τὸν Ισραηλ καὶ Ιερουσαλημ ἐρημωθῆναι ἐκάθισεν Ιερεμιας κλαίων καὶ ἐθρήνησεν τὸν θρῆνον τοῦτον ἐπὶ Ιερουσαλημ καὶ εἶπεν). The Vulgate has translated this superscript almost word for word, but adds before "he said," *amaro animo suspirans et ejulans* ("sighing and groaning with a raw spirit"). The tradition that Jeremiah wrote Lamentations appears also in the Syriac Peshitta and the Aramaic Targum, and it spread throughout the church, so that the English Authorized Version calls the book, "The Lamentations of Jeremiah."

We cannot say that the tradition authentically goes back to Jeremiah himself. It may be that since Jeremiah lived through and vividly described the last days of Jerusalem, he was thought to be the book's most likely author. Also, 2 Chronicles 35:25 states, "Jeremiah also made a lament for Josiah, and all the male and female singers have included Josiah in their laments to this day. They made [the singing of these laments] a rule in Israel. You can still find them in the [book of] Laments." But if this is the basis for ascribing the canonical book of Lamentations to Jeremiah, it is mistaken. The now lost book described in 2 Chronicles concerns King Josiah, but there is no allusion to Josiah in Lamentations.

Lamentations does have some similarities to Jeremiah. In both books, the poet's eyes overflow with tears (see Jer. 9:1, 18 [MT 8:23; 9:17]; 13:17; 14:17; and Lam. 1:16; 2:11; 3:48–49). Both books use the expression "terrors on every side" (Lam. 2:22, מְגוּרַי מִסָּבִיב; Jer. 6:25, מָגוֹר מִסָּבִיב). Lamentations 3:53–56 may allude to Jeremiah 38:6–8 (for more examples, see Driver 1920, 462; Salters 2010, 6). These similarities could mean that Jeremiah wrote the book or that someone who knew Jeremiah's messages wrote it. On the other hand, there are significant differences in vocabulary between Jeremiah and Lamentations (Lalleman 2013, 321).

Jeremiah lamenting the destruction of Jerusalem by Rembrandt (1630). Public domain.

Some objections to ascribing Lamentations to Jeremiah are not persuasive. For example, Lamentations 4:17 states that "we" looked for help from a nation that could not save Jerusalem (an allusion to Judah's alliance with Egypt). Jeremiah, however, condemns seeking help from other nations (Jer. 2:18), and thus he presumably would not have written these words. Against this objection, the poet behind Lamentations 4:17 could have opposed the alliance with Egypt, and yet out of a patriotic love for his country still hoped against hope that the Egyptians would turn back the Babylonians. As another example, Lamentations 4:20 grieves over the death of King Zedekiah, calling him "the breath of our nostrils, YHWH's anointed." But Jeremiah condemned Zedekiah (Jer. 21:3, 7; 24:8), and one might wonder how he could speak in such a way about a man he considered unworthy of the crown. Against this objection, the verse does little more than honor Zedekiah for being the heir of the Davidic covenant and YHWH's anointed (just as David honored Saul). The poet may have still believed Zedekiah to be a bad king.

Two objections to regarding Jeremiah as the author of Lamentations, however, are more substantial. First, the Hebrew text, unlike the LXX and other versions, does not ascribe the book to Jeremiah. The tradition that Jeremiah wrote Lamentations was widely accepted, but the Hebrew, not the later versions, constitutes the biblical text, and it makes no such claim. The superscripts in the versions may reflect a later unreliable tradition. Second, one detail of Lamentations makes it very difficult to ascribe to Jeremiah. Lamentations 4:19–20a states, "Our pursuers were faster than eagles in the sky! / They chased us over hills and ambushed us in the wilderness. // The breath of our nostrils, YHWH's anointed, was caught in their traps." This almost certainly alludes to Zedekiah's failed attempt to escape the Babylonians at the end of the siege (2 Kings 25:4–5), and it suggests that the author was with the king when he and his company were caught (Lam. 4:19, "They chased us"). But Jeremiah was not with Zedekiah on this occasion; he was in custody at the "court of the guard" when the city fell (Jer. 38:28; 39:13–14). Today, few scholars of any theological persuasion defend the position that Jeremiah wrote Lamentations. (For a massive survey of the literature on this question from an evangelical position—concluding tentatively that one person, not necessarily Jeremiah, wrote the book—see House 2004, 283–303.)

Little is gained by claiming that Jeremiah is the author, since the interpretation of Lamentations does not depend upon it being tied to the prophet. We do not know who the poet behind Lamentations is, or indeed if there was one or more than one. It may be that Lamentations, like the Psalms, is a composite book written by several poets. We do best to follow the Hebrew Bible and treat it as anonymous.

## PLACE AND DATE OF WRITING

Lamentations speaks of the calamity of the fall of Jerusalem as a recent and indeed ongoing event. Although it is possible that a later poet wrote as if he were an eyewitness, wanting to make the poems more vivid (Hillers 2008, 10), the text implies that the poet lived through the crisis and that it had recently occurred. Linguistic evidence suggests that the book was contemporary with Ezekiel and was composed in the sixth century (Dobbs-Allsopp 1998), although we must bear in mind that dating any part of the Hebrew Bible linguistically is a dubious practice, especially when trying to determine the date of a text that is in a narrow time frame, either in the exilic or in the first part of the postexilic era. It is almost impossible to fix linguistically the date of a text when we are working with a range of only

about two centuries. However, we know that the Jews took up the tradition of making ritual laments over Jerusalem almost immediately after its fall (see Jer. 41:5; Zech. 7:3–5), which suggests that there would have been a very early demand for a text of laments. As such, nothing demands that there were decades, much less centuries, between the fall of Jerusalem and the composition of Lamentations. We can posit that it was written about 550, and no later than 520 B.C. (see also Berlin 2004, 33–35). The book may have been written in Jerusalem or, as Psalm 137 apparently was, in Babylon.

## HISTORICAL SETTING

Because Lamentations is a liturgical text for remembrance, prayer, and mourning, it does not have a specific historical setting in the manner of Jeremiah (before, during, and immediately after the fall of Jerusalem), Daniel (in Babylon among the earliest Jewish captives taken for royal service), or Revelation (with John writing from the island of Patmos). Its setting is literary and liturgical, not historical, even though it focuses on a historical event. The poetry of Lamentations transports the worshiper to the terrible time of the fall of Jerusalem and enables an outpouring of prayer, grief, and reflection over that calamity.

## OCCASION FOR WRITING

Lamentations is a series of five dirges (lament poems) over the fall of Jerusalem in 586 B.C. Each poem takes up one chapter of the book. They self-evidently served as liturgical texts for rituals of mourning over the fall of the city (and such rituals began quite early; see Zech. 7:1–3). In this, there is no mystery about the meaning and purpose of the five poems. It is much more difficult, however, to determine what might be the implied message of the book in the canonical context, and to construct messages for Christian congregations that are both true to the book and relevant to contemporary life and worship.

## GENRE OF LAMENTATIONS

### *Background*

Lamentations has a number of parallels in the Bible, but it is also a unique work. No other book is made up entirely of lament poems—much less a series of laments that all concern a single event. On the other hand, we see many poems of mourning in the Bible. David composed a major lament over Saul and Jonathan after their defeat at Mount Gilboa (2 Sam. 1:18–27). A fair number of psalms include lamentation over a national catastrophe, and these typically make complaints directed toward God (for example, Pss. 74 and 89). We see both elements in Lamentations. The prophets regularly composed lament poems over Israel, Judah, and even over Gentile nations (Isa. 29:1–10; Jer. 4:23–31; 48:1–6, 28–33; Ezek. 27:1–36).

### *Ancient Near Eastern Parallels*

Notwithstanding the parallels it has with other biblical dirges and complaints, Lamentations is strikingly similar to a body of literature from elsewhere in the ancient Near East—the laments over a fallen city that first appear in Sumer. This was an ancient Mesopotamian culture that flourished in the third millennium B.C. Sumer predated Assyria and Babylonia, the great Semitic civilizations that dominated Mesopotamia in the second and first millennia. Their language was not Semitic (and thus was unrelated to Akkadian, Aramaic, or Hebrew), but their culture heavily influenced the societies that came after them (for example, they invented the cuneiform system of writing).

Five city-laments from ancient Sumer have survived: two over Ur (the second is often called the lament over Sumer and Ur), and one each over Nippur, Uruk, and Eridu (all of these cities were in lower Mesopotamia, not far from the Persian Gulf). The first lament over Ur, composed no later than 2000 B.C., is the most famous of the poems (for the text of this poem, see Hallo and Younger, Jr. 2003, 1.535–539). It begins by declaring that the city's patron gods have abandoned the city, so that it has fallen to its enemies (note that Ezekiel 10 describes how the glory of YHWH abandoned the Jerusalem temple prior to the fall of the city). The poem also describes how the goddess Ningal grieved over her city and pleaded for it before the other gods, and it gives a poignant account of the suffering of the people. Some metaphors found in the Ur lament reoccur in Lamentations. For example, Ur's warriors were like deer caught in a trap (line 220); in Lamentations 1:6, Jerusalem's commanders were like fleeing stags. Also, the second Ur lament grieves that those who once had sheep and bulls but now lie down hungry in the grass (line 313); Lamentations 4:5 makes a similar complaint.

Considering how much temporal and physical distance there is between Sumer and the Jerusalem of 586 B.C., how likely is it that the earlier body of texts influenced the latter? If this were all the information we had, we would indeed be justified in doubting that there was any connection between the two. There is, however, evidence that a tradition of "city lament" poetry and ritual persisted in the ancient Near East until as late the Seleucid period, well after the destruction of the first Jerusalem temple (see especially Gwaltney 1983). Although scholars may debate whether there was an identifiable "city lament" genre, some ongoing tradition of composing such laments certainly existed (for discussion, see Salters 2010, 13–15; Hillers 2008, 32–39). Biblical writers, both prophets and poets, would have known this tradition.

The existence of this tradition and the use of it by biblical writers is neither surprising nor troubling. It is foolish to think that Israel's inspired authors were never influenced by the literary conventions of the world around them. On the other hand, the extant Mesopotamian material is not especially illuminating when wrestling with the meaning of Lamentations. The biblical book does not allude to the earlier literature and never expects the reader to be aware of it (by contrast, biblical writers frequently do allude to earlier biblical texts and expect their readers to catch the allusions). The standard commentaries on Lamentations seldom cite the Sumerian laments as part of their exegesis.

### *The Poetry of Lamentations*

Lamentations, like Psalms, is a collection of liturgical poetry. Distinctively, all of its five poems follow a single theme, although there are portions of the Psalter in which a series of psalms all develop a common theme (for example, Pss. 77–80). Also, the first four poems of Lamentations are acrostic, and the fifth is quasi-acrostic. Although acrostics occur in Psalms and Proverbs, they are relatively rare. Finally, some scholars see distinctive metrical or stichometric schemes in Lamentations.

#### *The Acrostic Pattern*

In a typical acrostic, the verses are arranged in the order of the alphabet, with each verse in turn beginning with a successive letter. Thus, in chapters 1, 2, and 4, the first verse begins with א, the second with ב, the third with ג, and so forth. There are twenty-two verses in these acrostics because in ancient Hebrew the שׂ and שׁ were counted as a single letter. Lamentations 3 has sixty-six verses because in it, verses 1–3 all begin with א, verses 4–6 with ב, verses 7–9 with ג, and so forth. However, chapters 1, 2, and 3 are all roughly the same length. The Hebrew word count for each chapter is as follows: 1: 375; 2: 381; 3: 381; 4: 259; 5: 145. This is because each verse of chapters 1 and 2 has three lines, but each of these three lines is as long as an entire verse of chapter 3. Thus, three verses in chapter 3 roughly equals one verse in chapters 1 or 2. The lines are shorter in chapters 4 and 5. Chapter 5 is not acrostic, but it has twenty-two verses, as if it were following the acrostic pattern. It thus may be considered quasi-acrostic.

Another peculiar feature of these acrostics is that chapter 1 follows the normal order of the Hebrew alphabet, but chapters 2–4 deviate from this at one point. In the standard Hebrew alphabet, the letter ע is followed by פ, but the poems in chapters 2–4 reverse this order, so that פ is followed by ע. This suggests that two different poets, each with a different understanding of the order of the alphabet, composed the poems. But we cannot be sure that this the true explanation. It may be that a single poet composed all the poems, but for reasons lost to us changed the order of the letters.

The key questions are: Why does Lamentations employ acrostic poetry, and can anything account for the variations described above? Scholars have proposed several explanations. It could be a mnemonic device, meant to help worshipers memorize a poem. This would be helpful for a liturgy, since there was nothing like a Book of Common Prayer for a congregation to follow. Or, it could be a means of signifying that a topic has been treated thoroughly, like saying that we have touched upon every issue "from A to Z." Another possibility is that the acrostics impose order on a chaotic event: the fall of Jerusalem (Berlin 2004, 4–5). Or, it could be that the acrostic scheme is pure artistry, like the illuminations in a medieval manuscript, and serves no purpose at all other than to enhance the text by a display of poetic skill. Some have claimed that ancient people thought that acrostics had magical power, analogous to reciting a spell. This claim is highly dubious (for more discussion of ways to account for the acrostic patterns, see House 2004, 19–21; Salters 2010, 19–21).

The best way to resolve this is by looking at other acrostics in the Old Testament and seeing if they have something in common. Psalms 34, 37, 111, 112, 119, 145, and Proverbs 31:10–31 are all acrostic poems. Their most striking commonality is that they all have a didactic emphasis. Psalm 34:11 [MT 12] reads, "Come, children, listen to me, and I will teach you the fear of YHWH." Psalm 37:1 opens with direct instruction to the reader: "Do not get upset because of the wicked; / Do not be envious of those who commit iniquity," and it continues in a series of arguments and appeals on this topic. Psalm 111 lists the praiseworthy qualities of YHWH, while Psalm 112 is a catalogue of the virtues of those who fear YHWH. Psalm 119 is an extended lesson on the value of Torah. Psalm 145 is a hymn of praise and thus not so explicitly didactic, but it lists the praiseworthy qualities of YHWH and asserts that each generation in its turn will praise him (v. 4); the psalm is thus a guide to future generations. Proverbs 31:10–31 lists the qualities of the good wife and so instructs the young man concerning what to look for when seeking a woman to marry (see Garrett 1993, 248).

But how does this apply to Lamentations? The book is a liturgy for mourning Jerusalem's destruction, but the acrostic patterns suggest that readers should seek a specific message or theological lesson in the text. Indeed, all liturgy, properly done, instructs the worshipers. The implied lesson of the acrostics is that the Jewish mourners should learn some specific lesson from both the words of the text and the event itself, the fall of Jerusalem. But the fifth poem is not acrostic. Chapter 5, however, is entirely a prayer to God, and it may be that it was thought to be inappropriate to make it acrostic, as if implying that God needed instruction. However, it is "quasi-acrostic" to keep it in harmony with the rest of the book.

We cannot account for the variation in the alphabet order in chapters 2–4, but it may be possible to account for the peculiarity of chapter 3, in which each of every three verses begins with the same letter. This might be considered a kind of "super-acrostic." This poem focuses on a representative man's response to the disaster, and this may imply that readers should especially look for a theological lesson here.

### Other Features

The Hebrew term for "dirge" or "lamentation" is *qinah* (קִינָה). This is to be distinguished from the "complaint" or "appeal" one often encounters in the Psalms. For example, in Psalm 74 (a complaint), the psalmist speaks forcefully of how Israel has suffered, and yet he does so in the hope and expectation that God will soon act to defeat Israel's enemies and restore the nation. A *qinah* is sung over a dead person, for whom there is no hope (in this world, anyway) for a restoration of life. David sang a *qinah* over Saul and Jonathan (2 Sam. 1:17), knowing that they were dead and he would never see them again. When Amos sang a *qinah* over Israel (Amos 5:1), he knew that the northern kingdom was destined for destruction. Samaria was doomed, and once destroyed, would be gone for good (for further discussion, see Berlin 2004, 22–26). As will be explored below, Lamentations offers scant explicit hope for a restoration of Israel.

Many scholars believe that the *qinah* has a specific poetic meter, a bicolon containing first a line of three stresses and then a shorter line of two stresses (for full discussions of this issue, see House 2004, 308–10; Salters 2010, 15–17; Berlin 2004, 2–3; Hillers 2008, 16–19). In my view, there is no discernably consistent stress meter in Hebrew poetry, and the supposed "*qinah* meter" is an artificial, scholarly creation (see especially Hillers 2008, 18–19). But today, many translations render Lamentations 1–2 with verses that are each six lines long (three couplets per verse) to maintain the theory that the book has the supposed *qinah* meter. Against that, I believe that the verses in these chapters are three lines each. Thus, for example, I think 1:1 should be translated, "How she sits alone! / The city that had so many people has become a widow! / [The city that was] great among the nations [and] a mistress among the provinces has become a slave." This slightly differs from what the cantillation indicates but brings out the strong parallel between lines 2 and 3 (הָעִיר רַבָּתִי עָם הָיְתָה כְּאַלְמָנָה / רַבָּתִי בַגּוֹיִם שָׂרָתִי בַּמְּדִינוֹת הָיְתָה לָמַס, where רַבָּתִי עָם parallels רַבָּתִי בַגּוֹיִם and הָיְתָה כְּאַלְמָנָה parallels הָיְתָה לָמַס). By contrast, the NIV and ESV disregard the major division represented in the cantillation at "like a widow" (כְּאַלְמָנָה), translate the verse with six lines instead of three, and lose the principal parallelism. Readers should not assume that the poetry as presented in modern English Bibles corresponds to the lines in the Hebrew (for a good translation of the structure of the poetic lines in the Hebrew text, see Salters 2010, 33–35).

Many aspects of Hebrew poetry are debated today. For example, in classical Greek poetry, enjambment (a poetic line ending in the middle of a syntactical unit) is very common. A line of Greek poetry may end halfway through a prepositional phrase, or a line break may separate a verb from its subject. Thus, the first line of *The Bacchae* of Euripides translates to, "I, Dionysus, child of Zeus, have come to this land of Thebes," but in the Greek, "Dionysus" is actually in the second line (ἥκω Διὸς παῖς τήνδε Θηβαίων χθόνα / Διόνυσος . . .), rendering the poetic structure untranslatable into English. Some interpreters believe that enjambment exists in Lamentations as well (Dobbs-Allsopp 2001a; Dobbs-Allsopp 2001b; Parry 2010, 10–11). This is not correct. It depends on following a translation that artificially creates a *qinah* meter, one that does not represent properly the Hebrew verse structure. Also, even with the *qinah* structure, no true enjambment, such as we see in Greek poetry, exists.

A curious feature is that all five poems routinely refer to God as YHWH (יהוה), but chapters 1–3 fourteen times refer to him as "my Lord" (אֲדֹנָי; cf., e.g., 1:14). Eventually, the Jews would cease to pronounce the name יהוה altogether, and would say אֲדֹנָי instead, as is done to this day whenever Jewish cantors encounter יהוה when reading the Bible. It may be that the poems were written early in the transitional period, when Jews were just beginning to say אֲדֹנָי rather than יהוה.

## THEOLOGICAL EMPHASIS OF LAMENTATIONS

### *Overview of the Five Laments*

The structure of Lamentations is self-evident: It is divided into five parts, with each poem being one of the five. What is not self-evident is that each poem has a distinctive point of view and message. These can be summarized as follows.

*Lamentations 1: The Suffering of Lady Zion*: Throughout the first poem, Jerusalem is personified as a woman. In some lines, the poet grieves over what has happened to her (the poetry is in third person); and in other lines, Lady Zion herself speaks of her pain and sorrow (the poetry is in first person).

*Lamentations 2: The Prophetic Perspective*: The speaker voices the prophetic outlook on Jerusalem's fall. The city sinned, and YHWH responded with punishment. The poet has knowledge that only a prophet could possess: he knows of God's emotional state, his intentions, and his actions. But as the prophets often do, this chapter also voices deep sorrow over what has happened. Lamentations 2 has several parallels in the prophetic books, especially in Isaiah. For example, although fire is a standard metaphor for the wrath of God, it is heavily employed in Lamentations 2:1–9 and in the prophets (for example, Isa. 5:24; 9:19; 29:6; 30:27, 30; 33:14; 47:14; 66:15; Jer. 4:4; 15:14; 21:12; Ezek. 15:7; 21:31; Nah. 1:6). Also, God has thrown down Jerusalem from heaven to earth (v. 1; Isa. 14:12–15). The Jerusalem sanctuary is God's "footstool" (v. 1; Isa. 60:13). God has brought Jerusalem's fortifications down (v. 2; Isa. 25:12). God has come upon the "garden" that was Jerusalem and torn apart its "booth" (v. 6; Isa. 1:8; 5:5). God despises Israel's rituals of worship and has brought them to an end (vv. 6–7; Isa. 1:13–14). Jerusalem's gates are broken down and lie in the dirt (v. 9; Isa. 45:2). The prophet's eyes are exhausted from weeping (v. 11; Jer. 9:1). The prophet appeals for ritual mourning (vv. 18–19; Joel 2:12–17). Young and old, men and women, lie dead in the streets of Jerusalem (v. 21; Ezek. 9:6).

*Lamentations 3: The Representative Archetype*: Throughout most of this poem, a man serves as a representative archetype, reciting his suffering and his grief over the city, and also meditating on the ways of God (these lines are first-person singular). His poem is self-referential, beginning with, "I am the man who has seen affliction" (3:1a), and his language frequently echoes the psalms. He represents the ideal of Israelite piety in confrontation with this terrible event. The poet laments that God has shot him with arrows (Lam. 3:11–12; Ps. 38:2 [MT 3]). God's kindness and faithfulness are unending (Lam. 3:22–23; Ps. 36:5 [MT 6]). The poet declares that God is his "portion" (Lam. 3:24; Ps. 16:5). The faithful should wait quietly for God's salvation (Lam. 3:26–28; Ps. 62:1 [MT 2]). God's anger does not endure forever (Lam. 3:31–33; Ps. 103:9–12). The poet calls to God from the depth of the pit (Lam. 3:55; Pss. 88:6 [MT 7]; 130:1). The poet takes comfort in his past experience: When he has called on YHWH, God has heard his prayer (Lam. 3:55–57; Ps. 34:6, 17 [MT 7, 18]). In verses 42–47, however, a chorus of citizens prays to YHWH (these lines are first-person plural). These verses voice more anger and confusion over what has happened to the city.

*Lamentations 4: The Grim Reality of Jerusalem's Fall*: This section lacks any personal element. It is a stark account of how horrific has been the calamity that befell Jerusalem.

*Lamentations 5: An Outcry*: This is entirely a prayer, delivered by the Jews in first-person plural, and it recounts how horribly they have suffered.

### Interpreting Lamentations

Lamentations is difficult to interpret because it does not appear to have any core message beyond voicing the grief over Jerusalem's destruction and over the humiliation and suffering of her people. A cry of pain does not have a self-evident theology, and interpreters have suggested various approaches for making sense of the text.

Many aspects of the theology of Lamentations are implicit. Lamentations shares presuppositions with the rest of the Old Testament: God is in covenant with Israel and looks upon the nation with compassion, and yet God is also just. He is not willing to let sin go unpunished when the people refuse to repent but continue down a path of paganism and immorality. While these truths should not go unspoken, they should not be the focus of a series of sermons on Lamentations. They constitute background information. The covenant and even the idea of sin and punishment are not the explicit topics of the book. Lamentations never mentions or even clearly alludes to YHWH's covenant with Israel (contrary to the idea that "hope in a covenant context" is the central message of the book, as in Parry 2011, 31–33). Similarly, it is true that many in Jerusalem believed that their city was inviolable due to the presence of the temple and were no doubt shocked and appalled to see it in flames (see Jer. 7:4). But Lamentations does not in any manner raise this issue, and it cannot be the core of the book's message (against Albrektson 1963, 219–30).

Some recent interpreters assert that the book contains a challenge to traditional orthodoxy. Claus Westermann argues that Lamentations is dominated by accusations and complaints directed at God (Westermann 1994, 222). F. W. Dobbs-Allsopp asserts that Lamentations contains both "theodic" and "anti-theodic" elements (that is, it sometimes justifies the ways of God, and it sometimes rejects such justifications of God). He too notes that the book is replete with complaints against God, and that it routinely portrays God as a warrior (Dobbs-Allsopp 2002, 27–33). Kathleen O'Connor argues that the book presents God as loving but also as abusive, but she clings to Lamentations 3:33 as a way out of the contradiction ("For he does not willingly afflict or bring suffering on people"). She concludes that God is powerless to prevent evil (O'Connor 2002, 110–23).

Feminist interpreters, outraged that guilty Jerusalem is portrayed as a promiscuous woman, have adopted novel and indeed radical interpretations of the book. Carleen Mandolfo, approaching the Old Testament from a feminist and postcolonial perspective, argues that Lady Zion is in dialogue with, subverts, and refutes the standard prophetic ideal that YHWH is the righteous husband, Jerusalem is the sinful wife, and thus all that she suffered was right and proper. In this reading, Jerusalem does not deny the accusations against her but declares the system to be fundamentally unfair and based on twisted logic. Yes, she was unfaithful, but how does that compare to wholesale genocide that God carried out (Mandolfo 2007, 97)? Similarly, Elizabeth Boase argues that Lamentations enters into dialogue with the prophetic tradition but does not fully accept it. Instead, Lamentations subverts the prophetic outlook by its extensive expressions of grief, by the sympathetic portrayal of the suffering female figure of Jerusalem, and by refusing to specify or give extended attention to Jerusalem's sin (Boase 2006, 239–44). In this manner, the scales that balance divine justice against human sin are upended and the justification of God's severity is subverted.

Against this, Lamentations never alludes to or engages the prophetic texts that it supposedly opposes. Although Lamentations 2 is given from a prophetic perspective, it is not set against the rest of the book. Furthermore, the whole notion of "subversion" as a literary tactic, whereby one appears to agree with a point of view but undermines it with a series of qualifications or slyly introduced counterstatements, is alien to the Old Testament and to ancient literature generally. When biblical texts challenge traditional orthodoxy they do so openly, as in many of the speeches of Job (for a helpful, more general, critique of feminist readings of Lamentations, see Berlin 2004, 8–10). Even so, it is correct to say that Lamentations focuses heavily on the suffering of Lady Zion and that she is presented sympathetically.

Regardless of our presuppositions (whether evangelical Christian, feminist, or any other outlook), we should base our interpretation on what the text actually says. We should be aware of the message of the rest of the Bible, but we should not let our pre-understanding of Old Testament theology—a pre-understanding that comes entirely from other texts—dominate Lamentations. Although the book breaks the reader's heart with its portrayal of Jerusalem's anguish, it never challenges the validity of the prophetic denunciations of the city. The current attraction to Lamentations as the text of the bewildered and angry Israelite, shaking his (or her) fist at the YHWH the cruel God, does not accurately reflect the tone or message of the full book. Even so, words of despair, confusion, and sometimes anger do appear in the book, and this should not be dismissed.

Against a more traditional reading of the book, there is this: although Lamentations speaks of Jerusalem's guilt as a root cause of her suffering, it spends far less time on this topic than we might have expected. It never speaks of how the people violated the terms of the Sinai covenant, and in stark contrast to texts such as Ezekiel 16 and 23, it never explores the adultery and promiscuity of Lady Zion. Furthermore, it is shallow to read Lamentations and come away with no more than this as its message: Jerusalem sinned and so was punished, and yet God is loyal to the covenant and therefore is the people's hope. Someone with only a minimal familiarity with the Old Testament could easily draw such conclusions after giving Lamentations a superficial reading. The obvious, surface meaning is important, but there is more to the book than that.

We have observed that Lamentations 3 employs a single man, the poet, as a representative of the people who suffered so bitterly in the city's collapse. The distraught but pious poet acknowledges that this happened because of Jerusalem's sin, and he calls for faith and contrite prayer. In response, the people pray (3:42–47; the poem switches from the first-person singular to the plural here). Their prayer, however, is not what we might expect—a lengthy recitation of their guilt followed by a plea for restoration. Indeed, it is instructive to compare their prayer to the deep contrition of Daniel's prayer (Dan. 9:4–19). The prayer in Lamentations mentions only once and in passing that they had sinned (3:42a), and even here they complain that God has not forgiven them (3:42b). Instead, they give a recital of how badly God has treated them. He has only dealt with them in anger and has been pitiless in his slaughter of the people (v. 43). He cut himself off from their prayers (v. 44). He has made the nations treat the Jews like scum (v. 45). Their enemies swallow them down (v. 46), and on every side they see only terrors and snares (v. 47). In this, the assertion that Lamentations focuses heavily on airing complaints toward God is valid.

Four responses to this prayer are possible, but none is adequate: We could excuse their words, saying that Old Testament prayer is often quite blunt with God (see, for example, Pss. 44:23 [MT 24]; 74:1; 77:7 [MT 8]). Therefore, this kind of thing is to be expected. Although there is truth in this, it obscures the blatant fact that this prayer shows little contrition and complains fairly directly against God (again, the contrast with Daniel's prayer and other such prayers, such as Nehemiah 9:1–37, is remarkable).

Secondly, we could disregard the first-person plural forms in the prayer of chapter 3 (for example, 3:43: "You have wrapped yourself with anger and chased us down; / You have killed us without pity") and assert that all of the prayer comes from the one poet, who expresses much more pious sentiments in 3:21–28. From this point, we have two options. We could claim that his harsh complaints must be balanced against his other, more devoutly humble statements, and that the overall tone is one of faith and submission (House 2004, 421–22). Or, we could argue that the poet cannot quite maintain his confident faith and gives way to doubt and skepticism (Bier 2014). Either way, this erases a critical distinction the poem makes between the one man and the people, and it obscures the text rather than elucidates its meaning.

As a third option, we could celebrate the people as heroes speaking truth to power, telling God to his face that he is too harsh. But as noted above, the book never goes so far as to say that God is not just or that the prophetic ideal is wrong. If the text pulls back somewhat from saying what orthodox readers would expect, it certainly pulls back from saying what feminist and other deconstructive interpreters claim.

As a fourth option, we could assert that the people's prayer is impious, and that it is intended to serve as a warning to the reader, showing how we should *not* pray. But this is a canonical text for a liturgy of lament over Jerusalem. One does not, in a liturgical text, include examples of impious words that the reader should avoid when praying.

The prayer in 3:42–47 and similar outcries found elsewhere in the book (as in the whole of chapter 5; see especially 5:21–22) are not a "problem" in Lamentations, nor are they exceptional. They are an essential and conspicuous feature of the book. They represent the reality of the Jewish condition ever since the fall of Jerusalem and the beginning of the exile. The glory of preexilic Israel was gone. There would never again be an earthly, Davidic dynasty in Jerusalem. The great restoration had not come, and it seemed a long way off. The return from exile in 538 B.C. was a token; it was a true work of God, but it was not the restoration promised in Deuteronomy 30:1–10; Isaiah 60:1–7; Amos 9:11–15; and similar texts. To the contrary, the Jews continued to be dominated by the empires of the nations, and the Second Temple period ended with the Jews more scattered than ever. Lamentations may have been written soon after Jerusalem fell, but it gives voice to the Jewish tragedy as it has continued for some 2,500 years: the nations hound the Jews and inflict terrible suffering upon them, and the Jews find that their God is far away, leading them to wonder if he has abandoned them entirely (5:22). This is the true message of Lamentations: *The Jews and their city are prostrate, and the promised restoration is nowhere in sight; from their destitution, they wonder what God is doing and if or when the great work of salvation will ever come about.*

This is the same thing the anguished Paul wrestled with in Romans 9–11, as he confronted both the unbelief and the suffering of the Jews. It is what Jesus wept over, lamenting how Jerusalem killed the prophets and refused to be brought under God's wings (Matt. 23:37). Lamentations is the text for Israel in exile, estranged from their God. Understanding the book in this manner, we do not use it as an occasion to censure the Jews, but to join with Lamentations and with Jesus and Paul in sorrowing over their condition. Ultimately only a great work of God, an eschatological circumcision of the Jewish heart (Deut. 30:6), will bring an end to this sad lament.

How and when will God stop punishing Israel and save the nation? That is the question Lamentations asks. *And it does not answer the question.* In observing that this is the core of the book, we are not imposing an alien theology upon it. If we say that the account of salvation history as outlined in Romans 9–11 is the answer, we are claiming that a solution to the dilemma can be found, but not within Lamentations. It is to be found elsewhere in the biblical account of God's dealings with Israel and humanity.

Lamentations is focused on salvation history as it played itself out in the story of Israel. This does not mean that the Lamentations poet understood salvation history as we would understand it, but that in his concern for Israel's story as the people of God, he is engaged in what we would call salvation history. And the book voices grief and dismay over one of the greatest calamities of that history. That is why it is misguided to read the book abstractly as a treatise on tension between the "loving" and "abusive" nature of God, as in O'Connor's treatment; or to see "theodic" and "anti-theodic" elements, as in Dobbs-Allsopp's. The book is not concerned with theodicy as a theological or philosophical abstraction. And that is also why, when looking for a solution to the challenge Lamentations poses, it is valid to look elsewhere in biblical theology. Thus, we should distinguish these two things: the core message of Lamentations (grief, confusion, and despair over what has happened to Israel) and the biblical answer to Lamentations—which is, in a word, Christ. And a Christological element is strongly in evidence in chapter 3.

## OUTLINE

Lamentations may be preached in five sermons, with one sermon for each lament.

- First Lament (1:1–22)
- Second Lament (2:1–22)
- Third Lament (3:1–66)
- Fourth Lament (4:1–22)
- Fifth Lament (5:1–22)

## Lamentations 1:1–22

**EXEGETICAL IDEA**

The passage explores the suffering of Jerusalem under the personification of the city as a woman. The poem is divided between the parts where Jerusalem herself is the speaker and those where the poet is the speaker. The personification is meant to provoke compassion and sorrow in the reader: a beautiful mother has been ravished and laid low.

**THEOLOGICAL FOCUS**

Jerusalem the beautiful city of God is fallen and destitute. Although the text does not deny her guilt, it focuses on her suffering. When a society is brought down by sin and folly, much that is beautiful is destroyed alongside the ugly. Divine wrath is just, but it is still horrible.

**PREACHING IDEA**

We are invited to feel the hurt.

**PREACHING POINTERS**

The application of this book and this first lament will stretch most pastor/teachers. The image of a widow weeping was more intense in the ancient world because much of a family's welfare was dependent upon the husband. But even with the cultural difference the feelings of pain and grief still come through. At the funeral service for a faithful husband the feelings of grief are intensified when the widow is seated.

The poet is inviting us to share Israel's pain for her sins. We are not to stand on the sidelines and say "poor Israel." Rather we, by way of the genre of poetry, are invited to feel the pain with Israel. God, through this text, is asking us to feel something, and to let the feeling become a part of how we feel about the consequences of all sin—our sins and those of others.

# FIRST LAMENT (1:1–22)

## LITERARY STRUCTURE AND THEMES

Throughout this chapter, Jerusalem is personified as a woman. The text is divided between lines in which the poet laments over her, or in which she laments over what has befallen her. The structure is as follows:

- ***Laments over Lady Zion's Suffering (1:1–9b)***
- ***Lady Zion Laments (1:9c)***
- ***Laments over Lady Zion's Suffering (1:10–11b)***
- ***Lady Zion Laments (1:11c–16)***
- ***Laments over Lady Zion's Suffering (1:17)***
- ***Lady Zion Laments and Prays (1:18–22)***

## EXPOSITION

### *Laments over Lady Zion's Suffering (1:1–9b)*

**1:1–3**. Lamentations begins with the three words, "How she sits alone!" (אֵיכָה יָשְׁבָה בָדָד). The first thing that the book that describes about Jerusalem's suffering is not the burning of the city, the breach of the walls, or the defeat of her army. It is that she is alone. She has no people left to crowd her streets, no allies among the nations, and no help from God. Like any other fallen city, she is utterly bereft of aid or comfort. This contrasts with her former status, when she was filled with people and honored as a great city. As lonely people do, she weeps (v. 2). Her crying "at night" is a function of the personification; people in great distress cannot sleep, but lie in bed and sob. Zion's "lovers" and "friends" are the nations that were her allies and neighbors. Unlike the prophetic denunciation of Jerusalem as an adulteress, in which the "lovers" are often foreign gods whom the Israelites worshiped, the lovers here are nearby states who turned against her in time of crisis, such as Edom. Also, the word "lover" (אֹהֵב) often connotes no more than "friend" and does not necessarily have a sexual connotation (Esth. 5:10; Ps. 88:18 [MT 19]; Isa. 41:8; Jer. 20:4, 6), and thus an allusion to the adulteress metaphor is not necessarily implied. Verse 3 says that she went "from affliction and much hardship" (מֵעֹנִי וּמֵרֹב עֲבֹדָה) into exile. The preposition מִן cannot mean that she went into exile "with" suffering (against NRSV). The ESV translation that her exile was "because of" affliction, although grammatically possible, is logically incoherent. The word implies that she first suffered greatly and then went into exile (the NIV translation "after" is correct). The "affliction and hardship" includes all the time in which Judah was a vassal to Babylon, and then the time that the city was under siege and endured starvation and terror.

**1:4–7**. These four verses describe the sad conditions in Jerusalem after the destruction in this order: the cessation of temple worship, the Jewish people under the domination of foreigners, the loss of the glory and prestige for Judah's nobility, and the loss of Jerusalem's wealth. First, and foremost in the poet's mind, the temple has ceased to function (v. 6). This was the greatest calamity of all. Since all of the major festivals (and after Josiah's reformation, all sacrifices) took place at the temple, Jerusalem was the major pilgrimage city of Judah (although possibly other towns, such as Beersheba, were also pilgrimage centers if the situation described in Amos 5:5 still applied). The empty pilgrimage roads to the temple mount are portrayed as if they were in mourning. The priests, whether taken to Babylon or left behind in the land, groaned over the fall of the temple. The grieving women of verse 4 may refer to young women who participated in songs and celebration at the festivals or to women who served as assistants in the temple precincts (1 Sam. 2:22; Exod. 38:8). Second, the Israelite people were now fully under the control of the Gentiles; they were exiles in foreign lands (v. 5). Third, the glory of the royal house and aristocracy has vanished (v. 6). The city's leaders became like deer that could find no pasture and so, in their hunger and weakness, were unable to escape predators. Fourth, what was once a prosperous society was now desolate, homeless, and impoverished (v. 7). Other peoples, who may have once been trading partners with the Jews, refused to give them assistance and instead mocked them.

*THE MEANING OF* בַּת־צִיּוֹן

The construct chain בַּת־צִיּוֹן (e.g. 1:6) is routinely translated, "Daughter of Zion," implying that the metaphorical woman has Jerusalem as her parent (similarly, בַּת־יְהוּדָה is rendered "Daughter of Judah" and בַּת יְרוּשָׁלָם is rendered, "Daughter of Jerusalem"). But this is almost certainly wrong. The genitive relationship is not one of possession or origin; it is appositional. That is, the "daughter" *is* Zion, Judah, or Jerusalem; she is not their daughter. As Adele Berlin has demonstrated, the phrase should be translated "Lady Zion" or even "Fair Zion" (the word "fair" originally referred to a beautiful woman). The phrase "Daughter of Zion" should be abandoned, and we should just call her "Lady Zion" (see Berlin 2004, 10–12).

**1:8–9b**. The root of all this calamity was Jerusalem's sin. Translators often take line 8a to mean that Jerusalem "sinned greatly," but the noun and cognate verb (חֵטְא חָטְאָה) probably concerns not the magnitude of her sin but the certainty of it. She "truly sinned" (see Salters 2010, 60), and that is the reason she is defiled. Also, the meaning of נִידָה in 8a is disputed. Some take it to mean that she has gone into exile, others that she is the object of scorn, and others that she is unclean (see Parry 2010, 50–52; Lalleman 2013, 338; Berlin 2004, 53–54; Salters 2010, 60–61). But the latter is preferable, and the whole of 8a means that because she truly sinned, she is now defiled (נִידָה can refer to uncleanness from menstruation). The nakedness of the woman in line 8b could refer to the familiar prophetic denunciation of Judah's metaphorical adultery, but this is probably not the point. The standard prophetic word for denouncing Jerusalem as a metaphorical whore (זֹנָה; the word is highly derogatory) does not appear in Lamentations. The nakedness probably refers to the conquest of the city. When Babylon breached Jerusalem's walls, the city was metaphorically raped, and her people were left exposed to be exploited and abused. In line 8c, she "turns her back" (וַתָּשָׁב אָחוֹר) not simply from embarrassment but because she is trying to protect herself, as people often do when physically attacked.

The phrase, "Her impurity is in her skirts" (v. 9) is a complex metaphor. It probably relates to menstrual uncleanness. The idea may be that her sin made her impure before God, just as a woman in her cycle was ritually unclean and had to avoid the temple precincts until she had purified herself. The impurity (טֻמְאָה) could refer strictly to sexual immorality, but I doubt this. The term טֻמְאָה always refers to ceremonial uncleanness, whether of men or of women, and when used of a woman would naturally refer to menstruation, not promiscuity (against Berlin 2004, 54–55). If menstrual "impurity" is a metaphor for sin, it relates to all kinds of sin, not just to (literal or metaphorical) adultery. But the fact that it is visible on her skirts suggests something entirely different: people look at her and consider her disgusting, just as they would when seeing a woman on the street with menstrual blood visible on her skirt. The metaphor relates to how other nations despised the Jewish refugees and considered them dirty, refusing to have anything to do with them or help them. This, I think, is the main point (see also the comment at 1:17).

**Echoes of Lamentations 1 in Revelation**

We have already observed that in the ancient Near East there was a tradition of composing laments over fallen cities. Furthermore, in the Old Testament, it is common for cities to be personified as women. This metaphor connects the city to the feminine ideals of daughter, wife, and mother. She is protected by her parents, just as the leaders and soldiers of a city must protect her from being ravished by outsiders. She is the beloved of her husband, just as the citizens admire their city and its beauty. And she nurtures her children, just as the culture of a city shapes the minds of all who dwell there. But just as a woman can turn evil, so a city can be portrayed as a prostitute. Finally, a suffering woman can provoke great sympathy in observers. In Lamentations 1, Jerusalem the weeping woman is especially poignant; the scene recalls a tragedy many in the ancient world would have seen, a woman weeping over her deceased children. Lamentations thus draws heavily on motifs found in the ancient world and in the Bible.

In one sense, however, Lamentations is distinctive. Although the Old Testament has other poems that focus on fallen cities (Isa. 14; Nah. 3), these passages are often not laments but taunts. They *celebrate* the fall of an evil city; they do not *mourn* it.

In Revelation 18, we have another poem over a fallen city, the apocalyptic "Babylon." This poem does draw upon prophetic texts that rejoice over the fall of an enemy city (compare Nahum 3:4, a taunt against Nineveh, to Revelation 17:16; and compare Jeremiah 51:7, a taunt against Babylon, to Revelation 18:3). But aspects of Revelation 18 are also reminiscent of Lamentations. Jerusalem is a great lady, and Babylon is the great prostitute. Jerusalem was once a princess (Lam. 1:1), and Babylon called herself a queen (Rev. 18:7). Jerusalem lost all of its former wealth (Lam. 4:1–2), and Babylon suffered the same fate (Rev. 18:11–13). Both Jerusalem and Babylon fell under God's judgment. Both cities stood at the head of their respective typological ideals. Jerusalem was the apostate city of God, and Babylon was the mother city of paganism and imperial power.

While we could read Revelation's lamentation over Babylon simply as a taunt, it is probably more than that. Rather, like the lamentation over Jerusalem, the lamentation over Babylon is real. Babylon was sinful, but it was also a thriving and creative city, providing income and a home for many people. Revelation's Babylon prostituted her beauty, but she was beautiful. When the city fell, people suffered terribly. Reading Revelation 18, we should not suppose that God despises the culture and ingenuity within the great centers of human civilization, much less that he despises the individuals who live there. For all their sins, their achievements were great, and Revelation expresses deep sorrow over the corruption that undoes all the good that people achieved. Lamentations enables us to see that Revelation expresses grief over the fall of a great city; it does not simply rejoice triumphantly over the death of a sinful society.

### *Lady Zion Laments (1:9c)*

**1:9c**. Lady Zion interrupts the poet and cries out for God. Everyone else shuns her, so God is her only hope.

### *Laments over Lady Zion's Suffering (1:10–11b)*

**1:10–11b**. The poet resumes his lament over Lady Zion, declaring that the enemy has plundered Jerusalem, taken away everything of value, and entered the temple sanctuary.

The plundering of the city obviously relates directly to 11a–b, which speaks of how the impoverished, homeless refugees are starving. The enemy's penetration of the temple includes an implied appeal to God: he forbade the admission of Gentiles into the sanctuary, and therefore should punish those Gentiles. In addition, however, it further develops the idea of the sack of Jerusalem as the rape of Lady Zion.

### *Lady Zion Laments (1:11c–16)*

**1:11c**. Once again Lady Zion interrupts the poet, here echoing the appeal she made in line 9c. Again, the point is that all have turned against her, and only God can save her. Unlike the short interjection at 9c, however, she continues her appeal and lament through verses 12–16.

**1:12–13**. Surprisingly, in line 12a she turns to outsiders (Gentiles) and asks how they can look upon her without pity. This does not imply that she expects the Gentiles to change their attitude and be kind to her. Her apparent appeal to them is actually a statement of astonishment and anger that they could be so callous. After line 12a, verses 12b–15 recount how severely God dealt with her. She does this to show that others ought to feel pity for her. The analogy is to a man convicted of a crime and who receives a very severe punishment. Onlookers realize that the man was guilty, but still they say, "Wow, the judge was really harsh with him," and feel a measure of sympathy. This, she implies, is how the nations should have felt toward her. Her rhetorical question, "Is there any pain like my pain?" (line 12b) is not to be taken literally but is a form of hyperbole (it is impossible to objectively claim that the sufferings of one group outweigh any other people's suffering). Even so, Jerusalem's suffering was so great that one cannot easily think of a place that had it worse. Her declaration that YHWH inflicted this pain on her implicitly acknowledges her guilt, but the meaning in context is that her pain was exceptionally severe: God, with all his power and in all his anger, inflicted it on her.

In verse 13, she uses three images to convey how severely God afflicted her: fire, which is obviously excruciatingly painful; entrapment, which is terrifying; and desolation, which implies that the cities and farms are abandoned and ruined. The fire is in her bones, a vivid metaphor of extreme agony. The nets may refer not to nets used in hunting but to nets used by soldiers to capture defeated enemies, a tactic known from Assyrian art (Berlin 2004, 57). Afflicted so severely, she is "feeble all day" (end of line 13c). The word "feeble" (דָּוָה) means "faint" or "ill," but used of a woman it also implies menstruation (Lev. 15:33; 20:18). She is bleeding her life out, but people only look on her with disgust.

*THE TRANSLATION OF 1:13*

The MT מִמָּרוֹם שָׁלַח־אֵשׁ בְּעַצְמֹתַי וַיִּרְדֶּנָּה is difficult; it literally says, "He sent fire from on high into my bones, and he oppressively ruled her." The problem is the verb וַיִּרְדֶּנָּה, a qal *wayyiqtol* 3ms with a 3fs suffix from I-רדה, "to dominate, to rule (oppressively)." Conceivably, this means that YHWH forcibly managed the fire (a feminine noun), driving it throughout Judah. But this seems to be a desperate translation move. The LXX reads κατήγαγεν αὐτό ("he brought it down"), implying the root was ירד, not רדה. This suggests an emendation of the Hebrew to יוֹרִדֶנָּה, a hiphil *yiqtol* 3ms with 3fs suffix from ירד (Hillers 2008, 72; Salters 2010, 76–77). This implies that line 13a should be translated, "From on high he sent fire; he brought it down to my bones." This is followed by most translations.

**1:14–16**. The word "yoke" (עֹל) is generally used either literally for the yoke placed on an ox (Num. 19:2; Deut. 21:3; Job 1:3) or metaphorically to represent oppression by a governmental power (Gen. 27:40; Lev. 26:13; Deut. 28:48; 1 Kings 12:4, 10, 11, 14; Isa. 9:4;

14:25; Jer. 27:8, 11, 12). Less commonly, the yoke represents an obligation or duty (Hos. 11:4; Lam. 3:27). Here, quite unusually, it represents a burden of guilt. With such a weight on her neck, Jerusalem could not withstand her enemies. God therefore "rejected" (סִלָּה) her warriors (v. 15), meaning that he refused to treat them as his allies or subordinates, and he fought against them. As such, she has been trampled down by her enemies (v. 16).

*THE TRANSLATION OF 1:14*

This verse has two significant problems. The clause נִשְׂקַד עֹל פְּשָׁעַי is generally taken to mean "The yoke of my transgressions has been bound [on my neck]." The problem is that שׂקד is *hapax legomenon* (it is found only once in the Hebrew Bible), and so we cannot be sure what it means. The LXX has Ἐγρηγορήθη, "he was kept alert," from γρηγορέω. This suggests that the Hebrew root was שׁקד, "to watch over." The issue has vexed interpreters through the ages, and many explanations have been proposed (Salters 2010, 78–79). Against following the LXX (and other versions), no niphal of שׁקד is extant. But in any case, the Hebrew *Vorlage* for the LXX would have been unpointed (שקד), and thus the LXX may represent the translator's interpretation of the text, not an alternative text tradition. All in all, it is best to go with the traditional interpretation, taking נִשְׂקַד to mean "was bound." Another problem is נְתָנַנִי אֲדֹנָי בִּידֵי לֹא־אוּכַל קוּם, where the construct בִּידֵי ("in hands of") has no object. This is usually taken to be no more than ellipsis (omission of unnecessary words), and so it is translated, "The Lord gave me into the hands of [those before whom] I cannot stand." But if so, it is a severe ellipsis, omitting both אֲשֶׁר and לִפְנֵיהֶם. It may be that a word such as אֹיְבַי or צָרַי, ("my enemies") has simply fallen from the text. The LXX has ἔδωκεν κύριος ἐν χερσίν μου ὀδύνας ("The Lord has given pains into my hands"), which seems to reflect an original צָרַי, albeit with a mistranslation of the Hebrew. We should read it as, "The Lord has given me into the hands of [my enemies]."

**Echoes of Lamentations 1 in the Words of Jesus**

At several points, Jesus's words appear to reflect the outpouring of grief over Lady Zion in Lamentations 1. The most obvious example of this is in Jesus's sorrowful condemnation of Jerusalem in Matthew 23. After an extensive denunciation of the Jewish religious leadership, he personifies Jerusalem as a woman and declares that she "kills the prophets and stones those who are sent to her" and promises that the city will suffer desolation (vv. 37–38). We cannot say that Jesus intended an allusion specifically to Lamentations 1 here, but he clearly recalls a literary stream that runs through the Old Testament.

In one place, Jesus may deliberately allude to Lamentations 1. In Matthew 11:20–30, something unusual is going on, because Jesus appears to make a series of non sequiturs. He begins by lamenting the sin, unbelief, and approaching destruction of Chorazin, Bethsaida, and Capernaum, but then he abruptly thanks the Father because he hid the truth from the wise and learned but revealed it to small children—and then, with equal abruptness, declares that all who are burdened should come to him because his yoke is easy. The sudden shifts at verse 25 where Jesus begins his prayer, and again at verse 28 where Jesus begins his appeal to take up his yoke, are often attributed to a redactional process. "The text stands in sharp contrast to the woes pronounced on the Galilean cities. . . . It is an assured result of research that Matt. 11:25–30 is not a unitary text but that we have here three logia" (Luz 2001, 156). But it is possible that Jesus uttered all three sayings at one time, notwithstanding the apparent non sequitur.

As Lamentations 1 mourns over Jerusalem, so Jesus in Matthew 11:20–24 mourns over the destruction of Jewish cities as punishment for their refusal to repent. His sudden prayer in 11:25–27 asserts that God has hidden the truth from the wise, whereas Lady Zion asserts that God has cast aside the warriors who were defending her (1:15).

These two seem to have little in common, but the "wise" are supposed to protect the people from error just as the "warriors" are supposed to protect them from an enemy. In both cases, the men are the champions of the people but God has rejected them. Jesus also thanked God that he had revealed his truth to little children (Matt. 11:25). Here, Jesus was probably looking back to Psalm 8:2 (see Matt. 21:16). Even so, however, there is an ironic link to this section of Lamentations: Lady Zion mourned the deaths of her "children," representing her people (1:16), just as Jesus mourned the coming judgment on Chorazin, Bethsaida, and Capernaum. But Jesus also declared that, ironically, the youngest children in those cities were the only ones who could recognize who he was.

The metaphor of the yoke in Lamentations 1:14 may be behind Jesus's sudden appeal to take up his yoke at Matthew 11:28–30. In her outpouring of grief, Lady Jerusalem said that her sin was a yoke around her neck. This is an unusual metaphor. As noted above, the yoke frequently represents slavery or forced subordination to a person or nation (Lev. 26:13; Deut. 28:48; 1 Kings 12:10; Isa. 9:4; Jer. 27:8). It is peculiar to represent sin as a yoke. Normally, we take Jesus's appeal to mean that those who are burdened by a hard life and by many sorrows should come to him. But sin, as Lady Zion discovered, is a terrible yoke, and it brought ruin down upon Jerusalem. Jesus was calling upon the unbelieving cities of Chorazin, Bethsaida, and Capernaum to take up his yoke. Understood in this manner, the yoke they should cast off is not simply their hardships and worries. Jesus was willing to exchange his yoke, the obligations of discipleship, for the one they were already wearing, their profound guilt.

### *Laments over Lady Zion's Suffering (1:17)*

**1:17**. The poet portrays Lady Zion as prostrate, begging for pity from God and people, and getting no answer. Line 17c, "She has become uncleanness among them" (הָיְתָה יְרוּשָׁלַם לְנִדָּה בֵּינֵיהֶם), confirms that verses 8–9 primarily concern how the other nations regarded the Jewish refugees as defiled, so that they refused to give them any aid. Note that 1:8 also says Lady Zion has become unclean (לְנִידָה הָיָתָה), like a woman who is menstruating, and clearly the point is how other people react by shunning her.

### *Lady Zion Laments and Prays (1:18–22)*

**1:18–19**. Once again, Lady Zion admits she has sinned. Her admission that YHWH was right to punish her is not "subversive" speech, setting up the reader for an implied challenge to God's justice. It is sincere. At the same time, the bulk of her speech is not taken up with her confession but with insisting that the nations should have shown her compassion. Although this text naturally calls to mind prophetic denunciations of Israel the adulteress, "my lovers" (מְאַהֲבַי) does not necessarily imply sexual partners (whether literal or metaphorical). While there may well be an echo of the prophetic denunciation of Israel's apostasy as spiritual adultery, the passage does not develop this idea. It instead focuses on how those who should have provided succor did not. The NIV is arguably correct in translating this as "allies." She speaks of how those with the greatest dignity and authority (priests and elders) starved, which implies that all lower-ranking people starved too. Her erstwhile allies should have taken in refugees and rendered other material aid. Being compassionate to those whom God has punished is not defiance of God or equivalent to claiming that he had been unjust. To the contrary, Proverbs 24:17–18 states, "When your enemy falls, do not rejoice, and do not let your heart be glad when they stumble. Otherwise, YHWH will see it and regard your actions as evil and turn his anger from him."

**1:20**. Lady Zion speaks directly to God, calling on him to observe how severely she suffers and to punish the nations for their hostility. Calling on God to "look" (ראה) at her pain implies that he should do something about it and not just observe from a distance. She says God should do this "although I have been truly rebellious" (כִּי מָרוֹ מָרִיתִי). The word כִּי is here normally translated "for" (in the sense of "because"), but it has a wide range of meanings, including "although." The ambiguity of כִּי is significant here. She may be distressed *because* she has been thoroughly rebellious but, importantly, she is calling on God to look compassionately on her suffering *although* she has been thoroughly rebellious. She is not calling on God to show her compassion "because" she sinned but in spite of it. Furthermore, the text does not develop the theme of mourning over sin but the theme of appealing to God for help. She is surrounded by death; it is time for God to relent. Again, the confession is not ironic or subversive, but it is not the main point of her outcry. Rather, she wants God to help her.

**1:21–22**. Lady Zion believes that her treacherous neighbors are at least as deserving of punishment as she is, and she appeals to God to avenge her. The reader should not judge her, as though her prayer was unworthy. The Psalter has many texts like this; Psalm 83 is a particularly strong parallel: "God, do not be silent. . . . [The enemies say,] 'Come, let us obliterate them as a nation; let the name of Israel never be remembered again.' . . . O my God, make them like swirling dust, like chaff before the wind. . . . Let them be permanently put to shame and horrified; let them be chagrined and die" (vv. 1, 4, 13, 17). Such prayers should provoke fear among the Gentiles. If they persecute the broken and dispirited Jews, they will not escape punishment. The nations' joy over her downfall is the greatest indictment against them, and God will take notice. As for Zion herself, she has lost the ability to resist them; her heart is giving out (v. 22).

## THEOLOGICAL FOCUS

In interpreting Lamentations, we should focus on the emphases of the text and not on abstract theology—even if that theology is traditional (God's justice and human sin), and certainly not if it is driven by a postmodern agenda (challenging the justice of God). However, this does not require our interpretation to focus entirely on the historical setting. We should not dwell excessively on the events of 586 B.C., turning our exposition into a history lesson.

- This passage concerns especially the suffering of the Jews during and ever since the destruction of the first temple. From that time forward, they have been under the domination of the Gentiles. In ancient times, the province of Yehud (called "Judea" by the Romans) was under one empire after another. With the fall of the Second Temple, they have been at the mercy of Gentiles around the world and have often received brutal treatment. Christians have pointed out that their refusal to acknowledge their Messiah has been at the root of their sorrows, but this does not justify or excuse anti-Semitism among Christians. It is not our place to add to the sufferings of those whom God has punished. The sad laments of Lady Zion, that she has been abused by those she considered friends, has been repeated many times and in many places throughout history. To give but a single and very famous example: the reason that there were so many Jews in Germany in the early twentieth century is that they fled the pogroms in Russia and eastern Europe and were welcomed into Germany—but then the Germans turned on them.
- The curses that Lady Zion proclaimed against her Gentile persecutors have

not gone and will not go unfulfilled. As the twentieth century reached its midpoint, millions of Jews had been slaughtered, but Germany was in ruins as well.

- Who is Lady Zion?
  - She is first of all the personification of Israel, the chosen people through whom God would reconcile the world to himself.
  - She is secondarily the city of Jerusalem with its walls and houses and, above all, its temple. Those who loved YHWH and Israel also loved this city: "Walk around Zion, go all about it, count its towers, consider its districts; go through its grand structures, that you may tell the next generation that this is God, our God forever and ever. He will guide us forever" (Ps. 48:12–14 [MT 13–15]). Like a mother, she loves, encourages, and comforts her children.
  - Lady Zion is now the heavenly Jerusalem, and all who come to Christ come to her. "The Jerusalem above is free—she who is the mother of us all" (Gal. 4:26).
  - Ultimately, she is the heavenly city, where all the saints will dwell forever (Rev. 21:2–4).
- To the Jews of the sixth century B.C., the corruption and fall of Jerusalem seemed to have derailed God's plan. They thought he would use Israel as the means by which all the nations of earth would be blessed (Gen. 12:3), resulting in the exaltation of Zion above all the mountains of the earth (Isa. 2:1–4). All that seemed to have perished. It was especially hard to see how the Davidic king would claim sovereignty over all nations (Ps. 2). But God in his wisdom fulfilled these promises in a manner that no one could have imagined. Jesus is now raised to the right hand of the Father, and people from every nation and race come to honor the Jewish God and his Messiah. In the fullness of time, they will worship him forever in the New Jerusalem.

## PREACHING AND TEACHING STRATEGIES

### *Exegetical and Theological Synthesis*

This lament is full of pain. The images may be a little foreign to us, but the pain comes through. Our normal reaction is to distance ourselves from the poet's experience. But poetry is written to engage and invite the reader into the emotion. Each week we, pastors/teachers, strive to give a clear directive that comes out of a passage; normally it is something to do, or stop a certain way of thinking, or to start truly believing something. However, this passage calls us to an unusual application: to feel something.

This poem teaches us to feel the pain of sin. This pain is not the end of the application—rather, just the beginning. When we hurt with Israel, we should learn to hurt for the consequences of all sin, in our own lives and the lives of others. When we hurt with Israel over her sin, it should help us avoid or turn from our sin. God designed us to be moved by emotion, so the feelings of this poem should move us to action. But we begin with the pain.

### *Preaching Idea*

We are invited to feel the hurt.

### *Contemporary Connections*

#### *What does it mean?*

In the early 1990s Sarajevo was torn by racial and political conflicts. Thousands lost their lives. Snipers and mortars were common in the city as the two sides sought to destroy each other and only succeeded in destroying their city. The following took place in the midst of this tragic and needless conflict.

> On May 27, 1992, a long line of people had queued up at one of the still-functioning bakeries. A mortar shell fell into the middle of the line, killing 22 people and creating a bloody mess of body parts and rubble. Vedran Smajlović lived close to the bakery and was appalled by what he saw as he helped the wounded. He felt powerless as he was neither a politician nor a soldier—he was a musician, who could speak truth to the heart beyond any language.
>
> Smajlović took his cello to the spot where those waiting for bread had been butchered and began to plaintively play. He played in a daze but in an incredibly evocative way. In spite of the risk, people gathered to listen. When he was finished, he packed up his cello and went to a coffee shop. Quickly people came up to him expressing their appreciation, "This is what we needed." Smajlović went back the next day and the next 22 days, one for each person killed. Sniper fire continued around him and mortars still rained down in the neighborhood, but Smajlović never stopped playing. (Buttry 2011, 305)

Vedran Smajlovic was playing a melancholy composition, "Albion's Adagio in G Minor." It was his way of entering into a lament for these victims and for the city. The poet of chapter 1 of Lamentations is writing this poem as an invitation for us to enter into lament. How do we play our cellos to lament with Israel?

Do we only lament for ancient Israel? As we look at the treatment of the Jews throughout history and throughout the world, mistreatment and persecution always seem to follow them. There is cause to continue our lament for Israel. This lament is further widened by the parallels to Revelation 18, where God's angel laments a prosperous city that is destroyed because of sin. The call to lament is first focused in Israel's tragic destruction and seems to apply to any city or culture that is being destroyed. The lament here is very specific; it is not for the general difficulty of living in a fallen world. That lament is valid and should be done. The focus here is on lamenting because a culture has rebelled against God and is enduring the consequences of rebellion.

We should enter into a lament for Israel and for those around us whose lives are being destroyed. This is not a distant judgment of "oh, poor them." It is a deep grieving because of the loss. In *Dark Clouds, Deep Mercy*, Mark Vroegop speaks of feeling like an exile on Election Day in 2012 when three states voted to redefine marriage to include homosexual couples, and two other states legalized marijuana for recreational use (Vroegop 2019, 121). While national elections cause us to lament in a general way, it is the personal experiencing of our culture's decline that should bring tears of lament to our eyes.

There are tragic losses all around us. I talk with a friend whose marriage is in the final stages. He is dressed in work clothes and says he is heading home to move out. Do we know a teenager who tragically talks about escaping through suicide? And there are those who end up destroying their lives and others because they thought they could handle driving after a few beers. A churchgoing family man loses his job and his family because of an addiction to pornography. Years of conflict result in a grandmother being isolated from her family in her last years of life. We should lament when a culture, a city, a church, a family is being destroyed by the consequences of sin.

#### *Is it true?*

When we look at the history of the Jews, it is a long hard story—at times the harshest of stories, as in the Holocaust. There is a sad overtone in so many of the movies about Israel, and even their music often seems to be in a minor key. Jeremiah's lady Zion, the personification of the fallen Jerusalem, invites us to behold her misery. God through the appeal of a hurting woman is asking us to be a part of a funeral, mourning not the loss of a loved one but the loss of a joyful, prosperous, and at times God-honoring city. Lamentations is not just a lament over sin; it is the grieving over the painful discipline that Jerusalem is enduring because of her sin. God invites us to be a part of this focused lament. Certainly, there is a cathartic element as we hear the tragedy of their sin and the consequences, and as we reflect on our own sins and the pain that we endure. But that is the theme and applicational thrust of many other passages. Here God is calling us to lament with Israel.

*Now what?*

There is no resolution in this first lament, and much of our lamenting is the same. There is the wonderful hope of God's promised future, which is mentioned in later laments, but here we are left with just lament. So how do we do that?

We let the emotion have its effect on us. Our culture seems to quickly run away from the pain of lament. But this first lament calls us to the hurt. We certainly hurt when we experience those consequences because of our own sins. In a similar way, we should be grieved and upset when we see tragic consequences of sins in others. The genre of tragedy in plays and films doesn't seem to be a box-office draw. Who wants to watch a leading character destroy herself? Think back to that famous tragedy *Romeo and Juliet*. Audiences leave the theater hurting. Perhaps that cathartic experience of crying over the fictitious young lovers' deaths helps us release the real pain that is holed up within us. For some, the tragedy might lead to a desire to resolve a conflict; for most, it just hurts.

The temptation is to suggest specific actions or steps to take after reading this first lament. What does God want us to do? He wants us to hurt. God invites us to share the hurt, the pain of the tragic consequences of sin that result in the loss of so much in lives all around us. It is not so much that he wants us to do something; rather, he wants us to feel something.

### *Creativity in Presentation*

This unusual book calls for to explore some unusual presentations of the sermon. It would be good to read all twenty-two verses as a poem. An effective interpretive reading will require an in-depth understanding of the images and the flow of thought as well as practice. It might be that someone gifted in this area could help. Since the poem has a narrator and a metaphorical woman who speaks, perhaps two people could do the reading. If other persons are enlisted to read the poem, it would be good to coach them as to the meaning and the context.

Another possibility is to have the "Adagio" by Albion played either live or as a recording while the above illustration is being read. The emotional effect of music could help the congregation enter into the lament. This will need careful planning and rehearsal; to do something like this poorly is far worse than not doing it at all.

The exposition needs to be such that it doesn't become so analytical that it takes away from the emotion of the text. In trying to honor the intent of the text, the deep emotions that are present in the text need to be displayed as well as explained. Some images will need to be explained, while others can stand on their own. It will be important to highlight the Lady's invitation to *look upon her pain* (v. 12) and *behold her pain* (v. 18).

For those who are unsure of their salvation, or for those who have never come to trust the work of Christ on their behalf, the emotion that this passage generates can be greatly used by the Spirit. Perhaps God will work through the emotions to move a person to faith or use the pain to draw one of his children back to himself. The pain is an invitation to embrace what God has done for us.

- Present the text
  - Narrator (vv. 1–9b)
  - Lady Zion (v. 9c)
  - Narrator (vv. 10–11b)
  - Lady Zion (vv. 11c–16)
  - Narrator (v. 17)
  - Lady Zion (vv. 18–22)
- Application: We are invited to feel the hurt.
  - We should feel the pain of the consequences of Israel's sin.
  - We should feel the pain of the consequences of other's sins.
  - We should feel the pain of the consequences of our sins.
    - Turn form the sin.
    - Turn to Christ.

## DISCUSSION QUESTIONS

1. What are some tragedies in novels, films, or on stage? How does one feel after watching one of these productions?

2. Does it ever feel good to feel bad for someone?

3. Why do you think God wants us to enter into a lament for Israel?

4. Why do you think God wants us to enter into a lament for loss in others' lives?

5. How is lamenting over the consequences of sin different from lamenting over natural disasters or sicknesses?

## Lamentations 2:1–22

### EXEGETICAL IDEA

This poem approaches Jerusalem's calamity from a prophetic perspective, describing all that happened as the work of God. Although guilt and punishment are part of this, the focus is on God's control of events. One cannot complain to God while denying that he is the sovereign over all that happens in the world. This focus allows the poem to move toward prayer and intercession after the lament, since God remains sovereign over all things. He who struck Israel is the only one who can save Israel.

### THEOLOGICAL FOCUS

The reader should understand that Jerusalem's fall did not come about simply because of poor leadership in Judah or aggressive enemies in Babylon. These things, too, were orchestrated by God (not in a deterministic sense, but as a response to Israelite apostasy). Appreciating divine rule over all things, the readers can respond with a prayer for mercy, knowing that divine sovereignty does not contradict the need for prayer.

### PREACHING IDEA

When the pain comes in, the cry should go up.

### PREACHING POINTERS

There is no wondering about the source of Israel's pain. Clearly God is the one bringing disaster upon his people. God seems to be the enemy because the destruction is so severe. But the object of the lament is equally clear. God is the one to whom the people cry.

When we are in pain, no matter the cause or the reason, we cry out in some way. Perhaps it is a literal cry or silent cry within our minds and spirits. The passage does not explain why God allows or causes pain, but it does direct us to cry out to him. Crying out to him doesn't mean that the pain will go away. But when we cry out to him, it brings purpose and significance to our cries because he is the one who has a reason and a purpose, and we can trust him.

# SECOND LAMENT (2:1–22)

## LITERARY STRUCTURE AND THEMES

The second lament does not deny the guilt of the Israelites or excuse the atrocities committed by the Babylonians, but it steadily asserts that all of this happened according to the will and plan of God. The poem is almost an exposition of Amos 3:6b, "Does disaster befall a city if YHWH has not done it?" Acknowledging that God is the ruler of all things, the poem complains to him alone and seeks salvation from him alone.

- ***YHWH's Wrath Against Zion (2:1–10)***
- ***A Lament (2:11–16)***
- ***YHWH's Wrath Against Zion (2:17)***
- ***A Call to Prayer (2:18–19)***
- ***The Poet Prays (2:20–22)***

## EXPOSITION

### *YHWH's Wrath Against Zion (2:1–10)*

The poet here speaks as a prophet, declaring what God has done and even describing his mental state: that he was angry, and yet deliberate and purposeful, when he destroyed Jerusalem.

**2:1**. This is a general introduction to the account of the suffering that God inflicted upon Jerusalem. It opens with the same word as chapter 1, an exclamatory "How!" (אֵיכָה). But Lamentations 1:1 immediately launches into an account of Lady Zion's agony ("How she sits alone!), whereas 2:1 immediately speaks of the actions of God: "How the Lord has clouded over Lady Zion with his anger!" This signals to the reader that this poem will bring a prophetic perspective to the issue, giving insights into the actions and intents of God.

**2:2–5**. These verses focus on military aspects of the disaster. But the human actors who destroyed Jerusalem are only the agents of God, the actual destroyer of Jerusalem. In all the verbs of verse 2 ("he swallowed" [בִּלַּע]; "and he did not pity" [וְלֹא חָמַל]; "he destroyed" [הָרַס]; "he struck" [הִגִּיעַ]; "he brought into disgrace" [חִלֵּל]), God is the subject, and this continues through verses 3–4. Lamentations never mentions Babylon, the human entity that destroyed Jerusalem, treating that as an insignificant detail. God turned Judah into a dehorned bull, helpless to resist the predators around it (v. 3). The army of Judah failed because God was not fighting as their ally but "as an enemy" (v. 4, כְּאוֹיֵב and כְּצָר). He has burned the city with fire (for further discussion of the metaphor of fire here, see Labahn 2006).

**2:6–7**. God has even rejected Jerusalem's sacred institutions, including the temple and all its services. Line 6a should be translated, "And he tore down [Jerusalem] as though it were his booth in a garden; he destroyed its meeting place" (for another option, see Provan 254–255). This alludes to how ancient farmers would construct temporary shelters in the fields at harvest time so that they could remain with the crops until the whole harvest was taken in. They would then tear down the booths or leave them abandoned. But the word for "booth" (שֹׂךְ, a by-form of סֹךְ or סֻכָּה), also calls to mind Succoth (the Feast of Booths or Tabernacles), one of the sacred festivals of Israel's calendar. This association points toward the services of the temple, here called the "meeting place" (מוֹעֵד). Also, God made Zion forget her "festivals" (again מוֹעֵד), implying again that the temple is meant. The poet has exploited the two meanings of מוֹעֵד to imply that God rejected both the sacred place and the sacred events: the temple and its festivals. Without the temple, Israel can no longer properly observe its holy days or make the Sabbath sacrifices. Priests can no longer function. Verse 6 also says God has rejected the "king." We think of this as a secular function, but the Israelites would not have regarded the king, especially the Davidic king, in purely secular terms. He was YHWH's anointed, an integral part of the theological meaning of Zion. But now Zion was gone, and the king and priests were in exile. The temple and altar were taken by the enemy and left in ruins because God rejected them.

**2:8–9a**. The defensive structures around Jerusalem, its walls and towers, are in ruins. Again, the text stresses that this is a work of God: "YHWH deliberately tore down the wall around Lady Zion" (line 8a, חָשַׁב יְהוָה לְהַשְׁחִית חוֹמַת בַּת־צִיּוֹן). YHWH lays out a line, something normally done for construction work, but here done in preparation for a demolition. Again, the lament stresses that all of this was a considered work of God. Also, what chapter 1 described metaphorically as stripping Lady Zion naked and raping her is here presented in more literal, prosaic terms. With the walls breached, Jerusalem was defenseless. In line 9a, the desolate, broken-down walls of the city seem to be mute mourners.

**2:9b–10**. People of all classes in Jerusalem, if they survived the war, suffered terribly. The text focuses on the leadership classes (king, officials, priests [the teachers of "the Law"], prophets, and elders), but by implication all those of lesser status suffer as well. The text speaks of the sorrow of the "young women" (בְּתוּלֹת יְרוּשָׁלָםִ, literally "virgins of Jerusalem"), because their weeping evokes most powerfully the sympathy of the reader.

### *A Lament (2:11–16)*

The biblical prophets generally do not rejoice when the wrath of God befalls a people and fulfills their prophecies. They often mourn, and sometimes do so even when the calamity befalls one of Israel's enemies (Isa. 16:6–11). So here, the poet abruptly turns for declaring what God has done to grieving over the suffering it caused.

**2:11–13**. The poet expresses his own misery over the calamity, using intense biological terms to express the depth of his sorrow (he has wept till he has no strength; his stomach regurgitates acid into his mouth). He is especially distressed over the state of mothers and children. Although a master of language, the poet has no words to adequately describe the horrors all around him.

**2:14**. As is common when someone is grief-stricken, the poet issues an implied "If only!" He laments how false prophets brought this upon her, implying that none of it would have happened if only the prophets had not misled the people. While it is correct to see the doctrinal significance of this—that apostasy destroys a people—in context it is primarily an expression of grief and a wish that things had not gone so badly. It also illustrates the prophetic focus of this poem.

**2:15–16**. The poet grieves because the nations gloat over prostrate Jerusalem. Although Lamentations at several points calls on God to punish the nations, the focus here is again on the extreme suffering of the Jews. They have lost their home, their king, and their temple, and yet they receive only jeers from the nations around them.

### *YHWH's Wrath Against Zion (2:17)*

**2:17**. The poet once again asserts that all this is from God, who purposefully brought enemies down upon Jerusalem. God planned (זָמַם) all of this. This verse serves as an inclusion with verse 1, implying that the entire calamity (vv. 1–17) was brought on by God, and now the people must respond.

### *A Call to Prayer (2:18–19)*

**2:18–19**. As prophets typically call on the audience to do something in response to their message, the poet here urgently calls on his audience to pray for relief. The people should do this continuously until God responds and shows them mercy.

### *The Poet Prays (2:20–22)*

This text is a prayer. It is voiced by one person (the speaker mentions "my young women and men" and "my enemies" rather than "our enemies"). Although it is possible that Lady Zion is the speaker, it is more likely that the poet is his heeding his own call and praying for the city.

**2:20–22**. The essence of the prayer is that the city has suffered unspeakable horrors. God should look upon all the suffering and relent. By pointing to this most appalling situation—mothers cannibalizing their children, indiscriminate slaughter, priests slain in the sanctuary—the poet appeals to God to bring relief to the Jews. Verse 22 ironically looks back to verse 6, which says that God has put an end to every festival day (מוֹעֵד) in Jerusalem's temple. The metaphor relates to the high holy days at the temple, at which an enormous number of animal sacrifices would be made, creating something of a bloody spectacle (for example, 1 Kings 8:63–64). Now, God has made a festival day (מוֹעֵד) of his own—one involving the slaughter of Jerusalem. But the metaphor also alludes to Isaiah 34:1–7, in which an apocalyptic judgment on all nations, the day of YHWH, is described as though it were a great animal sacrifice. Lamentations 2:22 implies that the day of YHWH has come upon Israel. The people have seen "terror on every side," referring to the slaughter, rape, pillage, and destruction that engulfed the city. This phrase occurs in Jeremiah 6:25; 20:3, 10; 46:5; 49:29; Psalm 31:13 (MT 14). While this may support the claim that Jeremiah wrote Lamentations, it is not decisive. Lamentations alludes to other texts as well, especially Isaiah.

## THEOLOGICAL FOCUS

Once again, it is clear that Lamentations affirms that the people of Judah sinned grievously and brought disaster down on their own heads, and also that the enemies of Israel committed horrible atrocities. But neither of these is the focus of the liturgy. Rather, it is that God brought this disaster about, and it is an appeal for him to give the surviving Jews some mercy. From this, we can learn several lessons:

- God is sovereign over all human affairs. He punishes when he chooses, and he relents when he chooses. There is no point in praying to God if one does not think he is in control.
- When a terrible calamity strikes, some would defend the justice of God by saying, "God had nothing to do with this." This approach is as far from Lamentations as it can be. Did God have the ability to thwart the Babylonians when they attacked Jerusalem, or did he not? To give a modern example: Could God have stopped the Islamic terrorist attacks on New York on September 11, 2001, or not? But the Bible goes even beyond saying that God permitted these things. It says that they happen according to his purpose. But that does not mean that God punishes happily, or that he does not hold the perpetrators to be guilty.
- The true prophetic heart, as exemplified in this lament, never engages in *schadenfreude* over the destruction of sinners. It weeps bitterly and calls on God to be merciful.
- The greatest calamity of all, which God could have averted but did not, was the crucifixion. This event shows that even God's harshest actions have a greater purpose of mercy.

## PREACHING AND TEACHING STRATEGIES

### *Exegetical and Theological Synthesis*

When a disaster strikes, whether it is a flood from a hurricane or the flood of evil from warring nations, there is a natural reaction to ask why this happened. The answer given is seldom other than to explain the weather patterns that let the hurricane form, or the patterns of conflict that led up to the war. A more specific question that is also asked is, "Why did God let this happen?" While that question needs to be answered as best as we can, this passage answers another question.

The Jewish disaster is clearly described in this lament. The cry of the poet doesn't emphasize the content of his lament so much as it highlights to whom his lament is directed. When the pain of a disaster comes into our lives, our cry should go up to the one who can bring purpose and reason to our pain.

### *Preaching Idea*

When the pain comes in, the cry should go up.

### *Contemporary Connections*

#### *What does it mean?*

Why do we want to know? Perhaps it is so we can make things right, if possible. If our car's taillight is crunched, we would like the person who did it to fix it. When a virus is floating around the church nursery, we make sure the moms know and ask them to keep the even possibly sick kids at home. In the case of crimes, we want to bring those responsible to justice.

Lamentations describes the destruction of Jerusalem and Israel in such a way that we are appalled at the misery and pain, from the generalized metaphors of Israel being cast down from heaven (v. 1) to the specific image of mothers not having food for their children (v. 12). The only exhortation in the midst of this vivid picture of total destruction is that Israel should cry out to God. And we join Israel in crying out to God when pain enters our lives. This seems in keeping with numerous other scriptures, but the twist comes when we hear that God is the responsible party for the pain. The lament is overwhelmingly clear: God did this. It was His hand, and yet it is to him that we should cry out.

Why cry out to God if he is the one who caused this? If the pain is his fault, why should we cry out to him—other than to blame him and shake our fists at him like we would at the old pickup truck that drives off after smashing our taillight? When we think of God in this way, we impose the motives and irresponsibility of fellow humans on God. The pain cannot be God's fault, for he does not have faults. That means that he has somehow purposed the pain for good. He is the one who can bring purpose and even good out of the pain. It is not always ours to know all the reasons for the pain, but in this lament we know why. Israel had sinned greatly, both in number and in gravity.

Perhaps the pain in our lives is showing us sin of which we were unaware. Perhaps the pain is part of this fallen world and not related to our sin. The poet doesn't try to solve the problem of pain in the world. God, through this lament, is teaching us that when pain comes we should cry out to the one who is behind all that happens. Yes, God could have stopped 9/11; he could have stopped the wildfires, the hurricanes, the cancer, the divorce, even the virus. We often do not know *why*, but we know *what*: when we experience pain, we are to cry out to God.

#### *Is it true?*

After the shock of airliners crashing into the towers on 9/11, the first question we asked was, "Who caused this?" The same question is asked after a shotgun attack on worshippers in a church in Texas, or a machete-wielding maniac assaulting those at a Hanukkah celebration in New York. We cry out, "Who did this?" We are desperate to know who is behind the pain. Even when a virus is going around and we catch it, we ask, "Where did I pick this up? Was it that person behind us on that last flight, the handshake during the welcome time at church, or maybe the grandkids brought it home from school and shared it by way of a big hug?" It is even the basic plot of so many movies and TV series. Who is the responsible party? We want to know.

### *Now what?*

Crying out to God can take many forms. Everyone seems to have their own way of crying, which is affected by background and culture. Some are loud and extremely expressive, while others have a quiet intensity. This lament gives us at least three hints as to what it might look like to cry out the Lord: tears of weeping (v. 11), pouring out one's heart (vs 19), and the genre itself—a song.

Medical research has shown that an emotional response of tears can be a benefit. When we cry, certain chemicals are released in our brains that actually bring some comfort. The tears that come from emotion have a different chemical breakdown than that of the tears that moisten our eyes. Most of us have either had a good cry or have seen someone who did. Sometimes crying out to the Lord means letting the tears flow. The tears and physical response are a nonverbal form of crying out to the Lord.

Pouring out one's heart seems to be the verbal expression of crying out: pouring out your inner thoughts, questions, frustrations, confusion, and yet at the same time, praise. Recently a dear friend was diagnosed with liver cancer and was told he had two to four years to live. A day or so later he had to make a four-hour drive by himself. In that solitude he was fully honest with God. He asked everything from "Why me?" to "How will my family make it?" He spent the hours crying out to God. Another way that he cried out to God was through music, both listening and singing. Some of the old hymns that speak of God's care for us in times of pain became more real to him. It must not go unnoticed that God chose a musical genre for this book of lament. God has not healed my friend, but God has given him the four years and is using the pain in many ways to advance the kingdom.

Though not specified in this lament, another way to cry to the Lord is to write about the pain. Somehow putting the pain that is in your heart and life onto a piece of paper can help. Years ago, I went through a conflict which resulted in great misunderstandings and loss of a position. I poured out my heart to the Lord on a long walk on the shores of Lake Michigan. Afterward I wrote a poem about the walk. The poem ended with me throwing all of my confusion, frustration, and sense of betrayal into the lake of God's sovereignty. The walk and the poem were my cry to the Lord.

### ***Creativity in Presentation***

This lament highlights the hand of God in Israel's destruction, so let that govern the presentation. Perhaps start by walking through the passage, highlighting and explaining the suffering that Israel was experiencing. The passage is filled with references to God's hand, but these can be read without commenting on them. While doing this, keep asking or hinting at who is behind this. Let this question be the tension point. Perhaps even mention the Babylonians. Build the emotion of wanting to know who could have done a thing like this. This would be the first movement.

Then show the answer in the text, and how the poet is overwhelmingly clear that God is the responsible one. It might be tempting to give an apologetic as to why God would do this, but that is not what this passage is doing. This lament doesn't explain why God did this; it only tells us that he did.

The third movement is the directive to cry out. The command to cry out to God is the main application point, which can be expanded as mentioned above by describing and suggesting different ways of crying out. The gospel should fit into this section of the sermon/lesson, both using Christ's example on the cross and the sinner's cry for salvation. Here is one possible structure:

- Present the suffering of Israel (vv. 1–17).
  - Emphasis upon the suffering (the action portion of the stanza)
- Present who did this: YHWH (vv. 1–17).
  - Emphasis upon the one causing it (the subject of each stanza)
- Application: What we are to do—cry out to God (vv. 18–22)
  - Crying out to him can take many forms: speaking, crying, music, writing, etc.
  - Christ's example, when he died for our sins on the cross

## DISCUSSION QUESTIONS

1. Describe when a good cry was helpful to you or a friend. Describe how it was helpful.

2. What do you think about this C. S. Lewis quote: "God whispers to us in our pleasures, speaks in our conscience, but shouts in our pains"?

3. Why might we hesitate to cry out to God when a tragedy or pain comes into our lives?

4. On a scale of 1 (being just a little) and 10 (being unbearable), how would you rate the pain described in this lament?

5. What are some different ways to cry out to God?

## Lamentations 3:1–66

### EXEGETICAL IDEA

One single man serves as the voice of the people, and he is a paradigm of both suffering and faith. He laments over the city, expresses his extreme pain, declares his unwavering faith in God, appeals to the people to repent and pray, and himself prays in hope that God will set all things right. He is the ideal of how the devout should respond to the calamity.

### THEOLOGICAL FOCUS

The singular man of Lamentations 3 takes on the role of the suffering servant of YHWH. In this, he is a model for all readers, in that he maintains his righteousness and devotion to God while he suffers terribly and is fully aware of how badly the people have sinned. The ideal is especially fulfilled in Jesus, but all who belong to God should imitate the model set forth in this text.

### PREACHING IDEA

Embrace (accept) the suffering and the Savior.

### PREACHING POINTERS

This longest of the laments is like a solo sung by a righteous man who sings while Jerusalem crumbles around him. His song doesn't gloss over his suffering; in fact, he describes it with vivid and powerful images such as teeth grinding on gravel and tears flowing like a river. But his song also has the delightful expression of God's faithfulness in 3:22–23, which is made all the more precious when we see it in light of the suffering that is expressed in this lament and in the context of the other four laments. And while it gives us hope in suffering, that is not all that God wants us to know and do when we are suffering. This lament guides us through suffering to embrace the suffering, but more importantly to embrace the Savior.

# THIRD LAMENT (3:1–66)

## LITERARY STRUCTURE AND THEMES

Throughout this lament, a solitary man, whom I will simply call the "archetype," is the exemplar of Jerusalem's suffering. Although a devout man himself (not one of the apostates), he suffers along with everyone else and gives voice to their anguish. He believes in the goodness of God, but he does not in any manner understate the scope of the calamity.

- ***Introduction (3:1)***
- ***First Lament (3:2–16)***
- ***The Archetype's Emotional State (3:17–20)***
- ***A Confession of Faith in God (3:21–39)***
- ***An Appeal to Jews to Confess Their Sin and Seek God (3:40–41)***
- ***The Prayer of the Jews (3:42–47)***
- ***Second Lament (3:48–54)***
- ***A Prayer, Confident That God Will Again Save (3:55–66)***

## EXPOSITION

### *Introduction (3:1)*

**3:1**. The opening verse tells us that we are now looking at the calamity through the eyes of a single, representative citizen: the "archetype." It is not necessary to decide whether the poem describes the suffering of one man (even if that one man is a literary creation) or if the one man is representative of all the people; both are true. The people experience the calamity together, but everyone also suffers individually and privately. On the other hand, it is not wise to try to identify the man by name. The traditional view is that the man is Jeremiah, but others have proposed he is Jehoiachin or Zedekiah (Salters 2010, 185–86). But nothing is gained by attaching a name to the archetype. The opening words, "I am the man who has seen affliction," make for a strikingly powerful beginning. Also, the poem's very first words, "I am the man" (אֲנִי הַגֶּבֶר), call to mind Pilate's presentation of the bloody Jesus, wearing the crown of thorns, to the Jerusalem crowd, "Behold the man!" (John 19:5: ἰδοὺ ὁ ἄνθρωπος, or perhaps more memorably in the Vulgate, *ecce homo*). The parallel is intriguing, since Jesus is the one man who suffered as a representative of all.

### *First Lament (3:2–16)*

God has severely afflicted the archetype. Throughout the passage, although devout, he attributes his suffering to God. YHWH is the subject of almost every verb in this section, and almost every verb describes a hostile action.

**3:2**. God has led the archetype but has taken him into "darkness and not light" (חֹשֶׁךְ וְלֹא־אוֹר). This phrase appears in Amos 5:18, where the prophet warns those who seek the day of YHWH that it is "darkness and not light." Smug Israelites have now experienced the day of YHWH and discovered that it is indeed a day of judgment, and for themselves first of all.

**3:3**. This verse should be translated, "Truly he repeatedly turns (יָשֻׁב יַהֲפֹךְ, two *yiqtol* verbs describing ongoing action) his hand against me all day," meaning that the poet gets no respite and sees no end to his suffering. The imagery is powerful and disturbing; it presents YHWH as constantly slapping or beating the archetype.

**3:4**. Translating somewhat loosely, this means, "He has made my muscle and skin feeble; he has broken my bones." The word בָּשָׂר, often translated "flesh," generally refers to the meat or muscle of an animal or person. The verb בלה is used of clothing that is worn out (Josh. 9:13; Isa. 50:9); used of muscle and skin, it means that the body is frail and withered, as that of someone who is extremely old. YHWH's afflictions have left the archetype broken and feeble.

**3:5**. God has "besieged" him with "poison" (רֹאשׁ). This is a mixed metaphor, but it is effective. The archetype feels entrapped by events that pollute his body with sorrow and anger. Every time he hopes that the worst has passed, God adds a new affliction. The word for "affliction" (תְּלָאָה) is often associated with the troubles of Israel (Exod. 18:8; Num. 20:14; Neh. 9:32). This suggests that the poet, as archetype, is taking on himself the troubles of Israel.

*THE TRANSLATION OF 3:5*

The Hebrew of this verse is extremely terse: בָּנָה עָלַי וַיַּקַּף רֹאשׁ וּתְלָאָה, literally, "He built against [or "upon"] me and surrounded poison [or "head"] and affliction." Interpreters, both ancient and modern, have struggled with this and suggested a broad range of interpretations (Salters 2010, 197–99), and various emendations have been proposed (for example, Hillers 2008, 113). It appears that בָּנָה עָלַי describes a siege: "He built [siege works] against me." Connected to תְּלָאָה, the word רֹאשׁ is probably "poison" and not "head." In this elliptical text, a preposition בְּ is implied but not expressed. רֹאשׁ וּתְלָאָה therefore means "[with] poison and affliction." The verse means "He built [siege works] against me and has surrounded me [with] poison and affliction." Apart from the extreme terseness of the verse, interpreters have probably been confused by the mixed metaphor. Also, the text makes better sense if one disregards the MT cantillation.

**3:6**. The Israelites, like all ancient people, strongly contrasted the light of life with the bleak darkness of death. Sheol, like Hades, was thought of as a joyless, gloomy domain, situated somewhere between existence and nonexistence. The disaster the archetype has seen and the perceived hostility of God have left him as numb and despondent as a soul in Sheol.

**3:7**. Here, the metaphor is that he is chained up in a prison. He cannot escape the disaster or the pain it gives him. It is as though God has locked his head in place so that he must face the bloodshed and destruction all around him; he cannot turn away from it.

**3:8**. As far as the archetype can tell, God has abandoned him and refuses to hear his prayers. This can be thought of as a meditation on Psalm 22:1: "My God, my God, why have you forsaken me?"

**3:9**. The metaphor has again shifted: he is now a man on the road who finds that obstacles have been put in his path, and that even the road itself has been warped and made obscure. It is not clear where he is wanting to go; probably, he just wants to escape from the disaster. But he cannot; God is determined to force him to endure it all.

**3:10–11**. The archetype is still a man trying to make his way down a road, but now God is a bear or lion who leaps out from a hiding place and mangles his body. The imagery of a wild animal attacking a traveler as he goes down a path is straightforward, but what does it mean to say that God is behaving in this manner toward the archetype? Like verse 9, it implies that he cannot escape the experience of the disaster; he must endure the full wrath of God on Jerusalem. More than that, if he tries to escape the experience, God in some manner makes it all the worse for him, as though he were a lion ripping the man's flesh. He must endure the fiery pain to the full.

**3:12–13**. The poem now abandons the metaphor of the traveler and, having introduced the concept that God attacked the archetype as a bear or lion, now focuses solely on God as his active enemy. God is now an archer shooting arrows at him; perhaps it is a military metaphor, or perhaps God is now a hunter with a bow and the archetype is a wild beast. Since the poem now focuses on God's affliction of the archetype, rather than on the archetype's attempts to get away, the arrows probably represent disasters that continue to afflict him. Perhaps hope for some bit of comfort or relief fails, someone near to him perishes, he is insulted by a hostile Gentile, or he hears fresh news of some new tragedy that has afflicted his people. We should take note of the highly poetic language of verse 13: הֵבִיא בְּכִלְיוֹתָי בְּנֵי אַשְׁפָּתוֹ is literally, "He has brought the sons of his quiver into my kidneys." What he means: "He shot his arrows into my guts."

**3:14**. In a surprising turn, the archetype now declares, "I am the laughingstock of all my people." The verse does not explicitly say that God did this to him, but this is implied. Still, it is strange. Thus far, it seems that the archetype is the representative of the people of Jerusalem, enduring suffering as one of them. How is it that his own people now mock him? A few Hebrew manuscripts read עַמִּים, "peoples," instead of עַמִּי, "my people," and some scholars follow the alternate reading (for a survey of scholarly positions, see Salters 2010, 210–11). This removes the problem, as it changes the meaning to, "I am the laughingstock of all peoples." But the MT should be followed; it is supported by the LXX and Vulgate, and it is the more difficult reading. One could read the received MT differently: הָיִיתִי שְׂחֹק לְכָל־עַמִּי could mean "I am a laughingstock *for* all my people," meaning that he suffers as one of them and is a representative of what they all endure. Still, the line is at least ambiguous, and it would more naturally be taken to mean that he is ridiculed by his own people, the Jews. In my view, the ambiguity of the line is intentional. The archetype does endure scorn for all of his people but he is also, perversely, mocked by his own people. In no other verse does the individuality of the archetype come through so clearly. He is more than a representative "everyman" for the people of Jerusalem; he is an individual who suffers uniquely.

**3:15–16**. The metaphor shifts again: God is now a torturer finding different ways to afflict his prisoner. He makes the archetype drink a bitter, poisonous concoction; he puts rocks in his mouth and smashes the jaws together to break his teeth; he makes the archetype cower on the ground and tramples him down into the dirt. The archetype is not just a citizen who sees his home city suffering and shares in its pain. God is actively, deliberately afflicting him.

### The Theological Meaning of the Suffering Archetype

The man I call the archetype describes in excruciating detail how severely God has both afflicted him and forced him to confront the full measure of God's wrath, not allowing him to turn his face away or escape the calamities all around him. This carries two separate, although perhaps related, messages.

The first message concerns the archetype's inability to escape the experience of the intense brutality that was the destruction of Jerusalem and subsequent captivity. When people endure a painful experience, the natural response is to want to escape the pain. This is especially true if one is in some measure responsible for the suffering (everyone wants to escape powerful guilt). It can even be true if one is not personally responsible for the suffering (few people want to live in a community that is falling apart or spend time among the dying).

Pain is an inextricable part of human existence. We suffer because of what we have done, because of what others have done to us, and because sometimes things just go wrong. Suffering of itself produces only bitterness, depression, and desperate acts, but suffering endured with faith can be healing, edifying, and redemptive (James 1:2–5). The key here is that one must endure in faith. But understandably, people seek escape. Some seek escape by substance abuse, by sexual misconduct, or by turning their pain into rage against some supposed enemy. Some Christians seek to end the pain by abandoning the faith, supposing that the restraints imposed on them by Christian morality are the real source of their troubles (this is especially common if the former Christian's pain was brought on by guilt).

The critical lesson here is that suffering can be redemptive. Therefore, God will not allow the archetype to escape his suffering until it runs its full course. As the archetype faces the storm, he becomes more reliant on God. When the winds subside, he will emerge from the ordeal with a wiser and more stable faith. And the suffering will teach him compassion for those enduring their own storms.

The second lesson in the suffering of the archetype concerns what we observed at 3:1: that the opening words, "I am the man," have a striking echo in the words of Pilate to the Jewish crowds: "Behold the man!" (John 19:5). Of itself, this could be no more than a coincidence, but there is more to the issue.

A significant theme in the Old Testament is the suffering servant of YHWH. This is manifested in various places, such as in Moses's exasperating experiences with the Israelites, in David's appeals to God in the Psalms, and in the persecution and rejection experienced by Jeremiah. The most profound and direct statement on the suffering servant appears in the servant songs of Isaiah 42:1–7; 49:1–9; 50:4–11; 52:13–53:12. Within these passages, several figures might be identified as the servant: 49:3 explicitly calls Israel YHWH's servant, and yet 49:6 says that the servant has a mission to Israel and also to the nations, alerting the reader to the fact that the identity of the servant can be fluid. The servant of 50:4–11 is clearly prophetic; he hears YHWH's message, proclaims it, and endures persecution. Isaiah himself and many other prophets fulfilled this ideal. The servant of 52:13–53:12 suffers vicariously for the sins of other people, including those of all Israel, it seems, and indeed for those of all of humanity (as implied in 53:6, "All we like sheep have gone astray"). The vision of the servant in Isaiah 53 is messianic, as his vicarious suffering is unique; it is something that Israel or the prophets could never fulfill.

But it is not correct to say simply that the Old Testament's "suffering servant" is the Messiah, as though he were YHWH's only servant. YHWH's servant is a theological ideal—a pattern or "type"—that has many manifestations or fulfillments. Moses, David, Isaiah, Jeremiah, and indeed all Israel, among many others, were in different ways expressions of the ideal. Of course, some people fulfill the pattern more completely than others, and only the Messiah fulfills it perfectly. But when we speak of the servant of YHWH, we are speaking of an ideal and not exclusively of a specific individual.

This brings us back to the archetypal man of Lamentations 3. Self-evidently, he is an ideal; he has no distinctive identifying features and no name. His suffering, although ferociously intense, is nonspecific; it is presented in a series of diverse metaphors in which YHWH besieges him, poisons him, beats him, shoots arrows at him, or tears him apart. Although the metaphors are brutal, the text does not describe any actual historical events. He simply suffers YHWH's wrath and waits in faith for God to turn and save. He is in some sense a representative figure, and in that regard a personification of the suffering people of Jerusalem. On the other hand, he has recognizable individuality and is not just a collective representation of the Jews. He is mocked by his people (3:14), and he calls on them to return to YHWH (3:40–42). As is the case with the suffering servant of Isaiah, his identity is fluid; what matters is the theological ideal. Like the servant of Isaiah 49, he is Israel and yet he is an individual with a mission to restore Israel.

It would not be correct to say, "Jesus is the archetypal man of Lamentations 3," if by that one means that the text is exclusively messianic and predictive. It is, first of all, a presentation of the suffering of the Jews in the experience of Jerusalem's fall, and it that sense it is not predictive but retrospective. Even so, it deals with the calamity in a distinctive way: *It gives the reader another vision of the ideal of the suffering servant*. The applications of this ideal are diverse and not bound to a specific time or event. In the destruction of Jerusalem, the suffering of the archetype was to some degree experienced by all the Jews, but it was more profoundly and fully experienced by those who were devout, and especially by a prophet such as Jeremiah. However, the travails of the Jews in exile and diaspora also fulfilled the ideal. Later cataclysmic episodes, such as those Jerusalem experienced under Antiochus IV Epiphanes around 167 B.C. or during the destruction of Jerusalem by the Romans in A.D. 70, are yet more fulfillments. But it was, again, especially the righteous remnant who more completely fulfilled the ideal.

And this brings us back to Jesus, who is not the *exclusive* but the *ultimate* fulfillment of Lamentations' archetype, and of Isaiah's servant. He is the righteous and faithful man who endures the wrath of God to the full. He is the representative of all the Jews, suffering brutal treatment at the hands of the Gentiles, and yet he was also despised by his own people. Jesus himself was keenly aware that his suffering was tied to that of Jerusalem and foreshadowed its fall (Luke 23:27–31). Lamentations 3 presents a figure who is both Israel and a man seeking to save Israel—and who, although devout, experiences God's punishment to the full.

Some details are uncannily fulfilled in Jesus. As noted above, the "I am the man" of Lamentations 3:1 is echoed in the "Behold the man" of John 19:5. Jesus was mercilessly pummeled (as in Lam. 3:3) before the crucifixion. Near the end of his ordeal he was offered bitter gall (as in Lam. 3:15). He could not escape the ordeal God had set before him, although he sought it in prayers bathed in blood and sweat, just as the archetype could not escape (Lam. 3:7). He asked why God had forsaken him, just as the archetype felt that God had shut himself off to his prayers (Lam. 3:8). He was for a time laid to rest with the dead (as in Lam. 3:6).

Again, this is not to say that the lament specifically predicts the suffering of Christ. Lamentations 3:1–16 is highly metaphorical, and some details differ from what we see in the passion of Christ (for example, the archetype had all his bones broken [3:4], whereas none of Christ's bones was broken [John 19:33–36]). Lamentations 3 gives us a type, not a prediction. Nevertheless, Jesus is the ultimate fulfillment of the type, and the echoes of the passion narrative force us to look beyond the calamity of 586 B.C. to the crucifixion—the ultimate example of the archetype enduring the wrath of God and the hatred of men.

### *The Archetype's Emotional State (3:17–20)*

Here, the archetype describes not so much what God has done to him but how he has fared mentally and emotionally because of the experience.

**3:17**. He no longer knows what it is to be content. The word טוֹבָה generally refers to acts of kindness (1 Sam. 24:17) and personal happiness (Eccl. 6:6), and can be associated with prosperity (Eccl. 7:14). The archetype clearly is not prosperous; instead, he feels enduring deprivation. He has lost all happiness and never experiences the kindness of others.

**3:18**. He feels abandoned by God. The language is abstract; he says, "My splendor (נִצְחִי) and my hope (וְתוֹחַלְתִּי), [which come] from YHWH, have perished (אָבַד)." These refer to the feelings of radiant joy he had when he had felt that God was with him and was watching over him.

**3:19–20**. Even when he is not suffering some new calamity, he remembers what has happened to him, and this leaves him in a state of deep despair. In verse 18, he said that his splendor and hope perished; now he says, "my affliction (עָנְיִי) and my homelessness (וּמְרוּדִי)" are an abiding reality. Thus, whenever he thinks about all that has happened, his soul collapses within him (v. 20: וְתָשׁוֹחַ עָלַי נַפְשִׁי). In other words, he falls into severe depression.

*THE TRANSLATION OF 3:19*

The NIV has "I remember," following the LXX (ἐμνήσθην), but the MT has what appears to be the imperative "remember" (זְכָר), an appeal for God's help (followed by Berlin 2004, 78). A case can be made for following the LXX (Hillers 2008, 114) and emending to זכרתי, but the MT is not problematic and is to be preferred. On the other hand, the MT could be read as an infinitive construct. This is preferable. Otherwise, the final two words, "wormwood and poison" (לַעֲנָה וָרֹאשׁ), have no discernable grammatical function. However, if we take these words to be the predicate of זְכָר־עָנְיִי וּמְרוּדִי, the whole line means, "Thinking about my affliction and my homelessness is [like] wormwood and poison [for me]" (see also Salters 2010, 219).

### *A Confession of Faith in God (3:21–39)*

The archetype's piety is present in the earlier part of the chapter, although not in a form we might equally recognize. His dismay at how God treats him and his confidence that all things are governed by God are both obvious in the previous verses. These attest to the reality of his determined faith in God. However, in the following verses we see his piety presented in more obvious, conventional terms.

**3:21–24**. The archetype makes a confession of faith in the goodness of God. Verse 21 has no conjunctions; it tersely reads, "This I call to mind; on this I hope." The lack of conjunctions makes the text less discursive (that is, he is not saying, "Well, it is true that things are bad, but on the other hand, God is good"). Instead, it suggests a determined effort to persevere in faith, and the bluntness of it surprises the reader. The first words of verse 22, חַסְדֵי יְהוָה ("YHWH's acts of kindness") are the "this" of verse 21, the basis for his hope. The rest of the verse explains that though it seems to have vanished, mercy is in fact a permanent trait of God. The opening claim of verse 23, "They are new every morning" (חֲדָשִׁים לַבְּקָרִים), means that God never tires of showing mercy. He has, as it were, a fresh supply of grace each morning. So also, the archetype says to God, "Your faithfulness is abundant" (רַבָּה אֱמוּנָתֶךָ), meaning that God has an inexhaustible supply. Therefore, he confesses in verse 24, "YHWH is my portion" (חֶלְקִי יְהוָה), meaning that he chooses God to be his hope for deliverance and happiness. He will not turn to any anything else or to any other person. The last words of verse 24, "I will trust in him" (אוֹחִיל לוֹ), create an inclusion pattern with אוֹחִיל in verse 21, creating the boundaries of this section.

**3:25–28**. The archetype encourages patient endurance in the face of divine punishment. To "hope in" (I-קוה) YHWH, to "seek" (דרשׁ) him, and to "wait quietly" (יחל and דום) for his salvation are obviously parallel statements, and all imply that one should endure in faith when God seems distant and indifferent to our suffering (vv. 25–26). Verse 27 is somewhat different: a man should bear the yoke in his youth. The nature of the "yoke" is not defined, although it obviously implies hardship and suffering. It could be noble suffering, as when one is persecuted for the sake of righteousness. In the context of 1:14, however, it is suffering the repercussions of one's sins. Why is it good that one bear this yoke while he is young? The answer is not that he is stronger at this time and better able to tolerate it, but that by enduring such suffering in youth he will learn lessons that will protect him from a tragic moral downfall later in life. Verse 28 then asserts that he should sit in silence under this yoke, since God laid it on him. One may wonder at this recommendation of silence in light of how vociferously the archetype described his plight in verses 1–16. But the two attitudes are not really opposed to one another. One may openly speak of how severely God punishes while still clinging persistently to God and his mercy. The "silence" of verse 28 implies patience and enduring faith, but not necessarily being literally mute.

**3:29–30**. The text offers two specific actions that demonstrate faith in God while passing through trials: putting one's face (literally "mouth," פֶּה) in the ground as a sign of abject submission to God, and enduring the anger of those whom God has set against us. The command to offer the cheek to someone who would slap us recalls Jesus's command in Matthew 5:39. In Lamentations, the meaning is that when God punishes us, even if he does it through the hands of cruel people, we should endure it patiently and not resist or try to escape. It may be that Jesus, looking back to this text, spoke with the same intent.

**3:31–33**. God's punishment is temporary and does not reflect his true desires. The meaning of verses 31–32 is self-evident. God does not hold on to his anger forever or continually inflict punishment; even if he does punish, he will at some point relent and provide healing (this presupposes that the individual is repentant). Verse 33 is more surprising: he does not afflict people "willingly" (מִלִּבּוֹ; literally, "from his heart"). This does not mean that God punishes automatically, as though he had no control over the situation or his own actions. It means that he is fundamentally compassionate and takes pleasure in showing favor to people. This understanding of God's nature arises from Exodus 34:6–7, which implies that kindness is a primary aspect of God's nature but punishing, while sometimes necessary, is secondary.

**3:34–36**. God will punish those who afflict others. These verses give a list of heinous sins: treating cruelly people who have been taken captive (v. 34), denying people their basic rights in defiance of God's law (v. 35), and perverting the path of justice when someone is seeking redress for wrongs he has suffered (v. 36). God sees all this and will judge those who do evil. The list is a broad and general statement on how God avenges the abuse of the poor and defenseless, but in this context it is especially directed at both those who destroyed Jerusalem and those who exploited the Jews in the aftermath.

*THE TRANSLATION OF 3:36–38*

Verses 36–38 contain parallel clauses that are equally baffling. First, אֲדֹנָי לֹא רָאָה (v. 36) could be "The Lord does not see" or "Does the Lord not see?" It does not mean, "The Lord does not approve" (against Stone 2018, 94–96). Second, אֲדֹנָי לֹא צִוָּה (v. 37) could mean, "The Lord did not command [it]" or "Didn't the Lord command [it]?" Third, מִפִּי עֶלְיוֹן לֹא תֵצֵא הָרָעוֹת וְהַט

וּב (v. 38) could mean, "Troubles and prosperity do not come forth from the mouth of the Most High," or "Do not troubles and prosperity [both] come forth from the mouth of the Most High?" In every case, the clauses would definitely be rhetorical questions if the lines began with the interrogative ה, but none does. The last example is the simplest: it must be a rhetorical question because the first option, a simple negative statement, claims that God does nothing. This is not an Old Testament sentiment. This suggests that the other two clauses are also rhetorical questions. The whole of verse 37 reads, מִי זֶה אָמַר וַתֶּהִי אֲדֹנָי לֹא צִוָּה. The words מִי זֶה אָמַר can only mean, "Who is this [that] says?" and not "Who says this?" Thus, understanding the final clause to be a rhetorical question, verse 37 means, "Who is this [that] says [a word] and it happens? Isn't it the Lord who makes such commands?" By analogy, verse 36 is also a rhetorical question: "And as for the cheating of a man in his court case, doesn't the Lord see [that]?"

**3:37–39**. God is sovereign. This is implied in all the earlier complaints of the archetype, and it is made explicit here. The argument has two main points. First, because God is in control of all things, we ought to endure patiently when calamity strikes, knowing that he has a purpose for everything. Second, often our suffering is the result of our own sin, and we certainly have no claims against him in that case (see also 1 Pet. 2:20–23).

### *An Appeal to Jews to Confess Their Sin and Seek God (3:40–41)*

**3:40–41**. The archetype exhorts his people to prayer, and more specifically, to repentance. They should examine their ways and return (שׁוּב) to YHWH. This implies that they should acknowledge that their "ways" have been wrong; the verb שׁוּב often connotes repentance. The exhortation is not just that they ask for divine help, but that they look into what specific sins they had committed, confess and turn from them, and then appeal for grace.

### *The Prayer of the Jews (3:42–47)*

Interpreters routinely assume that this passage is a model prayer that the archetype has composed for the people (the NIV even adds the words "and say" at the end of verse 41). But the prayer found here is quite different from what the archetype recommended in verses 40–41. It begins with a brief acknowledgment that they sinned (v. 42a) but confesses to nothing specific (there is no examining of their ways). And from that point on it is a series of complaints against God. Also, in the prayer the speakers are plural (the archetype always uses the singular of himself). It is best to regard this as the people's response to the archetype; they pray, but not exactly as he recommended. This does not mean that the people are wrong in what they say (much of it echoes the archetype's earlier complaints). But it lacks the repentance he appealed for them to make. Speaking for the whole of the Jewish people and for the Jewish experience through history, this prayer voices their bewilderment over how God refuses to forgive them but instead continues to heap great suffering upon them. We will explore more fully how this prayer relates to the particular story of the Jews when we examine chapter 5.

**3:42**. The people both acknowledge their sin and complain that God has not forgiven. It is probably too much to call this a "backhanded confession," but clearly the complaint, not the confession, dominates the verse.

**3:43–47**. The people assert that God is implacably hostile. He is wholly angry and has slain them mercilessly (v. 43), he refuses to hear their prayers (v. 44), he provoked the Gentiles toward hatred of the Jews (vv. 45–46), and everywhere they turn things go wrong (v. 47).

### *Second Lament (3:48–54)*

**3:48–51**. The archetype's eyes are filled with tears over the suffering of his fair people (בַּת־עַמִּי). The people did not pray as he recommended, but he does not say that their words were false. Their agony is intense, but there is still a barrier between themselves and God. One cannot but recall here the tears of Jesus over Jerusalem (Luke 13:34) and the tears of Paul over the Jewish people (Rom. 9:1–3).

**3:52–54**. Enemies entrap and drown the archetype. Commentators often point out that this portion of the text is reminiscent of the so-called individual psalms of lament (for example, Lalleman 2013, 361; House 2004, 425). There are certainly many parallels to these verses in the Psalms (18:4–5 [MT 5–6]; 69:1–2 [MT 2–3]; 124:7; 130:1–2). What receives far less attention, however, is the identity of the enemies who pursue and seek to kill the archetype. Perhaps interpreters assume that the enemies are the Babylonians and other Gentiles, but after 3:14 ("I am the laughingstock of all my people") this is by no means certain. His enemies may very well include, or even be composed primarily of, his own people. This is coherent with the theme of the suffering servant, and it was realized in the lives of both Jeremiah and Jesus.

### *A Prayer, Confident That God Will Again Save (3:55–66)*

**3:55–57**. The archetype affirms that YHWH has heard his prayer. This implies that God is not wholly silent in Lamentations (see Gladson 2010), and it follows a pattern we see in many other psalms and prayers, where the individual laments his sad condition but asserts that God has heard him and will deliver him (for example, Ps. 31:11–20 [MT 12–21]). The third servant song of Isaiah (50:4–9) also follows a similar pattern. This again marks the archetype as another expression of the ideal of the suffering servant.

**3:58–66**. The archetype calls on YHWH to punish his enemies. These enemies plot vengeance against him (v. 60), constantly malign him (vv. 61–62), and find clever ways to mock him (v. 63). Again, it is by no means clear that these are Gentiles. An analogous text such as Jeremiah 20:7–10 suggests again that they are the archetype's fellow Jews. Indeed, the actions of the enemies consist primarily of mockery, which agrees with the archetype's complaint that he is a laughingstock to his people (1:14). Like Jeremiah, the archetype expects to be vindicated by God and for his enemies to fall into disgrace (Jer. 18:18–23; 20:11–12).

## THEOLOGICAL FOCUS

The distinctive feature of Lamentations 3 is the role played by the archetype.

- The archetype follows the model of the suffering servant. He is in one sense the embodiment of the whole people, especially in their suffering at the hands of the Gentiles, but he is also an individual who stands against them and seeks to call them back to God.
- The archetype experienced God's wrath to the full, but he was not himself apostate. Instead, he held fast to his faith in God and exhorted others to repent and pray.
- The archetype, like Isaiah's suffering servant, is fulfilled in various persons through history, but the ultimate fulfillment is in Jesus. He entered into the suffering of Israel at the hands of the nations when he was crucified by the Roman army. He was fully devoted to God and yet he suffered along with and for sinners.
- Jesus also exhorted us to embrace the archetype's role when he told us to "turn the other cheek" if slapped (Lam. 3:30; Matt. 5:39). This link to Lamentations suggests that Jesus had more in

mind than just putting up with people patiently. We are to engage in redemptive suffering in a world engulfed by guilt and brutality.

- The prayer of the people (vv. 42–47) does not rise to the level of faith exemplified by the one, the archetype, but it eloquently describes the historical suffering of the Jews.

The archetype continued to face hostility down to the end of the poem, but analogies in the Old Testament suggest that this hostility was primarily from fellow Israelites. This, too, is ultimately fulfilled in Jesus, but it also has many analogies from the lives of the prophets.

## PREACHING AND TEACHING STRATEGIES

### *Exegetical and Theological Synthesis*

The archetype is both an example of how to cope with present suffering and the ultimate fulfillment of the suffering servant archetype who suffers for our sins. The archetype shows us how to react and how to trust God in the midst of the suffering caused by sin around us and how to cope with our own pain.

This suffering of God's servant is clearly demonstrated for us by Christ suffering for our sins. We can embrace this poem of suffering as an example of how to suffer, and as a call to fully trust the fulfiller of the archetype of suffering for our salvation.

### *Preaching Idea*

Embrace (accept) the suffering and the Savior.

### *Contemporary Connections*

#### *What does it mean?*

"Life is hard and then you die." It is difficult to establish the source of this saying, but the sentiment or meaning has been around since the gate to the garden of Eden was shut. And yet, there is more to the biblical view of life being hard.

Buddy was an example to all. He led and loved his family, ran his own engineering firm, frequently competed in long-distance runs, faithfully taught the Bible, and loved those he taught. Then Buddy was in a major car accident. He found himself conscious but unable to move any part of his body. He could tell that more than likely he would be paralyzed. As the paramedics began to untangle him from the wreck, he told them, "Just let me die." They told him they could not do that. His worst fears were right; he was paralyzed from the neck down. The feeling of just wanting to die lingered for weeks, but as the months passed he began to accept his suffering and clung to hope in a sovereign Lord.

I was living out of state at that time, and by the time I could travel to see him several months had passed. I knew Buddy because we had taught a college Bible study class together. Though fifteen years my senior, he was always energetic and more full of life than I was. With this memory in mind, I stepped into the hospital room filled with a special bed, air-cooled mattress, and medical machines humming constantly and beeping occasionally. Buddy turned his head and greeted me with a smile revealing that though he was suffering, he was still Buddy. A therapist came in, so in keeping with ministerial etiquette, I began to step out of the room. But Buddy spoke up, "This is my friend who came a thousand miles to see me. Could we do the therapy later today?" The therapist was kind enough to reschedule.

Buddy and I talked about family and events as though we were in a coffee shop. Then after refreshing our relationship, we turned to the present struggle. Through shortness of breath, he told me the details of the wreck and his request to be left to die. He spoke of the long, hard journey in suffering. He paused, caught his breath, and then in a strong voice said, "I am glad this happened. No, really, because

I would have never known the intimate relationship with God that I have now. He is truly my only hope." Buddy embraced the example of the suffering servant, and fully trusted that servant in the midst of his own suffering.

### *Is it true?*

Elisabeth Kubler-Ross, in her 1969 book *On Death and Dying,* identified five stages of grief. This popular approach to grief helped to articulate different experiences when people suffer loss. Larry Sittser warns us that we must not take the stages as a pathway to get over the suffering (Sittser, 2004, 60). Suffering is part of living in this fallen world, and until God steps in we will never fully recover from suffering. To be sure there will be many moments of joy and even happiness, but suffering will not go away. Thus, this passage is all the more important. I have heard preachers say something like this for years: "We are either moving from suffering, or are in the midst of it, or will soon experience it." God, through this poem, doesn't give us an explanation; he gives us what we need far more: a way to approach suffering.

### *Now what?*

So how does a person endure suffering and come to the same conclusion, the same hope? The poet moves us through a progression of how to react in suffering: accept the suffering (vv. 1–20), hope in the suffering (vv. 21–39), repent while suffering (vv. 40–51), and trust through the suffering (vv. 52–66).

We must *accept* that we do suffer (vv. 1–20). Of course, the level of suffering varies with every person, but if we live in this world we will experience suffering. Often, we discount our suffering because it seems trivial when compared the suffering of others. Or, we pretend that it is not there, because we believe the lie given to Job by his friends: that suffering shows God's disfavor. Certainly, we must show compassion to those in extreme suffering, and not expect the same amount of care given to them, but this must not cause us to mask our suffering. Pain comes in many forms: a leg is broken by a harsh fall; a spirit is broken by a harsh word. We can't ignore the pain of a broken leg, but the pain of a broken spirit is often buried deep, and the suffering is there for years.

Only after we accept that we suffer can we realize the hope we have because of a faithful God who does give us grace even in the midst of suffering. We can *hope* in the suffering (vv. 21–39), but there is no need for hope if there is no suffering. The object of our hope is that God will bring an end to our suffering. However, we must be careful to remember that it is not the end of suffering that is the object of our hope; it is in the one who can bring an end. The setting for the poet was a great national sin that was linked to the suffering. Though our suffering may or may not be linked to sin, *repentance* is always in order this side of heaven. We need to repent even while we suffer (vv. 40–51). The last part of the poet's process is that of *trusting* that our Lord has heard our cry and that he will take action (vv. 52–66).

The poet gives us this personal example of how to suffer as a suffering servant, but far more. The greater theme of the suffering servant of YHWH points directly to Jesus, who suffered for us. He is the object of our hope and trust.

## *Creativity in Presentation*

Covering sixty-six verses in one sermon demands special care. If one is to read all of the verses, then care must be given to prepare the congregation to know how to listen. Summarizing the theme and explaining how the poet develops that theme before a section is read can enhance the ability to follow what is being read. Thus, the explanation could precede the reading rather than the more traditional way of reading the text first and then explaining it. The flow of the sermon/lesson could be: explaining the text, reading the text, and then applying the text. Another method to cover numerous verses in one session would be to summarize a section and read only key verses in that section.

The beginning example of Buddy is one of many of those who suffered and embraced the example of suffering and the Savior who gives hope in suffering. One that is well known is Joni Erickson Tada, who in her book *Joni: An Unforgettable Story* tells of being paralyzed as a teenager. A lesser known one is *Life, in Spite of Me* by Kristen Jane Anderson. Kristen tried to commit suicide, but God had other amazing plans for her.

It is best if the teacher/preacher relates an example that he/she knows personally, but it is very important to have a current example. If possible, an appropriate and personal testimony would add greatly to presenting the truth of this text. Here is one possible structure:

- Accept the suffering (vv. 1–20).
- Hope in the suffering (vv. 21–39).
- Repent while suffering (vv. 40–51).
- Trust through the suffering (vv. 52–66).

Embrace (accept) the suffering and the Savior.

## DISCUSSION QUESTIONS

1. Compare and contrast emotional, mental, and physical suffering.

2. When does one who suffers become self-absorbed?

3. What can help us from becoming self-absorbed when we suffer?

4. How does the suffering of others affect us? How should it affect us?

5. What can keep us from accepting our own suffering?

## Lamentations 4:1–22

### EXEGETICAL IDEA

This text is an unflinching presentation of the suffering, terror, and tragedy of Jerusalem's conquest and captivity. We must see the horrors of Jerusalem's fall for what they are, and not turn our heads and move on, simply saying that the people got the punishment they deserved. Although most of us are Gentile Christians, we read this as people who have been adopted into Israel and participate in both its promises and its tragedies.

### THEOLOGICAL FOCUS

The suffering of Jerusalem and the Jews for their apostasy is unspeakable, and yet must be spoken. We must not preach over this event coldly and clinically, and certainly not judgmentally, as though it had nothing to do with us. The poem calls on us to participate in their grief just as we would grieve some terrible shame and calamity that befell our great-grandparents.

### PREACHING IDEA

Really? Sin can do that?

### PREACHING POINTERS

This chapter contains some of the most horrifying images in the Bible, that of cannibalism. But the degradation plummets to depths that become unbelievably despicable: mothers boiling their children. In this lament the terrifying high cost of sin is graphically described.

The illustration of a frog in the pot of water over a flame which is gradually heated is often used to explain that little sins, uncorrected, can lead to a disaster, without the person even noticing that things are progressively getting worse. This chapter shatters the pot and lets the full heat of the results of sin come all at once. The horrific result of sin described in this passage should shock us and compel us to full obedience toward God, and to hold spiritual leaders accountable to do the same.

# FOURTH LAMENT (4:1–22)

## LITERARY STRUCTURE AND THEMES

Lamentations 1 focuses on the personification of Lady Zion. In Lamentations 2, the poet takes on the persona of a prophet. Lamentations 3 relates Zion's suffering through the eyes of the representative "archetype." But no such personal element is present in Lamentations 4. It is a simple, direct recounting of the horrors of Jerusalem's fall and the suffering of the Jewish people. This is the bleakest chapter of the book, and it forces the reader to look directly into the terrible abyss.

- ***The Plundered and Defiled City (4:1–10)***
- ***The Apostate Clergy (4:11–16)***
- ***The Distraught People (4:17–20)***
- ***A Warning to Edom (4:21–22)***

## EXPOSITION

### *The Plundered and Defiled City (4:1–10)*

**4:1–2.** Jerusalem has lost everything of value, including its gold, but especially its children. The tarnishing of the gold is probably metaphorical, not meaning that the gold has literally lost its luster but that it did its owners no good because plundering soldiers snatched it away. Interpreters wonder about the reference to "sacred stones," which would appear to refer to stones from the sanctuary or from the high priest's vestments (Exod. 28). Probably the sanctuary gems are those made doubly precious both because of their intrinsic value and because of their status as holy objects. But all Jerusalem's gems were plundered so violently and indiscriminately that some lie about in the streets. The invading hordes had no respect even for the sanctuary stones, and so they certainly had no respect for privately held wealth. Even so, the gold and gems serve primarily in juxtaposition to Jerusalem's most precious possession: its children (v. 2). The verses imply that Jerusalem lost her wealth but, even worse, lost her children, who are compared to clay vessels. Ordinary pottery was cheap, easily made, and disposable (something like paper bags today). In the crisis, the children were treated by the invaders as worthless, even though they were in fact Jerusalem's most precious possession.

**4:3–10.** This part of the poem focuses on the ravages of starvation. This could refer to the last days of the siege, when the city was starving, or to the aftermath of the siege, when the survivors in the plundered city struggled desperately for food. From verse 2, we might have supposed that it was only the invaders who despised the lives of the children, but it turns out that even their parents, made desperate by starvation and terror, turned against them. Jackals, because of their vicious demeanor and pack tactics, are presented as especially despicable predators (lions, by contrast, are sometimes presented as awesome animals or even as a metaphor for God). But even jackals know how to treat their young, while Jerusalem's people have abandoned parental duty and compassion. The ostrich is proverbial for its indifference to the well-being of its eggs ; this is the example the people of Jerusalem have followed (v. 3). The children perish from thirst and hunger, and no one shows them compassion (v. 4). Verse 5 states that even the most powerful and wealthy of citizens have been reduced to desperation. The wearing of "purple"

(עֲלֹות) does not necessarily refer to members of the royal family; it describes anyone who could afford very expensive clothing.

Verse 6 is difficult. It literally says, "The iniquity (עָוֹן) of my fair people is greater than the sin (חַטָּאת) of Sodom, / [which was] overturned seemingly in an instant, with no hands twisting [חול] in/against her (בָּהּ)." Does the verse mean that Jerusalem's sin was worse than Sodom's, or that her punishment was worse than Sodom's? And what is meant by hands twisting in or against Sodom? Regarding the second line, it probably means that Sodom fell without any human hands fighting against her. By analogy, Hosea 11:6 says, "A sword twists (חול) against (בְּ) his cities" (Salters 2010, 298–99). This implies that the whole verse means that Jerusalem's punishment was worse than Sodom's, because Sodom fell quickly and without any invading army to prolong the suffering of the people. Jerusalem, by contrast, endured a lengthy siege with mass starvation at the hands of a bitter enemy.

Verses 7 and 8 speak of the terrible effects of malnourishment upon the nobility. The word נָזִיר here means "leader" and not "Nazirite," as it makes little sense to speak of Nazirites in this context, and the word נָזִיר can mean "leader." In both Genesis 49:26 and Deuteronomy 33:16, for example, Joseph is called the נְזִיר אֶחָיו, the "leader of his brothers." The aristocrats, whose bodies fairly shined because they were in such good health, have become blackened, shriveled, and dry through famine. The starvation that wracked the city was so bad that those who were struck down by the sword were better off (v. 9). Their vitality flowed away (זוב) painfully slowly, as if in prolonged torture. The verb זוב can be used of some slow bodily discharge, such as an infection or menstruation (Lev. 15:4, 6–9, 11–13, 19, 25, 32). It here describes the extended ebbing of life in famine conditions. The most horrific example of what starvation means appears in verse 10, in which women cook and devour their own children. This forms an inclusion structure: verses 3–4 speak of people refusing to share food with their children, and verse 10 says they cannibalized their own offspring. This whole section, in fact, has a carefully developed structure:

Introduction: Jerusalem has lost everything (vv. 1–2)
A' Starving children receive no compassion (vv. 3–4)
  B Upper classes starving (v. 5)
    C Punishment by starvation is terrible because prolonged (v. 6)
  B' Upper classes starving (vv. 7–8)
    C' Punishment by starvation is terrible because prolonged (v. 6)
A" Children eaten by starving parents (v. 10)

### *The Apostate Clergy (4:11–16)*

**4:11–12**. The destruction of Jerusalem was a terrible work of God. These two verses are a fairly conventional description of such a calamity: YHWH's wrath was like a consuming fire, and the destruction was so complete that the surrounding nations were astonished and appalled.

**4:13**. This verse is distinctive for placing the blame for the disaster entirely at the feet of Judah's prophets and priests. The leadership, teaching, and example provided by these men determined the direction the populace would go, and for that the guilt of the clergy was all the greater. Of course, this does not mean that the poet regarded the aristocracy or the common people as blameless, but the strong focus on the guilt of the religious leadership is striking (by contrast, 1 and 2 Kings evaluate every generation of Israelites by the behavior of its kings). The poet asserts that if those who ministered in YHWH's name had remained faithful, they could have withstood the apostasy of the upper class and the superstition of the people. Instead, the clergy led the way into apostasy.

**4:14–16**. As retribution for their sin, Jerusalem's holiest men have now become the scum of the earth. They wander as if blind (v. 14)—an appropriate punishment for those who were once the guides of the people (Matt. 23:16, 24). It is difficult to know whether the "blood" that defiled them should be taken literally, meaning that the priests and prophets had committed acts of violence. It is certainly possible; a corrupt religious leadership will resort to thuggish behavior (as in the crucifixion of Jesus). However, the "blood" that defiled the clergy may refer to how their bad teaching and example enticed Judah into apostasy and thus into judgment. When ministers pervert the word of God, people will perish, and the clergy will have blood on their hands. Being defiled by the deaths they have caused, the priests and prophets, who ought to be the most holy of men, are the most defiled. Their own clothing pollutes them, and wherever they go, they shout (or ought to shout) that they are unclean, and that people should stay far away. Even the Gentiles, sensing something repugnant about them, are loath to have them in their presence (v. 15). We should note that this passage is metaphorical; they did not literally walk about covered in blood and shouting that they were unclean. The verse asserts that they are rejected by both God and people, as if all could see on their clothing the blood of the people whose lives they destroyed.

*THE TRANSLATION OF 4:14*

The second line of 4:14 is very difficult: בְּלֹא יוּכְלוּ יִגְּעוּ בִּלְבֻשֵׁיהֶם. The form בְּלֹא normally means "without" and is typically followed by a noun; here it is followed by a *yiqtol* verb. The only apparent parallel to this is in Jeremiah 2:11, but this is not a true parallel, since the בְּ in that verse is a בְּ of price; this cannot be the case in Lamentations 4:14. The verb יוּכְלוּ ("they should be able," from יכל) would be easy to work with if it were followed by an infinitive, as is normal, but it is followed by another *yiqtol* verb, יִגְּעוּ ("they should touch," from נגע). This has no clear parallel in biblical Hebrew. (Numbers 22:6 has a possible parallel, but its apparent *yiqtol* verb, נַכֶּה, is probably an otherwise unattested piel infinitive.) Thus, the line appears to be unintelligible: "Without they should be able they should touch their clothes." Scholars have sought to unravel the problem, but no solution is certain (Berlin 2004, 100; Salters 2010, 317–18; Hillers 2008, 142–43; Parry 2010, 130). Interpreters also differ over who cannot touch the garments, whether it should be the priests themselves or the common people. In my view, it means that the religious leaders cannot touch their own clothing. The verse, although highly elliptical, can be rendered, "They wander blind in the streets; they are defiled by blood to the degree that they are not able [even that] they could touch their [own] garments." In other words, the priests and prophets cannot touch their own clothes due to the extreme defilement of guilt they contain, and they certainly cannot allow anyone else touch them. This interpretation offers an expansive translation of בְּלֹא, taking the בְּ to mean "in [that]" and thus "to the degree that," but it does the least violence to the text.

### *The Distraught People (4:17–20)*

As verses 11–16 described the guilt and punishment of the clergy, so verses 17–21 describe the distress of the people. Here, for the first time in chapter 4, the perspective is first person. Up to this point, the account has been a quasi-objective, detached account of how severely Jerusalem has suffered. The switch to a first-person plural perspective communicates the despair and anger of the Jewish people. Doing so, it adds pathos to what is already a bleak and terrible account of Jerusalem's experience.

**4:17**. The nations have been brutal to the refugee Jews. The Jews continue to suffer and long for salvation (see translation note below). Verse 17 speaks of the betrayal they felt from nations who had promised them aid (Egypt had promised to rescue Jerusalem from the

Babylonians). Although they watched intently for signs of that their ally was coming to save them, no help was forthcoming. But Egypt is not named in the verse. Therefore, the verse probably speaks of more than the historical situation; it foreshadows a long history of Jews looking in vain for help from the nations.

*THE TRANSLATION OF 4:17*

The opening word of this verse has perplexed interpreters. The *kethiv* is עוֹדֵינָה, "Still she." The *qere* is עוֹדֵינוּ, "Still we." It is difficult to know what to make of the *kethiv*, although it is defended by some (Salters 2010, 324). Another possibility is to reject both readings and emend the text, changing the ד to ר and reading עָרְנוּ from II-עור. This is then interpreted to mean, "We stay alert" or "We kept watch" (Hillers 2008, 144). But this has little to commend it. The most reasonable course is to follow the *qere*. But this poses a problem. One would expect to see a participle, adjective, or some other complement after עוֹדֵינוּ, as in Genesis 46:30, עוֹדְךָ חָי ("you are still alive"); or 1 Kings 1:22, עוֹדֶנָּה מְדַבֶּרֶת ("while she was still speaking"). What are we to make of עוֹדֵינוּ by itself? First, "Still we . . ." makes for a powerful shift to the first person, which, as noted above, begins with this verse. Second, it is a case of anacoluthon, a rhetorical device in which a grammatical construction is broken off half-way through, as in "What do you mean by. . . . How can you say such a thing?" The first line of the verse thus means, "Still we . . . Our eyes have failed, [looking] in vain for help." The opening "Still we" also conveys a sense of ongoing suffering and longing for deliverance.

**4:18–19**. Indeed, instead of helping them, the Gentiles hunt them down. Verse 18 begins, "They hounded our steps" (צָדוּ צְעָדֵינוּ; note the assonance, the wordplay of similar sounds, in the Hebrew poetry). The hostility of the Gentiles was so intense that the Jews could not walk outside in their own neighborhoods (מִלֶּכֶת בִּרְחֹבֹתֵינוּ, "[preventing us] from walking in our open areas"). Although this may have had immediate application in the days immediately after the fall of Jerusalem, when both enemy soldiers and predatory scavengers flooded the city, it has continued to be true in the Jewish experience in cities around the world. The situation is so bad, the verse asserts, that they lose hope in their continued existence as a people: "Our end is near; our days are finished, for our end has come" (קָרַב קִצֵּנוּ מָלְאוּ יָמֵינוּ כִּי־בָא קִצֵּנוּ). Verse 19 adds that their enemies are powerful, relentless, and everywhere. Escape is not a possibility.

**4:20**. There are two problems here. First, which "anointed" does the text speak of? Candidates include (1) Josiah, who was slain by Pharaoh Neco in 609 (2 Kings 23:29); (2) Jehoiachin, who was taken captive by Nebuchadnezzar in 597 and remembered as Jerusalem's last surviving king (Jer. 52:31–34); and (3) Zedekiah, who was on the throne when Jerusalem fell in 586 and who, while fleeing, was captured by Nebuchadnezzar's forces (Jer. 52:5–11). The Targum identifies Josiah as the anointed king of Lamentations 4:20, but it almost certainly makes this claim because of Josiah's famous piety. Apparently the Targumist thought that only a righteous king could be spoken of in such glowing terms, but this is not correct. The verse speaks of the significance of the office of the "anointed of YHWH" and not of the virtues of a specific person. It is also unlikely that Lamentations looks back to the death of Josiah, an event that took place more than two decades before Jerusalem fell. And although Jehoiachin was taken captive, the city still stood and the temple still functioned, and a Davidic monarch (Zedekiah) still sat on the throne. To the extent that any specific king is intended in the verse, it must be Zedekiah (and only he was hunted down and violently captured). But as noted in the Introduction, this verse does not imply that the poet was a political supporter of Zedekiah. Second, the verse says, "The anointed of YHWH was captured in their pits (בִּשְׁחִיתוֹתָם)." Why is "pits" plural? Also, none of the aforementioned kings was taken in a pit. The plural probably points to the fact that this is a metaphor and that it is focused on a general truth: the end of the Davidic dynasty. The verse alludes to Zedekiah's capture, but it mourns the fall of the Davidic dynasty. Clinging to the promises of 2 Samuel 7, the people of Jerusalem believed that their city and king, however bad things may have looked, was effectively invulnerable. This sense of invulnerability was reinforced in the Assyrian crisis, when YHWH slew the army of Sennacherib (Isa. 36–37). God had after all chosen the line of David to reign forever and had promised that all the nations would submit to their king's authority, a point clearly made in Psalm 2. The son of David was YHWH's anointed, and no one could imagine how, in light of the divine promise, Jerusalem could fall and the dynasty could end. And yet this had happened. One need only read Psalm 89 to see what a crisis of faith this was for the Jewish people.

### *A Warning to Edom (4:21–22)*

**4:21–22**. Edom's triumph will be short-lived. They "rejoice" because Jerusalem, their historic enemy, has fallen. But soon they too will drink the "cup," a metaphor for being subjugated by a world-conqueror (see Jer. 25:15–29; Obad. 16; Hab. 2:15–16; Zech. 12:2). As Jerusalem was stripped naked and raped, so too will Edom be. What's more, Jerusalem's suffering will finally end, but Edom's will not. The Jews would survive and continue, whereas the Edomites, in the course of time, would be exterminated and cease to exist as a people. But it is surprising to us that Lamentations includes a harsh condemnation explicitly directed at Edom, a very minor state, and includes a prediction of its demise. And yet it never mentions Babylon, the enemy that destroyed Jerusalem, or Egypt, the nation that proved to be a false friend (although various passages imply accusations against these enemies). Why is Edom, alone of all the nations, made an *explicit* target in Lamentations? Historically, Edom and Israel were rivals from the beginning. The twin brothers Esau and Jacob struggled for supremacy, and Edom refused Israel passage into Canaan (Num. 20:21). David conquered Edom (2 Sam. 8:14), but they gradually gained independence, and late in the preexilic period Edom began to encroach on Judah's territory (Salters 2010, 335). Obadiah 11–14 implies that Edom exploited Judah's prostrate condition when Jerusalem fell (see also Ezek. 35:1–15; 36:5). For all of that, it is still strange that Edom is singled out for a direct attack while other states that were also historical enemies go unnamed. The answer seems to be that Edom occupies a peculiar position in the Old Testament: it represents all the nations in their hostility to Israel. Thus, for example, Isaiah 63:1 describes YHWH's great eschatological triumph over the nations as a slaughter of Edomites: "Who is this who comes from Edom [and] from Bozrah with his garments stained red? / His [bloody] apparel honors him; he moves forward with great power. / [Saying] 'I, [YHWH], speak with righteousness [and] am mighty to save.'" The use of Edom as a cipher for all nations is enhanced by the spelling of the name (אדם), which can also mean "humanity." Amos 9:11–12 makes use of this in a salvation oracle, in which the "remnant of Edom" represents all persons from every nation who will call on YHWH's name (see Acts 15:16–17). Here in Lamentations, therefore, the condemnation is in one sense directed at historical Edom but at the same time condemns all enemies of the Jews throughout history.

## THEOLOGICAL FOCUS

This text is a catalogue of Jerusalem's agony, and it is suggestive of the long-term suffering of the Jewish people. That, however, is a topic we will explore in the theological emphases of chapter 5. This chapter, with its stark depiction of human misery, allows us to look at the topics of suffering and the plan of God more broadly and generically.

- Sin and suffering create a downward spiral. The apostasy of Jerusalem led to the Babylonian siege, which in turn created starvation in the city, which in turn led people to commit horrible atrocities, including cannibalism. The people of the city were not crueler than all others, and they did not easily resort to eating their own children. But intense suffering leads to a kind of madness, in which people do what they otherwise would not. Examples of such downward spirals are all around us, even if they are not so dramatic as cannibalism. Conflict in families leads parents and children to say and do foolish things, which in turn leads to more anger, hurt, and further acts of evil folly.
- Apostasy by the clergy has far-reaching effects. If they fall away, society is sure to follow.
- Our hold on dignity and prestige is tenuous. The priests of Jerusalem were sacred persons; their need to avoid ritual impurity required all to treat them with utmost deference. But as the city collapsed they, like everyone else, became foul scavengers and were despised by outsiders as unclean. When we hold to a position of some dignity, we start to think of it as our birthright, little recognizing how quickly we could lose it all.
- The ancient Israelites thought that the plan of God could not possibly go forward without a strong Jerusalem under a Davidic king, just as the Jews of Jesus's time were sure that the messianic kingdom would involve the triumphant exaltation of the Jews and their city. Both were wrong, and in both cases the will of God involved taking the people through horrible suffering. We should always be cautious about thinking we know the plan of God—especially when our interpretation involves us escaping all suffering.

## PREACHING AND TEACHING STRATEGIES

### *Exegetical and Theological Synthesis*

When a person describes an event in their lives that is hard to believe, a common verbal response is "Really?" It is almost a challenge to the speaker that what they are saying couldn't really have happened. When the results of sin listed in this passage reach the deepest of pits, describing mothers boiling their own children, we can't help but say, "Yes, really." Surely this did not happen. But it did.

While being sensitive to our audiences, this passage must be proclaimed. Sin does lead to disaster. As teachers of the Word, we must not leave this as just a description of horrific effects of sin, but we must move to how this can and should motivate us to take sin seriously—even the so-called little sins.

### *Preaching Idea*

Really? Sin can do that?

### *Contemporary Connections*

#### *What does it mean?*

At my house we have a septic system that has three tanks. The first tank holds the foulest contents, the second is less harsh but still putrid, and the third amazingly has relatively clear water. I don't like it, but I have looked down into the third tank on occasion when chemicals or a routine inspection are necessary. It has a rusty pump, connection pipes, wires, a relatively mild smell, and that hollow sound of dripping water. It's nothing that bad, but I still don't like to look down into that pit, and I always close it up as quickly as I can.

When there is a more serious issue, I call the service technician. Most often, he must open the second pit. He opens the lid and looks deeply into the filth and stench. When that happens, I have no desire to look even for a moment into that pit of human waste. But the technician, being a good repairman, will call me over to show me the problem that he is about to fix. I'll look, but ever-so-quickly at the brown, smelly, utterly unpleasant pit of human waste. In chapter 4 the poet of Lamentations opens the pit for us to see the most catastrophic and horrific consequences of sin. And we must look.

### *Is it true?*

Can sin really lead us to such horrific depths? We can easily answer yes, but that usually only when we are looking at sin in the life of others, or when we look back on own long-past experiences. The drug addict can see that the recreational experimentation with drugs led to the addition. The habitual liar can see that so-called white lies led to bigger ones. The extremely obese person did not gain fifty pounds in one week. All these can be seen after the fact. This passage is telling us to see the disaster before it happens. Can sin really lead to something unthinkable? Paul Tripp, in his book *New Morning Mercies,* says, "Sin brings with it a functional insanity" (Tripp, 2014, reading for September 2). Sin can lead us to do things that we not only never thought we *would* do, but can even lead us to do things we never thought we *could* do. The illustration of the frog in the kettle mentioned above can be used, and then altered to say that God wants us to feel the devastating heat through the shocking images in this passage.

### *Now what?*

It is like a wake-up call. Talent shows are currently a popular form of entertainment. Part of the conflict and tension of such talent shows is that the hosts seem to enjoy making fun of the less talented or awkward performers. A delightful surprise took place some years ago when Susan Boyle appeared. She had a homely appearance and frumpy demeanor, which caused the hosts to raise eyebrows as though she had no right to be there. But when she opened her mouth, and her amazing voice came out, it stunned both the audience and the mocking hosts. One host said that it was a wake-up call to their smugness.

Wake-up calls don't come gradually. They are not like the dawn that gradually and gently brings in the light. Wake-up calls stun us. Chapter 4 continues in the presentation of the destruction of Jerusalem, but the cannibalism by mothers of their own children hits us like a 2 a.m. phone call to parents of teenagers. One reads it and can't believe what was just said. Really, this is where sin takes us?

When we take the time to look deeply into pain around us—child abuse, spousal abuse, human trafficking—the results of sin are horrific. We need to remember that we are just one choice away from causing or experiencing this painful pit of sin. Our response should be to run from any form of sin. But we like to play with it. So we flirt a little with a coworker; forgetting that the results can be horrific. We like to try just a little bit of sin, so we tell the off-color joke to fit in, just this once. We linger on a particular website because we like the short-lived satisfaction. God draws our attention to this pit and says, "Wake up! Look down into the pit of sin and be horrified!" In the closing section, when the poet addresses Edom, the poet is reminding us that there is an end to this horrific scene. The suffering and pain of sin have an end or purpose: to drive us to God. He doesn't want us to stay horrified; rather, he wants us to run from sin and be glorified in us.

## ***Creativity in Presentation***

This is perhaps the most difficult chapter in all of Jeremiah and Lamentations to read out loud. Depending upon how one handles the details of this chapter, it might be wise to alert parents of younger children as to the graphic nature of this chapter.

In keeping with the emotion of this text, the teacher/pastor should strive to let the shocking climax of the first section be felt in the preaching and/or teaching. In order to do this, there should be hints that this chapter goes from bad to worse. For example, the reference to children in verse 3 is a harsh foreshadowing of the corresponding horror of verse 10. The anticipation that the worst is coming creates an expectation in the congregation—for something bad, but not as bad as maternal cannibalism. When that is read, the expectation heightens the shock factor. We were expecting something bad, but not this horrific.

There are two subpoints that flow from the major image of the first section. The first concerns the spiritual leaders. Since the results of sin are so horrific, the leaders of that day and of our day must be held accountable. The last section, which is an address to Edom, has a word to Israel within it: there will be an end to the exile and the discipline of God. That end indicates a purpose for the harshness of this chapter. God wants us to see the horrific results of sin so that we will return to him, or perhaps turn to him for the first time. This is the call to repentance, to salvation for the lost and repentance of believers back to obedience to God. It is a harsh wake-up call.

The preaching idea is written as two questions; thus, when spoken, one should use a rising inflexion. At the end the idea becomes a statement which should be spoken with a falling inflexion of authority. Here is one possible structure:

- Really? Sin can do that?
- The results of sin are horrific (vv. 1–10).
  - Therefore, make sure that . . .
- Spiritual leaders must be held accountable for sins (vv. 11–16).
  - And, remember that . . .
- God has a purpose or end to the discipline of sin (vv. 17–22).
- Sin can do that much evil. Really.

## DISCUSSION QUESTIONS

1. When have you been shocked by an event or situation?
2. What were some of the responses you observed in others and in yourself during that time?
3. What are some appropriate ways to hold spiritual leaders accountable?
4. What are some of the foulest things we experience? How are these like the results of sin?
5. Why don't we instinctively run from sin like we run from these foul experiences?

## Lamentations 5:1–22

### EXEGETICAL IDEA

The poem is entirely a prayer, and it appeals to God to end the Jewish suffering. The interpreter must not emphasize ideas that are only slightly present, if present at all. The poem accurately reflects the grief and bewilderment of the Jewish people, but it says little about the apostasy that brought the disaster upon them. One should read the prayer sympathetically but not deny that something is missing in the prayer.

### THEOLOGICAL FOCUS

The Jews will continue to suffer abuse until the great day of their redemption occurs. This is not an occasion for triumphalist boasting against the Jews. It is a sad recognition, in the spirit of Romans 9–11, that Israel's travail will continue until they look upon him whom they have pierced (Zech. 12:10).

### PREACHING IDEA

When we suffer because of sin, seek God more than the end of the suffering.

### PREACHING POINTERS

"Lord, remember" and "Lord, restore"—these are the two prayers of this closing lament. In between these two short prayers is the description of Israel's sufferings and their confessions of the sin that led to the suffering. Israel cries out to God for help, and she cries out to God in confession.

The ending of this book of painful experiences is not what most of us would write. When we are hurting, our loudest cry is for the pain to stop. To be sure, there is physical pain that is so intense that every part of our being—mental, spiritual, and physical—will do everything to end the pain. But when there is pain that comes from God's hand due to sin, our cry should not be "Lord, stop the pain." It should be "Lord, restore me . . . to you."

# FIFTH LAMENT (5:1–22)

## LITERARY STRUCTURE AND THEMES

This is the shortest poem of Lamentations, and it is entirely a prayer. It is a "quasi-acrostic," being twenty-two verses long (equal to the number of letters in the Hebrew alphabet) but not acrostic. As mentioned in the Introduction, acrostics often are instructional, and it may have been thought improper to compose what might appear to be a set of instructions for God.

- ***The Opening Appeal to God (5:1)***
- ***An Account of the Suffering of the People (5:2–18)***
- ***The Closing Appeal to God (5:19–22)***

## EXPOSITION

### *The Opening Appeal to God (5:1)*

**5:1**. The prayer calls on God to pay attention to what has happened. Two specific focal points are the suffering they have endured ("what has happened to us" [מֶה־הָיָה לָנוּ]) and the shame that has come upon them ("our disgrace" [חֶרְפָּתֵנוּ]). The appeal for God to "remember" (זְכֹר) is also an appeal for him to act on their behalf (see Ps. 74:18–23).

### *An Account of the Suffering of the People (5:2–18)*

**5:2–6**. The starving refugees are exploited by the nations. First, their enemies took away their land and homes (v. 2). Second, they are like orphans and widows, meaning that they had no source of income (v. 3). In ancient Israel, the husband/father was responsible for providing for his family, and an orphan or widow was destitute. Now all the surviving Israelites, including the adult males who once owned property, are destitute. Third, no one will give them even the most meager charity, such as water to drink or wood for a fire; they must find some way to pay for it (v. 4). Fourth, hostile people continue to chase them down to exploit or abuse them, and they have no refuge or rest (v. 5). Fifth, they had to make humiliating agreements with their ancient enemies seeking help, but it did them no good (v. 6). It is surprising that this verse refers to Assyria, which was long gone by the time of the Babylonian captivity; but it is retrospective, looking back to how Judah had through the years sought aid from foreign powers. For example, Ahaz had sought the support of Tiglath-pileser of Assyria during the Syro-Ephraimite war. The Assyrians did defeat Damascus and Samaria, saving Judah from an immediate threat, but they soon turned on Judah and ravaged the country, as described in Isaiah 7.

**5:7**. We bear the price of our ancestors' sins, the prayer declares. Commentators routinely compare this verse to Jeremiah 31:28–29 and the more developed analysis in Ezekiel 18, which criticize the people for trying to shift all the blame for the calamity to earlier generations, saying, "The parents have eaten sour grapes, and the children's teeth are set on edge." The similarity is real and should not be downplayed; Lamentations 5:7 is not entirely different from the other texts. But we can make certain observations. First, in agreement with Jeremiah and Ezekiel, it is never wise to blame all of your problems on your parents or anyone else, acting as though you had no responsibility for the course of your own life. Second, however, it is true that the sins of the parents can have terrible repercussions on the children. Any parent who commits a crime and goes to prison brings many sorrows upon his or her children, for example. Third, this verse is a frank statement of the Jewish distress over their longstanding suffering and exile. The Jews of the last 1,900 years had no role in the events that led up to the first and second destructions of Jerusalem, but their exile and persecution have nevertheless continued.

**5:8–10**. The refugees face brutality, violence, and exposure. The claim that "slaves rule us" (v. 8) is most likely literal and not metaphorical (for a survey of views, see House 2004, 464). The term "slaves" does not refer to the Babylonians or any other nation, as though the poet were calling those nations "slaves" to show how he despises them. Instead, it speaks of how common slaves on estates viewed themselves as superior to the Jewish refugees who wandered from place to place seeking help. The slaves on estates owned by rich Gentiles serve as gatekeepers for their masters, and they spitefully enjoy the chance to domineer over someone else. Verse 9 speaks of the poverty and hunger of the Jewish refugees, but interpreters have puzzled over the expression "sword of the wilderness." Once again, this is probably to be taken more or less literally, referring to gangs of outlaws who haunted the roads in remote areas (against Berlin 2004, 121). The Jews of the diaspora, wandering from place to place in search of a homeland, are in danger even when trying to get from one hostile territory to another. In addition, they suffer from exposure to the elements when out on the road (v. 10). In the ancient Near East, this meant burning under the sun and suffering from hunger and thirst. This passage not only looks back to the Babylonian sack of Jerusalem but also forward to the Jewish experience of being wandering refugees, perpetual aliens in the lands they inhabit.

**5:11–14**. Refugees of every class suffer abuse. Jewish leaders, who ought to receive special respect, receive none; they suffer brutality instead. Jewish women are raped, suffering physical violence and the most profound humiliation (v. 11). Jewish aristocrats are treated like criminals (v. 12). They were hung up by their hands, implying the abuse, torture, and possible execution that might normally be reserved for criminals only. Their young men, normally the glory and strength of the nation and also the hope for a bright future, work as the lowest of slaves. They toil at millstones, grinding the grain, and carry wood meant to fuel fires. The normal activities of Jerusalem's social life have ceased (v. 14). Elders no longer sit at the city gate to adjudicate matters, and young men no longer play music and dance. In speaking of "women" and "virgins" (נָשִׁים and בְּתֻלֹת; v. 11), "officials" and "elders" (שָׂרִים and זְקֵנִים; v. 12), "young men" and "boys" (בַּחוּרִים and נְעָרִים; v. 13), and again "elders" and "young men" (v. 14), the passage alludes to an idealized portrait of how things ought to be, with people of every status fulfilling their roles in society with dignity and in security. Every group is now broken and humiliated.

**5:15–18**. All joy is gone from their lives. Verse 15 is a general statement, and verses 16–18 are more specific. The word "crown" (עֲטָרָה) sometimes refers to a king's crown (2 Sam. 12:30; 1 Chron. 20:2; Jer. 13:18), but it might be a garland worn by ordinary people at a time of celebration (Isa. 28:1) or a kind of tiara, either worn as a piece of jewelry or bestowed upon someone as a mark of honor (Ezek. 16:12; Esth. 8:15). It is sometimes used metaphorically for a person's glory (Job 19:9; Prov. 4:9; 12:4; 16:31). In Proverbs 17:6, grandchildren are the "crown" of the aged. Here in Lamentations 5:16, while the crown could be a metaphor for Zion (Isa. 62:3), it is probably a metaphor for one's dignity and happiness. In verse 17, the calamities that have befallen Jerusalem make the people's hearts weak and their eyes dim. By mixing a singular "because of this" (עַל־זֶה) with a plural "because of these things" (עַל־אֵלֶּה), the poet indicates that there is not some single, specific event that has caused sorrow. More broadly and generally, all the troubles that befell them have broken them. The weakness of the heart and darkening of the vision may be no more than a poetic expression of their grief, but it could imply that the burden of sorrow is so great that they are dying. There is, however, one specific event that has struck them more deeply than any other: the fall of Jerusalem and the temple (v. 18). To them, Jerusalem was the earthly city of God. Seeing it now as a desolation and the home of jackals is tantamount to it becoming the domain of demons.

### *The Closing Appeal to God (5:19–22)*

**5:19–20**. God's power is sufficient to end their suffering, but he seems to be paying no attention to the Jews. Verse 19 is a standard confession that YHWH is the eternal sovereign over the earth (Ps. 9:7 [MT 8]; 45:7; 102:12 [MT 13]). In this context, it is a profound confession of faith. An ancient person, by contrast, might assume that Babylon defeated Judah because it had stronger gods, but this passage rejects any such notion. Also, this verse affirms that the fall of the temple does not in any way weaken YHWH. "God is not physically or spatially limited to his temple, and his existence does not depend on a physical structure. Nor can he be carried off like the statues of pagan gods were when their countries were conquered" (Berlin 2004, 125). Even so, the main point of the verse is not to assert that God is in his heaven and all is well; it is, instead, the basis for the complaint in verse 20: since God is so powerful and yet has done nothing to save us, we can only wonder if he has abandoned us. In the Psalms, someone in deep distress may speak to God very boldly, as in the "My God, my God, why have you forsaken me?" of Psalm 22:1. Even so, there is more to Lamentations 5:20 than a powerful complaint. The verse takes a long view, asking if God has forgotten them forever. This suggests not just the tragedy of the Babylonian exile but the bewildered suffering of the Jews that has continued for generations.

**5:21–22**. If God does not restore them, the prayer suggests, perhaps he has completely rejected them. Verse 21 makes a simple appeal for God to restore and renew the Jewish exiles. The verb for "restore" (שׁוּב) can carry the connotation of repentance, so that 21a could be translated, "Bring us back to yourself, YHWH, so that we may repent." This alludes to the full restoration and repentance, including the circumcision of the heart, promised in Deuteronomy 30:1–10. This is the great day of Israel's eschatological salvation. In 5:22, however, the book has a surprisingly dark, open-ended conclusion. It could be translated, "But if you have completely rejected us / [and if] you are angry with us in the extreme . . ." This translation ends the book with a protasis that has no apodosis—an unanswered question (Linafelt 2001).

Lamentations has a bleak conclusion. The reason for this is that the book is not concerned primarily with individual, private piety. Its message is not like this: "When tragedy strikes, pray these prayers and put your faith in God, waiting for him to deliver you, and in due time all will be well." Plenty of Psalms have such a message and do relate to private and personal tragedies. Lamentations 5, however, is focused on the historical suffering of the Jewish people, not on private suffering. It looks across centuries and sees a repeated pattern of exile, persecution, and suffering. It therefore ends with an open question, wondering if and when God will do something to resolve this.

## THEOLOGICAL FOCUS

If we are to be true to the text of Lamentations, we must acknowledge that it is a book about Jewish suffering. It is not merely a historical reflection on how terrible the fall of Jerusalem was; nor is it a theological exposition of sin, punishment, and divine justice abstractly considered; nor is it a theological challenge to the justice of God. It is a lament for Jerusalem and the Jews.

- The severity of the punishment God inflicted on the Jews must make one wonder about God's justice, but to conclude that God is unjust is to disregard two important facts. First, all human life and happiness, and also the restraint of evil in the world, depend on the common grace of God. In a godless world, evil and suffering are the rule, not the exception. It is God's mercy that makes peace and safety appear to be normal. Second, the Jews are God's chosen people, and this implies great privilege and great responsibility: "You alone have I known of all the families of the earth; / therefore, I will punish you for all your iniquities" (Amos 3:2).
- The suffering of Israel does indeed show that God punishes evil, but using this as a simple lesson about sin and punishment neglects again the special place of Israel. God has punished some peoples by simply exterminating them (for example, the Assyrians). But this cannot be the case with the Jews, who have suffered everywhere, but endured. Their suffering may be exemplary, but it is also unique and contains elements that cannot be rendered abstract and applied generally to all.
- The prayer highlights how terribly the Jews have suffered, and it ought to evoke sympathy in the reader. All anti-Semitism is reprehensible, and no one has a right to add to Jewish pain on the grounds that they somehow deserve it. Christians must never attack Jews as "Christ-killers" or listen to rumors about Jewish conspiracies.
- The prayer issues a warning to nations that heap abuse upon the Jews. Indeed, anti-Semitism marks a people as particularly degenerate. As I write this, anti-Semitism is rising in America and throughout the west, particularly on the political left. This does not bode well for the future of these societies.
- The rhetorical question with which the book ends, asking if God has rejected them completely, can be answered with both a Yes and a No. They are God's people, but they have long existed as a people toward whom God seems especially hostile. Their alienation from God will persist until they mourn over the one whom they pierced and embrace Jesus as their Messiah (Zech. 12:10).

## PREACHING AND TEACHING STRATEGIES

### *Exegetical and Theological Synthesis*

When a physical pain becomes so great, we have the great benefit of going to an emergency room, be examined by a doctor, and often receive something to ease the pain. So it is understandable that we are conditioned to request that God make the pain stop. But that is not pattern of response given to us in this lament. After the acknowledgement of the pain and suffering that is Israel's (vv. 1–19), the poet cries out for the restoration to YHWH. It is the relationship that he is seeking to restore (v. 21), not merely the cessation of pain.

Just as God's nation disobeyed and he punished them for their disobedience, God still disciplines his people today. That doesn't mean that all pain is God's disciplining hand, but often God uses the pain that comes from sin to draw his children to himself.

### *Preaching Idea*

When we suffer because of sin, seek God more than seeking the end of the suffering.

### *Contemporary Connections*

#### *What does it mean?*

How do we respond when we find ourselves in the pain of God's disciplining hand? When we willfully step over a line into sin, the results loiter around our lives—be it a nonbiblical divorce, a foolish spending of money, or a lifelong unhealthy habit. While God certainly forgives, the pain of those sins can linger. What do we do with the residual pain? How do we cry out? And what do we say? The woman who cries at night because of the memory of an abortion, the young man who fights depression after spending two years in prison for vehicular manslaughter, the pastor who yearns to preach but his financial crimes with church monies prevents it . . . what do they say? Of course, our first response is to ask that the pain would stop: the pain of guilt, the pain of rejection, the pain of being so disappointed in ourselves, the pain of feeling we have no value. As with any pain, we want it to stop.

When the teenager in anger says that she hates her mother, God's spirit brings the pain of a broken relationship. The teenager runs to her room and as the anger subsides, still the tears flow because of the pain of guilt and a broken relationship. A young father chooses to stay late at work just to avoid the chaos of a household overrun with three preschoolers, but when he finally gets home and looks in on his now-sleeping children and his exhausted wife, he bows his head because of the pain of disappointment in himself. When a business owner lies to cover a mistake, the pain of that lie stays on his mind as he drives home, and later as he tries to go to sleep.

When pain comes because of sin, we need to seek for a restoration of our relationship to God, through repentance and confession, before we ask for the pain to be taken away. And then in the power of a restored relationship with God, we strive to correct the wrong and ask for forgiveness, and often the pain subsides. But if the pain still lingers, we need still seek the restoration of our relationship to God more than the relief from pain.

#### *Is it true?*

To better understand her husband, a wife read *Adult Children of Divorce* by Karen Sandvig. She knew that his parents' divorce thirty-five years earlier still affected him, but it would seem that after all this time the consequences of that divorce would no longer haunt him. Sandvig demonstrated to her that children will hurt all their lives because of a divorce by their parents. The focus of the book is on the children, but Sandvig's findings also point to the lifelong pain of the parents. The pain of divorce may subside in its intensity, but there is pain that never goes away this side of heaven.

Of course, we thank God for his forgiveness toward us. His sacrifice to take us out from under sin receives eternal gratitude. But in our culture, forgiveness can be equated with the taking away of the pain of sin and its current consequences. To say that forgiveness guarantees release from the consequences is to be presumptuous. God can use the extended pain of the consequences of sin to discipline us. This not only applies to divorce, but to any form of sexual sins. Teenagers who stepped over the line in this area in some way carry the pain all their lives. While the consequences of sexual sins are sometimes more noticeable, all sin has consequences. God often uses these consequences to discipline his children. In our rightful rejoicing over the forgiveness of sin, and the joy of the victory of the imputation of righteousness, we forget that God still disciplines His children (Heb. 12).

#### *Now what?*

When we are hurting, taking prescribed steps doesn't always appeal to us because of the complexities of regret, disappointment, guilt, and other unarticulated emotional pains. But there are some specifics that need to be mentioned, whether or not they are followed in this order. The closing petition is more descriptive than prescriptive, but we can still take some guidance from it.

1. Praise God's sovereign authority.
2. Acknowledge the pain of the discipline we are under. In this step, there are some implications that would accompany this action:
   a. confess (admit) the sin
   b. repent (turn from the sin)
   c. accept that the discipline is from God's good hand
3. Ask for restoration in humility.

As the poet closed the lament with the rhetorical question that shows his total submission to God's sovereignty, so we must not be presumptuous when we experience the disciplining hand of God. He clearly offers us forgiveness and a restored relationship through the work of Christ and the Spirit. But we should not demand that God stop the pain, for we are in no position to make demands.

In the garden, our Lord Jesus demonstrated this humble submissive spirit when he said, "not as I will, but as you will." He was in pain and facing even more excruciating pain—not because of his sin but because of ours. Asking for the pain to stop was affirmed by Jesus's request for the cup to pass, not as a demand but in submission to the relationship. The relationship to the Father was more important than the pain. C. S. Lewis stated it well in his essay "Petitionary Prayer": "The road may be hard but the map is clear" (Lewis 1967, 143).

### *Creativity in Presentation*

This passage has two short petitionary prayers (vv. 1, 19–22) with a summary of Israel's suffering in between them (vv. 2–18). The amount of sermon time given to the sections of this lament may be disproportionate. Though the prayers are only five of the twenty-two verses, they are the heart of the application and require more attention. The middle summary can be effectively presented by reading the text with some brief explanatory comments. The prayers at the beginning and the end can be treated almost as one point, for the tenor of the opening prayer is in keeping with the spirit of the closing rhetorical question. To honor the flow of the text, the opening prayer could be treated as a foreshadowing of the closing prayer. These examples of prayers in a time of pain are short in words, but long in application. Here is one possible structure:

- Summary petition: Lord, remember us (v. 1).
- Lord, here is our situation:
  - Israel's suffering (vv. 2–18)
  - Ways that we suffer today
- Lord, restore our relationship to you:
  - Praise (v. 19)
  - Acknowledge the pain (v. 20)
  - Ask for restoration (vv. 21–22)
- When we suffer because of sin, seek God more than seeking the end of the suffering.

## DISCUSSION QUESTIONS

1. What is the difference between pain and suffering?
2. What kind of pain do we experience because of our sin?
3. When you have physical pain that lingers, how do you cope with it?
4. Are relationships important when we are hurting? Why?

# REFERENCES


Ackerman, Jon. 2020. "Chiefs Claim Super Bowl LIV: Owner Clark Hunt Thanks the Lord, MVP Patrick Mahomes Aims to Glorify Him." Sports Spectrum, Feb. 3. https://sportsspectrum.com/sport/football/2020/02/03/chiefs-super-bowl-owner-clark-hunt-thanks-lord-mvp-patrick-mahomes-glorify-him.

Ackerman, Susan. 2006. "Queen of Heaven." In *The New Interpreter's Dictionary of the Bible*, edited by Katharine Doob Sakenfeld, 4.702. Nashville: Abingdon.

Ackroyd, Peter R. 1984. "The Book of Jeremiah: Some Recent Studies." *JSOT* 9 (28): 47–59.

Aejmelaeus, Anneli. 2002. "Jeremiah at the Turning-Point of History: The Function of Jer. XXV 1–14 in the Book of Jeremiah." *VT* 52 (4): 459–82.

________. 2017. "What Happened to the Text in Jer. 25:1–7?" *TC* 22 1–10.

Albrektson, Bertil. 1963. *Studies in the Text and Theology of the Book of Lamentations: With a Critical Edition of the Peshitta Text*. Lund: CWK Gleerup.

Allen, Leslie C. 2008. *Jeremiah*. Louisville: Westminster John Knox Press.

Althann, Robert. 1983. *A Philological Analysis of Jeremiah 4-6 in the Light of Northwest Semitic*. Rome: Biblical Institute Press.

Anderson, Kristen Jane. 2011. *Life, in Spite of Me: Extraordinary Hope after a Fatal Choice*. Colorado Springs: Multnomah.

Arnold, Patrick M. 1992. "Mizpah (Place)." In *The Anchor Bible Dictionary*, edited by David Noel Freedman, 4.879–81. New York: Doubleday.

Baker, David W. 1992. "Cushan (Place)." In *The Anchor Bible Dictionary*, edited by David Noel Freedman, 1.1219–20. New York: Doubleday.

Berlin, Adele. 2004. *Lamentations: A Commentary*. Louisville: Westminster John Knox Press.

Berridge, John M. 1992a. "Jehoiakim (Person)." In *The Anchor Bible Dictionary*, edited by David Noel Freedman, 3.664–66. New York: Doubleday.

Berridge, John M. 1992b. "Jehudi (Person)." In *The Anchor Bible Dictionary*, edited by David Noel Freedman, 3.674. New York: Doubleday.

Bier, Miriam. 2014. "'We Have Sinned and Rebelled; You Have Not Forgiven': The Dialogic Interaction Between Authoritative and Internally Persuasive Discourse in Lamentations 3." *Biblical Interpretation* 22 (2): 146–67.

Billings, J. Todd. 2010. *The Word of God for the People of God*. Grand Rapids: Eerdmans.

Blomberg, Craig L. 1992. *Matthew*. Nashville: Broadman.

Boase, Elizabeth. 2006. *The Fulfilment of Doom? The Dialogic Interaction between the Book of Lamentations and the Pre-Exilic/Early Exilic Prophetic Literature*. New York: T & T Clark.

Bright, John. 1963. *Jeremiah*. Lund: CWK Gleerup.

Buttry, Daniel. 2011. *Blessed Are the Peacemakers*. Canton, MI: Spirit Books.

Campbell, Robert C. 1933. *Modern Evils*. New York: Revell.

Carroll, Robert P. 1986. *Jeremiah: A Commentary*. Philadelphia: Westminster Press.

Charny, Israel W. 2018. "The Nature of Man: Is Man by Nature Good, or Basically Bad?" *Psychology Today*. https://www.psychologytoday.com/us/blog/warrior-life/201803/the-nature-man-is-man-nature-good-or-basically-bad.

Christensen, Duane L. 1990. "In Quest of the Autograph of the Book of Jeremiah: A Study of Jeremiah 25 in Relation to Jeremiah 46–51." *JETS* 33 (2): 145–53.

Craigie, Peter C., Page H. Kelley, and Joel F. Drinkard Jr. 1991. *Jeremiah 1–25*. Dallas: Word Books.

Crenshaw, James L. 1983. "A Living Tradition: The Book of Jeremiah in Current Research." *Interpretation* 37 (2): 117–29.

Crouch, Carly L. 2017. *An Introduction to the Study of Jeremiah*. London: Bloomsbury T & T Clark.

Dahood, Mitchell. 1975. "Emphatic Double Negative M'yn in Jer. 10:6–7." *Catholic Biblical Quarterly* 37 (4): 458–59.

Day, John. 1992. "Ashtoreth (Deity)." In *The Anchor Bible Dictionary*, edited by David Noel Freedman, 1.491–94. New York: Doubleday.

Dobbs-Allsopp, F. W. 1998. "Linguistic Evidence for the Date of Lamentations." *JANES* 26 1–36.

________. 2001a. "The Effects of Enjambment in Lamentations (Part 2)." *ZAW* 113 (3): 370–85.

________. 2001b. "The Enjambing Line in Lamentations: A Taxonomy (Part 1)." *ZAW* 113 (2): 219–39.

________. 2002. *Lamentations*. Louisville, KY: John Knox Press.

Driver, S. R. 1920. *An Introduction to the Literature of the Old Testament*. Edinburgh: T & T Clark.

Edwards, Jonathan, ed. 2006. *The Life and Diary of David Brainerd* (reprint of 1749). Peabody, MA: Hendrickson,

Eskenazi, Tamara C. 1992. "Hananel, Tower of." In *The Anchor Bible Dictionary*, edited by David Noel Freedman, 3.45. New York: Doubleday.

Feinberg, Charles Lee. 1966. "Jeremiah 31:22: Proverb, Promise, or Prophecy? (Part One)." *Bibliotheca Sacra* 123 (492): 315–24.

________. 1967. "Jeremiah 31:22: Proverb, Promise, or Prophecy? (Part Two)." *Bibliotheca Sacra* 124 (493): 16–21.

Fishbane, Michael. 1971. "Jeremiah IV 23-26 and Job III 3-13: A Recovered Use of the Creation Pattern." *VT* 21 151–67.

France, R. T. 2008. *Matthew: An Introduction and Commentary*. Downers Grove, IL: InterVarsity.

Frick, Frank S. 1992. "Rechab." In *The Anchor Bible Dictionary*, edited by David Noel Freedman, 5.630–32. New York: Doubleday.

Garrett, Duane A. 1993. *Proverbs, Ecclesiastes, Song of Songs*. Nashville: Broadman & Holman.

________. 1997. *Hosea and Joel*. Nashville: Broadman & Holman.

Garrett, N., Lazzaro, S., Ariely, D., et al. 2006. "The Brain Adapts to Dishonesty." *Nat Neurosci* 19, 1727–1732. (Accessed through https://doi.org/10.1038/nn.4426.)

Gesenius, Wilhelm, and E. Kautzsch. 1898. *Gesenius' Hebrew Grammar*. Oxford: Clarendon Press.

Gladson, Jerry A. 2010. "Postmodernism and the Deus Absconditus in Lamentations 3." *Biblica* 91 (3): 321–34.

Gordon, S. D. 1904. *Quiet Talks on Prayer.* New York: Revell.

Grant, Reg and John Reed. 2001. *Telling Stories to Touch the Heart*. Eugene, OR: Wipf and Stock.

Grudem, Wayne. 1994. *Systematic Theology.* Grand Rapids: Zondervan.

Gwaltney, W. C. 1983. "The Biblical Book of Lamentations in the Context of Near Eastern Lament Literature." In *Scripture in Context II: More Essays on the Comparative Method*, edited by W. Hallo, J. Moyer, and L. Perdue, 191–211. Winona Lake, IN: Eisenbrauns.

Hallo, William W., and K. Lawson Younger Jr. 2003. *The Context of Scripture*. Leiden: E. J. Brill.

Harper, Kyle. 2017. *The Fate of Rome: Climate, Disease, and the End of an Empire*. Princeton, NJ: Princeton University Press.

Hillers, Delbert R. 2008. *Lamentations: A New Translation with Introduction and Commentary*. New Haven, CT: Yale University Press.

Hobbs, T. R. 1985. *2 Kings*. Dallas: Word.

Holladay, William L. 1986. *Jeremiah 1: A Commentary on the Book of the Prophet Jeremiah, Chapters 1–25* (Hermeneia). Philadelphia: Fortress Press.

________. 1989. *Jeremiah 2: A Commentary on the Book of the Prophet Jeremiah, Chapters 26–52*. Philadelphia: Fortress Press.

House, Paul R. 2004. "Lamentations." In *Song of Songs and Lamentations*, edited by James W. Watts, 267–473. Nashville: Thomas Nelson.

Huey, F. B. 1993. *Jeremiah, Lamentations*. Nashville: Broadman.

Janzen, J. Gerald. 1973. *Studies in the Text of Jeremiah*. Cambridge, MA: Harvard University Press.

Jobes, Karen H., and Moses Silva. 2000. *Invitation to the Septuagint*. Grand Rapids: Baker.

Johnson, James Weldon. 1969. *God's Trombones*. New York: Viking.

Jones, Richard N., and Zbigniew T. Fiema. 1992. "Tahpanhes." In *The Anchor Bible Dictionary*, edited by David Noel Freedman, 6.308–9. New York: Doubleday.

Joüon, Paul, and Takamitsu Muraoka. 2006. "A Grammar of Biblical Hebrew." Rome: Editrice Pontificio Instituto Biblico.

Kellermann, D. 1974. "בצע." *Theological Dictionary of the Old Testament*. Grand Rapids: Eerdmans.

Kraus, Hans-Joachim. 1993. *A Continental Commentary: Psalms 60–150*. Minneapolis: Fortress Press.

Kruger, Paul A. 2008. "A Woman Will 'Encompass' a Man: On Gender Reversal in Jer. 31,22b." *Bib* 89 (3): 380–88.

Labahn, Antje. 2006. "Fire from Above: Metaphors and Images of God's Actions in Lamentations 2:1-9." *JSOT* 31 (2): 239–56.

Lalleman, Hetty. 2013. *Jeremiah and Lamentations: An Introduction and Commentary*. Nottingham, England: InterVarsity.

LaSor, William Sanford. 1979. "Nebuchadrezzar." In *The International Standard Bible Encyclopedia, Revised*, edited by Geoffrey W. Bromiley, 506–8. Grand Rapids: Eerdmans.

Lewis, C. S. 1967. *Christian Reflections*. London: Geoffrey Bles.

Liid, Dale C. 1992. "Horse Gate." In *The Anchor Bible Dictionary*, edited by David Noel Freedman, 3.290. New York: Doubleday.

Linafelt, Tod. 2001. "The Refusal of a Conclusion in the Book of Lamentations." *JBL* 120 (2): 340–43.

Ludwig, Köhler, Walter Baumgartner, M. E. J. Richardson, and Johann Jakob Stamm. 1994. *The Hebrew and Aramaic Lexicon of the Old Testament*. Leiden: E. J. Brill.

Lundbom, J. R. 1992. "Baruch." In *The Anchor Bible Dictionary*, edited by David Noel Freedman, 1.617.

________. 2008a. *Jeremiah 1–20: A New Translation with Introduction and Commentary*. New Haven, CT: Yale University Press.

________. 2008b. *Jeremiah 21–36: A New Translation with Introduction and Commentary*. New Haven, CT: Yale University Press.

________. 2008c. *Jeremiah 37–52: A New Translation with Introduction and Commentary*. New Haven, CT: Yale University Press.

Luz, Ulrich. 2001. *Matthew 8–20*. Minneapolis: Fortress Press.

Mandolfo, Carleen. 2007. *Daughter Zion Talks Back to the Prophets: A Dialogic Theology of the Book of Lamentations*. Atlanta: Society of Biblical Literature.

McCrosky, James. 2001. *An Introduction to Rhetorical Communication*. Boston: Allyn and Bacon.

McGuiggan, Jim. 1998. *Jesus, Hero of Thy Soul.* West Monroe, LA: Howard Publishing.

McKane, William. 1986. *A Critical and Exegetical Commentary on Jeremiah.* Edinburgh: T & T Clark.

Neighbour, Ralph. 1973. *The Seven Last Words of the Church.* Grand Rapids: Zondervan.

O'Connor, Kathleen M. 2002. *Lamentations and the Tears of the World.* Maryknoll, NY: Orbis Books.

Parry, Robin A. 2010. *Lamentations.* Grand Rapids: Eerdmans.

________. 2011. "Lamentations and the Poetic Politics of Prayer." *Tyndale Bulletin* 62 (1): 65–88.

Pixner, Bargil. 1992. "Copper Scroll." In *The Anchor Bible Dictionary*, edited by David Noel Freedman, 1.1133–34. New York: Doubleday.

Propp, William H. C. 1987. "On Hebrew Śāde(h), 'Highland.'" *VT* 37 (2): 230–31.

Provan, Iain W. 254–255. "Feasts, Booths and Gardens (Thr 2,6a)." *ZAW* 102 (2): 1990.

Rainey, A. F. 1979. "Mizpah." In *The International Standard Bible Encyclopedia*, edited by Geoffrey W. Bromiley, 3.387–88. Grand Rapids: Eerdmans.

Redford, Donald B. 1992. "Hophra (Person)." In *The Anchor Bible Dictionary*, edited by David Noel Freedman, 3.285–87. New York: Doubleday.

Ritmeyer, Leen. 2006. *The Quest: Revealing the Temple Mount in Jerusalem.* Jerusalem: Carta.

Robinson, Torrey. 2003. *It's All In How You Tell It.* Grand Rapids: Baker.

Sadler, Rodney S., Jr. 2006. "Cush, Cushite." In *The New Interpreter's Dictionary of the Bible*, edited by Katharine Doob Sakenfeld, 1.813. Nashville: Abingdon.

Sandvig, Karen, 1990. *Adult Children of Divorce.* Waco, TX: Word.

Salters, R. B. 2010. *A Critical and Exegetical Commentary on Lamentations.* London: T & T Clark.

Saucy, Robert L. 1993. *The Case for Progressive Dispensationalism.* Grand Rapids: Zondervan.

Sawyer, Deborah F. 1999. "Gender-Play and Sacred Text: A Scene from Jeremiah." *JSOT* 24 (83): 99–111.

Schmitz, Philip C. 1992. "Queen of Heaven (Deity)." In *The Anchor Bible Dictionary*, edited by David Noel Freedman, 5.586–88. New York: Doubleday.

Seow. C. L. 1992. "Ark of the Covenant." *The Anchor Bible Dictionary.* New York: Doubleday.

Shaw, Ian, and Paul Nicholson. 1995. *The Dictionary of Ancient Egypt.* New York: Harry N. Abrams.

Sittser, Jerry. 2004. *A Grace Disguised.* Grand Rapids: Zondervan

Smothers, Thomas G., Gerald Lynwood Keown, and Pamela J. Scalise. 1995. *Jeremiah 26–52.* Dallas: Word Books.

Soderlund, Sven. 1985. *The Greek Text of Jeremiah: A Revised Hypothesis.* Sheffield, England: JSOT Press.

Speiser, E. A. 1974. *Genesis: Introduction, Translation, and Notes.* New Haven, CT: Yale University Press.

Stone, Mark P. 2018. "Vindicating Yahweh: A Close Reading of Lamentations 3.21-42." *JSOT* 43 83–108.

Tada, Joni Erickson. 2001. *Joni: An Unforgettable Story.* Grand Rapids: Zondervan.

Thompson, J. A. 1980. *The Book of Jeremiah.* Grand Rapids: Eerdmans.

Toorn, Karel van der. 1986. "Judges 16:21 in the Light of the Akkadian Sources." *VT* 36 (2): 248–53.

Tov, Emanuel. 2012. *Textual Criticism of the Hebrew Bible.* Minneapolis: Fortress Press.

Tripp, Paul David. 2012. *Dangerous Calling.* Wheaton, IL: Crossway.

________. 2014. *New Morning Mercies.* Wheaton, IL: Crossway.

Unterman, Jeremiah. 1987. *From Repentance to Redemption: Jeremiah's Thought in Transition.* Sheffield: JSOT Press.

Vanhoozer, Kevin J. 1998. *Is There a Meaning in This Text?: The Bible, the Reader, and the Morality of Literary Knowledge*. Grand Rapids: Zondervan.

Vroegop, Mark. 2019. *Dark Clouds Deep Mercy*. Wheaton, IL: Crossway, 2019.

Westermann, Claus. 1994. *Lamentations: Issues and Interpretation*. Minneapolis: Fortress Press.

William, Joseph A. 2015. *Seventeen Fathoms Deep*. Chicago: Chicago Review Press.

Wray Beal, Lissa M. 2014. *1 & 2 Kings*. Downers Grove, IL: InterVarsity.

Würthwein, Ernst. 2014. *The Text of the Old Testament*. Grand Rapids: Eerdmans.